Glencoe

SCIENCE INTERACTIONS

Course 4

 Glencoe McGraw-Hill

New York, New York
Columbus, Ohio
Woodland Hills, California
Peoria, Illinois

A *GLENCOE* Program

Science Interactions

Student Edition

Teacher Wraparound Videodisc Edition

Teacher Classroom Resources

Laboratory Manual: SE and TE

Study Guide: SE and TE

Concept Mapping

Activity Masters

Basic Concepts Transparencies

Section Focus Transparencies

Critical Thinking/Problem Solving

Multicultural Connections

Tech-Prep Applications

Review and Assessment

Making Connections:

  Technology and Society

  Integrating Sciences

  Across the Curriculum

Performance Assessment

Computer Test Bank: Windows and

  Macintosh Versions

Spanish Resources

English/Spanish Audiocassettes

Science and Technology Videodisc Series

MindJogger Videoquizzes

Lesson Plans

The Glencoe Science Professional Development Series

Performance Assessment in the Science Classroom

Lab and Safety Skills in the Science Classroom

Cooperative Learning in the Science Classroom

Alternate Assessment in the Science Classroom

Exploring Environmental Issues

Series and Cover Design: DECODE, Inc.

Send all inquiries to:
GLENCOE/McGraw-Hill
8787 Orion Place
Columbus, OH 43240

ISBN 0-02-827607-8

Printed in the United States of America.

6 7 8 9 10 071/043 05 04 03

Authors

Robert W. Avakian, M.S.
Earth Science Teacher
Alamo Junior High School
Midland, Texas

Daniel J. Blaustein, M.A.
Biology Teacher
Waukegan High School
Waukegan, Illinois

Charles W. McLaughlin, Ph.D.
Coordinator of Science Education
Chemistry Teacher
Central High School
St. Joseph, Missouri

Kevin Reel, M.S.
Principal
The Westminster School
Atlanta, Georgia

Marilyn S. Thompson, Ph.D.
Assistant Professor
College of Education
Arizona State University
Tempe, Arizona

Julie Iris Wulff, Ph.D.
Adjunct Professor
William Rainey Harper
Community College
Palatine, Illinois

Paul Zitzewitz, Ph.D.
Professor of Physics
University of Michigan–Dearborn
Dearborn, Michigan

Contributing Writers

Linda Barr
Freelance Writer
Westerville, Ohio

Henry Carrigan
Freelance Writer
Westerville, Ohio

Mary Dylewski
Science Writer
Houston, Texas

Barbara Everett
Freelance Writer
Columbus, Ohio

Helen Frensch
Science Writer
Santa Barbara, California

Rebecca Johnson
Science Writer
Sioux Falls, South Dakota

Robert Landes
Freelance Writer
Hilliard, Ohio

Devi Mathieu
Science Writer
Sebastopol, California

Denise Minor
Science Teacher
Terre Haute, Indiana

Patricia West
Freelance Writer
Oakland, California

Consultants

Chemistry

Anne Barefoot, A.G.C.
Physics and Chemistry Teacher, Emeritus
Whiteville High School
Whiteville, North Carolina

Dorothy Gabel, Ph.D.
Professor of Science Education
Indiana University
Bloomington, Indiana

Rebecca King
Chemistry Teacher
New Hanover High School
Wilmington, North Carolina

Earth Science

Ralph M. Feather, Jr., M.Ed.
Science Department Chair
Derry Area School District
Derry, Pennsylvania

Dale Gnidovec, M.S.
Collection Manager, Museum
The Ohio State University
Columbus, Ohio

Mark Dennis Izold, M.S.
Adjunct Faculty–Geology
Rio Salado Community College
Phoenix, Arizona

Biology

David M. Armstrong, Ph.D.
Professor of Environmental, Population,
and Organismic Biology
University of Colorado, Boulder
Boulder, Colorado

Melissa Stanley, Ph.D.
Professor of Biology
George Mason University
Fairfax, Virginia

Physics

William J. Boone, Ph.D.
School of Education
Indiana University
Bloomington, Indiana

Patrick Hamill, Ph.D.
Professor of Physics
San Jose State University
San Jose, California

Environment

Robert Vasconcellos
Coordinator and Project Director
San Jose Unified School District
San Jose, California

Tech-Prep

Denise Minor
Teacher
West Vigo High School
Terre Haute, Indiana

Multicultural

H. Prentice Baptiste, Jr., Ed.D.
The Center for Science Education
Kansas State University
Manhattan, Kansas

Karen Muir, Ph.D.
Lead Instructor
Department of Social and Behavioral Sciences
Columbus State Community College
Columbus, Ohio

Reading

Elizabeth Gray, Ph.D.
Reading Specialist
Heath City Schools
Heath, Ohio
Adjunct Professor
Otterbein College
Westerville, Ohio

Assessment

Robert M. Jones, Ph.D.
University of Houston–Clear Lake
Houston, Texas

Safety

Peggy W. Holliday
Science Education Specialist
NIOSH Certified Lab Trainer
Raleigh, North Carolina

Reviewers

Albert Acierno
Science Teacher
Ft. Hayes Metropolitan
Education Center
Columbus, Ohio

Ellen Averill
Science Department Chair
Kendrick High School
Columbus, Georgia

Susan Parsons Booth
Science Teacher Specialist
Kecoughtan High School
Hampton, Virginia

David Bydlowski
Science Teacher
Stevenson Junior High School
Westland, Michigan

Candace L. Cline
Science Teacher
Etiwanda High School
Etiwanda, California

Rocky Allen Craft
Biology Teacher
Whitesburg High School
Whitesburg, Kentucky

Neil Evans
Department Head/
Science Teacher
Mission San Jose High School
Fremont, California

Lorena R. Farrar
Department Chairperson/
Science Teacher
Westwood Junior High School
Dallas, Texas

Sara Frances Hall
Science Teacher
Heritage High School
Conyers, Georgia

Diana Williams Harrison
Science Department
Chairperson/Teacher
Marion Abramson Senior
High School
New Orleans, Louisiana

Mary M. Kendall
Science Department
Chair/Teacher
Camden County School System
Kingsland, Georgia

Claudia Knippenburg
Physical Science/
Biology Teacher
Northshore High School
Slidell, Louisiana

Maruta Krastins
Department Chair/
Chemistry Teacher
Bartlett High School
Bartlett, Tennesee

Kenneth L. Krause
Science Teacher
Tubman Middle School
Portland, Oregon

Diane Lauritsen, Ph.D.
Consultant/Research Scientist
Aquatic Science Ventures
Mount Pleasant, South Carolina

Stephen C. Little
Department Chairperson
Indian Hill Junior High School
Clive, Iowa

Neil D. Michels
Physics and Earth
Science Teacher
Apple Valley High School
Apple Valley, Minnesota

Rocio Munoz
Science Department Head
North Shore Middle School
Houston, Texas

Jean Olson, Ph.D.
Science Department
Chair/Chemistry Teacher
Rutherford High School
Panama City, Florida

Walter A. Racynski
Science Department Head
Addison Trail High School
Addison, Illinois

Darrell Richter
Department Chair/
Science Teacher
Moorhead Senior High School
ISD # 152
Moorhead, Minnesota

Betty L. Schiddell, Ph.D.
Science Teacher
Morton East High School
Cicero, Illinois

Richard M. Schwalm
Science Department
Head/Teacher
Eastern Lebanon County
School District
Myerstown, Pennsylvania

Donna Gumulak Stempniak
Bilingual Science Teacher
Grover Cleveland High School
Buffalo, New York

Billie J. Thorson
Science Teacher
Peninsula High School
Gig Harbor, Washington

George Varga
Science Teacher
Sweetwater Union High School
National City, California

SCIENCE INTERACTIONS
CONTENTS OVERVIEW
Course 4

Food

Food is the means by which organisms obtain energy to live. But how does energy get into the food? How does an organism release that energy? How do plants obtain energy? How is food preserved to keep it safe to eat? The answers to these questions are served up in Unit 3.

Resources

Shiny black coal is one of the Earth's most abundant, important resources. What other resources does Earth hold? How are they extracted from Earth's surface? Can we make sure the supply of coal and other important resources will last? Dig into Unit 4 to find out.

Shelter

How do people solve the problems of providing shelter? In this unit, find out how sites are selected for buildings, what materials are used in construction, and how buildings are heated, cooled, and provided with electricity. Pick up your hammer along with Unit 5 and let's get started.

Disease

Y ou're sneezing. Your eyes are watering. Is it an allergy? The flu? The common cold? Maybe you were exposed to a toxic substance. How are diseases detected and classified? How are they prevented? Grab a tissue and turn to Unit 6 to find out.

Flight

W hat forces and fuels enable birds, planes, and helicopters to fly? How is flight a necessary part of the life cycle of some plants and fungi? What forces do rockets use to escape Earth's gravity? Unit 7 is a first-class ticket to answering these questions.

Cooler, denser fluid flows under warm, less dense fluid and pushes up

UNIT 3

Food   202

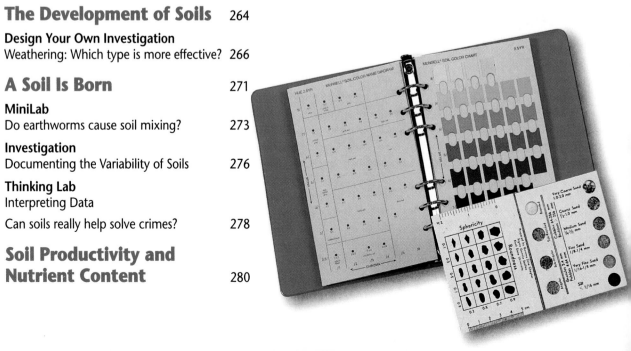

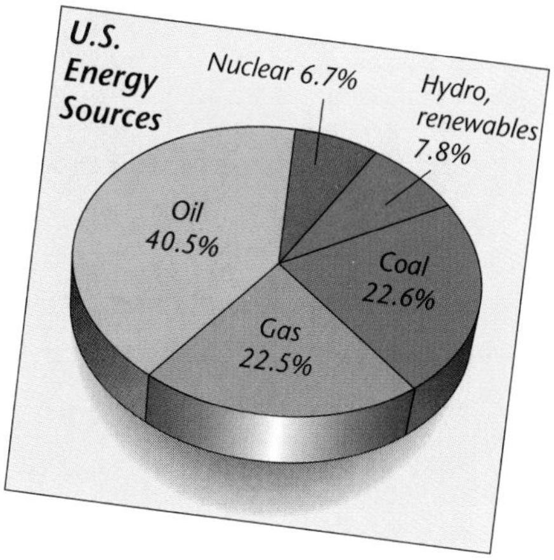

U.S. Energy Sources

Nuclear 6.7%

Hydro, renewables 7.8%

Oil 40.5%

Coal 22.6%

Gas 22.5%

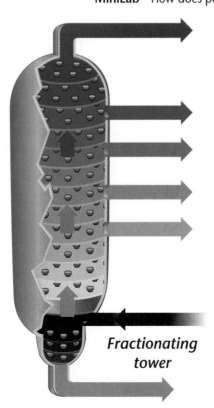

Fractionating tower

UNIT 5

Shelter   **444**

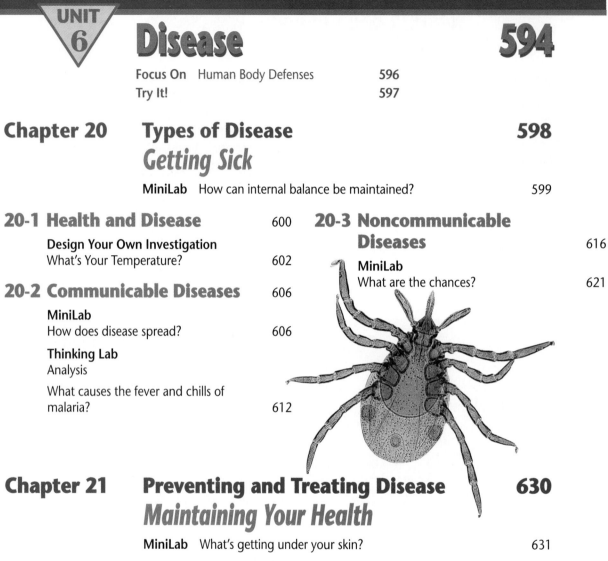
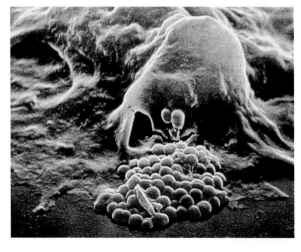
xx

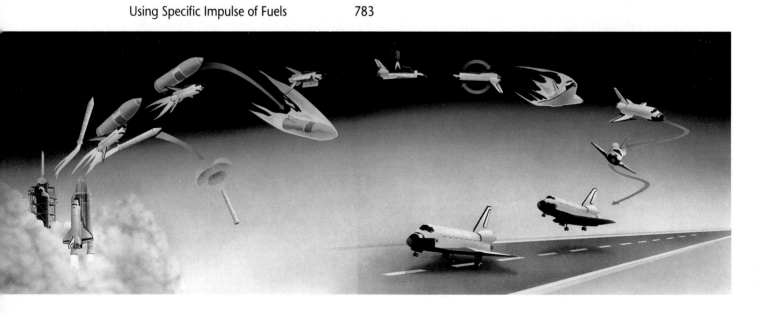

Appendices 796

Skill Handbook 816

Glossary 836

Spanish Glossary 845

Index 853

13	14	15
Al	**Si**	**P**
Aluminum	Silicon	Phosphor
26.981 54	28.0855	30.973 7

31	32	33	34		
Ga	**G**	**As**	**Se**	**Br**	**Kr**
Galliur		Arsenic	Selenium	Bromine	Krypton
69		216	78.96	79.904	83.80

			52	53	54
			Te	**I**	**Xe**
			Tellurium	Iodine	Xenon
		57	127.60	126.9045	131.29

SCIENCE CONNECTIONS

What will you do with the science principles you learn? In-Depth Look features help you recognize that scientific principles are a part of everyday things. Applying Technology features show that you can apply these principles to a career.

SCIENCE CONNECTIONS

How does science affect you and society? Consider some of the issues that have been covered by the media. In the Science and Society features, you'll be asked to think about science-related questions and technologies that will affect your life now or even fifty years from now.

Science and Society

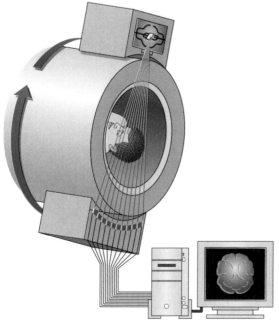

CAT scan technology

CROSS-CURRICULUM CONNECTIONS

Does science affect history? Can people become healthier through creative expression? The Art, History, and Literature Connections expand your view of science. What are scientists like? In the People in Science features you'll find out what excites them about science. Eyewitness Accounts give you perspectives on how scientific events have affected people.

ENVIRONMENTAL CONNECTIONS

How do we all affect the environment? Throughout each of the chapters below, you will learn more about how you interact with your environment.

Resources

Air and Water

Ecological Interactions

Science

A Tool for Solving Problems

Welcome to Science Interactions! *You are about to begin an exciting new year in which you investigate the wonders of science. In this year of science, you will learn about the world, from atoms to airplanes and from worms to weather. It will amaze you, amuse you, and challenge your thinking. In this course, you practice scientific processes while learning about the four major scientific disciplines—biology, chemistry, Earth science, and physics. But, what exactly is science?*

The Mystery of Elkhorn Lake

After a long, hot drive, José, Selena, and their parents finally made it to the mountains to begin their annual two-week vacation. The teens could hardly wait to try their luck at fishing in the crystal-clear waters of Elkhorn Lake.

The fishing was good, but the only type of fish they caught were catfish, carp, and other bottom-feeding species. The large trout that they had caught so easily in other years were strangely absent. The teens noticed other differences, as well. The water near the shore that had served as their swimming spot for so many years was now covered with algae and other water plants. What had happened to Elkhorn Lake?

Analyze the methods you use to solve problems in the following Mini-Lab.

MiniLab

How do you solve problems?

You encounter problems every day. Perhaps you lost your keys or a notebook. Usually, these problems are solved quickly, but have you ever stopped to think about the steps you take to solve such problems? In this MiniLab, you'll analyze how you solve everyday problems.

Procedure

1. Obtain a sealed box from your teacher containing three everyday objects.
2. Before touching the box, list three approaches you might take to figuring out what is in the box.
3. Try each method listed to identify the objects in the box. Do whatever you need to do to the box except open it.
4. Make a list of the specific steps you took.
5. Open the box. Were you right?

Analysis

1. Analyze the steps you took to identify the objects. Did they provide necessary information?
2. Did you change your ideas or add new approaches as you manipulated the box?

What is science?

Science Is an Ongoing Process

Science means different things to different people. You may think of science as a large body of information. Although you'll certainly learn a lot of information in science class this year, science isn't just a collection of isolated facts and ideas. Science is an ongoing, dynamic way of investigating the world.

Answers to complex problems take time. Jane Goodall, the scientist pictured below, has conducted research on the behavior of chimpanzees for an extended number of years. The results of her research will be added to the knowledge that scientists throughout the world have collected about chimpanzee behavior.

Dr. Goodall's results will not be the final word on chimpanzees. As scientists study her findings and make more observations of their own, they will ask new questions about chimpanzees that may modify previous conclusions. The changing of previous conclusions doesn't mean that a scientist's original research is wrong. This merely illustrates the temporary nature of scientific understanding. Modifying ideas, rather than rejecting them, is the norm in science.

Much of what we know about the behavior of wild chimpanzees comes from the pioneering efforts of Dr. Jane Goodall. Scientists like Dr. Goodall form conclusions about the world by conducting rigorous, long-term scientific research.

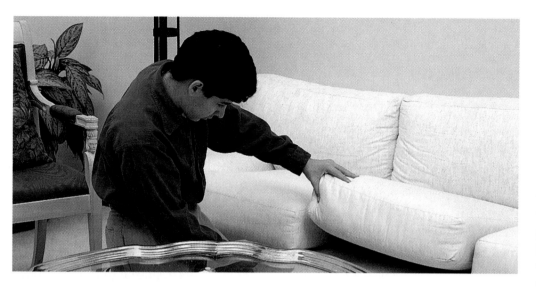

We all misplace items at times. How do we go about locating them? You probably first stop to think where you saw them last. Based on this you make an educated guess about where they may be. You then test your guess. If you haven't located them by this point, you revise your original guess and keep looking.

Scientific Processes

What methods do scientists use in their research? You use procedures similar to ones scientists use in research to solve problems every day. Have you ever lost your glasses or keys? How did you go about finding them?

Scientific methods are the common steps scientists apply to gather information and answer questions. These methods aren't any different from methods you use every day.

Scientists find problems to solve by simply observing the world around them and becoming curious about one particular problem. For example, a scientist observing several different species of fishes in a lake may become interested in the feeding behavior of one of these species. Jane Goodall became interested in the behavior of chimpanzees, which led her to spend numerous years in Tanzania studying them.

The Flex Your Brain strategy shown here will help you begin to think like a scientist. It gives you a way to define questions you may want to answer either in science or in your daily life.

Scientists often ask questions that have practical applications. For instance, think back to the problem faced by the teens at Elkhorn Lake.

FLEX YOUR BRAIN

1 Make an interesting observation.

2 What do I already know about this sort of thing?

3 How can I explain this based on what I know?

4 How sure am I that this explanation is accurate?

5 What evidence do I need to prove that the explanation is accurate?

6 How can I gather that evidence?

7 Just do it!
Make a plan to collect data, and carry it out.

8 Conclude & Communicate

My explanation isn't accurate because...

Communicate your results and return to step 3.

My explanation is accurate because...

Communicate your results and return to step 1.

I can't say because...

Communicate your results and return to step 6.

Finding Explanations for Problems

At the beginning of the chapter, when José and Selena discovered the disastrous changes at Elkhorn Lake, they tried to find some explanation for the problems. While walking through the forest a short distance from the water's edge, they noticed that what was once a dense forest of pine trees was now a cleared-out patch of tree stumps and muddy soil. Further along the road beyond the forest line, they also discovered a large pile of plant fertilizer that had been dumped on the dirt road.

To arrive at an explanation for the changes at the lake, the teens first suggested reasons for the damage to the lake.

Forming a Hypothesis

Based on the observations the teens made, they formed a hypothesis, a testable explanation for a question or a problem. They hypothesized that the chopped-down trees and the dumping of the fertilizer somehow caused the changes in the lake.

■ Inductive Reasoning

Sometimes, hypotheses made from observations can be simple, but often they may be complex. A hypothesis is usually not a random guess. Before a scientist makes a hypothesis, he or she has an idea what the answer to the question is based on observations, experience, research, and previous experiments. Using all this information, the scientist applies his or her own reasoning powers. Think back to the example of the lost keys. You made a hypothesis about where the keys were based on previous experience. In doing this, you used *inductive reasoning*. Inductive reasoning is reasoning that uses a set of facts to develop a general rule.

■ Deductive Reasoning

In some cases, a general rule is known before all the facts of a situation are known. For example, the plant in your room is wilting. You think, "If the plant is wilting, the soil must be too dry." When you check the soil, you find

What could have caused the changes in Elkhorn Lake? This complex problem is the type of question scientists tackle every day. There is no set way of solving a problem, but the first step in any scientific investigation is observing the world around you and asking questions.

Using deductive reasoning, the teens came up with testable hypothesis statements about the problems at Elkhorn Lake.

A If the removal of the trees caused the muddy soil, then similar conditions should exist in other cleared forest areas.

B If the fertilizer got into the lake and caused an overgrowth of algae, then fertilizer should affect other lakes in similar ways.

that it *is* dry. In this situation, you have used *deductive reasoning*. Deductive reasoning is reasoning that suggests something must be true about a particular case from known rules. In this case, the known rules were that plants need water. Deductive reasoning often leads to an "If . . . then" statement. This statement made from the plant example would be, "If I don't water my plant, then it will wilt."

In the Thinking Lab, you will practice using deductive reasoning to help solve a problem.

Thinking Lab   Making a Model

How do you use reasoning in solving the problems of everyday life?

Inductive and deductive reasoning are not just for scientists. You probably use some form of reasoning every day without even thinking about it.

Analysis
Imagine you are experiencing a common, every-day problem: a personal stereo that won't work. Use deductive reasoning to figure out what's wrong with the stereo. For example, you might say, "*If* the problem is with the batteries, *then* new batteries will make the stereo work."

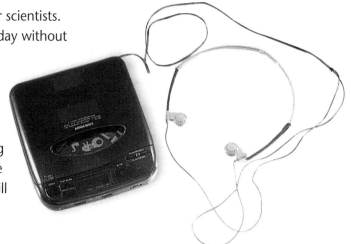

Thinking Critically
Use scientific modeling to help solve the problem. Prepare a list of three other "If . . . then" statements that could be tested directly to solve the problem.

Experiments—Testing the Hypothesis

What does the word *experiment* mean to you? Many people mistakenly think that "experiments" are only conducted by scientists. People do not always use the word *experiment* in their daily lives in the same way scientists do in their work. However, people experiment frequently without realizing it. Have you ever experimented with a new hair or clothing style? Perhaps you've experimented with a cookie recipe by substituting raisins for chocolate chips. To a scientist, an experiment is a procedure used to test a hypothesis or prediction. One experiment may not always provide the solution to a problem, so scientists continually rethink their experiments. Simple experiments can solve a variety of everyday problems. Try this next activity to see how even simple experiments can have useful applications at home.

MiniLab

Which is the best clear plastic wrap?

What if you wanted to find out which brand of plastic wrap is the most effective at keeping foods from drying out? Do all brands have the same capacity to keep air out? Make a hypothesis that predicts which wrap works the best. Do this simple experiment to test your hypothesis.

Procedure

1. Choose three different brands of plastic wrap and follow steps 2–5 for each brand. Be sure to identify the brand for each set of packets.

2. Soak one paper towel with water and place it on one of the pieces of plastic wrap.

3. Wrap the towel and plastic tightly. Squeeze the air out of the packet and tie it tightly with string.

4. Soak a fourth paper towel in water, but do not wrap it in plastic. Place this towel with the other packets.

5. Put the packets in a dark area at room temperature and let them sit overnight.

6. Open the packets and compare the moistness of the paper towels.

Analysis

1. What hypothesis were you testing in this experiment?

2. Which brand of plastic wrap left the paper towel the wettest?

3. What was the purpose of the fourth towel?

4. How could you make this experiment quantitative?

In the MiniLab activity, you hypothesized, then experimented to determine whether a particular brand of plastic wrap was airtight. The experiment you carried out is known as a *controlled* experiment because it involves two groups: an experimental group and a control group. The control is the standard—the part of the experiment in which all conditions are kept the same. The experimental group is the group that is tested. In the MiniLab, what was the control? Which was the experimental group?

What are variables?

As you saw in the activity, you kept the plastic wrap in the experimental group under the same conditions as the control except for the single condition you were testing—the ability of the plastic wrap to keep out air. In a controlled experiment, only one condition is changed at a time. The condition in an experiment that is changed is the independent variable. What was the independent variable in the MiniLab?

By changing the independent variable, a scientist can observe or measure the effects of the change. The dependent variable is any change that results from manipulation of the independent variable. The dependent variable in the MiniLab was the wetness or dryness of the paper towels. The illustration below shows a simple controlled experiment developed by the teens at Elkhorn Lake.

The experimental procedures scientists use to solve problems depend on the difficulty of the questions being investigated. Some experiments, as you've seen, are simple and may involve only one independent variable and one dependent variable. Sometimes, though, a scientist is interested in more than one effect of an independent variable. Such questions require more complex experimental procedures. In the following Investigation, you will use scientific methods to perform an experiment.

To determine whether fertilizer affects plant growth, José and Selena developed a simple controlled experiment to test the hypothesis that fertilizer makes plants grow faster. What is the control group in this experiment? What is the independent variable? The dependent variable?

9

INVESTIGATION

Using Scientific Methods

Well over 100 years ago, French scientist Louis Pasteur carried out a simple, but famous, experiment to test the hypothesis that bacteria arise spontaneously from air. In this Investigation, you will test whether bacteria are, in fact, present in the air by performing a simple, controlled experiment similar to Pasteur's.

Preparation

Problem

Are microorganisms present in the air?

Objectives

In this Investigation, you will:
- *Demonstrate* scientific methods to determine whether bacteria are found in air.

Materials

beaker (400-mL)
chicken bouillon soup
cotton balls
graduated cylinder (50-mL)
hot plate
labels
test-tube holder
test-tube rack
test tubes (4)
distilled water

Safety Precautions

Use care when handling hot objects. Be sure to use a test-tube holder when moving the hot test tubes.

Data and Observations		
Tube	Appearance	Odor
Soup, open		
Soup, sealed		
Water, open		
Water, sealed		

INVESTIGATION

Procedure

1 Make a copy of the data table shown on page 10.

2 Add 15 mL of chicken bouillon soup to each of two test tubes. Add 15 mL of distilled water to the remaining two test tubes. Label the test tubes with the date and whether they are water or soup.

3 Place the four test tubes into a beaker that is filled halfway with water. Place the beaker on a hot plate. Allow the test tubes to remain in boiling water for at least 15 minutes.

4 Use a test-tube holder to remove the test tubes from the hot water. Place them in a test-tube rack. **CAUTION:** *Use care when handling the hot test tubes.*

Step 4

5 Quickly seal one bouillon tube and one water tube with cotton balls. Let the other test tubes remain open to the air.

6 Make a hypothesis about what will happen to the test tubes. Write your hypothesis *in your Journal.*

7 After one week, examine the test tubes. Compare the appearance of the test tubes containing soup to each other. Are they clear or cloudy in appearance? Hold them near a bright light source to help you decide. Record your results in your data table.

8 Examine the appearance of the two water tubes. Record your observations in your data table.

Step 7

9 Carefully observe the odor of each test tube using the fanning method. Record in your data table whether the tubes smell spoiled or have no odor.

Analyze and Conclude

1. Identifying Variables What was the independent variable in this experiment? What were the dependent variables?

2. Using Constants and Controls Which test tubes represented the control group in this experiment?

3. Interpreting Data Make a statement explaining how your data did or did not support your hypothesis.

Going Further

Changing Variables
Design an experiment that involves the manipulation of other independent variables. See what happens to the test tubes if they are subjected to different environmental conditions, such as cold or very warm temperatures.

At Elkhorn Lake, José and Selena were able to show that cleared land is *associated* with increased soil erosion by making comparisons between different areas. Experimental tests that involve observation and comparison can be valid tests of hypotheses, but a more complex experiment would have to be planned to test whether cleared land *causes* an increase in soil erosion. How might you plan an experiment to test this hypothesis?

After gathering data from their fertilizer and plant growth experiment, the teens organized it by plotting the numbers on a line graph. How does a line graph make the data easier to understand?

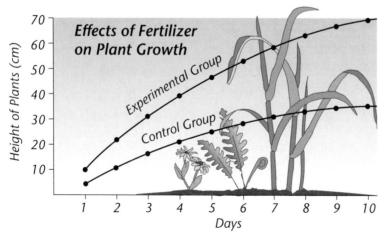

Effects of Fertilizer on Plant Growth

Experimental Group

Control Group

Height of Plants (cm)

Days

The testing of a hypothesis doesn't always have to involve an elaborate laboratory procedure in which controls are used and measurements are made. Collecting and interpreting data through observation are valid procedures, as well. Consider another experiment José and Selena carried out at Elkhorn Lake. Because they hypothesized that cutting down trees affects soil erosion, one of their first experiments involved observing soil in other areas where trees had been cleared.

Whether an experiment is simple or complex, it always involves the gathering of data, which are pieces of information obtained during a scientific experiment. When data have been gathered from an experiment, scientists may organize the data into a more understandable form, such as a table, graph (as shown at the left), chart, or a clear statement of their observations. Organizing data in this way helps scientists during the analysis process.

Data Analysis—Thinking About What Happened

Having data from an experiment does not end the scientific process. Data then have to be analyzed and interpreted. After data have been reviewed and analyzed, a conclusion must be made. Was the hypothesis supported by the data, or was it not supported? Sometimes, a scientist may even feel that more data are needed to test a hypothesis. Other times, a scientist may decide that the data are invalid due to errors in the experimental design. Only when repeated experiments yield similar results can data be considered confirmed and reliable.

No scientist could possibly read all the information published each day in scientific journals. How do you think the computer technology available today can benefit a scientist researching a problem?

The Final Step—Reporting Results

The conclusions and results of scientific investigations are reported in weekly and monthly scientific journals like those shown below. When a scientific article is published, it is open to examination and review by other scientists. Reporting results is one of the most critical steps in the scientific process. It allows scientists to verify the results and work of other scientists.

Information shared between scientists is also useful when related to data published by other scientists. If a scientist considers a particular published investigation valid and acceptable, he or she may use the results for the development of a hypothesis, planning an experiment, or in the final analysis of an experiment. Working in this manner is useful for tackling the big questions that may require results from different scientific disciplines. For example, the modern theory of evolution is actually the culmination of more than 150 years of shared research in such fields as biology, geology, mathematics, and chemistry.

Theories—Well-tested Hypotheses

People use the word *theory* in everyday life differently from the way scientists use this word. When people say they have a theory about something, it means that they are guessing that something will happen based on past experience.

Scientists use the word *theory* much differently. As you can see below, a theory is an explanation of a natural phenomenon that is supported by a large body of scientific evidence obtained from different experiments and observations.

When a scientific conclusion reaches the level of a theory, it is usually accepted by most scientists in the scientific community. Validated theories enable scientists to predict events and develop solutions to complex problems.

In this chapter, you have learned how scientists investigate facts about the world. As you proceed through this course and learn the scientific facts presented, pay particular attention to the science process involved and ask yourself questions about how the evidence was gathered. Remember, whether or not you pursue a career in science, it will most certainly play a part in shaping your future. Only by understanding how scientists arrive at conclusions will you be able to make critical decisions in your life.

Scientific Methods

Question

Hypothesis

Experiment

Results

Conclusions

Additional hypothesis

Reject and revise hypothesis

Confirm

Publication

Theory

Other scientists experiment and react

In science, a hypothesis that is supported by many separate observations and experiments, usually over a long period of time, becomes a theory.

Read the statements below that review major points presented in the chapter. Using the concepts that you have learned, answer each question *in your Journal.*

1 The four major disciplines of science—biology, chemistry, Earth science, and physics—are bodies of knowledge that contain facts about the natural world. *Why is it important to learn facts about the things that happen around you?*

2 Scientists investigate nature by using scientific methods, which are step-by-step processes developed to reveal facts about living and nonliving things. *How are scientific methods similar to methods you use to solve everyday problems?*

3 Results of scientific investigations are reported in professional journals, where they can be evaluated and verified by other scientists. When results are accepted, they become incorporated into a body of scientific knowledge. *Why is the reporting of results a key step in the scientific process?*

15

Understanding Ideas

Using complete sentences, answer the following questions in your Journal.

1. What is a scientist's next step likely to be if data support the hypothesis?
2. If a scientist's experimental data do not support the hypothesis, what would be the next likely step for a scientist?
3. A student plans an experiment to test the growth of bean plants under three temperatures ranging from 10°C to 60°C. What are the dependent and independent variables in the experiment?
4. Why is the word *process* often used in describing science?
5. Explain why science can be thought of as both a body of scientific information and as a way of investigating.

Developing Skills

Use your understanding of the concepts developed in this chapter to answer each of the following questions.

1. **Experimenting** Design a controlled experiment to test the hypothesis that clearing forests speeds up soil erosion.
2. **Sequencing** Think about an item that you recently lost and then found again, such as your keys. Sequence the steps you took to locate the object. How was your procedure similar to the methods used by scientists?
3. **Predicting** In the Investigation on pages 10 and 11, what experimental results would you expect if both tubes of soup were boiled and sealed?

4. **Concept Mapping** Use the following terms and phrases to complete the concept map about scientific methods.

theory, hypothesis, independent variable, data, dependent variable, conclusion, experiment, control

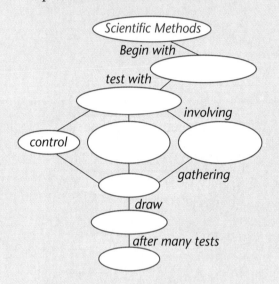

5. **Making and Using Graphs** The following data are taken from an experiment about plant growth and fertilizers. Do these data support the hypothesis that fertilizer enhances the growth of plants?

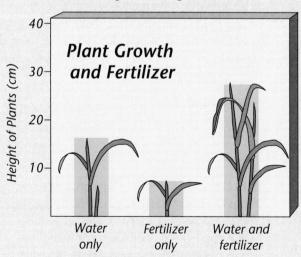

CHAPTER REVIEW

Critical Thinking

In your Journal, *answer each of the following questions.*

1. You and your friend have a theory about who will get the highest grade on the science test. Explain why this use of the word *theory* differs from the way scientists use the word.

2. Inductive reasoning is reasoning from a specific set of facts to a general rule. Describe how you have used inductive reasoning in your everyday life.

3. Describe the importance of scientific journals to the process of science.

4. Scientists often try to repeat, or replicate, the work of other scientists. Describe at least one reason why a scientist would do this.

5. One of the most important parts of any scientific article is the section entitled "Methods and Materials." Explain the importance of this section in the scientific process.

Problem Solving

Read the following problem and discuss your answers in a brief paragraph.

One summer morning, a group of teens swimming at a lake near their homes noticed a large number of dead fish, crabs, and other aquatic organisms floating in the water near the west end of the beach. What was interesting to them was the fact that the water at the east end of the beach was clear and free of dead fish.

Describe in words a step-by-step procedure the teens could follow to find out what was happening at the lake. Make sure your procedure follows a correct scientific process.

CONNECTING IDEAS

1. **Theme—Nature of Science** If scientific concepts can change, why is it necessary to sit through a whole year of science class?

2. **Theme—Unity Within Diversity** Scientists investigate information in a variety of fields from cell biology to geology. What characteristics do you think scientists have in common?

3. **Theme—Stability and Change** Explain why it is necessary to repeat an experiment with a change in the independent variable.

UNIT 1

Storms

It's 4:00 P.M. Lightning flashes across a blackening sky. Gusts of wind drive sheets of rain against the windows, and the lights you've had to turn on now flicker. The sirens of a tornado warning wail and the wind seems to make them come first from one direction, then from another. Within the hour, the wind is calm. The sky has cleared. How did the storm change so suddenly? Where is it now? Did it do any damage? The information in this unit will help you understand both the causes of storms and their effects.

Severe storm conditions often create dramatic cloud formations. Careful observation of these formations enables meteorologists to predict the next move that a severe storm might make.

Weather is notorious for causing changes in plans. At many sporting events, rain checks are issued that can be used for another game if the current game is rained out.

Accurate prediction depends on data collected by earthbound instruments, such as this weather station on top of a mountain, and weather satellites.

Focus On

··

Television Weather Forecasting

Whether it's the early morning news and weather broadcast or the cable weather channel, television is a major source of information that tells you whether you need to carry an umbrella or whether you'll be able to shed your coat by the end of the day. The technology that goes into a televised weather forecast changes each year.

Television stations rely on several sources of information to make forecasts. The National Weather Service provides general information and issues warnings and watches about dangerous storms.

Television weather forecasters use a process called *chroma key* in which the forecaster stands in front of a special, single-color backdrop. A blank space is created into which computer-generated maps and other graphics are projected onto the television screen.

There is no map or graphics on the backdrop. The forecaster looks at TV monitors showing weather information located on either side of the screen to see where to point on the backdrop. Skillful forecasters make it appear that they are pointing to changing information on the backdrop itself.

Try It!

Try your hand at predicting the weather for your area of the country a week from now. Study the information on the weather page of a newspaper.

What To Do

1. Look at the conditions predicted for areas of the country west of where you live. Read the five-day forecast.

2. Make a prediction about whether the five-day forecast will hold true.

3. In five days, check out the validity of your prediction.

Try It Again

After you've learned more about weather forecasting and its accuracy, look again at a five-day forecast and see whether you can make a more accurate prediction for your area.

Tony's Five Day Forecast 6

WED	THU	FRI	SAT	SUN
63	60	50	60	65
37	35	30	30s	40

Specific weather forecasts for 48 hours in the future are made using data from around the world. Five- and six-day forecasts, however, are based on weather trends.

UNIT 1 PROJECTS

During your exploration of storms, you may discover new questions or wish to explore related topics. **Design a School Weather Station** and **Produce Your Own Television Weather Report**, found in the Unit 1 Projects section on pages 108-109, will give you the challenge of predicting weather. Read through these projects. By the time you finish this unit, you'll know what you need to successfully complete both of these projects.

CHAPTER 1

Weather Prediction
The Approaching Storm

What do unmanageable hair, a postponed cross-country meet, and a farmer's feelings of relief have in common? They are all the result of those rain clouds moving in. The weather influences many things in your life—from the clothes you decide to wear in the morning to the food you eat for dinner at night. That's why many decisions and plans depend on the weather forecast. Predicting the weather depends on careful observations, measuring instruments—some centuries-old—and space-age technology.

▶ *In the following activity, explore how successful your local weather forecaster is at predicting the weather.*

How accurate is your weather forecaster?

When weather information comes into the newsroom, your local weather forecaster summarizes the data and may even do some personal interpreting to reflect local conditions. In this activity, determine how successful he or she is at doing the job.

Procedure

1. Choose a weather forecaster on a local television station or in the newspaper.

2. Watch the nightly weather forecast each day for three days.

3. Each day, record *in your Journal* the weather prediction for the following day and then record the actual weather that develops.

Analysis

1. What weather observations and measurements seemed to be associated with certain weather patterns?

2. How accurate was the weather forecast each day? List predictions that were correct and those that were incorrect. Infer why the predictions might have been incorrect.

Observing Weather from the Ground

Objectives

- Measure and record weather data.
- Predict weather conditions based on observations and measurements.

Key Terms

relative humidity
dew point
barometric pressure

The Elements of Weather

What signals a change in the weather? Think about it. How do you tell when a storm is moving in? Does your hair droop or start to frizz? Do you feel a drop in temperature or a sudden shift in the wind? Does the sky suddenly fill with dark clouds? The activities in this section will show you how you may be able to depend on your own powers of observation and measurement skills to predict what the day-to-day weather in your area will be like.

■ What's the temperature outside?

One of the first things you probably notice when you step outside is how hot or cold it is. To describe the weather and predict changes, you need to accurately measure the air temperature.

When measuring air temperature, resting the thermometer on an object will simply result in measuring the temperature of the object rather than the air. And placing the thermometer in sunny spots will result in higher temperatures than if the thermometer were placed in shaded spots. For purposes of weather reporting and forecasting, air temperature must be measured under standard conditions. Thermometers used by weather forecasters are placed in shaded, well-ventilated places about 2 m above the ground.

B Meteorologists use thermometers protected from direct sunlight.

A A standard thermometer is a glass tube filled with liquid mercury or alcohol. When the temperature increases, the liquid expands more rapidly than the solid glass, so the level of the liquid rises in the tube.

Figure 1-1

Thermometers are used to measure temperature.

How does a thermometer measure temperature? It makes use of thermal expansion. Thermal expansion is the characteristic of matter that causes it to expand as its temperature increases. As the temperature increases, the liquid in the thermometer expands more than the glass, causing the level of the liquid to rise. You can see some thermometers in **Figure 1-1**.

■ How humid is it?

The amount of moisture in the air is called the humidity. Knowing the humidity outdoors can give you a clue about how comfortable the weather will be and whether your hair will droop or frizz.

You will determine the relative humidity of several areas in your school by doing the next activity.

MiniLab

How wet is the air?

By making and using a psychrometer and a special table of numbers, you can directly determine the relative humidity.

Procedure

1. Gather together the following materials: Celsius thermometer; cotton shoelace, gauze, or cotton; rubber band; container of water; small piece of cardboard to use as a fan.

2. Each lab group should pick a different area of the school to measure, for example, the library, the locker room, the cafeteria, the gym.

3. Hold the thermometer at shoulder height until it adjusts to the air temperature in your classroom. Record this temperature *in your Journal* and call it the *Dry Bulb Temperature.*

4. Slide a 1-cm length of the shoelace over the thermometer bulb and secure it with the rubber band. (Gauze or cotton could be attached to the bulb similarly.) Thoroughly wet the material with water at room temperature.

5. Holding the thermometer in one hand, use the cardboard fan to fan the bulb rapidly for about

1 minute. Be careful not to hit the thermometer. Record *in your Journal* the temperature on the thermometer as the *Wet Bulb Temperature.*

6. Subtract the wet bulb temperature from the dry bulb temperature and record the result *in your Journal* as the *Temperature Difference.*

7. Use the values from steps 3 and 6 and the relative humidity table in Appendix N to determine the relative humidity in your area.

Analysis

1. What is the relative humidity in your area today?

2. Would you expect the relative humidity to be higher in the locker room or the library? Why?

Connect to...

Biology

Many organisms that live in the Namib Desert depend on dew as their only source of water. Investigate where the moisture comes from and some of the ways various organisms collect the dew.

The relative humidity you measured in the MiniLab is one of the observations that helps describe weather conditions. But what is relative humidity? Air can hold only so much moisture at a given temperature, and warm air can hold more moisture than cold air. **Relative humidity** is a measure of the amount of water vapor in the air compared with the amount of water vapor the air can hold at that temperature. Relative humidity is always expressed as a percent and is calculated as follows:

$$\text{relative humidity} = \frac{\text{amount of water vapor in the air}}{\text{amount of water vapor the air can hold at that temperature}} \times 100\%$$

Before doing rigorous exercise, it is important to know the relative humidity. As your muscles contract, the heat they produce raises your body temperature. To keep your body from getting too hot, you sweat. Evaporation is a cooling process, so as the sweat evaporates, it takes heat from your skin and your skin cools. This system works well when the relative humidity is low, but what do you think happens when the relative humidity is high? The air is already nearly saturated with water vapor. It's like trying to sop up water with a sponge that's already soaked. That's what happens when you sweat at high humidity. The sweat evaporates at a much slower rate, so your skin cools less efficiently. To try to compensate, your body perspires more. There is no additional cooling, but your body loses large amounts of fluids. So when the relative humidity is high, it's a good idea to take it easy when you exercise and to drink plenty of water.

The time of year affects the amount of moisture in the air. The ability of warm air to hold more water vapor than cold air explains why the air is generally drier in the winter than in the summer. It also explains why doors tend to stick more in the summer.

■ What's that dew doing there?

Look at **Figure 1-2.** Have you ever accidentally left something outside overnight, only to find it damp with dew the next morning? Dew is the moisture that sometimes forms on grass, cars, and other surfaces at night. Why does dew form only on certain nights? The following activity will help you understand why.

Figure 1-2

As the ground loses heat at night and cools, it cools the air in contact with it. When air reaches its dew point, water vapor condenses into water droplets, condensing on spider webs and other objects.

Why does the grass get wet at night?

Cool air holds less water vapor than warm air. At night, temperatures usually cool down. Use these two facts in this activity to produce some dew of your own.

Procedure

1. Collect the following materials: steel or aluminum can with the top cut off, thermometer, glass stirring rod, crushed ice, water at room temperature.

2. Pour water into the can until it is half full. Gently lower the thermometer into the can and read the temperature. Do not let the thermometer rest on the bottom of the can. Record the temperature.

3. *Slowly* add crushed ice to the can and stir with the stirring rod. *Don't stir*

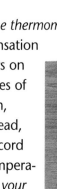

with the thermometer. When condensation appears on the sides of the can, stop, read, and record the temperature *in your Journal.*

Analysis

1. Where did the water on the outside of the can come from?

2. How does the addition of ice simulate the cooler air temperature at night?

3. Based on your findings, give an explanation for why grass becomes wet at night.

As you saw in the MiniLab, as the air cooled it could hold less moisture than warm air. For a given amount of moisture in the air, as the temperature decreases, the relative humidity increases. When air is cooled to the temperature at which it can hold no more water, the water vapor in the air condenses and dew forms. At this temperature, the **dew point** has been reached. You discovered the dew point of the air in your classroom when water drops condensed on the can in the last activity. For dew, frost, or fog to form, temperature needs to drop sufficiently. If you know the dew-point temperature, you can predict dew, frost, or fog.

■ The Highs and Lows of Barometric Pressure

Most outdoor plans are made with fair weather in mind—blue sky and sunshine. The best indicator of such weather is high barometric pressure. The **barometric pressure** is the measure of the pressure caused by the weight of the atmosphere. Air pressure exerted on you is caused by Earth's gravitational force pulling on the column of air above you. This column extends from wherever you are to the outer edge of the atmosphere.

At any one time, one area of the United States may be covered by high-pressure air while areas surrounding it are covered by low-pressure air masses. Because these masses of air are almost always moving, meteorologists measure the pressure changes in an area to make weather forecasts.

High pressure is usually associated with fair weather. Cooler, denser air aloft sinks and warms, and any clouds evaporate. If the barometric readings are high, you are probably experiencing blue skies and sunshine. On the other hand, low pressure is associated with gray, cloudy skies and sometimes precipitation. Less dense air is being pushed up from the surface until it cools to its dew point. The water vapor in the air then condenses and forms clouds. If the barometric readings are low, the weather has probably been overcast. **Figure 1-3** explains why this is so.

Figure 1-3

The vertical movement of air masses affects the weather.

A A mass of air with high pressure is dense and sinks toward Earth's surface. As it sinks, it warms up. Remember that warmer air can hold more moisture than cooler air. Therefore, because the amount of moisture in the air is constant, the relative humidity of the sinking, warming air decreases. The water droplets that were present in the air mass evaporate, and you get a beautiful day.

B A mass of air with low pressure has low density and rises. As it is pushed up, it cools. Remember that cooler air can hold less moisture than warmer air. Therefore, the relative humidity of the rising, cooling air increases. The air reaches its dew point, and the water vapor that was present in the air mass condenses, forming clouds. Not only do you get a gray day, you may get rain or snow.

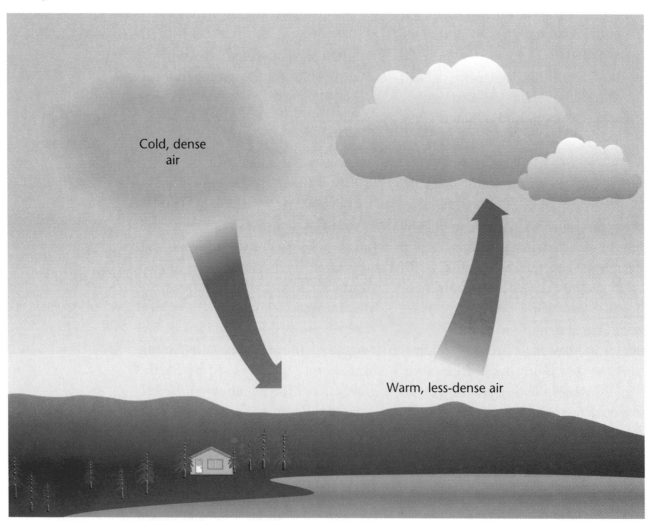

Cold, dense air

Warm, less-dense air

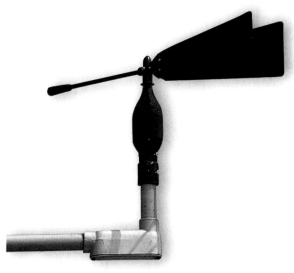

Figure 1-4

When fixed on a pole, a vane spins freely in the wind. As the tail end is caught by the wind, the arrow or head end points in the direction from which the wind is coming. Compass directions may be added to define the wind direction more precisely.

■ Describing the Wind

You can't directly sense atmospheric pressure in the same way you can sense temperature and humidity. But you *can* directly sense the result of changing air pressure. When molecules in an area of high pressure flow into an area of lower pressure, you feel the rush of molecules through your hair and against your skin as wind. The greater the difference in pressure, the faster the wind blows.

Winds are described by the direction from which they come and their speed. For example, southerly wind comes from the south. There are many ways to tell from which direction the wind is blowing. Have you ever tried dropping a few pieces of straw to see which way they blew? Another method uses a wind vane like that pictured in **Figure 1-4.**

Wind speed near the ground is measured by an anemometer, illustrated in **Figure 1-5.** Because winds are often changeable, speeds are recorded as the average over a five-minute period or a one-minute period, or as the shortest time it takes the air to move 1 mile. Anything lasting a shorter time is called a gust.

In most places on Earth, wind speeds average 5 to 15 knots. A knot, a unit used to measure wind speed, equals about 1.15 miles per hour. Friction, the force between two moving objects, plays a large role in slowing down wind. There is less friction over water, so winds blow faster over the oceans. Winds high off the ground are strong. In the high-altitude river of air called the jet stream, they may be greater than 250 knots.

Figure 1-5

An anemometer measures the speed of wind. The force of the rushing gas molecules in air causes the anemometer to rotate as the molecules collide with the cone-shaped cups. The faster the wind blows, the faster the cups rotate. Wind speed is measured by the number of rotations in a certain period of time.

To Find Out More About . . .

Air Pressure and Wind
read *The Weather Book* by Jack Williams, published by Vintage Books, 1992, pages 29-43.

Figure 1-6

Knowing what different kinds of clouds indicate helps us to predict what weather is headed our way.

Ⓐ As the storm approaches, a thin layer of cirrus clouds moves in.

■ Clouds

Clouds form when water vapor in the air reaches its dew point and condenses into water droplets. To most people, clouds are either shapes parading across the sky or nuisances that block the sunlight and bring rain and snow. To meteorologists, though, clouds are giant clues to what's happening in the sky. Clouds can also give us a hint of upcoming weather. **Figure 1-6** shows some typical cloud shapes and how they can be used to predict a storm.

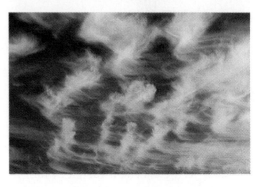

Ⓑ Cirrus clouds are delicate, fibrous clouds found in high, cold altitudes. They are carried by fast-moving winds. These clouds are often the first hint that a storm is on its way.

Microclimates

If you've ever had to cancel plans for a fun day because of an unexpected change in weather, someone has probably tried to console you by saying "You can't change the weather." Is this really true?

While you can't stop a thunderstorm, people can and do change the weather daily. This may seem like an outrageous claim, but the construction of a city can have a major impact on the local weather by creating what is known as a microclimate.

The Heat Is On

Microclimates are isolated areas where the weather is different in some way from the surrounding weather. Think about the last time you stood in the middle of a crowd of people. You probably felt that it was warmer there than near the edge of the crowd. Likewise, the center of a city is usually warmer than the surrounding suburbs or farmlands. These so-called *heat islands* are

E Altocumulus clouds are a cloud type that indicates a thunderstorm may be on its way. They are small, heaped-up clouds that are found at middle altitudes when warm air is pushed upward by approaching cold air.

C As the storm gets closer, a parade of thickening stratus (sheetlike) clouds passes. Altostratus clouds look like fibrous sheets. They are thin, and often the sun or moon can be seen through them. They usually appear after the higher, thin clouds just before a storm moves into the area.

D Nimbostratus clouds are the dark gray clouds you see when the storm has arrived. They are low clouds and bring with them snow or rain.

F Cumulonimbus clouds are large, tall clouds that are gray at the base and have a whiter, anvil-shaped top. These clouds bring heavy rain, snow or hail, and thunderstorms.

related to the solar energy that is absorbed and reradiated, heat produced by the area itself, and to the blanket of pollutants that often hovers over a city.

In the summer, the buildings, streets, and other concrete structures in a city absorb and store the large amounts of solar energy that reach Earth and, as a result, warm the overlying air. Even during the winter, the energy generated by human activities, such as heating buildings, warms the air above a city.

Pollutants from motor vehicles, factories, and other such sources also contribute to the microclimates associated with large cities. This blanket of particles and gases absorbs some of the sun's energy that's reflected from Earth's surface. This factor keeps the air above a city warmer than it would be if the air were clean.

Humidity

The amount of moisture in the air, or humidity, is another factor that is affected by the human activities in an urban area. The relative humidity in a city is generally lower than that in a rural area because of two factors. First, the heat islands created by cities lower the relative humidity of cities com-

pared to nearby undeveloped areas. Second, the lack of vegetation in cities when compared to rural areas results in lower amounts of moisture in urban air.

Thinking Critically

1. *Describe* a microclimate.
2. You have just learned that the formation of a heat island depends on many factors. Suggest a *hypothesis* that explains how wind and cloud cover affect the temperatures of a large city at night.

Forecasting

The elements of weather—temperature, humidity, barometric pressure, wind—are like the pieces of a jigsaw puzzle: Put them together, and you have a picture of the weather for the day. But as you saw in the chapter opener, knowing what the weather will be like tomorrow, the day after that, and even during next week is important, too.

The goal of most scientific undertakings is to be able to make accurate predictions. Weather science is no different. Knowing the elements of weather in your particular area, however, is often not enough to predict the weather, even in the short term. Weather changes because weather moves around the globe, so a good forecast requires data from other geographic areas as well. Examples of sources of data are shown in **Figure 1-7.** As you'll see in the next section, modern observational and measuring instruments give weather forecasters the information they need.

Figure 1-7

Three sources of weather data are weather buoys in the oceans (A), weather balloons in the upper atmosphere (B), and land weather stations (C).

check your UNDERSTANDING

Understanding Concepts

1. What information do you need in order to determine the dew point?
2. What type of weather does low barometric pressure bring?
3. A westerly wind is predicted. In which direction would a weather vane point?

Skill Review

4. **Thinking Critically** During what time of year is air generally moister? Why? For more help refer to Thinking Critically in the *Skill Handbook.*

Using Technology to Measure Weather

Observing Weather from Above

With practice, ground-based weather observations can be used to predict weather with fair accuracy. But to get even more accurate forecasts, you need a little more information from space. Weather systems are huge masses of air, sometimes hundreds of miles across. To get all the essential data for describing such a phenomenon, you must step back for a larger perspective. How do meteorologists step back from the ground? One way is by sending the latest technology into space to look back at Earth's surface and inner atmosphere.

You've no doubt seen pictures taken by artificial satellites orbiting thousands of miles above Earth's surface. A **geostationary satellite** is one that remains over the same spot on Earth.

From 35 000 km above Earth's surface, geostationary satellites scan disk-shaped sections of Earth and send pictures back every 30 minutes. These pictures are received at weather stations around the world. Information from these pictures is collated to help in making weather predictions.

■ What does the incoming information tell us?

Satellites provide us with overall views of entire weather systems. Satellite pictures indicate the extent of cloud cover and the location and size of storms. By combining reports from different satellites, such as the series shown in **Figure 1-8,** meteorologists can also predict the direction in which a system will move and its speed. Can you see how this information is important for storms in which people must take shelter or evacuate?

Objectives
- Explain how satellites provide weather data.
- Describe how radar provides weather data.
- Explain how Doppler radar works.

Key Terms
*geostationary
  satellite*
Doppler radar

Figure 1-8

Viewing a sequence of satellite pictures over a period of days reveals a moving picture of a storm's activity.

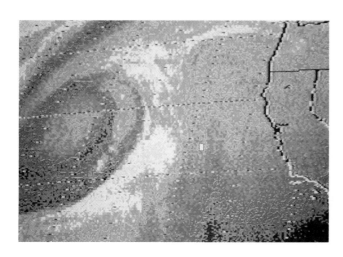

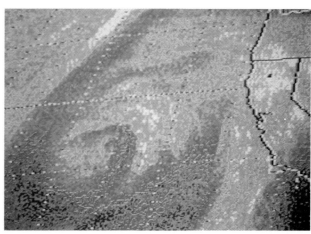

How does a weather satellite work?

Photographs are relayed every half-hour from weather satellites to receiving stations on Earth. During the day, light is provided by sunlight reflected from Earth and clouds. At night, the satellites sense infrared radiation. Warmer objects give off more infrared radiation than cooler objects.

Figure 1-9 shows how differences in radiation are used to produce a satellite picture of cloud cover and how a computer presents the information.

This capability of weather satellites is so refined that differences in ground and clouds and in land and water can be detected. Also differences in water temperature and types of land surfaces can be distinguished.

Figure 1-9
Satellites make use of temperature differences and the resulting differences in radiation from Earth and clouds to reveal where clouds are.

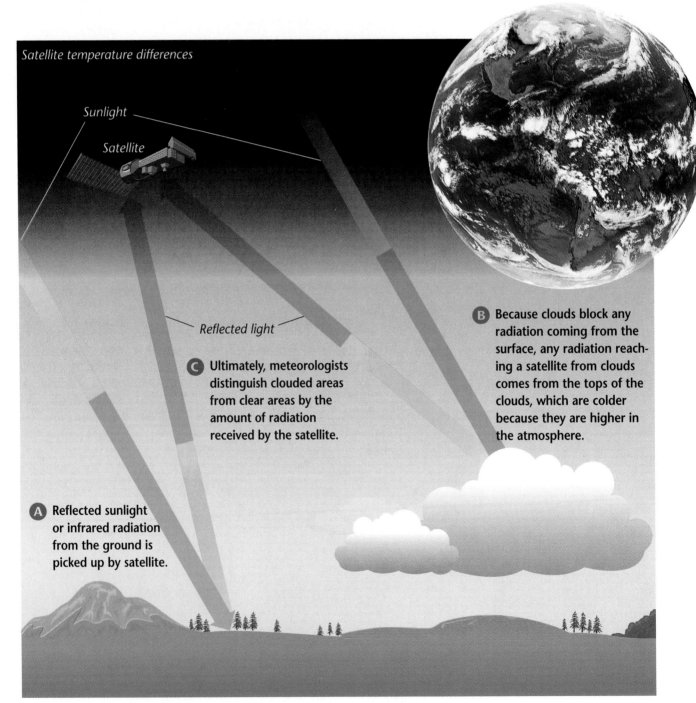

Satellite temperature differences

Sunlight

Satellite

Reflected light

C Ultimately, meteorologists distinguish clouded areas from clear areas by the amount of radiation received by the satellite.

B Because clouds block any radiation coming from the surface, any radiation reaching a satellite from clouds comes from the tops of the clouds, which are colder because they are higher in the atmosphere.

A Reflected sunlight or infrared radiation from the ground is picked up by satellite.

Using Radar to Observe Weather

Satellites are used by weather forecasters to determine where clouds are. Radar, on the other hand, is used to determine where clouds producing precipitation are. How does radar make this distinction?

When an object is hit by a radar beam of microwaves, it intercepts the beam and scatters it. A receiver picks up the returning beam, revealing the location of the object.

Radar sweeps horizontally, giving information on the location, intensity, and direction of a storm's movement. It can also sweep vertically, giving information on cloud height and the altitude at which snow and ice are melting. Why is this information important to know?

■ Doppler Radar

If you watched the local weather forecast in the chapter-opening Mini-Lab, you may have noted that the forecaster referred to Doppler radar. The **Doppler radar** system can detect wind velocities and clear air disturbances, not just precipitation. The next activity illustrates the main principle on which Doppler radar works.

MiniLab

Why does the sound of a moving object change as it passes you?

It's the Doppler effect! You'll need the following materials to demonstrate the Doppler effect: foam ball with small slit cut into it, small sound source (a smoke detector beeper works well), and a battery for the sound source.

Procedure

1. Connect the battery to the sound source so that sound is emitted.

2. Stuff the source into the slit in the foam ball.

3. Gently toss the ball around your classroom and note what happens to the noise.

Analysis

1. What is happening to the sound as the ball is tossed from one classmate to another?

2. How do you think the returning sound waves would change as the beeper moves toward you and then away from you?

Figure 1-10

The foam ball assembly demonstrates the Doppler effect.

A As the ball approaches, the sound waves from its beeper are squeezed together and produce higher-pitched sounds to an observer standing ahead of the ball. In fact, the faster the ball is moving, the higher the pitch.

B The opposite occurs as the ball moves past and farther from the observer. This Doppler effect characterizes sound and light waves.

■ How does the Doppler system work?

Did the sound in the activity become higher-pitched as its source approached you, then lower as it moved away? This change in pitch is due to a change in the sound waves. The wavelength of a sound becomes shorter as it approaches you and longer as it travels away. This wave phenomenon is illustrated in **Figure 1-10.** This apparent change in the pitch of the sound (or frequency of the wave) is called the Doppler effect, and can be used to determine whether objects are moving toward or away from us. How is it used in the Doppler radar system?

Just as with the conventional weather radar system, a Doppler radar signal is sent out, intercepted, and returned to the station. However, radio signals, as opposed to microwaves, are used, and the pitch or wavelength is received back differently. If it comes back with a higher pitch, meteorologists know the object that intercepted the signal is approaching. If the signal returns at a lower pitch, the object is moving away from the station.

The signals are then analyzed to determine the location, movement, and speed of the object, as illustrated in **Figure 1-11.** In the case of Doppler radar, the objects it locates are storms.

■ What are some capabilities of the system?

Doppler radar can detect anything from dust storms to hurricanes. It is able to bounce off raindrops up to 140 miles away from the detector. Because raindrops and snowflakes are carried by winds, Doppler radar can "see" into clouds to detect precipitation and give information about the winds there. It can indicate the direction of wind and storm movement and measure the speed of moving objects. This is an improvement to conventional radar, which indicates only movement.

However, if the wind is moving at right angles to the radar station, the wind shows up as having zero velocity. In this situation, the Doppler system could miss detecting a tornado in a squall line that is moving at right angles to the station. Therefore, more than one Doppler radar is used to complete the picture. **Figure 1-11** shows how Doppler radar images give information about the intensities and movements of storms.

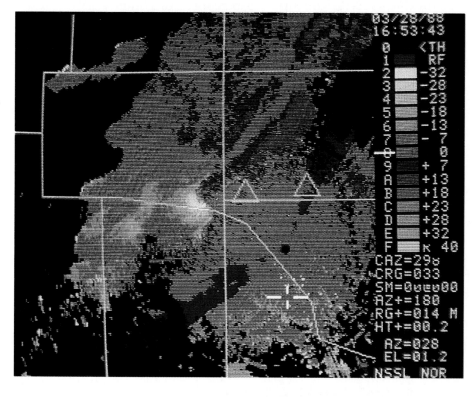

Figure 1-11

High-speed computers analyze the returning frequencies of the Doppler radar and translate the data into color patterns on display screens.

A Increasing degrees of red on the screen indicate increasing velocities from objects moving away from the station.

B Increasing intensities of green colors indicate objects moving with increasing velocities toward the station.

check your UNDERSTANDING

Understanding Concepts
1. What types of satellites are used for weather forecasting? Why are they called what they are?
2. How does a satellite photograph Earth at night?
3. What do radar units primarily detect?

Skill Review
4. **Comparing and Contrasting** How does Doppler radar differ from conventional radar? For more help refer to Comparing and Contrasting in the *Skill Handbook.*

Mapping and Using Weather Data

Objectives
- Interpret a weather map.
- Predict weather using a weather map.

Key Terms
station model
isobar

Weather Maps

Imagine you're a weather forecaster who has just received weather data for your area from satellites, Doppler radar, and ground instruments. What do you do with it all? How can you organize it so that it becomes useful? You could construct a weather map.

A road map can show you where you are and how to get where you're going. A weather map shows where weather systems are and where they are likely to go. Surface weather stations report temperature, dew point, barometric pressure, and wind speed and direction. The barometric pressure is adjusted to show what it would be if the station were at sea level. Stations may also report horizontal visibility if less than ten miles, type and amount of precipitation, and sky cover and types of clouds. Once data have been organized and placed on a weather map, the map can be used to show areas of high and low pressure and the location of fronts, and to predict the weather for the local area. In the following Thinking Lab, you will decide what data are necessary on a weather map to make predictions.

Thinking Lab   Evaluate the Relevance of Data

What information should be represented on a weather map?

Weather data are gathered from ground and aerial instruments. Yet in order for the data to be useful to forecasters, the information needs to be organized and mapped.

Analysis
Think of all the elements of weather you have studied and know about. Think of both the elements that help describe present weather and the factors that determine where weather might move next.

Thinking Critically
Which weather data must be represented on a weather map in order for the map to be useful in predicting the weather? Could any data be left off of a weather map?

Even though you may have decided that some weather data may be left off a map, the information essential for accurate forecasting is still substantial. To present the information in a concise way—small enough to be put on a map—forecasters use symbols to represent weather elements. You can see these symbols in Appendix M on page 812. You can also see that the weather elements you learned about in the first two sections of this chapter are included in the symbols, along with other weather factors. These symbols are the same for any weather map, anywhere in the world.

■ Mapping the World's Weather

Every six hours, stations all over the world measure local weather conditions. The data are translated into an international code and sent to central collection centers all over the world. These worldwide centers then exchange the information with one another.

Meteorologists at each center prepare weather maps from the data using the international symbols in Appendix M. Each set of data describes the weather at one of the reporting stations and becomes a cluster of symbols around that station's location on the map. This cluster is referred to as a **station model,** which you can see close up in **Figure 1-12.** Use Appendix M to help you read the symbols. Station models on maps are revised as new data are received.

Figure 1-12

The photograph shows the weather in New York one day. The station model below shows that same weather represented by symbols. Translate the information given in the station model using Appendix M and relate it to the photograph.

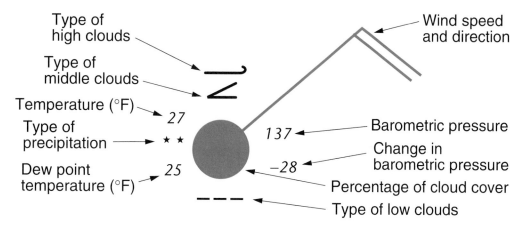

Type of high clouds

Type of middle clouds

Temperature (°F)

Type of precipitation

Dew point temperature (°F)

Wind speed and direction

Barometric pressure

Change in barometric pressure

Percentage of cloud cover

Type of low clouds

27

★ ★

25

137

−28

In addition, lines called **isobars** are drawn to connect areas of equal atmospheric pressure as determined from the station models. The prefix *iso* means "same" and the root *bar* indicates pressure. You can see these isobars, along with station models, on the weather map in **Figure 1-13.**

Meteorologists study isobars to determine wind direction and speed. Because wind flows from areas of high pressure to areas of low pressure, you can use isobars to show what the wind will do. The wind will flow from one isobar to the one closest to it. The closer together the isobars, the greater the pressure difference between two air masses and the faster the wind will blow.

The construction of isobars gives meteorologists other important information. Isobars show the location of high-pressure and low-pressure areas. From this information, plus the change in wind direction shown in the station models, meteorologists can determine the location of fronts.

Figure 1-13

A surface weather map of the United States.

A Fronts occur where one air mass meets another. The side of the line on which the identifying warm symbols (semicircles) or cold symbols (triangles) appear shows the direction in which the front is moving. Stationary fronts are stalled fronts. Precipitation often occurs at fronts.

B An isobar marks off areas with the same atmospheric pressure.

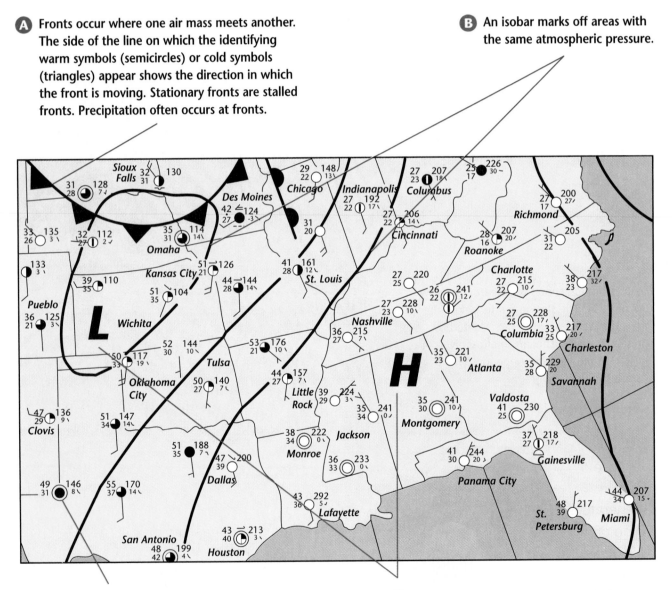

C A station model gives relevant weather data for a specific location.

D H marks the center of an area of high atmospheric pressure; L, an area of low pressure.

■ How to Read a Weather Map

Once weather data are collected and translated into station models and isobars on a weather map, you can tell what the weather is like at any spot on the map. The following activity will give you a chance to do that using the weather map in **Figure 1-13.**

What is the weather like around the country?

Meteorologists use a series of symbols to provide a picture of local and national weather conditions. You've learned about station models, isobars, and pressure systems. Now you will interpret weather information from a weather map.

Procedure

1. Use the information in Appendix M and **Figure 1-13** captions to study the weather map in **Figure 1-13.**

2. Locate the city of Gainesville, Florida, on the map. Find the temperature, dew point, barometric pressure, wind speed, and wind direction there.

3. Determine what kind of front is over the state of Illinois and in which direction the front is moving.

Analysis

1. What is the weather like in the city of Gainesville? Be as detailed as possible.

2. What kind of front is over the state of Illinois? In which direction is it moving?

3. What parts of the country are generally having fair weather?

■ Forecasting Weather from a Map

In the last activity, you were able to describe and report weather conditions using a weather map. But predicting the weather is more useful to most people. And earlier in this chapter, you learned that local ground-based weather observations are generally not enough to make a prediction. However, with a surface weather map in hand, you're better able to accurately predict the weather, and produce a forecast map like the one in **Figure 1-14,** just as your local TV weatherperson does. The next activity will give you a chance to use what you have learned to forecast the weather.

Figure 1-14

Meteorologists use maps of current conditions to make maps like this one showing predicted weather in newspapers and on television.

Can you predict the weather?

Forecasting the weather accurately depends on careful measurement and mapping of weather conditions over a large geographic area. It also demands an understanding of the movement of fronts. Because of Earth's rotation, winds are deflected eastward in the United States. Therefore, weather systems here move in a general west-to-east path.

Preparation

Problem

What will the weather be like in your community tomorrow? What about the day after tomorrow? Obtain a weather map from a local weather station, a local television station, or a newspaper, or make your own observations.

Hypothesis

Study the weather map or your observations. Then decide on a weather prediction for tomorrow. Be as specific as possible, including details on as many weather elements as possible. Do the same for the day after tomorrow.

Objectives

In this Investigation, you will:
- *Analyze* data on a weather map.
- *Predict* the weather.

Possible Materials

weather map for today
weather maps or reports for next two
    days, or measuring instruments:
    thermometer
    barometer
    anemometer
    vane
    rain gauge
    data table

Plan the Experiment

1 Decide on a way to test your prediction. Will you actually observe and measure the relevant weather conditions for the next two days? Or will you rely on the local television or newspaper weather report?

2 Record your predictions *in your Journal.* Prepare a table for each day in which you record the predicted temperature, wind speed and direction, cloud cover, possibility and kind of precipitation, and presence of high or low pressure. Add a second column in each table in which you can record the actual conditions as you measure them or get them from each day's weather report.

Check the Plan
Discuss the following points with other group members to decide the final procedure for your experiment.

1 Who will be responsible for measuring or obtaining the data about each of the weather elements over the next two days?

2 How will you summarize how accurate your predictions were?

3 *Make sure your teacher has approved your experimental plan before you proceed further.*

4 Carry out your plan.

Analyze and Conclude

1. **Checking Your Hypothesis** How accurate was your overall prediction for the following day? For the day after that?

2. **Comparing and Contrasting** For which weather elements were your predictions the most accurate? The most inaccurate?

3. **Evaluating** Were some data more useful in predicting the weather than others? If so, which?

Going Further

Application
Do library research to find out how meteorologists make long-range forecasts for the next month and even the next year.

Science and Society

Issue: Lorenz's Butterfly

One evening in 1961, Edward Lorenz, a meteorologist at the Massachusetts Institute of Technology, was trying to figure out why long-range weather forecasts were so often wrong. These forecasts are important to many people. Perhaps, thought Lorenz, if we just knew a few more facts, the accuracy of these long-range weather forecasts could be improved.

The Issue

We know that many events in the universe can be described by mathematical equations, and weather is no exception. Lorenz was playing around on his computer with a set of equations that describe weather patterns.

The Background

Computers in 1961 were rather slow, and Lorenz decided he would take a shortcut to speed things up a bit. One of the numbers he was working with was 0.506127, so Lorenz lopped off the last three digits and typed 0.506 instead. He thought that such a small change wouldn't make much of a difference, and he wouldn't have to wait so long for the computer to make its calculations. Lorenz ran the program, and found that the small change he had made in the number had made a big difference in the results.

What Lorenz had discovered was that the equations that describe the weather are extremely sensitive to initial conditions. Small changes in the initial conditions become greatly amplified over time and can completely alter the final result. For example, if you start out using a certain value for wind velocity, the equations might predict clear skies for next week, while if you change the value for wind velocity only slightly, the forecast may be for rain. Lorenz called this the "butterfly effect" because the equations showed that the weather was so sensitive that the tiny breeze from a butterfly's wings one day might change the weather three or four days later from a sunny day into a thunderstorm.

No wonder long-range weather forecasts were wrong so often! In fact, Lorenz came to the conclusion that making accurate long-range predictions about the weather, and maybe a lot of other things, was impossible.

The Question

Many scientists thought that if they could discover enough facts about a system, they would be able to predict exactly what would happen in the future. But here was evidence that sometimes predicting the future is impossible, no matter how many facts we know.

GRAPHING CALCULATOR

To show the effect a small change can make, use a graphing calculator to graph $Y = 0.506127 \times X$ and $Y = 0.506 \times X$. Use a large range, such as $-10\,000$ to $10\,000$, for both X and Y. Can you see any differenecs in the graphs of the lines? For each line, use the trace function to find the Y value that corresponds to an X value of about 6000. Do the Y values differ?

The Importance of Forecasting Weather

As you may have discovered in the Investigation, predicting weather is not always easy to do. That's why meteorologists collect as much information as possible and continue to study weather patterns. Many people depend on accurate weather forecasts. Airplane pilots need to know how storms in their area are moving, as seen on the cockpit radar in **Figure 1-15.** Construction workers need to know if the weather will be warm or cold so they can pour concrete. Farmers need to know when the danger of frost has passed in the spring before they plant crops.

Weather forecasting plays a critical role in saving lives. Predicting severe weather in time for people to prepare depends on the science and latest technology of weather forecasting. A misjudgment in the prediction of a storm can be a matter of life and death. In the next chapter, explore severe weather and how storms are formed.

Figure 1-15

Many airplanes have weather radar in their cockpits. Farmers need to schedule planting and harvesting around the possibility of storms.

check your UNDERSTANDING

Understanding Concepts

1. What types of weather information does a weather map show?
2. What does an isobar designate on a weather map?
3. Where do meteorologists get their weather information?

Skill Review

4. **Representing Data** Draw a station model for the following conditions: sky 0.1 covered, SW wind at 10 knots, dew point 10°C, barometric pressure 1089.8 mb, rising 10 millibars in the last 3 hr., fair weather cumulus and scattered cirrus clouds, and temperature 25°C. For more help, refer to Representing Data in the *Skill Handbook*.

Art Connection

Wind Vanes as Folk Art

The wind vane is one of the oldest instruments used to predict weather. In the 1800s, farmers built these devices to help determine wind direction. Wind vanes usually have two parts: a piece shaped like an arrow that points into the wind, and a plate below the arrow marking the direction from which the wind is blowing. The earliest vanes were wooden and made by hand. As the demand for wind vanes as decoration grew, though, these weather devices were often forged from iron in factories.

Practical and Pretty

In addition to serving as weather instruments, wind vanes often were used to advertise the purpose of the building on top of which they were set. So, a wind vane in the form of a cow might indicate a dairy farm, while a vane in the form of a ram would signal a wool factory. Church steeples usually had vanes in the form of an angel. Makers of weather vanes became less concerned with how well a vane could predict wind direction and more concerned with how beautiful and pleasing to the eye these objects were.

Collector's Items

By the early 1900s in America, wind vanes became more folk art than weather tools. Because hand-crafted vanes

were being replaced by mass-produced vanes, many people tried to collect the hand-crafted vanes as a means of preserving the past. Also, these earliest wind vanes preserved the great artistry of the people who made them. Today, wind vanes are seldom seen on buildings to mark wind direction.

interNET CONNECTION

Visit the Glencoe Homepage, **http://www.glencoe.com/**, for the Chapter 1 link to the Digital Library of the Earthlab Project, for information about weather instruments and weather forecasting. Research two weather instruments, and then draw a diagram to illustrate how the instruments work.

Read the statements below that review major points presented in the chapter. Using the concepts that you have learned, answer each question *in your Journal.*

1 Many observations can be used to predict weather, such as temperature, air pressure, relative humidity, wind speed and direction, and cloud types. *What air-pressure data would you expect on a sunny day?*

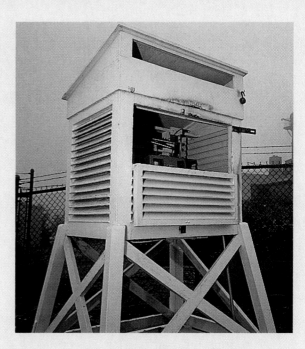

2 Technology such as radar and satellites improves our ability to accurately predict weather. *What information can you get from Doppler radar?*

3 Weather maps organize weather data so that it can be used to predict weather. *What information can be found on a weather map?*

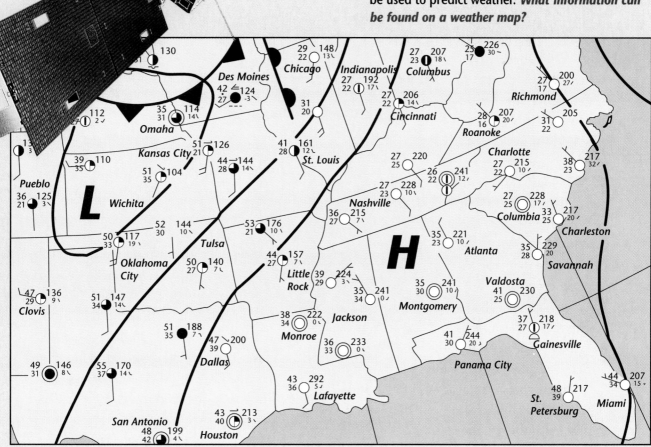

chapter 1
CHAPTER REVIEW

Using Key Science Terms

barometric pressure   isobar
dew point   relative humidity
Doppler radar   station model
geostationary
   satellite

Relate one of the terms from the list above to each concept below.

1. approaching or retreating storm systems
2. water vapor in the air
3. isobars on weather maps
4. weather satellites
5. moisture forms on cool surfaces
6. international weather reporting

Understanding Ideas

Using complete sentences, answer the following questions in your Journal.

1. Why does the level of mercury rise or fall in a thermometer?
2. In measuring air temperature, why should a thermometer be raised approximately 2 m above the ground?
3. Why does rising air usually mean cloudy weather?
4. What happens at the dew point?
5. Why is wind speed faster over water?
6. What are the light sources for satellite photography?
7. What happens when a radar beam hits an object?
8. What is different about the signal that returns from Doppler radar?
9. What are the advantages of Doppler radar?
10. How can a current weather map be used to predict future weather?

Developing Skills

Use your understanding of the concepts developed in this chapter to answer each of the following questions.

1. **Concept Mapping** Create an events chain concept map showing the operation of a weather satellite. Use the following phrases: *scattered beam returned to satellite; beam hits object; coded information sent to weather station; beam scattered.*

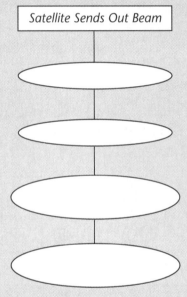

Satellite Sends Out Beam

2. **Hypothesizing** Review the Investigation on predicting the weather. What would the relative humidity value be if the temperature and dew point were the same? What weather condition would you expect?
3. **Organizing Data** Make a station model for the following data: sky overcast, SE wind at 20 knots, dew point 62°F, moderate rain, barometric pressure 969.5 mb, falling 12 millibars in the last 3 hr., temperature 72°F, and fractostratus clouds.
4. **Comparing and Contrasting** What are the benefits of a published weather map versus a recorded telephone weather report?

Critical Thinking

In your Journal, *answer each of the following questions.*

1. Why is it important to know the direction from which the wind is coming?
2. Where would wind speeds possibly be greater—across a large parking lot or across a park with trees and playground equipment? Why?
3. Why are weather satellites geostationary?
4. Conventional radar can detect the movement of storms, but Doppler radar can tell the speed of the storm as well. Why is Doppler radar's ability to detect speed an improvement over conventional radar?

Problem Solving

Read the following problem and discuss your answers in a brief paragraph.

A severe storm has been reported just 100 km from your weather station. Your Doppler radar screen picks up the storm. It appears as bright red areas. Some visitors to the station ask if you are going to recommend evacuating the area. You tell them what you will do and explain your actions by answering the following questions.

With reference to your station, in which general direction is the storm moving? How do you know?

CONNECTING IDEAS

1. **Theme—Systems and Interactions** For the same amount of moisture, how does temperature influence relative humidity?
2. **Theme—Energy** How is weather related to solar energy?

3. **Theme—Scale and Structure** What weather observations would you expect to record as a storm moves into your area?
4. **In-Depth Look** How do automobiles contribute to the formation of a micro-climate?

5. **Science and Society** Why did Lorenz call the phenomenon he observed the butterfly effect?

Severe Weather
The Storm Center

To say that dark clouds, howling winds, and torrential rain are nothing more than the products of warm air and water seems far-fetched. Yet the warm, moist air that swirls around you as you take a hot shower is the same substance that supplies the energy that powers a hurricane.

The source of energy that heats the water in the warm springs and geysers in Yellowstone National Park is the molten material beneath Earth's crust. Can you guess what might be the energy source that warms Earth's surroundings enough to cause violent storms?

▶ ***In the activity on the next page, you will explore how the sun warms the air over different surfaces.***

50

How does sunshine affect air?

Does air warm differently over land and water? Find out in this activity.

Procedure

1. Obtain two 1-L clear, plastic bottles; 2 pieces of modeling clay; 2 pieces of aluminum foil, and 2 thermometers.

2. Half-fill one bottle with room-temperature water.

3. Cover the top half of each bottle with aluminum foil.

4. Punch a hole in the foil covering the mouth of each bottle and insert a thermometer 2 cm. Hold the thermometer in place with modeling clay.

5. Place both bottles in direct sunlight.

6. Measure and record *in your Journal* the temperature of the air in the bottles every two minutes for 16 minutes.

Analysis

1. Compare the rates at which the air in the bottles warmed.

2. How can you account for any differences?

2-1 Moving Air

Objectives

- Explain how energy is moved through the atmosphere.
- Explain how solar energy causes the formation of global winds.
- Describe the circulation patterns of global winds.

Key Terms

weather
heat
conduction
radiation
convection
convection cell
evaporation
Coriolis effect

Figure 2-1

In this model of a solid, the particles are connected by a network of imaginary springs. The springs allow each particle to vibrate in three dimensions. The temperature of a solid material is a measure of the average kinetic energy of the vibrating particles. As the energy of the particles increases and they vibrate faster, the temperature of the solid increases.

The Sun and Weather

It's nice to see the sun after the dark clouds of a storm have passed. You might say that the sun brings fair weather. Unfortunately, that statement diminishes the role that the sun plays in weather. It is better to say that the sun brings all weather—both fair and foul.

Weather is the condition of Earth's atmosphere at any particular place and time. There are many kinds of weather, some seemingly unrelated to others. You might think that the conditions of the atmosphere on a cool, crisp day, a hot, humid night, and during a thunderstorm have nothing in common. However, they do. These conditions are the result of solar energy reaching Earth.

■ The Sun's Energy and Earth: Conduction

If you have ever tried a barefooted dash across the sands of a sunny beach, you felt one effect of the sun's energy. The sun's energy makes things hot! You sensed the hotness of the sand when energy from the sand was transferred to the cooler soles of your feet. The total thermal energy transferred from an object at a higher temperature to an object at a lower temperature is called **heat.**

In each step of your dash, heat was transferred to the sole of your foot as it touched the sand. The transfer of heat between objects that are in contact is called **conduction.** Your feet became hot by conduction.

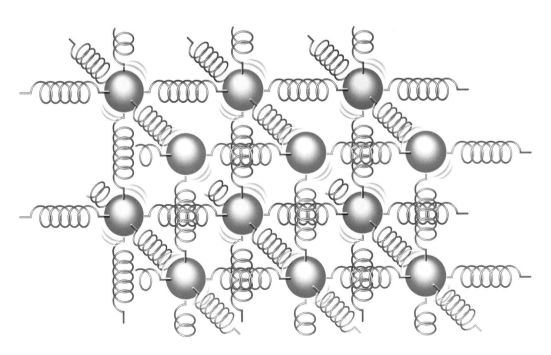

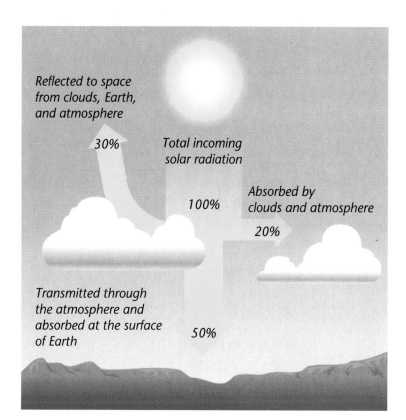

Figure 2-2

The atmosphere modifies the amount of solar radiation reaching Earth's surface through absorption and reflection. Solar radiation is made up of electromagnetic waves. These energy-carrying waves radiate in all directions from the sun, varying in wavelength from long radio waves to very short X rays and gamma rays. Solar radiation reaching the ground contains only 1 percent of wavelengths shorter than visible light and contains no X rays or gamma rays.

You can understand heat transfer by conduction if you recall that matter is made up of particles that are in constant motion. In solid materials, such as skin and sand, the particles vibrate around fixed positions within the structure of the material. **Figure 2-1** shows how you can picture the particles as if connected to each other by springs.

When a cooler material, such as the skin on the sole of your foot, is brought in contact with a warmer solid material, such as sand on a beach, the more violently vibrating particles of the hot sand bump against the particles that make up your skin. The motion of the particles in your skin increases as energy is transferred to them from the vibrating particles in the warmer sand. The transfer of energy results in increased motion of the particles in your skin that is measured as an increase in its temperature as it stimulates receptors in your skin.

■ Radiation

You can explain the heating and cooling of your feet by conduction. However, you can't use conduction to explain how the sand got hot to begin with because the sun and sand aren't in contact with each other. As you know, the sun isn't even close to Earth's atmosphere. Millions of kilometers of almost-empty space separate the sun and Earth. The warming of Earth by the sun is explained by another type of heat transfer called radiation. **Radiation** is the transfer of energy in the form of electromagnetic waves. As you can see from **Figure 2-2,** only half of the solar radiation reaching Earth's atmosphere is eventually absorbed by Earth's surface. As materials such as sand absorb the electromagnetic waves that reach the surface, the materials warm.

In the following Investigation, you will observe how substances in the atmosphere affect the amount of radiation that reaches Earth's surface.

What affects solar radiation on Earth?

Weather runs on energy from the sun. This energy must reach Earth's surface, where it heats and evaporates water. Both dust and water in the form of clouds affect the amount of solar energy reaching the surface. In this activity, you will design and carry out an investigation about the effect of dust and water droplets on energy reaching Earth's surface.

Preparation

Problem
How do dust and water droplets in the atmosphere affect the amount of solar energy that reaches Earth's surface?

Hypothesis
Work with your group to form a hypothesis to be tested. Record the hypothesis.

Objectives
- Experimentally *verify* how dust and water droplets affect the amount of solar energy that reaches Earth's surface.

Possible Materials
thermometers
transparent plastic wrap
tape
water
spray bottle
dust sources such as talcum powder
shoe boxes or similar-sized boxes

Safety Precautions

Treat thermometers gently. If a thermometer breaks, beware of broken glass. Notify your teacher at once.

Plan the Experiment

1 Examine the materials provided by your teacher. As a group, make a list of the possible ways you might test your hypothesis.

2 Agree on one way your group could investigate your hypothesis. Design an experiment that allows for the collection of quantitative data.

3 Write out the steps you will follow in your experiment. What do you think will happen if you add water droplets or dust to the atmosphere? Do not forget standard scientific practices such as controls and repeated trials.

4 Design and construct a table *in your Journal* for recording your data.

Check the Plan

Discuss the following points with other group members to decide the final procedure for your experiment.

1 Determine how you could use the boxes. Explain how your experiment will model the real world and what effects you expect to see.

2 Where would be the best place to locate the thermometer to obtain the most accurate reading?

3 *Make sure your teacher has approved your experimental plan before you proceed further.*

4 Carry out your experiment.

5 Decide how to present your data.

Analyze and Conclude

1. **Measuring in SI** How did you determine the effect of dust and water on solar heating of the atmosphere?

2. **Comparing and Contrasting** If you used a shoe-box model setup, which setup showed the greatest variation in temperature? What was the significance of this?

3. **Drawing Conclusions** As a meteorologist, how would you use the results of your experiment to help make weather predictions?

4. **Analyzing the Procedure** Does your experiment accurately model the real world? Why or why not? What could you do to improve the experiment?

Going Further

The amount of dust in the upper atmosphere varies over time. Name several natural processes that might introduce dust into the upper atmosphere. Which do you think might have the greatest effect?

Convection

Particles in the atmosphere affect the amount of radiation that reaches Earth's surface. Once the radiation is absorbed by the surface, part of it is transferred by conduction back to the air in contact with it. The remainder is transferred to the atmosphere and the space beyond by radiation. However, little heat is transferred from one part of the atmosphere to another by conduction because the rapidly moving molecules of the gases that make up the atmosphere aren't in contact long enough for much heat transfer to take place.

Gases and liquids are called fluids because they flow. Heat transfer in fluids such as air and water occurs mostly by convection. **Convection** is the transfer of heat within a fluid by movement of the fluid from warmer areas to cooler areas. Warm water rises in a beaker heated from below, much like warm air rises over a campfire. Both occur because the heated fluid becomes less dense and is pushed upward by the cooler surrounding fluid, whose density hasn't changed. The constant replacement of the warmer fluid by cooler fluid that moves in beneath it maintains a flow of warmer fluid upward, as shown in **Figure 2-3.** How does such a flow take place?

MiniLab

How does convection occur in a fluid?

Convection transfers heat by the flow within a heated fluid. How can you account for the flow?

Procedure

1. Fill two small beakers with hot water and two with ice water.

2. Pour hot water into a large beaker until it is about half-full, and pour cold water into another large beaker until it is about half-full.

3. Mix a few drops of red food coloring into the two small beakers of hot water. Mix a few drops of blue food coloring into the two small beakers of ice water.

4. Using a dropper, carefully add two drops of red-tinted water from one of the small beakers to a small beaker of blue-tinted water. Observe the red-tinted drops.

5. Set the two beakers aside.

6. Using another dropper, carefully add two drops of blue-tinted water from the other small beaker to the beaker of red-tinted water. Observe the blue-tinted drops.

7. Carefully pour the small beaker of red-tinted water into the large beaker of hot water. Observe the contents of the large beaker.

8. Repeat step 7 using the small and large beakers of cold water.

Analysis

1. Explain your observations of steps 4 and 6.

2. Predict the direction of the flow of warmer water in a beaker of cold water if the beaker were being heated from below.

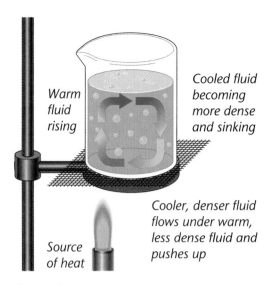

Figure 2-3

Warming part of a fluid reduces its density, and it begins to rise, buoyed upward by the surrounding cooler fluid, whose density has not changed. If the quantity of fluid is large, a convection current will form in which the fluid warms and rises and then cools and sinks.

The region of a fluid in which a convection current, such as the one shown in **Figure 2-3,** is maintained is called a **convection cell.** The water in the beaker and the air above a campfire are examples of convection cells. As you will see, other examples of convection cells are nearly global in size.

Global Heating

Half of the solar radiation that strikes Earth is absorbed at its surface. This amount of heat is then transferred by conduction and radiation to the atmosphere. As you can see in **Figure 2-4,** the solar radiation and Earth's radiation are not balanced over much of the globe.

A much greater amount of radiation reaches Earth's surface at the equator, 0°, than at the north and south poles, 90° north and south. Even more important, the graph shows that between approximately 40° and 90° in both hemispheres, the amount of energy radiated *from* Earth's surface exceeds the amount radiated *to* Earth from the sun. Between 40° and the equator, the radiation *to* Earth's surface is greater than the energy radiated *from* the surface. Why don't the equatorial regions grow continually warmer, and the poles become more and more frigid? To answer this question, look at the interplay between solar radiation and Earth's oceans at the equator.

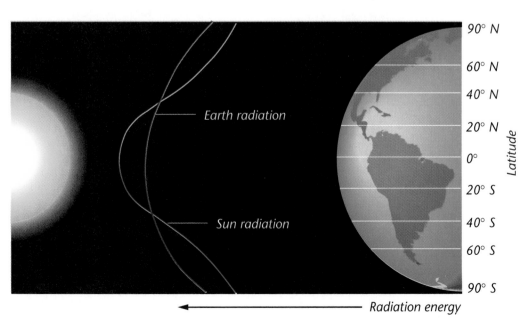

Figure 2-4

The orientation of Earth and the sun causes the amount of solar radiation reaching Earth's surface to decrease toward the poles.

■ Evaporation and Oceans

Solar radiation striking Earth's oceans not only heats the water, it also causes a great amount of evaporation. **Evaporation** is the change of a liquid into a gas. When molecules of a liquid evaporate, they absorb energy from their surroundings because work has to be done against the forces of attraction that hold the molecules together as a liquid. As a result, a molecule of gaseous water has more energy than a molecule of liquid water at the same temperature.

Water in the form of a gas is called *water vapor.* Air that contains water vapor is often called *moist air. Moist air* sounds like it should be dense because water is dense. But as you can see in **Figure 2-5,** moist air is less dense than dry air at the same temperature.

■ A Rising Bubble of Air

When a bubble of air warms and absorbs moisture, its density decreases and it rises, pushed upward by the surrounding cooler air rushing in to take its place. The air expands as it rises because air pressure decreases with elevation. As the bubble of air expands, it cools. If you have ever used a can of aerosol spray paint, you may have felt the cooling of the can as the gas escaped the nozzle. As the gas escaped from the can, it expanded, pushing outward on the can, and requiring the gas to do work. Doing work requires energy. The can and its contents transferred energy to the expanding gas, causing the temperature of the can and its contents to fall.

Apply this experience to the rising bubble of warm air. As it rises, there is

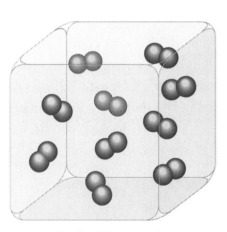

Total = 288 mass units

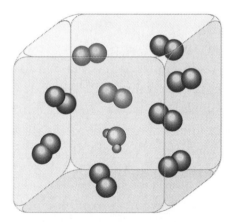

A water molecule replaces a nitrogen molecule.
Total = 278 mass units

Figure 2-5

In a fixed volume of air, the number of molecules is constant at any given temperature and pressure. If a water molecule replaces a nitrogen or oxygen molecule in the air, the mass of that volume of air will decrease. As a result, air containing water vapor is less dense than dry air under similar conditions.

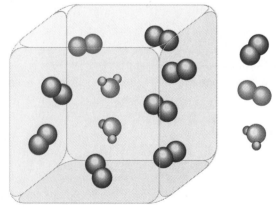

A water molecule replaces an oxygen molecule.
Total = 264 mass units

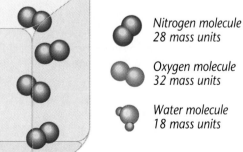

Nitrogen molecule
28 mass units

Oxygen molecule
32 mass units

Water molecule
18 mass units

no energy transfer from the outside air into the bubble because the bubble is at the same or a slightly higher temperature than its surroundings. So, the energy to do the work must come from the bubble of air itself, causing it to cool. The bubble of air cools to its dew point, and the water vapor it contains condenses into liquid water in the form of tiny droplets. The energy absorbed by the molecules of water when they evaporated from the ocean is now released. The energy released raises the temperature of the bubble of air, so it continues to be buoyed upward, sometimes to altitudes of 25 km.

Global Winds

Once the rising air reaches its maximum height, it cools and becomes too dense to stay aloft. It moves outward and sinks to the surface again. This sets up a convection cell just like the small ones described on page 57. You can see how global convection cells are formed in **Figure 2-6.**

Figure 2-6

The heating and cooling of air causes global convection cells.

A Convection cells are formed in the polar regions. Dense, frigid air at the poles sinks and moves toward the equator along the surface, warming as it moves south. At about 60°N and 60°S latitudes, this polar air meets the air moving poleward from the equator and rises. Some of the rising air flows back toward the poles, completing a polar convection cell.

B Warm air rising at the equator moves northward and southward, cooling as it moves. Eventually, the density of the air causes it to fall toward Earth at latitudes of 30°N and 30°S. Some of the air returns to the equator, completing the convection cell. Some of the air continues to move poleward at the surface, warmed by contact with the ground.

C Part of the air flows back toward the equator, cooling and sinking at latitudes of about 30°N and 30°S, completing midlatitude convection cells.

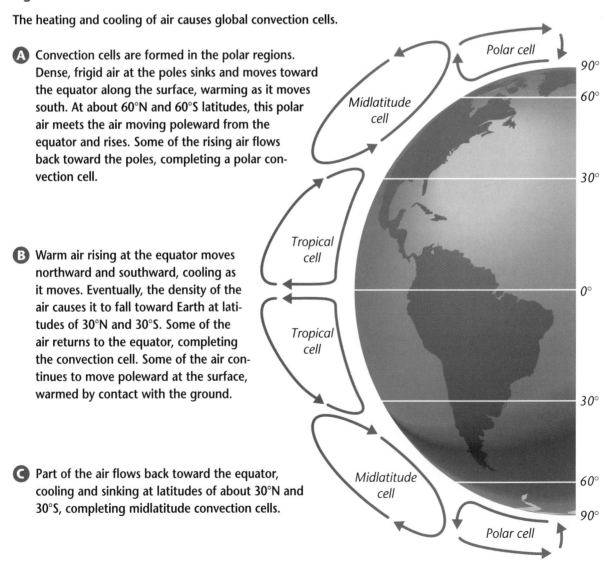

To Find Out More About . . .

The Coriolis Effect
read "The Coriolis Force," by Neil de Grassi Tyson, in *Natural History,* Vol. 104, number 3, March 1995, page 76.

As shown in **Figure 2-6,** the global movements of air, which are called global winds, should be either northward or southward. As you can see in **Figure 2-7,** however, global winds don't move like this. How can the deflection of the global winds from their northward and southward treks be explained?

■ Coriolis Effect

The turning motions of the global winds are examples of the Coriolis effect. The **Coriolis effect** is the deflection of a moving object from its original position as seen by observers on Earth's surface. To understand the Coriolis effect, you have to think about the fact that observers who are standing on Earth's surface are moving along with Earth as it rotates. Not only are these observers moving, but they are also

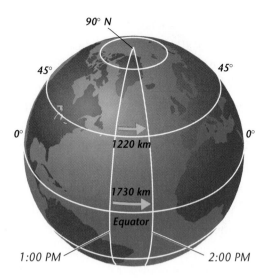

Figure 2-8

In one hour, a person standing on the equator has moved eastward 1730 km. In the same amount of time, a person standing at a latitude of 45°N has traveled only 1220 km. Where would a person move at the slowest speed?

moving at different speeds depending on their latitude. You can see a comparison of their speeds in **Figure 2-8.**

To see what might happen to the path of a moving object, suppose that a person at the equator throws a ball northward hard enough for it to land at a latitude of 45°N one hour later. Where will the ball land? To answer this question, you have to recall that objects have the property of inertia. Inertia is the tendency of an object at rest to stay at rest and an object in motion to continue moving at the same speed and in the same direction. So a ball at the equator will be moving eastward at a speed of 1730 km/hr. With inertia in mind, you can see where the ball thrown northward will land by looking at **Figure 2-9.**

Both observers would say that the ball's path wasn't straight but veered to the east as the ball moved northward. This apparent deflection is an example

Figure 2-7

Global winds don't blow directly north or south because of the Coriolis effect.

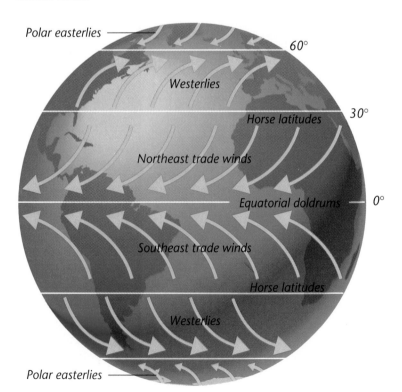

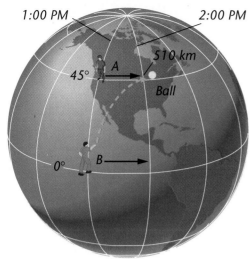

Figure 2-9

In the hour that the ball is in flight, the horizontal speed of the ball thrown at A is greater than that of the observer at B. The ball falls 510 km east of the observer.

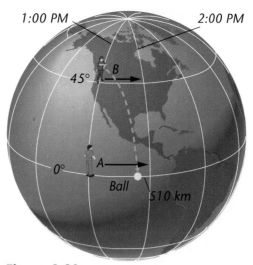

Figure 2-10

In one hour, because the ball's eastward speed is less than that of Observer A, the ball falls to the west of the observer.

of the Coriolis effect. The effect is a consequence of the observers not being able to detect the straight-line motion of the thrown ball because they are traveling along with Earth at two different speeds. **Figure 2-10** shows the path of a ball being thrown from 45°N southward to the equator.

Moving air behaves in the same way as the ball. Its path in the northern hemisphere will always appear deflected to the right. Because the path always veers to the right, the global winds of the northern hemisphere always appear to be turning clockwise, as shown in **Figure 2-7.** In the southern hemisphere, the paths of the global winds veer left. Therefore, the global winds in the southern hemisphere appear to be turning counterclockwise.

The global winds of Earth are produced by giant convection cells, powered by the sun. In the next section, you will see how vertical air movements on a more local scale can produce some spectacular weather.

check your UNDERSTANDING

Understanding Concepts

1. What causes warm, moist air to rise?
2. Describe the three global convection cells in the northern hemisphere.
3. What is the Coriolis effect?

Skill Review

4. **Inferring** Using the direction of vertical movement in the global convection cells, suggest the latitudes of two areas of surface high pressure and two areas of surface low pressure in the northern hemisphere. For more help, refer to Inferring in the *Skill Handbook.*

people in SCIENCE

Meet Margaret LeMone, Meteorologist

It's mid-January in Boulder, Colorado, but instead of the expected snowdrifts and freezing winds, the area is experiencing the mildest winter it has had in decades—at least so far. Meteorologist Margaret LeMone looks out her office window and heaves a small sigh. The weather is just too *perfect. Perhaps she'd prefer to be in California, where storm clouds are gathering, or in Iowa, which is having a blizzard.*

In the following interview, Dr. LeMone tells about her personal and professional involvement with severe weather.

On the Job

Q Dr. LeMone, could you tell us something about your work?

A Right now, I'm using some new equipment, Doppler radar, that actually lets you see the wind in clear air. What excites me most is trying to figure out how the atmosphere and the land and sea of Earth's surface interact. There are lots of specific questions that intrigue me, such as this one: Does a huge city like New York slow down the passing of a cold front? And I'm especially interested in clouds.

Q How big is a cloud?

A I like to ask people, "How much do you think a cloud roughly 1 km in diameter weighs?" People tend to think of clouds as light, fluffy things floating in the sky, so they are amazed by the answer: about 550 tons. A neat thing about clouds is that you don't need money or any fancy equipment to enjoy watching them.

Q Does your work frequently take you out of your office?

A In the last few years, I've been involved in two field programs. One was in the Midwest, and the other was in the Solomon Islands, where we studied how the air and the ocean interact. To do that, we flew a plane just 100 feet above the ocean and measured evaporation rates and heating rates. The data we gathered will help meteorologists make computer models of Earth's climate.

Early Influences

Q When did your interest in weather begin?

A When I was in the third grade, in Missouri, lightning struck our house while we were eating dinner one night. The chimney basically exploded and the roof was blasted into splinters. Smoke filled the house. The fire department sent several trucks, but the driving rain put out the fire right away. It was pretty exciting. I remember thinking how lucky I was that the next day was my group's turn for show-and-tell time!

Q What did you do to follow that interest?

A Around seventh grade, I began keeping records of the weather. I built a simple rain gauge and put it in the yard. But my real interest—even then—was cloud formations, so I spent hours drawing and photographing them.

Personal Insights

Q Since your childhood encounter with lightning, have you had other close calls with severe weather?

A Many! Recently, I was hiking up Long's Peak with a group of cloud physicists. I was wearing a dark wool cap, and suddenly the person next to me yelled, "Peggy, you're giving off a coronal discharge!" I could hear the

You can get weather forecasts from many different sources: TV, radio, newspaper, and telephone (from the National Weather Service). Use each of these, and others if you can find them, and compare the content of their weather forecasts. Investigate the following professions and determine which forecast would be of most use to you if you held that job.

▶ *farmer, fisher, building contractor, park director, astronaut*

sparks flying out of my hair, which was standing straight up. Everyone found this so interesting that it took a moment for us to realize we were in imminent danger of being struck by lightning and to throw ourselves flat on the ground.

The Anatomy of Thunderstorms

Objectives
- Explain the stages of a thunderstorm.
- Describe some of the consequences of thunderstorms.

Violent Storms

In the first section, you saw how the vertical movement of air in convection cells causes global winds. Most violent weather is caused by the vertical movement of warm, moist air. In terms of damage, the two most dangerous storms are thunderstorms and hurricanes. Thunderstorms come and go quickly, affecting a relatively small area. However, a thunderstorm's high winds, damaging hail, and potential for tornadoes make it a storm to be feared.

Hurricanes affect large areas. Much of a hurricane's damage is due to wind, large amounts of rain, and flooding. If this were not enough, hurricanes can spawn thunderstorms and tornadoes.

A major effect of thunderstorms and hurricanes is the redistribution of energy within Earth's atmosphere.

Thunderstorms

Rising moist air does not have to create a storm. Puffy, white clouds are the result of small parcels of warm, moist air rising. However, large sections of warm, moist air rising into cool, dry air create the most violent weather event most of us will ever see—the thunderstorm. To understand why thunderstorms create so much damage, we need to see how they work.

Figure 2-11

There are three characteristic stages in the life cycle of a thunderstorm.

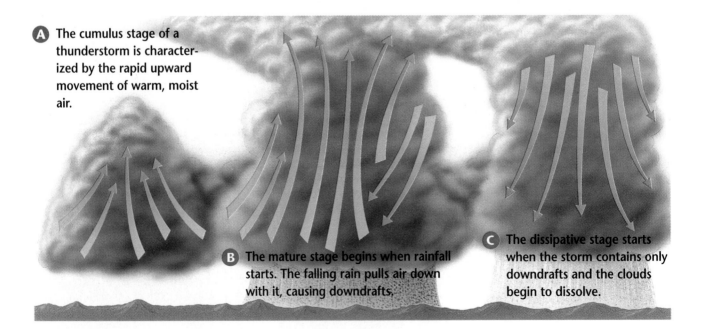

A The cumulus stage of a thunderstorm is characterized by the rapid upward movement of warm, moist air.

B The mature stage begins when rainfall starts. The falling rain pulls air down with it, causing downdrafts.

C The dissipative stage starts when the storm contains only downdrafts and the clouds begin to dissolve.

■ Cumulus Stage

Figure 2-11 shows that all thunderstorms have three stages: cumulus, mature, and dissipating.

The cumulus stage involves a large bubble of upward-moving, moist air, as described in Section 2-1. The temperature within the bubble is higher than that of the surrounding air at any level. The familiar thunderhead clouds develop rapidly. There is no lightning or chance of tornado formation during this stage. Any rain formed will be light. The upward-moving air in this stage can approach speeds of 160 km/hr.

■ Mature Stage

As the cloud extends upward, enough water condenses, as described on page 59, to provide a strong rain. The rain signals the start of the storm's mature stage. The falling rain pulls air downward with it, and the storm develops regions of downward-moving air. At the same time, air still rises at the top of the storm, achieving its maximum upward speed of more than 300 km/hr. The upward-moving air can reach heights of 25 km. Temperatures of the upward-moving air are warmer than those outside the cloud, while the downward-moving air is cooler than the rest of the storm. Large, mature thunderstorms can produce large amounts of rain in a short time. Hail is also common. However, one of the most common occurrences is violent lightning with accompanying loud thunder. Why do thunderstorms produce lightning?

■ Lightning

Lightning occurs when the charges in a thundercloud become separated. The bottom of the cloud becomes nega-

Figure 2-12

Lightning heats the surrounding air up to 30 000°C, causing it to expand. As it expands, it cools and contracts. This rapid expansion and contraction sets up a sound wave that we hear as thunder.

tively charged; the top becomes positively charged. The mechanism of this separation is not totally understood. It is generally believed that large raindrops and hail become charged by friction as they fall through the cloud. The negative cloud bottom attracts positive charges to Earth's surface. When there are enough charges, the air, which is normally an insulator, becomes a conductor, and charges flow between a cloud and Earth, as shown in **Figure 2-12.** The charges surge upward from the ground at an amazing speed of 129 000 000 m/s. Lightning may also take place within a cloud or between two clouds. In the United States alone, lightning strikes account for about 7500 forest fires, an average of 200 deaths, and 550 injuries to humans each year.

Technology: Raindrops on Radar

On April 25, 1994, a massive tornado devastated the town of Lancaster, Texas. Within minutes, more than 175 houses were turned into a pile of rubble. Fortunately, the National Weather Service's new $4.4 billion modernization program had put a new radar unit in place in Lancaster. It no doubt saved many lives.

The Technology

When finally completed, the new system will be made up of a network of domed radars reaching across the country to forecast severe storms. NEXRAD, or Next Generation Radar Network, has Doppler radar units arranged at stations 400 km apart. By 1995, 116 NEXRAD units were in place. There will be 175 Doppler radar stations when the network is completed. The units already functioning have doubled the average warning time for tornadoes to nine minutes. Actually, the inhabitants of Lancaster had even longer and were able to reach safe havens. The death toll was held to four people.

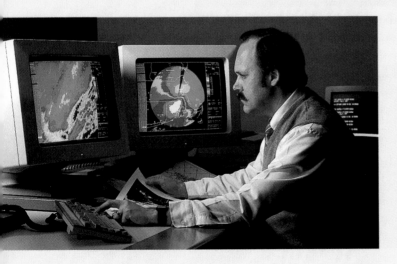

The Background

Radar is an acronym for "radio detection and ranging." Weather radar works this way: Microwaves are sent into the atmosphere from a radar antenna. Raindrops and other kinds of precipitation in the atmosphere reflect the microwaves back to the antenna. The radar's computer calculates the direction from which the reflections come and produces a map on the display terminal. Areas of heavier precipitation have a different screen color from an area of lighter precipitation. The radar screen also shows how far the precipitation extends. This information is useful, but it is not enough for severe storms such as tornadoes. Ordinary radar provides only half the information needed to predict a severe storm.

Doppler Radar to the Rescue

Doppler radar furnishes the other half—information about the direction and speed of the winds in the storm. It is able to detect whether precipitation is moving with the wind toward or away from the radar station.

According to the Doppler principle, waves from an approaching source have a higher frequency than waves that are moving away. Meteorologists use this principle to track storms. You can verify the Doppler principle by listening to the high pitch of the whistle of an approaching train change to a much lower pitch as the train moves away.

When a radar pulse bounces off a rain droplet or snowflake, its frequency is raised or lowered, depending on which way the droplet is moving. By measuring the Doppler shift, NEXRAD's computers can determine the wind speed toward or away from the radar facility from a distance of up to 120 nautical miles. A computer can also overlay maps of highways, towns, and airports directly on the radar screen.

The Questions

With the network of Doppler radar increasing across the country, forecasting is improving. It has become more of a science. Warning times have more than doubled, and false alarms have been cut in half. Although NEXRAD has a good record so far, it isn't perfect. It cannot detect every storm. NEXRAD has a 140-mile range for detecting winds. This is only half as far as its range for spotting precipitation. All major cities will lie within the shorter wind-spotting range when the network is complete, but many rural locations will fall outside that range. They will only be within the precipitation-spotting range.

Furthermore, near the limits of its range for detecting winds, the radar's resolution—and hence its ability to detect tornadoes—becomes fuzzy. For that reason, towns in the tornado belt want their own Doppler radars. For example, Huntsville, Alabama, which is about 100 miles from the nearest NEXRAD site, has raised concerns about dangerous weather warning times.

Another complaint focuses on NEXRAD's blind spots. Distant, dangerous storms may be hidden behind less destructive weather that is closer. The radar cannot distinguish between reflections from close by and those sent from a greater distance if both arrive at the same time.

These problems must be addressed. Should the National Weather Service have waited until it could afford to cover every area in the United States with Doppler radar? How would you feel if you lived in the tornado belt? Would you feel differently if you lived in a rural area?

The fiberglass radome protects the Doppler radar antenna from the weather.

NEXRAD is not cheap to build or operate. Not only is it costly to construct and install, but also, specially trained personnel are necessary to operate it. Is the additional information that we get from NEXRAD worth the considerable money it costs in all cases?

*inter*NET CONNECTION

Visit the Glencoe Homepage, **http://www. glencoe.com/**, for the Chapter 2 link to the National Weather Service to get current weather forecasts. Compare the forecasts on the World Wide Web with forecasts from newspapers and TV. Compare the accuracy of the different types of forecasts. In your journal, discuss the advantages and disadvantages of the NEXRAD system.

Figure 2-13

Tornadoes and funnel clouds are basically the same kind of phenomenon.

A Funnel clouds extend down from the base of a severe thunderstorm.

B Tornadoes move across the ground surface.

by their high winds and twisting motion; see **Figure 2-13.** These winds may reach 400 km/hr but often are less than 150 km/hr. Because of the shape of the land and the summer heating, tornados are seen most often in the central, southeastern, and midwestern parts of the United States.

■ Dissipative Stage of a Thunderstorm

The last stage of a thunderstorm is the dissipative stage. All air movement is downward. All air within the storm has become cooler than the air outside of the storm. Deprived of its energy source of warm, moist air, the storm soon splits into a series of disorganized layers of clouds. The storm is finished.

Even as one storm dies, however, weather conditions may be right for the formation of new thunderstorms in the area. Although an individual storm may last for only a few minutes, severe weather related to thunderstorms can continue for several hours. During its short life, a thunderstorm can wreak havoc with lightning and winds at speeds exceeding 160 km/hr. Violent hail may cascade down on the land below, and severe downdrafts—downward-moving, cool air traveling at speeds of more than 300 km/hr—may flatten crops and slam aircraft into the ground.

■ Tornadoes

Tornadoes may form during the mature stage of the most violent thunderstorms. They are winds that rotate rapidly around an area of low air pressure. Tornadoes are called funnel clouds before they reach the surface of Earth. They cause most of their damage

check your UNDERSTANDING

Understanding Concepts

1. What causes most violent weather?
2. What causes lightning to form?
3. Describe the stages of a thunderstorm.

Skill Review

4. **Inferring** Why might the rain from the mature stage of a violent thunderstorm cause flooding? For more help, refer to Inferring in the *Skill Handbook.*

2-3 Hurricanes: The Heavyweight Storms

Objectives
- Describe the formation of a hurricane.
- Explain how a hurricane moves and weakens.

Key Terms
air mass
tropical depression
blocking high

Conditions for Hurricane Formation

The hurricane, also called a typhoon in the Pacific Ocean, is by far the largest storm in terms of area covered. In terms of energy, this is the biggest engine on Earth, changing billions of joules of thermal energy into mechanical energy each second. This is equivalent to the power of 300 electrical power plants.

Your best chance of observing the formation of a hurricane in the northern hemisphere is in the summer and fall in the Atlantic Ocean between the latitudes of 5° and 20°. Such a specific time and place is a clue to how hurricanes form.

■ Air Masses

If you look back at **Figure 2-4,** you'll recall that the solar radiation in these latitudes exceeds the energy radiated by Earth. In the summer and fall, this imbalance is even greater. Solar radiation produces vast quantities of warm, moist air during summer and fall. A large quantity of air that has similar characteristics throughout is called an **air mass.** Each air mass has the same characteristics of temperature and moisture as the area over which it formed, **Figure 2-14.** For example, a tropical air mass may be warm and dry or warm and moist.

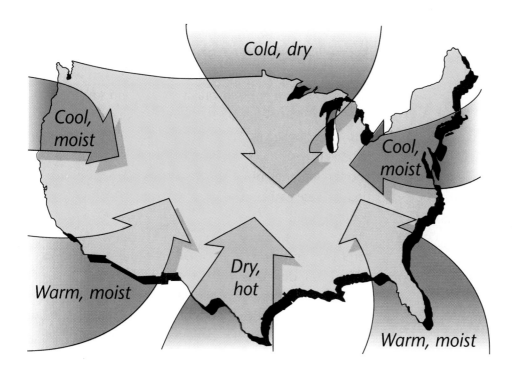

Cold, dry

Cool, moist

Cool, moist

Warm, moist

Dry, hot

Warm, moist

Figure 2-14

These are the six major air masses that affect the United States.

Air masses are also characterized by their air pressure. For example, the convection of warm, moist air in the tropics produces a central region that has strong ascending winds and lower pressure. You can see how the lower pressure occurs in **Figure 2-15.** A tropical air mass of low atmospheric pressure is called a **tropical depression.**

The Hurricane Itself

The exact conditions required for a tropical depression to form a hurricane are still not entirely understood. Only about ten percent of tropical depressions develop into hurricanes. However, high humidity, light winds, and warm water are necessary for a tropical disturbance to grow into a full-blown hurricane with winds of at least 120 km/hr. The large areas of warm ocean water found in the tropics can provide a storm with almost unlimited energy for growth. The warm air evaporates water, which rises at the center of the storm and condenses, releasing thermal energy. The growing storm pulls air in from surrounding areas, heats it, and sends it rushing skyward in the storm's center. As the storm grows, the Coriolis effect sets the air spinning, and the arms of clouds associated with the storm spiral around the center in the familiar pinwheel pattern.

Sudden Desert Downpours

IN-DEPTH LOOK

Heavy rains are not limited to thunderstorms and hurricanes. Some deserts may get no rain for years and then get several inches in one day. How does a sudden downpour affect a desert?

Beware of Flash Floods

Arroyos, or dry creek beds, suffer flash floods during downpours. These flash floods carve the arroyos deeper as they carry sand and rocks, which scour down the creek bed. But the floods also help arroyo plant seeds germinate.

The seeds of most arroyo plants and shrubs have thick, protective coats. When they are left without water, seeds such as this won't germinate for years. During a flash flood, however, the seeds are tumbled with grains of sand and small rocks, so the protective covering gets deep scratches. Water can then enter the seed, causing it to swell and sprout.

Desert Plants and Animals

Desert plants and animals have many adaptations that allow them to survive long periods of drought broken by short periods of intense rain.

Figure 2-15

Hurricanes form over the warm tropical oceans.

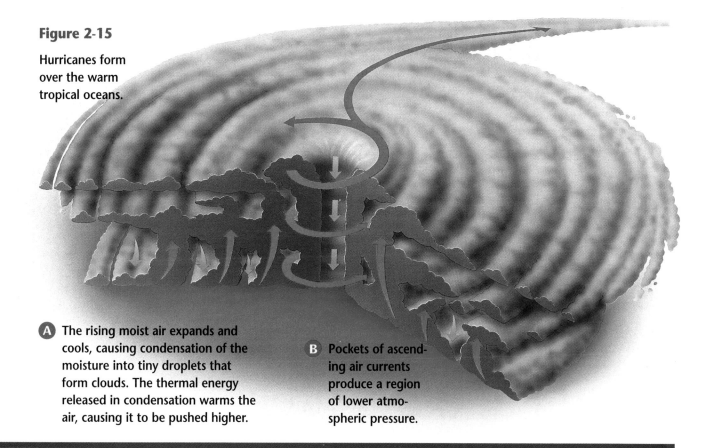

A The rising moist air expands and cools, causing condensation of the moisture into tiny droplets that form clouds. The thermal energy released in condensation warms the air, causing it to be pushed higher.

B Pockets of ascending air currents produce a region of lower atmospheric pressure.

Annual plants—plants that live for only one year—survive in deserts because they have short life spans. Their seeds don't germinate until they get at least an inch of rain, which washes away a coating on the seed that prevents germination. Then they grow quickly, flower, and produce seeds in only two to eight weeks, while the desert is still wet. In that time, the plants produce millions and millions of seeds per acre, and more than half of the seeds germinate. During their brief season, desert annuals cover the ground in a breathtaking array of flowers. For the rest of the year, their ungerminated seeds are food for many desert animals.

But a hard rain triggers the emergence of more than flowering plants in the desert. Harvester ants have adapted to use this time for their mating flights, while spiders, birds, and lizards prey on the ant swarms.

The Spadefoot Story

Spadefoot toads survive in the dry desert conditions by secreting a waterproof coating and burying themselves in the drying mud of desert lakes. When it rains, they emerge, find mates, and produce as many as 4000 eggs per pair. The eggs hatch in two days, and the tadpoles develop into adults in a month. The new adults then bury themselves in the rapidly drying mud and

remain dormant until the next rain. Every year, some tadpoles don't become adults quickly enough to reach safety underground. They either become food for larger animals or die from exposure.

Thinking Critically

1. *Describe* how annual plants survive in the desert.
2. Suppose you lived in a desert and had to obtain water from once-yearly rains. *Infer* whether you would try to tame flash floods. How would you collect a year's supply of water and keep it from evaporating?

Figure 2-16

A graph of the air pressure in a tropical depression and a hurricane.

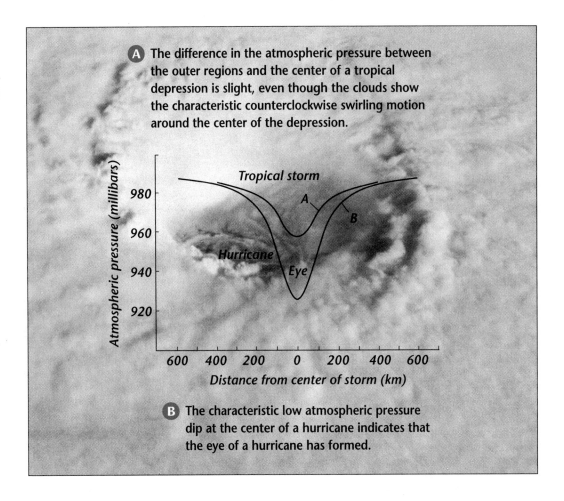

A The difference in the atmospheric pressure between the outer regions and the center of a tropical depression is slight, even though the clouds show the characteristic counterclockwise swirling motion around the center of the depression.

B The characteristic low atmospheric pressure dip at the center of a hurricane indicates that the eye of a hurricane has formed.

■ The Eye

A curious feature of a full-grown hurricane is the eye. This clear center of the storm may be as large as 65 km in diameter and have little or no wind. Ocean waves in the eye are high but lack the menacing, mountainous form of those elsewhere in the storm. The hurricane consists of rings of heavy thunderstorms with strong winds and atmospheric pressure that decreases as you approach the center. Just outside the eye, however, the howling fury of the storm is at its maximum, with winds in excess of 250 km/hr and waves 50 m high. You can compare the atmospheric pressure of the center of a tropical storm and a hurricane in **Figure 2-16.**

You may be wondering why the eye of a hurricane doesn't collapse if the pressure at its center is so low. The answer is that the inertia of the winds makes them likely to blow in a straight line. An inward force is needed to keep an object moving in a circle. If you were ever in the passenger seat of a car making a sharp turn, you felt the inward push of the door on you keeping you moving in a circle instead of flying off in a straight line. The air moving in the circle at the edge of the eye of a hurricane must have a force keeping it moving in a circle, too. That force is the force of the air at higher pressure surrounding the eye and pushing inward.

After the hurricane forms, the swirling winds bring more moist air into the storm, and its energy increases. Meteorologists can easily locate the hurricane from its beginning as a tropical depression with the pinpoint accuracy of a weather satellite photograph. Predicting where the hurricane is headed is harder.

Hurricane Movement

Once formed, an average hurricane covers an area of about 50 000 square kilometers. What causes such an enormous mass of swirling air and moisture to move?

■ Prevailing Winds

The balmy breezes of a tropical island may seem gentle. Would you think these breezes may be the movers of hurricanes? Strong storms formed off the African coast may take more than a week to cross the Atlantic, growing in strength as they travel. If you look at **Figure 2-17,** you'll see the path of a typical hurricane. The global winds, called the *prevailing winds,* match the typical path of a hurricane. These winds—the trade winds and the prevailing westerlies—are often responsible for pushing the hurricane along its path. Local weather conditions determine the actual track.

■ Blocking Highs

Along with prevailing winds, air masses also affect the path of a hurricane. As you recall, an air mass is a region of air having consistent characteristics. What would happen if a hurricane encountered a completely different type of air mass, such as a polar air mass having high atmospheric pressure? Before you try to answer that question, you may want to observe some effects of atmospheric pressure in the MiniLab on the next page.

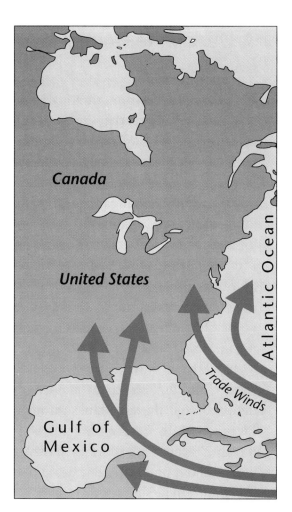

Figure 2-17

Shown here are some typical tracks of hurricanes approaching the east coast of the United States. An average tropical storm formed in the western Atlantic travels westward and northwestward on the tropical trade winds. If it reaches as far north as 30° latitude, it gets caught in the prevailing westerlies and then moves northeast. However, local conditions make it difficult to predict a hurricane's exact path.

Air pressure is invisible, yet it exerts a large force. Pressure differences in the atmosphere can help change the direction of even the largest storm. The following activity demonstrates how air pressure pushes on a glass of water.

Procedure

1. Obtain a glass and a cardboard square cut larger than the opening in the glass. Pour water into the glass until it is full to the brim.

2. Place the square of cardboard on top of the glass.

3. Holding the glass and cardboard over a sink, quickly turn the glass upside down.

4. Let go of the cardboard and observe what happens.

Analysis

1. What happens to the water in the glass when the glass is turned upside down?

2. What is keeping the cardboard square in place?

Figure 2-18

A blocking high causes the hurricane to continue moving westward.

As you noted in the MiniLab, air pressure exerted over an area produces great force—so much, in fact, that an air mass containing high pressure produces strong winds blowing outward and can keep a hurricane from advancing. Such air masses are called **blocking highs. Figure 2-18** shows you the effects of a blocking high on the path of a hurricane.

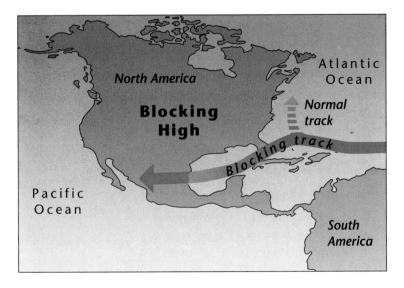

A Hurricane Comes to Its End

Throughout its life, the hurricane has been giving energy back to the ocean in the form of waves. As hurricane winds blow over the ocean, there is friction between the water surface and the wind. The wind drags the water into waves, and, in doing so, the wind loses some of its speed and energy to friction and the movement of massive amounts of seawater. As you might imagine, a great amount of energy is needed to build and maintain 20-meter high waves.

Luckily, all hurricanes eventually weaken and die. Eventually, the clouds disappear and the sun shines through, **Figure 2-19.** In fact, in human terms, most hurricanes are short-lived, existing for about nine days. The death of a hurricane can be simple or complex.

■ A Hurricane Ends at Sea

If a hurricane stays in open ocean, it moves, blown by prevailing winds, into the North Atlantic. There the water is cool and evaporation is slower. Even though the storm draws energy from a wide area, the cooler water does not provide enough energy to keep the storm going. The hurricane loses energy, its winds slow, it is downgraded to a storm, and it eventually breaks up into a series of rain showers. At sea, the death of a hurricane is a slow process resulting in its fading away. Hurricanes that die by moving over the coasts of the continents meet a different fate.

■ A Hurricane Hits Land

A hurricane hitting land is a victim of multiple processes. When a hurricane hits land, friction dramatically increases. Instead of an almost-flat ocean of water, the winds encounter hills, trees, power lines, and other objects sticking out above the surface. These obstacles easily absorb wind energy. They also disrupt the winds' even, rapid, spiral flow. It is this flow that distributes the energy carried by warm, moist air throughout the storm. The airflow becomes even more critical to the storm as it moves over land.

Figure 2-19

After an average of nine days, a hurricane dies, the clouds dissipate, and the sun becomes visible again.

■ A Lack of Energy: Too Far from the Sea

As the hurricane makes its way over land, there is less and less of the storm left over the ocean with its readily available energy. The winds that would normally channel warm, moist air to the front of the hurricane are disrupted by the irregular land surface. The combination of increased friction and loss of fuel causes the hurricane to become disorganized and reduced to a series of thunderstorms called squall lines. Even these squall lines, however, can dump large amounts of rain on coastal areas as they move inland.

check your UNDERSTANDING

Understanding Concepts
1. Describe the eye of a hurricane.
2. What causes hurricanes to rotate?
3. List two main reasons for a hurricane to end.

Skill Review
4. **Inferring** The Gulf Stream is an ocean current that carries warm water north along the east coast of North America. What effect does the Gulf Stream have on hurricanes? For more help, refer to Inferring in the *Skill Handbook.*

Weather and Folklore

Long before people could watch the television weather forecaster to find out what the next day's weather would be like, they watched nature carefully to predict the weather. The shapes of clouds in the sky, the color of the moon or sun, the appearance of a rainbow, or the behavior of animals were utilized in forecasting weather. When these signs led to an accurate prediction of weather conditions, people made up sayings about how certain natural phenomena could help predict what kind of weather to expect. Such folklore—stories (lore) told by the people of the community (folk)— taught everyone who heard it the weather wisdom learned by keeping a keen eye on the world of nature.

Rhymes and Weather

Here are a few rhymes that people still use to predict weather.

The crow with loud cries
A sudden shower foretells;
In single file they fly
Up and over the hills.

Crows feed in groups but roost and look for shelter individually. So, when a storm is on its way, they fly away in single file.

When bees far away
Make their flight,
Days will be warm and skies bright.
But when their flight
Ends near home,
Stormy weather is sure to come.

Many insects are sensitive to changes in temperature, humidity, and air pressure. When rain is near, bees feel the drop in barometric pressure levels and the increase in humidity, and they stay near their hives.

Weather Folklore Today

Much of this folklore can be found collected in a book called *The Old Farmers' Almanac.* While many people might think such stories are just superstitions about the weather, these stories still influence the ways that forecasters and farmers predict the weather and reflect the observations of farmers over hundreds of years.

Thinking Critically

1. *Infer* how weather folklore gets started.
2. *Collect data* to make a class scrapbook of rhymes and stories about the weather. Have each class member ask family members such as parents and grandparents for weather folklore. Then gather the stories and information into a book.

Read the statements below that review major points presented in the chapter. Using the concepts that you have learned, answer each question *in your Journal.*

1 Evaporation and condensation move energy throughout the atmosphere to create weather. *What is the original source of the energy that fuels weather?*

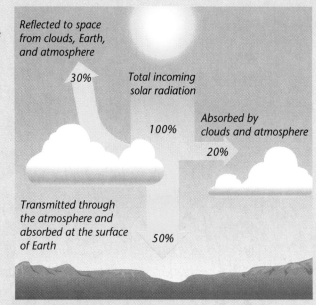

Reflected to space from clouds, Earth, and atmosphere

30%

Total incoming solar radiation

100%

Absorbed by clouds and atmosphere

20%

Transmitted through the atmosphere and absorbed at the surface of Earth

50%

90° N

45°   45°

0°   0°

1220 km

1730 km

Equator

1:00 PM   2:00 PM

2 Global wind patterns caused by Earth's rotation and regional heating and cooling of air are responsible for moving storms over Earth's surface. *Why do TV weather forecasters always talk about the weather to the west of your area?*

3 Storms die from loss of energy to Earth's surface through wind friction and as they move away from a source of energy. *Why does the creation of waves actually help dissipate a storm?*

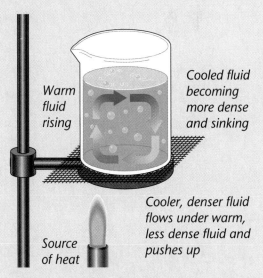

Warm fluid rising

Cooled fluid becoming more dense and sinking

Source of heat

Cooler, denser fluid flows under warm, less dense fluid and pushes up

4 Warm, moist air fuels storms by carrying energy upward from the surface. Storms come in several types, depending on the source of rising air. *Why do thunderstorms usually form in the summer?*

Using Key Science Terms

air mass

blocking high

conduction

convection

convection cell

Coriolis effect

evaporation

heat

radiation

tropical depression

weather

Relate one of the terms from the list above to each concept below.

1. Hurricane winds move in a counterclockwise direction in the northern hemisphere.
2. Warm, moist air buoyed up by colder, denser air.
3. Cooling process when water changes from a liquid to a gas.
4. A low-pressure area forming in the Atlantic Ocean near the equator.
5. A large parcel of air that causes a hurricane to change directions.

Understanding Ideas

Using complete sentences, answer the following questions in your Journal.

1. Compare and contrast the thunderstorm and the hurricane.
2. What might the Coriolis effect do to air rising straight up from the surface of Earth?
3. Why do hurricanes get so much bigger and cover more area than thunderstorms?
4. Describe what conditions on Earth might be if convection did not carry energy from the surface into the upper atmosphere.
5. Why does adding moisture to air make it lighter?

6. Why is the sun responsible for our having weather on Earth?
7. Why do hurricanes always form in the tropics?
8. Why are the poles colder than the equator?
9. Why is the Coriolis effect important to the eye of a hurricane?
10. Some scientists think the amount of energy the sun gives off changes over the years. What would happen to hurricanes if the sun were to give off more energy than it does now?

Developing Skills

Use your understanding of the concepts developed in this chapter to answer each of the following questions.

1. **Concept Mapping** Complete the cycle concept map using the following phrases: *air expands and cools; droplets collect, forming raindrops; surface water evaporates; raindrops fall back to surface; warm, moist air rises; water vapor condenses.*

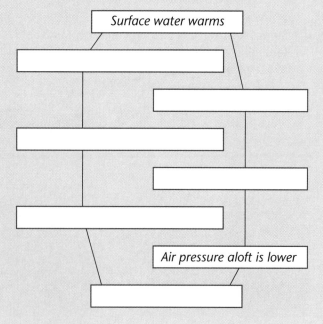

Surface water warms

Air pressure aloft is lower

2. Classifying How might you classify thunderstorms?

3. Predicting What kind of violent storm would be most likely to affect your area? Why, and what would be its likely effects?

4. Making and Using Graphs Create a graph of outside temperature every hour for at least one 24-hour day. You may take readings yourself or use hourly data from your local weather bureau, newspaper, or other sources. Next, mark the hours of sunrise and sunset on the graph. How do the times of maximum and minimum temperature relate to those of sunrise and sunset? Does this surprise you? Explain this relationship.

Critical Thinking

In your Journal, *answer each of the following questions.*

1. What do you think storms might be like if Earth did not rotate?

2. Would a convection cell operate on an orbiting space shuttle? Explain.

3. Do you think a storm could develop from rising dry air? What might such a storm be like? Why?

4. Describe what global weather would be like if every place on Earth received the same amount of solar energy.

Problem Solving

Read the following problem and discuss your answers in a brief paragraph.

You are chief forecaster for the Florida Citrus Growers Association. It is February and the jet stream is being pulled southward by a large low-pressure system located southeast of the Florida coast. A blocking high holds the low pressure in position and the situation should last at least a week.

Do you issue a freeze alert to your members? Why or why not? In your answer, draw a sketch of the situation. Enter both the sketch and your answer *in your Journal.*

CONNECTING IDEAS

1. Theme—Energy Both the atmosphere (in storms) and an automobile engine convert energy and move it from one place to another. Compare and contrast the ways in which each accomplishes this.

2. Theme—Systems and Interactions Explain why storms are referred to as "weather systems" and how they are indeed large-scale systems.

3. Science and Society How is Doppler radar differ-

ent from regular radar?

4. In-Depth Look How do seeds of arroyo shrubs adapt to life in the desert?

5. Literature Connection List three things in nature that are used to predict weather.

CHAPTER 3

The Effects of Storms
Aftermath of the Storm

Imagine the feelings that run through people's minds as they sit in a high school gym where they have taken shelter, waiting for a hurricane to finally stop. Even inside the brick and concrete building, it is too easy to hear the screaming wind and driving rain.

Fear is replaced with relief when the storm's fury subsides and people begin to leave the shelter. Anticipation may turn to dismay as they get their first look at the damage done by nature. Then, shock settles in as they view trees and buildings that have been destroyed. For many, almost every material possession they own is gone.

Within a few short hours, nature's fury can alter your life and the stability of the ecosystem of which your home was a part. In this chapter, learn how storms and other natural disasters affect local environments and how these environments recover.

▶ **In the activity on the next page, explore how you can prepare for a natural disaster.**

MiniLab

Are you prepared?

People who live in areas where natural disasters such as tornadoes, hurricanes, blizzards, earthquakes, or floods are common often have supplies set aside in case of an emergency.

Procedure

1. Choose one of the disasters from those listed above.

2. Read about the following situation and then list what supplies are needed.

   The electricity goes out and the phones are dead. You need to keep in contact with local authorities, provide light and heat, and provide food and drink.

Analysis

1. If you lived in an area subject to blizzards, what items might you want in a standby disaster kit?

2. What other supplies might be useful?

3-1

The Moving Storm

Objectives
- Identify those natural disasters that people can be forewarned about.
- Determine the source of a hurricane's energy and what happens when the storm leaves its energy source.

Key Terms
evacuate

Natural Disasters

The outcome of historical events has sometimes been influenced by acts of nature. In the 1500s, a fierce westerly gale destroyed many of the ships of the Spanish Armada, thus ushering in England's domination of the oceans and the spread of its colonial empire. And one hypothesis is that the pilgrims landed in Massachusetts instead of Virginia because a hurricane blew their ship off course.

Storms and other natural disasters not only change the events of history, they also affect the daily lives of all sorts of people and change the economy and ecology of an area. Let's find out what can happen to an area that is hit by a major natural disaster such as Hurricane Andrew in August of 1992, and

how modern forecasting methods help lessen storm damage.

■ Warnings of Impending Danger

Today, scientists are trying to improve ways of forecasting the specific times and locations of severe weather. By using modern weather radar equipment, large computers, as shown in **Figure 3-1,** and satellites, they can warn the public about approaching hurricanes, tornadoes, and floods.

One important piece of information in issuing warnings about a hurricane is its forward speed. In the next MiniLab you will investigate the relationship between wind speed and forward speed.

Figure 3-1

In 1992, scientists at the National Hurricane Center in Coral Gables, Florida, were able to track the development of Hurricane Andrew from its modest beginnings off the coast of West Africa to its full fury as it hit the Gulf Coast of the United States.

How fast do hurricanes move?

Hurricane wind speed changes as the storm passes over water, then land. Does the forward speed of the storm change in the same way? In this MiniLab you will determine the answer by calculating Hurricane Andrew's forward speed as it traveled from the open ocean to the state of Mississippi.

	DATE	TIME	WIND SPEED	
A -	Aug 23	5:00 pm	150 mph	
B -	Aug 24	5:05 am	145 mph	
C -	Aug 24	8:00 am	125 mph	
D -	Aug 24	8:00 pm	130 mph	
E -	Aug 25	7:00 am	130 mph	
F -	Aug 25	7:00 pm	140 mph	
G -	Aug 26	3:30 am	120 mph	
H -	Aug 26	1:00 pm	60 mph	- Tropical storm
I -	Aug 27	1:00 am	35 mph	- Tropical depression

Adapted from National Geographic

PATH OF HURRICANE ANDREW

SCALE
150 km

Procedure

1. Examine the map of Hurricane Andrew's path above, and locate its path over land from 5:05 A.M. to 8 A.M. on August 24.

2. Using the scale on the map, determine the distance between these two points.

3. Calculate the speed at which the storm was moving using the equation $v = d/t$, where v = speed, t = time elapsed, and d = distance. Record your answer *in your Journal.*

4. Repeat steps 1 to 3 for the hurricane's path over water from 8:00 P.M., August 24, to 7 P.M., August 25.

Analysis

1. What happens to the wind speed of the hurricane as it travels over land and water?

2. Is the forward speed of the hurricane affected by whether it's over land or water?

3. *In your Journal,* describe what happened to Hurricane Andrew as it left the Gulf of Mexico and moved across Mississippi.

As you saw in the MiniLab, storms have two kinds of wind movement that are not necessarily related to each other. One is the horizontal movement of the whole storm across the surface of Earth. The other is the speed of the winds within the storm itself. With conventional radar it is difficult to distinguish between the two types of motion. The development of Doppler radar has made it possible to separate the two kinds of motion. The ability to more accurately measure the horizontal speed of a storm has allowed meteorologists to give people a much longer warning time before a storm arrives.

Figure 3-2

Weather satellites easily pick up the characteristic spiral shape of a hurricane. Hurricane winds in the northern hemisphere spiral in a counterclockwise direction. In the southern hemisphere, the winds spiral in a clockwise direction. The motion in hurricanes helps redistribute the heat from the warm, tropical ocean waters into the atmosphere and then over large, more temperate areas of Earth.

■ The Birth of a Monster

The warm tropical ocean west of Africa is the birthplace of most Atlantic hurricanes. Hurricane Andrew was no different when it started as a wave of low pressure in the middle of August in 1992. Recall from Chapter 2 that hurricanes form over the warm ocean as warm, moist air is drawn into the low-pressure center and forced aloft into the cooler upper atmosphere. Thermal energy is released as water vapor condenses. This energy warms the surrounding air. Cool, dense air from above rushes down and under the warm air, pushing the warm air aloft. These updrafts carry thermal energy and water vapor high into the atmosphere. As warm air is forced up, the Coriolis Effect gives it the characteristic spiraling pattern shown in **Figure 3-2**. These spiraling winds are in contrast to the straight-line winds of a thunderstorm. A hurricane's forward motion is measured by the progression of the low-pressure system in the center. The speed averages about 12 to 14 mph. Warm air plus the relative absence of winds aloft blowing in opposite directions allowed Hurricane Andrew to develop and intensify rapidly. Andrew's traveling speed across the ocean was about 20 mph.

■ Heading Toward the Coast

Hurricanes are the largest and most destructive storms on Earth. As they travel over a warm ocean, they gain energy by evaporation and conduction and build in strength. The amount of energy such a storm contains is often compared to atomic bombs. A fully developed, large hurricane can move more than 3 billion tons of air per hour and spend its energy at the rate of several large atomic bombs every minute.

As a hurricane approaches the coast, changes occur in its overall character. Energy carried by the wind is

Figure 3-3

Officials went from door to door warning people of the coming storm. Officials at the National Hurricane Center, however, were caught in the fury of Andrew. The Center's wind gauge recorded a speed of 264 km/hr just before it was blown away.

transferred to the shallower water, resulting in huge waves that batter the shore. Once the storm reaches land, this energy is no longer used to form waves, but blows directly onto the land, causing great property damage. When Hurricane Andrew traveled over the tip of southern Florida, it brought 242 km/h (150 mi/h) winds and left a path of destruction 100 km long and 50 km wide.

Fortunately, when a hurricane moves over land, it gets cut off from its energy supply—the warm ocean water. Consequently, the storm starts to die out. Rarely do hurricanes get far inland. However, many smaller storms such as tornadoes can spin off of the dying hurricane and cause damage.

■ Following a Hurricane

Weather forecasters had tracked Hurricane Andrew for several days as it grew in strength. When it became apparent that it was heading for land, warnings were issued telling people to prepare for a devastating storm. Thousands left the area when officials asked residents to evacuate, **Figure 3-3.** To **evacuate** means to move people away from a dangerous place in an orderly way. Thousands of others boarded up their windows; filled their bathtubs with water for later use; and stocked up on food and other storm supplies and stayed on. As you will learn next, these preparations were no match for Andrew's power.

check your UNDERSTANDING

Understanding Concepts

1. Explain why a hurricane dies when it moves over land.
2. Where does a hurricane get its energy?
3. Why were people told to evacuate the area where Hurricane Andrew was predicted to hit?

Skill Review

4. **Inferring** Why would you be unlikely to experience a hurricane in Idaho? For more help, refer to Inferring in the *Skill Handbook.*

Agents of Destruction

Objectives

- Explain the different ways that wind associated with a storm causes damage.
- Determine the other forms of damage associated with the passage of a storm.

Key Terms

gust
storm surge

Damage by Wind

Violent storms and flooding aren't limited to the United States. They occur throughout the world. Hurricanes originate in the tropical Pacific Ocean as well as the Atlantic. In the Pacific Ocean, they are called typhoons or tropical cyclones and batter the eastern coast of Asia.

Most physical damage caused by hurricanes results from wind and water. In fact, extremely strong wind is probably the first characteristic that comes to mind when these storms are discussed. Complete the MiniLab to find out how wind can damage buildings.

We know that when hurricanes reach land, coastal areas are the first to sustain damage. But not all coasts are the same. The overall geometry of a coast can significantly increase a hurricane's destructive powers. Winds tend to pile water up where coasts bend inland, such as the corner created by New Jersey and Long Island. Here, resulting high water levels could be as much as 15 to 19 feet above normal. No matter what the coastal geometry is, hurricane winds are devastating. Hurricane Andrew's winds were strong enough to suck the

MiniLab

How strong is a house?

Contemporary building codes in south Florida require new construction to be able to withstand the intensity of a severe storm. Unfortunately, we still cannot predict the intensity of any given storm. Thus, even the newest buildings may not hold up. This situation is not unlike attempts at earthquake-proof construction. In this Lab, you will see how well your "hurricane-proof" building will hold up under severe storm conditions.

Procedure

1. Examine the building materials supplied by your teacher.

2. Using paper and pencil, design a hurricane-proof structure that will be

made out of your choice of the materials. (Remember, more is not necessarily better!)

3. Construct your building according to your plan.

4. Once finished, devise a plan for testing your building and carry it out.

Analysis

1. Which held up best, solid or open walls? Why?

2. Why are skyscrapers designed to bend in the wind?

Figure 3-4

People search for their belongings in homes ripped apart by the winds of Hurricane Andrew.

outer walls off of buildings. They damaged 275 small airplanes at one airport and blew a 44-foot sailboat one-half mile inland.

■ Destruction from the Air

What can be done to make buildings less subject to destruction by hurricanes? After living through Hurricane Andrew, people learned the wisdom of following stringent building codes. Building codes are specifications for contractors telling them how to construct buildings with structural reinforcements so that they will be able to survive storms with minimal damage. Of the 125 000 homes destroyed or damaged by Andrew, wind caused much of the destruction. As a hurricane sucks up air, the air spirals around the eye at speeds from 120 to 321 km/h. The velocity of these winds is about 16 times more than an average thunderstorm. Sudden increases in the wind, called **gusts,** tear off parts of buildings and uproot huge trees.

The actual force the wind exerts depends on its speed. If the wind speed doubles, the force the wind exerts is four times as strong. This means that even small increases in wind speed result in large increases in force. A 30-knot wind makes walking difficult; a 50-knot wind can knock a person down. At 110 knots, wind can even pick up a person. Continuous strong winds can gradually weaken buildings until they begin to tear apart as shown in **Figure 3-4.**

Hurricanes aren't the only source of damaging winds. Tornadoes and thunderstorms can generate winds strong enough to blow down trees and damage buildings. Sometimes, fallen trees or branches knock down power lines, making hazardous situations.

■ Tornadoes Spawned by the Hurricane

You learned in Chapter 2 that tornadoes form during the mature stage of thunderstorms. These deadly phenomena regularly form from about 25 per-

Figure 3-5

Once hurricanes hit land, they are capable of spawning tornadoes along their outer edges. Much of the damage done to this trailer park was caused by a tornado that formed after the hurricane came ashore, not by the hurricane itself.

cent of hurricanes. While there might be an average of ten tornadoes for each of these hurricanes, some storms produce many more than the usual number. Hurricane Beulah, in 1967, gave birth to between 115 and 140 tornadoes. Counting the actual number of tornadoes is difficult as they are often undetected in the chaotic swirl of hurricane winds. Scientists now know that these violent by-products of a hurricane usually form along the larger storm's outer edge. Hurricane-produced tornadoes are not as big or long-lasting as those formed by violent thunderstorms. As shown in **Figure 3-5,** however, they still are capable of inflicting considerable damage.

Damage by Water

Damage by water sometimes is greater than that caused by the wind. Although we do not usually think of

floods as violent weather, it is a fact that floods occur more often than any other type of natural disaster and account for the greatest number of weather-related deaths around the world.

In 1979, Hurricane Claudette dropped about 108 cm of rain near Alvin, Texas, in one 24-hour period. Rainfall from both hurricanes and thunderstorms may ultimately lead to flooding. Extensive damage results from floodwaters from either source, as shown in **Figure 3-6.** Like wind, the force exerted by moving water increases as the speed increases. That's why flooded rivers are so dangerous. Imagine standing in a river that's up to your knees, exposing about a square foot of your body to the current. If the water moves at 4 mi/h, you would feel a force of about 66 pounds. If the water moves at 8 mi/h, the force jumps to about 264 pounds. This means that every square foot of an object submerged in water moving at 8 mi/h would experience a force of 264 pounds. Imagine the total force moving water would exert on a house or a car. Just as in the case of wind, as the speed of the water doubles, the force increases by a factor of four.

■ Flash Floods

Sometimes floods happen suddenly. In mountainous areas with little soil to absorb rainfall, the water runs directly into streams, making them raging rivers. This can happen so quickly that a wall of water sweeps through the valley. The force of the rushing water is so strong that boulders the size of a car are carried far downstream. Think about the destruction that can be done with such a force. The following activity shows how some flood damage may occur.

Figure 3-6

During a flood, bridges are often washed away. Often, people have to travel 100 or more kilometers to find a road that is still open and connecting one side of the river with the other.

MiniLab

Why do bridges fail in high floodwaters?

Flooding is a serious side effect of heavy rain. During high-water stages, erosion increases around bridge supports. In this activity, you will explore the reasons why this increased erosion endangers the strength of bridges.

Procedure

1. Work with a group. Set up a stream table with 5-8 cm of sand filling the bottom.

2. Start the water flowing rapidly and observe any erosion that occurs. Record your observations.

3. Stop the water and smooth out the sand.

4. Insert a marker into the sand halfway downstream from the water's source and in the stream flow. The marker represents a bridge support.

5. Start the water flowing again and observe any erosion that occurs. Record your observations.

Analysis

1. What direction is the water flowing in step 2? Why?

2. In what part of the stream is the water flowing fastest in step 5? The slowest? How can you tell?

3. Based on your results, why do bridges become unsafe during a flood?

Storm Surge: A Deadly Wall of Water

You may not realize that about 90 percent of the deaths and much of the damage credited to hurricanes results from storm surges. A **storm surge** is an unusually high rise in the level of the ocean that creates a wall of water, as shown in **Figure 3-7.** A storm surge forms as winds push water toward the center of a hurricane.

■ Damage from a Storm Surge

When the storm surge from Hurricane Andrew pushed ashore in south Florida, the east coast of Florida record-ed a water level 5.2 m above normal—about the height of a small house. The Gulf Coast had a smaller surge measur-ing 4.6 m. On the northern coast of a Bahamian island, the storm surge was up to 29 m.

A storm surge is damaging when it hits the wide-open area of a flat coast-line. Now try to imagine how much more damage is done if the surge is forced into a confined space such as a narrow bay or riverbed. Such a place is the country of Bangladesh. Bangladesh is located at the head of the funnel-shaped Bay of Bengal. Bangladesh has had a history of storm surges that have resulted in the deaths of thousands of people at a time.

Figure 3-7

The action of hurri-cane winds and low pressure combine to form a storm surge.

A The winds play the greatest role in forming the mound of water. The mound is not directly below the eye, because the wind speeds are commonly greatest in the right-hand quadrant. Open-ocean surges are not high because the deep water allows the water to flow away.

B When the surge reaches shallow water, however, there is no place for the water to go. The mound builds higher as it approaches the shore. The effect of a storm surge is magnified if it slams into the coast at the same time as the normal high tide.

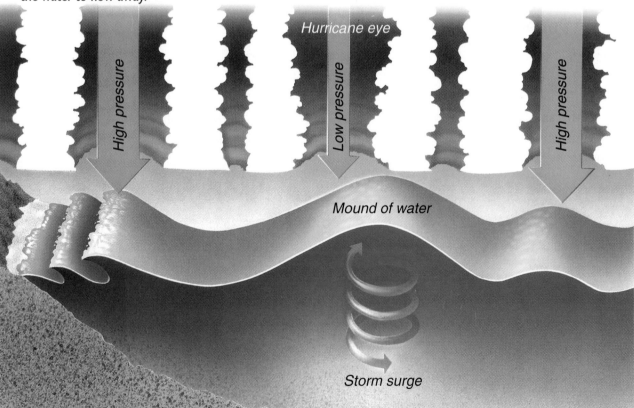

Hurricane eye

High pressure

Low pressure

High pressure

Mound of water

Storm surge

Lightning and Hail

In addition to wind and water, there are two other storm-related natural agents of destruction. These are lightning and hail. Recall from Chapter 2 how lightning forms. The power that is released by this electrical display is immense. With temperatures up to five times those on the surface of the sun, about 30 000°C, lightning can melt metal objects or cook crops, such as potatoes, that have not yet been harvested. It can spark forest fires as well as fires in homes and other buildings. Economic losses caused by the fires or electrical outages can be substantial. About 100 people are killed by lightning each year in the United States.

Hail is formed as a particle of ice bounces between the updrafts and downdrafts in a storm cloud. Hailstones cause great damage to crops and personal property each year. They fall from altitudes that are several kilometers above Earth. It is possible to accumulate a layer of hailstones several centimeters deep from one hailstorm. While their size usually is about that of peas or marbles, in rare instances hailstones have grown to the size of baseballs or grapefruits, as in **Figure 3-8**. Most of the severe damage is caused by the large hailstones.

Figure 3-8

Hailstones add a layer of ice each time they ride the updrafts and downdrafts in the clouds.

1 cm

Connect to...
Physics

Refer to **Figure 3-7**. Compare and contrast a storm surge and a tsunami (wave created by an earthquake on the ocean floor) from a physical and a destructive point of view.

---

check your UNDERSTANDING

Understanding Concepts

1. Rain itself may not cause damage to an area. Why, then, should people be concerned about prolonged or heavy rainfall?
2. At what part of a coastline might hurricane winds produce a great amount of damage?
3. Weather forecasters usually warn people in the path of a hurricane to be on the lookout for tornadoes. At what point during the hurricane should people be most concerned about a tornado forming?

Skill Review

4. **Inferring** Suppose that you live more than 500 km from where a hurricane first comes ashore. Infer how most of the damage done to your home probably occurred. For more help, refer to Inferring in the *Skill Handbook*.

Science and Society

Issue: A Burning Question

Some natural disasters are not directly related to wind or water. The year was 1988. It was a warm July evening in Yellowstone National Park, located in northwestern Wyoming. Lightning flashed in the distance as a fast-moving thunderstorm approached, and soon jagged bolts of lightning and crashing thunder were all around. Somewhere in the forest a tree was struck by lightning, and glowing sparks fell onto the forest floor. A small fire started in the underbrush. Lightning bolts struck other trees, and several more fires began burning. There had been very little rain that summer, and the dead leaves, fallen limbs, and grasses were dry. The fires spread quickly. The animals in the forest hurried to escape the flames.

The Issue

At first, park officials took a "let it burn" approach, and did not try to put out the fires. They thought that allowing a few small fires to burn would clear away the dry, thick underbrush and prevent an even bigger, more dangerous fire that might occur later if large amounts of underbrush were allowed to accumulate. This is a strategy that had been tried before in other forest fires, and seemed to be effective.

Unfortunately, the 1988 Yellowstone fires quickly got out of hand. The smoke and flames moved close to the towns on the border of the park, and officials decided the fires must be put out. Hundreds of people had to be evacuated, and firefighters and smoke-jumpers (firefighters who parachute into the forest from airplanes) were called in. But it was too late. The wildfires burned out of control all during that summer until snow fell in September. More than one million acres of woodlands were incinerated, buildings were destroyed, and two people lost their lives.

Widespread forest fires occurred again in the western United States in 1993 and 1994, with extensive destruction of property and loss of life.

These events focused attention on the question as to what is the best way to handle large, destructive forest fires.

The Background

For as long as there have been forests, lightning has been igniting forest fires. In the past, these fires simply burned themselves out because there was no way to stop them. With the development of modern technology (airplanes, powerful water pumps, chemicals) we now have the means to put out many of these fires. But it has raised the question whether we should put them out. In fact, since it has been found that small, contained fires may prevent larger fires later by burning away accumulated debris, many experts recommend setting some fires intentionally ("prescribed" fires). These fires would be carefully tended to try and make sure they didn't get out of control.

There are also ecological arguments for allowing forest fires to burn. Natural wildfires play an important role in establishing the balance between plant and animal species in an ecosystem. As shown in the photographs, burned out forests quickly start to regenerate. Contrary to what many may think, few animals lose their lives in forest fires. Most are quick enough to escape the flames. Some species actually depend on forest fires to survive. A bird called the Kirtland warbler builds its nest only on low, burnt tree branches. The cones of the lodgepole pine lie dormant on the forest floor for many years until the heat from a wildfire pops open the cones to release the seeds. And ash from burned vegetation falls onto the ground, returning nutrients to the soil. Preventing forest fires from occurring or putting them out before they've had a chance to burn can upset an ecosystem that has developed over thousands of years, and perhaps lead to the elimination of species that depend on fires for their survival.

However, naturally occurring fires and intentionally set fires, no matter how closely watched, can sometimes get out of control. For example, an unexpected change in wind direction can suddenly blow a fire toward a residential area, endangering lives and property.

The Question

As population increases, and people build more and more houses in wooded areas, the danger that forest fires present to human lives and property becomes greater. Finding the best way to control these fires is a very important issue.

Discussing the Issue

1. *Identify* three arguments for allowing forest fires to burn.
2. Stage a *debate* to discuss the pros and cons of the proposition "Forest fires should be put out immediately using all methods available."

After the Storm

3-3

Objectives

- Explain the effects of natural disasters on the local economy.
- Describe how periodic disturbances can alter the ecosystem.
- Identify possible health hazards resulting from the disasters.

Key Terms
salinity

Some Common Problems

Imagine surviving a hurricane, flood, blizzard, or any other natural disaster, only to face the overwhelming task of getting back to life as it was before the storm. Whatever the type of storm, people face similar adjustments. The problems they must solve fall into the following broad categories: economic damage, ecological damage, and health concerns.

■ Economic Damage

Hurricane Andrew and the 1993 flood of the Mississippi River are both considered the most destructive disasters of their type to hit the United States. In Florida alone, almost 8000 businesses and 120 000 jobs were affected by Hurricane Andrew. About $25 *billion* is the estimated loss caused by the storm.

How would you feel returning to a home that is destroyed or so badly damaged that you are told you can't enter it? All of your personal possessions have disappeared or are beyond repair. Your job is lost because the building it was in is also destroyed. You have no money because the bank's branch offices are closed. Even if you had the money, there is almost no place left to buy food, clean clothes, or other necessities.

Thinking Lab   Using Reference Materials

How have storms affected your local economy?

You don't have to live near the coast or in tornado alley to experience severe weather or to have crops and businesses damaged by a natural disaster.

Analysis
Use your library's resources to find out how and when your local economy has been severely affected by weather.

Thinking Critically

1. What is the most common agent of damage in your area?

2. Are there any ways to prevent or limit the extent of the damage?

3. Based on what you know about your local economy, how essential are these businesses or crops to the community's economic survival?

Figure 3-9

Farmers lost not only the crops of 1993, but also the crops for the following year because the fields did not drain or dry out soon enough to be replanted.

■ Recovering from a Storm

After a severe storm passes, businesses that have only minor damage can usually reopen quickly. If, however, many factories are severely damaged, thousands of people may lose their source of income. Recovery is more difficult when many people have no jobs.

Figure 3-10

Hurricanes and floods cause great economic damage.

Ⓐ Florida crops were damaged by Hurricane Andrew. How would this affect the price of these products in other parts of the country?

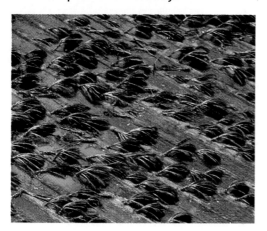

Agricultural profits can be severely damaged or wiped out if the area's crops are flooded as shown in **Figure 3-9.** Hurricane Andrew destroyed at least 25 percent of Louisiana's sugarcane crop. It destroyed almost every crop in Dade County, wiping out 15 percent of Florida's $6 billion in citrus and vegetable revenue. See **Figure 3-10A.**

■ Lower Tourist Dollars and Higher Fuel Costs

One of Florida's main industries is tourism. Luckily for the Florida economy, the major tourist attractions and hotels suffered only minor damages during Hurricane Andrew. They were able to serve the few tourists that continued to come to south Florida. However, income from tourism did decrease. Some vacationers thought that the attractions had been badly damaged. Others were concerned that

Ⓑ The barge industry was also hit hard. High waters and flooding made it difficult for barges to travel up or down the river. This industry lost up to $2 million a day in 1993.

Figure 3-11

Businesses are often damaged or destroyed by floodwaters, as near Fargo, ND, in 1997.

another hurricane would hit. A reduction in the number of tourists and closed or damaged businesses can seriously hurt a local economy, as shown in **Figure 3-11.**

The Gulf Coast area is also dependent on income from the petroleum industry. Because offshore drilling is a major source of fossil fuels, when drilling rigs are damaged, the supply of fuel and the ability to deliver that supply are upset. While Andrew caused minimal damage to the drilling rigs, it did disrupt pipelines. Thus, the cost of natural gas and other fuels increased.

One industry that benefited from Hurricane Andrew was the construction industry. Rebuilding began almost immediately. Stores that were able to

A Summer to Remember

"I was only 14 then, but I didn't think twice about helping," says John Leufray of St. Louis, Missouri. A mountain of sand had been dumped in the middle of the street. John and his friends from the YMCA formed an assembly line with people from other groups. Some shoveled the sand into burlap bags, some tied the bags shut, and some heaved them onto trucks. "The National Guard took the bags where they were needed most," John says.

Fighting the Flood

And they definitely were needed. This was the summer of 1993. Months of heavy rain had sent the Mississippi River surging over its banks. With more than 17,000 square miles of land underwater, John and thousands of other volunteers rushed to help. He met people

open and sell construction materials flourished. Contractors had more jobs than they could handle, especially after the insurance companies processed claims and paid out money.

■ Ecological Damage

Ecology is the study of interactions between organisms and their environments. Economic concerns may be foremost in the minds of people who live through a disaster, but damage to the ecosystem, the living populations in a community and the nonliving factors with which they react, is also a major problem. Various environments are affected when hurricanes hit. Obvious damage to the plant life can be seen in

Figure 3-12, which shows whole trees that were stripped of their leaves. Many trees were uprooted or bent so badly that their branches broke, and even huge trunks cracked or split.

Figure 3-12

Leaves from defoliated trees and plants will regrow, but trees with badly cracked or split trunks may take up to a year to die. Sufficient amounts of water and other nutrients cannot move within the tree. Some of the lost trees could take 50 to 100 years to replace.

of all ages who had come from many states to do whatever they could. The sandbags they filled were stacked into dams to try to direct the water away from homes.

But in many areas the water was unstoppable. Thousands of families in nine states along the river fled to Red Cross shelters and friends' homes to wait out the flood.

John's home in North St. Louis escaped the flooding, but he saw some of the destruction. "Houses looked like islands in the water," he recalls. "I could only see the tops of trees in some places. It was amazing to see all that water." In some areas, the Mississippi was ten miles wide.

St. Louis and other towns had built soil dams called levees to control the river's flow. In many places even the levees could not stop the raging water. Sometimes a levee burst, and the torrent of water swept away everything in its path.

Getting Back to Normal

Still, by the time John started Metro High School that fall, the flood waters had retreated and life was getting back to normal again. "People weren't discouraged by the flood," John reports. "They just worked together to make things better."

In St. Louis, the levees were rebuilt higher. Sandbag dams were reinforced to protect against more flooding. Some smaller riverside towns decided to relocate to higher ground, but others are rebuilding on the same spot. People who had always lived by the river intend to stay. They will rebuild their houses and reclaim their land and try to build more protective structures to control the waters.

*inter*NET CONNECTION

Visit the Glencoe Homepage, **http://www.glencoe.com/,** for the Chapter 3 link to the Red Cross. What are some safety tips to prepare for floods? What advice does the Red Cross offer about repairing a flood-damaged home?

There are other factors that may damage the ecosystem. Storm surges and high tides are important factors in coastal erosion. Entire sections of beachfront sand and property can be washed out to sea in a few hours. While artificial defenses such as seawalls may help slow the rate of erosion, they are not foolproof.

■ Habitats Under Attack

A habitat is the physical location in which an organism lives. Organisms are adapted to specific conditions within their habitats. Some organisms live in fresh water, some live in salt water, and some live in marine environments where the concentration of salt may vary with the tides. The damage caused on land by severe storms is usually self-evident. The damage to biological communities may be harder to see and measure. Delicate ecosystems are easily disrupted by changes in **salinity,** which is the concentration of salt in the environment. The influx of polluting chemicals from ground runoff, burial by debris or settling dust, and other factors can harm living organisms. Habitats may be vastly changed or even destroyed, causing the organisms that usually live there to relocate or die. Carry out the MiniLab to find out how a change in salinity may affect plants.

MiniLab

What happens when salt water floods a freshwater environment?

A severe storm may cause flooding or may force ocean water back into the mouth of a river. Either situation dramatically alters the salinity. The following activity may help you predict the effect that higher-than-normal tides can have on a fresh water ecosystem.

Procedure

1. Use a wax pencil to mark each of three test tubes into three equal parts.

2. Pour fresh tap water into each tube until it is two-thirds full.

3. Pour 1/8 teaspoon of salt into tubes 1 and 2. Label the tubes S for salt.

4. Add one drop of food coloring (made with fresh water) to tubes 1 and 3, and do not shake the tubes. Add one drop of food coloring to tube 2, but shake before observing. Observe and record the results.

5. Place the stem of a white carnation into tube 2. Observe the results, making sure to note the length of time involved.

6. Shake the third test tube and add another carnation. Observe any results and note the time involved.

Analysis

1. What happens when food coloring (fresh water) is added to the salt water?

2. What effect did shaking have on the water in test tube 2?

3. How does shaking the test tube represent what happens during a storm?

4. What happened to the two carnations? How does this represent what happens when ocean waters are forced into freshwater habitats?

Flood Contamination

Flooding, whether it is caused by hurricanes or continuous rains as in a river basin, brings the special problem of chemical and waste contamination. Farmers use chemical fertilizers and pesticides to increase their crop yields. As floodwaters spread out over the fields, they mix with the chemicals. Flooded industries may also contribute to the chemical levels of the river. These chemicals then move down the swollen rivers, contaminating the environment and the drinking supplies of people who live further downstream.

■ Damage to a Marine Ecosystem

Most of the damage discussed so far deals with changes in land ecosystems. Storms also disrupt marine ecosystems.

The physical characteristics of the ocean, such as salinity and mineral content, are fairly constant, so even small changes in its chemistry or temperature can significantly disrupt the ecosystem. In addition, the living organisms can be physically destroyed.

Because reefs grow in shallow ocean water, high winds and waves can cause hard corals to break. When Hurricane Andrew struck, strong currents stripped the bottom of the ocean of sponges, corals, and sea whips as seen in **Figure 3-13.** These organisms were thrown up along the shore with other debris. Scientists think that even the delicate coral reefs of the Florida Keys will recover from Hurricane Andrew's damage. They have seen coral larvae successfully settling on ocean floor newly exposed by storm action. In the following Investigation you will study how a storm can damage an ecosystem.

Figure 3-13

Wind and water currents are only some of the dangers faced by coral reefs. The increase in the deposition of rock, plant and animal remains, plus debris moved by the storm, can smother the corals. A change in salinity because of the rain may harm some organisms that live in the reef. In addition, dead, dying, and decaying organisms attract other organisms that feed on them.

How sensitive is an ecosystem?

Natural disasters often alter the living and nonliving conditions within an ecosystem. Sometimes the conditions are changed so much that the area may have difficulty recovering. In this Investigation, attempt to alter a simple ecosystem by simulating the damage caused by severe weather.

Preparation

Problem
How much change can an ecosystem tolerate?

Hypothesis
Have your group agree on a hypothesis to be tested. Record the hypothesis.

Objectives
In this Investigation, you will:
- **Determine** which factors cause permanent damage to an ecosystem.
- **Observe** how organisms adapt to changes in their environment.

Possible Materials
large test tubes
test-tube rack
beakers
dropper
stirring rods
vinegar
fine-grained sediment
fertilizer

salt water (several different concentrations)
fresh water
litmus paper
pH standard solutions
electric fan with variable settings
freshwater plants in individual cups
freshwater microorganisms in individual cups
flashlights
food coloring
thermometer
hot plate
microscope
microscope slides

Safety Precautions

The solutions used to adjust pH may burn your skin. Wash your hands immediately after the lab. Wear your safety goggles.

DESIGN YOUR OWN
INVESTIGATION

Plan the Experiment

1 Examine the materials provided. As a group, make a list of possible ways you can modify the ecosystems provided to model the effects of a storm on the ecosystems.

2 Decide which variables you will change (salinity, temperature, pH concentration, amount of suspended sediment, and so on) in order to test your hypothesis.

3 Design an experiment that will allow for the collection of qualitative and quantitative data. Prepare a list of numbered directions. Include a list of materials and the amounts you will need.

4 Make a data table *in your Journal* that will enable you to conduct your experiment and record your data in an organized manner.

Check the Plan
Discuss the following points with other group members to decide the final procedure for your experiment.

1 Read over your entire experiment to make sure it is logical and that you can carry it out in the time allotted.

2 What will be your control? State how you will gather and measure the data. How often will you observe the ecosystems? How will you make sure they are not disturbed for the duration of the experiment?

3 *Make sure your teacher has approved your experimental plan before you proceed further.*

4 Carry out your experiment. Complete your data table and write a paragraph or two summarizing your results.

5 Compare your results with those of the other groups.

Analyze and Conclude

1. Comparing and Contrasting Did any one variable seem to cause the most damage? If so, which one and why do you think it did?

2. Drawing Conclusions Were all of the organisms affected the same way?

What can you say about their abilities to adapt to stressful conditions?

3. Analyzing the Procedure In what way did this experiment simulate real-life situations? In what ways was it different?

Going Further

Changing Variables
Suppose you were given a desert ecosystem to use. Would the variables change and if so why?

Figure 3-14

People often wait in long lines to pick up supplies of fresh water following hurricanes and floods. Army and National Guard troops provide food, water, housing, and medical treatment for the victims.

■ Health Concerns

You may take the supply of clean water for granted. But, suppose it was disrupted and you had none to drink. You would have to travel far to take a shower, and finding toilet facilities would be difficult. That's exactly what it is like for the people living in the aftermath of hurricanes and floods. See **Figure 3-14.**

■ Disease May Follow Storms

Natural disasters cause broken water lines, flooded water-treatment plants, like the one in **Figure 3-15,** and contamination of the water supply by chemicals, human and animal wastes, and disease-causing agents called pathogens. Unless measures are taken immediately to clean up the dirt and debris, the number of pests such as rodents, scavengers, and insects such as mosquitoes increases quickly. The pests and contaminated water can lead to the spread of infectious diseases. The fact that there were no major

outbreaks of disease following Hurricane Andrew or the 1993 Mississippi River flood can be attributed to the quick setup of medical facilities in both areas.

Figure 3-15

When water-treatment plants like the one in the picture couldn't operate because of flooding, people had to boil all of their water or find other safe sources for drinking, cooking, bathing, and even washing their clothes.

Figure 3-16
Emergency medical facilities are quickly set up to take care of hurricane victims. Not only do medical personnel treat people injured in the storm, they also work to combat the spread of disease by giving immunizations and helping to establish safe and sanitary temporary living conditions.

■ Danger from Injuries

Injuries account for a large number of visits to the medical facilities, **Figure 3-16.** While many injuries occur as a direct result of a disaster, many more occur as people try to clean up and rebuild. The risk of contracting tetanus, a deadly disease caused by bacteria that live in the soil, is very real because of the contaminated environment. Getting a tetanus shot is part of the medical treatment.

■ What benefits come from storms?

Storms help distribute the energy from the sun that reaches Earth. Globally, they help even out the atmosphere's temperature so that there are no great extremes as there are on planets with no atmosphere. As a result, more areas of Earth can support life. The precipitation from storms provides water for plants and animals and washes pollutants from the air.

check your UNDERSTANDING

Understanding Concepts
1. What seems to be the biggest danger to freshwater environments from a hurricane?
2. Speculate why broken water lines could lead to the spread of disease.
3. Why might farmers be asked to limit the amount of chemical fertilizers and pesticides they use on fields in flood-prone areas?

Skill Review
4. **Inferring** How could the destruction of crops in the fields cause the price of produce already in the stores to go up? For more help, refer to Inferring in the *Skill Handbook.*

Emergency Preparedness

No matter where you live, you have most likely experienced severe weather conditions at some time. For the worst storms, survival can be a matter of being prepared in the case of an emergency. Shelter, food, water, and medical supplies can mean the difference between being a statistic and survival.

You're the Emergency Preparedness Director

Imagine you have been asked to develop an emergency weather plan for your school. Your budget is limited, so building a separate shelter should be avoided, although it may be necessary, depending on your situation. Consider how to provide each of the following for all of the students in your building—shelter, food, clean water, medical supplies.

Drawing on Experience

1. Find out what your school's current emergency weather plan is. How does it address each of the necessary elements?

2. Walk through your school looking for a strong part of the building that could serve as a shelter for everyone at the school. Do you think the building is strong enough to withstand high winds and heavy rains or snow from a severe storm? If not, how could it be strengthened?

3. Make a list of the provisions you would need for the survival of everyone at your school for a week.

4. Make a plan for informing your school about emergency procedures for severe weather so everyone knows what to do.

You may want to use a combination of posters, special classes, radio commercials, or other ideas.

Testing...Testing

1. Outline your emergency weather plan for your school. Describe where people should go and how the shelter would be supplied.

2. Carry out your information plan telling people what to do in the case of an emergency during school hours. Present your plan to the rest of the class.

How Did It Work?

What was the most difficult part of developing an emergency weather proposal? How does it compare with the plan your school currently uses? Develop an emergency weather plan for your home.

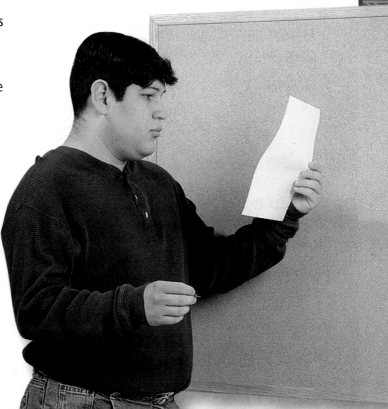

Read the statements below that review major points presented in the chapter. Using the concepts that you have learned, answer each question *in your Journal.*

1 While large, violent storms can be catastrophic, some benefits are linked to their occurrence. *Explain how a hurricane helps even out Earth's atmospheric temperature.*

2 Most damage done by hurricanes is caused by the forces of strong winds and flowing water. *Explain two ways that wind can destroy a building during a hurricane.*

3 Damage from natural disasters can be placed in the following categories: economic, ecological, or health-related. *How could you help lessen the impact of a natural disaster on your own home?*

Using Key Science Terms

evacuate

gust

salinity

storm surge

Answer the following questions using what you know about the science terms.

1. What is the relationship between wind and storm surges?
2. Why would government officials want to evacuate people ahead of a flood?
3. Describe how salinity and pathogens can cause damage after a natural disaster.
4. How does the force of the wind change if a sudden gust triples its speed?

Understanding Ideas

Using complete sentences, answer the following questions in your Journal.

1. How does a change in available energy cause a change in a hurricane?
2. How does wind raise the level of a storm surge?
3. How do hurricane winds differ from thunderstorm winds?
4. Why might rain be more damaging than wind during a severe storm?
5. What helped keep deaths to a minimum during Hurricane Andrew?
6. How does the containment of human and animal wastes help limit the spread of disease?
7. What type of business is most likely to suffer major damage during a hailstorm?
8. Why is it difficult to make hurricane-proof buildings?

9. Why would local governments want to restrict the amount of construction that can be done on a beach?
10. Why would some of the trees that remained standing after Hurricane Andrew passed by die a year later?

Developing Skills

Use your understanding of the concepts developed in this chapter to answer each of the following questions.

1. **Concept Mapping** Using the listed phrases, complete a concept map that follows the progress of a hurricane:

   wave of low pressure forms, hurricane breaks up into isolated thunderstorms, increasing energy, tropical storm forms, storm becomes a hurricane

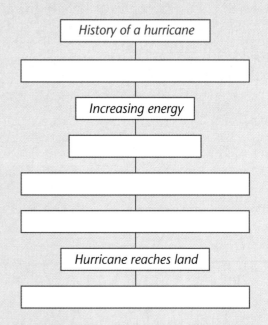

History of a hurricane

Increasing energy

Hurricane reaches land

2. **Predicting** Reviewing the data you collected in the MiniLab about salt water and organisms on page 98, predict what would happen if fresh water were added to salt water.

3. **Comparing and Contrasting** Think about damage that would be caused by a major earthquake. How would this damage compare to the damage caused by major floods?

4. **Inferring** Lives are saved because many people listen to and follow evacuation orders issued before a hurricane. Explain why some people might refuse to leave their homes even when threatened by a natural disaster.

Critical Thinking

In your Journal, *answer each of the following questions.*

1. Why do branching corals and delicate sea fans most often grow where waves do not break over them?

2. Compare the abilities of hurricanes, tornadoes, and floods to cause damage over a large area.

3. Why is a hailstorm potentially more devastating than a drought?

4. Why would government officials be concerned about rounding up stray animals after a disaster?

Problem Solving

Read the following problem and discuss your answers in a brief paragraph.

You have the opportunity to build a new home on the beach. The isolated site is on a high bluff. You notice that the bluff has been sharply undercut by wave action and wind erosion. The builder tells you that in the event of a hurricane, your home will be safe from harm. You question this assurance.

What side effects from a hurricane could contribute to increased erosion? What problems might wind cause for an isolated house on top of the bluff?

CONNECTING IDEAS

1. **Theme—Energy** How does the energy in ocean waves, lightning, and severe storms compare? In what way does the energy produced by each of these affect humans?

2. **Theme—Stability and Change** Some scientists think that a warming of the oceans, caused by the greenhouse effect, will cause more hurricanes to have the same high winds as Hurricane Andrew. While not all scientists agree, what factor would cause some to make this prediction?

3. **Theme—Systems and Interactions** Scientists closely study an ecosystem that is recovering from an environmental disaster. How can the data from these studies help us better understand the original ecosystem?

4. **Eyewitness Accounts** What was done with the sandbags that John Leufray and his friends filled?

5. **Applying Technology** What is the single most important item you should provide when preparing for survival in case of a natural disaster?

DESIGN A SCHOOL WEATHER STATION

Problem

Weather forecasters use data from instruments designed to report conditions in Earth's atmosphere. Build a weather station on your school grounds to obtain daily weather conditions for a daily school bulletin.

Materials

2 identical alcohol
   Celsius thermometers
piece of gauze
   (2 cm²)
string
tape
cardboard

beaker of water
3 or 4 small plastic
   or paper cups
small coffee can
6 drinking straws
large rubber balloon
construction paper

transparent tape
scissors
rubber band
pin
pencil with eraser

Getting Started

1. Using library resources, construct instruments and collect weather data for several weeks.

2. Construct a cup anemometer to take measurements of wind speed.

3. Construct a wind vane (a flag on a flagpole may be used) to take measurements of wind direction.

4. Construct a barometer to measure increases and decreases in air pressure.

5. Use a thermometer to record daily morning and afternoon temperatures.

6. Using a wet and dry thermometer, measure relative humidity.

7. After recording the data from your instruments for two weeks, hypothesize what weather conditions lead to cloudy, rainy weather. Monitor weather conditions to see if your hypothesis is supported by data.

8. You will want to build a protective box to place around your instruments when they are not in use. Be sure to keep thermometers stored in a safe place until you are using them and remember not to place thermometers in the sunlight.

Resources

The USA Today Weather Book. Williams, Jack. New York, NY. Vintage Books, 1992.

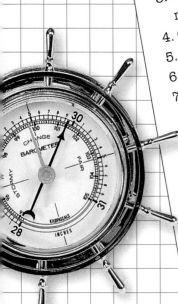

PRODUCE YOUR OWN TELEVISION WEATHER REPORT

Problem

Have you ever been caught in a surprise storm? How do weather forecasters make predictions about the weather? Imagine you are the television weather reporter. You and your production team have been given the job of producing weekly weather reports to be broadcast over your school television or radio station. You will need to collect data for two weeks and then use the data to predict weather conditions near your school.

Materials

video camera or tape recorder

videotape or audiotape

daily weather reports from the newspaper (your own weather data from instruments in your school weather station would be better)

appropriate costumes

Getting Started

1. Set aside a portion of the room and decorate it as your weekly weather report station. You should include weather maps and other props.
2. Using data from your school weather station or the local newspaper, write a script for the weekly weather report for your school.
3. Several students should be in charge of setting up and operating the video or audio equipment.
4. Decide qualifications then audition your weather broadcasters.
5. Select a weather program producer from your group.
6. Select a name and theme for your weather program.
7. In addition to reporting factual weather information, predict what will happen over the next few days. In other words, forecast the weather.
8. Use a taped segment from "The Weather Channel" to enhance your weather report. Be sure to obtain permission from "The Weather Channel" to use film footage of weather conditions.

Resources

Nightly weather reports from local radio and television stations.
Weather report from "The Weather Channel" programming.

Ecology

All organisms have a particular place in which they live. The beautiful, clear, emerald-green water of a coral reef seems to be a perfect environment for any fish. But, is it the perfect place for your pet goldfish? The tranquil woodland setting is a great place for a chipmunk, but could chipmunks survive in a city environment? What are the parameters that define the "best place" for an organism? In this unit, you'll explore the world of living things and the conditions in which they live.

The wide variety of corals that form coral reefs provide habitats for many organisms.

Chipmunks live on the forest floor of eastern woodlands like the one shown here. They are small, ground-loving mammals that feed on nuts, seeds, and fruits.

Focus On

•••••••••••••••••••

Habitats

Shelter, an abundant supply of food and water, and other members of your species—these are some of the requirements of the "perfect" place for an organism to live. Do all organisms have the same requirements? Do some "perfect" environments have hidden problems? Perfect peregrine falcon habitat includes lots of ledges for nesting, lots of open space to fly, and lots of birds to eat. Where is this habitat? Would you imagine downtown Los Angeles? What are the factors that make a place suitable for a particular organism? In this unit, you'll explore the complex web of interrelationships between organisms and their environment.

Downtown Los Angeles

The pristine-looking coastal cliffs of California's Big Sur look like a perfect habitat for peregrine falcons. In reality, the pesticides in the area have caused the birds to lay eggs with such thin shells that they cannot withstand the conditions of incubation. This reproductive failure has caused a decline in the population in that area.

112

Try It!

Many factors determine the correct environment for a particular organism. You've seen the conditions necessary for peregrine falcons. In the case of a coral reef, the correct water temperature, the right minerals in the water, the right organisms, and the right weather conditions are all important. In this activity, you'll discover the conditions required by the organisms that inhabit a rotting log. For what organisms is the rotting log a habitat? What are some of their characteristics?

What To Do

1. Examine your rotting log and record *in your Journal* the different living and nonliving things you find.

2. Next to each item on your list, write down what conditions you think organisms need to live in that habitat. What conditions are necessary in order for that habitat to form?

Try It Again

After you've learned more about habitats and the interactions of the living and nonliving things in them, try this activity again to see if you can see more.

One way biologists are trying to save the peregrines is to gather the thin-shelled eggs, hatch them safely in a laboratory, and then return them to the nest. In the nest, the real eggs are replaced by dummy eggs that mimic the real thing. The parents are fooled and later accept the laboratory-hatched chicks.

UNIT 2 PROJECTS

During your exploration of organisms and their environments, you may discover new questions or wish to explore more about how organisms respond to environmental pressures. **The Salt Pollution Project** and **The Micro-environment Project**, found in the Unit 2 Projects section on pages 200-201, will give you the challenge of examining the effect of a pollutant in a plant's environment. Read through these projects. As you explore this unit, think how you could apply what you discover to your projects.

CHAPTER 4

Biotic and Abiotic Factors
Organisms and Their Environments

magine talking with two friends who have just returned to the city from their summer vacations. One friend visited the Rocky Mountains; the other traveled to the Florida Keys. The visitor to the Rocky Mountains took long hikes through the forest and went swimming in cold, deep lakes. The Florida traveler lounged on sandy beaches and took in a snorkeling tour of a coral reef. What were the living and nonliving features that made the environments your friends described different from one another?

▶ *In the following activity, you will explore the living and nonliving features of an environment.*

MiniLab

What are the living and nonliving features of an environment?

Every region on the surface of Earth includes living organisms and nonliving or physical features that affect those organisms. All living things interact with the nonliving features of their environment. Nonliving features include objects such as rocks and ponds and factors like sunlight and temperature, all of which have an effect on living organisms.

Procedure

1. *In your Journal,* make two columns, *Living* and *Nonliving.*
2. Examine the environment provided, and record the living organisms and nonliving features you observe.

Analysis

1. For each item on your *Nonliving* list, write down at least one way in which it affects the living organisms.
2. Select one organism from your *Living* list and suggest one or more ways it might affect another organism.

Biotic Factors in Ecosystems

Objectives

■ Recognize that some ecosystems include a larger variety of species than others.

■ Demonstrate that populations of living organisms differ in size and composition.

Key Terms

ecosystem
biotic factor
population
species
diversity
community

The Living Ecosystem

What living organisms did you find in the environment you observed? There were probably some plants, a few insects or earthworms, and maybe some mold or fungus. Your list of non-living features probably included air, light, soil, water or moisture, and perhaps a few pebbles or rocks. The interactions of all the living organisms with the nonliving factors in a given area powered by a flow of energy are called an **ecosystem**. Ecosystems can be as small as an aquarium or a petri dish or as large as a rain forest or ocean. The size or location of an ecosystem is not as important as the interactions of the organisms within the ecosystem.

■ Populations

Many types of ecosystems can be found on Earth, each characterized by different organisms and physical features. The organisms that make up the living portion of an ecosystem are known as **biotic factors**. For example, the biotic factors in a forest ecosystem include trees, shrubs, birds, insects, chipmunks, and bears. The biotic factors in an ocean ecosystem include fishes, whales, jellyfish, and many kinds of microscopic plants and animals.

The organisms living in an ecosystem make up **populations**. A population is a group of organisms of the same species living in a specific area.

Figure 4-1

These flowering plants, called Alpine avens, represent a population of organisms adapted to the arctic-like conditions of the high elevations of the Rocky Mountains. They have low woody growth that protects them from the wind and rolled leaves that prevent water loss. In addition, they are evergreen so they are able to begin food production as soon as the snow melts.

The plants in **Figure 4-1** form a population as do all the students in your school. The particular type of plant that makes up the population in **Figure 4-1** is a species. A **species** is a group of closely related organisms that are able to breed with one another to produce fertile offspring. Members of a population compete for food, water, space, mates, and other resources. The ways in which members of a population utilize and share the resources in the environment determine how large a population can be.

An ecosystem such as a forest, which contains a large number of populations of different species, has a high diversity. **Diversity** is a measure of the number of species that dwell in an ecosystem. For example, a large supermarket has a greater number of different items than does a small convenience store. The supermarket has a high diversity and the convenience store a low diversity. A crack in the sidewalk that is populated by a dandelion plant, a few blades of grass, and a few insects is an example of an ecosystem with a low species diversity. A tropical rain forest is an ecosystem with a high diversity. Species diversity is higher in areas closer to the equator. Diversity tends to be less in areas that are stressed due to overpopulation or a lack of resources.

Thinking Lab   Interpret the Data

Comparing Diversity in Different Ecosystems

What is the diversity of an ecosystem? The higher the diversity of an ecosystem, the more complex are the interactions among the organisms found there. Knowing how many species are present is an important step in learning how these populations interact with each other.

Analysis
Observe the following three photographs, which show approximately the same area each of coral reef, forest, and urban ecosystems. *In your Journal*, make a table with one column for each ecosystem. In the appropriate column, list each kind of organism you see in the photograph. Then, total the number of species you observed in each ecosystem.

Thinking Critically
According to your observations, which ecosystem shows the greatest diversity? The lowest diversity? Do you think you might get different results if you were to actually travel to make observations of each ecosystem rather than relying on a photograph? Why or why not? How could you change the design of this activity to make certain your results were as accurate as possible?

■ Diversity in Forest Ecosystems

Forest ecosystems occur on all continents except Antarctica. Tropical forests are found in the warm-weather regions that lie near the equator. Deciduous forests—forests made up of trees that lose their leaves each autumn—occur in North America, Europe, Asia, and other temperate regions. Many of the high slopes of the Rocky Mountains are covered with a third type of forest, the coniferous forest.

Coniferous forests are found in North America on both the east and west coasts. On the east coast of the United States, large coniferous forests can be found in Maine, New York, and New Hampshire. In the west, Montana, Colorado, Northern California, and Wyoming are places to see these forests. They are also found in England, Scandinavia, and across Europe and the former Soviet Union to the Bering Sea. Coniferous forests of the world are named for the cone-bearing trees that are a major

Figure 4-2

A Rocky Mountain coniferous forest has a high species diversity.

Ⓐ The primary feature of this Rocky Mountain forest is the dense growth of coniferous trees, including several species of pine, fir, spruce, and juniper.

Ⓒ Groves of aspen trees are commonly found in Rocky Mountain forests. These groves occur in areas where fire has opened the forest and in areas lower on the mountain. Fireweed covers the floor of this aspen grove.

Ⓑ The northern pygmy owl, commonly found in Rocky Mountain forests, is no larger than a sparrow. These owls nest in holes in trees in the coniferous forest.

feature of this ecosystem. Because these trees bear their seeds in cones, they are called conifers. These trees are well adapted to a wide variety of environments and are one of the most abundant types of tree on Earth. Like all forests, coniferous forests have a high species diversity. Porcupines, wolves, and lynx are a few of the animals that can be found in coniferous forests. Thousands of species can be found in a coniferous forest in the Rocky Mountains. A few of these are shown in **Figure 4-2.**

F Elk browse in clearings and less dense areas of the forest. Herds of elk are widely distributed in mountain forests of the West. Native Americans in the Rockies referred to elk as *Wapiti*—a term that is still used today.

E The habitats of the mountain bluebird are the open, high-elevation areas. These birds nest in old woodpecker diggings, as well as holes in cliffs and banks. They feed on insects, catching them as they fly. They also feed on seeds and berries.

D Plants that need a constant supply of water—such as sedges and berry bushes—grow along the banks of streams in these forests.

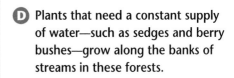

■ Diversity in the Coral Reef Ecosystem

Coral reefs are another example of ecosystems with a high species diversity. Coral reefs, such as the one in **Figure 4-3,** can be found in warm, shallow, tropical ocean waters. Reefs are common in the waters along the coast of Florida, the islands of the West Indies, parts of Africa and Australia, and the islands of Indonesia and the South Pacific Ocean. It has taken thousands and thousands of years to form some of the massive coral reefs found in today's oceans. Large coral formations are made up of many individual soft-bodied animals related to jellyfish. A single individual, called a polyp, may be only a few millimeters in size, but as **Figure 4-4** shows, thousands grow

Figure 4-3

These photos show a few of the organisms commonly found in and around a coral reef.

Ⓐ Coral colonies grow in a variety of shapes, sizes, and colors. The complex shape of a coral reef provides nooks and crannies that shelter many other organisms. Hundreds of species of fishes, crabs, shrimp, and snails live in or on the reef. The reef also provides a hard surface on which algae and sponges can grow.

Ⓑ Moray eels such as this white mouth moray are nocturnal and generally secretive by nature. They hide in crevices in coral and under ledges.

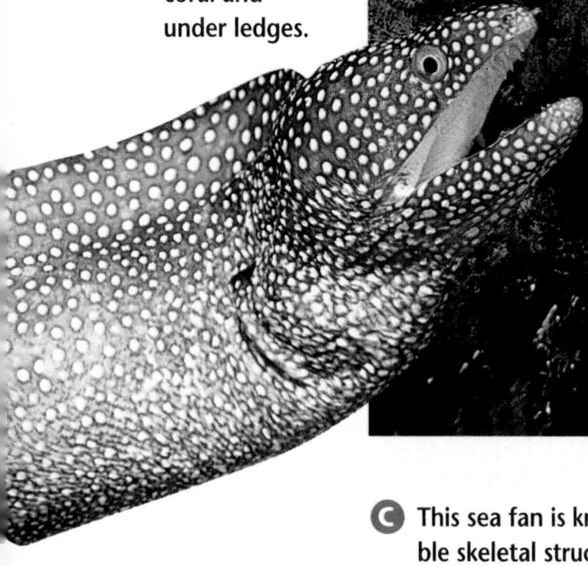

Ⓒ This sea fan is known as a soft coral due to its flexible skeletal structure. Sea fans have a flat, compressed surface and may grow to be five feet tall.

together to form reefs. Each polyp has a mouth opening surrounded by tentacles that have stinging cells. These cells are used to sting and trap prey. Corals use minerals from the ocean water to build a hard protective skeleton that develops from the cells on the lower side and bottom of the polyps. When the polyp dies, the hard outer skeleton is left. The next generation of polyps attaches to the skeletons of the preceding generation. The reef is built up slowly, as generation after generation adds another layer. Only the top layer of a reef contains living polyps. Each species of coral has its own unique pattern of growth. An example of one type of coral is shown in **Figure 4-5.**

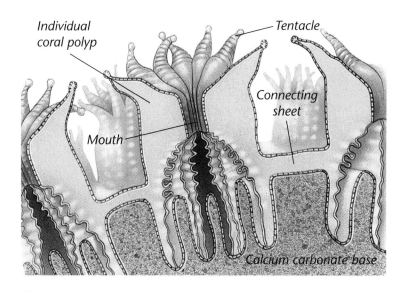

Figure 4-4

The polyps of corals that form colonies are all connected by a horizontal sheet of tissue.

Figure 4-5

This lettuce coral forms semicircular, ruffled or flat sheets, arranged in an upright position. This coral is often found growing at the base of elkhorn coral. Its color can be yellow-brown or purple-brown, splotched with green. The close-up photo shows individual polyps in this colony.

To Find Out More About ...

Urban Ecosystems
read "A Scientist in the City" by James Trefil, Doubleday, New York, 1994.

■ Diversity in the Urban Ecosystem

Humans are the organisms we most readily associate with an urban ecosystem. What other kinds of organisms live in this environment? Dogs, cats, and goldfish, as well as potted plants are obvious, but there are many organisms living in this environment that we don't think about. An old piece of bread can be the habitat for bread mold, and a damp shower can provide the perfect environment for mildew. Silverfish, a type of insect, can often be found feeding on old books and clothes.

What about the occasional spider in the corner of the ceiling, or the pigeons roosting on the roof of an apartment building? Sometimes we find ourselves sharing our homes with mice, ants, roaches, and termites. What does the urban environment have that would attract these organisms? Do you think an urban ecosystem has a higher or lower species diversity than a forest? **Figure 4-6** provides a few more examples of organisms common to urban ecosystems. What other organisms can you think of that may inhabit an urban environment?

Figure 4-6

The species diversity of a city may seem low compared to a coral reef, but urban environments are the home of many organisms besides humans. The trees, shrubs, flowers, and other ornamental plantings we use around our homes contribute to the species diversity of a city.

A The common house centipede, a scutigeromorph, is usually found trapped in bathtubs and sinks.

B A crack in the pavement is an example of a tiny urban ecosystem. What other organisms might you find here in addition to the dandelion plant?

Populations Form Communities

When you conducted the MiniLab at the beginning of this chapter, you speculated about ways in which one organism might influence another. You might have observed that a snail living in a terrarium eats the leaves of one of the plants, and a caterpillar uses the plant's stem as a resting place. Or you may have noticed that some species of insects burrow into the fungi that break down rotting logs. In doing so, they make a shelter for themselves, and at the same time they have a source of food.

A single population could not survive without some type of interaction with other populations in the ecosystem. Just as a group of organisms makes up a population, a group of populations makes up a community. A **community** is a group of populations in an area that interact with one another. **Figure 4-7** shows some examples of interacting populations in a pond community.

Figure 4-7

Communities are composed of populations of organisms that depend upon one another for food, shelter, or other survival needs. Cattails and yellow pond lilies growing in shallow water provide a sheltered nursery ground for the young of several species of fishes and frogs. Great herons and other birds depend on the fish and frog populations for their food.

check your UNDERSTANDING

Understanding Concepts

1. Compare the diversity of a coral reef ecosystem to the species diversity of an urban ecosystem.
2. List several biotic factors found in a forest ecosystem. Describe how two of these factors influence each other.
3. Explain why it is necessary that ecosystems contain populations of many species.

Skill Review

4. **Comparing and Contrasting** Compare the species diversity of an urban ecosystem with that of a forest ecosystem. Be sure to consider all organisms that may be found in each. For more help, refer to Comparing and Contrasting in the *Skill Handbook*.

Science and Society

Issue:
National lands, whose are they?

"We need the tonic of wildness,—to wade sometimes in marshes where the bittern and the meadow-hen lurk, and hear the booming of the snipe. . . and the mink crawls with its belly close to the ground. . . ."—Henry David Thoreau (1854) *Walden*.

The Issue

The words of the American writer Thoreau awakened many people to a new appreciation of nature. Today, an intimate moment in the wilderness is becoming more rare than it was in Thoreau's day. Still, many people are fortunate enough to visit a national park, one of the last areas of wilderness left in the United States.

Most people are surprised to learn that as citizens of the United States, they own the national parks. These lands are managed by a combination of federal agencies. Of course, with so many owners, not everyone agrees on how these lands should be managed or even what their primary purpose is. Early on, an important goal of the national parks and forests was natural resource management. One spokesperson for resource management described this goal to be the use of the natural resources now existing on this continent for the benefit of the people who live here now.

The resource management view disturbs preservationists, those who want to keep the wilderness as it is now, for future generations. Sustainable-earth conservationists go one step further and state that the nation's wilderness must be protected and expanded on the grounds that the wild species it contains have a right to exist without human interference.

Some national forests are used for commercial logging.

The Background

Trappers in the early 1800s returned from what is now Yellowstone National Park with tales of spectacular geysers and steaming springs. By 1872, the federal government declared Yellowstone the first national park in the world. More than a century ago, some people were concerned about protecting the nation's unique places.

Today, more than 32 million hectares of federal lands have been designated by Congress as national parks. Seventy-four percent of the major parks are in Alaska and in the western United States.

The Question

A wilderness area is a roadless and otherwise *unimproved* area within a national park, wildlife refuge, or forest. Only about 49 percent of the national parks have protected wilderness areas. In these areas, grazing, timber harvesting, mining, and commercial activities are prohibited. Hiking, nonmotorized boating, fishing, and camping are allowed. Studies by the Wilderness Society reveal that, to be effective, a wilderness area should comprise at least 400 000 hectares. This much land insures that air, water, and noise pollution from surrounding areas will not impact the wildlife in the park. It also insures that large predators have sufficient territory in which to find food.

Since 1950, visitors to the national parks have increased by 1200 percent. Over the same period, the numbers of wolves, bears, and other large predators have dropped sharply. Often, when animals are disturbed, they leave an area or suffer interruptions in breeding patterns. A decrease in predators results in a disastrous increase in the number of prey. The prey then overgraze the vegetation, causing a further upset in the balance of nature. Does this mean that access to the parks should be restricted?

National parks are used by many for rest and relaxation.

What about people's need to be out in nature? Wilderness satisfies many human needs. One is the need to see beauty and uniqueness and at the same time to escape the bustle of the city. Another is the need to prove that one can survive in a place not yet tamed by civilization. Compare these needs with the needs of wildlife and the need for resources found on national lands. Are America's national parks for people, for wildlife, for development, or for all these purposes?

*inter*NET CONNECTION

Follow the link for Chapter 4 on the Glencoe Homepage, **http://www.glencoe.com/**, for information about the U.S. park system. Visit Nature Net, the park service's website. How does the National Park Service monitor air and water quality in the nation's parks? How does it monitor the status of plants and animals?

Abiotic Factors in Ecosystems

4-2

Objectives

■ Identify some of the abiotic factors that affect life.

■ Describe how water is essential for life.

Key Terms

abiotic factor, solution, solute, solvent, polar molecule, acid, base, pH

The Nonliving Environment

Suppose you are a biologist who has set out to discover why a certain species of tree grows in some parts of South America but not in others. Do you think a study of organisms living in and around the tree would provide a complete answer to the question? How could the biologist find out what environmental factors determine where the tree is likely to be found? Taking a close look at your own surroundings may give you some ideas.

Not all organisms need exactly the same physical conditions for life as human beings do, as you can see in **Figure 4-8**. Organisms have adaptations that allow them to survive in a variety of conditions. The nonliving features of an environment are called **abiotic factors**. Examples of abiotic factors include air, temperature, moisture, light, and soil. Abiotic factors have direct effects on the living things in an environment; in fact, they often determine what organisms can live in a given environment. The following MiniLab will help you determine how abiotic factors affect living things.

MiniLab

Do nonliving features help determine which species live in an ecosystem?

The abiotic factors in an ecosystem determine what species of organisms can survive there. What are the nonliving features important for humans?

Procedure

1. Make a list of all the abiotic, or physical, features of your environment that you have encountered since you woke up this morning.

2. *In your Journal*, make two columns—one labeled *Essential* and one labeled *Nonessential*.

3. List the nonliving features you consider necessary for a human being's physical survival in the *Essential* column. List all others in the *Nonessential* column.

Analysis

1. Explain why you think each feature listed in your *Essential* column is necessary to the survival of a human being.

2. List several other organisms that share the same essential needs for survival.

3. List some organisms that require different nonliving factors for their survival.

Figure 4-8

Abiotic factors help determine which species are present in an ecosystem.

A *Oxygen* Some types of bacteria will die if exposed to the oxygen in the air.

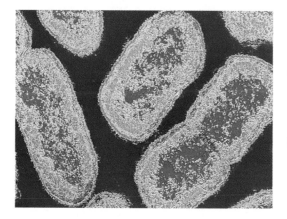

B *Temperature* Polar bears and penguins survive and reproduce in conditions far colder than humans can withstand.

C *Light* This blind cave fish, *Characidae astganax fasciatus,* has adaptations to survive in the dark.

D *Water* Mesquite trees have long, deep roots that enable them to thrive in extremely dry regions.

Sunlight and Temperature

Have you ever noticed that grass growing in the shade of a tree is often not as lush or healthy as grass growing in an open field or lawn? If you've ever done any digging in garden soil, you've probably observed that earthworms exposed by your shovel immediately begin working their way back into the darkness of the soil. Although some organisms are better adapted for darkness and others for bright sunlight, virtually all life on Earth depends on sunlight as its ultimate source of energy. Green plants use energy from sunlight to manufacture food in a process known as photosynthesis. Photosynthesis will be discussed in more detail in Chapter 8. All organisms need energy to live. Human beings and other animals obtain energy by eating food. Energy from the sun also influences living organisms in other ways.

4-2 Abiotic Factors in Ecosystems **127**

■ Sunlight Is Reflected, Transmitted, and Absorbed

What is it like to climb into an automobile that has been sitting in the bright sun with its windows closed? In the wintertime, you might welcome the warmth, but in the summer it is miserable and can be dangerous. In the summer, the temperature in a car with its windows rolled up can reach a dangerously high level in a very short time. Why does the air inside the car become so much warmer than the air outside it? The following MiniLab will let you explore the answer to this question.

MiniLab

How does sunlight affect temperature?

Some objects on Earth absorb more of the sun's energy than others. Either the sunlight is blocked because the object is in the shade, or the object itself reflects some of the sunlight back into the atmosphere.

Procedure

CAUTION: *Alert your teacher if a mercury thermometer breaks.* **Do not touch it.**

1. Pour about ½ cup of water into each of two small, clear glass or plastic jars or beakers.

2. Use a thermometer to measure the temperature of the water in each jar. Record the measurement *in your Journal.*

3. Cover the top of one jar with clear plastic wrap; leave the other container open.

4. Put both containers in bright, direct sunlight or under a bright lamp for at least one hour; then measure and record the water temperature in each one.

Analysis

1. Did the temperature of the water in the two containers change by the same amount? If not, explain.

2. Use the results of this experiment to explain why the interior of a car parked in the sun with windows closed soon becomes hotter than its surroundings.

As you found in the MiniLab, if Earth were like a car with its windows closed or a covered container of water left in the sun, temperatures would soon become unbearably hot for humans and most other organisms. But Earth does not absorb all of the sun's energy. Study **Figure 4-9** to find out what happens to the energy of the sun that strikes Earth.

Figure 4-9

Several things can happen to the radiant energy from the sun that reaches Earth's atmosphere.

A Part of the energy is reflected back into space by dust particles and water vapor in the upper atmosphere.

B Part of the energy is absorbed by clouds or reflected and scattered throughout the atmosphere.

C A layer of ozone gas in the upper atmosphere absorbs much of the harmful ultraviolet portion of the sun's energy, preventing most of it from reaching Earth's surface.

D Part of the sun's energy is transmitted by the atmosphere to Earth's surface. Some is absorbed by landmasses and some radiates back into the atmosphere.

E Sunlight that reaches the ocean is reflected back into the atmosphere or is absorbed by the water. Sunlight penetrates only about the top 200 m of even the clearest ocean water. Many ocean organisms, including corals and algae, are able to survive only in the well-lighted surface water of the ocean.

129

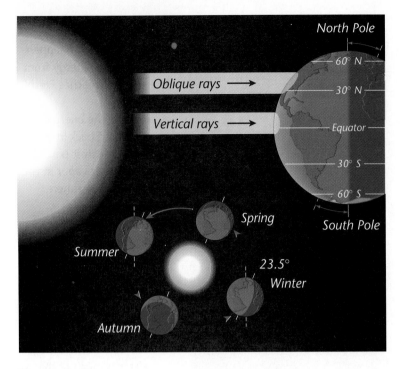

Figure 4–10

Sunlight at the equator is five times more intense than sunlight at the poles. Because Earth is curved, rays of sunlight that fall on the regions near the poles are spread over a larger area than the rays that fall near the equator. As a result, equatorial regions receive more radiant energy from the sun and have a warm climate. As you move toward the poles, less of the sun's energy reaches the surface, and climates get progressively colder. Temperature is an important abiotic factor.

■ Temperature

Walking barefoot across a hot sidewalk on a hot summer afternoon can be quite an experience. The hot pavement sends you running to the nearest patch of shade, where the ground is cooler. Sunlight is a form of energy, and matter, like the sidewalk, heats up when it absorbs energy. There is a direct relationship between the amount of sunlight that falls on an object and the object's temperature. Because Earth is curved, not all parts of Earth receive the same amount of sunlight. As shown in **Figure 4-10**, the equator receives more energy from the sun than the regions near the poles; therefore, the tropics are warm and the poles are cold.

The range of temperatures that occurs in an area helps determine what species will be able to survive there. You wouldn't expect to find a tropical rain forest in New York or polar bears on the Hawaiian Islands. Some organisms survive only in regions where temperatures remain fairly stable. Others are adapted for wide variations in temperature, and a few can tolerate extreme heat or cold. **Figure 4-10** gives a few examples.

A This desert lizard is active during the early morning, then seeks protection from the heat of the sun under a rock for the rest of the day.

B A thick layer of fat under the feathers of these Adélie penguins acts as an insulator that helps them survive in the frigid Antarctic.

The Importance of Water

How much water do you drink every day? It has been estimated that about two-thirds of the weight of a human body is water. The bodies of most organisms contain 50 to 95 percent water. Earth is often called the "Water Planet" because about three-fourths of its surface is covered by water. Water is necessary for plants to be able to photosynthesize, and for the thousands of chemical reactions that take place inside the cells and tissues of organisms. What is it about this common liquid that makes it so important? Water has at least two properties that are necessary to life. First, it resists changes in temperature. Second, its molecular structure enables it to dissolve many substances.

■ Water and Temperature

Water is another factor that influences the temperature of an environment. If you put a paper cup of water at the edge of a campfire, the edges of the cup will burn down to the water level, then stop. The rest of the cup will not burn until the water boils away. Why? Water has a high thermal capacity, which means an ability to absorb and retain heat. It takes far more energy to heat water than to heat paper, wood, metal, and many other substances. For example, it takes nine times as much energy to raise the temperature of water by one degree as it does to raise the temperature of the same volume of iron by one degree. The high thermal capacity of water helps regulate the climate in many areas of the world. Because the water in an ocean or large lake can hold so much of the sun's heat, it helps keep the nearby land cool during hot seasons. High thermal capacity also means that water releases its heat slowly, so nearby land stays warmer during cold seasons. **Figure 4-11** shows an example of an organism for which the high thermal capacity of water is very important.

Suppose you live in an area that has four distinct seasons. This year, the fall has been extremely mild. Temperatures have been above normal and rainfall has been normal. These mild conditions continue well into the winter months. With these weather conditions, you expect the trees to begin blossoming and seeds to begin sprouting any day. In the next activity, find out how abiotic factors affect the growth of plants.

Figure 4-11

Temperature-sensitive crops like these wine grapes can be grown in the mild coastal climates of California or France, but cannot survive the more extreme winter and summer temperatures that occur farther inland at the same latitude.

Temperature and Seed Germination

Seeds remain dormant until temperature, light, and moisture conditions are right for germination. Germination is the process in which a seed sprouts into a new plant. Some seeds, such as lettuce, will germinate if only exposed to light. They will not germinate if buried too deeply in the soil. The seeds of desert wildflowers germinate immediately after a rainstorm and develop and flower before conditions become too dry once again. In this activity, you will investigate the effect of temperature on pea seed germination.

Preparation

Problem
Does temperature have an effect on the germination of pea seeds?

Hypothesis
Make a hypothesis regarding how you think temperature will affect the germination of pea seeds. Consider both high and low temperatures. You will also want to consider other abiotic factors. Record the hypothesis *in your Journal.*

Objectives
In this Investigation, you will:
- *Analyze* the results of experimental groups of pea seeds.
- *Draw conclusions* about temperature and its effects on seed germination.

Possible Materials
water
pea seeds
plastic bags
paper towels or potting soil
refrigerator
oven or other heat source
thermometer

Safety Precautions

Use caution near heat sources to avoid burns. Use care when handling mercury thermometers. Mercury is a poisonous material. Alert your teacher if a mercury thermometer breaks. **Do not touch it.**

Plan the Experiment

1 Decide on a way to test your group's hypothesis.

2 Keep available materials in mind as you plan your procedure. How many seeds will you need? How much water will you use?

3 *In your Journal*, record your procedure and list the materials and quantities you will need.

4 Design and construct a data table for recording your observations. Include a place to record temperature, number of seeds included in each trial, and the number of seeds that germinate. Decide how long you will observe your seeds.

Check the Plan
Discuss the following points with other group members to decide on the final procedure for your experiment.

1 What data will you collect, and how will you record it?

2 What factors should be controlled?

3 What temperatures will be tested?

4 How will you get and maintain these temperatures?

5 *Make sure your teacher has approved your experimental plan before you proceed further.*

6 Carry out your experiment.

Analyze and Conclude

1. Checking Your Hypothesis Was your hypothesis supported by your data? Use your data to explain how temperature did or did not affect pea seed germination.

2. Analyzing Data Use the following formula to calculate the percentage of seeds that germinated from each of your trials: number of seeds germinated divided by the total number of seeds × 100 = percent germinated.

3. Thinking Critically Do you think performing the same experiment with other types of seeds at the same temperature would yield the same results? Why or why not? Describe an experiment you could conduct to find out.

Going Further

Changing Variables
Design an experiment that you could perform to test whether other abiotic factors affect pea seed germination. If you have the materials you would need, carry out this experiment.

■ Water Is the Universal Solvent

Do you put sugar in your iced tea? Why do the sugar crystals dissolve when you stir them into the liquid? When one substance is dissolved in another, the resulting mixture is called a **solution**. The substance that dissolves—such as sugar in tea—is called a **solute**. The liquid in which the solute dissolves is called the **solvent.** Water is known as the universal solvent because many substances can be dissolved in it.

What is it about water that makes it such a good solvent? As the molecular structure in **Figure 4-12** illustrates, the water molecule is polar. A **polar molecule** is one that has a negative charge at one end and a positive charge at the other. The polarity of water molecules is a major reason water is so important to life on Earth.

Remember that ions are atoms that have lost or gained an electron and therefore have a positive or negative charge. Ionic compounds—compounds made up of atoms or groups of ions that have a positive or negative charge—dissolve readily when placed in water. For example, in the case of table salt, sodium chloride, the negatively charged chloride ion is attracted to the positive poles of water molecules, and the positively charged sodium ions are attracted to the negative poles of water molecules. The salt is dissolved when all the ions of the solute—the sodium and chloride ions—have been pulled apart and surrounded by molecules of the solvent—water.

IN-DEPTH LOOK

Bamboo Havens

When someone mentions the word *bamboo,* what comes to mind? Many people associate bamboo with pandas, some of which can eat as much as 50 kg of the leaves and stems each day. Others think of the furniture and baskets made from this woody grass. Still others might envision the stringy but tasty shoots used in some types of Asian cooking. For most people, however, the term does not bring to mind the complex ecosystems supported by this unique plant.

Katydids, et al.

In the lowland tropical rain forests of Peru, in the Peruvian Biosphere Reserve, small brown katydids have been found that cut tiny slits into bamboo shoots. The katydid makes

Figure 4-12

Each water molecule is made up of two hydrogen atoms and one oxygen atom arranged in an angular shape. Each atom has its own orbiting electrons, but oxygen attracts all the electrons—even those belonging to hydrogen—more strongly. As a result, the oxygen end of the atom has a negative charge and the hydrogen end has a positive charge.

these microscopic cuts to deposit its many eggs in the bamboo. As the woody grass quickly grows, the slits become longer and wider. Into these elongated windows, other types of insects and small organisms move to make the 10- to 20-m tall shoots their homes. In fact, in addition to mosquitoes, damselflies, and cockroaches, researchers have also observed yellow-striped dart frogs and brown and white chunk-headed snakes emerge from these slits.

Water, Too

Water, as you know, is essential to every ecosystem on this planet. In the bamboo shoots, water is stored in the internodes, which are the hollow areas between the joints of the stem. Where the water that accumulates to form these small pondlike bodies comes from is unclear. Researchers hypothesize that the bamboo, *Guadua weberbaueri* of Peru, along with the thousands of other species of bamboo, secrete their own water and, in turn, form these life-supporting havens. This water allows the bamboo and its inhabitants to survive the dry season.

Hidden Food Source

Many species of organisms depend on the hidden water chambers of the bamboo. The Cebus monkey, a brown capuchin, depends on the bamboo for food. The monkey does not eat the bamboo, but rips it open to feed on the hoard of organisms living inside. There are also at least three species of birds that feed primarily on the organisms living in the watery pools within the Guadua.

Thinking Critically

1. *Identify* how the windows are first made in the bamboo shoots.
2. *Hypothesize* what you think might happen to the organisms that depend on the bamboo if a disease wiped out a large percentage of the population.

■ Water and pH—Acids and Bases

Water has another property that makes it an important abiotic factor. This property, called pH, has to do with the number of hydrogen ions in a solution. As **Figure 4-13** shows, the water molecule can break apart into one positively charged hydrogen ion and a negatively charged hydroxide (oxygen plus hydrogen) ion. Pure water has an equal number of hydrogen and hydroxide ions and has a neutral pH. Water in a liquid form has a tendency to form ions. A very small but constant number of ions are always present in any given volume of pure water. The number of H^+ ions and OH^- ions remains exactly equal because as some molecules of water are breaking into ions, others are joining. This keeps pure water in a state of equilibrium. Most water on Earth contains dissolved substances as well as water molecules. These substances can change the balance of hydrogen and hydroxide ions. A solution that contains more hydrogen than hydroxide ions is called an **acid**. A solution containing more hydroxide than hydrogen ions is called a **base**. **Figure 4-13** illustrates how acids and bases are measured in units called **pH**. A solution that has a pH lower than 7 is acidic. A solution with a pH above 7 is basic. As you can see, ocean water has a pH of 8, which is slightly basic. If the pH were much lower, the chemical reactions involved in the formation of coral reefs could not take place. Most chemical reactions take place within a limited pH range.

MiniLab

How can solids form in water?

Ionic compounds dissolve easily in water, yet reef-building corals use dissolved calcium and carbonate ions in ocean water to build their hard, protective outer skeletons. In this activity, you will see how ions dissolved in water can come together to form a solid.

Safety Precautions

CAUTION: *You will be working with solutions of chemicals. Work carefully to avoid spills, and put on goggles to protect your eyes from splashes.*

Procedure

1. Put 40 mL of water into a 100-mL beaker. Add 0.2 g of sodium carbonate and stir until it dissolves.

2. Put 40 mL of water into another 100-mL beaker. Add 0.2 g of calcium chloride and stir until it dissolves.

3. Pour the contents of one beaker into the other. Observe what happens.

Analysis

1. Explain what happened to the sodium carbonate and calcium chloride compounds when you stirred them into the water.

2. If you allowed the water in the final mixture to evaporate, what would happen to the chemicals you added to the beakers?

3. How is this chemical reaction similar to the reactions that take place in reef-building corals?

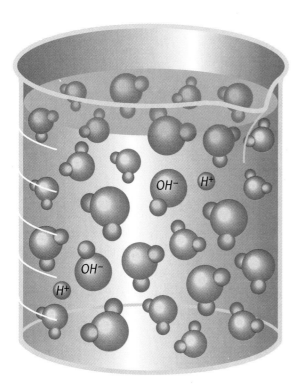

Figure 4-13

A solution can be acidic or basic depending on the amount of hydrogen and hydroxide ions that are contained in the solution.

A In pure water, a small fraction of water molecules breaks apart into hydrogen (H^+) and hydroxide (OH^-) ions. When other substances dissolve in water, the balance of hydrogen to hydroxide ions can change, making the solution acid or basic.

B The pH scale is used to measure how acidic or basic a solution is. A lower pH means the solution contains more hydrogen ions and so is more acidic. A higher pH means the solution contains more hydroxide ions and is more basic.

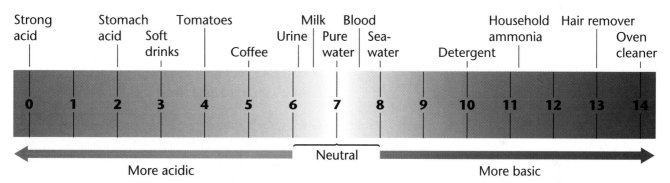

Strong acid | Stomach acid | Soft drinks | Tomatoes | Coffee | Urine | Milk | Pure water | Blood | Sea-water | Detergent | Household ammonia | Hair remover | Oven cleaner

0 1 2 3 4 5 6 7 8 9 10 11 12 13 14

Neutral

More acidic ← → More basic

check your UNDERSTANDING

Understanding Concepts

1. Describe an imaginary ecosystem with a combination of abiotic factors that are ideal for life, and explain why you think they are ideal. Describe a second imaginary ecosystem with abiotic factors that you think would prohibit life, and explain.

2. Describe two ways in which sunlight supports life.

3. How does the thermal capacity of water benefit aquatic organisms living in a pond in New England in the winter?

Skill Review

4. **Making and Using Graphs** Create a bar graph using the pH data from **Figure 4-13**, then add the following data to the graph: unpolluted rain, 5.6; apples, 3.3; lemons, 2.2; lye, 14; eggs, 7.8; vinegar, 3.0. For more help, refer to Making and Using Graphs in the *Skill Handbook*.

Literature Connection

The Everglades: River of Grass

In this chapter, you have studied what ecosystems are, and what interaction makes them work. Listen to Marjory Stoneman Douglas as she describes the uniqueness and irreplaceable value of America's last great ecosystem, the Everglades.

"There are no other Everglades in the world. They are, they have always been, one of the unique regions of the earth, remote, never wholly known. Nothing anywhere else is like them. . . . They are unique also in their simplicity, the diversity, the related harmony of the forms of life they enclose. The miracle of light pours over the green and brown expanse of saw grass and of water, shining and slow-moving below, the grass and the water that is the meaning and the central fact of the Everglades of Florida. It is a river of grass."

The Everglades

Marjory Stoneman Douglas wrote these words in 1947. In her book, *The Everglades: River of Grass*, Douglas describes in great detail the overwhelming beauty of the land that the Native Americans called "Pa-hay-okee," or "Grassy Water." Douglas tells the exciting, and sometimes sad, story of this great river of grass by focusing on the relationships between the animals and plants that share the ecosystem. She shows the negative impact that the building of housing developments in South Florida, the attempted construction of the Florida jetport, and the draining of chemical herbicides from large farms in central Florida have had on the Everglades.

Saving the Everglades

The Everglades: River of Grass helped convince government officials that the 1927 charter placing the Everglades under protection of the National Park Service should be enacted. In 1947, the river of grass became the Everglades National Park. Douglas's final words in her book cause us to think more deeply about the ways humans can interact with the natural world: "The capacity of the earth for compensation and forgiveness after repeated abuses has kept the planet alive, but it has also encouraged more abuse. The Everglades is a case in point."

Aerial view of the Everglades

Thinking Critically

1. *Explain* how the development of Florida affected the Everglades.
2. *Write* an essay about the history of an ecosystem in or near the place you live. Write about the ways that human intervention has had both positive and negative effects on that ecosystem.

Read the statements below that review major points presented in the chapter. Using the concepts that you have learned, answer each question *in your Journal.*

1 Diversity, the measure of the number of species that live in an ecosystem, is an important biotic factor of ecosystems. *What can the number of different species tell about a given ecosystem?*

2 Populations of organisms differ in size. *What are some key factors in determining the size of a population?*

3 To survive in an environment, organisms need to adapt to the abiotic factors in that environment. *List several abiotic factors of a desert and how organisms can adapt to them.*

Using Key Science Terms

abiotic factor	pH
acid	polar molecule
base	population
biotic factor	solute
community	solution
diversity	solvent
ecosystem	species

For each set of words below, choose the one term that does not belong and explain why it does not belong.

1. solvent, species, solute, pH
2. temperature, light, water, population
3. ecosystem, population, community, acid
4. pH, polar molecule, solvent, diversity

Understanding Ideas

Using complete sentences, answer the following questions in your Journal.

1. List two reasons that might explain why a particular ecosystem has a low species diversity.
2. Compare the most abundant species of forest, reef, and urban ecosystems. How are these species alike? How are they different?
3. List at least five important abiotic factors.
4. Describe how water's thermal capacity influences life on Earth.
5. Describe how the availability of sunlight and water affect a cactus in the desert and a pine tree in the Rocky Mountains.
6. Explain the difference between communities, populations, and ecosystems.

Developing Skills

Use your understanding of the concepts developed in this chapter to answer each of the following questions.

1. Concept Mapping Use the following terms and phrases to complete the concept map about ecosystems: *biotic factor, abiotic factor, microorganism, temperature, whale, forest, sunlight, water.*

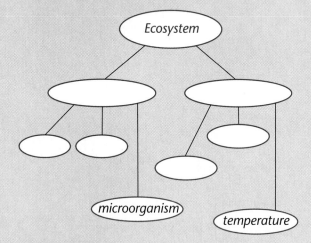

2. Interpreting Illustrations At the right is an illustration of the sulfate ion. To which pole of the water molecule is it most attracted?

Sulfate ion SO_4^{2-}

3. Measuring in SI A biologist measures the sea anemone population along a line on a coral reef and finds there are about eight anemones/m^2. If the total area of the reef is 200 000 m^2, what is a reasonable estimate for the entire anemone population on the reef?

Critical Thinking

In your Journal, *answer each of the following questions.*

1. Suppose an ecosystem in Africa has received less than normal rainfall for ten years. What effect do you think such a long drought would have on the species diversity of that ecosystem? Explain.

2. If you place a 2-g piece of aluminum in the freezer along with 2 g of water in a cup, which will reach the temperature of the freezer first? When you remove them from the freezer, which will come to room temperature first? Use the concept of thermal capacity to support your answer.

3. Describe how a greenhouse creates an environment that has a higher temperature than the surrounding air.

Problem Solving

Read the following problem and discuss your answers in a brief paragraph.

A resort on a small Caribbean island needs to install a sewage-treatment plant so that its waste does not contaminate its source of drinking water. The most likely place to install the treatment plant is at the mouth of a stream, where it flows into the ocean. Nitrate ions, which are a final product of sewage treatment, act as a fertilizer to green algae. Releasing treated sewage here would cause the population of green algae to increase rapidly in size, and prevent much of the sun's energy from reaching the organisms in a nearby coral reef.

Devise a plan to dispose of the sewage without endangering the coral reef.

CONNECTING IDEAS

1. **Theme—Energy** Use your understanding of thermal capacity to explain why areas close to bodies of water have a milder climate than inland areas at the same latitude. (Compare Washington state with North Dakota, for example.)

2. **Theme—Stability and Change** Explain why an ecosystem with greater diversity would have a better chance of maintaining life after a storm, disease, or famine than an ecosystem with a lower diversity.

3. **Science and Society** The use of national parks is increasing every year. With this increase in use, pollution, commercial development, litter, and traffic congestion have all become problems. Trails in parks are also deteriorating due to overcrowded conditions. List several ways to solve some of these problems of national parks.

4. **In-Depth Look** How do the organisms that live in the bamboo benefit from living there?

5. **Literature Connection** How might books such as Douglas's lead to the conservation of lands destined for development?

CHAPTER 5

Cycling of Matter and Energy
Ecosystems in Balance

Sunlight filters through leafy branches of willow trees. Deer rustle through tall reeds on their way to a pond for a drink. Ducks dip and splash as they nibble on tender water plants. Dragonflies hover over the water, and a turtle crawls onto a half-submerged log to bask in the sun.

We often associate scenes like this with peaceful inactivity. However, when you examine this pond ecosystem more closely, you discover it is anything but inactive. In any ecosystem—whether it's a tropical rain forest, a coral reef, or the local park—there are hundreds, even thousands, of such interactions taking place every moment.

▶ **In this chapter, investigate the dynamic interactions between organisms and the environment, and find out how all organisms play a key role in the balance of nature. The MiniLab on the next page will get you started.**

MiniLab

How do organisms interact within ecosystems?

Have you ever carefully watched the different types of organisms you encounter daily in your environment? In this activity, you will observe and record the interactions of organisms in your community over a five-day period.

Procedure

1. Identify an area around your school, home, or in a park where you know you can observe different types of plants and animals such as birds, rabbits, squirrels, or insects.

2. Observe at least two types of plants and two types of animals over a five-day period.

3. Make observations about how the organisms interact with each other and with the abiotic factors of the environment. Record all observations *in your Journal.*

Analysis

1. Where did you make your observations? List the types of plants and animals you observed.

2. What kinds of interactions did you observe between organisms? Between organisms and the abiotic factors?

Interactions Among Organisms

5-1

Objectives

■ Describe the components of an organism's habitat and niche.

■ Relate feeding relationships of organisms to the flow of energy in ecosystems.

■ Identify the different trophic levels in an ecosystem.

Key Terms

habitat
niche
autotroph
heterotroph
decomposer
symbiosis
food chain
trophic level
food web

Every Organism Has a Home Address

A street address and an apartment number often provide the information you need to locate the home of a friend. When you meet someone for the first time, you're probably interested in finding out what kind of work he or she does or in what kinds of weekend activities he or she participates. Biologists are interested in obtaining similar information about the organisms that make up an ecological community. Every species has a home address—a specific place where it can usually be found—and a set of tasks it performs. You can gather information about the organisms that live on the forest floor by taking a close look at a sample of leaf litter in the following Minilab.

MiniLab

What kinds of organisms live in leaf litter?

In this activity, you will investigate some of the organisms in a pile of leaf litter. Leaf litter includes leaves, needles, and twigs that fall to the ground, as well as the organisms that live on and under them.

Procedure

1. Locate an area around your home, school, or a nearby park that has a lot of leaves covering the ground. Measure a 20-cm × 20-cm section of the ground. Use gloved hands or a trowel to scoop up all the leaves and organisms from your section, including the topmost layer of soil. Place your sample in a sandwich bag and seal it.

2. In your classroom, pour the contents into a shallow pan. Sort the contents,

identifying the different types of organisms. Use a hand lens to identify small organisms such as seeds, insects, and worms. Return the soil to the plastic bag and seal it for later use.

3. Use field guides or other reference sources to identify the different types of organisms you found. List them *in your Journal.*

Analysis

1. Where does a community of leaf-litter organisms begin and end? What are the boundaries of any community?

2. What roles do you think insects play in this community? What roles do plants play?

Even a small amount of leaf litter can contain a wide variety of organisms. Perhaps you identified worms, ants, snails, millipedes, or sow bugs in your leaf-litter sample. Maybe you discovered new plants sprouting from the soil or collected a small patch of moss. If you examined portions of your sample under a microscope, you would also discover many species of bacteria and fungi that thrive in the soil and on decaying leaves.

The organisms in the sample have many differences, but they do share one thing in common—their habitat. A **habitat** is the physical location in which an organism lives. You can think of a habitat as the home address of a species. For example, ferns are often found on the moist, shady forest floor, while the habitat of the tropical parrot fish is the warm, clear water of a coral reef. The leaf litter you looked at is a habitat found in a forest community. **Figure 5-1** shows some examples of other forest habitats.

■ How Organisms Live

As you've seen, many species can share the same habitat. A coral reef is home to hundreds of species, from fishes and crabs to sponges and seaweeds. A single tree may be the habitat of several species of birds, a family of squirrels, untold numbers of insects and spiders, and some patches of moss. How can a single habitat support so many different organisms? Each species makes use of

Figure 5-1

Common forest habitats include leaf litter, hollow logs, leafy branches, and the underside of rocks.

A American beech trees are commonly found in lowlands and on slopes in the eastern and midwestern United States. The branches of this tree are a habitat for many species of birds and squirrels.

B The leaf litter of this forest floor provides an ideal habitat for these mayapple seedlings.

C Hollow logs are common hiding places for animals such as this red fox. Other animals that might be found here include skunks, raccoons, and opossums.

its habitat in a different way. For example, both caterpillars and beetles are found in trees. Caterpillars chew leaves for food and crawl out in the open, while some species of beetles remain in burrows they make as they chew through the bark.

Beetles and caterpillars have different roles to play in the community of organisms living in the tree. Similarly, warblers and finches can feed in the same tree because warblers eat insects and finches eat seeds. The way in which a species uses the resources of its habitat and what it does in the community is called a **niche.** A niche includes food, living space, methods of obtaining food and finding mates, and other conditions necessary for a species to survive and reproduce. Several species can share the same habitat, as long as they have different niches, as shown in **Figure 5-2.**

Energy Cycles in Ecosystems

What did you eat for breakfast this morning? Cereal? Fruit? Toast? Eggs? You probably ate this morning because you were hungry. Hunger is one way your body has of telling you that it needs energy. All organisms need energy to carry out their life processes. Try this next activity to discover how energy is obtained by freshwater snails.

Cape May warbler

Bay-breasted warbler

Myrtle warbler

Figure 5-2

These three species of warblers live in the same habitat—the branches of a spruce tree—but they occupy three different niches. The Bay-breasted warbler forages for insects in the central branches of the tree, the Cape May warbler prefers the top branches, and the Myrtle warbler spends its time in the lower branches. By using different parts of the tree, these three species share a habitat without competing for foraging space.

MiniLab

What do pond snails eat?

Most snails—whether they live on land, in freshwater ponds, or in the ocean—feed on plants, algae, or bacteria. You may have noticed that a green film often grows on the sides of glass aquariums. The film is made up of microscopic organisms. Having a few snails in the aquarium can help keep the aquarium glass clear of this film.

Procedure

1. Observe the activities of snails in an aquarium tank. Record your observations *in your Journal.*

2. Use a toothpick to scrape some of the green film from the inside of the aquarium glass. Transfer the scraped material to a microscope slide.

3. Add a drop of water to the material on the slide. Carefully place a cover-slip over it.

4. Record the appearance of any organisms you see on the slide. There will probably be several kinds.

5. Using reference books, try to identify

some of the organisms. The green color you see is a pigment called chlorophyll. Chlorophyll is found in organisms that are capable of photosynthesis. Algae and similar organisms possess chlorophyll in cell organelles called chloroplasts. Chloroplasts will appear as small, dark green spots within an algal cell. Bacteria that contain chlorophyll will be much smaller in size and a uniform green color.

Analysis

1. What did the organisms making up the scraped material look like? Did they all contain chlorophyll?

2. Based on your observations, what statement can you make about the feeding habits and food choices of aquarium snails?

3. Based on your observations, what kinds of abiotic conditions are required by the organisms that snails eat?

As you discovered in the activity, pond snails feed on microscopic organisms that grow in sunlight. Chemical reactions that take place within the cells of these chlorophyll-containing organisms capture energy from sunlight and store it in the form of chemical bonds. This energy becomes available for life processes when the bonds are broken through the process of cellular respiration. You will learn more about chemical reactions in Chapter 8.

■ Producers Make Food

You may not be a big fan of spinach or broccoli, but humans, as well as most other organisms, owe their lives to green plants. Why? The sun is the source of all energy available to most ecosystems. Green plants are capable of transforming energy from sunlight into food during photosynthesis. Humans and other organisms are not capable of photosynthesis and depend on plants, directly or indirectly, for their energy.

Plants are examples of organisms that make their own food. An **autotroph** is an organism that can manufacture its own food. The term *autotroph* means "self-feeder." Plants are known as photoautotrophs because they use light energy to produce food through photosynthesis. They are the most common land autotrophs, but algae and many single-celled organisms are also capable of photosynthesis. Some autotrophs do not use sunlight as their energy source. Instead, they use energy stored in chemical compounds in manufacturing their food. These organisms are known as chemoautotrophs. Examples of both types of autotrophs are shown in **Figure 5-3.**

Figure 5-3

Ultimately, all of the energy available to organisms in an ecosystem can be traced to autotrophs. Can you see why autotrophs are also known as producers?

B Microscopic algae are the main producers in most marine ecosystems.

C Green plants, like this jade plant, are autotrophs.

A Some of the bacteria living in this deep-sea vent community are chemoautotrophs. Rather than using sunlight as their energy source, they use the energy stored in chemical compounds that rise from openings in the ocean floor.

Figure 5-4

Heterotrophs, also called consumers, obtain energy by feeding on other organisms. Examination of a heterotroph's teeth can reveal information about its diet.

A Plant-eating heterotrophs such as mice and other rodents are limited to a diet of autotrophs. Their teeth are adapted to shred and grind tough plant fibers.

■ Consumers Rely on Producers

If an organism can't manufacture its own food, it must obtain energy in some other way. You've seen how snails obtain food by grazing on algae. Snails are **heterotrophs,** which are organisms that depend on other organisms for nutrients and energy. What other organisms would be classified as heterotrophs?

There are several types of heterotrophs, as shown in **Figure 5-4.** Organisms that consume only plants or other producers are called herbivores. Organisms that eat only consumers are called carnivores. Those that eat both producers and consumers are known as omnivores.

B Carnivores such as this coyote eat other heterotrophs. Their teeth are adapted for slicing meat.

C Omnivores are organisms that feed on both plants and animals. Humans, bears, and raccoons are examples of omnivores. How are the shapes of human teeth adapted for processing a variety of foods?

■ Decomposers

Have you ever seen an orange or some other fruit get moldy? Perhaps you've seen an old, fallen tree branch crumble at the slightest touch. You were witnessing the important ecological process of decomposition, the breaking down of organic substances. Decomposition is an essential process in ecosystems because it recycles nutrients back into the soil so that they may be used again by other organisms. In ecosystems, this process results from a type of heterotroph called a decomposer. **Decomposers** break down the complex compounds of dead and decaying organisms into simpler molecules. Decomposers include microscopic bacteria and the turkey-tail fungi pictured in **Figure 5-5.** In the Investigation that follows, you'll discover how soil microorganisms decompose some familiar organic materials.

Fungi and bacteria are the major organisms of decomposition on Earth. Mushrooms, molds, and yeasts are all types of fungi that feed on living and nonliving organic matter. Most species of fungi feed on nonliving things such as fallen trees, dead organisms, and leaves. Other types of fungi feed on living things. Athlete's foot is a common infection of a living organism caused by a parasitic type of fungi. The reproductive structure is the visible part of a fungus. The rest is composed of a tangled mat of individual strands called hyphae that invade the food source.

Decomposers: The Key to Life

What happens to organisms when they die? When a tree is blown over in a storm and dies, what happens to it over time? Where does it go?

A Fallen Tree

When a tree falls, some of the first things that start to grow on it are bacteria, slime molds, and various kinds of fungi—decomposers. These organisms obtain nutrition by secreting chemicals to break down a food material so they can absorb the nutrients. Often, their first effect is to loosen the bark, and soon it falls away from the wood. Decay has begun.

Moss begins to cover the fallen log, and soon chemicals produced by the fungi and moss have softened the wood enough that other organisms

A fallen log covered with mushrooms and moss

Figure 5-5

Fungi such as these mushrooms may resemble plants, but they are heterotrophs and do not produce their own food. Fungi feed by secreting digestive fluids that help break down dead or decaying plants and animals so the nutrients they contain can be absorbed into the cells of the fungus.

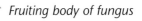
Fruiting body of fungus

Mass of fungal hyphae

can begin to live on it. These plants send their roots drilling into the log and loosen the wood even more.

Ants bore tunnels through the wood under the loosened bark. As the wood softens more and more, other animals that live in the soil—millipedes, pill bugs, staghorn beetle larvae, scavenger beetles, carrion beetles, springtails, mites, protozoans, and earthworms—move in and consume the stored food in the wood.

Nutrient Cycling

As the soil organisms continue to break down the plant cells, the valuable mineral nutrients that were bound in the wood are returned to the soil.

Nitrogen, phosphorus, sulfur, calcium, iron, and magnesium, among others, are released. The nutrients can now enter a new plant through the roots, and take their places in the new plant's cells. When an animal eats the new plant, the minerals may become part of the animal's cell structure until they are again returned to the soil when the animal dies.

What would happen if there were no decomposers? Dead trees and other dead organisms would pile up. The minerals and nutrients needed for life would remain locked inside dead cells and would not be available for new plants and animals. Without decomposers, there would be no life on Earth.

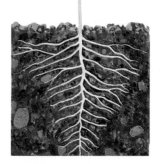

Thinking Critically

1. *Describe* how decomposers help break down dead organisms.
2. In some areas of the world, decomposition takes much longer than in others. *Identify* areas in which decomposition would happen quickly. Why?

The Role of Decomposers in Ecosystems

The primary decomposers in any ecosystem are bacteria and fungi. In this Investigation, you will examine how microorganisms that live in the soil affect the decomposition of some common foods.

Preparation

Problem

How are microorganisms important for the decomposition of organic materials?

Hypothesis

Have your group agree on one hypothesis to be tested. Record your hypothesis.

Objectives

In this Investigation, you will:
- Carry out a *controlled experiment.*
- *Observe* the effect of soil microorganisms on decomposition of organic materials.

Possible Materials

non-sterile soil
balance
2 glass pickle or jelly jars
cheesecloth
rubber bands
organic materials such as old fruit, vegetables, bread, or cheese (finely chopped)

Safety Precautions

Remember to wash your hands immediately after handling soil and food waste. Do not use any meat products. Be sure to dispose of materials as directed by your teacher.

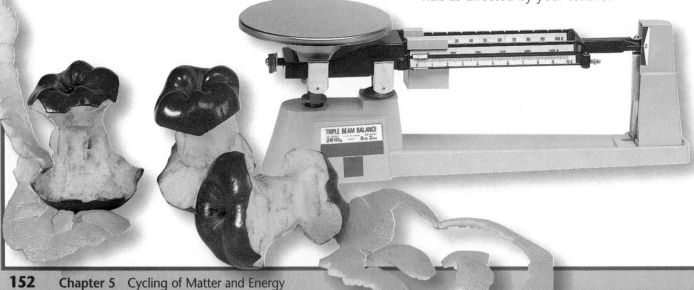

Plan the Experiment

1 Examine the materials provided by your teacher. As a group, make a list of some of the ways you can test your hypothesis.

2 Agree on one way that your group will test your hypothesis. What variable or variables will you manipulate? Design an experiment that will allow you to collect quantitative data.

3 Prepare a list of numbered directions for your experiment.

4 Design and construct a data table for your experiment.

Check the Plan
Discuss the following points with other group members to decide the final procedure for your experiment.

1 What variable is being manipulated? Determine how you will set up your jars. How many jars will you use? What will you add to them?

2 Where will you carry out the experiment?

3 What kinds of observations will you make? How often will you make observations?

4 *Make sure your teacher has approved your experimental plan before you proceed further.*

5 Carry out your experiment. Design a visual presentation of your results.

Analyze and Conclude

1. **Observing and Inferring** Describe any changes you observed taking place in your jars. Were there any differences from one jar to another? If so, describe them and suggest one or more reasons to explain them.

2. **Making Inferences** Do your observations support your hypothesis? Why or why not?

3. **Thinking Critically** Why did you use non-sterile soil? Based on your results, what statements can you make about the importance of microorganisms for decomposing organic substances?

Going Further

Changing Variables
Find out what types of environments are best suited for decomposition. How do abiotic factors affect the rate of decomposition? Design a new experiment to investigate an additional variable.

■ Organisms That Live Together

Close relationships aid survival. Have you ever gained some valuable assistance from a friend? Perhaps your friend helped you build a special project for school or gave you a ride to the mall. Maybe you teamed up to prepare food for a party.

In a similar way, many species in nature have complex relationships that provide benefits for survival. This type of interaction is an example of symbiosis. **Symbiosis** is a close, long-term relationship between two or more species.

In lichens, two species benefit from the relationship. The fungus receives food from its autotrophic partner. The alga or cyanobacterium benefits because the fungus provides it with a protected environment in which to grow. But not all symbiotic relationships benefit both partners. As you can see in **Figure 5-6,** different types of symbiotic relationships exist between many different types of organisms. Symbiosis occurs in virtually every ecosystem on Earth.

Figure 5-6

Symbiotic relationships are common in nature. Because energy is essential to survival, many symbiotic relationships involve getting or conserving energy.

Ⓐ The relationship between humans and mosquitoes is an example of *parasitism,* a symbiotic association in which one species benefits by harming another. Female mosquitoes feed on the blood of humans and other mammals. The harm done to the human might be limited to the discomfort of an itchy mosquito bite. But certain species of mosquitoes can also transmit the organisms that cause serious diseases such as malaria.

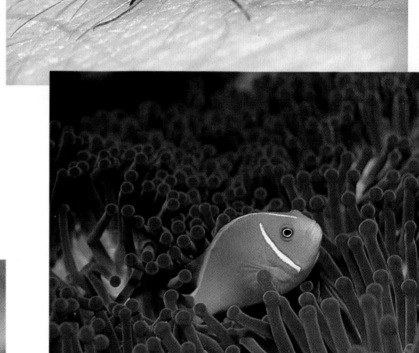

Ⓑ The yucca plant and yucca moth represent a symbiotic relationship called *mutualism.* In mutualistic relationships, both species benefit. The yucca moth is the yucca plant's only pollinator. The yucca moth depends on the yucca plant for food for both the larvae and adults.

Ⓒ The clownfish and sea anemone represent a type of symbiosis called *commensalism.* In this type of symbiosis, one partner benefits but the other is not helped or harmed. The fish receives protection from predators by hiding among the stinging tentacles of the anemone. The anemone is unaffected.

Matter and Energy in Ecosystems

When you observed the feeding behavior of a pond snail, you saw that all organisms need energy. Energy is transferred from one organism to another in a feeding relationship. In the same way, when you eat an apple, you are consuming energy from the sun that has been captured by a plant.

When you eat a steak, you are consuming energy from the sun that was captured by grass plants, then transferred to the animal that ate the grass. To understand how energy flows through ecosystems, biologists construct models to trace the feeding relationships. These models show the transfer of energy from one organism to another. Do the following MiniLab to find out how energy flows through a leaf-litter community.

MiniLab

How does energy flow in a leaf-litter community?

When heterotrophic organisms such as snails, humans, and fungi feed upon something, energy is transferred. In this activity, hypothesize about the flow of energy through a leaf-litter community.

Procedure

1. Make a list of the organisms you identified earlier in your leaf-litter community. Add to the list bacteria, fungi, and other leaf-litter organisms you have read about.

2. Check reference sources to learn about the niches of the organisms on your list. In particular, you will need information about the types of food each species eats.

3. Rearrange your list of organisms. Start by writing the names of the autotrophic organisms at the top of the list. Next, list the heterotrophs that feed on the autotrophs. Did you find any additional consumers that feed on the other consumers? If so, add them to the list.

Autotroph
• leaves
• moss
• flower
Heterotroph
• sowbug
• spider
• mushroom

Analysis

1. What producers did you identify in the community? What consumers did you identify?

2. Explain how the list you just created illustrates a pathway of energy flow.

Matter and energy are continually being cycled through ecosystems. You have just learned that feeding relationships can describe some ways in which organisms interact. Organisms also interact to obtain energy or protection in symbiotic relationships. By studying these types of relationships, models can be made to trace the flow of matter and energy through ecosystems.

Food Chains Indicate Energy Flow

A **food chain** is a model scientists use to indicate how energy flows through ecosystems. The kelp forest community pictured in **Figure 5-7** illustrates many examples of ocean food chains. In all ecosystems, energy flows from plants and other autotrophs, through heterotrophs, and eventually to decomposers.

When drawing a food chain, arrows are used to indicate the path of energy transfer. For example, one possible food chain for the kelp forest community would be:

algae $\longrightarrow$ sea urchin $\longrightarrow$ sea otter.

Food chains can consist of three or four organisms or links. Most have no more than five links. This is due to the decrease in the amount of energy available at each link, and the small amount of solar energy that is fixed by plants in the first place. The amount of energy left by the fifth link is only a small portion of the amount available at the first.

Figure 5-7

In any ecosystem, energy flows from autotrophs to heterotrophs. Follow the steps of the path of energy in the kelp forest ecosystem shown here.

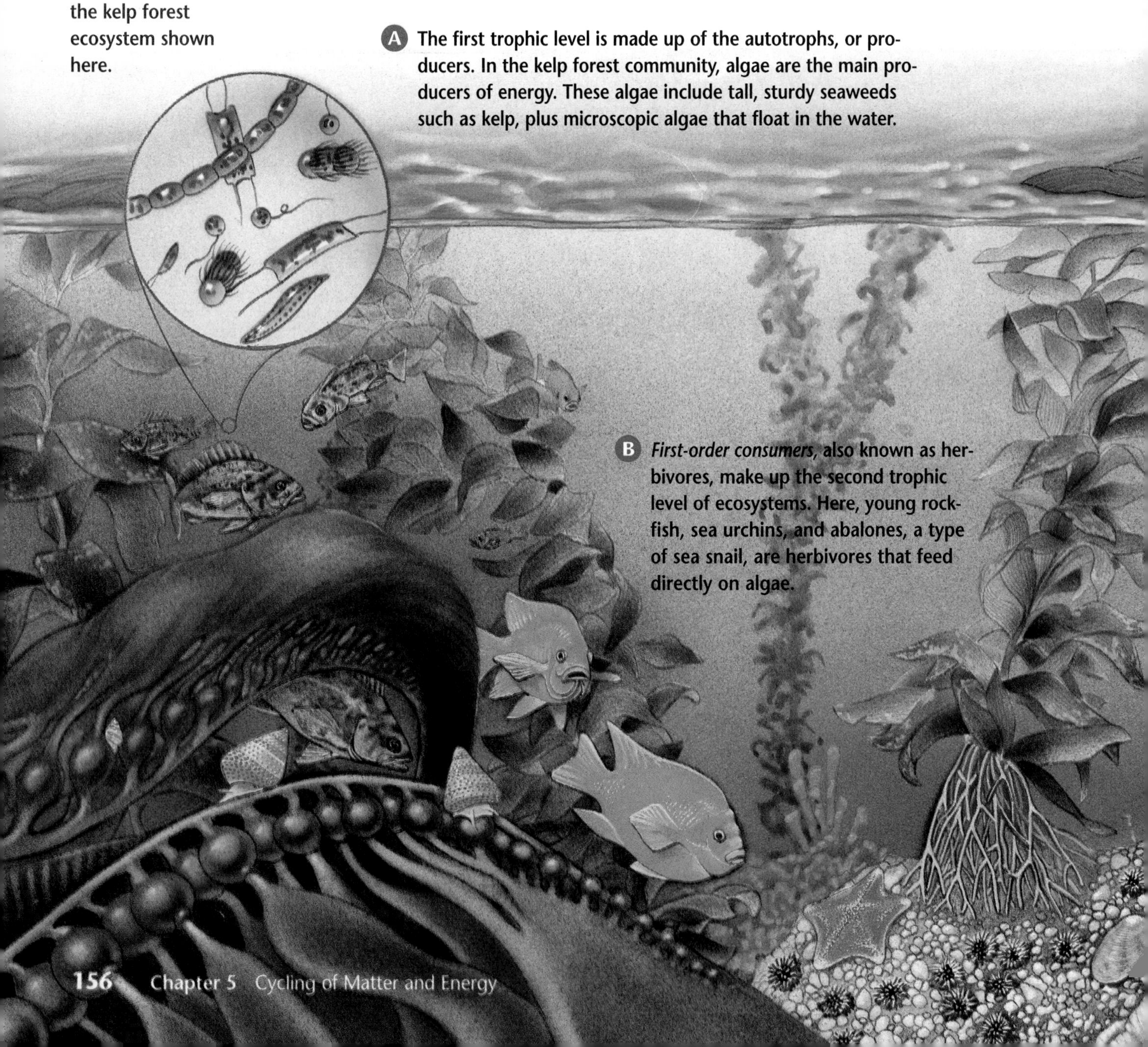

A The first trophic level is made up of the autotrophs, or producers. In the kelp forest community, algae are the main producers of energy. These algae include tall, sturdy seaweeds such as kelp, plus microscopic algae that float in the water.

B *First-order consumers*, also known as herbivores, make up the second trophic level of ecosystems. Here, young rockfish, sea urchins, and abalones, a type of sea snail, are herbivores that feed directly on algae.

Why is this the case? At each level, a portion of the energy is lost as heat.

■ Energy Flows from Producers to Consumers

To follow the movement of energy through an ecosystem, ecologists assign each organism to a trophic level. A **trophic level** is a feeding step of a food chain and consists of species that obtain energy in similar ways. As you can see in **Figure 5-7**, rockfish, abalone, and sea urchins feed directly on autotrophic algae, and therefore belong to the second trophic level of the food chain. A food chain represents only one possible route for the transfer of matter and energy in an ecosystem. Many other routes can be found in a given community.

On what trophic level are you? Most people, except for those who are vegetarians, eat a variety of foods, including plants and animals. In the same way, other organisms eat different foods, so it's not uncommon to find a single species, such as yourself, at several trophic levels.

C *Second-order consumers,* or carnivores, occupy the third trophic level of ecosystems. Carnivores, such as the California sea lion and many species of adult rockfish, are meat eaters and feed on first-order consumers. Sea otters eat abalone and sea urchins and also occupy this trophic level.

D *Third-order consumers* such as the great white shark feed on second-order consumers and make up the fourth trophic level of ecosystems.

E When organisms die in a marine ecosystem, bacteria act to decompose the body. Can decomposers function on any trophic level?

157

Figure 5-8

Food webs are complex networks of interconnected food chains. In the forest community of organisms shown here, how many different food chains can you identify?

Connect to...

Physics

The Law of Conservation of Mass states that matter is neither created nor destroyed during a chemical reaction. Look at the chemical equation for photosynthesis in Chapter 8 on page 254. Make a chart showing that the number and types of atoms (C, H, and O) on both sides of the chemical equation are equal.

Food chains are convenient models to illustrate energy flow. However, they don't represent the total picture of ecosystems. Because many organisms feed on more than one trophic level, a more realistic model for energy flow is the food web, as shown in **Figure 5-8.** A **food web** is a model that expresses all of the possible feeding relationships within an ecosystem.

Some of the energy that flows through a food chain is released in the form of heat. Plants, as you know, capture the sun's energy to make food. However, only about one-half of the sunlight captured by a plant is actually stored in the plant as food. Some of the remaining energy is used by the plant for its own growth, and the rest is lost as heat.

Losses also occur every time energy is transferred from one trophic level to another as shown in **Figure 5-9.** For example, the herbivores in an ecosystem receive only about 10 percent of

Figure 5-9

A pyramid of energy shows how energy decreases at each trophic level. Only about 10 percent of the energy available on one trophic level is transferred to the next level. The loss of energy at each transfer limits the number of trophic levels that are possible. As a result, few ecosystems contain more than five trophic levels.

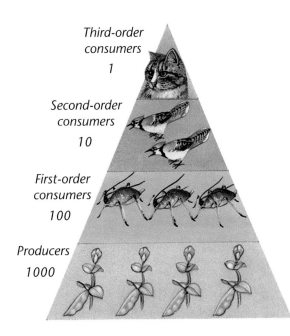

Third-order consumers
1

Second-order consumers
10

First-order consumers
100

Producers
1000

Forming a Hypothesis

How does a pyramid of biomass reflect feeding relationships in ecosystems?

A pyramid of biomass is an ecological model that expresses the mass of living material at each trophic level.

Analysis

Biomass at a trophic level is calculated by finding the average mass of each organism and multiplying this value by the estimated number of organisms in a population. Shown here is a pyramid of biomass for a forest ecosystem.

Thinking Critically

Use your knowledge of food chains and food webs to explain what you observe in this pyramid of biomass.

Second-order consumers

First-order consumers

Producers

the energy present in the producers. What happens to the rest of the energy? Some is lost as heat. Some remains at the producer level because herbivores do not eat all of the producers available. And some of the energy is used up by the processes of feeding and digestion.

In this section, you've seen how organisms interact with each other to obtain the critical resources for survival such as food, shelter, and protection. You've seen how feeding relationships between species determine how energy flows through an ecosystem. But, organisms need more than energy to survive. In the next section, you'll investigate how other important substances cycle through ecosystems.

check your UNDERSTANDING

Understanding Concepts

1. Food items important to brown-headed cowbirds include ticks and other blood-sucking parasites the birds pluck from the hides of cows and other herbivores. On what trophic level would you place the tick? The cowbird?
2. What is the habitat and niche of the tick in the cowbird-cow-tick relationship?
3. Use your knowledge of trophic levels to explain why there are fewer cheetahs than gazelles on the African plains.

Skill Review

4. **Sequencing** Think of a meal you had recently that included either meat or fish. Sequence a possible food chain for this meal. Put yourself at one end of the food chain. For more help, refer to Organizing Information in the *Skill Handbook*.

Issue:
Of Moondust, Catfish, and Kudzu

"The Eagle has landed!" It was July 20, 1969, and the U.S. space mission *Apollo 11* had reached the moon. A short time later, astronaut Neil Armstrong climbed out of the lunar lander and became the first human to get moondust on his feet.

The Issue

Are there any organisms in moondust that could cause diseases on Earth? Nobody was sure, so when the *Apollo 11* astronauts returned to Earth, they were kept in quarantine for three weeks to see whether they developed any symptoms of illness. Fortunately, there were no organisms in moondust. The moon turned out to be a lifeless place.

The Native Americans who greeted Columbus and his crew in 1492 were not so fortunate. The sailors from Europe brought diseases such as smallpox and measles for which the Native Americans had no immunity. Exotic species, which are organisms that are introduced into an ecosystem, can cause serious problems when they interact with the plants, animals, and humans within that ecosystem.

The Background

Many examples can be found of unwelcome exotic species that have invaded the United States—Africanized killer bees, zebra mussels, and noisy, pesky English sparrows to name a few. In central Florida, walking catfish can be seen flip-flopping in the dust of the road looking for food. These fish can live out of water for up to 12 hours and can actually walk using their pectoral fins as legs. This strange creature

originally lived only in Asia. In the 1960s, a pet-store owner brought a few specimens into the United States to sell to his customers. Some of the fish escaped into the countryside, where they made themselves at home and reproduced rapidly. Now, walking catfish are a common sight in some parts of Florida, competing with species of native fish.

Plants introduced from other areas can also be harmful exotic species. For example, the kudzu vine was introduced into the United States from the Orient around 1900. In the 1930s, with encouragement from the government, farmers began planting kudzu as a ground cover to help

prevent soil erosion. With abundant rain and sunshine, kudzu vines can grow at the almost-unbelievable rate of up to a foot a day. It didn't take long for kudzu to spread over the landscape like a thick green blanket as shown on page 160. Today, in many parts of the southeastern states such as Alabama and Georgia, the thick blankets of kudzu cover the trees. The vines climb high into the branches, damaging the trees by breaking off small limbs and keeping sunlight from reaching the leaves.

Upsetting the Balance

Why do exotic species so often cause trouble in a new habitat? We know that in an ecosystem, a balance is maintained among the various species. This natural balance can be upset when a new species is introduced. The new arrival may consume plants that other species need for food. If no natural predators keep them in check, the newcomers may multiply quickly until they overrun the area. Or, the introduced species may itself be a predator, wiping out a previously existing population.

The Global Village

The problem has become more critical since rapid transportation has made the world a global village. Jet planes carry passengers around the world to faraway lands in short amounts of time. When these travelers return home, they often bring with them, intentionally or unintentionally, foreign organisms. For this reason, many countries have laws against the introduction of species that are known to be troublemakers. The United States, for example, has a list of more than 100 plants and animals that are not allowed into the country. Passengers and their baggage are inspected when they enter at the border to make sure they aren't carrying any undesirable or illegal "hitchhikers."

Walking catfish

The Question

Visiting another country and becoming acquainted with a different culture and people can be a valuable experience. However, it can also lead to the introduction of exotic species. While some of these species may have no great effect, or may even be helpful, others may cause great harm to local ecosystems. It is often difficult to predict what kind of effect a newly introduced organism will have.

In view of these facts, is it realistic to try to prevent the introduction of exotic species, given that the world has become a global village? Because not all exotic species are harmful, some authorities suggest that it might be a better use of time and money to wait and see what kind of effect an introduced species has, then take measures to destroy the species if it turns out to be harmful. Would this be a better solution to the problem?

Discussing the Issue

1. *Identify* three places where exotic species have caused problems. What were the problems?
2. Zebra mussels are a species of small mollusk introduced to the United States from Europe. They multiply rapidly and are causing problems in freshwater lakes and streams. If a predator to this mussel is found, *explain* advantages and disadvantages there might be in introducing it to the ecosystem.

Cycles in Ecosystems

5-2

Objectives

■ Compare and contrast the ways carbon, water, and nitrogen cycle through ecosystems.

Key Terms

transpiration

Figure 5-10

The carbon cycle shows how carbon moves through an ecosystem. Carbon dioxide is released into the atmosphere as a waste product of cellular respiration, from the burning and decay of organic compounds, and from the burning of fossil fuels such as oil. Autotrophs remove carbon dioxide from the atmosphere during photosynthesis. The carbon then moves through the food chain as organisms eat or are eaten.

The Cycling of Matter

What do humans have in common with dinosaurs? Did you know that the atoms of carbon, nitrogen, and other elements that make up your body are the same ones that have been part of Earth since life began? Some of the atoms in your body could once have been in a dinosaur. How can that be?

In the last section, you learned how energy flows through ecosystems. Matter such as water, oxygen, carbon, and nitrogen, also moves through the trophic levels of ecosystems. The sun provides a constant input of energy into Earth's ecosystems, but the amount of matter on Earth never changes. As a result, it must be recycled constantly.

When an organism dies, the matter that makes up the organism is broken down by decomposers. As a result, atoms from the elements that make up matter become available to other organisms.

■ The Carbon Cycle

Carbon is essential to all life. It is a chemical element that is a major component in the composition of all living things. At one time, compounds containing carbon were thought to be found only in organisms and so were called organic compounds. The natural cycling of carbon through an ecosystem is called the carbon cycle, as shown in **Figure 5-10.**

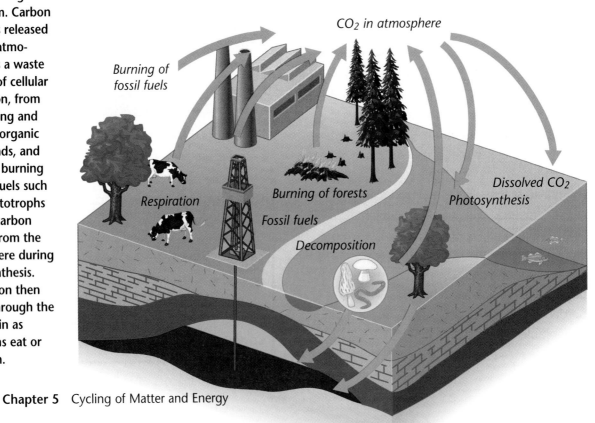

CO$_2$ in atmosphere

Burning of fossil fuels

Respiration

Burning of forests

Fossil fuels

Decomposition

Dissolved CO$_2$
Photosynthesis

Today, almost any compound containing carbon is called an organic compound, whether or not it is associated with life. Chemists have now learned how to make organic compounds in the laboratory. Carbon exists in the atmosphere as carbon dioxide gas (CO_2), which is made up of carbon and oxygen. During photosynthesis, plants and other autotrophs use carbon dioxide. Inside the autotroph's cells, the carbon is combined with other elements to form the complex organic compounds that make up the organism's body. Through this process, O_2 is released to the environment.

A second important life process that involves carbon dioxide is cellular respiration. During cellular respiration, the chemical bonds in food are broken down to release energy in the presence of oxygen. You will learn more about this process in Chapter 8. In the process, carbon dioxide is released into the atmosphere. Many organisms, heterotrophs and autotrophs alike, undergo cellular respiration. In the next MiniLab, you will see some of the effects of this process.

MiniLab

Do germinating seeds produce carbon dioxide?

All organisms need energy to fuel their activities and life processes. Many organisms release energy through cellular respiration, the process in which sugar and oxygen are combined to release energy. A waste product of this process is carbon dioxide gas. In this activity, you will investigate whether germinating seeds produce carbon dioxide gas.

Procedure

1. Pour pinto beans into an Erlenmeyer flask until it is one-third full.

2. Pour distilled water over the beans until covered. Let the beans soak overnight.

3. Insert a flexible drinking straw into the mouth of the flask. Use cotton or clay to secure the straw and close the flask.

4. Insert the free end of the straw into a small container of bromothymol blue indicator. Bromothymol blue turns from blue to green to yellow in the

presence of carbon dioxide.
CAUTION: *Use care when handling chemicals. Bromothymol blue may stain clothing.*

5. Wait about 10 minutes, then observe the color changes in the bromothymol blue solution.

Analysis

1. Did the beans produce carbon dioxide gas? How do you know?

2. What might this experiment tell you about a source of carbon dioxide for the atmosphere?

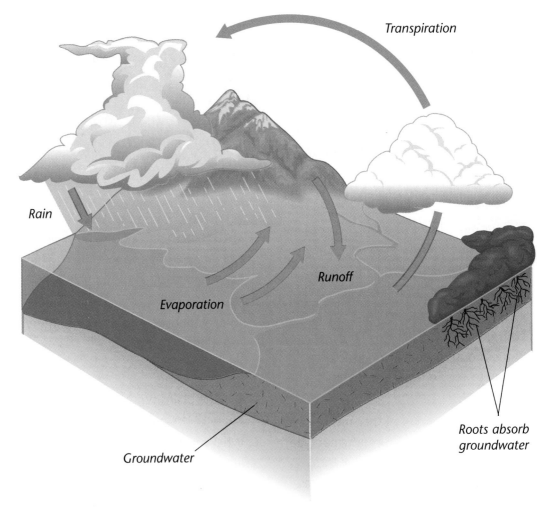

Try It!

Plants and the Water Cycle

Place plastic sandwich bags over several large leaves of a houseplant. Secure the bags with rubber bands or twist ties. Be sure the entire leaf is enclosed. Let the plant stand undisturbed overnight. Observe the plastic bags the next day for the presence of small water droplets.

■ **The Water Cycle**

Water is perhaps the most important nonliving component of ecosystems. Water occurs on Earth as a liquid or solid and in the atmosphere as a gas. How does water cycle through ecosystems? Organisms need a constant supply of water. In Chapter 4, you saw how the availability of water determines, to a large degree, the diversity and adaptations of organisms in an ecosystem.

As you know, animals, including humans, obtain water through drinking or from the foods they eat. Some animals, such as desert rodents, rely on the water produced through metabolism. Excess water is released back into the environment as a by-product of cellular respiration and excretion.

Figure 5-11 shows that plants are even more important than animals in the cycling of water. Water begins its cycle through the ecosystem when plants absorb it through their roots. Some of this water is used during photosynthesis. Some is cycled back into the environment as it evaporates from plant leaves.

Have you ever noticed water collecting on the inside of the windows of a greenhouse? If you have you have witnessed the results of the process of transpiration. **Transpiration** is the evaporation of water from the leaves of a plant. Through the process of transpiration, much of the water absorbed by plant roots is eventually returned to the environment.

Figure 5-11

The water cycle illustrates how water cycles through ecosystems. When water evaporates from plants, oceans, lakes, and other bodies of water, it enters the atmosphere as water vapor. It condenses and returns to the ground as rain, snow, and other forms of precipitation. Water is taken in by plants, animals, and other living organisms. Water is also released back into the atmosphere by living organisms.

Transpiration

Rain

Runoff

Evaporation

Groundwater

Roots absorb groundwater

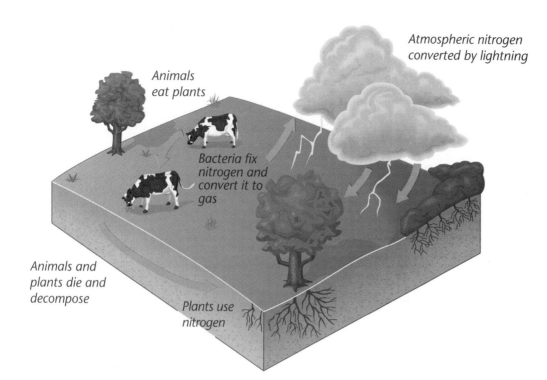

Animals eat plants

Bacteria fix nitrogen and convert it to gas

Atmospheric nitrogen converted by lightning

Animals and plants die and decompose

Plants use nitrogen

Figure 5-12

Although nitrogen gas makes up about 80 percent of the atmosphere, living organisms cannot use nitrogen in its gaseous form. Life would not be possible if it weren't for soil bacteria that fix atmospheric nitrogen by converting it into a form that can be used by all forms of life.

■ The Nitrogen Cycle

The chemical element nitrogen is an essential component of several substances that make up living organisms. Nitrogen is needed to form protein molecules. It is also an important ingredient in nucleic acids, such as DNA, which guide the growth and life processes of any organism. Like other forms of matter, the supply of nitrogen on Earth is fixed. It must be recycled, as shown in the illustration of the nitrogen cycle in **Figure 5-12.**

In this chapter, you've seen how the interactions between organisms and the physical, nonliving aspects of the environment make up a functioning ecosystem. Ecologists model these interactions and associations to trace how energy and matter flow through ecosystems. But what happens when ecosystems are disturbed? In the next chapter, examine how natural and human-induced disturbances affect ecosystems, and learn how ecosystems respond to change.

---

check your UNDERSTANDING

Understanding Concepts

1. Describe the relationship between biotic and abiotic factors in the water cycle.
2. In what way are bacteria important in the nitrogen cycle?
3. What effects might deforestation have on the carbon cycle?

Skill Review

4. **Design an Experiment** Design an experiment to test whether or not broad-leaved plants, such as those in a tropical rain forest, have more of an impact on the water cycle than plants with smaller leaves. For more help, refer to Practicing Scientific Methods in the *Skill Handbook*.

John T. Biggers

As a young boy growing up in Gastonia, North Carolina, in the 1930s, African-American muralist John T. Biggers (1924-   ) never gave much thought to becoming an artist. At 17, he enrolled at the Hampton Institute in Virginia with every intention of studying heating and sanitary engineering, and becoming a plumber. But during his first year at Hampton, he took a night class in drawing. That class, and the teacher who taught it, changed the course of Biggers's life.

The instructor was Viktor Lowenfeld, a Jewish artist who came to the United States as a refugee. He believed that artistic self-expression was a way to create self-esteem in his young pupils. Under Lowenfeld's guidance, John Biggers developed his artistic talents and gained new respect for his African heritage.

After receiving both his bachelor's and master's degrees from Pennsylvania State University, Biggers was invited in 1949 to join the faculty of Texas Southern University in Houston and set up an art department there. At TSU, Biggers quickly established his artistic reputation as a mural painter. Through both his art and his teaching, he promoted the identity of African-Americans and black culture in the United States.

In 1957, Biggers spent six months living and traveling in West Africa, something he had dreamed of doing for many years. Visiting Africa was a revelation for the artist. He was inspired by the close relationship many West Africans had with nature and how their lives were intimately interwoven with those of the animals and plants around them. One plant in particular—the cassava—became for the artist a symbol of nature as a nurturing force in human life.

Since retiring from TSU in 1983, Biggers has had more time to paint. His recent murals and paintings are more abstract than his earlier works, but they continue to depict the ties that link African-Americans to their ancient heritage and the world of nature.

interNET CONNECTION

Visit the Glencoe Homepage for the Chapter 5 link to find out about poet/author Maya Angelou, another African American artist. Read her poem, "A Brave and Startling Truth." What event does the poem commemorate? How does she link natural imagery to social and political issues? List some examples.

Read the statements at the right and below that review major points presented in the chapter. Using the concepts that you have learned, answer each question *in your Journal.*

1 Every species plays a unique and key role in the functioning of an ecosystem. No two species can occupy the same niche. *Why can't two species occupy the same niche at the same time?*

Cape May warbler

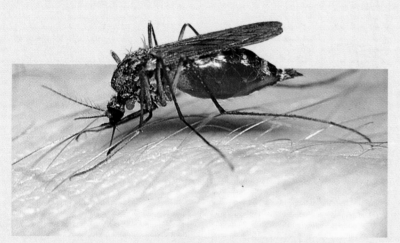

2 Many organisms conserve energy and gain other benefits by engaging in symbiotic relationships with other organisms. *How is the lifestyle of a mosquito an example of symbiosis?*

3 Energy needed to fuel the life processes of organisms flows through ecosystems by way of the food web, the complex network of feeding relationships in an ecosystem. *How do food webs illustrate the delicate balance of nature that exists in ecosystems?*

Grizzly bear

Goshawk

Berries

Grouse

Elk

Chipmunk

Marmot

Grasses

Insects

Seeds

Using Key Science Terms

autotroph   heterotroph

decomposer   niche

food chain   symbiosis

food web   transpiration

habitat   trophic level

For each pair of terms below, write a sentence that reflects your understanding of the relationship of both science terms.

1. autotroph, food chain
2. symbiosis, niche
3. heterotroph, carbon cycle
4. decomposer, food web
5. trophic level, pyramid of energy

Understanding Ideas

Using complete sentences, answer the following questions in your Journal.

1. What trophic level do humans occupy? Explain.
2. Why can't an ecosystem contain 20 trophic levels?
3. In an ocean ecosystem, what organisms make up the first trophic level?
4. How is the niche of an organism similar to the job of a person in a community?
5. What happens to energy as it flows through a food chain?
6. Which is a more realistic model for feeding relationships in ecosystems: a food chain or a food web? Explain.
7. Describe the role of autotrophs in the carbon cycle.
8. Fleas and ticks feed on the blood of mammals. This is what type of symbiotic relationship?

Developing Skills

Use your understanding of the concepts developed in this chapter to answer each of the following questions.

1. **Concept Mapping** Use the following terms and phrases to complete the concept map about ecosystems: *autotroph, heterotroph, food chains, habitats, abiotic factors*

Ecosystem
includes
organisms
occupy
niches
such as
interact in

2. **Observing and Inferring** The pyramid of biomass shown here reflects the biomass of organisms in a forest ecosystem. Based on this model, do you think this is a stable, healthy ecosystem? Why or why not?

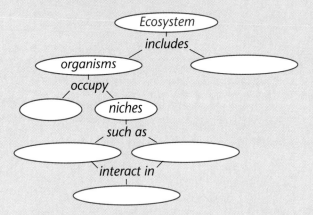

Second-order consumers

First-order consumers

Producers

3. **Hypothesizing** What effect would a lack of decomposers have on an ecosystem? Formulate a hypothesis, then describe an experiment you might perform to test your hypothesis.

Critical Thinking

In your Journal, *answer each of the following questions.*

1. How would you describe the habitat and niche of humans?
2. The graph below represents energy stored in the bodies of the producers in three different ecosystems. How might the difference in available energy reflect the amount of carbon cycled through each ecosystem? Explain.

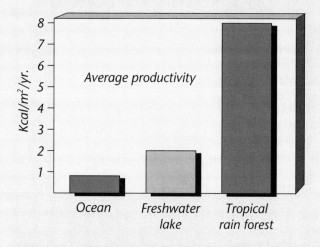

3. Why do plant fertilizers contain nitrates?
4. The chemical element phosphorus is important for the maintenance of cells. Plants absorb phosphorus through their roots and animals obtain phosphorus by eating plants and animals. Draw a diagram that shows this nutrient cycle.

Problem Solving

Read the following problem and discuss your answers in a brief paragraph.

An ecologist investigating the effects of air pollution on lichen populations determined that the numbers of lichens were much lower in polluted areas than in nonpolluted areas.

How might the destruction of lichens affect the food web of a community?

CONNECTING IDEAS

1. **Theme—Energy** Explain how the symbiotic relationship between fungi and algae in lichens involves energy.
2. **Theme—Stability and Change** During experiments on forest ecosystems, it was found that the amount of nitrogen entering a healthy ecosystem was about the same as the amount leaving it. Explain why these experimental findings reflect the fact that there is a fixed amount of matter on Earth.
3. **Theme—Systems and Interactions** A keystone species is one whose niche affects many other niches in an ecosystem. Why do you think it is important for conservationists to pay particular attention to keystone species?
4. **Science and Society** Some plants and animals are considered pests. Choose one and describe the possible effects to the ecosystem if the pest were destroyed by an introduced species.
5. **In-Depth Look** How might weather and temperature affect the rate of decomposition?

CHAPTER 6

Changes in Ecosystems
Upsetting the Balance

The bulldozers and construction crews have come and gone. A new building rises from what was once a grass-covered lot. Most of that grass is gone now—dug up when a huge hole was made for the building's foundation. At first, all that piled-up dirt seemed lifeless. But, since workers first broke ground a little more than a year ago, new weeds and grasses have sprouted. Patches of ground near the edge of the new building have become the home of mosses and other moisture-loving species.

Why do some plants pop up in areas that seem uninhabitable, such as sidewalk cracks and construction sites? In this chapter, you will examine some of the factors that regulate population size and growth. You will also learn how balance is maintained even when ecosystems undergo constant change.

▶ *In the following activity, you'll explore ways that plants are adapted to grow in harsh places.*

MiniLab

Why can some plants grow in harsh areas?

Most plants we consider weeds are those that are able to survive in harsh conditions that the majority of cultivated plants can't tolerate. Look at the characteristics of dandelion plants and determine their adaptations to harsh conditions.

Procedure

1. Locate an area near your school or home where dandelions or other weeds grow.
2. Using a small shovel or garden trowel, remove several dandelion plants from the soil. Remove the entire plant.
3. Find a few dandelions that are in the puffball stage.
4. In the classroom, examine the leaves, roots, and seeds.

Analysis

1. What kind of root do dandelion plants have? What advantage is this root to the dandelion plant?
2. What are the characteristics of a dandelion leaf? How do these characteristics help the plant?
3. What do the seeds tell you about the reproductive adaptations of the dandelion?

6-1 Population Growth

Objectives
- Compare and contrast linear growth and exponential growth.
- Describe how environmental factors place limits on population growth.
- Recognize how species' interactions regulate population size.

Key Terms
exponential growth, biotic potential, carrying capacity, interspecific competition

Growth of Populations

Streams of people bustle along the crowded city streets, squeezing into every available inch. Consider some of the largest cities of the world, such as New York City, Tokyo, and Mexico City. According to the most recent statistics, cities such as these already contain tens of millions of people and are still growing. In fact, in just the ten-year period between 1980 and 1990, the Los Angeles metropolitan area grew by a whopping 27 percent—an increase of 3 million people.

The growth of human populations is similar to the growth of populations of other species. How fast do populations grow?

Populations Can Explode

Millions of humans live in New York City, but that number is relatively small compared to the billions of ants that probably dwell within those same city limits. As shown in **Figure 6-1,** some species are characterized by large populations, while populations of other species are small.

You've probably noticed that it doesn't take long for dandelions to transform an untended lawn or a patch of bare soil into a blanket of yellow flowers. When environmental condi-

Figure 6-1

Population sizes can range from enormous to tiny. Bees living in a single hive may number in the tens of thousands, while the population of ducks nesting along the shores of a pond may include only a few individuals. What other populations can you think of that are very small? Very large?

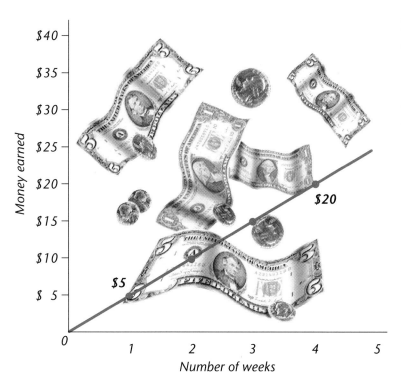

Figure 6-2

This graph shows how your savings will grow if you put away the same amount of money each week. Because the increase occurs at a steady rate, it can be represented by a straight line, and so is called linear growth.

tions are suitable, the size of a population can increase rapidly. How does a population of dandelions grow from a few plants to several dozen plants in just a few weeks? To answer this question, think about the mathematics of population growth.

The rate at which a population increases is not the same as the rate of growth of other familiar items. Take a weekly allowance, for example. Suppose you receive $5 every week for completing certain chores around your home. If you save this amount in a jar under your bed for two weeks, you will have a total of $10 to spend. If you save your allowance for ten weeks, you'll have $50. As **Figure 6-2** shows, if you plot this information on a graph, the result is a straight line that shows a steady rate of growth.

Living populations don't exhibit linear growth. A graph of any growing population of organisms resembles a J-shaped or exponential curve. **Exponen-**

tial growth occurs when a population increases by a fixed percentage each year. As you can see in **Figure 6-3,** the increase in the number of organisms is slow at first. That's because the number of potentially reproducing individuals is small. The rate of population growth increases quickly because the number of individuals capable of reproducing increases.

Figure 6-3

Unlike the linear growth of a weekly allowance, populations of organisms grow exponentially. Because of this pattern, organisms that reproduce rapidly, such as the common housefly, *Musca domestica,* have the potential for explosive growth. Houseflies produce nearly 120 eggs per year. If each egg develops into an adult and half of the eggs of each generation are female, then 120 eggs could produce nearly 6 trillion flies in only one summer.

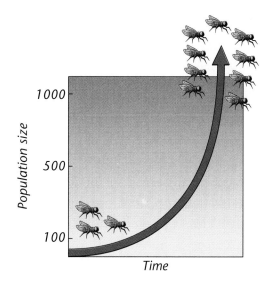

Population Size Has Limits

If rapidly reproducing organisms like houseflies and weeds have the potential for explosive population growth, why isn't Earth covered with them? What causes a population of organisms to explode? How many organisms can the environment support? Why don't populations of elephants explode the same way populations of flies, mosquitoes, or rats do? Do the next MiniLab to see the potential number of offspring one organism can produce.

MiniLab

How many offspring can a single dandelion produce?

One of the defining characteristics of weeds is that they have a high reproductive potential, which is the ability to reproduce in large numbers. In this activity, you will determine the reproductive potential of one dandelion plant.

Procedure

1. Locate a field of dandelions around your school, home, or town.

2. Carefully remove three to five dandelion plants from the ground. Be sure each plant you collect has at least one seed head. A seed head is a flower that has reached the puffball stage of development.

3. Count the number of flowers on one dandelion plant. Although each bloom may appear to be a single flower, it's actually a mass of tiny, closely packed flowers known as a composite flower. Next, count the number of individual, parachute-like seeds on each seed head. Or, if some of the seeds have come off the seed head, you could count the number of small depressions on the seed head that indicate where each seed was attached.

4. Multiply the total number of seeds by the number of composite flowers to calculate the reproductive potential of one dandelion plant.

5. Repeat the procedure for the other plants you collected.

Analysis

1. What is the average reproductive potential of one dandelion plant?

2. How might you estimate the reproductive potential of a population of dandelions in a grassy field or lawn?

As you observed in the MiniLab, one dandelion plant has the potential for producing several hundred new dandelion plants. If every dandelion seed developed into an adult plant, the numbers would reach the hundreds of thousands. This would be the highest rate of reproduction under ideal conditions and is known as the **biotic potential** of the population.

Do populations of organisms ever reach their biotic potential? Obviously, they do not. If they did, Earth would most certainly be covered with dandelions, insects, and other species with high reproductive potential.

Limiting factors, such as availability of food and water, temperature, light, and other biotic and abiotic factors, keep organisms from reaching their biotic potential. Consider, for example, the data from a population growth study of yeast cells shown in **Figure 6-4.** As you can see from the data, the yeast population grows exponentially for a few hours, then levels off. Eventually, the population stops growing. When a population is no longer increasing or decreasing in size, it has reached the carrying capacity of the environment. The **carrying capacity** is the largest number of individuals an environment can support on an ongoing basis.

Regulating Population Size

As you've seen, the limit imposed on a population's growth is the carrying capacity of the environment. What environmental factors determine the carrying capacity?

In Chapter 3, you learned that severe weather can temporarily affect ecosystems by damaging the habitats of organisms living there. In Chapter 4, you learned how abiotic factors such as temperature, rainfall, and sunlight help determine which species will thrive in a particular habitat or ecosystem. Population sizes are not only regulated by environmental factors, but are also limited by interactions among organisms.

Figure 6-4

According to the data, the growth of this yeast population skyrockets between the sixth and tenth hours of the study, then begins to slow. By the 18th hour, growth has leveled off because the carrying capacity of the environment has been reached. There is not enough food or other resources to support a larger population of yeast cells.

Ⓐ Populations can follow an S-shaped curve. There is an initial slow growth phase, a period of exponential growth, and a plateau where the number of organisms the environment can support is reached.

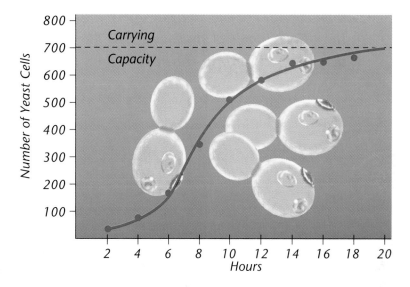

Ⓑ As the yeast population grows, the liquid medium becomes cloudier as the number of yeast cells increases. Each tube represents a portion of the growth curve. Which tube shows the period of exponential growth?

INVESTIGATION

Population Growth in *Paramecium*

Paramecium *is a unicellular species of protist that lives in freshwater environments. It feeds on bacteria and decaying material in the environment. The growth of* **Paramecium** *populations, like any living population, is regulated by a variety of factors. In this activity, you will investigate how the availability of food affects growth of a* **Paramecium** *population.*

Preparation

Problem

How does the availability of food affect population growth in *Paramecium?*

Objectives

In this Investigation, you will:
- *Calculate* the population size of a *Paramecium* culture.
- *Compare and contrast* the growth of a *Paramecium* population with models of population growth.

- *Demonstrate* how the availability of food affects *Paramecium* population growth.

Materials

microscope
microscope slides
coverslips
dropper
10-mL graduated cylinder
plastic cup
yeast culture
Paramecium culture

Safety Precautions

Use care when handling the microscope.

Data and Observations

Number of *Paramecium* in culture	Slide 1	Slide 2	Slide 3	Average	Total in culture
Monday					
Tuesday					
Wednesday					
Thursday					
Friday					

INVESTIGATION

Procedure

1 Make two copies of the data table *in your Journal.* Label one data table "food," and the other data table "limited food."

2 With the graduated cylinder, measure 10 mL of *Paramecium* culture and pour it into each plastic cup. Label one cup "food" and the other cup "limited food."

3 Add one drop of yeast culture to the plastic cup labeled "food." Yeast cells are a food source for *Paramecium.*

4 Prepare three wet mount slides of the "food culture" by placing one drop of the *Paramecium* culture on each slide. Be sure to correctly label all slides.

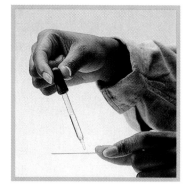

Step 4

5 Observe the slides under low power of the microscope. Count the total number of *Paramecium* on each slide. Average the count for the three slides from each group, then enter the data in the appropriate data table.

6 Two hundred drops equal 10 mL, so multiply your average by 200 to estimate the total number of *Paramecium* in the culture.

7 Repeat steps 4 through 6 for the "limited-food" culture.

8 Repeat steps 4 to 6 every school day for three weeks for each culture.

9 For each culture, use a graphing calculator to create a scatter plot of your data with the total number of paramecia on the vertical axis and the number of days on the horizontal axis.

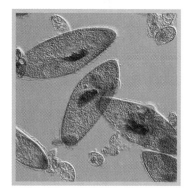

Step 5

Analyze and Conclude

1. **Collecting and Organizing Data** Why was it necessary to prepare three slides of each *Paramecium* culture?

2. **Analyzing the Procedure** Was the total number of *Paramecium* in your culture an estimate or an actual number? What are the limitations of this technique?

3. **Making and Using Graphs** Compare and contrast the shapes of the graphs. How do the graphs compare to models of population growth?

4. **Thinking Critically** Based on your data, would you conclude that availability of food affects population growth in *Paramecium?* Explain your answer.

Going Further

Project
Develop an experiment to observe the growth of Paramecium *populations under different environmental conditions. Carry out this experiment. How long does it take for the population to reach its carrying capacity in each environment?*

■ Predation Regulates Population Size

As the previous Investigation showed, given ideal environmental conditions, a population will grow until it reaches the carrying capacity of the environment. What other factors may regulate the size of a population? Predator-prey relationships are one important factor.

As shown in **Figure 6-5,** both predator and prey populations increase and decrease over time. What's interesting is that the predator-prey feeding relationship affects the population size of both the predator and its prey. Suppose an unusual cold spell reduces the availability of grass and seeds that a population of hares depends on for food. The hare population would decline. What would happen to a population of lynx that depends on these hares for food? It too, would decrease in size.

A similar kind of decline might also occur if the lynx population became so large that virtually all of the available hares were consumed. This type of graph can't identify the factors that cause shifts in population size, but it does show how predator-prey relationships are important to the regulation of both populations.

■ Environmental Limits to Population Size

As you read, population size can be limited by factors in the environment such as a limited food or water supply, severe weather, or disease. Scientists have divided these environmental factors into two groups: density-dependent factors and density-independent factors.

Figure 6-5

Predator-prey relationships regulate both predator and prey populations. Notice how the total numbers of lynx and hares fluctuate together. What would happen if the lynx population suddenly declined due to disease?

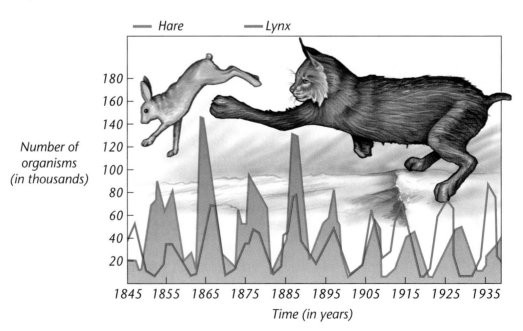

Figure 6-6

By defending its home territory against other fish species, the brook trout can preserve the food, shelter, and other resources for its own use. The sunfish and perch shown here must move to other areas to feed and seek shelter.

Perch

Sunfish

Brook trout

Density-dependent factors are factors that have an increasing effect as a population grows. These factors include disease, competition, and parasites. A disease, for example, spreads more quickly through a population whose members live closer together than in a population whose members are spread out. Think of how a cold virus or the flu affects the population of your school. In many cases, a large percentage of the school is affected.

Density-independent factors are things that affect all populations, regardless of their size. Most density-independent factors are abiotic factors. Some of these include temperature, floods, and habitat destruction. When a new shopping mall is built, all the organisms living in that area are affected, regardless of the size of each population.

■ Competition for Resources Limits Population Size

In the last chapter, you learned that no two species can occupy the same niche. Different species may, however, rely on the same resources in an environment, such as food, water, and space.

Constant competition occurs in nature among different species for the same limited resources. Organisms compete for such things as living space, food, and water. Brook trout, shown in **Figure 6-6,** are highly territorial fish. If other fish come too near, the trout will fight to defend its territory. This type of behavior helps the trout avoid competing with other fish species for the food, shelter, and other resources available in its territory. Competition between species is called **interspecific competition.** Interspecific competition

How can competition be demonstrated?

When two populations of organisms compete for the same food source, what happens to the two populations? In a demonstration of interspecific competition, biologist G.F. Gause showed that when two species of *Paramecium* are forced to compete for the same resources, one species always dies.

Analysis

The graphs shown here represent population counts of two species of *Paramecium*. One count was made when each was grown alone. The other was made when the two populations were mixed. Analyze the graphs to answer the following questions.

Thinking Critically

1. Compare and contrast population growth in *P. aurelia* and *P. caudatum* in each graph.

2. According to the graphs, which species was more successful in obtaining resources? Why do you think this occurred?

Paramecium aurelia

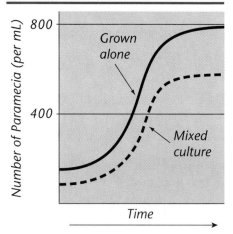

Paramecium caudatum

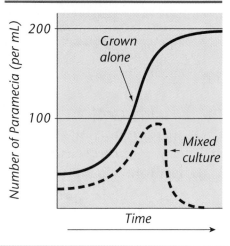

can have a significant effect on the population size of competing species. Competition also directly affects the distribution of organisms. A species that successfully prevents intruders from entering its territory may have more food, shelter, and other resources available for growth and reproduction. As a result, its population could increase in comparison with that of its less successful competitors. The species that is outcompeted has to occupy less favorable areas with fewer available resources.

Variations within a species allow the species to adapt to competition from other species, or to changes in the environment. These variations within a species provide the basis for the theory of evolution. Individuals with variations favorable for a particular environment are more likely to survive and pass those variations on to the next generation than individuals with variations less favorable for a particular environment. When a species changes through time, scientists say that is has evolved.

■ Crowding Affects Population Growth

As you have probably observed, the population densities of weeds tend to be high. Weed species can survive easily in crowded conditions, but this is not true for many other species of organisms.

As shown in **Figure 6-7,** when populations become crowded, individuals may experience stress. Animals under stress may become aggressive and fight more readily. They may stop taking adequate care of their young or become less resistant to disease. They may produce fewer offspring or stop reproducing altogether. All of these factors can lead to a decline in population size.

In this section, you investigated how populations of organisms grow, as well as the ecological factors that tend to regulate population size. As you have seen, predation, competition, and crowding are natural limiting factors that maintain a balance in ecosystems.

Figure 6-7

The effects of crowding have been well documented in laboratory populations of mice. When mice are crowded together, older and weaker individuals die because they are less able to obtain food, water, and other resources. Other individuals may experience symptoms of stress, including an increase in aggressive behavior, reduced fertility, and a higher incidence of disease. These responses of crowding are natural mechanisms that help regulate population size.

check your UNDERSTANDING

Understanding Concepts

1. Draw a graph that would represent the population growth of a rapidly reproducing species with high reproductive capacity.

2. Mice are an important prey species for forest owls. Predict what might happen to an owl population if the population of mice suddenly experienced a drastic decline due to disease.

3. Why is it unlikely that a species would ever reach its full biotic potential?

Skill Review

4. **Making and Using Graphs** The table below shows the growth of a population of unicellular organisms. Prepare a graph of these data. What information about the population does the graph give you? For more help, refer to Thinking Critically in the *Skill Handbook.*

Time (days)	0	1	2	3	4	5	6	7	8	9	10	11
Number of organisms	10	18	40	63	80	125	125	137	121	138	145	124

people in SCIENCE

Meet Louidajean Holloway, Chemical Engineer

The billboard shows a happy young couple, hand-in-hand, splashing in the lake. It's an ordinary scene except for the color of the water—bright magenta. A speech balloon over the young man's head reads, "Hey, Sue, that looks like the paint we dumped down the storm drain last week."

Ms. Holloway, who works for the Ohio Environmental Protection Agency, believes that most people care about the environment but aren't always aware of the consequences of their actions.

On the Job

Q Ms. Holloway, what do you find is a frequent ecological misunderstanding among the people you talk to?

A People often don't understand that many older cities have separate sewage systems and storm drains. Storm drains are built to carry off rainwater quickly and prevent flooding. This water doesn't pass through a sewage-treatment plant but goes directly to a bay, lake, or river.

Q What sorts of pollutants do you see going into storm drains?

A Construction debris, paint, oil, Styrofoam peanuts—you name it!

I don't think people intentionally pollute the water system; they just don't think about the possible consequences.

Q How do you try to deal with the problem?

A I give presentations to groups, such as contractors' groups. I also provide technical assistance by answering upwards of 50 phone calls a week from contractors and developers. My people skills get used a lot as I help folks understand that in dealing with pollution problems, preventive measures are almost always less costly than corrective measures. And the possibility of a $10,000 per day fine gets their attention, too!

Early Influences

Q Since your college degree is in chemical engineering, did your childhood years involve a lot of playing with chemistry kits?

A I certainly did a lot of experimenting. It was fun to see how something I'd learned about in science classes had applications in real life, such as making the water for pasta boil faster by adding a little salt. I was lucky enough to have teachers who made science fascinating, such as a physics teacher who sent us to a big amusement park to answer questions about the acceleration of roller coasters and other rides.

Personal Insights

Q Science and math can be tough for kids. What do you say to encourage them?

A Since I've tutored several students and often visit the classroom

Look in the yellow pages of a phone book under "Environmental, Conservation and Ecological Organizations." Choose an organization and contact it to learn about volunteer opportunities. Then make a brochure to interest classmates in one of the following careers.

▶ *forestry technician, park ranger, naturalist, wildlife photographer*

where my mom teaches, I get many chances to talk to kids. I tell them that lots of things in life are hard and remind them that catching a pass or making a free throw is hard, too. Learning any kind of skill requires work. I played varsity basketball in college, so I'm able to compare studies to sports. I'm also proud to tell kids that I was the first African-American woman to graduate from the chemical engineering program at the University of Toledo in Ohio.

6-2 Ecosystem Change

Objectives

- Sequence the events that occur in ecological succession.
- Describe some effects of human activity on ecosystems.

Key Terms

succession
primary succession
climax community
secondary succession
pollution
particulate
acid precipitation

All Ecosystems Change Over Time

Ecosystems show the effects of storms, fires, and floods. Trees can lose branches or be uprooted and fall over. Frigid temperatures kill plants. Heavy rains flood worms and other underground organisms out of their homes. But ecosystems usually recover from disruptions. Studying how ecosystems change over time and respond to disturbances helps us understand how human activities affect the environment and how the environment responds.

■ Change Comes Naturally

Changing conditions sometimes make it more difficult for certain species to continue to survive in an area. A severe storm, extended cold period, or drought can affect the habitat of the organisms living there. A lack of water or a limited food supply causes problems for most organisms. In the next MiniLab activity, find out whether changes to an environment can also create conditions that make an area more suitable for other species.

Figure 6-8

Primary succession is the gradual colonization of a barren area by organisms.

Ⓐ The first organisms to colonize a new, rocky site are hardy species—species that can survive harsh environmental conditions. These organisms, such as lichens and mosses, are known as *pioneer species.* As some members of the lichen or moss populations die, they are broken down by bacteria and other decomposers.

Ⓑ Weathering of rocks over time can cause small cracks to form. Materials like decaying lichens, tiny particles of rocks, and even airborne dust settle into the cracks, initiating the process of soil formation.

Ⓒ Further work by decomposers enriches the soil, making it possible for the seeds of herbaceous plants, ferns, and small shrubs that have been brought to the area by wind or animals to sprout and grow.

How does a changing environment make conditions more suitable for certain species?

As populations of organisms grow and reproduce, they cause changes in the environment. Over time, species that cannot tolerate these changes disappear, to be replaced by other species that are adapted to the new conditions. In this activity, investigate how this process works.

Procedure

1. In a beaker add ½ teaspoon of powdered milk to 20 mL of tap water.

2. In another beaker add ½ teaspoon of dry yeast to 20 mL of warm tap water.

3. Mix the two solutions in a 100-mL beaker. Let the mixture sit for one hour.

4. Prepare a wet mount slide of the mixture and observe the yeast cells under low power of the microscope.

5. Cover the beaker loosely with plastic wrap for three to five days.

6. Make a wet mount slide of the mixture and observe under low power of the microscope. Observe the tiny bacterial cells now present.

Analysis

1. What was the odor of the solution after it sat for a few days? What might this indicate?

2. Why do you think the bacteria were able to survive in the solution?

As you observed in the MiniLab, when yeast cells use sugar to release energy, they change the environment. The odor you noticed was alcohol, a by-product of the energy-making process in yeast. The new environment created by the yeast cells made conditions favorable for bacterial populations to grow and survive.

D As shrubs, ferns, and grasses grow taller, they crowd out the pioneer species, which die and decay, further enriching the soil. The environment then supports larger species such as aspens and birches.

E As the forest matures, maples, beeches, and shade-tolerant species begin to appear.

Most ecosystems change gradually over a longer period of time. A gradual change in the structure of an ecological community is known as **succession.**

■ Primary Succession

As you could see in **Figure 6-8,** new communities begin when hardy species such as lichens first populate barren, rocky areas that have little soil. **Primary succession** is the formation of a new community in an area that started out as bare land. Diversity in the ecosystem increases gradually over hundreds, perhaps thousands of years as organisms change the environment and make conditions suitable for other species.

After some time, primary succession slows down, and the community becomes fairly stable. A stable, mature community that changes very little is called a **climax community.**

■ Secondary Succession

During the summer of 1988, large forest fires burned huge expanses of one of the country's great national parks, Yellowstone. As firefighters struggled to contain one of the greatest blazes in recorded history, few people realized that they were witnessing the beginning of a new forest community. **Secondary succession** is the sequence of changes that takes place when a community is disrupted by natural disturbances or human actions, as shown in **Figure 6-9.**

The Yellowstone fires burned nearly 20 percent of the biotic community of the park and gave ecologists an excellent opportunity to study secondary succession. Secondary succession occurs more rapidly than primary succession. Seeds are usually present, and soils are already fertile. The community has not started from scratch.

Figure 6-9

Secondary succession

A Secondary succession occurs when a climax or near climax community is destroyed by a natural event such as a fire, drought, or flood, or human action such as mining or farming.

B Wildflowers and other plants that require plenty of sunshine were among the first to germinate in the ash-covered soils following the fires in Yellowstone National Park.

Human Disturbances to Ecosystems

Ecosystems are resilient and can recover after severe disturbances like hurricanes, fires, and volcanic eruptions. Even some human activities, such as logging, shown in **Figure 6-10,** and construction, usually aren't devastating enough to transform lush ecosystems into barren wastelands. Ecosystems rebound from disruptions through the process of succession. However, some human activities can more radically alter the environment.

As you learned in Chapter 5, a delicate balance between living organisms and the physical environment makes up a stable ecosystem. As a result of our

Figure 6-10

Logging of forests is one example of the ways in which human actions can directly affect other organisms. More often, though, human activities affect ecosystems indirectly by polluting air and water, and by interfering with the natural cycling of nutrients throughout ecosystems.

Figure 6-11

Motor vehicles are a major source of air pollution in large cities. Improved mass-transportation systems, such as trains and buses, reduce dependence on automobiles and cut down on smog and other pollution.

increasingly industrialized and technological society, humans have placed great stress on this delicate balance. How do human activities disrupt ecosystems?

■ Effects on Air Quality

Today, you may have taken a bus rather than walk five blocks to the store. Perhaps you ate fast food from a foam container or threw an aluminum can away with the regular trash rather than in the recycling bin. These activities contribute to **pollution,** the contamination of the environment by excess waste material.

Many pollutants affect the air. Pollutants can enter the air from a variety of sources, including natural fires and volcanic eruptions. However, the burning of fossil fuels in homes, in transportation, and in factories, is by far the greatest source of air pollutants.

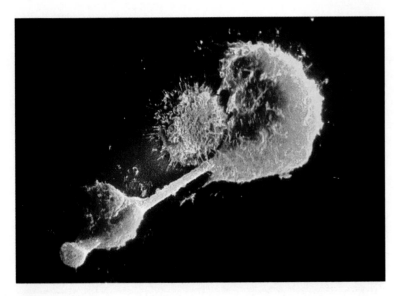

Figure 6-12

Asbestos, a type of mineral fiber used in insulating materials, can be a dangerous air pollutant. These fibers are easily dislodged, float in the air, and may be inhaled. Here in the lungs, asbestos fibers rupture white blood cells, which are trying to engulf and destroy them. Scar tissue builds up in the lungs due to the enzymes released from the ruptured cells, which injures healthy lung tissue.

The efficient burning of fossil fuels releases carbon dioxide and water into the atmosphere. However, because most car engines and furnaces are not efficient enough to completely burn fuels, other substances are also released, including carbon monoxide, nitrogen oxides, sulfur oxides, hydrocarbons, and soot. Soot is an example of a particulate, which is a small, solid particle that has been released into the air. Many types of particulates are extremely harmful to humans and other animals. When some types of particulates enter the lungs, they adhere to the lining of the air passages and can ultimately interfere with the normal functioning of these important organs. **Figure 6-12** shows one possible response of the body to an air pollutant.

Beauty on the Wing

Ro Vaccaro says she migrated to Pacific Grove, California, just like the monarch butterflies that drew her there. One day while she was working in an office in an eastern city, she noticed a monarch stop to rest on the ledge outside her window.

The sunlight shimmering on the black and orange wings fascinated Ro. During an earlier trip to California, she had learned that millions of monarchs spend the winter in a town called Pacific Grove. Inspired by the beauty of the monarchs, Ro moved to Pacific Grove.

Moving West

"But when I got to Pacific Grove," Ro says, "I found out the monarchs were in trouble." During winter, the butterflies

Monarch butterflies cover trees in Pacific Grove

■ Air Pollutants Can Cause Acid Precipitation

One of the most serious effects of air pollution caused by the burning of fossil fuels is acid precipitation. **Acid precipitation** is precipitation that is more acidic than unpolluted precipitation. It forms when nitrogen and sulfur oxides dissolve in atmospheric water vapor to form nitric and sulfuric acids.

Acid precipitation can corrode metal structures, such as bridges, and can dissolve limestone structures. More important are the effects of acid rain on ecosystems, as shown in **Figure 6-13.** Acid rain increases the leaching of important minerals, such as calcium and potassium, from the soil. Try the next Investigation activity to see how acid rain also disrupts the cycling of nitrogen throughout ecosystems.

Figure 6-13

Acid rain has damaging effects on ecosystems. Decreased fertility of soils devastates trees, and lower pH in lakes and ponds kills fish and other aquatic organisms.

---

cluster in one grove of trees that provides the precise environment they need. The butterflies need the insulating effect provided for them by the trees. The trees also protect them from storms and drying winds. The grove's owner intended to cut it down and build condominiums. Ro led a hard-fought campaign that enabled the town to purchase and preserve this unique butterfly sanctuary.

Now Ro visits her butterflies nearly every day from their arrival in October to their departure in February. "When temperatures reach 55°," she says, "the butterflies clinging to the trees in the sanctuary open

their wings. They bask in the sun to let their bodies warm up. Then they do a little shimmy-shake to loosen up their wings. With a hundred or more butterflies clustered together, the whole branch shakes."

Doing Lunch

Then the monarchs fly to nearby "hospitality zones" to sip energy-giving nectar from flowers. Each monarch makes this trip every week or so until the end of December, when the butterfly becomes nearly dormant.

The longer, warmer days of February bring the butterflies to

life again. "About Valentine's Day, the monarchs mate and the whole grove becomes very active," Ro reports. After mating, the males die, but the females fly north to lay 400 or more eggs on milkweed plants, the only food that monarch caterpillars will eat.

Thinking Critically

1. *Explain* why the groves of trees are so important for the monarchs.
2. *Infer* how Ro's fight to protect one species of organism can be important to all organisms.

Acid Rain and the Nitrogen Cycle

As you learned in Chapter 5, nitrogen is an important chemical for living things. Nitrogen is abundant in the atmosphere, but most organisms can't use it until it has gone through the process of nitrogen fixation. Nitrogen fixation occurs as part of a symbiotic relationship between bacteria and legumes, which are plants such as beans, peas, and clover. Nitrogen-fixing bacteria live within the roots of legumes and produce swellings called nodules. In this Investigation, you will design an experiment to test the effects of acid rain on the nitrogen-fixing capabilities of plants. You will also investigate how acid rain affects nearby plants that depend on legumes for nitrogen.

Preparation

Problem
Does acid rain interfere with the nitrogen cycle?

Hypothesis
Discuss the possible evidence you could collect that would answer the problem question. As a group, decide on a hypothesis that you can test to answer the question, and write the hypothesis *in your Journal.*

Objectives
In this Investigation, you will:
- *Determine* whether acid rain affects the nitrogen-fixing capabilities of clover.
- *Determine* the effect of acid rain on non-nitrogen-fixing plants.

Possible Materials
small packet of rye grass seed (a non-nitrogen-fixing plant)
small packet of clover (inoculated with nitrogen-fixing bacteria)
nitrogen-free nutrient media
small plant pots
distilled water
acid solution adjusted to a pH of 4.0
plastic wrap
bag of vermiculite

Safety Precautions

Use care when handling the acid solution. Acid can cause minor burns to skin. Be sure to wash your hands thoroughly after the experiment.

Plan the Experiment

1 Review the list of possible materials. Have your group decide on a procedure to test your hypothesis.

2 Your teacher will help you prepare the simulated normal rain and simulated acid-rain solutions using the nitrogen-free nutrient media.

3 Record your procedure and list the materials and quantities you will need.

4 Design and construct a data table for recording your data. What do you think will happen to the plants? How will you make your observations or measurements?

Check the Plan
Discuss the following points with other group members to decide the final procedure for your experiment.

1 How many groups of plants will you use? How many seeds will you plant? What precautions will you take to prevent contamination of your plant pots?

2 What observations will you make? How often will you make your observations?

3 *Make sure your teacher has approved your experimental plan before you proceed further.*

4 Carry out your experiment. Make your observations and complete your data table.

5 Design and complete a graph or other visual representation of your results.

Analyze and Conclude

1. **Analyzing the Procedure** How important was the presence of clover to the rye grass?

2. **Comparing and Contrasting** How well did the rye grass in the acid-rain group grow compared with the other two groups?

3. **Drawing Conclusions** Does it appear that acid rain has an effect on the nitrogen-fixing process, or is it inconsequential?

Going Further

Application
Conduct a similar experiment to test a range of pH levels. Prepare a chart that shows the effect of various pH levels on nitrogen fixation.

Figure 6-14

The pesticide DDT cannot be broken down by the organisms that consume it. Instead, it becomes concentrated in the organisms' tissues. As a result, DDT is passed along the food chain in increasingly higher concentrations in a process known as biological magnification. In small amounts, DDT is not harmful to animals. However, the gradual buildup of the chemical in the fatty tissues of an animal can ultimately affect the health of the animal.

A Once DDT enters the water supply, it slowly builds up within the tissues of algae and other microorganisms living in the water. As a result, the concentration of DDT in algae is nearly 100 times greater than the concentration in the water.

B Small fish feed on algae. The concentration of DDT in the fish is now 1000 times greater than in algae.

■ Effects on Water Quality

Water covers more than two-thirds of Earth's surface, but the fresh water of our lakes, rivers, and underground wells represents about 0.3 percent of all the water on Earth. This is also the water that humans and other organisms depend on for survival. When water supplies are affected, it often has serious consequences for ecosystems.

One of the most damaging problems resulting from water pollution occurs when contaminants get washed into lakes, ponds, and rivers. This occurs due to runoff from farm fields, discharge from industry, and dumping. As you recall, food chains are the feeding relationships among organisms. When poisonous substances enter the food chain, they can be passed from one organism to another.

The use of DDT, discussed in **Figure 6-14,** was banned in the United States in 1972. Even though it was banned in the United States, DDT is still used in other countries that supply produce to the United States. One of the discoveries that led to the ban of DDT in the United States was the thinning of the eggshells of birds that are top carnivores, such as falcons, eagles, and pelicans. Birds that had high levels of DDT in their bodies produced eggs with shells so thin that they broke long before the embryo had a chance to develop and hatch from the egg. This reproductive failure resulted in a sharp decrease in the populations of many of these organisms—so much so that they were threatened with extinction.

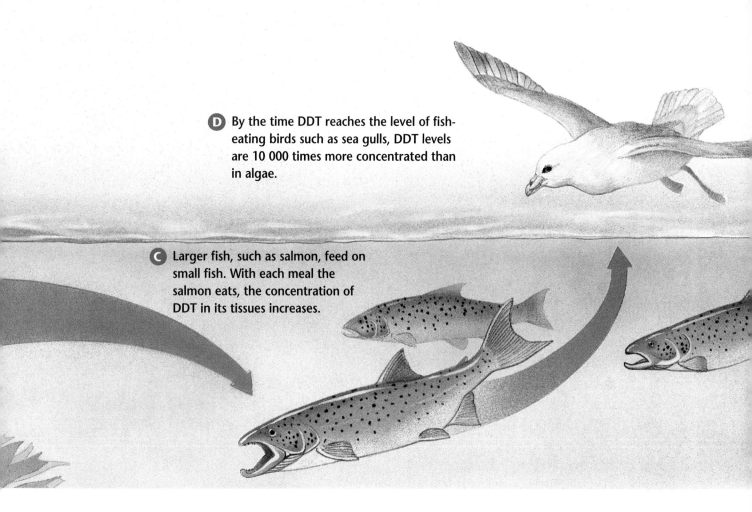

D By the time DDT reaches the level of fish-eating birds such as sea gulls, DDT levels are 10 000 times more concentrated than in algae.

C Larger fish, such as salmon, feed on small fish. With each meal the salmon eats, the concentration of DDT in its tissues increases.

In this chapter, you've learned how populations grow and how natural mechanisms help regulate population growth. You've also seen how communities change during the process of succession. The growth of human populations has similarities to the population growth of other organisms. However, crowding, competition, and other natural mechanisms do not seem to exert the same level of control on human populations as they do on populations of other species. In the next chapter, you'll find out how human use and misuse of Earth's natural resources can affect the quality of human lives.

check your UNDERSTANDING

Understanding Concepts
1. Why do ecosystems naturally change over time?
2. Describe the role of decomposer organisms in primary succession.
3. Discuss how human activity can disrupt the functioning of ecosystems.

Skill Review
4. **Sequencing** Sequence the steps that occur when a forest community develops in an area covered with bare rock or cooled lava. For more help, refer to Organizing Information in the *Skill Handbook.*

Science and Society

Wetlands are not what most people call attractive. As their name implies, they are lowlands covered at least periodically by shallow water. They are muddy, not suitable for walking or boating, and often a-buzz with the sound of mosquitoes. So, why worry about wetlands?

The Issue

We should worry—a lot. Some wetlands produce more than 50 times as much plant material as the same size grassland area, which makes them important to large numbers of wildlife. Many commercial fish and shrimp begin life in coastal wetlands and estuaries, where they find abundant food and shelter. Wetlands also provide vital rest stops for migratory ducks and

Wetlands include marshes, swamps, and bogs. These areas are home to many different species of plants and animals.

geese and longer stopovers for herons and king-fishers. Wetlands are also used by these birds as breeding grounds and nurseries.

The Background

Wetlands are a wonderful place to observe nature. They can also be put to work to dispose of industrial, agricultural, and sewage wastes. A wastewater plant that meets federal standards costs close to $5 million to install. Wetlands are a natural filter of wastes and a controller of floods. To avoid the high cost of a new treatment plant, some towns, such as Arcata, California, have created artificial wetlands of about 154 acres between the town and the bay to do the job.

In wetlands, water moves slowly through the thick vegetation, allowing time for solid wastes to fall to the bottom. Microbes transform polluting nitrogen and phosphorus compounds in the water into simpler substances. These

substances are absorbed by wetland plants such as cattails and reeds.

The number of wetlands has been declining due to the development of coastal areas and the draining of these lands for planting crops. The Office of Technology Assessment estimates that between 30 and 50 percent of the wetlands that existed within the lower 48 states at the time of colonization have been lost.

The Question

If wetlands are so useful, why not create artificial wetlands to take the place of natural wetlands being lost? That is what is happening in many places. When developers or farmers wish to drain an existing wetland area, they are usually required to obtain a permit that requires them to create new wetlands of equal size in another location. However, no guidelines and no formal training exist for installers of artificial wetlands. Unless those responsible for the grading, seeding, and planting have an understanding of the purpose of the project, the wetlands will fail.

Some experts say a system as complex as a natural wetland cannot be duplicated. Follow-up studies to date have been short-term—no longer than ten years. Natural wetlands are the result of thousands of years of accumulation of soil and the populations of organisms that inhabit them. Many ecologists believe that artificial wetlands cannot possibly duplicate these precise conditions.

Projects Continue

In spite of these drawbacks, some wetlands are easier to create than others. For example, coastal wetlands develop more quickly than inland wetlands. Fewer plant species are involved at the coast, and the water requirements of the ecosystems are more easily duplicated. Artificial wetlands may never develop the biodiversity of natural wetlands. Preserving existing wetlands may be the best solution.

inter**NET**
CONNECTION

Visit the Glencoe Homepage, **http://www. glencoe.com/,** for the Chapter 6 link to the National Park Service's Water Resources Department to learn more about wetlands. Research how wetlands are classified. What is being done to protect them?

Oil Spill

One of the hazards of living in a technological society is industrial pollution. No matter how careful people are in handling toxic wastes and other hazardous materials, accidents happen. Cleaning up after these accidents is critical to reducing the amount of environmental damage done.

You're the Hazardous-Waste-Emergency Manager

A tanker truck has overturned on a local highway, spilling thousands of gallons of oil. The oil has run down a steep slope and is starting to flow into a nearby river. You want to assess the situation and develop a plan for keeping the oil out of the river and for cleaning up the land near the highway.

Drawing on Experience

❶ With a group, brainstorm ways to stop oil from flowing down the slope, clean up oil-soaked soil, and remove oil from a moving stream.

❷ You may contact a local hazardous-waste-management company to find out how they would handle such a spill.

❸ As a group, decide how you would clean up the oil spill.

Testing...Testing

❶ Fill two long containers with soil and a third with water. In the first container, spread vegetable oil across the soil and allow it to soak into the soil. Use your chosen method to clean up the spill.

❷ In the second container, raise one end to form a slope. Test your method of preventing oil from flowing down a slope to keep the oil from reaching the lower end of the pan.

❸ Pour some oil in the water. Use this container to test your water cleanup method.

❹ If necessary, revise your methods so they clean up the spill as completely as possible.

How Did It Work?

How well did each of your methods work? Were you able to restore each of the containers to the way it was before the oil spill? Make an action plan that describes how you would clean up oil spills and prevent them from spreading.

Read the statements at the right and below that review major points presented in the chapter. Using the concepts that you have learned, answer each question *in your Journal.*

1 Under ideal conditions, populations grow exponentially until they reach the carrying capacity of the environment. *How does population growth compare to the growth of a weekly allowance?*

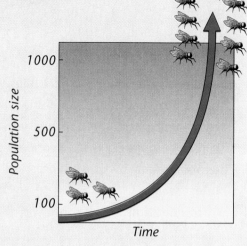

2 In addition to abiotic factors, population size is also regulated by interactions between species, such as predation and competition. *How might a decline in the size of a prey population affect the population size of predators, such as foxes?*

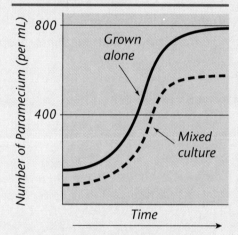

Paramecium aurelia

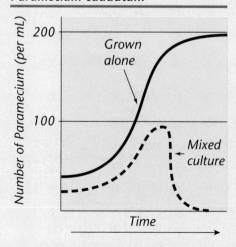

Paramecium caudatum

3 Ecosystems change naturally over time, or after a major disturbance such as fire. *How are primary and secondary succession similar? How are they different?*

Using Key Science Terms

acid precipitation   particulate

biotic potential   pollution

carrying capacity   primary succession

climax community   secondary succession

exponential growth   succession

interspecific
  competition

For each set of terms below, choose the one term that does not belong. Provide an explanation for why it does not belong with the other terms.

1. succession, exponential growth, pioneer species
2. pollution, particulates, primary succession
3. biotic potential, acid precipitation, carrying capacity
4. particulates, biological magnification, climax community

Understanding Ideas

Using complete sentences, answer the following questions in your Journal.

1. How does the growth of a weekly allowance by saving it under your mattress differ from the growth of a population?
2. How does the availability of resources relate to the carrying capacity of a particular environment?
3. How do predator-prey relationships regulate populations?
4. What features of weeds make them well-suited for their role in primary succession?
5. How does primary succession differ from secondary succession?

Developing Skills

Use your understanding of the concepts developed in this chapter to answer each of the following questions.

1. **Concept Mapping** Make a concept map that demonstrates your understanding of the following terms and phrases. Supply the appropriate linking words for your map.

   climax community, succession, pioneer species, primary succession, secondary succession, natural disturbance, human-induced disturbance

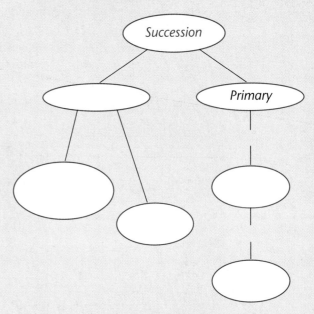

2. **Predicting** What steps would you take if you wanted to estimate the biotic potential of a field of dandelions?
3. **Thinking Critically** Suppose you were investigating the population growth of a *Paramecium* species. After tracking population size for five hours, you notice a drastic decline in the number of *Paramecium*. What signs might you look for to determine whether overcrowding was the cause of the population decline?

4. Predicting Acid precipitation can have disastrous effects on the cycling of nitrogen throughout an ecosystem. Discuss the effects that an acid-rain-disrupted nitrogen cycle might have on plants, animals, and other organisms.

Critical Thinking

In your Journal, *answer each of the following questions.*

1. What environmental factors would most affect the growth of the human population?
2. The following food chain occurs in a forest community: plants → mice → owls. How might an increase in the owl population affect the plant population?
3. In some regions, a grassland would be considered a climax community. In other regions, grassland is an earlier stage in succession. Discuss some factors that might result in different climax communities in different areas.
4. How might the addition of a new food source into an environment change the carrying capacity of that environment?

Problem Solving

Read the following problem and discuss your answers in a brief paragraph.

As a park manager in a famous national park, part of your job includes tracking the populations of all the mammals in the park. Near the end of spring one year, you notice that the fox population is no longer growing. Further research shows that many young foxes are dying from a respiratory disease.

What might happen to existing food webs in the park if the foxes continue to die? Is the population being affected by a density-independent or density-dependent factor? Explain.

CONNECTING IDEAS

1. **Theme—Stability and Change** How can an ecosystem undergoing succession be both stable and changing at the same time?
2. **Theme—Systems and Interactions** Why are predator-prey relationships important for the healthy functioning of ecosystems?
3. **Eyewitness Accounts** How do the monarchs obtain food while in Pacific Grove?
4. **Science and Society** What are some of the disadvantages to creating artificial wetlands?
5. **Applying Technology** Why is it important to clean up an oil spill as quickly as possible? What hazards can it pose to a nearby water supply?

THE SALT POLLUTION PROJECT

Problem

Most land plants cannot tolerate salty water. In areas that have ice and snow storms, salt used on the roads washes into the soil and can damage nearby plants. This is also why seawater, which is about 3.5% salt, cannot be used to irrigate plant crops. Design an experiment to determine the salt concentration range that can be tolerated by a specific plant species.

Materials

young plants
   (grass, corn, bean, etc.)
water

salt
balance
graduated cylinder

beakers
test tubes
labels

Getting Started

1. Hypothesize the effect of various salt concentrations on the normal growth and appearance of a specific plant. Record your hypothesis in your Journal.

2. Design an experiment to test your hypothesis. Be aware of the fact that a salt concentration of 3.5% is usually harmful to most land plants when designing your experiment.

3. Carry out the experiment. Keep a daily log of your observations. Prepare a report of your findings. How did your results compare with your hypothesis? Offer an explanation as to why salty water is harmful to plants. Describe how you could determine which type of plant is most resistant to salt water.

Resources

Bottle Biology. Williams, Paul.
   Kendall/Hunt Publishing Company,
   1993.

THE MICRO-ENVIRONMENT PROJECT

Problem

Place a sample of pond water in a small glass jar. Observe samples of the pond water using a microscope over a period of weeks. What will happen to the populations of organisms in this environment over time?

Materials

glass jar
pond water sample
microscope

glass slides and coverslips
medicine droppers
guides for identification of microorganisms (optional)

Getting Started

1. Hypothesize whether changes may occur over time in the populations of organisms present in this environment. Record your hypothesis *in your Journal*.

2. Design an experiment to test your hypothesis. Try to make the recording of your observations both qualitative (names of organisms present) and quantitative (number of each organism type present). Make diagrams of any organism you are unable to identify. Observe this pond environment for a period of no less than 8 weeks.

3. Check your plan with your teacher. Conduct the experiment and prepare a report of your findings.

4. How did your results compare with your hypothesis? Why was the suggestion of using **colored** diagrams important in the identification of organisms? How do your qualitative observations relate to the term *succession*? How might your quantitative observations support the concept of population growth and decline?

Resources

<u>Biology: An Everyday Experience</u>. Kaskel, Albert. Glencoe/McGraw-Hill Publishing Company, 1995, pages 263-264.

<u>Probing Levels of Life</u>. Hummer, Kaskel, Kennedy, and Oram. Merrill Publishing, 1989, pages 224-226.

Food

What drives some animals to forage most of the day, while others search through the refrigerator at all hours for something to eat? Whether food is served "fast" or at the kitchen table at home, it supplies energy and nutrients for life. In this unit, learn about the nutrients that all organisms compete for in the web of life.

Green algae and green plants, such as this corn plant, capture energy from the sun and turn it into food through the process of photosynthesis. The health of the soil in which corn and other crop plants grow also makes a difference in the nutrients that become available for other organisms in the food chains of life.

Throughout the world, the food supply of most organisms depends on the energy and nutrients stored in green plants. Those who cultivate food crops must be certain that the plants receive proper nutrients from the soil and have adequate water. They must protect the plants from insects, microorganisms, weeds, and rodents that compete with humans for the food supply. Adequate methods of preservation must be used to keep the food from spoiling before it can be used.

Many foods contain the same basic ingredients—carbohydrates, lipids, and proteins. These components, in turn, are made up of smaller units linked together, such as the glucose molecules that chemically combine to form carbohydrates. The chemical bonds holding these units together store energy. Creative approaches to food preparation result in this energy's being served up in a variety of ways.

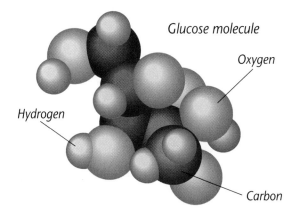

Glucose molecule

Oxygen

Hydrogen

Carbon

Green Plants

A green plant plays an important role between the sun and most of Earth's organisms. Green plants and green algae are uniquely adapted to take the sun's energy and use it to power reactions to make food that supplies energy for almost all of Earth's life-forms. The individual parts of a corn plant illustrate where the sun's energy is trapped, where food is made, and where food is stored.

Food is manufactured in the leaves of plants in the form of a carbohydrate, glucose.

Food is stored in the roots of plants and sometimes in other parts of the plant, such as in the kernels of corn that form on the "ear."

Try It!

Where in a green plant might food be manufactured? Remember that all green parts of the plant contain a substance that can capture energy from sunlight.

What To Do

1. Look at an entire potted plant. Observe all the parts that are green. If necessary, use a magnifying glass to find some green parts.

2. Compare the sizes of the various parts of the plant (i.e., stem, leaves, etc.), to the overall size of the plant and predict which parts of the plant play the most important role in capturing sunlight.

3. Illustrate your predictions in a bar graph.

Try It Again

After you have learned more about the role plants play in manufacturing food, try this activity again and see whether your predictions change.

Energy from the sun is captured by chlorophyll, a green pigment in the chloroplasts contained in the cells of green plants.

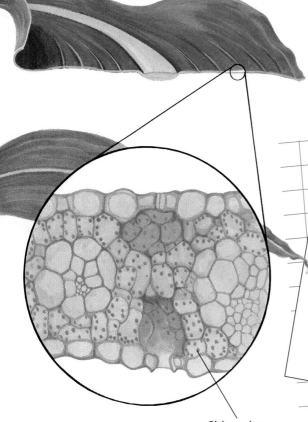

Chloroplast

UNIT 3 PROJECTS

During your exploration of food and food-related chemistry, you may discover new questions or wish to explore one of these topics further. **Chilling Seeds to Help Break Dormancy** and **How much fertilizer is enough?**, found in the Unit 3 Projects section on pages 322-323, will give you the challenge of learning more about the importance of healthful food as a source of energy. Read through these projects now. By the time you finish this unit, you'll know all you need to know to successfully complete both of these projects.

CHAPTER 7

Biochemistry

What's in the food you eat?

A great way to celebrate a special occasion is eating out. While you're waiting for a meal at a restaurant, do you think of how various ingredients are being put together in the kitchen to make a finished dish? Do you consider how various dishes are combined for a complete meal? Probably not; you're just too hungry to think about preparing food!

No matter how dishes are prepared, you will find that meals contain three major types of organic compounds. These compounds supply your body with the important components you need to grow, move, and stay healthy.

▶ *In the following activity, you'll explore one way that a variety of foods can be similar.*

Is it a matter of taste?

Bread, crackers, cooked pasta, cooked rice, and tortillas are different in shape and texture. In this activity, you will discover one characteristic that is common to all of these foods.

Procedure

1. Report to your teacher any food allergies you may have.

2. Place a sample of one of the foods in your mouth and chew it slowly for several minutes before swallowing.

3. As you chew, identify any taste changes you may notice.

4. Repeat steps 2 and 3 with each of the remaining samples.

5. Clean up your work area. Dispose of any wastes according to your teacher's instructions.

Analysis

1. Compare and contrast the taste of each food as you began to chew.

2. How did the taste of each sample change as you chewed?

7-1 Food Chemistry and Food Energy

Objectives
- Explain how the basic laws of chemistry apply to life processes.
- Relate Calories to the energy content of foods.

Key Terms
calorie

Back to the Basics

Whether you're running in a race, reasoning out the answer to a question, or eating popcorn, your body is actively carrying out many different processes. These processes are the result of a variety of chemical reactions, just like other chemical reactions that occur around you. Materials used in your body's chemical reactions come from food you eat and are made up of different elements and compounds.

■ Atoms and Elements

Recall from other science courses that the basic building blocks of all matter are atoms. The core, or nucleus, of an atom is made of protons, which are positively charged particles, and of neutrons, which are particles without any charge. As shown in **Figure 7-1,** electrons are negatively charged particles that move around the nucleus.

Elements are substances that cannot be broken down into simpler substances by ordinary chemical means. They are composed of atoms that have the same number of protons. Of the 112 currently known elements, carbon, oxygen, hydrogen, and nitrogen are the most important for living organisms. Other elements are still crucial for an organism even though they may be present in limited quantities, as shown in **Table 7-1.**

Electron cloud

Nucleus

Figure 7-1

A cross section of an atom shows its internal structure.

A Most of the mass of an atom is in its nucleus. Electrons move around the nucleus in an area called the electron cloud. The electron cloud area makes up most of the volume of an atom.

B If the nucleus of an atom could be scaled up to the size of a grape, its electrons would be about 1.6 km (1 mile) away.

■ Compounds

As you study **Table 7-1,** notice that oxygen is the most abundant element in the human body. Yet, you may have heard that the living cells that make up your body are 70 to 95 percent water. Why isn't water listed in the table?

You can see the answer to this question by examining **Figure 7-2.** Water is not an element. Water is a compound. Compounds are substances that can be broken down into two or more different elements by ordinary chemical means.

Scientists use chemical formulas to show the makeup of compounds. For example, the chemical formula for water is H_2O. Because water is a compound and compounds are made up of atoms, the formula indicates that the smallest unit of water that has the properties of water is a combination of two hydrogen atoms and one oxygen atom. How do elements combine to form compounds?

Some Elements in the Human Body		Table 7-1
Element	Symbol	Percent by Mass
Oxygen	O	65.0
Carbon	C	18.5
Hydrogen	H	9.5
Nitrogen	N	3.3
Calcium	Ca	1.5
Phosphorus	P	1.0
Potassium	K	0.4
Sulfur	S	0.3
Sodium	Na	0.2
Chlorine	Cl	0.2
Magnesium	Mg	0.1
Iron	Fe	trace
Iodine	I	trace
Copper	Cu	trace
Manganese	Mn	trace
Molybdenum	Mo	trace
Cobalt	Co	trace
Boron	B	trace

Figure 7-2

Water is a substance made of specific numbers of hydrogen and oxygen atoms. It can be broken down into two simpler substances—the elements hydrogen and oxygen. If it's not an element, what is water?

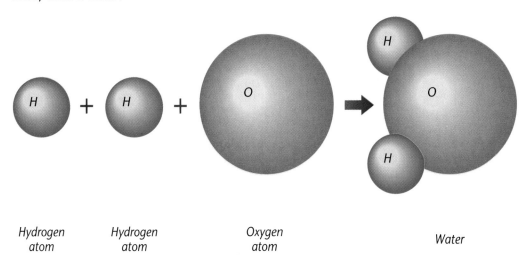

Hydrogen atom   Hydrogen atom   Oxygen atom   Water

How Atoms Interact

Individual atoms are rarely found alone because most of them are chemically unstable and will react with other atoms. Atoms may interact in several ways to become stable; they either lose, gain, or share electrons. These interactions all result in chemical bonds between atoms. **Figure 7-3** shows how atoms form chemical bonds. Chemical energy is stored in these chemical bonds and is released in some chemical reactions.

If you look at a campfire, you can see that light and thermal energy are released in the chemical reaction of burning. To start the fire burning, however, energy was supplied. In any chemical reaction, energy known as activation energy must be supplied to break bonds present in the reactants. As the reaction proceeds and products form, new chemical bonds form. Usually, these new bonds contain less energy than the original bonds contain, and excess energy is released, usually as heat or light. The running of the engine of a family car, the warmth of your skin, and the light and sound of a fireworks display are examples of energy that is being released when chemical bonds are broken and re-formed in chemical reactions.

Figure 7-3

Usually an atom has the same number of protons, which are positively charged, and electrons, which are negatively charged. The charges balance each other, and the atom has a neutral charge.

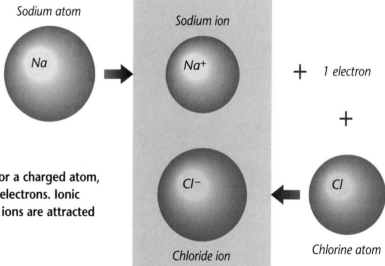

A A neutral atom can be made into an ion, or a charged atom, when it gives up or receives one or more electrons. Ionic bonding occurs when oppositely charged ions are attracted to each other.

B Most chemical bonding in living organisms involves the sharing of electrons. When atoms share electrons, covalent bonding occurs.

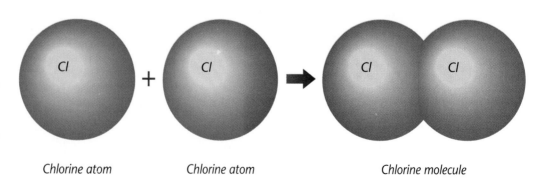

Food—Packaged Energy

No one expects the engine in an automobile to operate without fuel. This fuel contains energy-filled bonds. Humans need energy from fuel to function, too. The most common definition of *energy* is "the ability to do work." Scientists also define *energy* as "the ability to transfer heat." Many chemical processes, such as burning, break and reform chemical bonds and release energy in the form of heat. **Figure 7-4** illustrates a human body's reaction to the release of heat from food.

Traditionally, scientists use either joules or calories to indicate the amount of energy change in a chemical reaction. One **calorie** is the amount of energy needed to increase the temperature of 1 g of water by 1°C.

Mostly due to tradition, the energy content of food listed on a food label is in units of Calories. A Calorie has a value of 1000 calories. Because the metric prefix for 1000 is *kilo*, one Calorie is actually one kilocalorie of energy.

Notice that a capital letter is used to show energy value for foods.

Heat is also released and transferred by chemical reactions in your body. The food you eat is the source of the energy that fuels all of the chemical processes that occur within your body.

Figure 7-4

Think about what happens as you exercise vigorously. As you exercise, many chemical reactions are needed to make your muscles move. Energy from food fuels the reactions. Your body becomes warmer. Eventually, you may sweat, which evaporates and carries away some of the excess heat that is generated as you exercise.

check your UNDERSTANDING

Understanding Concepts

1. Study the following chemical formulas. Which formulas represent elements and which represent compounds? Explain.
   H_2O (water) H_2 (hydrogen gas)
   C_2H_2 (ethyne) CO (carbon monoxide)
2. Sodium fluoride, NaF, is a compound composed of sodium ions and fluoride ions. What type of bonding forms this compound?

3. If a bag of pretzels lists 110 Calories in a serving, how many kilocalories would a serving of the snack contain?

Skill Review

4. **Inferring** Why do you feel warmer when you are exercising? For more help, refer to Inferring in the *Skill Handbook*.

What have you eaten lately?

Objectives
- Identify three categories of nutrients.
- Compare the chemical structures of carbohydrates, lipids, and proteins.

Key Terms
carbohydrate
lipid
protein
amino acid

Filling Your Empty Fuel Tank

Think about the last time you ate. Maybe you had orange juice and cereal with milk. Or you may have had a hot dog, fries, and a soft drink. Whatever the menu, most of the different components of your food can be placed into one of three categories based on its chemical composition. All three categories—carbohydrates, lipids, and proteins—contain the elements carbon, hydrogen, and oxygen. Differences arise in the ratio of one element to another, the arrangement of atoms, the type of bonds, and the size of molecules formed.

■ Carbohydrates

Your body's main source of energy comes from foods that contain high percentages of carbohydrates. A **carbohydrate** can be a simple sugar or it can be a polymer composed of simple sugars. Simple sugars contain either five or six carbon atoms. A polymer, such as the carbohydrate starch, is a large molecule made of smaller molecules that are covalently bonded. The formulas of carbohydrates show that the compounds contain carbon and also contain one oxygen atom for every two hydrogen atoms.

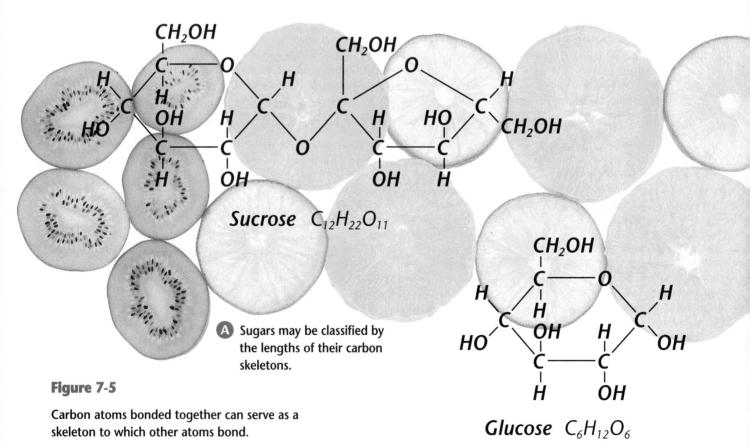

Sucrose $C_{12}H_{22}O_{11}$

A Sugars may be classified by the lengths of their carbon skeletons.

Figure 7-5

Carbon atoms bonded together can serve as a skeleton to which other atoms bond.

Glucose $C_6H_{12}O_6$

■ Sugar

Glucose, $C_6H_{12}O_6$, a common simple sugar, is a carbohydrate that provides the main source of energy for most organisms. Even your body's cells use energy that is stored in the chemical bonds of molecules of this sugar. Look at **Figure 7-5A**. A complex sugar is formed when two simple sugars combine, such as when glucose and fructose, which is fruit sugar, combine to form sucrose, common table sugar.

When you examine a food label, be aware that if *sugar* is listed as an ingredient, it usually means that sucrose is present. Examples of other sugars that are commonly present are fructose, maltose, and dextrose, as well as those listed as corn syrup or corn sweetener. This information is especially important for those who have sugar-related health concerns, such as diabetes or hypoglycemia.

■ Starch

Another type of carbohydrate is starch. Many of the foods you commonly eat contain starch.

How does the structure of a starch differ from that of a sugar? Do you recall ever seeing a freight train made of a long string of cars hooked together? In one way, a starch molecule can be compared to the train. Instead of train cars, starch is composed of glucose units strung together.

Sometimes the glucose units form a straight chain, as in the starch shown in **Figure 7-5B**. More complex starches, such as glycogen, have a branched structure. Your body stores glycogen in its muscle cells and liver. When necessary, your body breaks the bonds between the units of glucose in the starch and uses the energy released. Cellulose, which provides structure for plants, is another complex starch.

B Starch is a polymer made up of glucose molecules.

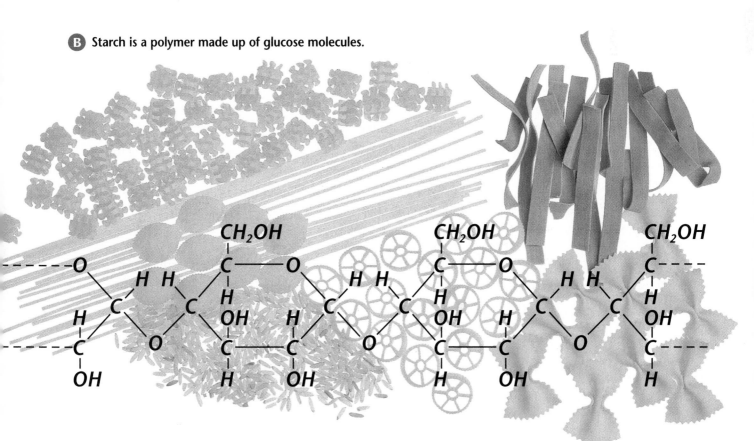

Lipids

Ah-ah, what a meal! While you may be daydreaming about a double cheeseburger, a large order of fries, and a thick milkshake, a nutritionist is having a nightmare. Your ideal meal is filled with fat, fat, and more fat.

What exactly is a fat? Fat belongs in a category of compounds called lipids. Lipids include oils as well as fats. Fats are lipids that are generally solids at room temperature and come from animals. Oils are lipids that are liquids at room temperature and usually come from plants.

Like the more complex carbohydrates, **lipids** are compounds made by connecting smaller units, one of which you can see in **Figure 7-6**. Lipids are different from carbohydrates because the chemical bonds that are in lipids result in a more concentrated form of energy storage. One gram of fat stores twice as much energy as a gram of starch stores.

Figure 7-6

In fats, the smaller units that are connected include the molecule glycerol, $C_3H_8O_3$, and fatty acids.

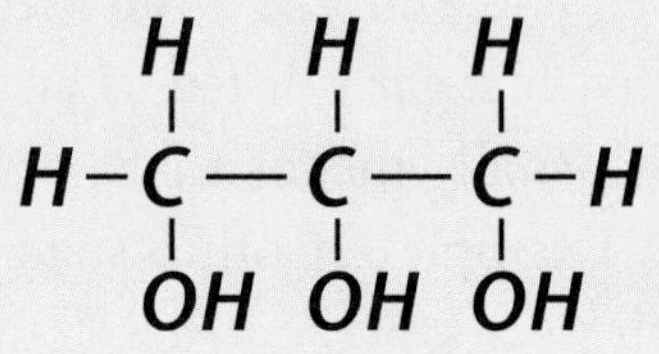

Glycerol, also known as glycerine

MiniLab

Where's the fat?

You have probably noticed food labels listing the nutritional value of food. One entry shows the fat content of the food. Usually, total fat content is listed, as well as the amount of each type of fat. In this activity, explore some features of fat found in butter and margarine.

Procedure

1. Read the labels for both the butter and margarine. Record the fat content and type for each sample.

2. Place one teaspoon of margarine in a small glass container.

3. Cover the margarine with three teaspoons of fingernail polish remover that contains acetone. Stir and mash the margarine with a fork.

4. Fold a coffee filter to make a cone shape. Place the filter in the funnel and rest it inside a beaker. Pour two teaspoons of the liquid into the filter.

5. Wait a few minutes and observe the coffee filter.

6. Repeat steps 2 through 5 with butter.

Analysis

1. Record your observations *in your Journal.*

2. Based on your observations about the residue in the paper, are there differences between butter and margarine?

Saturated or Unsaturated

As you saw in the MiniLab, there are different types of lipids. One common way to classify lipids is to identify each as being either *saturated* or *unsaturated*. Health-conscious individuals try to limit the total intake of lipids in their daily diet, especially the saturated fats. Scientists and doctors regard saturated fats, which are animal fats, as an important factor in the heart disease known as atherosclerosis. Patients with this disease have fatty deposits in their blood vessels that slow down or block the flow of blood. But how do saturated and unsaturated fats differ chemically?

Look at **Figure 7-7** and you will see that lipids differ in the bonding that occurs between the carbon atoms. Single bonds between carbon atoms allow the greatest number of hydrogen atoms to bond with the carbon atoms. The molecule is full, or saturated, with hydrogen atoms.

Wherever a double bond occurs in unsaturated fats, two fewer hydrogen atoms are bonded to the carbon atoms that are connected by the double bond. You might say that the fat is not holding as many hydrogen atoms as it could if it did not contain the double bonds.

The molecules of these unsaturated fats do not pack together easily. Thus, they melt at lower temperatures and do not collect as easily as deposits in blood vessels.

Connect to...

Biology

The bodies of caribou, which are arctic animals, contain mostly saturated fats. The parts of their legs that are near the hooves, however, contain many unsaturated fats. Infer why it is beneficial for the caribou's lower legs to contain unsaturated, rather than saturated, fat.

Figure 7-7

A single molecule of fat is made up of a molecule of glycerol and three fatty acids. Fats are classified as saturated or unsaturated based upon whether carbon atoms are bonded to each other by single or double bonds.

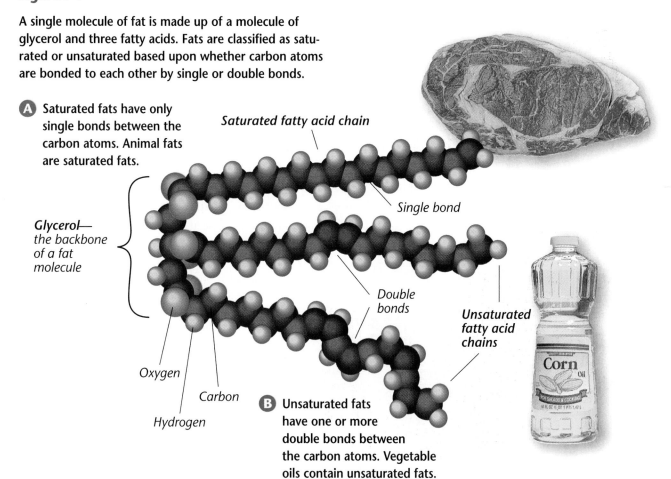

A Saturated fats have only single bonds between the carbon atoms. Animal fats are saturated fats.

Saturated fatty acid chain

Single bond

Glycerol—the backbone of a fat molecule

Double bonds

Oxygen

Carbon

Hydrogen

Unsaturated fatty acid chains

B Unsaturated fats have one or more double bonds between the carbon atoms. Vegetable oils contain unsaturated fats.

How many words can you make?

s h p w t o a

See how many words you can make using only the letters listed above. The English language has words made of 26 different letters. Imagine how many words can be made from that number!

Proteins—Versatile and Diverse

Food labels don't just list the fat content of foods. They also tell the consumer how much protein the food contains. What are proteins, and why are they important to your body?

What do proteins have in common with letters of the alphabet? Just as all English words are combinations of 26 letters, all proteins are composed of combinations of 20 different units called amino acids. In fact, **proteins** are polymers of amino acids. An **amino acid** forms when a carbon atom is covalently bonded with a hydrogen atom, an amino group, a carboxyl group, and an R group, as shown in **Figure 7-8A.** The R group may be a single hydrogen atom or a complex carbon skeleton. It is differences in the structure of the R group that determine which of the 20 amino acids is formed.

Your body can make 12 amino acids. The other eight are called *essential amino acids* and must be obtained from protein in food. Thus, a diet deficient in protein can cause serious health problems. Your body combines amino acids to make thousands of different proteins for many uses, as shown in **Figure 7-9** on page 218. In addition, some proteins are enzymes that increase the rate of chemical reactions within your body. You will learn more about enzymes in the next section.

Animals, Vegetables, and Minerals

Researchers around the globe have found that diets high in grains, fruits, and vegetables and low in saturated fats and cholesterol greatly reduce a person's risk of developing heart diseases and certain types of cancer. The United States Department of Agriculture has designed a food pyramid to help Americans make food choices that provide necessary nutrients. Most of the pyramid is made of breads, pasta, rice, cereals, fruits, and vegetables. These foods are supplemented by dairy products, meats, fish, and other proteins. Fats, sweets, and oils comprise the top of the pyramid and should be eaten in small amounts.

Do all cultures eat according to these guidelines? What is a typical meal like in different parts of the world?

IN-DEPTH LOOK

Key: 💧 Fat (naturally occurring and added during cooking)   □ Sugars (added to foods)

USE SPARINGLY

2-3 SERVINGS   2-3 SERVINGS

3-5 SERVINGS   2-4 SERVINGS

6-11 SERVINGS

Figure 7-8

Amino acids are the building blocks of proteins.

A The R groups of some amino acids are indicated here by the color red. Notice how some R groups are more complex than other R groups. The amino acids are symbolized by three-letter abbreviations.

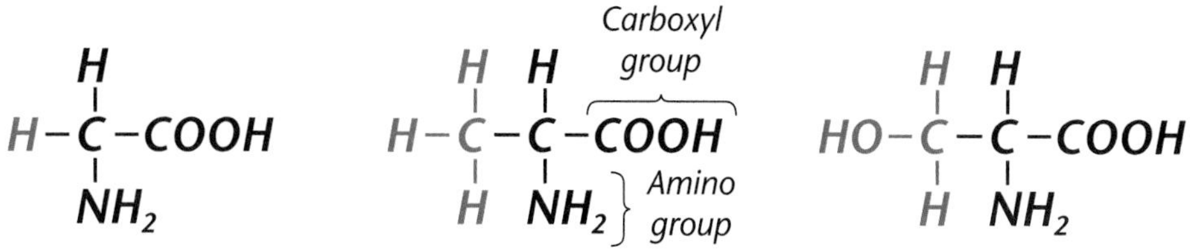

$$H-\underset{\underset{NH_2}{|}}{\overset{\overset{H}{|}}{C}}-COOH$$

Glycine (Gly)

Carboxyl group

$$H-\underset{\underset{H}{|}}{\overset{\overset{H}{|}}{C}}-\underset{\underset{NH_2}{|}}{\overset{\overset{H}{|}}{C}}-COOH$$

Amino group

Alanine (Ala)

$$HO-\underset{\underset{H}{|}}{\overset{\overset{H}{|}}{C}}-\underset{\underset{NH_2}{|}}{\overset{\overset{H}{|}}{C}}-COOH$$

Serine (Ser)

B Protein structure is determined by several factors. One factor is the amino acid sequence.

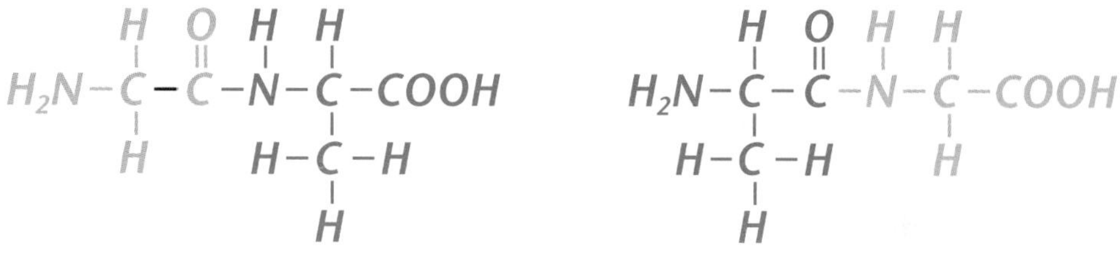

$$H_2N-\underset{\underset{H}{|}}{\overset{\overset{H}{|}}{C}}-\overset{\overset{O}{\|}}{C}-\underset{\underset{H-\underset{\underset{H}{|}}{\overset{\overset{|}{}}{C}}-H}{|}}{\overset{\overset{H}{|}}{N}}-\underset{}{\overset{\overset{H}{|}}{C}}-COOH$$

Glycylalanine (Gly-Ala)

$$H_2N-\underset{\underset{H-\underset{\underset{H}{|}}{\overset{\overset{|}{}}{C}}-H}{|}}{\overset{\overset{H}{|}}{C}}-\overset{\overset{O}{\|}}{C}-\underset{}{\overset{\overset{H}{|}}{N}}-\underset{\underset{H}{|}}{\overset{\overset{H}{|}}{C}}-COOH$$

Alanylglycine (Ala-Gly)

Chapatis and Chutneys

Indian cuisine consists mainly of grains such as millet, wheat, and rice. Chapatis are thin, flat wheat breads that accompany most meals. Dal, another common dish, is a thick soup made of beans, lentils, or peas. Meat makes up a relatively small portion of the Indian diet. Chutneys, which are fruit relishes, often top these meats.

Blini and Borscht

Breads, meats, and vegetables, much like those found in the American diet, are common in the Russian diet. A typical dinner might include roast beef, potatoes, cooked cabbage, and bread and butter. Stewed apples or plums are often eaten for dessert. Blini, which can be filled with warm, sweetened fruits and sour cream, are thin pancakes often found on the Russian dinner table. Borscht, a deep red soup made from beets, is a common Russian appetizer.

Rice and Tofu

Noodles made from rice and wheat are the staple of northern Chinese cuisine. People in the southern regions eat mainly rice. These grains are supplemented with a variety of vegetables including cabbage, bean sprouts, broccoli, mushrooms, water chestnuts, and bamboo shoots. Sometimes, small pieces of meat are added to a mixture of vegetables. Much of the protein in the Chinese diet comes from tofu—a white, spongy curd made from soybeans. Soups, dumplings, and egg rolls often complement the main Chinese meal.

Thinking Critically

1. *Compare* what you ate during the last 24 hours to what you might have eaten if your diet were strictly based on the food pyramid.

2. Based on your knowledge of nutrition, *infer* which of the diets discussed here seems the most healthful. Explain.

Figure 7-9

Proteins play important roles in animals' bodies because they perform many functions. In addition to those roles shown, proteins are important for growing hair and nails, maintaining healthy cells, muscle movement, and many other processes.

Ⓐ *Digesting food*—a snake eating a deer

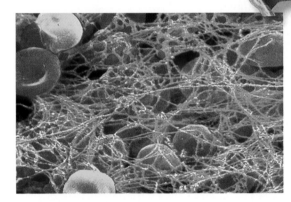

Ⓑ *Fighting infection*—a white blood cell engulfs a yeast cell

Ⓒ *Healing cuts*—blood cells and fibrin in a blood clot

Ⓓ *Carrying oxygen to tissues*—red blood cells in a capillary

check your UNDERSTANDING

Understanding Concepts

1. Carbohydrates and lipids both consist of carbon, hydrogen, and oxygen. What causes them to be different?
2. How are the structures of carbohydrates and some proteins similar?
3. Is the fat in a pork chop saturated or unsaturated? How do you know?

Skill Review

4. **Making and Using Tables** Prepare a table that lists the building blocks present in each of the three food categories described in this section. For more help, refer to Making and Using Tables in the *Skill Handbook.*

7-3 Speeding Up Your Body's Chemical Reactions

Enzymes: Chemical Motivators

Objectives
- Operationally define the lock-and-key model for enzyme activity.
- Explain how enzymes increase the rate of chemical reactions.
- Identify how enzyme reactions can be controlled.

Key Terms
enzyme
substrate
lock-and-key model

If you're like most people, the chore of cleaning your room usually proceeds at what can be best described as a snail's pace. But, amazingly, your pace will quicken if you're motivated to finish the chore by being offered money or the opportunity to go out on the weekend.

Chemical reactions sometimes need "motivation," too. At any given time, thousands of chemical reactions occur within your body. In a test tube, these reactions would occur too slowly to sustain life. In the body, the reactions are speeded up by enzymes. **Enzymes** are proteins that catalyze, or speed up, chemical reactions. They can be thought of as chemical motivators.

All enzymes share common characteristics. They speed up only the reactions that would normally occur at a slower rate; they don't make new reactions occur. Enzymes are not permanently changed or used up during reactions; they can be used over again. Try the following activity to learn a third characteristic of how an enzyme functions.

MiniLab

How does an enzyme function?

Speeding up one chemical reaction can be an easy task if only one reaction is occurring. Your body, however, has many thousands of reactions occurring at the same time. The reactions involve thousands of molecules and many different enzymes. In this activity, make a model showing how enzymes "recognize" the molecules with which they react.

Procedure

1. Your teacher will give you one bag holding five keys and another bag with five locks.

2. Carefully study the five keys. Record any differences you find.

3. Using the keys, try to open the locks.

Analysis

1. What happened when you tried to open the locks?

2. What had to happen for the locks to be opened?

3. Could any lock be opened by more than one key? If so, what did you notice about those keys?

The Lock-and-Key Model

You saw in the MiniLab that a lock could be opened only by a key that was shaped to fit that particular lock. In the same manner, an enzyme reacts only with a **substrate,** which is a specific molecule that the enzyme chemically recognizes. The term that is often used to describe enzyme-assisted reactions is the **lock-and-key model.** Follow the steps that show how an enzyme interacts with a substrate according to the model shown in **Figure 7-10.**

You can use the lock-and-key model to understand how enzymes affect a chemical reaction. To understand how enzymes speed up reactions, you have to recall from Section 7-1 that during a chemical reaction, chemical bonds are broken and new bonds are formed. As you recall, energy is needed to break chemical bonds. Enzymes speed up reactions by lowering the amount of energy needed to break the bonds.

The relationship between a chemical reaction and an enzyme is like the relationship between making baskets in a basketball game and the height of the hoop. A player could make baskets with the hoop high, but it takes less energy to make baskets when the hoop is lowered.

Controlling Enzymes

To maintain balance in the body, chemical reactions must occur at a steady rate. This rate can be altered by controlling enzymes. Control can be accomplished in several ways. One way is to control the actual number of enzymes available for reactions. Your

---

Figure 7-10

Each enzyme acts on a specific molecule or set of molecules called substrates.

A Each substrate fits into an area of the enzyme called the active site.

B The enzyme and substrates form an enzyme-substrate complex that allows the substrates to react with each other.

C The chemical reaction produces a new substance from the substrates but leaves the enzyme unchanged.

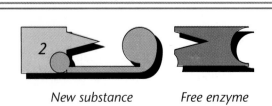

body has ways to slow down or speed up enzyme production.

Adjusting the environment is another way. Enzymes work best within specific temperature ranges. If the body temperature becomes too high or too low, enzymes are no longer able to function. A person with a high fever or hypothermia (greatly lowered body temperature) is at risk of dying because the enzymatic reactions within the body stop.

A third way to control enzymes is for another molecule, known as an inhibitor molecule, rather than a substrate molecule, to bind with the enzyme. This process is shown in **Figure 7-11.** This binding either ties up the enzyme so that it cannot serve as a catalyst or changes the shape of the active site. Either way, the enzyme can no longer react with the substrate and speed up the desired reaction.

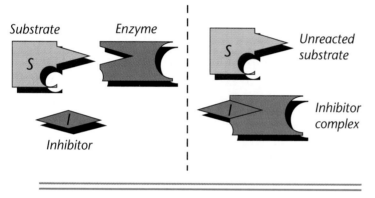

Figure 7-11

Under normal circumstances, an enzyme binds with the correct substrate and the chemical reaction can occur. Sometimes an inhibitor molecule and the enzyme form an inhibitor complex that interferes with this process.

A Some inhibitor molecules have a shape similar to that of the substrate, and these molecules compete for binding.

B Some inhibitor molecules bind to the enzyme at a place other than the active site, thus forcing a change in the shape of the active site and making the enzyme useless.

check your UNDERSTANDING

Understanding Concepts

1. Why is the term *lock-and-key* used to describe the model that shows how an enzyme works?
2. Explain the relationship between enzymes and energy.
3. Some of the most powerful poisons work by permanently inhibiting enzymes. What happens when an enzyme is permanently inhibited? How might this affect a person's body?

Skill Review

4. **Concept Mapping** Complete an events chain to describe how an enzyme works. For more help, refer to Concept Mapping in the *Skill Handbook*.

Science and Society

Issue: Food Additives

Warning: Food may be dangerous to your health.

You've probably heard more than a few lectures on how a diet that contains things like too much sugar, cholesterol, saturated fats, and sodium can cause health problems. More and more, people are likely to have an unhealthy diet because they tend to eat a lot of so-called junk food. But even if you are careful to watch what you eat, you may still be taking in some unnecessary and potentially toxic ingredients with your meals. *Toxic* means that those ingredients may be poisonous.

The Issue

Much of the food you buy in stores has had chemical substances added to it. These chemicals are called food additives, and they are used for a variety of reasons. Some of them preserve food so that it will keep longer in the store or in your home without spoiling. Flavorings and colored dyes are added to make food look and taste better. Other additives are used to change the consistency of the product (for example, to make cookies more crunchy or puddings creamier) or to keep the food from drying out too fast.

The Purpose

Most of these additives serve a useful purpose. For example, preservatives keep food fresh longer and reduce the chances of getting food poisoning from spoiled food. Artificial colors and flavorings make the food more tasty and appealing and encourage an adequate intake of nutrients.

However, these food additives also carry with them certain risks. These risks include the potential to cause health problems such as sudden changes in blood pressure, headaches, allergic rashes, hyperactivity, and even cancer. It is often difficult to decide whether the advantages offered by a given food additive are worth the risks it presents.

The Background

The use of food additives is not new. In the 1700s, bakers added white lead to bread dough to make the bread look whiter. Today, we know that lead is highly toxic. However, there are still an estimated 10 000 chemicals that food suppliers can add to their products, and the average American

Per Gram:
8 • Carbohydrate 4 • Protein 4

INGREDIENTS: CORN MEAL, SUGAR, OAT FLOUR, CORN SYRUP, SOYBEAN OIL (PARTIALLY HYDROGENATED TO PROTECT FLAVOR), WHEAT STARCH, SALT, YELLOW #5, NATURAL ORANGE, LEMON, STRAWBERRY, GRAPE AND OTHER NATURAL FLAVORINGS, RED #40, YELLOW #6, BLUE #1, BLUE #2.
VITAMINS & IRON: ASCORBIC ACID (VITAMIN C), FERRIC ORTHOPHOSPHATE (IRON SOURCE), VITAMIN A PALMITATE, NIACINAMIDE (a B VITAMIN), PYRIDOXINE HYDROCHLORIDE (VITAMIN B6), RIBOFLAVIN (VITAMIN B2), THIAMIN MONONITRATE (VITAMIN B1), FOLIC ACID (a B VITAMIN), CYANOCOBALAMIN (VITAMIN B12), VITAMIN D.

eats about 150 pounds of these food additives every year. Just what kind of chemicals are these food additives?

Common Additives

Among the most common food additives are the nitrites. They help preserve meat so it stays fresh longer. But now there is scientific evidence that when meat is cooked, any nitrites present are converted into nitrosamines, which have been shown to cause stomach cancer in humans.

Another food additive you may have heard about is monosodium glutamate (MSG). It is used as a flavor enhancer to make food taste better. MSG, however, has the potential to cause blood-pressure changes, chest pain, headaches, and numbness in some people, and it is known to cause brain damage and birth defects in animals.

Artificial coloring agents are chemical dyes that are used to make food look more attractive. These chemicals have common names such as Yellow No. 5, Red No. 3, and Blue No. 2. Many dyes have already been banned as food additives because they were shown to be toxic. Others, however, are still found in foods such as breakfast cereals, puddings, gelatin desserts, candy, ice cream, fruits, soft drinks, and frosting. Some scientists hypothesize that large amounts of the artificial coloring agents still allowed in foods can cause serious illness, and research is being done to see whether or not this is true.

The Question

The fact that food additives are chemicals is not the concern. Everything in the physical universe, including food itself, is made up of chemicals. But when chemicals that are not necessary for good nutrition are intentionally added to food, we must ask whether the advantages offered by these additives are important enough

to balance the possible bad effects. If we stop using nitrites to help preserve meat, more people may get sick from food poisoning. Is this a good argument for continuing to put nitrites in meat? Is it okay to inject a yellow dye into the skin of oranges to make them look better if it encourages people to eat more fresh fruit? These questions are not always easy to answer.

Most scientists suggest that the risks from using food additives in limited amounts are relatively small, and that the benefits outweigh any negative effects. But should a person take on any risk, however small, if it isn't really necessary?

inter NET CONNECTION

Follow the link for Chapter 7 on the Glencoe Homepage, http://www.glencoe.com/, for information about the International Food Information Council. IFIC keeps the public informed on food-related issues, including food additives. Collect data on which types of food contain the greatest number of additives. Weigh the advantages and disadvantages of several different food additives.

7-4 Food: The Journey from Mouth to Body Cells

Objectives
■ Explain the process of digestion.
■ Classify the breakdown products of carbohydrate, fat, and protein digestion.

Key Terms
digestion
hydrolysis

Digestion: An Experiment You Can Live With

You know that food provides nourishment for your body. What happens to food after you place it in your mouth? How does the food get changed into the kinds of materials needed by your body's cells? What chemical processes occur?

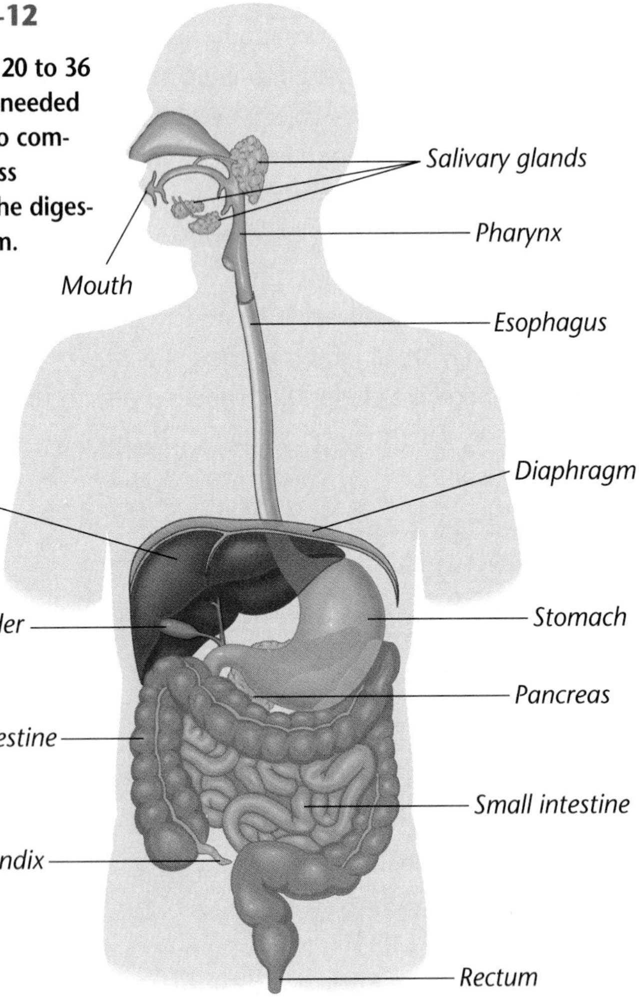

■ Digestion—Breaking Down Food

It may not seem that lunch is an experiment. Yet many chemical reactions take place as you eat. The process of digestion involves some of these reactions. **Digestion** is the process of breaking down food into smaller molecules that body cells can absorb.

Recall from Section 7-2 that food is made mostly of carbohydrates, fats, and proteins. These molecules are too large to move from the small intestine into the bloodstream and then into the cells. Also, your body cells can't actually use molecules of these materials without some changes. The cells, tissues, and organs of your body aren't made of the same carbohydrate, fat, and protein molecules that make up your food.

Needed changes occur during digestion. Different processes of digestion take place in different parts of your body. Follow the path that food travels as it goes through the digestive system, as shown in **Figure 7-12.** At each stage in the digestive system, food undergoes specific chemical changes, many of which are explained in this section. Generally, however, each of these specific reactions involves the use of water and enzymes to break down carbohydrate, fat, or protein molecules.

Figure 7-12

Normally, 20 to 36 hours are needed for food to completely pass through the digestive system.

Salivary glands
Pharynx
Mouth
Esophagus
Diaphragm
Liver
Gallbladder
Stomach
Pancreas
Large intestine
Small intestine
Appendix
Rectum

Figure 7-13

The chemical process called hydrolysis splits a polymer into its smaller units. It is the reverse of the process that results in a polymer being made from several smaller molecules.

A Polymers form when an enzyme action splits an H^+ ion away from one molecule and an OH^- group from another molecule. The two molecules form the polymer and the H^+ and OH^- ions form water.

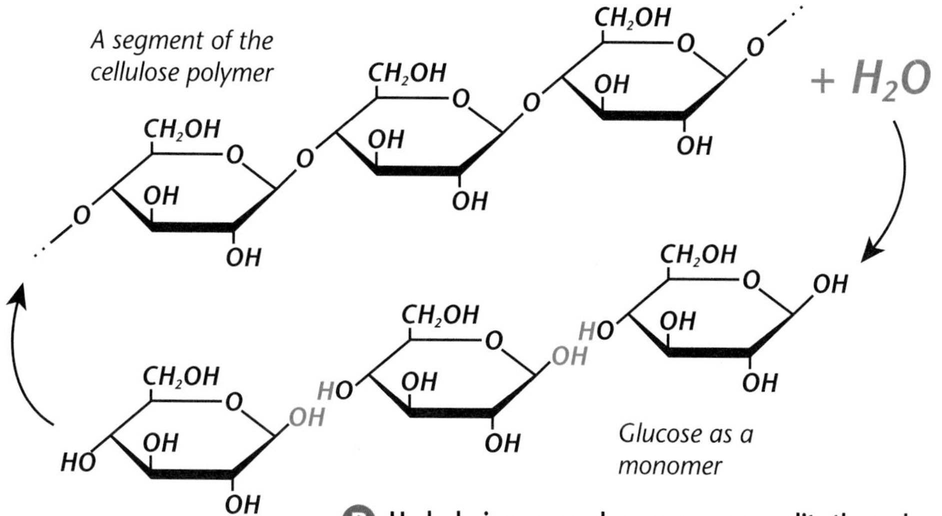

A segment of the cellulose polymer

$+ H_2O$

Glucose as a monomer

B Hydrolysis occurs when an enzyme splits the polymer into its smaller molecules and H^+ and OH^- ions from water reattach to the molecules.

■ Enzymes and Water: Two Factors in Digestion

In Section 7-2, you saw that molecules of carbohydrates, fats, and proteins are polymers that are composed of smaller units linked by chemical bonds. During digestion, these polymers are split apart by a chemical process called hydrolysis. **Hydrolysis** is the splitting apart of a molecule by a chemical reaction that involves the addition of water, as shown in **Figure 7-13B.** Enzymes also play an important role in speeding up the process of hydrolysis.

Study **Figure 7-13** to see that the formation of polymers and hydrolysis are opposite and necessary processes in the human body. The products of one reaction become the reactants for the other process.

Starch Digestion: Changes from the First Bite

Remember that at the beginning of this chapter you chewed samples of breads, pastas, and crackers. The sweet taste that developed was a signal that the starch in these foods was being broken down into a complex sugar by an enzyme called amylase. Amylase is found in saliva. Digestion of the complex sugars from starch and other complex sugars is then completed in the small intestine when hydrolysis splits them into molecules of the simple sugar glucose.

The role of enzymes is not limited to digestion of carbohydrates. The following Investigation shows how enzymes are involved in the digestion of proteins.

Do enzymes influence protein digestion?

The process of digestion uses specific chemical reactions to break down food into smaller units that can then be reassembled by your cells. The enzyme papain is used in some meat tenderizers to break down protein, such as that found in gelatin, into smaller amino acid units. Similar enzymes are present in certain fruits. Let's find out how these enzymes assist in the breakdown of protein.

Preparation

Problem
What will break protein molecules into smaller units?

Hypothesis
Hypothesize as to how each item tested will affect the protein in prepared gelatin dessert.

Objectives
In this Investigation, you will:
- *Observe* some of the chemical changes taking place when protein is digested.
- *Determine* the effect of temperature changes on the reaction.

Possible Materials
meat tenderizer containing papain
prepared gelatin dessert
samples of various fruits, including fresh and canned pineapple
small glass containers
refrigerator or ice chest
clock or watch

Safety Precautions

Do not eat any food from this Investigation.

Plan the Experiment

1 Examine the materials listed. Decide how you can use the protein-containing gelatin, the meat tenderizer, and the fruits to test your group's hypotheses. Be sure to include a control. Determine how any variables will be controlled.

2 Write down the agreed-upon steps. Be sure to include how you will record your observations. Will you have a data table? Will you have diagrams?

Check the Plan
Discuss the following points with other group members to decide the final procedure for your experiment.

1 How much meat tenderizer will be added to the gelatin?

2 How long will you wait to check the results?

3 What appears as a visible indication of protein breakdown?

4 *Make sure your teacher has approved your experimental plan before you proceed further.*

5 Carry out your Investigation. Make any needed observations, and record your results. Dispose of materials according to your teacher's instructions.

Analyze and Conclude

1. **Comparing and Contrasting** At the end of the testing time, which of the gelatin samples showed the most protein breakdown? How do you know?

2. **Predicting** Assume that a gelatin dessert is prepared according to package directions except that some meat tenderizer is added. The mixture is then placed in the refrigerator to set. Do you think the gelatin dessert will set? Explain.

3. **Drawing Conclusions** Which broke down more protein, the enzymes in fresh pineapple or those in canned pineapple? Relate your answer to how temperature can affect an enzyme.

Going Further

Project
Design a testing procedure that will determine the relative level of protein-breaking enzymes present in different fruits. Rank the fruits tested in order of increasing enzyme level.

Breaking Down Proteins

You observed in the Investigation that certain enzymes break down proteins. Do you know where this happens in your body? Protein digestion doesn't begin until protein reaches the stomach. Once in the stomach, the enzyme pepsin helps to break down the large protein polymers into smaller chains of amino acids. Further digestion occurs when the amino acid chains move into the small intestine. Here, enzymes called proteases work together to completely break down the amino acid chains into individual amino acids. The hydrolysis of the amino acid chains can be completed much more quickly when more than one enzyme is involved in the process. These amino acids are absorbed through the walls of the small intestine. The circulatory system then carries them to cells in the body that use the amino acids to make proteins.

Figure 7-9 on page 218 listed some functions that are carried out by proteins. You already know several foods that contain protein. Now use the Thinking Lab to find out how you can test for protein in foods and other types of materials.

Thinking Lab   Interpreting Data

What substances contain protein?

Because they are so important in the functioning of a healthy body, it's important to know which foods contain proteins. The following substances were treated with sodium hydroxide and placed in contact with a dilute solution of copper(II) sulfate. A positive test for protein is the formation of a violet color in the solution.

Analysis

Substance	Test Results
egg albumin	violet color
turkey	violet color
celery	no change
apple	no change
cracker	violet color

Thinking Critically

Carefully study the results. What common characteristic can you find for the substances that test positive for protein? Negative? What other substances do you think would test positive for protein? Why did egg albumin test positive, but the celery did not? If human hair were tested, what do you think the result would be?

Chemical Reactions in Fat Digestion

In the Thinking Lab, a solution of copper(II) sulfate was used to identify proteins. This solution is made by dissolving a small number of copper(II) sulfate crystals in water. As you can see in **Figure 7-14,** not all substances dissolve in water.

In the same way, fat molecules don't dissolve in water. This characteristic of fats means that their hydrolysis is more difficult than those of carbohydrates and proteins. It also means that little fat digestion occurs in the stomach, which contains mostly water.

Before fats can be digested, larger droplets must be broken into smaller droplets. This happens at the beginning of the small intestine. Then bile salts, produced by the liver, prevent the small droplets from joining together again by keeping them in a suspension of small droplets. Breaking the fats into smaller droplets exposes more of their surface area to the enzyme lipase, found in the small intestine. Lipase is used in the hydrolysis of the fats, which chemically breaks them down into smaller units of glycerol and fatty acids. These molecules can then enter into other chemical reactions, some of which involve the storage of energy.

If you thought about this chapter, did the activities and Investigation, and carried the book around, you used many Calories. Keep on eating nutritious meals. All that good food will supply you with the energy that you need. But what supplies all this food with energy? You will investigate this question in Chapter 8.

Figure 7-14

Have you ever observed an oil-and-vinegar salad dressing before it is mixed? You may remember that two distinct layers of liquids are visible. The dressing had to be shaken before it could be used. Shaking is necessary because the upper oil layer does not dissolve in the lower vinegar layer.

---

check your UNDERSTANDING

Understanding Concepts

1. In order that carbohydrates be digested properly, why is it important that food be chewed well?
2. Compare and contrast the digestion of carbohydrates, fat, and proteins.
3. Why is water necessary for hydrolysis to occur?

Skill Review

4. **Classifying** Study the following list of final products that result from digestion. Classify the products according to their original food categories. For more help, refer to Classifying in the *Skill Handbook.*

   glucose   fatty acids
   amino acids   glycerol
   complex sugar

people in SCIENCE

Meet Maria Valazquez, Apprentice Pastry Chef

Warning: Don't read this interview if mealtime is hours away! Pastry chef Maria Valazquez works in a bake shop that supplies several large hotels with desserts for their menus. She's also a student at El Centro Community College, a renowned culinary academy in Texas. Maria understands that successful cooking is more than a worthwhile skill—it's a science.

On the Job

Q What sorts of cooking classes have you taken?

A To get my associate degree in food service, I've taken nutrition, sanitation, safety, equipment, dining room service, and many more classes. In the lab course, students take turns cooking a weekly meal for 100 people. Doing that, I've found that cooking takes more planning time than preparation time.

Q Why do you have to take classes in sanitation to be a pastry chef?

A For the simple reason that when you work with eggs and cream, you often have to cool a product down quickly to prevent salmonella from growing and causing food poisoning.

Q What did you learn in nutrition classes?

A Nutrition classes deal with how to prepare a balanced meal. These classes aren't specifically for pastry. The classes let you know what nutrients are important and how to deal with deficiencies. We need knowledge of fats, sugars, and sodium, in particular. If someone needs a dessert that is low in sodium, you have to know what to do to provide it.

Q The chemistry of baking doesn't allow multiplying, say, a recipe for six people by a factor of 20, does it?

A In converting a recipe, you have to take into account that the materials that make cakes and breads rise—such as baking soda, baking powder, and yeast—can't simply be tripled or quadrupled. A baker has to have a lot of experience and then be willing to experiment. Our instructors tell us all the time that baking is a science.

Q Could you give us an example of baking as a science?

A Baking is unlike, for instance, cooking pork chops in a sauce. For that dish, you can throw together a few onions, some chopped bell peppers, a pinch of spices, and the chops and have it come out just fine. You have to use exact measures in baking or you could have a disaster.

Q I understand that your recipes are not really recipes, but formulas. How are pastry formulas different from regular recipes?

A With a regular recipe for a sauce, you can wing it—change it a little to make the flavor or consistency right. But with pastry, especially if it contains baking soda, everything needs to react in a particular way.

Early Influences

Q What made you want to become a pastry chef?

A A cousin of mine wanted to take a course in cake decorating. She didn't want to go alone, so I said that I would go with her. That's how I became interested.

 Two aspects of careers in food are planning meals and cooking and serving. Investigate the following food-related careers and decide which of these aspects each career emphasizes.

▶ *chef, dietitian, nutritionist, weight-management specialist*

Personal Insights

Q Would you encourage students to explore the careers offered in the food industry?

A Yes. It's fun, although there is stress, like on any other job.

Q Besides culinary aptitude, what other skills does a job in the food industry require?

A You need to be good at math and be able to plan ahead. For instance, if I don't keep on hand enough cake circles—they're those cardboard forms I put a cake on before decorating it—I'll find myself cutting them out with scissors and get behind in my cake decorating.

Sir Hans Adolf Krebs and the Krebs Cycle

How many times has someone told you to eat a good breakfast so you would have plenty of energy for school? The process by which food and other nutrients are converted to energy is called *metabolism*. For many years, scientists observed that the body somehow used, or metabolized, carbohydrates, fats, and proteins to produce energy, but they could not describe how this process happened. In 1937, Sir Hans Adolf Krebs discovered exactly how cells use oxygen, enzymes, and other chemicals to convert carbohydrates to energy.

The Krebs Cycle

Before Krebs made his discovery, most scientists thought that food was converted into energy all at once. Through his experiments with various animal tissues, Krebs discovered that carbohydrate metabolism happens in stages. He studied the ways that food in cells is broken down in a complex cycle of chemical reactions involving oxygen and various acids. This process involves a type of chemical reaction known as *oxidation*. Krebs showed in his studies that these reactions follow circular pathways in their constant conversion of carbohydrates to energy. Because one of the products of this cycle is citric acid, the Krebs cycle is also called the *citric acid cycle*.

The Impact of Krebs's Discovery

Krebs's discovery is important in several ways. First, Krebs introduced new experimental techniques in his study of metabolism. Second, his discovery of how carbohydrates were converted into energy led others to discover how proteins and fats were converted into energy. Finally, Krebs helped us understand the ways in which the body converts food into materials needed by reactions that produce energy in the body. In 1953, Krebs won the Nobel prize for medicine for his discoveries.

Thinking Critically

1. *Explain* why the Krebs cycle is also known as the citric acid cycle.
2. *Research* the relationship between food and energy. Present the results of your research in a short written report, on a poster, or in an oral presentation.
3. *Research* other scientists who have studied the ways that the body converts food into energy. Write a short essay about the life and work of one of these scientists.

Read the statements at the right and below that review major points presented in the chapter. Using the concepts that you have learned, answer each question *in your Journal.*

1 Foods contain carbohydrates, lipids, and proteins. *Carbohydrates include what two types of compounds?*

2 Chemical energy is stored in chemical bonds. *How is this energy released?*

3 Enzymes are proteins that speed up chemical reactions in the body. *How does the lock-and-key model explain how an enzyme works?*

Enzyme-substrate complex

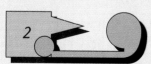

New substance   *Free enzyme*

4 Digestion is the process of breaking down food into smaller molecules that body cells can absorb. *How does hydrolysis help the process of digestion?*

Using Key Science Terms

amino acid   hydrolysis

calorie   lipid

carbohydrate   lock-and-key model

digestion   protein

enzyme   substrate

Answer the following questions about science terms used in this chapter.

1. What are the meanings of the root words of the word *carbohydrate*?
2. How many Calories are present in two kilocalories?
3. Is amylase a carbohydrate or a protein?
4. What is the relationship among an enzyme, a substrate, and the lock-and-key model for chemical activity?
5. What is the relationship between fat and hydrolysis?
6. In what part of the body does most lipid digestion occur?

Understanding Ideas

Using complete sentences, answer the following questions in your Journal.

1. Starch and glucose are both carbohydrates. What is the relationship between them?
2. If you have a substance that is either a compound or an element, how can you use the chemical formula of the substance to determine which type of substance you have?
3. Why are some amino acids called *essential* amino acids?
4. How many calories would be required to warm 10.0 g of water 2°C?
5. Explain what role an enzyme can play in a chemical reaction.

6. Often, after a high-fat-content meal, people have a full feeling for a long period of time. Explain.
7. What compound must be present during hydrolysis in order for the reaction to be completed?
8. How does an inhibitor molecule control enzyme reactions?
9. Some brands of peanut butter have been hydrogenated. That means hydrogen has been added to make the lipids saturated. What advantage might this have for the consumer?

Developing Skills

Use your understanding of the concepts developed in this chapter to answer each of the following questions.

1. **Concept Mapping** Complete the following concept map of digestion.

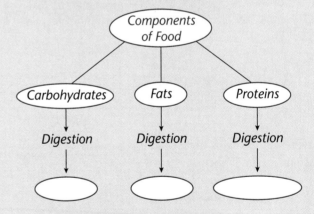

2. **Modeling** Explain how adjusting the height of a football goalpost can be used to model the relationship between enzymes and energy.
3. **Predicting** A person becomes ill with a liver-destroying disease. Predict how the disease might affect the digestive process.

Critical Thinking

In your Journal, *answer each of the following questions.*

1. Look at the following formulas and determine which is a carbohydrate.
   a. $CH_3(CH_2)_{16}COOH$
   b. NH_2—CHR—COOH
   c. $C_6H_{12}O_6$

2. Reactions that form carbohydrates, fats, and proteins involve the formation of water. Why does it make sense to call these reactions *condensation* reactions?

3. Why should you thoroughly chew all of your food, even carbohydrates and proteins, before swallowing?

4. Trace a piece of bacon through the digestive process.

5. If you were competing in a lengthy footrace, would it be better for you to eat a pasta dinner or a cheeseburger before the race? Explain.

Problem Solving

Read the following problem and discuss your answers in a brief paragraph.

The U.S. Department of Health and Human Services recommends the following number of servings per day for a balanced diet.

Bread, pasta, and
grains .... 6–11 servings
Vegetables .... 3–5 servings
Fruits .... 2–4 servings
Milk, cheese, and
yogurt .... 2–3 servings
Meat, poultry, fish, dry beans,
and eggs .... 2–3 servings
Fats, oils, and sweets .... sparingly

Analyze your food intake for yesterday. How did you classify your food? How many servings in each category did you have? In what ways could you improve your diet?

CONNECTING IDEAS

1. **Theme—Patterns of Change** How is the digestion process similar for carbohydrates, fats, and proteins?

2. **Theme—Systems and Interactions** Describe the interaction of the circulatory system with the digestive system.

3. **In-Depth Look** Explain why the biggest part of the food pyramid is made up of foods that are high in carbohydrates.

4. **History Connection** Infer why the steps in carbohydrate metabolism were discovered before the steps in protein metabolism and lipid metabolism were discovered.

5. **Science and Society** What are some advantages and some disadvantages of adding artificial sweeteners instead of sugar to certain foods?

6. **People in Science** Compare baking a cake to conducting an experiment.

CHAPTER 8

Photosynthesis
Solar-Powered Recycling

A completed book coming off the assembly line looks nothing like the raw materials used in its production. Only after many manufacturing processes have occurred can the paper, ink, and other materials be assembled into a final product. In general, factories receive raw materials, use energy to reassemble the materials, and produce new products that may not look anything like the original components.

▶ *In the following activity, learn how green plants function as food factories. They take in raw materials and reassemble the component parts into food for the plant and any organism that eats the plant.*

236

How are a factory and green plants similar?

Have you ever toured a factory? If so, you probably saw that raw materials were changed into the parts needed to assemble the final product. In this activity, you will model a green plant's raw materials and finished products.

Procedure

CAUTION: *Do not eat any candy used in the lab.*

1. Use several gumdrop models of the raw materials carbon dioxide, CO_2, and water, H_2O. Green plants use carbon dioxide and water as raw materials. Decide which color of gumdrop represents atoms of each element.

2. Separate the individual model atoms of the raw materials. Reassemble them into models representing one molecule of glucose, $C_6H_{12}O_6$, and six molecules of oxygen, O_2.

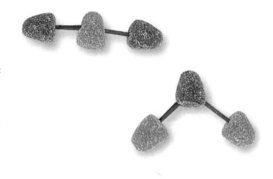

Analysis

1. How many molecules each of carbon dioxide and water are needed to make the molecules of glucose and oxygen?

2. Compare and contrast the raw materials and the products in this reaction.

8-1 Plants—Recycling Raw Materials

Objectives
- Demonstrate the law of conservation of matter through a balanced equation.
- Describe how carbon is cycled through the environment.

Key Terms
law of conservation of matter
cellulose

A Balancing Act

In the MiniLab, when you used the gumdrops to show how carbon dioxide and water combine to form glucose, several factors became apparent. More than one molecule of each raw material was needed to make one molecule of glucose. Another product, in addition to glucose, was formed. That product was oxygen. All the atoms from the raw materials were used, and no extra atoms were left over.

Scientists know that in this or any other chemical reaction, atoms are never created, nor are they destroyed. They are simply rearranged. This observation that atoms are neither created nor destroyed during chemical reactions is called the **law of conservation of matter.**

Recall from Chapter 7 that chemical formulas are used to represent the type and number of atoms that are in a molecule. Chemical reactions can be represented by using the chemical formulas in chemical equations, as shown in **Figure 8-1.** Because the law of conservation of matter states that matter can't be created or destroyed, a correctly written equation will have the same type and number of atoms on both sides of the equation. The equation is then said to be *balanced.*

Figure 8-1

The balanced chemical equation for the reaction that produces water from hydrogen and oxygen is $2H_2 + O_2 \rightarrow 2H_2O$.

A The formulas to the left of the arrow show the beginning substances, called reactants. The formulas to the right show the ending substances, called products.

B The numbers, called coefficients, in front of the formulas indicate how many units of each substance are present. If no coefficient is written, there is one unit present.

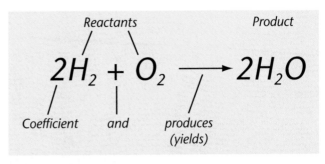

$$2H_2 + O_2 \xrightarrow{\text{}} 2H_2O$$

Reactants / Product / Coefficient / and / produces (yields)

C The + sign reads "and" and the ($\rightarrow$) reads "produces" or "yields."

Finding the Raw Materials

Before a chemical reaction can take place, reactants must be present. For example, potatoes store the carbohydrate starch in their cells for future energy use. Look at **Figure 8-2.** When energy is needed, the plant, or animals that eat the plant, first break down starch into glucose, which is then broken down and used as fuel by cells. Where do the carbon, hydrogen, and oxygen atoms in glucose come from originally? Where are some of these raw materials found in the environment?

Figure 8-2

If you keep a record of all the foods you eat in one day, you will probably find that more than 50 percent of your daily intake of carbohydrates comes from starch directly produced in green plants.

MiniLab

Take a Deep Breath!

Where do the carbon atoms used by plants come from? Think about what gases are in the air you breathe. Then look at the following chemical equation.

$$Ca(OH)_2 + CO_2 \rightarrow CaCO_3 + H_2O$$

Calcium carbonate is a white solid that is formed in the reaction between calcium hydroxide and carbon dioxide.

Procedure

1. Place a straw in a solution of calcium hydroxide, $Ca(OH)_2$.

2. Take a deep breath and slowly exhale through the straw. **CAUTION:** *Be careful not to draw any of the solution into your mouth.*

Analysis

1. What changes do you see in the solution when you exhale through the straw?

2. From your observations, what might you infer is a ready source of carbon for plants?

■ Out of Thin Air

Using your observations from the reaction in the MiniLab, you can infer that the carbon dioxide you exhale is released into the atmosphere. Carbon dioxide is an important part of a cycle that constantly reuses carbon atoms.

Just as water moves in a cycle, carbon moves in a cycle through the living and nonliving parts of the environment. Carbon atoms in the atmosphere are recycled through living organisms and nonliving objects such as certain rocks and fossil fuels. Remember that matter cannot be created or destroyed. Thus, some of the carbon atoms in the air breathed by the earliest land animals may now be found in the loaf of bread your family will eat this evening. Study **Figure 8-3** as you trace the cycling of carbon.

Figure 8-3

Carbon atoms are constantly being recycled within the ecosystem. Some carbon atoms, such as those in compounds in your body, are part of a short-term cycling process. Other carbon atoms may be part of a long-term cycling process when they are tied up for millions of years in deposits of fossil fuels. They are released when fossil fuels are burned.

Plants—One Part of the Carbon Cycle

Plants are supplied with carbon dioxide when this gas moves into the leaves through openings called stomata. Once in the leaves, the carbon dioxide becomes one part of a chemical process that reorganizes the atoms and forms glucose. This chemical process will be explained in Section 8-3. Some of the newly formed glucose is used to produce starch.

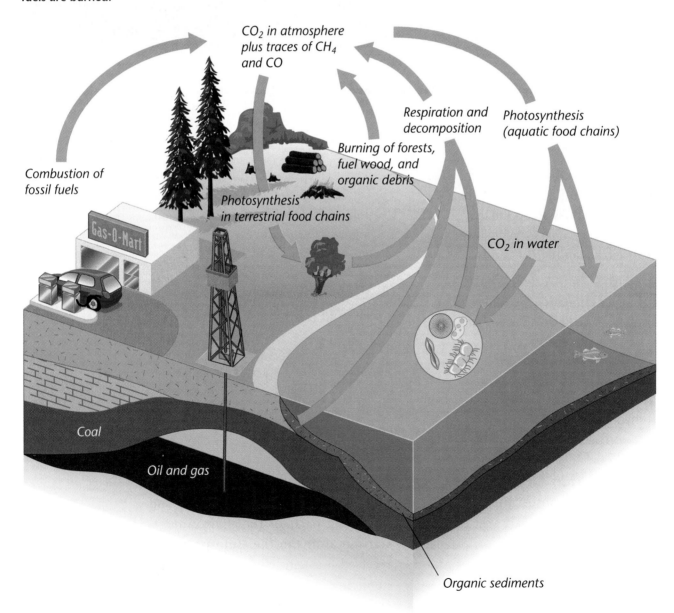

CO_2 in atmosphere plus traces of CH_4 and CO

Respiration and decomposition

Photosynthesis (aquatic food chains)

Combustion of fossil fuels

Burning of forests, fuel wood, and organic debris

Photosynthesis in terrestrial food chains

CO_2 in water

Gas-O-Mart

Coal

Oil and gas

Organic sediments

Figure 8-4

This micrograph shows cell walls that contain fiberlike cellulose. Cellulose is like steel reinforcing rods in concrete. Certain enzymes are needed for cellulose to be digested by animals. Cows contain microorganisms that have an enzyme needed to digest cellulose, but humans lack them. What does this tell you about your ability to digest cellulose? In spite of the fact that humans can't digest cellulose, foods rich in cellulose are an important part of the human diet because they help maintain a smooth passage of food through the digestive system and they absorb large quantities of excess water.

■ Cellulose

Plants also use glucose to form another carbohydrate called cellulose. **Cellulose** molecules form a tough, rigid structure that makes up the cell walls of plants. Cellulose provides structural support for plants, as shown in **Figure 8-4.** Its strength comes from the way the glucose molecules are bonded together. In cellulose, the glucose molecules lie in long, side-by-side chains similar to the rows of desks in a classroom. Just like rows of desks would be difficult to separate if students in side-by-side rows held hands across the aisles, the bonds connecting the glucose chains give cellulose its strength.

Carbon atoms in starch and cellulose molecules of plants become part of the food supply in an ecosystem because they are eaten by animals. When animals eat plants, they convert starch and cellulose, if they can digest it, back into glucose through the process of digestion. Glucose is then either used for energy or stored for later use in the animal's body. As you eat a hamburger, you are taking in many of the same atoms that once made up a plant.

A part of the carbon cycle is completed when carbon atoms are returned to the atmosphere as carbon dioxide. This gas is a product of the process of combining glucose and oxygen in the body and also decomposition as bacteria and fungi break down dead organisms or their wastes.

check your UNDERSTANDING

Understanding Concepts

1. Compare and contrast starch and cellulose.
2. What role do decomposers play in the carbon cycle?
3. Why are grains, such as corn and wheat, an important part of your diet?

Skill Review

4. **Classifying** Study the following equations and determine whether or not they are balanced. If not, balance them.
   a. $CH_4 + 2O_2 \rightarrow CO_2 + 2H_2O$
   b. $C_2H_5OH + O_2 \rightarrow 2CO_2 + 3H_2O$

   For more help, refer to Classifying in the *Skill Handbook.*

Technology: Industrialized Agriculture

A trip to the supermarket will convince you that modern agriculture is a technological success. Daily, the stores are stocked with displays of fresh produce, frozen vegetables, and an assortment of processed food.

The Technology

You are probably more than satisfied with the varieties of foods available to you. You may not realize that approximately 80 000 species of plants are edible! A closer look may reveal that the thousands of food items in the store are all based on just 20 food crops. That's right, only about 20 species of plants produce 90 percent of the food you eat. And four crops—wheat, rice, corn, and potatoes—are the main staples around the world. Even such foods as meat, milk, eggs, and cheese come from only a few species of livestock. This situation is due mainly to industrial-

ized agriculture, in which each industrialized farm produces large quantities of just one food crop or one kind of livestock for sale.

The Background

Plant and animal breeders are hard at work trying to develop the perfect crop—one that will provide each kind of food that you are used to eating. Their aim is to produce a product that has the right appearance and is the least perishable. They also need to keep ahead of diseases and pests that attack both the crops and animals that are used for food. This part of their job is far from easy. After a plant has been successfully bred to resist attack by a fungus or insect, it may not take long for a different fungus or insect to attack the plant. Once again, the plant becomes defenseless against its enemies and a source of food is lost.

Intercropping wheat and soybeans

Maintaining crop diversity helps solve this problem. Crop diversity relates to the number and variety of species cultivated by farmers. Because of plant and animal breeding, the number of species used for food and other economic products is rapidly decreasing. Fewer kinds of plants are cultivated. These plants occupy increasingly larger areas of farmland and are the basis of more of the human diet. As a result, many thousands of edible species that could feed millions of people are disappearing from Earth. Limiting the variety of plants being cultivated makes those cultivated plants less likely to adapt. As this tendency is lost, it increases the chance that a natural disaster could one day destroy the present supercrops.

The Question

Before industrialized agriculture became widespread, food was grown by subsistence farmers. These farmers grew almost all the goods required by their families with only a small surplus for sale. They had to grow a variety of crops to meet their families' needs for food and clothing. They also usually engaged in several methods of farming.

A return to some of these neglected methods could not only provide safeguards against the loss of species, but would also help the environment by reducing the use of pesticides. For example, one method of planting is known as *intercropping,* which means growing rows of two or more different crops at the same time on a plot. It is a creative way to keep plants from being devoured by insects. Many insect pests feed on only one kind of plant. Their feeding is interrupted by rows of plants that they do not find appetizing.

Another subsistence farming method involves *polyvarietal cultivation,* in which several varieties of the same crop are planted together on a plot of land. This is like taking out an insurance policy on a crop. If conditions are not right for one variety, they may be beneficial for another variety. Plant diversity goes a step further with the planting of several different crops together. Adjusting planting times so that insect pests have starved before the crop is ready to be harvested is another way to control pests and reduce the need for pesticides.

Although subsistence farming methods have been proven to work, they would increase the cost of food because more time and labor would be required to produce the same amount of food. Can people afford to pay higher costs for food? On the other hand, can we afford the increased loss of species of many edible plants?

*inter*NET CONNECTION

Visit the Glencoe Homepage for the Chapter 8 link to the U.S. Plant Variety Protection Office. Agriculturalists often work to develop different varieties of seeds with a goal of growing hardier crops. If you developed a new variety of seed for a particular plant species, what steps would you need to take to ensure that the results of your research were recognized?

8-2 Recycling Other Important Elements

Objectives

- Discuss the importance of nitrogen and phosphorus atoms to organisms.
- Explain how nitrogen and phosphorus atoms are recycled in the ecosystem.

Key Terms

nitrogen fixation
Haber process

Following the Nitrogen Cycle

The spectators at the soccer field wait anxiously for play to begin. Both teams are ready, the field is prepared, and the officials have arrived. But a key component of the game is missing. Without a ball, the game can't be played. Trying to play soccer without a ball is similar to a plant's trying to make proteins without nitrogen. It can't be done.

■ A Change in Form

Now suppose someone brought a football to the field. Could a soccer game be played? To have a proper game of soccer, the ball must be the right size and shape. A football is not suitable to use for soccer. The same is true for nitrogen and protein production in plants. Nitrogen in the air is not in a usable form.

Plant Root Hitchhikers

It takes a great deal of energy and other resources to manufacture nitrogen fertilizers. And once these chemical fertilizers are applied to the fields, crops take up only about half of the nitrogen available in the fertilizer. It's been found that unused fertilizer builds up in soil and runs off into water supplies.

Nature's Fertilizer Manufacturers

Instead of spreading chemicals, some farmers rely on nitrogen-fixing plants called legumes to provide usable nitrogen for their crops. Legumes include clover, peas, beans, alfalfa, peanuts, and lupines. Bacteria live inside the

Legume roots showing nodules

Nitrogen gas, N_2, is an abundant resource. It makes up about 78 percent of air and can be separated readily from the other gases present in air. But gaseous nitrogen, as shown in **Figure 8-5,** can't be used directly by plants. Nitrogen in the air is in a stable form.

Only after the triple bond holding the atoms together is broken can nitrogen be incorporated into compounds that plants can use. The process of changing nitrogen gas to compounds that can be used by plants is called **nitrogen fixation.**

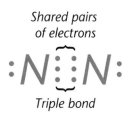

Shared pairs of electrons

Triple bond

Figure 8-5

In a nitrogen molecule, two nitrogen atoms share three pairs of electrons. The chemical bond formed is stable and strong, so nitrogen gas does not react readily with other atoms. Nitrogen gas is so unreactive that it is sometimes used to surround materials that would react with the oxygen or water vapor found in the air.

■ Fixing Nitrogen

A summary of the many processes that occur during nitrogen fixation is shown in **Figure 8-6** on page 248. A specific example of one type of nitrogen fixation is studied in the In-Depth Look feature below. The following Investigation will help you detect one of the nitrogen compounds that is formed during nitrogen fixation.

roots of the legumes and form swellings called nodules. Inside these nodules, which are shown in the photo, the bacteria "fix" nitrogen gas, N_2, from the atmosphere by converting it into ammonia, which the plants can use to synthesize amino acids and proteins. To help boost the nitrogen-fixing ability of legumes, farmers may dust their legume seeds with *Rhyzobium* bacteria just before planting.

In contrast to chemical fertilizers, bacteria deliver nitrogen straight to the plant with no runoff. Another advantage is that the bacteria can secrete extra nitrogen into the soil,

which increases fertility for the next crop.

Nonlegumes, Too!

In the early 1990s, agricultural researchers at Australia's University of Sydney announced that they had succeeded in introducing nitrogen-fixing bacteria called *Azospirillum* into the roots of wheat plants. Other researchers are using genetic engineering to do the same thing with corn and rice, as well.

If the three main grains of the world—corn, wheat, and rice—can become self-fertilizing, the world's people may all eat better.

Thinking Critically

1. The other natural kind of nitrogen fixation occurs in lightning storms. It's estimated that six pounds of nitrogen per acre per year are deposited by rain and snow. *Explain* why some farmers in the 1880s plowed under any snow that fell when their fields weren't frozen.

2. *Infer* why farmers frequently plant legumes in a field one year and a nonlegume crop the next year.

Can you test for ammonia?

Ammonia is a colorless gas that can be identified by a characteristic sharp odor. It also causes moist, red litmus paper to turn blue when contact is made. In this Investigation, test various substances for the presence of nitrogen by producing a chemical reaction that results in the release of ammonia.

Preparation

Problem

What substances contain nitrogen?

Hypothesis

Have your group agree on the substances to be tested and develop a hypothesis about which substances will test positive for ammonia.

Objectives

In this Investigation, you will:

- *Determine* a positive test for ammonia.
- *Distinguish and compare* those substances that contain nitrogen.

Possible Materials

small beakers
solution of lye, NaOH
plant fertilizer
lime (solid calcium oxide, CaO)
red litmus paper
various food samples
household ammonia cleaner
gloves

Safety Precautions

Ammonia fumes are hazardous and irritating. Avoid inhaling them. Hold the samples several centimeters away from your nose and gently wave the fumes toward your nose. Exercise caution and wear gloves when handling lye. Contact with skin results in severe burns. Wash your hands immediately after completing this activity. Do not eat any materials used in this activity.

Plan the Experiment

1 In the presence of a strong base such as lye, lime, or a combination of both, ammonia is released from many nitrogen-containing substances. Examine the materials provided by your teacher and decide on a way to test your group's hypothesis.

2 Design an experiment that will allow for collection of data about which substances release ammonia. It can then be inferred that these compounds contain nitrogen.

3 Write a list of procedure steps.

4 Design and construct a data table that includes a place for the identity of each tested substance and the results of the tests.

Check the Plan

Discuss the following points with other group members to decide on the final procedure for your experiment.

1 How will you ensure that only the color change in the litmus paper caused by ammonia is being tested?

2 How will you visually represent the data?

3 *Make sure your teacher has approved your experimental plan before you proceed further.*

4 Carry out your experiment. Record your observations *in your Journal* and complete the data table.

Analyze and Conclude

1. **Using Controls** How was household ammonia used to compare other substances?

2. **Comparing and Contrasting** How did the ammonia odor produced from fertilizer compare to the odors produced by other substances tested? Infer how much nitrogen the fertilizer contains compared to the other tested substances.

3. **Recognizing Cause and Effect** The combination of lime and lye makes the solution more basic. What substances gave a positive test only after the addition of both lime and lye? Why might it be necessary to use both substances?

Going Further

Analyzing
Visit a garden store and read the labels of several different plant fertilizers. Note the number of nitrogen-containing compounds in the fertilizers. Which type of nitrogen-containing compound is the most common?

Other Forms of Nitrogen Fixation

As you saw in the Investigation, many materials contain nitrogen. In a usable form, nitrogen can be absorbed by plants to make foods that contain protein. Look at **Figure 8-6.** The nitrogen is eventually returned to the atmosphere, and is available again for nitrogen fixation.

The increasing human population demands an ever-increasing amount of food. Unfortunately, the natural process involving bacteria in nitrogen fixation doesn't provide enough product to support the demand. Neither does a second naturally occurring method shown in **Figure 8-6A.**

The Haber Process

In the early 1900s, Fritz Haber, a German scientist, developed a process that enabled scientists to make ammonia in a laboratory. This process greatly increased the amount of fixed nitrogen available for agricultural and other uses. Named for its inventor, the **Haber process,** shown in **Figure 8-7,** utilizes high temperatures, high pressures, and a catalyst to make ammonia directly from the elements nitrogen and hydrogen. The ammonia is then used in fertilizer and added to nitrogen-deficient soils. The increased food production benefits people throughout the world.

Figure 8-6

A simplified version of the nitrogen cycle

Ⓐ Nitrogen fixation occurs naturally through the processes involving bacteria in the root nodules of some plants and the reaction resulting from lightning in the atmosphere.

Ⓒ Nitrogen is returned to the atmosphere when decomposing bacteria attack animal wastes, such as urea, that contain nitrogen compounds.

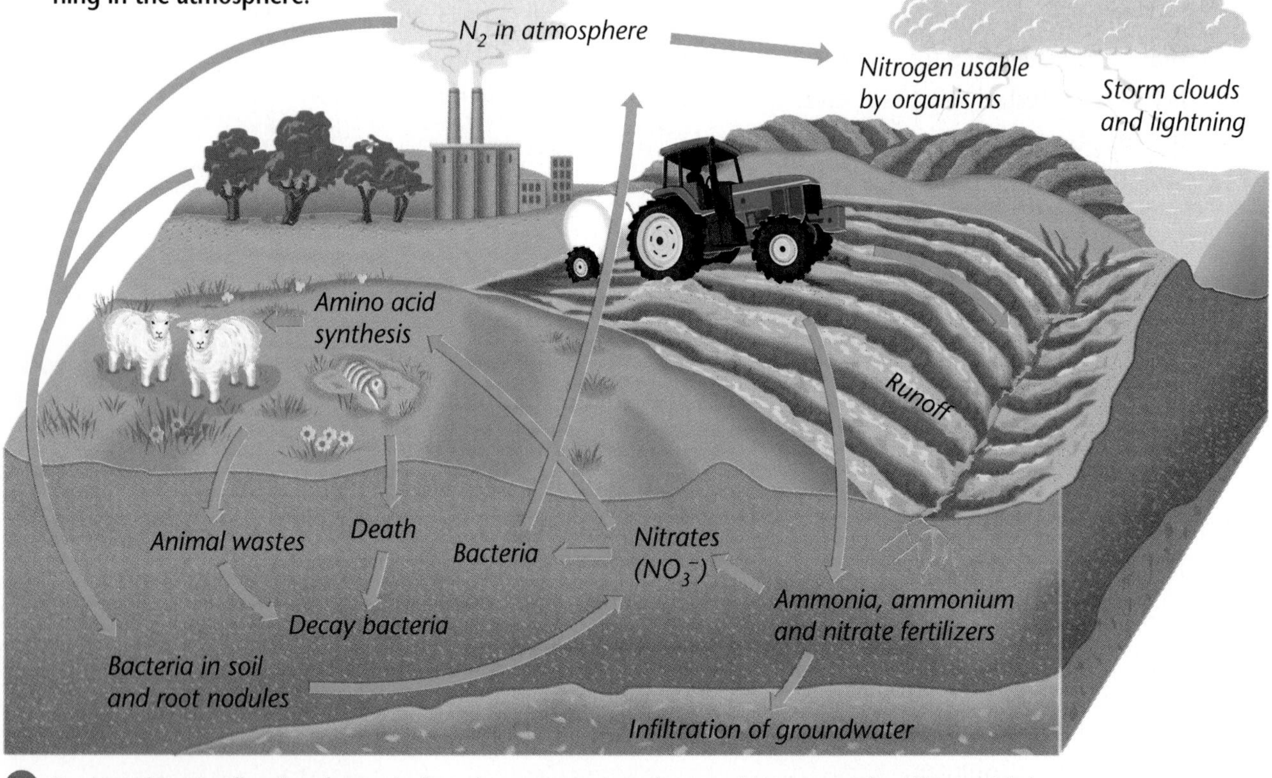

Ⓑ During nitrogen fixation, bacteria first change gaseous nitrogen into ammonia, NH_3, which is then changed into the ammonium ion, NH_4^+, by the addition of a hydrogen ion, H^+. Other bacteria then change some of the ammonium ions into nitrate ions, NO_3^-. Both the ammonium and nitrate ions are forms of nitrogen that can be used by plants.

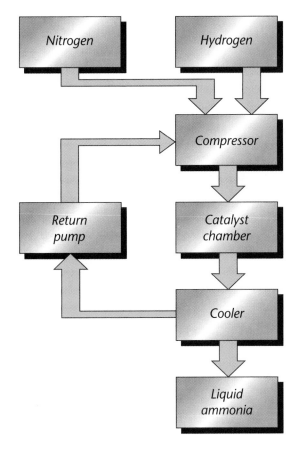

(A) In the compressor, the mixture of nitrogen and hydrogen is forced to go into a smaller volume, increasing the pressure.

(B) In the catalyst chamber, the compressed gases react to form ammonia gas.

(C) The cooler condenses most of the ammonia gas into liquid ammonia.

(D) Any uncondensed gases are returned to the compressor.

Figure 8-7

The Haber process was developed during World War I to allow Germany to produce the materials needed to continue manufacturing explosives. Today, the process allows farmers to grow much more food than could otherwise be produced.

■ Using Nitrogen

Once nitrogen is in usable form, plants absorb it through leaves and roots and begin synthesizing proteins that are necessary for life. In Chapter 7, you learned that proteins are made from amino acids, which contain nitrogen. The amino acids and proteins are then incorporated into your body when you eat either the plants or other animals that have eaten the plants.

Looking for Phosphorus

There are other elements that are as important as nitrogen is to the human body. Phosphorus is needed for the formation of your bones and teeth. It is contained in DNA, as shown in **Figure 8-8** on page 250. It is also important in the transfer of energy within your cells.

Typically, if you consume well-balanced meals, the meats and vegetables you eat will supply you with the amount of this element that your body needs. But how do the animals and plants that you eat obtain phosphorus?

■ Unlock a Rock

Unlike nitrogen and carbon, phosphorus is not typically found in a gas. Most phosphorus is found in rocks, much of it in the form of calcium phosphate, $Ca_3(PO_4)_2$. Weathering of the rocks releases phosphorus compounds, which become part of the soil. Often, the element is released in the form of phosphate. The phosphate ion, PO_4^{3-}, is the form in which phosphorus is absorbed by plant roots.

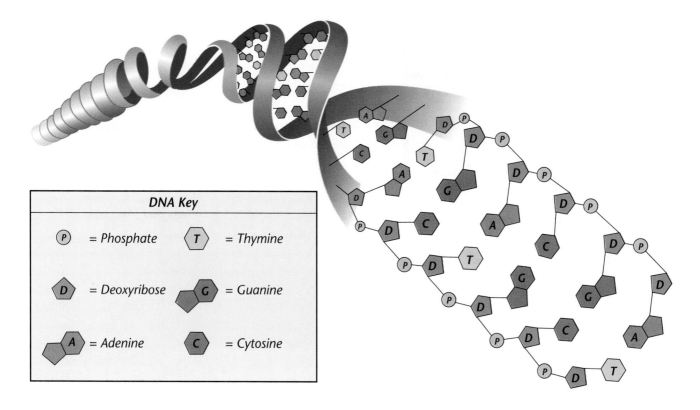

DNA Key

P = Phosphate		T = Thymine	
D = Deoxyribose		G = Guanine	
A = Adenine		C = Cytosine	

Figure 8-8

Phosphorus is an important element in the formation of DNA. Each of the four basic units that make up DNA contains phosphorus in the form of a phosphate group.

When animals eat plants, they take in phosphorus that was once part of a rock formation. Phosphorus is returned to the ecosystem when it is eliminated by organisms as waste. Bacteria and other decomposers in the soil return the element to the soil. There it can be absorbed by plants and used over again. Or, it can be dissolved in groundwater and eventually be carried to the ocean. Ocean sediments will then form rock that may be uplifted above ground at a future date.

■ **Adding to the Supply**

Most soil contains an adequate amount of phosphorus to maintain plant growth. However, poor management of land may lead to the loss of phosphates through erosion. Thus, farmers replace the loss by adding phosphate-containing fertilizers.

In this section, you learned how nitrogen and phosphorus are important in food production. In the next section, learn about the importance of energy in this same process.

check your UNDERSTANDING

Understanding Concepts

1. What property of gaseous nitrogen makes it difficult for plants to use?
2. How might farmers increase the amount of nitrogen available for their crops?
3. What role do decomposers play in the nitrogen and phosphorus cycles?

Skill Review

4. **Predicting** How might our world be different today if the Haber process had not been invented? For more help, refer to Predicting in the *Skill Handbook*.

8-3 The Energy Flow

Energy for Life

A cat lying next to the window can detect its presence. You detect it as you move into the sunshine. You can't really see it or touch it. Yet, in a variety of ways, you feel the effects of the radiant energy that travels from the sun to this planet, as shown in **Figure 8-9.** If you were able to follow energy as it moves through the universe, you would find that it changes from one form to another. But you'll find that energy cannot be created or destroyed by ordinary chemical means. Scientists call this observation the **law of conservation of energy.** How is the law of conservation of energy similar to the law of conservation of matter?

Think back to the newly printed book at the beginning of this chapter. When the presses run, electrical energy changes into thermal and mechanical energy. No energy is lost; one form of energy just changes to another form of energy.

■ An Energy Cycle

Let's look at what energy changes occur when food is broken down. As food is digested, chemical bonds in the food are broken and formed, and a large supply of energy becomes available for immediate use. However, not all of the energy can be used at one time. Energy-storing molecules called ATP are formed. When energy is needed, cells use energy from the breakdown of these molecules to carry out chemical reactions. Continuous formation and breakdown of energy-storing molecules are part of an energy cycle used in green plants.

This energy cycle is an important part of the series of chemical reactions utilized by green plants to make food. These reactions are more fully explained on pages 254-255 in this section. In the activity that follows, learn about another energy factor that affects these food-producing reactions.

Objectives
■ Sequence the steps that occur in photosynthesis.
■ Distinguish between anabolic and catabolic reactions.
■ Compare and contrast photosynthesis and respiration.

Key Terms
law of conservation of energy
photosynthesis
chloroplast
chlorophyll
light reactions
Calvin cycle
anabolic reaction
catabolic reaction
metabolism
cellular respiration

Figure 8-9

Energy from the sun travels 160 million km to Earth. Once here, solar energy is transformed into other forms of energy.

Light and Oxygen Production

Green plants are able to use certain colors of light to complete several biologically important chemical reactions that produce food and release oxygen gas. You can infer the connection between the different-colored light energy and food production by measuring the amount of oxygen produced. In this Investigation, the green aquatic plant **Elodea** *will serve as a model for testing the relationship between different-colored light and oxygen production.*

Preparation

Problem

How can you demonstrate that some colors of light result in a greater production of oxygen by plants?

Objectives

In this Investigation, you will:
- *Recognize the cause and effect* of light on certain reactions.
- *Experiment* with the variable of light color.

Materials

small test tubes (3)
beakers, 600-mL (3)
ring stand and test-tube clamps (3)
gooseneck lamps (3)
metric ruler
fresh *Elodea*
wooden splints (3)
matches or butane lighter
heat-resistant plastic filters:
   red, blue, green
cardboard boxes (3)
water

Safety Precautions

Use care when handling hot objects.

Data and Observations		
Filter used	Amount of gas in tube	Reaction of glowing splint
red		
blue		
green		

INVESTIGATION

Procedure

1 Work in three groups of two students each. Each group will follow all of the steps of the Investigation in the same way except at step 6, when each group will use a different-colored filter.

2 Add water to the beaker until it is two-thirds full.

3 Place a fresh sprig of *Elodea* under the water and into the test tube. Be sure sprigs are the same size and condition, and have the same number of leaflets. Fill the test tube to the brim with water.

4 Place your thumb over the top of the test tube. Invert the tube, and place it under the surface of the water in the beaker.

5 Remove your thumb and clamp the inverted tube so that its open end remains under the water and no air gets in.

Step 5

6 Place a colored filter over the lamp. Place the lamp 25 cm away from the test tube.

7 Then place an inverted cardboard box over the lamp, beaker, and tube assembly.
CAUTION: *Be sure the box does not touch any hot surfaces.*

8 Make a copy of the data table *in your Journal.*

9 After 24 hours, measure, in centimeters, the height of the column of gas collected in the test tube.

10 Remember that oxygen is necessary for fire to burn. Holding your finger over the end of the tube, remove the tube from the beaker. Invert the tube to an upright position. Remove your finger from the end of the tube. Slowly insert a glowing wooden splint into the mouth of the tube. Observe what happens.

11 Record your data and that of the other two groups in the data table.

Step 6

Analyze and Conclude

1. Comparing and Contrasting Which colors of light resulted in the most gas from the plant? How is this oxygen production evidence of food production in the plant?

2. Inferring If you had placed the *Elodea* in total darkness, infer what would have happened to the gas production. Why?

3. Sequencing Based on the data from all groups, sequence the light colors, starting with the color that resulted in the most gas production.

Going Further

Thinking Critically
How would your results be different if you used a plant grow lamp instead of a regular lamp? What would you consider if you manufactured a plant grow lamp?

Place a green, leafy plant next to a sun-lit window or a lamp with a grow-bulb for two days. Observe the position of the leaves and stems. Rotate the plant 180°. Wait two more days and observe the position of the leaves and stems again. What do you notice about their positions?

Photosynthesis

While green plants were producing oxygen in the Investigation, they were also producing food. A unique feature of organisms such as green algae and green plants is their ability to produce their own food. This process ultimately provides the nourishment, oxygen supply, and energy for almost every living organism on Earth. The process, known as photosynthesis, is actually several different chemical reactions. During **photosynthesis,** light energy is absorbed by green algae and green plants and is converted into chemical energy. This chemical energy is stored in glucose molecules in the cells of these organisms.

■ Chloroplasts—Nature's Light Catchers

You can infer from doing the previous Investigation that green plants need light to carry on photosynthesis. Green plants have specific cell parts designed to absorb the sun's energy. **Chloroplasts,** shown in **Figure 8-11,** are the plant cell structures that contain the green, energy-absorbing pigment **chlorophyll.**

Chlorophyll absorbs only certain forms of energy. As **Figure 8-10** shows, even some waves of light are not the right types to be absorbed by chlorophyll. Green light and some yellow light are reflected back to you. This is why most plants appear green. Why did green light produce the least amount of photosynthesis in the Investigation?

■ Following the Light Reactions

Photosynthesis involves a series of different chemical reactions. The sum of all the reactions is usually expressed in the simplified equation:

$$6CO_2 + 6H_2O \xrightarrow[\text{chlorophyll}]{\text{light energy}} C_6H_{12}O_6 + 6O_2$$

The process of photosynthesis is separated into two distinct groups of reactions: those known as light reactions and a set of reactions known as the Calvin cycle.

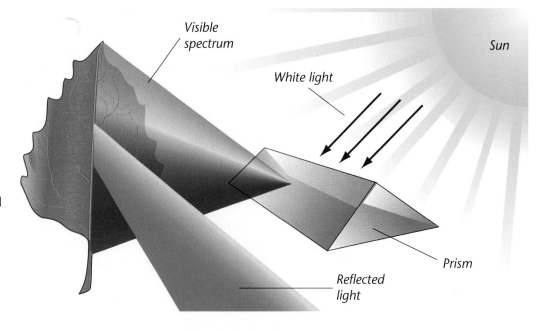

Figure 8-10

Each type of energy has its own characteristics. Chlorophyll in green leaves absorbs blue and red wavelengths of light and reflects green and some yellow light.

Visible spectrum

Sun

White light

Prism

Reflected light

The **light reactions** result in the conversion of light energy to chemical energy. As chlorophyll absorbs energy from the sun, some electrons become energized and are released from the chlorophyll molecule. The electrons are passed along a series of molecules, releasing a little energy at each molecule. Much of this extra energy is contained in the bonds of energy-storing molecules.

In the light reactions, water molecules are split. Hydrogen ions from this water eventually become part of glucose. Oxygen from the water is released from the plant as waste.

■ The Calvin Cycle

The **Calvin cycle** is the set of chemical reactions during photosynthesis in which simple sugars are formed. The light reactions also provide the energy, in the form of energy-storing molecules, necessary to drive the reactions of the Calvin cycle. The light reactions also provide the raw material hydrogen. Carbon and oxygen needed to produce sugars come from carbon dioxide from the air.

Initially, Calvin cycle reactions produce an unstable 6-carbon molecule from a 5-carbon molecule and carbon dioxide. Using energy from energy-storing molecules and hydrogen ions from the light reactions, each of these 6-carbon molecules splits immediately into two 3-carbon molecules. These 3-carbon molecules are then changed into 3-carbon sugars. Eventually, some of these sugars leave the cycle and form more complex sugars, starch, and cellulose.

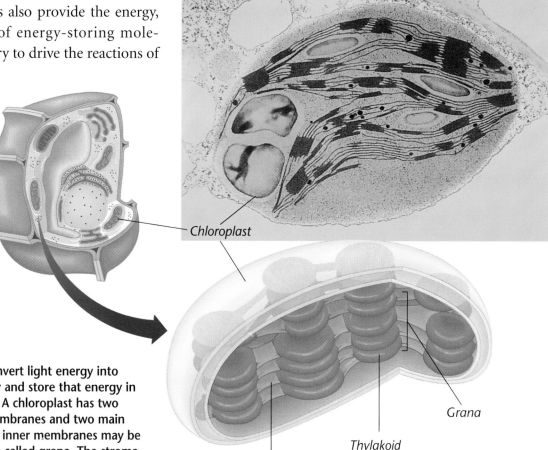

Chloroplast

Grana

Thylakoid membrane

Stroma

Figure 8-11

Chloroplasts convert light energy into chemical energy and store that energy in food molecules. A chloroplast has two surrounding membranes and two main inner parts. The inner membranes may be arranged in sacs called grana. The stroma is the material that surrounds the grana.

Building Up and Tearing Down Molecules

As you study the chemical reactions involved in the production and digestion of carbohydrates, fats, and proteins, you find a cycle of building up and tearing down of molecules. Scientists place these chemical reactions into two groups.

■ Classifying Biological Reactions

Reactions that build up complex molecules, such as the production of starch from glucose, require the input of energy and are called **anabolic reactions.** Energy-storing molecules provide the energy to drive anabolic reactions.

Catabolic reactions are the opposite of anabolic reactions. During **catabolic reactions,** energy, stored in the bonds of high-energy molecules, is released because complex molecules are broken down. Both anabolic and catabolic reactions are needed for the completion of the energy cycle, which is discussed on pages 254-255 of this chapter. The sum of all the anabolic and catabolic chemical reactions within an organism is called **metabolism.** Metabolic rate varies with temperature. The rate increases as temperature increases to about 50°C. At that temperature, the enzymes needed to control reactions have been destroyed. Now let's take a closer look at one particularly important catabolic reaction.

■ Cellular Respiration

In most organisms, the process used to convert the stored energy in glucose to usable energy is called **cellular respiration.** Most organisms use oxygen as one of the reactants in this catabolic process. Like photosynthesis, cellular respiration is a series of reactions. A simplified equation for the whole process is:

$$C_6H_{12}O_6 + 6O_2 \rightarrow 6CO_2 + 6H_2O + energy$$

How does this equation compare to the equation for photosynthesis on page 254? A key factor in the cellular respiration process is that energy is released a little at a time. One effect of cellular respiration rate on the human body is shown in **Figure 8-12.**

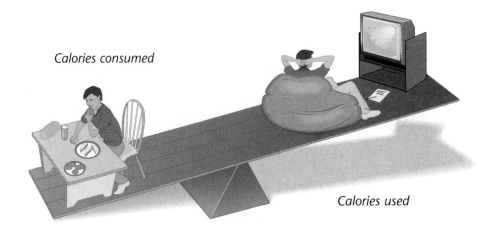

Calories consumed

Calories used

Figure 8-12

If a person eats more Calories than the body can metabolize, the body will store the extra energy as body fat. If a person eats fewer Calories than the body can metabolize, the body will use energy from stored fat.

Keeping the Balance

As forests are cleared and oceans become polluted, there are fewer green plants and algae to produce oxygen and use carbon dioxide. In addition to the carbon dioxide produced by cellular respiration, it is also produced as fossil fuels are burned for energy. Can an imbalance in these two processes affect the environment? There is no clear answer to this question, but the following Thinking Lab offers one opinion.

Thinking Lab   Interpreting Data

What is happening to the level of atmospheric carbon dioxide?

Much has been written about the relationship between increasing temperature of Earth's atmosphere, known as global warming, and the amount of carbon dioxide present in the air. Scientists have been studying evidence that will prove or disprove the existence of this relationship.

Analysis

The graph shown here represents the levels of atmospheric carbon dioxide in the northern hemisphere for the 30 years from 1958 to 1988. Notice the peaks and troughs that appear each year in the levels of carbon dioxide. These highs and lows are represented by the black line. Also notice the direction of the red midline. This midline represents the overall average level of the gas.

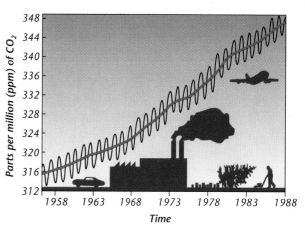

Thinking Critically

Based on what you know about photosynthesis and cellular respiration, explain why the levels of atmospheric carbon dioxide fluctuate during a year. If global warming is related to the amount of carbon dioxide in the air, how does the midline support or not support the theory that global warming is actually occurring?

check your UNDERSTANDING

Understanding Concepts

1. How does your exhaled CO_2 benefit plants?
2. In terms of energy, distinguish between an anabolic and a catabolic reaction.
3. Explain what happens during an anabolic reaction in terms of the law of conservation of energy.

Skill Review

4. **Recognizing Cause and Effect** How would the reactions in the Calvin cycle be affected in areas that experience long periods of darkness, such as Alaska during winter? For more help, refer to Recognizing Cause and Effect in the *Skill Handbook*.

Scurvy and Its Cure

During the winter of 1535-36, three ships under the command of the French explorer Jacques Cartier became frozen in ice in the St. Lawrence River, near where the Canadian city of Montreal is located today. For several months, the 110 men under Cartier's command endured the bitter cold and subsisted on little else but the dried and salt-cured sea rations that were on board the ice-bound ships. By mid-March, 25 men had died from scurvy, which we now know is caused by a lack of vitamin C in the diet. The rest were critically ill from the disease. It looked as if Cartier's entire crew would perish from scurvy before the spring thaw could free the ships from the ice.

Treatment Close at Hand

An encounter with the Iroquois nation changed the fate of Cartier's expedition. The Iroquois had a wealth of knowledge about local plants. As a result of centuries of careful observation and experimentation, they knew which plants to use to treat a variety of illnesses. The Iroquois recognized in the crew the symptoms of a disease that they knew how to cure.

The Iroquois women collected branches from several kinds of native evergreens, including eastern hemlock and black spruce. They boiled bark and needles in water to make a hot, strong-smelling tea that they gave to the dying sailors. After a few treatments, the sailors began to make a rapid recovery.

Cause and Cure

More than 200 years later, a British navy doctor, James Lind, read an account of the incident. He carried out experiments that eventually proved that scurvy was caused by a dietary deficiency. It was also shown that scurvy could be prevented by eating certain types of foods—something that the Iroquois had discovered in North America centuries before. As a result of Lind's work, British sailors were given limes to eat as part of their daily rations. This practice earned the sailors the nickname "Limeys," but it kept them scurvy-free during long sea voyages.

The Iroquois' "herbal tea" would have worked just as well. Some types of spruce and pine needles have five times more vitamin C than lemons or limes contain. The fruits of wild roses, called rose hips, were eaten by many Native American peoples as part of their health care. Rose hips have 60 times the vitamin C of most citrus fruits.

Hemlock

Thinking Critically

1. *Explain* why the members of Cartier's expedition developed scurvy.
2. *Research* the traditional diet of another Native American culture and make a list of foods or plant extracts that were used to treat health problems or cure disease.

Read the statements below that review major points presented in the chapter. Using the concepts that you have learned, answer each question *in your Journal.*

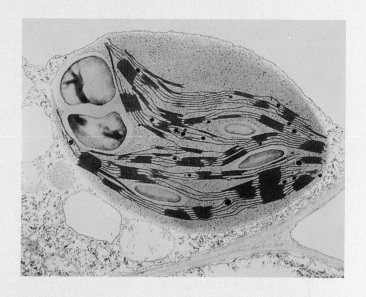

1 Green plants can be described as biological factories through which raw materials such as carbon, oxygen, nitrogen, hydrogen, and phosphorus are recycled into new products or returned to the ecosystem. *In what ways are these nutrient cycles a part of both living organisms and nonliving compounds?*

2 Matter and energy are continuously cycled. Additional amounts are not created and none is destroyed; however, atoms are reorganized by chemical reactions and energy changes from one form to another. *What laws summarize these statements?*

3 During photosynthesis, organisms use light energy to produce sugar molecules that store chemical energy. Cellular respiration reverses this process and releases the stored energy. *How do the reactants and products of photosynthesis compare to those of cellular respiration?*

Using Key Science Terms

anabolic reaction
Calvin cycle
catabolic reaction
cellular respiration
cellulose
chlorophyll
chloroplast
Haber process

law of conservation
    of energy
law of conservation
    of matter
light reactions
metabolism
nitrogen fixation
photosynthesis

Answer the following questions about science terms used in this chapter.

1. Look up the meaning of the word *photosynthesis*. Use a dictionary to find out the meanings of the main parts of the word. Explain why the word is appropriate.

2. Compare and contrast the use of glucose in cells and the use of cellulose in cells.

3. Explain the relationship between the light reactions and the Calvin cycle.

4. Compare and contrast the two types of reactions that, when taken together, make up metabolism.

Understanding Ideas

Using complete sentences, answer the following questions in your Journal.

1. Phosphorus cycles are both long term and short term. Explain.

2. Explain what happens to some electrons in chlorophyll as they absorb energy from the sun.

3. Compare plants that fix nitrogen with plants that don't fix nitrogen.

4. Why is nitrogen fixing so important to many animals?

5. What takes place during the Calvin cycle?

6. Describe two ways that bacteria are important components of the cycles discussed in this chapter.

7. Suppose you hear the statement: "People are solar-powered." Take a position on the statement and explain your opinion.

8. Explain how cycles can be both global and localized.

Developing Skills

Use your understanding of the concepts developed in this chapter to answer each of the following questions.

1. **Concept Mapping** Complete the cycle map with the following terms that deal with nitrogen fixation.
   atmospheric nitrogen, amino acids, ammonium and nitrates, nitrogenous wastes, proteins.

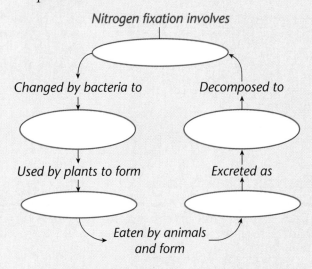

Nitrogen fixation involves

Changed by bacteria to   Decomposed to

Used by plants to form   Excreted as

Eaten by animals
and form

2. **Predicting** Predict what would happen if you repeated the *Elodea* investigation using a light with frequencies in the ultraviolet range.

3. Comparing and Contrasting What similarity do you find as you compare the laws of conservation of matter and energy?

Critical Thinking

In your Journal, *answer each of the following questions.*

1. Rates of cycling materials vary greatly depending on the ecosystems involved. What do you think is the rate of cycling carbon within the rain forest? Explain.
2. Green plants are often compared to factories. Explain how green plants are different from factories in terms of their energy supply.
3. When a cube of sugar is burned, energy is released. How is the process of burning a cube of sugar to release energy different from cellular respiration?
4. How are plants and animals both involved in the process of photosynthesis?

5. The Haber process uses high temperatures and pressures to change atmospheric nitrogen to a usable form. Hypothesize as to why these high temperatures and pressures are necessary.

Problem Solving

Read the following problem and discuss your answers in a brief paragraph.

Scientists hypothesize that average atmospheric temperatures and the percentage of carbon dioxide, CO_2, in the air will continue to rise above current levels well past the year 2000.

How might increased carbon dioxide levels influence photosynthesis? How might increased temperatures affect the survivability of plants?

CONNECTING IDEAS

1. **Theme—Energy** How does energy needed for body functions get to where it is needed?
2. **Theme—Systems and Interactions** Use one of the cycles mentioned in this chapter to discuss the relationships among humans, plants, and bacteria.
3. **Theme—Systems and Interactions** What is the relationship between the intensity of light and the amount of photosynthesis that occurs at different depths of the ocean?
4. **In-Depth Look** What are some possible problems with making nonlegume crops self-fertilizing?
5. **Science and Society** Seed banks classify and store seeds from many varieties of plants. Why are seed banks becoming more important as industrialized agriculture increases?
6. **History Connection** A sample of lemon, a citrus fruit, was found to contain 5 mg of vitamin C. How much vitamin C is in an equal mass of rose hips?

CHAPTER 9

Soil Formation
The Life-Giving Earth

Have you ever walked along an old cracked and crumbling sidewalk? Perhaps you have seen pictures of the ancient pyramids of Egypt. What is happening to the sidewalk and the pyramids? Large pieces are being broken into smaller pieces. The breaking up of a sidewalk or the blocks of rock making up a pyramid is caused by the same forces that cause rocks to break in nature. Cracks form in rocks, and small and large pieces begin to break off. Eventually these rock pieces can be broken even further, forming very small particles. These small particles of rock become a large part of what makes soil. In this chapter, you will examine not only how soils form, but different soil types as well. You will also look at the importance soil has for society.

▶ *The MiniLab on the next page will get you started.*

MiniLab

Is this soil?

Soil comes in many colors and types. All soils contain organic matter and are capable of supporting life. Observe the characteristics of several soil samples.

Procedure

1. *In your Journal,* construct a data table with the following column and row headings. Columns: Unaided eye, Hand lens, and Microscope. Rows: Sample 1, 2, 3, etc.

2. Carefully put approximately ¼ cup of each sample into separate, labeled petri dishes.

3. Observe each sample and record your observations.

4. Discuss your observations and conclusions with your class.

5. Return your samples for reuse or disposal.

Analysis

1. Why is it helpful to use a microscope in this study?

2. Which samples do you think would be the most productive soils? Why?

The Development of Soils

Objectives

- Describe soil.
- Explain the role of weathering in soil development.
- Describe how physical and chemical weathering differ.

Key Terms

soil
weathering
physical weathering
ice wedging
chemical weathering

What is soil?

To some, a soil is any loose, broken material covering the surface of Earth. Most of us think of soil as the substance seen in **Figure 9-1**. It is something for growing plants in, or the rich, dark colors in a freshly plowed farmer's field. We will use the term *soil* in this way throughout this chapter.

But there is a lot more to soil. Soil forms where much of Earth's surface is in contact with the atmosphere. **Soil** is a combination of broken-down rock and mineral matter, organic matter, air, and water. It may or may not be capable of supporting plant growth. Some soils are only a few tens to hundreds of years old, while others are hundreds of thousands to millions of years in age. How is new soil made? You can see how it happens in **Figure 9-2.** What are the conditions and processes that cause soil to form?

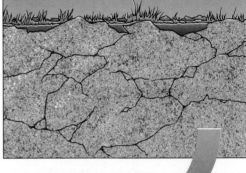

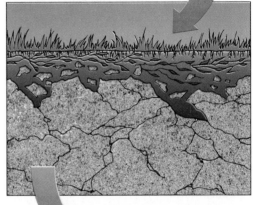

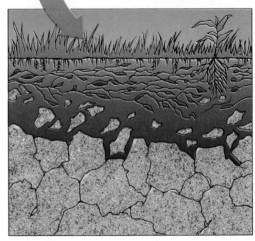

Figure 9-1

To geologists, soil is the blanket of loose, decayed rock debris that forms over solid bedrock as the result of weathering.

Figure 9-2

Soil evolves over time from weathered rock. This process occurs rapidly or slowly depending on location and weather conditions.

Weathering—The First Step in Soil Formation

What causes a brick building to begin crumbling, a sidewalk to break apart, or a rock in nature to begin cracking? Environmental conditions and processes act on rock and cause it to break apart. Processes by which rock and mineral matter are broken into pieces mechanically or changed chemically are called **weathering.** Weathering affects all things around us slowly, over long periods of time. It affects naturally formed structures as well as human-

Figure 9-4

The effects of weathering are seen wherever rocks are exposed. The materials that made up the Parthenon are now worn from weathering.

made ones. Soils are the result of weathering. Soils form a blanket over solid bedrock and are the basis for most life on land. There are two major kinds of weathering—physical and chemical.

In the following Investigation, you will see how weathering takes place and determine if physical or chemical weathering is more effective.

Figure 9-3

Weathering wears down large, jagged mountains into smooth, rolling mountains and hills.

Ⓐ Steep, jagged mountains with little vegetation represent relatively young mountains.

Ⓑ Older mountains, subjected to weathering over millions of years, have developed soils that support a large amount of plant life.

Weathering: Which type is more effective?

You have just read that two types of weathering can occur in nature. Physical weathering occurs from a number of things, including the friction due to the action of water and freezing and thawing. Chemical weathering occurs when water, air, and other substances react with minerals in the rocks and change the chemical composition of the rocks. Do they operate independently or together? In this Investigation, see firsthand how weathering takes place. Think about observations you've made of the weathering of buildings, sidewalks, and rocks in your neighborhood as you observe weathering in action.

Preparation

Problem
Which weathering agent or agents are most effective in breaking down rocks?

Hypothesis
Discuss the problem with your lab partners and decide what hypothesis you will test.

Objectives
In this Investigation, you will:
- **Determine** which agents of weathering are most effective in breaking down rocks.
- **Compare** the effects of agents from the same category (i.e., physical or chemical).

Possible Materials
rocks to be weathered
scale for weighing samples
tape measure
dilute HCl and H_2SO_4
distilled water
shower attachment
stream table (so that water can be reused)
fan with variable speeds
large tubs
freezer
oven

Safety Precautions

DESIGN YOUR OWN
INVESTIGATION

Plan the Experiment

1 Examine the materials provided by your teacher. Decide which materials you will test. Make a list of these materials. Form a hypothesis.

2 Design an experiment that will enable you to test your hypothesis.

3 Prepare a list of numbered procedure steps that you will follow, as well as your list of materials needed, including glassware, amounts needed, and time allowed.

4 *In your Journal,* prepare a table for recording data.

5 Prepare graphs or charts for displaying your quantitative data.

Check the Plan
Discuss the following points with other group members to decide the final procedure for your experiment.

1 What will the control be for your experiment?

2 How long will you need for your experiment to run its course?

3 When will you collect data?

4 Should all samples be the same size?

5 *Make sure your teacher has approved your experimental plan before you proceed further.*

6 Carry out your experiment. Record all observations and data throughout the lab.

Analyze and Conclude

1. Comparing and Contrasting Which seemed to cause more weathering—chemical or physical agents? Why? How can you tell?

2. Drawing Conclusions If different rock samples had been used in this experiment, would the results have been the same? Explain.

3. Interpreting Data Based on the quantitative data, if the experiment had run longer, would you expect the results to be different? Why?

4. Analyzing the Procedure How closely does this lab simulate real outdoor weathering? How does it differ?

Going Further

Application
The steps and handrails outside of our nation's capitol building are made of sandstone. Based on your results and observations, what sorts of situations should the grounds-keepers be on the lookout for in order to minimize weathering damage?

A Repeated ice wedging is a major force at work in physical weathering. Water that gets into cracks in rocks expands and contracts as it freezes and thaws. Eventually, pieces of rock are loosened and fall off.

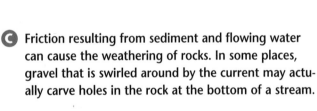

B As plant roots grow, they can exert enough pressure to split rocks.

C Friction resulting from sediment and flowing water can cause the weathering of rocks. In some places, gravel that is swirled around by the current may actually carve holes in the rock at the bottom of a stream.

Figure 9-5

Water and living organisms are two important elements of physical weathering.

■ Physical Weathering

Physical or mechanical **weathering** causes the breaking down of rock and mineral matter into smaller pieces without changing their chemical composition. Physical weathering occurs in a variety of different ways. Have you ever frozen a can of soda? If you have, you probably noticed that the can bulged out at the top and bottom after the soda froze. The water in the can expanded as it froze, causing the can to expand. When water gets into the cracks of rocks and freezes, it also expands. This process is known as **ice wedging.** Ice wedging repeated over and over as water melts and refreezes forces rocks to split apart. Other types of physical weathering seen in **Figure 9-5** include the action of moving water on rock in the form of rain or a flowing river or stream. Plants also cause mechanical weathering. As trees grow, their roots spread and expand. The pressure of these roots on a sidewalk, driveway, or foundation of a house can cause the concrete to break, resulting in cracks and bumps.

Chemical Weathering

The second major type of weathering is chemical weathering. **Chemical weathering** occurs when water, air, and other substances react with the minerals in the rocks and change the chemical composition of the rock. The reactions involved include oxygen, carbon dioxide, and water. Water is the main agent of chemical weathering. Some of the minerals that make up rock are dissolved by water. As the water dissolves the minerals, they are carried away, and the rock that remains is now slightly different in composition.

In some parts of the world, water from rain adds greatly to the process of chemical weathering. As you will remember from Chapter 4, a solution with a pH of 7.0 is neutral. Nonpolluted rainwater usually has a pH of 5.6 to 5.7, which is slightly acidic. This acidic nature of rain works to dissolve minerals in rocks, which weakens the rock, causing it to break down into smaller and smaller pieces.

Weathering occurs all over the world. Areas that have climates with a high average rainfall and high average temperatures have a higher rate of chemical weathering. Why would temperature be such an important factor in chemical weathering? Think about how an increase in temperature influences the rate of a chemical reaction. In what areas of the world would there be a high rate of physical weathering?

In most areas of the world, chemical and physical processes are both at work weathering Earth materials into soil. A common way physical and chemical weathering work together is illustrated in **Figure 9-6.**

Figure 9-6

As a rock is broken into more and more pieces by physical weathering, the total surface area exposed to the atmosphere is increased. This expansion in a rock's surface area greatly increases the amount of rock area being exposed by chemical weathering; therefore, the rate of chemical weathering increases.

■ Weathering by Organisms

Physical and chemical weathering are often caused by the work of organisms. An example of weathering caused by organisms is the breakdown of rocks by lichens. Lichens expand when wet and contract when dry. They also produce acids that work to break down the rock. The net effect is weathering similar to ice wedging and chemical decomposition combined. Cracks in the rock spread apart, increasing the surface area available for chemical weathering. The acids then decompose the rock.

Burrowing activities and overturning of soil by earthworms and other burrowing animals are also effective in causing weathering. The burrows made by earthworms allow more air and water to move down into the soil. These actions, as seen in **Figure 9-7,** loosen the soil and also allow plant roots to penetrate further and more easily into the soil.

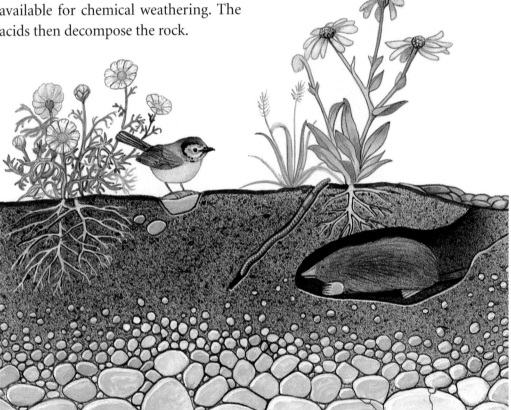

Figure 9-7

Many organisms, both microscopic and macroscopic, live in the soil and contribute to its formation. Plant roots help to loosen and aerate the soil. Earthworms, moles, and other soil-dwelling animals help to mix up the soil as they burrow for food.

check your UNDERSTANDING

Understanding Concepts
1. Describe the process of ice wedging. How does it help weather rock?
2. Why is weathering necessary for soil formation?
3. Explain how physical weathering allows chemical weathering to be more effective.

Skill Review
4. **Comparing and Contrasting** Compare and contrast the processes of physical and chemical weathering. For more help, refer to Thinking Critically in the *Skill Handbook.*

9-2 ◆ A Soil Is Born

Controls of Soil Formation

Objectives

- Describe the important factors in soil formation and composition.
- Compare and contrast the different soil horizons.

Key Terms

parent material
topography
humus
soil profile

The characteristics of a soil found in a given area depend on several factors such as climate, parent material, topography of an area, and the length of time it has taken the soil to form.

The parent material may be rock or loose material such as sediment. Over time, the result is a soil that is different both physically and chemically from the original parent material.

■ Climate

Climate is an important factor influencing the formation of a soil because rainfall, temperature, and seasonal change all directly affect soil development. In tropical areas that have a high average temperature and a large amount of rainfall, thick soils develop. Temperature greatly influences how fast chemical reactions take place. Increases in temperature of 10°C can double the rate of chemical reactions. Soils develop at a rapid rate due to the higher rate of chemical weathering. In arctic and desert regions, thin soils are formed due to limited rainfall and the dominance of mechanical weathering. The difference in soils in these two areas can be seen in **Figure 9-8.**

Figure 9-8

There is a major contrast between soils in tropical equatorial regions and arctic and desert regions.

Tropical soil

B Very thick soils are found in tropical regions.

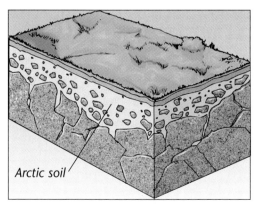

Arctic soil

A Partly decomposed rock and thin soils are seen in arctic and desert regions.

Figure 9-9

Different types of rock weather into different types of soil.

A The rock quartzite is resistant to chemical weathering. In areas where there is an abundance of quartzite in the parent material, thin, poorly drained soils are formed.

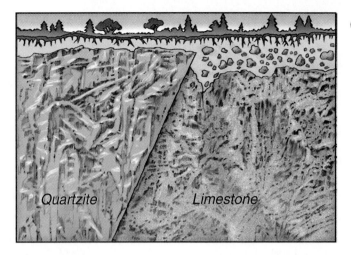

Quartzite   Limestone

B When a parent material contains limestone, thicker soils form because limestone weathers rapidly by chemical means.

■ Parent Material

Any type of Earth material can be changed into a soil by weathering. The kinds of rocks and minerals present in the parent material can influence the nature of the soil's composition. The **parent material** is the type of rock the soil originates from. Sandstone parent material weathers into sandy soils, while fine-particled shale rocks produce a soil with a high clay content. The parent material also affects whether the soil is acidic or basic in nature. Limestone produces a soil that has a neutral pH. Rocks such as granite produce soils that are more acidic. **Figure 9-9** shows two types of parent materials and the soils that may result from their weathering.

■ Topography

The lay of the land also affects soil development. The **topography,** which is the configuration of the surface of the land, affects the rate at which weathering occurs and how quickly water drains from the soil. What types of soils do you think develop on steep slopes? Water rushing down a steep slope does not allow much weathered material to accumulate; therefore, only thin soils form. The types of soils that form in different areas and the types of vegetation supported by those soils can be seen in **Figure 9-10.**

B Valleys typically have well-developed, fertile soils that are excellent for growing crops.

Figure 9-10

These photos illustrate how vegetation changes due to elevation. Just as soils change across the plains due to climate, they also change as elevation changes. This results in different vegetation and ultimately in different types of soils from valleys to the tops of mountains.

A These mountain plants have adaptations for growing in the thin soils and harsh conditions of high elevations.

Life in the Soil

Organisms play an important role in soil formation and development. Their presence is necessary for the good health and productivity of a soil. Soil that has few organisms in it can have a very different character from one that has many burrowing organisms. Examine the effect one type of living organism has on soil in the following MiniLab.

MiniLab

Do earthworms cause soil mixing?

Earth is teeming with organisms big and small, each carrying out its day-to-day life activities. Eating as they go, earthworms change a soil's characteristics.

Procedure

1. Obtain three to four samples of different-colored soils, a transparent plastic box, and three or four live earthworms.

2. Decide on an arrangement of soil and worms (for example, soil layer 1, soil layer 2, worms, and soil layer 3; or other combinations).

3. Fill your plastic box with soil layers about 2 cm thick. The worms should be against the sides of the plastic box so that at the beginning, you can see how they move.

4. Set the box in a warm place for 24 to 48 hours. Note any changes that take place.

Analysis

1. Did the spacing of the worms influence the amount of burrowing?

2. How would this burrowing affect the soil?

3. Predict whether the results would be the same if you packed down the soil or watered it more heavily. If possible, test your prediction.

As you saw in the MiniLab, earthworms move soil a lot and can have a great effect on the character of a soil. Microscopic organisms such as some fungi, bacteria, and protists are continually hard at work in soil, decomposing organic matter and returning nutrients to the soil. Many other organisms both dead and alive contribute to the formation of soil. An important part of soil is **humus,** shown in **Figure 9-11.** Also known as organic materials, humus consists of matter in an advanced state of decomposition.

Figure 9-11

Humus is the dark-colored organic material composed of partially decayed plant and animal matter. A large part of humus begins as litter. Litter consists of dead leaves, branches, and other plant parts.

Figure 9-12

This ancient Mayan temple was discovered buried up to its uppermost level with rain forest litter. Excavation revealed a huge temple.

■ Time

The changing of a parent material into soil can take a long time. The time needed for soil formation varies with the intensity of weathering and the characteristics of the parent material. Most soil-forming factors act on parent material over millions of years. Biological and chemical activities are slow in cold regions and in dry regions. As a result, these areas have thin, rocky soils with little organic material. The warmer temperatures and high rainfall of tropical areas speed up the weathering of parent material into soil. Over time, great thicknesses of soil can accumulate as can be seen in **Figure 9-12.** In these areas, the abundant rainfall has washed away soil nutrients. The many organisms living in these forests use available nutrients at an extremely rapid rate. These factors, combined with the high rate of weathering, form thick but not extremely fertile soils. **Figure 9-13** shows how many factors combine to form soils.

Figure 9-13

The type of weathering and the extent of its effects vary with the climate of a given area. The largest amount of weathering is seen in the tropics. There is a minimum of weathering in deserts and polar regions.

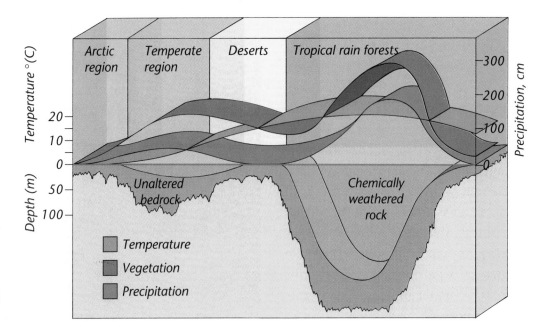

Soil Characteristics

The decay of organic matter, continued chemical and physical weathering, and the work of organisms result in most soils becoming layered. These layers, or horizons, make up a soil's profile. The **soil profile** is a vertical section through the soil that shows the layers of the soil or the soil's horizons, and the parent material it was derived from. A soil profile can give a picture of the environment in which the soil formed. **Figure 9-14** gives an example of a soil profile.

The most important features in a soil that distinguish horizons and define a profile are color, organic matter content, amount of moisture, and texture.

During a trip across the country, you may see soils of varying colors. Depending on the climate and the parent material the soil is derived from, you could see soil that is black, brown, red, yellow, tan, white, or gray. A high content of organic matter in soil is indicated by dark gray or black colors. Yellow-brown to red soils mean that the minerals in it formed when iron combined with oxygen from the atmosphere. Light gray to white soil contains silicon dioxide, calcite, or clay minerals.

Figure 9-14

A soil profile is divided into layers called horizons. Each horizon is affected as weathering continues.

Decaying vegetation

A-horizon

B-horizon

C-horizon

Bedrock

A-horizon This uppermost layer is thin and usually dark-colored due to a large content of organic material. This layer is also called the *topsoil*. Plant roots are concentrated in this layer. The A-horizon is the most fully evolved soil layer in a soil profile. This layer has changed the most since it was just weathered rock.

B-horizon This layer is often called the *subsoil*. The chemically dissolved material from the A-horizon above gets transported and concentrated here. Calcite or clays may build up, forming a distinct layer, often of a lighter color than the A-horizon.

C-horizon Partly weathered parent material makes up this layer. It is the C-horizon that has characteristics partway between parent material and the developing soil. Below the C-horizon is parent material.

INVESTIGATION

Documenting the Variability of Soils

What makes one soil different from another? How do these differences come about? Is a soil in Illinois different from one in Florida? You have just learned that several factors work together to make a soil. The combination of climate, vegetation, parent material, and time results in soil types that are associated with many different geographic regions. In this Investigation, analyze five specific characteristics of soils and try to interpret how they formed.

Preparation

Problem

What physical and chemical properties are present within a soil?

Objectives

In this Investigation, you will:
- *Test* soil samples for various chemical properties and *predict* which soil might be the most productive.
- *Describe* the physical properties of the samples.

Materials

petri dishes or other glass observation dishes (6 per lab group)
small spoons or spatulas for sampling
soil (6 to 8 samples)
hand lens
microscopes
microscope slides
grain-size chart for soils
GSA color chart for soils
dilute HCl
distilled water
droppers
pH papers and pH chart
graduated cylinder (25 mL)
stirring rods
goggles

Safety Precautions

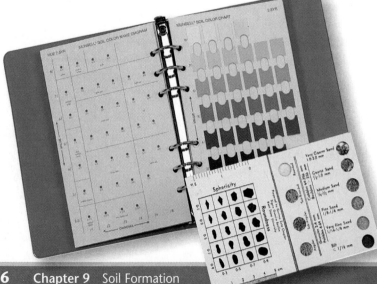

INVESTIGATION

Procedure

1 *In your Journal,* construct a data table with the following row and column headings. Rows: Sample 1, Sample 2, Sample 3, Sample 4. Columns: sorting, grain size, color, organic matter content, HCl reaction, and pH.

2 Analyze any four of the soil samples. Fill in the rows of your data table with the appropriate sample numbers.

3 Place 2 teaspoons of one sample in each of four separate dishes.

4 Describe the range of size of the particles in the sample. Record your observations as poorly, moderately, and well sorted.

Step 3

5 Compare the sample to the grain-size chart and describe the grain size.

6 Use the color chart to describe the sample's color. Report only the color; there is no need to worry about the proportions listed on the chart.

7 Note the color again and determine the approximate amount of organic matter in the soil. Record this observation.

8 Put 5 drops of dilute HCl into one sample dish. Observe and record what happens. **NOTE:** If there is a reaction, state whether it is vigorous, quiet, sustained, short, etc.

Step 8

9 Pour 10 to 20 mL of distilled water into another sample dish. Stir to mix well. Put one end of the pH paper into the water. Compare the color to the chart provided and record the value.

Analyze and Conclude

1. **Observing and Inferring** Do any of the samples have a high organic content? How did you determine this? Is your testing method scientifically accurate?

2. **Thinking Critically** Lime is used to neutralize acidic soils. Which sample would have the lowest acidity?

3. **Predicting** Permeability refers to the ability of water to move through a substance. Which soil sample do you think is the most permeable?

Going Further

Project
Design an experiment to test the permeability of your soil samples. Why might the permeability of the soil be important?

A Sandy soils contain a majority of sand particles. These particles are large and irregularly shaped. Water and dissolved nutrients drain rapidly out of these soils; therefore, they are relatively infertile.

B Soils that contain a lot of clay have mostly small, flat particles that pack closely together. Water does not drain easily from this type of soil. These soils are so dense that plant roots cannot grow easily in them.

C Silty soil is characterized by medium-sized, irregularly shaped particles. It has characteristics of both sand and clay.

Figure 9-15

The texture of a soil can determine what plants would best grow in it. Which soil type would be the most productive?

Thinking Lab   Interpreting Data

Can soils really help solve crimes?

You may not have thought much about soils helping to solve a crime. But they can and do add information that is often helpful to police. Their analysis can sometimes tell us much about the most likely places a crime may have been committed.

Analysis

It was a hot day. The usual afternoon rain typical of the tropical island had not made its way to the city. A crime had been committed. Detectives working the case were surprised to find two different kinds of soil at the crime scene. One was a dark soil with lots of organic matter. The other was a red soil rich in clay. Detective Smith wanted to just pass them off as dirt, but Detective Jones knew better. She called in the crime investigation team for help. A prime suspect had arrived only hours before from his home in Kansas. Use what you have learned about soils to set up the events of this crime.

Thinking Critically

How can you explain the presence of a soil that is different from one developed in the local area? What features would you look for to help you determine more about the soil?

■ Texture

When rock breaks down into soil, it forms smaller and smaller pieces. The smallest pieces are called soil particles and are 2 mm in size or less. Scientists usually classify soil particles into three groups, depending on the size of the particles—sand, silt, and clay. Texture refers to the different sizes of particles making up a soil. The percentages of each of these particles determine the texture of the soil. **Figure 9-15** illustrates soils with various textures.

■ Differences in Soil Types

Soils are different throughout the world. This is due to differences in climate, plants, and parent material. **Figure 9-16** summarizes soils from different regions of the world. Where does the soil in the area where you live fit in?

Figure 9-16

A survey of soil types.

Ⓐ In the northeastern United States, the cold, wet weather conditions form acidic soils.

Ⓑ Many places in the tropics have red soils developed by intense chemical weathering over a long period of time.

Ⓒ The midwest plant life is dominated by grasslands. The resulting soils are dark in color, indicating that they are rich in organic matter.

Ⓓ In the desert, the plants are mostly grasses, shrubs, and cacti. Due to the warm climate and high evaporation of moisture, the B-horizon is often rich in calcite.

check your UNDERSTANDING

Understanding Concepts
1. What is a soil profile? How does it form?
2. How is a soil from the desert of New Mexico different from soil present in a forest with a humid climate?
3. Discuss how soil layers or horizons are recognized.

Skill Review
4. **Interpreting Scientific Illustrations** Use **Figure 9-13** on page 274 to make a table summarizing the information found in the illustration. For more help, refer to Interpreting Scientific Illustrations in the *Skill Handbook*.

9-3 Soil Productivity and Nutrient Content

Objectives
■ Describe three methods that can be used to maintain soil fertility.
■ Explain deforestation and its effects.
■ List the essential elements needed for productive soil.

Key Terms
erosion

What makes a healthy soil?

Soil is one of the most economically important resources on Earth. It is the material that supports plant life and therefore all terrestrial life.

Most plants make their own food. But soil is the main source of nutrients and water that keeps plants healthy and growing. Soil scientists have determined that 16 chemical elements are essential for plant growth. Air and water provide hydrogen, oxygen, nitrogen, and carbon. Some of the other elements are provided by minerals present in the soil. These yield phosphorus, potassium, and calcium.

How do we make sure the soil remains healthy and productive? How do we use soil wisely for growing the food on which society is so dependent? Erosion-control and soil-conservation programs are two ways to keep soils healthy and productive. Such programs decrease nutrient loss and conserve water in soils. Crop rotation, contour farming, and terracing, as seen in **Figure 9-17,** are three ways to maintain healthy soils.

A Crop rotation is an easy way to recycle soil nutrients. Each crop removes different nutrients from the soil and each crop replaces different nutrients. Rotation goes from a cultivated crop to a small grain to grasses, then back to the cultivated crop. In the northeastern United States, one rotation scheme might include potatoes to oats to red clover and back to potatoes.

B Contour plowing helps to keep wind erosion and water runoff to a minimum by following the level lines that follow the contours of the land. By planting across the direction of water flow, runoff and erosion are decreased.

Figure 9-17

Several methods are used in farming to preserve the soil.

■ Deforestation

In many countries around the world where large tropical forests exist, farmers clear the jungle in order to grow crops. This practice can result in disaster to the soil. Unlike deciduous forests, tropical forests' organic matter such as fallen leaves, dead plants, and animal wastes are decomposed rapidly on the forest floor and are used by the existing vegetation. In fact, almost all of the organic and inorganic nutrients are tied up in the plants of tropical forests. Chemical weathering is so intense and there is so much rain that many of the remaining minerals and nutrients are lost from the soil. Often, only iron and aluminum remain, the other nutrients having been washed away. Growing plants in such soil is nearly impossible. The soils in these areas, when cleared, are easily eroded. When crops are grown in these soils, the available nutrients are quickly used, and the soils are

Figure 9-18

The deforestation of large areas of rain forest is destroying soil.

useless in one or two years. Farmers then move on to clear-cut more forest, repeating the cycle. **Figure 9-18** shows the effects of clear-cutting.

C Growing crops in terraced fields, such as these rice paddies in China, also keeps erosion and runoff to a minimum. Any water that does run off gets caught by the next lower terrace.

Boosting Soil Productivity

Often, farmland needs to be artificially fertilized because crops are harvested and little plant material is left to decay and return needed nutrients to the soil. Artificial measures are necessary to maintain soil productivity, resulting in an increased crop yield.

Fertilizers containing necessary nutrients may be applied on top of the soil or plowed into the ground, **Figure 9-19.** If a certain compound is needed only in small amounts, it can be sprayed directly onto the leaves of the plants.

Soils that contain too much acid are a common problem in many areas. An excessive amount of acid can inhibit crop growth. The acid can be neutralized by applying lime, a neutralizing element, to the soil.

Nitrogen is an extremely important element for plants and all living things because it is a major component of proteins and nucleic acids. Without plants that are able to fix nitrogen in the soil, sufficient amounts for optimal crop growth may not be present. This deficiency can be corrected by applying nitrogen compounds to the soil. Nitrogen can be replenished in the soil by applying organic fertilizers such as cow and chicken manure or human sewage to the soil. These natural fertilizers have been almost completely replaced by chemical ones because of transporta-

Mud-Free Farming?

Muddy, aching knees and weed-stained hands—is that what comes to mind when you imagine gardening? Then you may be meant to work on a hydroponics farm or garden.

Hydroponics

Hydroponics is the art or science of growing plants in a solution of water and nutrients instead of soil. The plants' roots are supported by a substance other than soil, called an aggregate. Many things can serve as the aggregate, but lava rocks or pea gravel are commonly used. Plants rooted in aggregate sit in tubes or trays across which the water-nutrient solution continually flows. Some systems, instead of providing a constant flow of water, have a timer that floods and then drains the aggregate several times a day.

tion problems and the possibility of contamination.

Phosphorus is another important element to living things. It is a major component of cell membranes in all living things. It is most available to plants when it is combined with organic matter, calcium, or magnesium. Although phosphorus is present in some minerals, it is not available to plants unless it is released from the rock by weathering. This can be accomplished by artificially adding certain types of acid to a soil.

Figure 9-19

Big machinery is necessary to apply fertilizers to large fields.

How Plant Needs Are Met

To replace sunlight, hydroponics systems use artificial lights. Fluorescent lights are commonly used as they provide a maximum light spectrum without generating an excessive amount of heat. Nutrients must be bought, measured, finely ground, mixed, and dissolved into the water supply. Nitrogen, phosphorus, and potassium are the basic nutrients for plants, but here even trace elements must be supplied. These include sulfur, iron, manganese, zinc, copper, boron, magnesium, calcium, chlorine, and molybdenum. Hydroponics systems offer a balance of nutrients, and the plant root hairs absorb what the plant needs from the mixture.

Advantages

Using an inert aggregate instead of soil makes weeds, diseases, and harmful insects much easier to eliminate. A well-managed hydroponics system is essentially a closed environment. The workers may even wear surgical gloves to protect the plants.

Hydroponically grown crops mature about 25 percent faster than crops grown in soil because the plants are never stressed. Outdoor crops may wait weeks for rain or endure poor soil, but hydroponically grown plant roots are bathed in nutrient-rich oxygenated water.

Another advantage is space efficiency. An acre of greenhouse space may grow in a year what would take 60 acres to grow outdoors. Remember that hydroponic farming can proceed all year long.

GRAPHING CALCULATOR

Use a graphing calculator to graph $Y = 0.75 \times X$, where Y is the time to maturity for crops grown in soil, and X is the time to maturity for crops grown hydroponically. Use the graph to determine the time to maturity for a hydroponically grown crop if the same crop would take 3.26 months to mature if grown in soil.

Our Dependence on Soil

Soils are an important, necessary part of our lives. It sounds drastic to say that our survival depends on healthy soil, but almost everything we use and consume has its origins in soil. Can you imagine life without blue jeans? The denim fabric from which they are made comes from cotton that grows in soil. Tortilla chips are a favorite snack of many people. The main ingredient of these chips, corn, is grown in soil. Years ago, paper was often hard to come by and students had to do their schoolwork on slate boards with chalk. All of us take for granted our seemingly endless supply of paper. Where does that paper come from? It comes from trees grown in soil. Without soil, we could not grow food and many other resources. Because we are so dependent on soil, management to prevent soil loss and nutrient depletion is crucial.

Figure 9-20

Many products we use and depend on come from resources grown in soil.

A Cotton is one of the most widely produced types of fabric in the world.

C Silviculture is the growing of trees. It includes growing trees to produce lumber for paper products, as well as for food products such as nuts and oranges.

B Through genetics and crossbreeding, corn, like many other crops, can be bred to be disease-, drought- and insect-resistant. This results in large crop harvests.

Figure 9-21

Unless soil conservation techniques are used when this wheat crop is harvested, large expanses of soil could be subject to erosion and soil loss.

The field in **Figure 9-21** shows a healthy crop of wheat. When the crop is harvested, the soil will be completely exposed to wind, rain, and erosion. **Erosion** is the process that moves weathered rock from one place to another. Wind and rain are silent eroders, taking away as much as 1 mm of topsoil with each heavy rain. In the United States alone, wind and water erosion cause croplands to be eroded an estimated 17 tons per hectare per year. Over time, this adds up, and in a few planting seasons, the soil in a field may be unable to support a crop.

As you have read, farmers use techniques such as contour plowing and terracing to help prevent soil loss. Another technique, called minimum tillage, which is the practice of not plowing a field after a crop is harvested, can decrease the rate of erosion by up to 90 percent. By preventing erosion, soil nutrients can be preserved also.

check your UNDERSTANDING

Understanding Concepts
1. Why is terraced farming a good method for maintaining soil productivity?
2. What are some naturally occurring sources for nitrogen to use in farming?
3. Why are farm fields in deforested areas good for only a few seasons?

Skill Review
4. **Separating and Controlling Variables** In an experiment testing how well a particular fertilizer works, which variable, the soil or the fertilizer, would you change and why? For more help, refer to Thinking Critically in the *Skill Handbook.*

Issue:
Organic Farming— Is Natural Better?

Without healthy soil, no living thing on Earth could survive. Therefore, keeping soil viable and productive is an important task. Many acres of farmland are being lost every day as cities and towns increase in size, and new office buildings, residential areas, and shopping malls are constructed. It is vital that efficient use is made of the cultivable land that remains.

The Issue

Modern methods of farming include the application of commercial fertilizers, pesticides, and herbicides. Such products have frequently been misused, resulting in pollution of water, land, air, and food. This has led some people to question whether the benefits gained from the use of these chemicals are worth the risk. Is it possible to maintain healthy, productive soil and adequate supplies of food without using these potentially harmful substances?

Yes, say proponents of organic farming. Organic farming is the raising of crops without the use of chemicals. Instead, natural organic materials such as animal manure, grass clippings, and peat moss are applied to the land. Some claim that these methods improve the condition of the soil, result in higher crop yields, and reduce the amount of environmental pollution.

The Background

During the Dust Bowl years in the early 1930s, large areas of land in the western United States were rendered unfit for farming. This catastrophe focused national attention on the necessity of developing sound practices of soil management and crop production.

Scientists in government, academia, and industry carried out intensive research and developed better ways to manage soils and produce crops. For example, in 1930, the average cornfield in the United States produced 20 bushels per acre. By 1985, the average yield had risen to 118 bushels per acre. Similar increases in production occurred with other crops such as wheat, oats, and cotton.

A major factor responsible for this increase in crop yield was the introduction of commercial fertilizers, which could be tailor-made to meet the specific requirements of a given soil and crop. Another factor was the use of pesticides. The success of these methods led to their widespread acceptance by farmers. Millions of pounds of agricultural chemicals are now dusted, scattered, and sprayed on farmland every

Organically grown produce is available at many markets.

year. Organic farming proponents argue that such practices cause environmental pollution problems and fail to provide the soil with essential organic matter.

Scientists agree that the soil needs more than just inorganic commercial fertilizer; it must be provided with some form of organic material in order to remain healthy. Just how this organic matter should be supplied, however, is a subject for debate. Organic farmers believe that natural organic materials such as peat moss, manure, and grass clippings are best. But there are 383 million acres of cropland in the United States. Finding, collecting, transporting, and applying enough natural organic material to fertilize such a large area is, at present, not feasible. The possibility of using human sewage as fertilizer is being explored, but problems involving odor, heavy metal toxicity, and the potential for spreading disease have hindered its general acceptance.

Conventional farming techniques do return organic matter to the earth. Periodically plowing the plants under instead of harvesting them is a common practice that supplies organic matter and nutrients to the soil. Commercial fertilizers produce large plants with large roots, so the amount of organic material supplied to the soil in this manner can be substantial.

The dangers of environmental pollution by agricultural chemicals can be minimized by using them correctly. Low levels of these substances are sometimes found in fruits and vegetables and in the meat, milk, and eggs of animals who feed on treated crops. The amounts are usually below the levels that many authorities consider to be a health hazard. But some persons don't like the idea of having any amounts of these chemicals, however small, in the soil, water, air, or food.

The issue of organic versus conventional farming practices may not be an either/or proposition. The solution may lie in combining the best and most practical organic farming methods with the intelligent, reasonable use of agricultural chemicals.

The Questions

Growing crops without the use of commercial fertilizers and pesticides certainly reduces the amount of these potentially toxic chemicals in our food and environment. This reason alone is enough for some people to favor organic over conventional farming methods. But there are also limits to organic farming. Organic fertilizers may not replace all the phosphorous and potassium needed by plants. Also, organic methods of returning nitrogen to the soil may not be enough.

But are the amounts of agricultural chemicals in our food and environment high enough to worry about? And is the widespread adoption of organic farming methods really necessary to keep our environment safe and to maintain a healthy, productive soil? Our survival may depend upon arriving at the correct answers to these questions.

*inter*NET
CONNECTION

Are pesticides dangerous to human health? Follow the link for Chapter 8 on the Glencoe Homepage, **http://www.glencoe.com/**, for information about pesticides in foods. Based on information provided at the International Food Information Council on the web and in your textbook, infer what might happen if pesticides were completely banned in the United States.

Recipe for Soil

Just as bread is made of a mixture of flour, water, and yeast, soil is a mixture of minerals, water, air, and organic matter. You can make different breads by changing the amounts of the basic ingredients or by adding others. Soils also vary in the amounts of their basic ingredients and sometimes have extra ingredients. Farmers, gardeners, and landscapers pay attention to the soil composition and adjust the ingredients to help their plants grow the best.

You're the Landscaper

Your school has plans for new athletic fields to be ready for next fall's games. As the landscaper, you need to recommend what adjustments should be made to the soil near your school to make the best soil for growing grass. You will need to choose a variety of grass that's suitable for your climate, and find out what soil conditions are best for that grass. After testing the local soil and experimenting with a couple of new mixtures, you'll be ready to suggest what additives would help make the new grass grow the healthiest.

Drawing on Experience

1. Obtain two plastic trays, a bucket of soil from the area around your school, several sheets of newspaper, and a soil test kit. Soil test kits are available from your local lawn and garden center and test soil pH, nutrient content, and drainage.

2. Examine the soil from your school. What materials can you observe in the soil? Is it sandy, or does it have clumps of clay? Is it wet or dry? Is it packed tightly or loosely?

3. Test the soil with the soil test kit. Record the results.

4. Predict what you should add to the soil to make the grass grow the best.

Testing...Testing

1. Mix your suggested additives into a sample of the school soil. You may want to make several samples, adjusting the amounts of the additives in each sample. Make a recipe for each of the soils you mix. Record what you add and how much of each ingredient you add.

2. Test each of the new soils with the soil test kit.

3. Plant the same amount of grass seed in each sample. As a control, also plant a sample of the school soil with no additives.

4. Place the trays near a window and keep the soil samples moist. Allow the grass to grow for two to three weeks.

How Did It Work?

Compare and contrast the soils you mixed. Which of the soil types encouraged the best plant growth? Based on your results, what soil recipe would you recommend for the athletic fields?

Read the statements below that review major points presented in the chapter. Using the concepts that you have learned, answer each question *in your Journal.*

1 Physical weathering is a major process causing the breakdown of rock into smaller pieces, ultimately forming soil. *How do physical weathering and chemical weathering differ?*

2 A soil profile can show the environment in which the soil formed. *What can you tell about the climate of an area by studying a soil profile?*

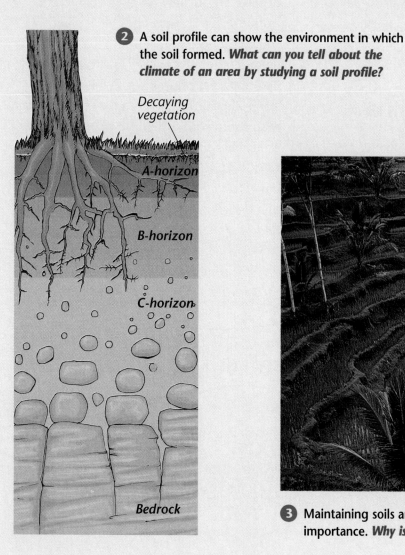

Decaying vegetation

A-horizon

B-horizon

C-horizon

Bedrock

3 Maintaining soils and their productivity is of great economic importance. *Why is it important to keep soils healthy?*

Using Key Science Terms

chemical weathering	physical weathering
erosion	soil
humus	soil profile
ice wedging	topography
parent material	weathering

For each set of terms below, write a sentence that reflects your understanding of both science terms.

1. physical weathering, chemical weathering
2. soil, soil profile
3. organic matter, humus
4. fertilizer, nitrogen
5. soil profile, humus

Understanding Ideas

Using complete sentences, answer the following questions in your Journal.

1. How do animal burrows help in the development of soils?
2. Explain how soil evolves from rock.
3. Why are valleys good places to grow crops?
4. Why does freezing and thawing of water cause rocks to break apart?
5. What factors are key in the development of soils in tropical areas?
6. How do horizons form in a soil?
7. What is the importance of humus in soil?
8. Compare the overall effects of physical weathering versus chemical weathering.
9. Nitrogen, phosphorus, and organic matter, when applied to soil, are known as what?

Developing Skills

Use your understanding of the concepts developed in this chapter to answer each of the following questions.

1. **Predicting** Predict what would happen if you used larger worms in the MiniLab on burrowing organisms. Repeat the MiniLab and compare the results to your original prediction.

2. **Observation and Interpretation** While watching a new road being built in your neighborhood, you notice that the dirt exposed in the new roadbed is different from the dirt in your backyard. What could you determine about the parent material the soils in each area came from?

3. **Concept Mapping** Use the following terms and phrases to complete the concept map about soil formation: *chemical weathering, physical weathering, growth of plant roots, water dissolves minerals, acids break down rock, areas with significant freezing and thawing, areas with high temperatures and rainfall, rain.*

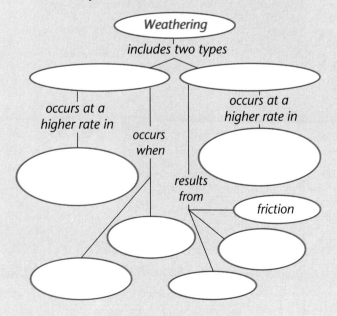

Critical Thinking

In your Journal, *answer each of the following questions.*

1. Explain how a row of trees planted at the edge of a field is a method of soil conservation similar to contour plowing.
2. Explain the relationship between soil productivity and plant growth using tropical rain forests, midwestern forests, and deserts as examples.
3. Explain what President F. D. Roosevelt meant when, in 1937, he said, "A nation that destroys its soils, destroys itself."
4. Think about a soil profile from a temperate, humid area and one from a dry, temperate climate. A major difference exists in the A-horizon of each sample. Why is this so?
5. Why is a combination of techniques, such as crop rotation, minimum tillage, strip cropping, and fertilizing, the best way to manage soil?

Problem Solving

Read the following problem and discuss your answers in a brief paragraph.

The Acme Steel Company is planning to build a new steel plant at one of two locations. Residents of the first location, which is an industrial area, are against the plant, protesting more pollution and waste. Steel mills produce phosphorus-containing slag as a by-product as well as air pollution. The second location for the plant is a farming community. This community would welcome the plant.

Which location would be the best for the plant in terms of the environment? Why?

CONNECTING IDEAS

1. **Theme—Energy** How is the sun's energy part of the soil-formation process?
2. **Theme—Systems and Interactions** France is known worldwide for its wine production. Utilizing what you know about soil types, plant growth, and climate, explain why certain regions of France only produce certain types of wine.
3. **In-Depth Look** What might be some negative aspects of growing plants hydroponically?
4. **Science and Society** Growing plants organically can produce fruits that can look less perfect but taste the same as crops grown with synthetic fertilizers and pesticides. How might this offset the future of organic farming?
5. **Applying Technology** If the soil you tested at the school was clayey, what could you do to improve it for growing grass?

CHAPTER 10

Chemistry of Food

From Field to Table

*F*ood gathering and preparation have always been essential to human survival. In earliest times, people simply ate whatever they could whenever they found it. Later, they learned to cultivate crops and domesticate animals. They found ways to cook and preserve foods. Even so, early peoples were in danger of starvation because of the possibility of crop losses caused by pests or the rotting of stored food. In the last century, great strides have been made in crop production and in food preparation and preservation. Many of the advances are the result of our understanding and utilization of chemicals and chemical processes.

▶ *In the activity on the next page, learn about one method of food preservation.*

How much water is the right amount?

Reducing the water content in food can limit the growth of organisms that cause food to spoil.

Procedure

1. Light a candle that has been placed in a candleholder.

2. Drop a raisin into a test tube.

3. Using a test-tube holder, hold the test tube about 3 cm above the flame. Move the test tube back and forth to evenly heat the raisin and keep it from burning.

4. Continue to heat the raisin in the test tube for 5 to 10 minutes. Carefully blow out the candle.

5. Record your observations *in your Journal.*

Analysis

1. What did you observe on the walls of the top of the test tube? What do you think is the source of this material?

2. Make a hypothesis about why most foods that have been preserved by drying still contain some water.

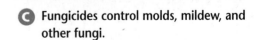

Fighting the Pests

Objectives
- Differentiate among various types of pesticides.
- Compare and contrast the benefits and risks of pesticide use.
- Compare and contrast organic and nonorganic pest-control methods.

Key Terms
pesticide
selective
biological control

Chemical Defenses

"In March of 1982, the majority of milk on Hawaii's most populous island, Oahu, was found to be contaminated with the pesticide heptachlor. Following this discovery, approximately 36 million pounds of milk were removed from the market. The incident frightened consumers, who now live with the uncertainty that their exposure to heptachlor may have future health consequences. It damaged the image of the local dairy industry and resulted in a wide range of cleanup costs, including $8, 551, 515 in indemnity payments made by the federal government to dairy producers for the milk that they had to dump." This quote was the opening statement at a seminar given on *Ethics and the Food System* presented by Michigan State University in May, 1987. Case studies continue as scientists consider the risks and advantages to consumers and the environment of pesticide use.

■ What is a pesticide?

A **pesticide** is a chemical agent that controls or kills a pest. Four major types of pesticides are described in **Figure 10-1.** Each type is designed to be used on a particular pest, called the *target.* The product

Figure 10-1

Pesticides are classified according to the pests they are designed to control. The most common types of pesticides are described here.

Ⓐ Insecticides control insects.

Ⓒ Fungicides control molds, mildew, and other fungi.

Ⓑ Herbicides control weeds or other unwanted plants.

Ⓓ Rodenticides control rodent populations.

that is being protected is called the *host.* For example, if field mice are eating wheat from a field, the mouse is the target, and the wheat is the host.

Some pesticides are **selective,** which means that they are effective only on specific pests. An example of a selective herbicide is one that will kill broadleaf weeds, such as dandelions, but won't harm other plants. Other pesticides are nonselective, and they will affect a large range of pests as well as organisms that are not pests. By law, selectivity must be shown on the label of a pesticide, as shown in **Figure 10-2.**

■ Types of Pesticides

Most pesticides being used now are synthetic-organic pesticides. That means that they are composed of organic materials, but they are made, or synthesized, in a laboratory. Before this type of pesticide came into use, farmers relied on pesticides that occur naturally in plants. Nicotine, which is usually associated with tobacco products, is an example of a pesticide that occurs in nature. Nicotine was extracted from tobacco plants and was used to control populations of insects, such as aphids. These natural pesticides were effective, but they required frequent use because they were unstable, which means that they were active for only a short time. Therefore, they had to be reapplied frequently.

Because so many of the organisms on Earth are insects, many pesticides are insecticides. Insecticides vary in how they affect insects. Some insecticides are stomach poisons, many attack the nervous system, some affect breathing, and some affect the formation of the hard outer covering of the insect.

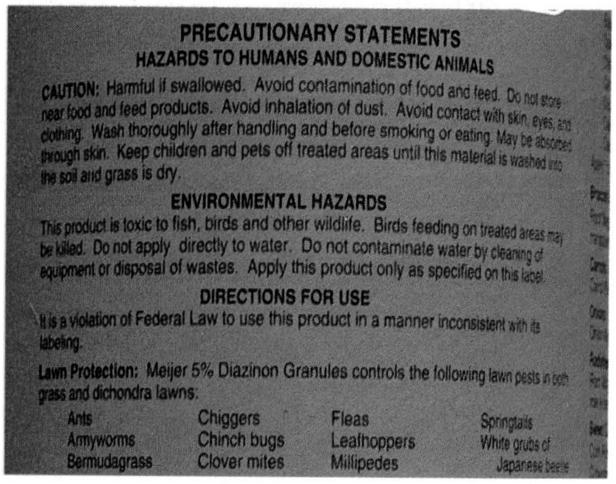

PRECAUTIONARY STATEMENTS
HAZARDS TO HUMANS AND DOMESTIC ANIMALS
CAUTION: Harmful if swallowed. Avoid contamination of food and feed. Do not store near food and feed products. Avoid inhalation of dust. Avoid contact with skin, eyes, and clothing. Wash thoroughly after handling and before smoking or eating. May be absorbed through skin. Keep children and pets off treated areas until this material is washed into the soil and grass is dry.

ENVIRONMENTAL HAZARDS
This product is toxic to fish, birds and other wildlife. Birds feeding on treated areas may be killed. Do not apply directly to water. Do not contaminate water by cleaning of equipment or disposal of wastes. Apply this product only as specified on this label.

DIRECTIONS FOR USE
It is a violation of Federal Law to use this product in a manner inconsistent with its labeling.

Lawn Protection: Meijer 5% Diazinon Granules controls the following lawn pests in both grass and dichondra lawns:

Ants	Chiggers	Fleas	Springtails
Armyworms	Chinch bugs	Leafhoppers	White grubs of
Bermudagrass	Clover mites	Millipedes	Japanese beetle

Figure 10-2

To correctly use any pesticide, the label must first be read and understood thoroughly. Directions for mixing and applying the chemicals are clearly stated. The selectivity of the product is explained, as are any needed safety precautions.

Pesticide Dangers

Each pesticide has at least one method of killing a pest. If pesticides that use the same method are widely used in an area, eventually the pest may become resistant to all pesticides that use that same method of action.

For example, assume that a farmer sprays a crop with the same insecticide for ten years. Each year, only some of the insects are killed by the insecticide. Why aren't all the insects killed? In many cases, these insects were genetically resistant to the insecticide. The chemical did not affect them. These resistant insects reproduced, and the new generations were also genetically resistant to that specific insecticide and other insecticides that use the same method of action.

The development of pesticide resistance is an example of the selection principle of evolution. This process shows how many pesticides, from years of misuse and overuse, have encouraged the evolution of "super bugs" that are resistant to insecticides and "super plants" that are resistant to herbicides. Many of the most commonly used pesticides are now ineffective to some extent because of this increased resistance.

■ Responsible Use of Pesticides

As mentioned earlier in this section, natural organic pesticides are unstable and therefore require frequent use. Look at the chemical structures shown in **Figure 10-3**. The bonds in natural organic pesticides are not as difficult to break as those in synthetic pesticides. Therefore, synthetic pesticides don't break down as easily and are more stable than natural organic pesticides. Is increased stability always a good thing? The following example shows how stability can be a problem when a stable pesticide is introduced into a food chain.

■ Stable Pesticides

In 1945, the synthesized pesticide dichloro-diphenyl-trichloroethane, also called DDT, was used to kill malaria-transmitting mosquitoes in the South Pacific and typhus-transmitting body lice in Europe. The world was provided for the first time with a long-lasting, effective insecticide that killed insects on contact. Because DDT was new and was the first chemical of its type, early use of DDT was not controlled. DDT was overused and misused unknowingly. The following MiniLab will help you find out what can happen when a stable pesticide, such as DDT, is used.

MiniLab

What happens when pesticides are passed along a food chain?

Farmers often treat their crops with pesticides and, as a result, have an increase in yield at harvest. Some chemicals break down quickly after application. Others stay in the environment long after their initial introduction. In this activity, explore how amounts of the chemicals may accumulate in higher-order consumers of a food chain.

Procedure

1. Work with the entire class to complete this activity.

2. Your teacher will pass out the following paper animals to individual members of the class:

    a. one insect to each student.

    b. one frog to each of eight students.

    c. one hawk to each of two students.

3. Each student with a frog must capture and eat at least four insects. Use tape to attach the prey (each insect) to the predator (the frog).

4. Each hawk must now capture and eat at least three frogs. Again, use tape.

Analysis

1. Notice that some of the paper insects have red dots on their bodies. These insects ate wheat that had been sprayed with a stable pesticide. What happens to the total amount of pesticide in the animals' bodies as it proceeds through the food chain?

2. How could a compound that was harmless to plants turn out to be harmful to other organisms?

3. This activity provides a model that shows how pesticides accumulate in organisms. How could the accumulation be stopped?

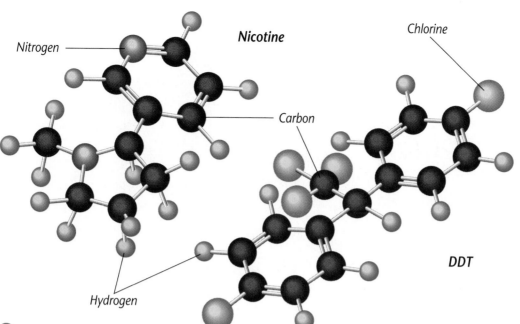

Nitrogen

Nicotine

Chlorine

Carbon

Hydrogen

DDT

Figure 10-3

The chemical structures of organic pesticides differ from those of synthetic-organic pesticides.

A Molecules of naturally-occurring pesticides such as nicotine contain mostly single bonds between the carbon atoms. These bonds are fairly easily broken, making the molecule relatively unstable.

B Molecules of synthetic pesticides such as DDT contain more double and triple bonds between the carbon atoms. Because these bonds are stronger than single bonds, the molecules are more stable and resist breakdown in nature.

Pesticides that are stable, such as DDT, can accumulate in the tissues of the organisms that come in contact with them. Think back to the Hawaiian milk problem on page 294. The milk contamination was traced to pesticides used in Oahu's pineapple fields. The pineapples were infested with mealy bugs. Mealy bugs secrete a substance that ants eat. The presence of the ants protected the mealy bugs from any natural predators. It was thought that if the ants could be eliminated, natural predators would eat the mealy bugs and the pests would be controlled. The pesticides DDT, mirex, and heptachlor—all of which are stable—were used on the fields. Look at the pineapple plant shown in **Figure 10-4.** Heptachlor, in particular, accumulates in the base of the pineapple plants and remains stable for years after its application.

Figure 10-4

A pineapple plant like that shown in the photo can accumulate the insecticide heptachlor in its base.

Figure 10-5

Birds of prey are especially harmed by increasing concentrations of DDT. This compound causes the thinning of the eggshells, which greatly reduces the number of eggs that remain unbroken. Thus, the number of young birds that hatch is reduced.

Connect to...

Biology

Pheromones are substances that may be used to bait insect traps. Find out why pheromones are effective in this role.

The pineapple plants were harvested and used as feed for dairy cattle. After eating the heptachlor-treated pineapple plants, dairy cows produced milk that also contained heptachlor. This substance was then passed to the consumer in dairy products made from this milk.

Just as the red dots were passed along that simple food chain in the MiniLab, heptachlor was passed along the real food chain in Hawaii. Other pesticides can also be passed along the food chains of Earth's ecosystems.

Just because some pesticides have been overused and misused does not mean that pesticide users are irresponsible. When DDT entered the market as the wonder pesticide, little was known about its long-term effects, one of which is explained in **Figure 10-5.** It was easy to apply, readily available, effective, and long-lasting, and it resulted in increased crop yields. It wasn't until many years later that the side effects of using such a stable chemical were understood.

■ Pesticide Regulations

In 1972, DDT was banned in the United States. As of 1978, heptachlor could no longer be used. Pesticide approval and use is now highly regulated by government agencies.

The Food and Drug Administration (FDA) and the U.S. Environmental Protection Agency (EPA) are responsible for the approval of new pesticides. These agencies specify the rate at which the pesticide is to be applied and the number of days before harvest that the use of a pesticide must stop, as shown in **Figure 10-6.** Certain pesticides require extra care to apply; the EPA and FDA certify qualified people to do these applications. Laws also control the labeling of pesticide containers and the disposal of pesticides and their containers. Each new pesticide may take several years to develop and may cost several million dollars from the beginning of its development to its approval. Only one synthetic pesticide is approved out of several thousand that may be developed.

Alternatives

What can be done to make pesticide use safer for consumers and the environment without greatly limiting our food supply? In recent years, some food producers have used pest management that is called *integrated pest control* (IPC). IPC uses several different tactics at the same time in controlling pests.

Some practices used in IPC involve methods of planting. Examine the fields shown in **Figure 10-7**. When fields are plowed, unwanted plants and weeds have ready access to water and nutrients in the soil. No-till planting, in which seeds are planted on unbroken soil, requires less herbicide. Certain insects prefer to eat certain crops, and a percentage of the insect population remains in the field after the crop is harvested. Rotating crops, so that the same crop is not grown in the same field each year, reduces the need for insecticides. As you learned in Chapter 7, crop rotation can also increase the amount of usable nitrogen present in the soil. This increased nitrogen reduces the need for chemical fertilizers, which may promote the growth of pest populations.

Other methods involve making wise decisions about when or whether to use a pesticide. There is close monitoring of pest populations. The pest is controlled only when its population rises to a certain level. Sometimes the economic and environmental cost of applying a pesticide is greater than the cost of lost produce if the pest population is small.

In IPC, if it is shown that a pesticide is needed, several different pesticides may be used all at once. Each pesticide used operates by a different method so the chance that a pest develops resistance is lessened.

■ Biological Controls

Plants that have a genetic resistance to certain pests may be planted instead of plants that have no resistance. Other **biological controls** include the use of

Figure 10-6

Farmers may safely harvest crops only after carefully tracking the number of days since the application of pesticides. Information on the label of the pesticide container indicates how long it takes for the chemicals to break down into harmless residues.

Figure 10-7

Crops may be planted on untilled land or on tilled (plowed) land.

Ⓐ No-till planting requires less herbicide.

Ⓑ Planting in plowed fields requires more herbicide.

Figure 10-8

Many different organisms can serve as biological controls.

A Frogs and ladybird beetles are two examples of biological controls. Both of these animals eat destructive pests.

B Certain plants can be biological controls. For example, the scent of a marigold plant and a chemical produced by its roots will help keep insects away from vegetable plants that are growing near the marigold plant.

living organisms, such as predators, parasites, and microbes, or their products, to control pests. Care should be taken when introducing a biological control. If the food supply is plentiful and natural predators are few, the control itself may become a pest. Examples of currently available biological controls are shown in **Figure 10-8.**

One alternative to existing pesticides is *insecticidal soap.* It kills an insect on contact and does not actually enter the insect, so resistance does not develop. It is biodegradable, does not accumulate in other organisms in the food chain, and can be safely used on crops up to the time of harvest. Unfortunately, insecticidal soap is selective and is not effective on all insects.

Why not ban pesticides altogether? The answer is simple—pesticides are important. As you have seen, agricultural pests damage crops in many ways. They may eat the actual plant or the produce from the plant. Weeds use water and nutrients that are needed by crops. Many studies have been made that compare the risks associated with using pesticides and the risks associated with not destroying the pest. Few clear-cut answers have been found.

---

check your UNDERSTANDING

Understanding Concepts

1. If you were debating the benefits and risks of pesticide use, explain why all pesticides should not be banned.

2. Your tomato plants are covered with a white mold. What class of pesticide would eliminate the problem?

3. Organic farming involves methods that use no synthetic fertilizers or pesticides. For crops to be considered organically grown, what IPC farming techniques are followed?

Skill Review

4. **Cause and Effect** How can pesticides be present in a mountain stream? For more help, refer to Cause and Effect in the *Skill Handbook.*

10-2 ▸ Food Preservation

Freshness Counts

Have you ever opened a container of food and been surprised to find that its contents had an unusual color, odor, or appearance? Changes in the food may signal that bacteria or oxygen have begun to act on the food and it has begun to spoil. Some foods, such as potatoes, retain their freshness for weeks or months. Others, such as meats, can show signs of spoilage within a few hours.

Figure 10-9

Several methods are commonly used to preserve food.

■ Keeping It Fresh

Food spoilage is not a new problem. In earliest times, people hunted and gathered food and ate it whenever it was found. There were no ways of preserving food—keeping it fresh for later use. As a result, excess food spoiled, and when food was scarce, starvation was a problem.

People began to respond to the need for having food available when it was difficult to acquire. They began to develop ways of obtaining more food than was immediately needed and preserving it to use later. Crops were cultivated, and animals were domesticated. Excess pro-

Objectives

- Classify chemical preservatives as inhibitors or antioxidants.
- Explain the process and purpose of pasteurization.

Key Terms
antioxidant
Delaney Clause
inhibitor
pasteurized

A Bacterial growth is greatly restricted in frozen food because the temperature is too low.

B Water can promote bacterial growth. Drying foods removes the water.

C Canning foods destroys bacteria in the food and protects food from oxygen in the air.

One Rotten Apple
Carefully slice an apple into small pieces. Put one piece in each of three small bowls. Leave the first piece exposed to the air. Cover the second apple piece with water. Cover the third piece with a solution made from a dissolved vitamin C tablet and water. After 20 minutes, observe the apple pieces. What changes occurred in the apple pieces? What evidence do you have that something in air caused the change? How can the change be prevented?

duce and animal products were preserved by methods that included adequate cooking of food, drying it, or keeping it cool by placing it underground or in cool water. Some food still spoiled, but it could be kept for a longer period of time before it lost its freshness.

■ New Methods

As time passed, new methods of preservation were developed and those in use were improved. Examine **Figure 10-9** on page 301. Cooking methods became easier and safer. Refrigerators and freezers replaced root cellars and cold springs. Safe canning methods were perfected.

These methods are used not only in homes, but also by industries specializing in preserving food and selling it to others. How much of your own food do you raise and preserve yourself? Most people buy at least some of their food from these industries.

If you purchase food from a store, how can you know if the food is really

fresh? Labels often have expiration dates printed on them. Some labels display *sell-by* instructions. Others display *use-by* information. Which type of information might be more useful to the consumer?

Just as pesticides are applied to crops in the fields for protection, other chemicals are sometimes applied to foods during processing to prevent them from spoiling. Complete the Try It activity to find out what role oxygen plays in the spoiling of some foods.

■ The Role of Oxygen

Remember from Chapter 7 that oxygen is able to chemically bond with many other substances. For example, oxygen from the air combines with iron to form rust. Oxygen is part of the chemical reaction that occurs in fire. It is also an important part of cellular respiration and other chemical reactions that occur within your body.

But oxygen is capable of causing some unwanted reactions in the food you eat. The apple in the first bowl chemically changed when it was exposed to the oxygen in the air in the Try It activity. This change is an example of how reacting with oxygen causes changes in certain foods. Other foods, such as dairy products and those with fats, are also susceptible to oxidation.

■ Food Additives

Because it is not always possible to seal food away from the air, chemicals that prevent reactions with oxygen may be added to the food. Compounds that prevent or slow down reactions with oxygen are **antioxidants.** Find the letters BHT and BHA on the pizza label in

Figure 10-10

BHT and BHA are added to cereal, crackers, and other foods to retard spoilage.

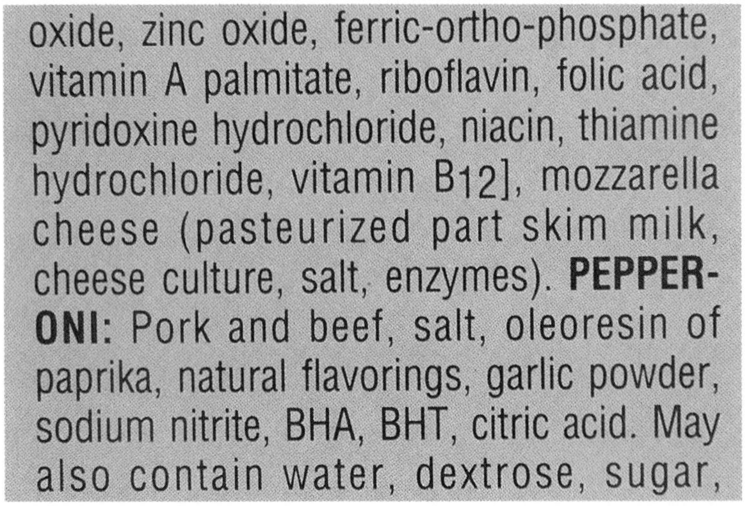

oxide, zinc oxide, ferric-ortho-phosphate, vitamin A palmitate, riboflavin, folic acid, pyridoxine hydrochloride, niacin, thiamine hydrochloride, vitamin B12], mozzarella cheese (pasteurized part skim milk, cheese culture, salt, enzymes). **PEPPERONI:** Pork and beef, salt, oleoresin of paprika, natural flavorings, garlic powder, sodium nitrite, BHA, BHT, citric acid. May also contain water, dextrose, sugar,

Contains inhibitor

Contains no inhibitor

Contains inhibitor

Contains no inhibitor

Figure 10-11

Foods such as salsa and cheese may eventually spoil after being opened even when they contain inhibitors, but the spoilage will be less.

Figure 10-10. These chemical preservatives are antioxidants that are added to food to slow down spoilage.

Antioxidants are not the only chemicals added to foods. Foods processed in the United States are subject to federal regulation under a law known as the **Delaney Clause.** Enacted in 1958, this addition to the Food, Drug, and Cosmetics Act closely regulates the use of chemicals in food processing. No chemical that has been shown to cause cancer may be used in the processing of food.

While the number of substances that must be tested under the Delaney Clause is large, some chemicals are considered to be safe and are exempted from further testing. Chemicals such as salt, sugar, certain vitamins, and other ingredients that have shown no ill effects over several years are added to the GRAS list. *GRAS* stands for "Generally Regarded as Safe."

■ Inhibitors

Inhibitors are common food additives. Substances such as BHT and BHA that slow down a chemical process are called **inhibitors.** Inhibitors are not limited to antioxidants. Have you ever opened a loaf of bread or a package of cheese and found mold? Mold inhibitors are sometimes added to these foods to preserve freshness. Even though an inhibitor slows a process, it may not entirely prevent it, as shown in **Figure 10-11.** Bread containing an inhibitor, for example, may mold, but it will not mold as quickly as bread that contains no inhibitor, assuming conditions are the same for both. Do the following Investigation to test for the presence of the mold inhibitor calcium propionate.

INVESTIGATION

Testing for Preservatives

Most of the bread sold in stores contains some form of preservative. One type of preservative is calcium propionate, which is used to retard the growth of mold. Small amounts of this preservative are considered safe for humans to ingest. In this Investigation, you will test a variety of breads for the presence of this preservative.

Preparation

Problem

How can you determine the presence of calcium propionate, a preservative, in breads?

Objectives

In this Investigation, you will:
- *Analyze* bread samples for the presence of calcium propionate.
- *Infer* which breads will stay fresher longer.

Data and Observations

Sample	Odor present or not
1	
2	
3	
4	
5	

Materials

3 to 5 samples from different types or brands of bread
hot plate
beaker, 400-mL
beaker, 600-mL
ethyl alcohol
small beakers (3 to 5)
wire gauze
large test tubes (3 to 5)
6*M* sulfuric acid, H_2SO_4
thermometer
10-mL graduated cylinder

Safety Precautions

Do not allow flammable alcohol or reaction products to come in contact with an open flame.

Use care when working with sulfuric acid so it does not come into contact with eyes, skin, or clothes.

Be sure to clean your work area and dispose of the materials as directed by your teacher.

INVESTIGATION

Procedure

1 *In your Journal,* make a copy of the data table shown.

2 Break up one sample of bread into several pieces and put them in a 400-mL beaker. Label this beaker *Sample 1.*

3 Add enough water to cover the bread. Using a hot plate, heat the contents until warm.

4 Leaving the bread particles behind, transfer 10 mL of solution from the beaker to a test tube.

5 Carefully add 3 mL of $6M$ H_2SO_4 to the solution in the test tube.

6 Add 5 mL of ethyl alcohol to the solution in the test tube. Using a hot water bath and the hot plate, warm the contents to just under the boiling point.

7 Use your hand to fan the vapors coming from the test tube toward your nose. **CAUTION:** *Do not inhale directly from the test tube.* A familiar, sweet smell indicates the presence of calcium propionate. Record any odor you smell.

8 Repeat steps 2 to 7 with the other samples, numbering each beaker with the appropriate sample number.

Step 3

Step 7

Analyze and Conclude

1. Observing and Inferring
What characteristic odor was present? Based on your observations, which breads contain calcium propionate?

2. Analyzing Why was the bread first soaked in water?

3. Recognizing Cause and Effect
Why do you think the solution in the test tube was not allowed to boil?

Going Further

Thinking Critically
Read the ingredients of the breads. Explain why testing for the presence of calcium is not sufficient to determine the presence of calcium propionate.

Spoiled Milk

As you discovered in the Investigation, any calcium propionate present in bread can be chemically changed to a substance that has a pleasant, fruity odor. But not all chemical changes are indicated by pleasant odors.

One of the most unpleasant characteristics of spoiled milk is its odor. The rancid odor results from the breakdown of long fat molecules into smaller fatty acids that evaporate into the air around the milk. Bacteria and enzymes in the milk, and to some extent exposure to sunlight, can bring about these undesirable changes.

Another characteristic of spoiled milk is its lumpy consistency. As shown in **Figure 10-12,** an increase in bacterial activity causes a rise in the milk's acidity level. Recall that a numerical scale, called the *pH scale,* is used to determine the acidity level of a solution. A pH reading below 7 indicates an acid. A reading above 7 indicates that the solution is alkaline or basic. If the pH is 7, the solution is neutral.

Sometimes people find ways to make undesirable changes become desirable ones. The production of yogurt is one example. As you complete the Thinking Lab, consider how factors involved in the spoilage of milk are utilized to produce yogurt.

Thinking Lab — Using Variables

What affects the thickness of yogurt?

Yogurt is made by adding certain bacteria to milk. The bacteria change milk sugar into lactic acid. The lactic acid then uncoils proteins in milk. Once uncoiled, the proteins interact with each other to form large clumps, increasing the overall thickness of the yogurt.

Analysis
The amount of clumping can be increased by adding an ingredient or removing all or part of an ingredient.

Thinking Critically
How could you increase the amount of clumping without changing the kind or amount of milk in the original recipe? The thickness of yogurt is determined by the ratio of clumps to water. What could you do to the milk before adding the bacteria to result in more clumps per unit of water?

■ Retarding the Spoilage
Preventing milk from spoiling was less of a problem when most people lived on farms or near herds of cows. Fresh milk could be obtained simply by milking a cow. When most people began living far from the dairy herds, they found a way to slow down bacterial activity in milk and thus slow its spoiling.

Figure 10-12

Low pH levels are associated with spoiled milk.

A Acids form as bacteria digest carbohydrates found in milk. The acids cause milk proteins to coagulate, which means to clump.

B Indicators change colors in relation to the acid level of a solution. Notice that the color of the left side of the indicator paper by the spoiled milk is a slightly darker orange. Compare the pH levels of fresh milk and spoiled milk.

The next time you have milk for lunch, read the label on its carton. You will likely notice that the term *pasteurized* is used. Milk that has been **pasteurized** has been treated with high temperatures to retard spoilage and prolong its shelf life.

Increased temperature is one way the body kills disease-causing bacteria or viruses, as when fevers accompany some illnesses. In the 1800s, the French scientist Louis Pasteur discovered the effects of heat on bacteria. During pasteurization, milk is heated to 62°C for 30 minutes. Almost all of the bacteria are killed, and several enzymes that react with the fat molecules in milk are also destroyed.

A newer, improved process of pasteurization called Ultra High Temperature, or UHT, raises the milk temperature to 138°C for 1 second. This process destroys more bacteria than regular pasteurization does. Although the newer UHT process raises the temperature above the boiling point, the short amount of time involved does not cause the milk to clump.

check your UNDERSTANDING

Understanding Concepts

1. A substance that stops a chemical reaction with oxygen has been added to your meat marinade. Is this substance most likely classified as an antioxidant or an inhibitor?

2. The pH of fresh milk is approximately 6.5. If the milk began to spoil, would you see the pH value rise or drop? Would this indicate an increase or decrease in acidity level?

3. Zinc propionate is used as a preservative on medical bandaging. If zinc propionate is similar to calcium propionate, what type of organism does it inhibit?

Skill Review

4. **Recognizing Cause and Effect** Explain why pasteurization requires relatively high temperatures.

Y ou are probably used to seeing logos on cars, letterheads, and packaged products. Logos serve to advertise the company responsible for the product. Most people pay little attention to one logo that has been appearing at the supermarket. Look at the figure on the next page. It looks like a flower in a broken circle and is accompanied by a label reading "Treated with irradiation." It appears on some packages of strawberries and certain other foods.

The Issue

The Food and Drug Administration (FDA) approved the use of irradiation to treat wheat in 1963. Later, the FDA gave its approval for irradiating spices (1983), pork (1985), fruits and vegetables (1986), and poultry (1990). The World Health Organization and more than 30 countries around the world have also approved the use of irradiation as a means of lessening food spoilage.

Some people, however, fear that irradiation leaves radioactive material in foods. This fear seems to be without scientific foundation. Just as dental X rays do not make parts of your body radioactive, neither does irradiation make food radioactive. For that to happen, you'd need radiation three times more energetic than the radiation that is actually used.

Critics of irradiation point out that when rays pass through tissues, they create free radicals, which are chemicals that can damage cells and sometimes form carcinogens. However, according to scientists at the FDA, compared with the changes in foods caused by canning, broiling, and ordinary cooking, changes caused by irradiation are small. Foods irradiated under conditions approved by the FDA are considered to be safe, nutritious, and tasty, according to the American Council on Science and Health. Irradiation delays ripening and controls bacteria, parasites, and insects that spoil food or harm people. Look at the photo on this page, and notice the difference in the irradiated strawberries and those that weren't irradiated.

The Background

Food irradiation uses high-energy electrons or electromagnetic waves in the form of gamma rays, ultraviolet rays, or X rays. When these high-energy particles or rays penetrate matter, they ionize it. The resulting electrically charged atoms, or ions, combine to form new chemical compounds. Subjecting bacteria and other living cells to ionizing radiation disrupts their normal chemical activity and often kills them.

Strawberries picked at the same time

Irradiated   *Not irradiated*

In an example of how the irradiation process operates, meat packers in Florida irradiate poultry with gamma rays, using the radioisotope cobalt-60 as the source of radiation.

Food to be irradiated is mounted on a carrier that moves slowly around the cobalt-60, exposing one side and then another to radiation. Controlled doses of gamma rays can be used to ionize atoms in important molecules in bacteria. When the atoms lose electrons, the way they bond to other atoms changes. These changes in bonding can also change the function of certain molecules, which could kill the bacteria.

The length of time a food carrier stays in the irradiation cell depends on the kind of food to be irradiated. Frozen chicken may take 20 minutes to be irradiated. Berries, on the other hand, take about eight minutes. At the end of those time periods, the unwanted organisms present in the foods usually have been destroyed. Irradiation does not kill all spores or break down all toxins. Heat is required to achieve these goals.

When it is not in use, the cobalt-60 rests in a tank of water 8.5 m deep that is lined with stainless steel and surrounded by a thick concrete slab. The cobalt-60 is 3.0 m below the surface of the water, which acts as a protective shield to block the gamma rays from entering the room.

The Question

If irradiation does such a good job of destroying bacteria, parasites, and insects, what does it do to the food itself? Experts at the University of California have done studies that prove that one problem with irradiation is that it can cause multiple vitamin losses, particularly of vitamins C and A, beta carotene, and the B vitamins. However, other experts point out that regular cooking has similar effects on water-soluble vitamins.

Irradiation symbol

Salmonella bacteria cause 10 million cases of food poisoning and 9000 deaths in the United States every year. Irradiation can eradicate this kind of food poisoning. However, a different approach is being tried in Sweden. Instead of using irradiation to prevent food poisoning, they eliminate contaminants in chicken feed, get rid of rats on chicken farms, and enforce stricter cleanliness standards at food-processing plants.

In this country, Maine and New York have outlawed the sale of irradiated food. And some companies have said that they will not use irradiated foods in their products. What do you think? Would you eat irradiated food? Is food irradiation safe? Is it necessary?

Discussing the Issue

1. *Research* why some states have prohibited the sale of irradiated foods.
2. Irradiation extends the shelf life of fruits and vegetables by a week or two. Higher doses kill most disease-causing microorganisms in poultry. Still larger doses sterilize foods, extending their shelf life for years. *Infer* how irradiation on a larger scale might affect the food industry.

Preparing for Dinner

10-3

Objectives
- Recognize the effects of heat on food.
- Compare and contrast methods of heating food.

Key Terms
denaturation

Cooking—Causing Chemical Changes

For some people, a breakfast with scrambled eggs is a delicious way to start the day. Think about how desirable that meal would be if the eggs were not cooked. A comparison of cooked and raw eggs sums up three reasons food is usually cooked: safety, texture, and taste. Raw eggs may carry *Salmonella* bacteria, a dangerous pathogen. The slippery texture and bland taste of raw eggs usually are not appealing. When we add heat to food, chemical bonds are broken and new ones are formed. The rate of molecular movement within the food increases, and liquid water in the cells changes to a gas. A good example of changes occurring when food cooks happens when popcorn is popped. Use the MiniLab to help you find out how this happens.

MiniLab

How does popcorn pop?

Commercial popcorn producers spend much time and money trying to find varieties of corn that produce large, fluffy, delicious-tasting popcorn. Popcorn pops when liquid water in the kernel rapidly expands as it changes into a gas. In this activity, explore what happens if the water within the kernel has more room to expand.

Procedure

1. Place one kernel of popcorn into a test tube.

2. Carefully pierce the shell of a second kernel with a pin. Place this kernel into a second test tube. Put a cotton ball in the top of each tube.

3. Carefully position each tube near the flame of a laboratory burner. Observe what happens.

Analysis

1. What difference did you notice about the popping?

2. Did creating a small opening in the shell make a difference? Explain.

■ Changing Appearance

Not only the taste and texture of the popcorn in the MiniLab changed. The appearance also changed. Observe the change in appearance of the peas shown in **Figure 10-13** after they have been cooked. Part of the change is due to the evaporation of water within the peas, and part is due to a chemical reaction in the chlorophyll molecules.

Figure 10-13

Food colors usually change during cooking.

A The green color of chlorophyll is dulled when trapped air sticks to plant cells. The gases diffuse light and make the color less intense. Heat drives away the trapped gas from between the cells, revealing a more intense green color.

B Prolonged cooking, however, causes chlorophyll to decompose. Heat releases acids from the cell walls, resulting in a loss of the element magnesium from the chlorophyll molecules. This chemical change brings about the loss of the intense green color.

■ Losing Nutrients

Just as the disruption of cell walls causes a color change in cooked vegetables, it also causes a loss of vitamins. Vitamins are organic compounds that are essential for good health. Humans get many of their vitamins from food. Nine of the 13 essential vitamins are water-soluble. When cooked in water, the water-soluble vitamins dissolve out of the food into the water, as shown in **Figure 10-14.** Thus, the food's nutritional values are diminished.

■ Producing a Gas

Baking bread involves some important chemical reactions. In Chapters 7 and 8, you learned about the chemical structures of foods and the way glucose and other sugars are converted to useful substances. When water is added to flour to make dough, carbohydrates soften and protein strands stick together to form gluten. Yeast and sugar are added to the dough. Carbon dioxide, which is released as the yeast converts the sugar into ethanol, causes the dough to rise, resulting in a light, porous product.

A Vitamin C, found in broccoli, is an example of a water-soluble vitamin. It will dissolve out of food into cooking water.

B Carrots are rich in vitamin A. Vitamin A is fat-soluble and does not dissolve out of foods during the cooking process.

Figure 10-14

Some vitamins are water-soluble and some are fat-soluble.

■ Altering Proteins

The changes discussed so far involve foods from plants. Meat also changes in color and texture when it is cooked. Most changes in meat occur because of changes in protein structure.

Choosing meat for a cookout may mean buying ground beef for hamburgers. You try to choose a fresh package containing beef with a bright red color. But what happens to that red color as the hamburgers cook? One kind of protein in the beef contains iron. The iron is also attached to molecules of oxygen. At high temperatures, an iron atom loses an electron and can no longer hold onto the oxygen. As the iron and oxygen separate, the meat's color changes from red to light brown.

Heat also causes a change in the texture of meat. Cooked meat is more firm and less spongy than raw meat. Remember from Chapter 7 that some proteins are made of long, coiled amino acid chains. Heating causes the amino acid chains in proteins to uncoil in a process called **denaturation.** The long chains then begin to attach to each other. As a result, water is forced out of the meat and its color changes. **Figure 10-15** shows what happens when the protein in an egg is denatured.

Meat texture can be changed another way by cooking. Meat contains a fibrous protein that strengthens connective tissues. Gently pinch the skin on the back of your hand. The skin does not tear apart because of these protein

Serving Up Good Health

Losing a job or surviving the destruction of your home by a natural disaster usually makes people worry about how they will maintain a warm place to live. A second concern for many is often how to feed the family. Major stresses such as these have been shown to impact health in a negative way, so finding a reliable source of healthful food becomes important.

In many large cities, community organizations have ongoing programs in the form of soup kitchens where people can go to obtain regular meals. The meals are free and enable people who eat there to maintain health. Many of these kitchens are staffed by volunteers as shown in the photograph.

Sophomore Service

High school student Lela Ostrander volunteers two Saturdays a month at

Figure 10-15

Proteins in a raw egg maintain their natural shapes. As the temperature rises, the proteins lose their shapes. The uncoiled chains attach to each other and cause clumps to appear. The egg white turns opaque.

fibers. Similar fibers are present in meats. Long, slow cooking softens and breaks down this protein and makes tough meats more tender.

Temperature plays an important role in the proper preparation of food. In the Investigation on pages 314-315, you will have the opportunity to evaluate the role of temperature in the preparation of one kind of food.

Community Kitchen. The kitchen is a program in her hometown that provides food, clothing, and other kinds of help for anyone who needs it.

As a volunteer, 15-year-old Lela is the service coordinator for her class at school. Every other Saturday, she organizes a team of four students to work at the kitchen.

"Almost everyone who comes in looks ordinary," Lela says. "There are tons of families with adorable kids. Some of them have homes and I guess some don't. I have often wondered why they come to the kitchen, but they don't talk about it, and I don't ask." Lela does know, however, that the nutritious food served at the kitchen makes a difference in the health of the people who come, especially the children.

Supplying Nutrients

During the week, the kitchen serves lunch to about 65 to 70 people. Much of the food is donated by local supermarkets once an expiration date has been reached. Although stores cannot sell food after a certain date, the food still contains the nutrients to keep people healthy. Lunch almost always includes a salad, "and desserts," Lela says—"The kids like desserts best." The cooks do not use many prepared foods or mixes, and many of the vegetables are fresh. Lela reports that she is "getting really good at peeling potatoes."

Lela plans to continue volunteering because she enjoys helping people. She says, "I'm getting paid better for this than if I were getting money."

Thinking Critically

1. *Explain* why you think stress can cause health problems.
2. *Research* community kitchens in your area. Find out whether they have a volunteer or staff member who plans and supervises the nutritional value of meals.

DESIGN YOUR OWN INVESTIGATION

How sensitive are enzymes to temperature?

Cheese making depends on enzymes to control the production of curds (coagulated proteins) and their separation from the liquid whey. Acid-producing bacteria are also needed for the cheese-making process to work. Some warming of the materials may be necessary to help the bacteria reproduce and produce acid. In this Investigation, you will determine how temperature affects the cheese-making process.

Preparation

Problem

How does temperature affect the production of cheese?

Hypothesis

Have your group agree on a testable hypothesis about how temperature affects the enzyme used in the production of curds.

Objectives

In this Investigation, you will:
- *Compare* the effectiveness of the enzyme rennet at various temperatures.
- *Observe* the production of curds and whey.

Possible Materials

hot plate
buttermilk
graduated cylinder, 100-mL
filter paper
beaker, 400-mL
whole milk (with buttermilk added)
rennet
funnel
thermometer
balance

Safety Precautions

Use care when working around heated materials. Wash your hands with soap after completing the Investigation.

Plan the Experiment

1 Examine the materials provided. As a group, design ways to test the hypothesis. Try to keep the actual cheese-producing time to 15 minutes.

2 Decide on one way to test the hypothesis. Make sure the experiment allows for the collection of quantitative data.

3 Prepare a list of materials and numbered steps. Design a data table that will allow you to record your findings.

Check the Plan

Discuss the following points with other group members to decide the final procedure for your experiment.

1 What will the control be and what are the variables?

2 Determine how much rennet will be used per 100 mL of milk.

3 Determine how many temperature variations will be tested.

4 Decide how you will determine which temperature presented the best results.

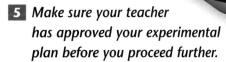

5 *Make sure your teacher has approved your experimental plan before you proceed further.*

6 Carry out your Investigation. Record the data in the data table.

7 Clean up your laboratory area and dispose of wastes according to your teacher's directions.

Analyze and Conclude

1. Inferring Why might it be best to allow the curds, or cheese, to dry overnight before determining mass?

2. Comparing and Contrasting After 15 minutes, which temperature resulted in the most cheese?

3. Drawing Conclusions What happens to the enzyme if the temperature gets too high?

Going Further

Project
Find a recipe for cheese and make some. Research cheese making to find out how aging affects cheese.

Methods of Cooking

In the Investigation, you found out that proper temperature is important for some types of food preparation. The enzyme rennin, contained in the rennet, caused the milk to clump according to the temperature used. Cooking also depends on temperature.

■ Conventional Cooking

Today's modern kitchen, shown in **Figure 10-16,** may use a variety of ways to cook foods. Stoves, conventional ovens, and grills are commonly found in the same cooking area. One characteristic of each of these cooking appliances is that they transfer energy in the form of heat to the surface of the food. Through conduction, the heat is then transferred, molecule by molecule, to the inside of the food, and it gradually cooks.

Sometimes, special cooking thermometers are inserted into the food being cooked and are used to measure the internal temperature of the food. For meats and other foods that must be completely cooked for safety or taste, the internal temperature indicates when the food is cooked on the inside.

■ Pressure Cooking

It is often difficult to use a stove, oven, or grill to reach the temperatures needed to kill microorganisms. These temperatures are especially important during processing of some non-acidic, home-canned products, such as green beans or pumpkin. Pressure cooking can achieve these needed temperatures.

In pressure cooking, water and the food to be cooked are placed in a specially designed cooker that can be sealed. You may remember from previous science courses that pressure, temperature, and volume depend on each other in relation to gases. In a pressure cooker, the volume of the air and water vapor it contains stays the same because the container is sealed. Thus, as the temperature increases, so does the pressure. With increased pressure, temperatures considerably higher than those achieved by using a stove or oven can be reached. Food cooks faster and at a higher temperature.

Figure 10-16

Modern cooking appliances can carefully control the amount of heat used to cook foods. Foods are less likely to be undercooked or overcooked.

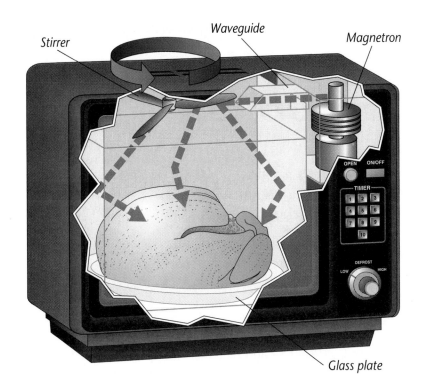

Stirrer

Waveguide

Magnetron

Glass plate

Figure 10-17

Within a microwave oven, microwaves that are produced by a magnetron bounce off the metal sides and into the food. Within the food, they cause molecules of water to vibrate. Other types of molecules, such as those found in some plastics and glass, do not vibrate, so dishes stay cool.

■ Microwave Cooking

Inside a microwave oven, shown in **Figure 10-17,** a pattern of invisible electromagnetic waves penetrates the food and causes the water molecules in the food to vibrate. As these molecules vibrate and bump into each other, friction causes heat to be generated and the food begins to cook from the inside out.

If you have used a microwave oven, you may have stopped the oven and rotated the food, or you may have used a turntable. One reason this process is needed is because microwaves, like other waves, can interfere with each other. One type of interference occurs when the same parts of different waves overlap. This type of interference increases the height of the wave and causes hot spots in the microwave oven. If wave parts cancel each other, interference causes cold spots in the oven.

Whatever cooking method you use, controlling temperature is a critical factor. Undercooking may not kill bacteria that cause illness or spoil food. Overcooking can burn food and destroy its nutritional value and its appeal.

check your UNDERSTANDING

Understanding Concepts

1. Explain how heat causes the clumping of protein fibers in cooked meat.
2. How can cooking vegetables too long in water decrease their nutritional value?
3. Why does it take several hours to cook a large turkey in a conventional oven?

Skill Review

4. **Sequencing** Describe and explain the color changes that occur as a raw green bean is overcooked. For more help, refer to Sequencing in the *Skill Handbook.*

APPLYING TECHNOLOGY

Solar Cooker

Depending on the climate where you live, you might rely on a heating system at some time during the year. All heating systems have a source of heat, such as fuel or electricity. Due to the limited supply of fossil fuels, solar energy is becoming a more and more attractive source of heat.

You're the Engineer

Imagine you live in a desert community and, in order to capitalize on the supply of sunshine in your geographic region, you are designing an outdoor solar cooker. Your job is to design a solar cooker to cook a hot dog without the use of fuels.

Drawing on Experience

1. Obtain a posterboard strip 30 cm × 100 cm from your teacher.

2. Cut aluminum foil to fit the posterboard and glue the two together.

3. Bend the board into an arc (like a parabola) so that the ends of the board are nearly parallel to one another.

4. Hold the board in this shape with string stretched between its corners.

5. Use wire coat hangers to make a mount that will hold the board with its arc pointed directly at the sun.

6. Use another wire hanger to construct a device to hold the hot dog. Position the hot dog at what you think will be the hottest region within the arc.

Testing...Testing

1. Move your solar cooking device to the outdoors, in an open area.

2. Position the cardboard to the sun and cook a hot dog or similar food item.

How Did It Work?

1. What area of the arc was most effective in heating the food? Why was it hot?

2. How quickly were you able to heat your food using the solar cooker?

*inter*NET CONNECTION

Visit the Glencoe Homepage for the Chapter 10 link to the Florida Solar Energy Center. List some applications of solar-powered technology. How might solar power be used in times of disaster? How might it be used to aid developing countries?

This large solar mirror in France operates on the same principles as your solar cooker uses.

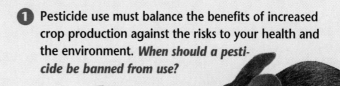
Read the statements at the right and below that review major points presented in the chapter. Using the concepts that you have learned, answer each question *in your Journal.*

1 Pesticide use must balance the benefits of increased crop production against the risks to your health and the environment. *When should a pesticide be banned from use?*

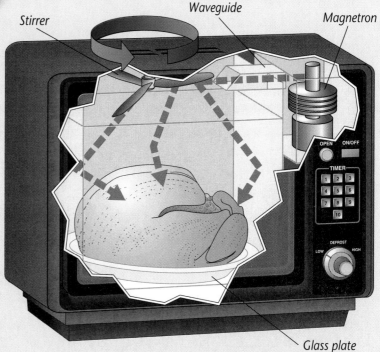

2 Certain chemicals or processes are used to prevent food from spoiling before it can be consumed. *How does irradiation preserve food?*

Stirrer

Waveguide

Magnetron

OPEN   ON/OFF

TIMER

DEFROST
LOW   HIGH

Glass plate

3 Cooking causes chemical reactions that change the appearance, texture, and nutritional value of foods. *Why should many foods be cooked before being eaten?*

Using Key Science Terms

antioxidant   inhibitor

biological control   pasteurized

Delaney Clause   pesticide

denaturation   selective

Answer the following questions about science terms used in this chapter.

1. Which of the terms applies to a chemical that is used to rid crops of insects, weeds, or rodents?
2. To what type of food does the Delaney Clause apply?
3. How does the denaturation of proteins affect the color of cooked meat?
4. How are biological controls used in farming?
5. What is the main benefit of milk pasteurization?

Understanding Ideas

Using complete sentences, answer the following questions in your Journal.

1. What is one factor that must be considered when choosing a pesticide to apply?
2. How are crops able to withstand the effects of certain herbicides?
3. What other consideration, besides its ability to kill pests, should be accounted for before using a pesticide?
4. What group of workers could be in the most danger from pesticides? Why?
5. Why does spoiled milk contain lumps?
6. Within which part of the pH scale would a sample of spoiled milk register? Why?
7. How would a preservative, such as calcium propionate, get on the GRAS list?

8. How does the denaturing of meat protein cause water loss during cooking?
9. Why do microwave ovens cook food from the inside out?
10. Why do some meats become more tender during cooking?

Developing Skills

Use your understanding of the concepts developed in this chapter to answer each of the following questions.

1. **Predicting** Scientists know about a synthetic compound that has a chemical composition similar to DDT. How stable do you think this compound would be in the environment? Explain your answer.
2. **Analyzing** An organic compound has one fluorine and two hydrogen atoms attached with single bonds to a carbon atom. How many more bonds would you expect the carbon atom to form?
3. **Observing and Inferring** When you isolated the calcium propionate from the bread sample and converted it into a different compound, you were directed not to boil it. What problem might boiling cause?
4. **Hypothesizing** Why do you suppose that steamed vegetables retain more vitamins than those that are boiled in water?
5. **Using Variables** Buttermilk contains bacteria that change lactose into lactic acid. In the cheese-making activity, how might the results be changed if milk that had not been pretreated with buttermilk had been used?
6. **Concept Mapping** Draw an events chain sequencing the steps that occur from when a stable insecticide is applied to when it accumulates in humans.

Critical Thinking

In your Journal, answer each of the following questions.

1. Explain how grasshoppers may benefit when a pesticide that is selective for beetles is applied to a crop.
2. The Delaney Clause was specifically directed at additives used in processed foods. What type of food is overlooked by this law?
3. Adding baking soda to fresh milk does not cause it to clump as vinegar does. What can you conclude about the pH level of a baking soda solution? Why?
4. Besides killing bacteria with heat, what other preserving action does pasteurization bring about in milk?
5. What other factor, besides piercing the shell, might alter the size or texture of popped popcorn? Explain.

Problem Solving

Read the following problem and discuss your answers in a brief paragraph.

You and a friend buy identical plastic containers of milk from the store. Both containers have the same sell-by dates. After a few days at home, your milk spoils while the milk your friend bought remains fresh.

Name at least three variables that could influence the spoilage of your milk. Describe how each variable could differ between your house and your friend's house.

CONNECTING IDEAS

1. **Theme—Energy** How is heat produced by a microwave oven?
2. **Theme—Scale and Structure** The structure of many pesticides produces molecules that do not dissolve easily in water. Explain why, if the pesticide is ingested by humans, this property could cause problems.
3. **Theme—Systems and Interactions** Sometimes proteins that have been denatured can return to their original shape if they are returned to their original environments. Explain whether this could happen to a denatured egg white.
4. **Eyewitness Account** If you were cooking a meal for 70 people, what would you do to make sure that the food was nutritious?
5. **Applying Technology** List an example of how energy changes from one form to another in a solar cooker.
6. **Science and Society** Explain why there is a need to irradiate spices.

CHILLING SEEDS TO HELP BREAK DORMANCY

Problem

Dormant seeds are those that are alive but show no signs of life. Provide the proper conditions and most seeds will break dormancy and germinate into new, young plants. Certain seeds must first be subjected to cold temperatures before they can break dormancy. Which seed types need these cold temperatures? How long must the seeds be kept at a cold temperature?

Materials

refrigerator
plastic bags
paper towels
labels
seeds, such as apple, orange, bean, grass, wheat, and lettuce

Getting Started

1. Make a hypothesis about the effect of different lengths of cooling time on breaking dormancy for several seed types. Record your hypothesis in your Journal.

2. Design an experiment to test your hypothesis. Keep in mind that different seed types may or may not need cooling to break dormancy and that the time needed might vary from hours to weeks for those types that do require cooling.

3. Check your plan with your teacher. Conduct the experiment and prepare a report of your findings.

4. How did your results compare with your hypothesis? If cooling did increase the breaking of dormancy for a specific seed type, how would you design an experiment to determine the ideal time length needed for cooling? If cooling did not increase the breaking of dormancy for a specific seed type, can you conclude correctly from your experiment that cooling was not effective?

Resources

<u>Biology: Exploring Life, Volume 2: Form and Function of Plant Life.</u> Brum, Gil, Larry McKane, and Gerry Karp. John Wiley & Sons, Inc., 1994.

<u>Eyewitness Books: Plants.</u> Burnie, David. Alfred A. Knopf, 1989.

<u>The Nature of Life.</u> Postlethwait, John H. and Janet L. Hopson. McGraw-Hill, 1992.

HOW MUCH FERTILIZER IS ENOUGH?

Problem

Adding minerals or fertilizer to the soil is a well-accepted practice by farmers and home gardeners. Growth, crop yield, and lawn health increase when plants are fertilized. So, if certain amounts of fertilizer are good for a plant, shouldn't more fertilizer added to the soil be even better?

Materials

young plants, such as bean, corn, geranium, or grass

plant containers

sand or vermiculite

water-soluble fertilizer

water

labels

Getting Started

1. Make a hypothesis about the effect that different amounts of fertilizer will have on the growth of a young plant species. Record your hypothesis *in your Journal.*

2. Design an experiment to test your hypothesis. Use the directions on the fertilizer container for the recommended solution strength normally used. Use this strength as the basis for preparing other solution strengths that are higher than those normally called for.

3. Check your plan with your teacher. Conduct the experiment and prepare a report of your findings.

4. How did your results compare with your hypothesis? Explain why excessive amounts of fertilizer may or may not be helpful to the growth of a plant. Can you conclude from your experiment whether all plant species will respond in a similar manner to excessive fertilizer strengths? Explain. Design an experiment that would determine the best fertilizer strength for a specific plant species.

Resources

Chemistry in the Marketplace. Selinger, Ben. Harcourt Brace Jovanovich, Publishers, 1989.

The Nature of Life. Postlethwait, John H. and Janet L. Hopson. McGraw-Hill, 1992.

Resources

Y ou may not think of large items, such as cars, as something to be reused. That's part of the reason why this version of Stonehenge, built of cars, is so unusual. There are also many more practical ways to reuse and recycle the parts of cars. In this unit, you can learn about where the resources and energy to build cars come from and how those resources can be reused and recycled.

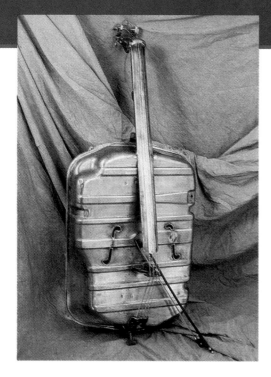

In recent years, reuse of car parts has resulted in some unusual pieces of art, such as this double bass made from a discarded gas tank.

In an effort to keep auto "graveyards" from becoming unsightly, cars are now crushed and compressed into easily stacked shapes after being stripped of usable parts.

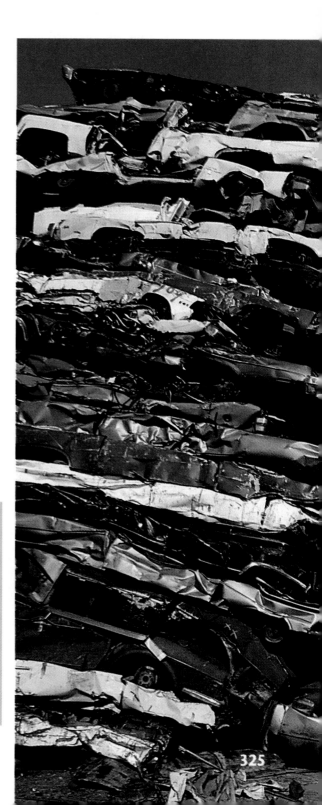

Unit Contents

Focus On

A Cross Section of a Car

A cross section of a new car gives you a glance at the body structure and the car's internal parts. In this unit, you'll learn about where the materials that go into making a car come from. You'll be surprised at the "rocky" start many of these materials have.

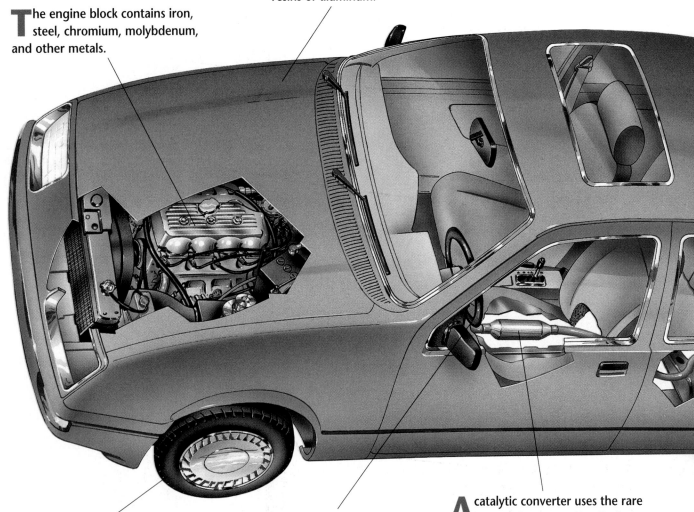

The body panels of the car are made of plastic resins or aluminum.

The engine block contains iron, steel, chromium, molybdenum, and other metals.

Tires contain rubber, sulfur, carbon black, steel, and nylon.

Steering wheels and seats are sometimes upholstered with leather.

A catalytic converter uses the rare metals platinum and palladium to change dangerous exhaust compounds to less harmful materials.

Try It!

The auto repair business relies heavily on used and rebuilt parts to curtail costs. Many people are not aware of the extensive use of these parts when a car is repaired after an accident.

What To Do

1. Interview the owner of a local auto body shop that repairs cars.
2. Find out how much of their repair business depends on used and rebuilt parts.
3. Ask for costs involved for using rebuilt parts in comparison to using new parts.

Try It Again

After you have learned more about resources and their many uses, look at the information from the above interview. Find out about the uses of recycled motor oil.

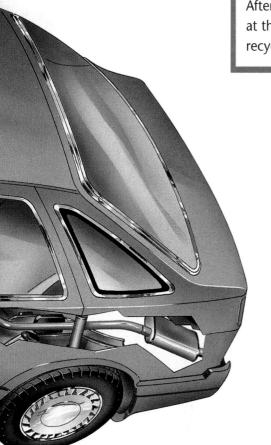

UNIT 4 PROJECTS

During your exploration of resources, you may discover new questions or wish to explore related topics. **Let's All Go (Re)Cycling** and **Around and Around We Go,** found in the Unit 4 Projects section on pages 442-443, will give you the challenge of tackling some actual recycling projects. Read through these projects now. By the time you finish this unit, you'll know all you need to know to successfully complete both projects.

CHAPTER 11

Resources
Earth's Limited Treasures

T*ake a look at the objects around you right now. Think about the materials they are made of and where those materials came from. Is the chair you're sitting on made of wood? Plastic? Metal? What covers the floor? Vinyl tile? Carpet? Do the light fixtures contain glass or plastic? What are your shoes made of? Your clothes? This book? The items you use every day are made from the many natural materials or resources that are found in and on Earth.*

▶ ***In the following activity, you'll explore what kinds of natural resources are used in cars.***

What natural resources are used in cars?

Millions of cars are on our roads today. What are they made of?

Procedure

1. Make a data table with columns and the following headings: *metal, plastic, cloth and leather, rubber, glass.*

2. After obtaining permission from the owner, carefully examine a parked car.

3. List as many car parts as you can that fit into each of the natural resource categories. Add additional columns as needed.

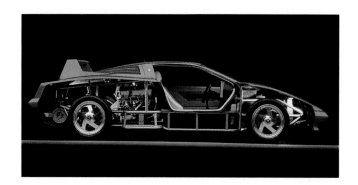

Analysis

1. Which category contains the largest number of car parts?

2. Which of the categories do you consider examples of resources that can be replaced easily by nature? Which resources are not easily replaced? Explain.

3. Predict which parts of the car could be recycled or used again after this car has outlived its usefulness. Explain.

11-1 Nonrenewable and Renewable Resources

Objectives
- Distinguish between renewable and nonrenewable resources.
- Describe ways in which the sun's energy can be used to generate power.

Key Terms
nonrenewable resource
fossil fuel
energy resource
renewable resource
solar energy

Types of Resources

Your examination of a car probably resulted in a long list of auto parts, from spark plugs and fan belts to seat covers and bumpers. Unless you have some experience working on cars or trucks, there were undoubtedly many parts that you couldn't name, but you could probably guess whether they were made of plastic, metal, glass, or some other material. Some of these materials come from natural resources that are classified as renewable, whereas other materials come from resources that are classified as nonrenewable. Did you know which parts are renewable and which are nonrenewable?

Supplies of some natural resources, such as wood for furniture and cotton for clothing, are considered renewable because they can be replaced by natural processes. Other natural resources, especially petroleum products such as oil and gas, are not easily replaced and are considered nonrenewable. In this chapter, you'll learn more about renewable and nonrenewable resources and begin to think about how resources can be reused and recycled.

Figure 11-1

Nonrenewable resources shown on these two pages include metals, fossil fuels, and some minerals.

A Earth's supply of metals is limited by the number and size of ore deposits. The ore that is being taken from this aluminum mine will not be replaced.

B Many companies encourage people to recycle goods, such as aluminum cans, by paying for them.

Nonrenewable Resources

As you may already know, the law of conservation of matter and energy states that matter cannot be created or destroyed by any ordinary physical or chemical methods. This law is important in helping to understand that there is just so much matter on Earth and that amount does not change. In Chapter 5, you learned that through the action of natural cycles, Earth's supply of water, carbon, and nitrogen is used over and over again. But, many of the substances we use every day, as shown in **Figure 11-1,** are not replenished by natural cycles. Natural resources that are not recycled or replaced by nature are called **nonrenewable resources.** This term also describes natural resources that are recycled or replaced so slowly that they are consumed faster than nature can recycle or replace them.

C Some minerals, such as phosphorus, are nonrenewable resources. Phosphorus, which is essential to plant growth, is one of the major components of fertilizers being applied to this farmland and houseplant to keep both healthy.

D It takes millions of years for the decaying bodies of marine organisms to form deposits of oil and gas. Even though fossil-fuel deposits are constantly being formed, humans are consuming them far faster than they can be replaced.

■ Nonrenewable Ores and Nonmetals

How many different kinds of metal do you use in a day? Aluminum is used to manufacture many items including soft-drink cans, cooking pots, foil, window frames, and airplanes. Copper is used to make electrical wires and pipes. Silver is used in jewelry and in some photographic processes, while lead is used in car batteries. These and other metals—including tin, gold, uranium, zinc, mercury, and nickel—are examples of nonrenewable resources that are not replaced by natural processes. **Figure 11-2** discusses an important type of nonrenewable metal mixture. Once a deposit of metal ore has been mined, it is gone forever. Other natural resources that belong in this category include nonmetals like limestone, calcite, sand, gravel, quartz, and sulfur. These materials may seem to be in abundant supply now, but eventually they could be used up.

Figure 11-2

Metals are sometimes combined to make new materials that possess unique qualities.

A Iron and chromium are combined to make steel girders, which are used to support large structures such as bridges, dams, and high-rise buildings.

B Metals and nonmetals used in building such structures are called *construction resources.*

■ Energy Resources

Petroleum deposits—underground accumulations of oil and natural gas—are formed from the remains of marine organisms buried beneath layers of earth for millions of years. Oil and natural gas, as well as coal, are known as *fossil fuels.*

Fossil fuels are made of decayed remains of ancient plants and animals and make up a major part of natural resources called **energy resources.** These include all materials used to produce energy. **Figure 11-3** shows energy sources and energy use in the United States.

Figure 11-3

The amount of fossil fuels consumed in the United States has nearly doubled every 20 years since 1900. Between 1960 and 1990, total energy demand rose by 140 percent.

A Fossil fuels provide more than 85 percent of the energy used in the United States, while renewable and nuclear sources make up 14.5 percent.

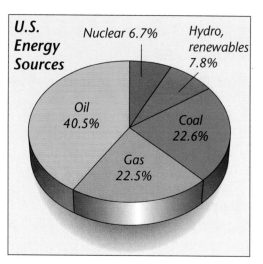

U.S. Energy Sources

Nuclear 6.7%
Hydro, renewables 7.8%
Oil 40.5%
Coal 22.6%
Gas 22.5%

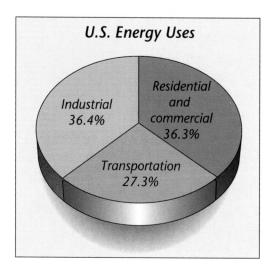

U.S. Energy Uses

Industrial 36.4%
Residential and commercial 36.3%
Transportation 27.3%

B Transportation—including cars, trucks, and airplanes—accounts for more than 27 percent of total energy use. This measurement has been steadily increasing. Why?

Although petroleum formation is always taking place, today's dying marine organisms won't become usable oil for several million years. According to current estimates, oil and natural gas reserves in the United States total about 27.7 billion barrels. World reserves total about 999.1 billion barrels. A barrel of petroleum, or 42 gallons, is a unit of measurement used within the petroleum business. What is likely to happen if the human population continues using up the world's reserves?

■ Using Petroleum Resources

What does a plastic grocery bag have in common with a gallon of gasoline? Our use of petroleum resources is not limited to energy production. Oil and natural gas contain chemicals that are essential for the manufacture of many materials we take for granted today, including dyes, solvents, and plastics of many kinds. Keeping this in mind, take another look at the list you created in the MiniLab activity at the beginning of this chapter. What automobile parts originate from natural resources that are replaced so slowly they are considered nonrenewable?

There are other types of natural resources in addition to energy resources that are equally at risk. Some of these nonrenewable resources may be overlooked when considering immediate needs such as energy. However, they too are important and have long-term consequences if ignored.

Was it appreciated before it was gone?

Has your neighborhood gone through any changes lately? How about the outskirts of your town? Perhaps a grass-covered field has been turned into a parking lot, or some nearby farmland has become a new subdivision.

Analysis

Suppose traffic in your neighborhood has become so congested that it is necessary to build a new road. The city council is planning to extend the existing expressway into open land. Right now, some of this open land is used for farming. The rest is undeveloped wetlands that serve as the home of many species of fishes, frogs, birds, other animals, and plants. Building the new road will help solve the traffic problems, but it will mean that the land can no longer be farmed and much of the wetlands habitat will be destroyed.

Thinking Critically

What effects could the new road have on the plants and animals in the area? What ideas do you have that might make it possible to solve the traffic problem and preserve as much of the farmland and wetlands as possible? Use your ideas to develop an alternative to the city council's plan. Write a description or draw a diagram that describes your alternative plan.

Figure 11-4

Tough choices are being made daily to balance the preservation of natural resources and the needs of growing populations.

Figure 11-5

Renewable resources are recycled or replaced by natural processes, without the need for any human intervention.

A Sunlight provides a constant supply of energy for this forest and all life on Earth and is the source of energy for all renewable resources.

B Plants grow in soil, a renewable resource, and extract nutrients from it. In return, dead plants and other organisms decompose and return nutrients to the soil. Topsoil, however, is considered to be a nonrenewable resource because it can take 500 to 1000 years for a 2.5-cm layer of topsoil to develop from decaying plant material and weathered rock fragments.

■ Land Resources

Sometimes we don't realize the value of a natural resource, such as a park or large expanse of open land, until it is changed. Had you even considered land as a natural resource? Take a look around your town or neighborhood to see whether there are land resources that you or your neighbors tend to take for granted. For example, you could spend some time investigating the pond in your local park. Do any fish live in it? What kinds of birds use it? As illustrated in **Figure 11-4,** decisions concerning the use of land must be weighed carefully.

Renewable Resources

We don't usually worry about running out of natural resources such as oxygen or sunlight. Plants produce oxygen during photosynthesis, providing a constant supply for animals to breathe. The sun is always shining on some part of Earth's surface, providing heat and the light needed for photosynthesis. A natural resource that is recycled or replaced by natural processes in less than 100 years is generally considered a **renewable resource.** Renewable resources are replenished at about the same rate as they are used. Examples of renewable resources include trees, food crops, and other plants and animals, as shown in **Figure 11-5.** Some elements that are important to life cycles, such as nitrogen and carbon, are also considered to be renewable resources.

Organic materials, such as the renewable resources listed above, eventually break down or decompose. The end product that most of us see is usually a moldy, foul-smelling substance that may or may not resemble the original material. However, some material from decomposed organic material can be made that is beneficial to growing plants. In the following Investigation, discover how to make compost.

Connect to...

Chemistry

Find out how fungi decompose substances on which they grow.

Replenishing the Soil

Compost is made when organic materials decompose under moist, warm, and aerated conditions. It is rich in nutrients essential for plant growth. How is compost made?

Preparation

Problem

What do you get when organic waste is allowed to decompose under specific conditions? Consider conditions such as moisture, temperature, aeration, materials used, and time.

Hypothesis

In your group, brainstorm possible hypotheses and discuss the evidence on which each hypothesis is based. Select the best hypothesis from your list.

Objectives

In this Investigation, you will:

- *Observe* how different organic materials decompose under specific conditions.
- *Design* a working method for composting.

Possible Materials

aluminum cans, black

steel cans, some shiny and some black

covers for the cans, some transparent and some opaque

organic material, large variety

thermometers

gloves and tongs (for handling garbage)

high-intensity light

oven

scale

graduated cylinders

measuring cups or beakers

Safety Precautions

Do not use any meat or dairy items.

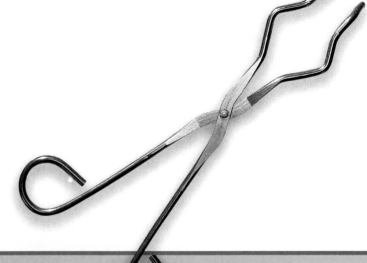

Plan the Experiment

1 Examine the materials you have chosen and review the introductory paragraph. As a group, make a list of the possible ways you might test your hypothesis.

2 Narrow down your list to one method, based on the materials and amount of time available. Design an experiment that will result in successful testing of your hypothesis and that will answer the previously stated problem.

3 Prepare a list of numbered directions, including a list of materials needed.

4 Create a table for recording any quantitative data you may collect. Think about the amount of material you start with and what you may have at the end.

Check the Plan
Discuss the following points with other group members to decide the final procedure for your experiment.

1 Determine how many setups you will need. How about a control? What variables will you change?

2 How many days will you need to run this experiment? How often will you check it?

3 *Make sure your teacher has approved your experimental plan before you proceed further.*

4 Carry out your experiment. Record any observations and data throughout the experiment. Complete your data table.

Analyze and Conclude

1. **Comparing and Contrasting** Which types of organic materials broke down the fastest?

2. **Measuring in SI** How did the volume and weight of the materials change throughout the experiment? Which was more dramatic: volume or weight change?

3. **Making and Using Graphs** Graph the results of your Investigation. What kind of graph would work best?

4. **Determining Cause and Effect** Which can worked best? Why would a shiny or dark can be better? (Hint: Think of a black car on a hot day.)

Going Further

Thinking Critically
Could you grow a plant in the material resulting from this lab? Why or why not? What steps would you take to test your answer?

Trees

Is a mature, old-growth forest an example of a renewable resource? An individual tree is renewable. If one tree dies or is harvested, it can be replaced by a new seedling. The death of a single tree would not result in major changes to the forest. But, the forest itself is not renewable. If many or all of the trees were removed, it could take centuries for the land to go through the process of succession and again become a mature forest. It's also possible that the forest might never grow back. The

A Clear-cutting forest land followed by replanting the land with seedlings is one way of harvesting trees. Clear-cutting can increase erosion problems, however, when soil becomes exposed after the mature trees are removed.

Figure 11-6

Trees are harvested to provide firewood for fuel, pulp for paper, and lumber for buildings and furniture.

Renewable Rain Forests?

Moist rain forests contain more biodiversity than any other ecosystem. Tropical rain forests are home to an estimated 50 percent of Earth's life-forms. Is such an important ecosystem a renewable or a nonrenewable resource?

Competing Demands

Much rain forest land is government owned but is used by many different groups. In many areas, the forest is the homeland of indigenous hunters and gatherers. As demand for farmland and trees for export increases, parts of the forest are being cleared or destroyed. Loggers alone clearcut the rain forest at a rate of 1600 hectares (about 4000 acres) per hour. Gold miners, tree poachers, cattle ranchers, and game hunters also compete within the rain forest habitat.

How can rain forests be managed so that the ecosystem is maintained?

B In a method known as *selective harvesting,* a small number of trees are selected for harvesting, leaving the rest of the forest undisturbed. This technique helps preserve both the forest ecosystem and a future supply of timber.

removal of the trees could alter the ecosystem so much that succession might result in a completely different climax community. **Figure 11-6** shows how proper harvesting methods can help preserve the forest ecosystem.

Such methods of harvesting will extend the life of these important natural resources. A continuing cycle of removal and replacement of trees helps to guarantee the presence of forests. Any natural resource can become non-renewable if it is overconsumed without replacement or if it becomes polluted by human activities. Natural resources, whether classified as renewable or non-renewable, should be treated with care in order to extend our present supply for future use.

Cooperative Solutions

Rain forest management may include clear-cutting in strips. Experiments in Peru and Costa Rica show that forest gaps 20 to 50 m (50 to 150 feet) wide will grow and close in 30 years and then the older trees will be ready to be clear-cut in strips. If only 1/30 of the rain forest is clear-cut in strips every year, the forest can be self-sustaining. While it is regenerating, the strip needs to have undesirable (not commercially valuable) tree sprouts removed and parasitic climbing vines chopped down. This approach maximizes the commercial value of the habitat for logging.

Ecotourism

Ecotourism, or ecology-minded tourism, is another approach. The key to ecotourism is to save an area's plant and animal life from destruction for short-term profit and preserve it by having it provide a steady income in the long run.

Some ecotourists are botanists hunting for rare plants for pharmaceutical applications, but many are simply interested people. They take seminars, guided tours, and photographs. In some reserves, aerial walkways, as pictured in the photograph on p. 338, up to 125 feet above the forest floor enable tourists to closely examine the canopy habitat. In some areas, indigenous people serve as rangers and caretakers.

Thinking Critically

1. *Explain* ecotourism.
2. Discuss different ways to turn rain forests into renewable resources. *Compare and contrast* the various concerns of those involved: indigenous hunters and gatherers, plants, animals, loggers, farmers in need of cleared land, ecotourists, tree poachers, and pharmaceutical researchers.

Figure 11-7

Solar energy is Earth's most important source of renewable energy. Using it to generate heat or electricity does not create the air pollution problems associated with burning fossil fuels.

A Heat from the sun, or *solar heat,* warms water contained in the collecting panels on this roof. This type of system could be used to replace a conventional gas or electric water heater in a home.

B Heat from the sun also creates wind, which can be used to turn wind turbines that generate *wind-powered* electricity.

■ What about water?

On Earth, water is found underground, in surface lakes, streams, and oceans; as ice at the poles and elsewhere; and as water vapor in the atmosphere. Because there is a limited amount of water on Earth, water is usually classified as a nonrenewable resource. However, water is constantly moving from the ground to the atmosphere and back again, so in some ways it acts as a renewable resource. Water can also be considered a reusable resource. Water will be discussed in more detail later in this chapter.

■ Energy from the Sun

As you learned in previous chapters, energy from the sun contributes to climate, weather patterns, and plant growth. It helps to speed the decomposition of organic matter and can be used to fuel chemical reactions and generate electricity. The sun's energy is called **solar energy.** Some researchers think that the amount of solar energy

that reaches Earth is enough to supply all of the power needed for human activities, from heating homes to fueling cars. So why don't we power all human activities using solar power?

There are problems also associated with solar energy. Because solar energy is spread over so much of Earth, there are difficulties in harnessing much of this energy. Also, what happens at sunset? The rate at which any place receives solar energy depends on many different conditions, including the time of day, the season, location on Earth, and whether the skies are cloudy or clear. Extensive and expensive energy storage is needed to sustain solar-powered homes and industries.

Until recently, technologies needed for converting solar power into usable energy have been somewhat unreliable and costly compared with conventional sources of energy, such as petroleum. Photovoltaic cells, one method for harnessing the sun's energy, are reported to be about 37 percent efficient in con-

To Find Out More About ...

Reclaiming Water, research how desalination of sea water takes place and where this process is most needed in the world.

C In a *hydroelectric power plant,* electricity is generated by giant turbines that are turned by torrents of water flowing over a dam. Heat from the sun drives the water cycle; it causes water to evaporate and rise into the atmosphere as water vapor. The water vapor eventually condenses and falls back to the ground, where it flows downhill. Hydroelectric plants transform the energy of flowing water into electricity.

D By combining thin layers of light-sensitive materials, scientists have been able to create *photovoltaic cells*—devices that produce electricity directly from sunlight. The energy source of a public telephone on this pole is the sun. The photovoltaic cells at the top convert the sun's heat into usable energy.

verting the sun's energy into a usable form. Photovoltaic cells and other methods of harnessing solar power are described in **Figure 11-7.**

To raise the funds needed for improved technologies, there must be a large enough market for solar power to justify the amount of money needed to expand this process to a practical scale for wider use. Unless the negative effects of fossil-fuel usage on the environment are considered seriously, the problems associated with conversion to solar power will not be addressed.

Perhaps the immediate solution to this problem would be using solar energy, supplemented with fossil-fuel energy. Power plants in southern California have been built that run on 75 percent solar energy and 25 percent natural gas. The result is reliable power all year long.

Nonrenewable and *renewable* are broad terms describing two groups of natural resources. Two additional classes are *recyclable* and *reusable,* both of which will be discussed in the next section.

check your UNDERSTANDING

Understanding Concepts
1. What does time have to do with whether or not a resource is renewable?
2. How can the sun's energy be used to generate power?
3. Discuss why fossil fuels are considered nonrenewable even though they are constantly being formed.

Skill Review
4. **Making and Using Tables** Construct a table that lists construction resources and energy resources. Which are renewable? Which are nonrenewable? For more help, refer to Making and Using Tables in the *Skill Handbook.*

Issue: Minerals and Mining

"Thar's gold in them thar hills!"

There are also other minerals in "them thar" hills, such as copper, coal, tin, silver, uranium, oil, and gas. We need these materials to build our houses, run our cars, heat our homes, construct our highways, and support our modern way of life.

The Issue

But, to obtain these valuable mineral deposits, trees and other vegetation on the surface of Earth must be cleared away, holes must be dug deep into Earth, and large quantities of toxic waste materials may be produced. Mining operations have the potential to cause great damage to the environment, disrupt ecosystems, and destroy some of our scenic areas. An important current issue, therefore, is how to obtain these necessary minerals in a way that is least harmful to the environment, and how best to restore the land after mining operations have been completed.

The Background

Back in the 1800s in the state of Montana, there was a mountain that was found to contain large amounts of gold, silver, and copper ores. It was known as the "Richest Hill on Earth," and mining companies tore the mountain apart to get at the valuable minerals. Not only was the mountain destroyed, but also dangerous waste materials were produced, including cyanide, arsenic, and radioactive trash. These toxic substances are still there, polluting the land and contaminating water supplies. Now it's known as the "Most Toxic Hill on Earth."

Mining companies today realize that the environment must be protected. These compa-

In the 1800s, Butte, Montana, was extensively mined for valuable minerals. The hill and part of the original town became the Berkely Pit and is known as the "Most Toxic Hill on Earth."

nies are working hard to develop mining operations that result in as little harm as possible to the land. And, the land that is damaged during mining operations is repaired so that it looks much like it did before the mining began. This process is called *reclamation.* To reclaim land that has been strip-mined, piles of dirt and rocks must first be leveled. The area may then be reseeded and the resulting vegetation is left to grow. A reclamation project is not considered complete until full vegetation growth is present.

Reclaimed areas can eventually be used for such things as farming, growing trees, or recreation. Often, but not always, the reclaimed land is more useful for these purposes than it was before mining began. However, it can take from 15 to 1000 years or more for a severely damaged area to recover, especially in the western United States where the climate is dry and plant life is fragile. Even after reclamation, the original ecosystem may have been changed forever, native species have been disturbed, and endangered species may have been exterminated.

To make sure that the environment is protected, laws have been passed to control mining operations. For example, a federal law was enacted in 1977 to regulate coal mining and reclamation procedures. Each state must make sure that its own state regulations are in agreement with those of the federal law; otherwise, the federal government may assume authority over this.

The Questions

Protecting and restoring the environment from damage done by mining operations is not inexpensive. Approximately 6 million acres of land in the United States have already been mined, and millions of dollars have been spent in reclaiming these lands. Reclamation can cost up to $8000 per acre. Some smaller mining

The smelters and surrounding hills in Butte, Montana in August, 1890, when it was called the "Richest Hill on Earth"

companies, for example, can't afford to undertake such an expensive task, and so they go out of business. This can cause unemployment and financial hardship for families in that locality.

Another difficulty is that many of the mining companies operating in the United States are foreign companies with overseas headquarters. These mining activities are not easily regulated. It is important for all concerned that these procedures not lead to adverse effects on the environment.

*inter*NET
CONNECTION

To view the reclamation project, follow the link for Chapter 11 on the Glencoe Homepage, **http://www.glencoe.com/**, to the U.S. Office of Abandoned Mine Lands & Reclamation. Analyze the steps taken during the reclamation process.

11-2 Recyclable and Reusable Resources

Objectives

■ Identify ways of reusing and recycling items to conserve natural resources.

■ Describe the benefits of recycling natural resources.

Key Terms

reusable resource
recyclable resource

Using Resources Again

What kinds of items have you thrown into the trash so far today? Cereal boxes, milk cartons, gum wrappers, broken shoelaces, breakfast leftovers? Each of us throws away about 1.6 kg (3.6 pounds) of trash every day. That amounts to 584 kg (1314 pounds) per year, and about 44 percent of this is paper. All this trash represents a waste of natural resources and also presents a disposal problem. In the MiniLab below, examine one alternative to this waste problem.

■ Reducing Trash

One way to reduce the amount of trash we throw away is to reduce the amount of material we purchase. The

MiniLab

Can you redesign this package?

Paper, cardboard, plastic, and glass are used to package the goods we buy. Sometimes the package is actually much larger than the item we're purchasing. Do we really need to use our resources this way? Can you create a package that is attractive without using unnecessary resources? This activity gives you a chance to find out.

Procedure

1. Choose one food item and one non-food item that, in your opinion, contain a lot of packaging materials.

2. Sketch the unopened packages, record their dimensions, and describe the packaging materials.

3. Using either new materials or some of the original material, redesign a package that will adequately preserve and/or protect your item.

Analysis

1. Is your package more recyclable or reusable than the original?

2. Does your package take up less room on the store shelf than the original?

3. Does it weigh less than the original? Is this an important point in terms of shipping and ease of transport?

4. Does your package look as attractive as the original? Would this affect whether or not you would buy it?

5. Does your package keep the enclosed item clean, sanitized, and tamper-proof?

packaging used to wrap almost everything we buy—from toys to TV dinners—makes up a large percentage of our garbage. The United States is the world's top producer of waste, generating nearly 200 million tons per year. That's enough to fill a string of garbage trucks stretching eight times around the world. One-third of our trash comes from packaging. Choosing to buy products that are not marketed with excess packaging is one method of reducing this volume of trash.

We can cut down on the amount of trash we produce by purchasing only what we really need and by reusing items as long as possible before throwing them away, then recycling them. For example, instead of discarding an empty pickle jar, you can use it for storing leftovers in the refrigerator or extra nails on the garage workbench. When the jar finally breaks, the glass can be recycled. A **reusable resource** is one that can be used over and over again in its original form. A **recyclable resource** can be reprocessed and used again rather than being thrown away. **Figure 11-8** gives a few more examples of reusable and recyclable resources.

Figure 11-8

Many items can be considered as both a reusable and a recyclable resource.

A Scrap iron and waste paper are the most abundant exports leaving New York Harbor. Taiwan, a large island off the coast of China that does not have the land to grow large forests for harvest, buys used paper to make more. Japan reprocesses our discarded iron and steel to manufacture cars that may be sold in the United States.

D Yard clippings and other organic materials are turned into compost for fertilizing farms and gardens.

B This expressway was repaved by using the old roadbed as the base for the new one. This type of construction helps reduce waste from construction sites, which is one of our biggest sources of solid waste.

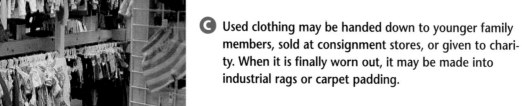

C Used clothing may be handed down to younger family members, sold at consignment stores, or given to charity. When it is finally worn out, it may be made into industrial rags or carpet padding.

Figure 11-9

What Goes Around Comes Around

Nearly everyone knows about recycling. Your community may have a curbside-collection program, as shown in **Figure 11-9,** that lets you separate recyclables like glass, plastic, tin cans, newspapers, and yard clippings and put them out to be picked up like the rest of your garbage. An average American family of four recycles 499 kg (1100 pounds) of recyclable materials every year. But, that same family still sends 2405 kg (5300 pounds) to the landfill.

Table 11-1

United States Recycling Data (in millions of tons)				
Resource	Amount Recycled	Amount Not Recycled	Percent Recycled	Comments
Steel	1.9	10.4	15%	100% recyclable; reusable almost indefinitely; long shelf life; ideal for food storage
Aluminum	1	1.7	37%	Recycling aluminum requires only 5% of the energy needed to process it from ore; car parts and home siding could be recycled too.
Paper	20.9	52.4	28%	Corrugated boxes, newspaper, and office paper amounts to about 44% of U.S. waste
Plastic	0.4	15.8	2%	The many varieties make it difficult to sort; recycling hampered by concern about contamination from use or improper storage; amounts to 8% of our trash
Glass	2.6	10.6	20%	"Glassphalt," used to pave streets, is a mixture of recycled glass and asphalt.

Figure 11-10

Corrugated cardboard is a major component of trash. Cardboard boxes can be used again and again to store or carry items. When they become too worn for use, they can be recycled much like other paper products.

Table 11-1 summarizes data on some of the recycling we have managed to accomplish in the United States over the past few years.

Reusing materials is the most promising and probably the least expensive way to conserve our natural resources. Whenever we reuse something instead of discarding it and buying a replacement, we avoid consuming raw materials. Reusing and recycling materials, as demonstrated in **Figures 11-10** and **11-11,** are responsible methods of extending the use of natural resources.

Figure 11-11

Crushed lightbulbs can be recycled into floor tiles.

Thinking Lab Interpreting Data

Are there treasures in the junkyard?

Is anything ever salvaged from a junkyard? Junkyards are filled with discarded cars. A look at some of them might show that before they were junked, some of the parts were in fairly good condition.

Analysis
Do some investigating to find out just how much material is taken out of a junkyard and put to good use. Could junkyards be a source of reusable or recyclable materials? Contact some junkyard operators to find out.

Thinking Critically
Based on the results of your research, do you think an organized effort to recycle junkyard material could result in a reduction in the size and/or number of junkyards? Could the cost of an automobile possibly go down if it were made from recycled steel and glass?

Figure 11-12

Water-treatment plants employ several steps in which many different water-purification methods are used in series.

Water Is a Reusable Resource

We've already stated that the amount of water on Earth is limited. More water cannot be made, but it can be reused. The water cycle recycles our water naturally, but what about water that has become polluted or contaminated? We can't put it into the ground untreated. It must be cleaned, purified, or treated before we return it to the water cycle so that it may be safely reused.

The greatest causes of water pollution include everyday activities such as flushing toilets, cleaning teeth, and watering lawns. Among other directives, the 1987 Clean Water Act, passed by the U.S. Congress, gave money to the states for building sewage- and waste-water-treatment facilities. Such treatment plants, as shown in **Figure 11-12**, provide clean drinking water for millions of people.

A Chlorination, which is the addition of chlorine gas, kills harmful bacteria and destroys offensive organic matter, including dead leaves, human refuse, and sewage.

C The water then flows into a settling basin, in which precipitated sludge settles at the bottom and is removed through pipes.

C SETTLING BASIN

A CHLORINATION

D FILTRATION

Sand

Gravel

Chlorine inlet

Water inlet

Chlorinator

B FORMATION of FLOC

Scraper blades

Sludge discharge pipe

Chemical feed line

Rapid mix

Slow mix

B This solution is mixed with chemicals to form floc—a light, loose mass—that combines with impurities and forms a solid precipitate.

D The water then passes through a rapid sand filter. The water passes through layers of sand and gravel and is finally drained off.

Figure 11-13

An *earthship*, located in Taos, New Mexico, was built with resource conservation in mind. Constructed out of aluminum cans, this building employs photo-voltaic cells to provide electricity, contains solar toilets, and utilizes a catch-water roof system to collect and filter runoff from snow and rain.

Earth contains many materials called *natural resources*. Whether renewable or nonrenewable in nature, these natural resources have been used over the years to supply food, shelter, and clothing for people. But, what would happen if people carelessly lost these treasures through overuse and pollution? Recycling and reusing such resources is a responsible alternative to excessive waste and will extend the life of Earth's limited treasures. The office building shown in **Figure 11-13** is an example of using resources wisely.

In the following chapters, you'll examine two types of nonrenewable resources. Chapter 12, *The Formation of Resources,* will cover rocks, and Chapter 13, *Petroleum Chemistry,* will present petroleum and fuels. How are these nonrenewable resources formed in nature? What are they composed of? What types of products are formed from these resources? Chapter 12 and Chapter 13 will address these issues. In Chapter 14, *Recycling,* the advantages and problems of recycling will be addressed in more detail.

Try It!

Car Parts Revisited Go back over your list of car parts from the MiniLab at the beginning of this chapter. Which parts do you think might be reused? Recycled? Reused *and* recycled? Label each car part appropriately and then explain your reasoning.

check your UNDERSTANDING

Understanding Concepts
1. Explain how recycling helps to cut down on our use of natural resources.
2. Name four different items in your home that can be recycled.
3. Compare and contrast reusable and recyclable resources.

Skill Review
4. **Making and Using Tables** Create a table that suggests ways of reusing at least four different household items. For more help, refer to Making and Using Tables in the *Skill Handbook.*

people in SCIENCE

Meet Terry Smith, Geologist

Geologist Terry Smith felt his first earthquake in Indiana in the late 1980s. He wasn't entirely surprised, though, because his training had taught him that Earth is potentially restless almost everywhere. The vast tectonic plates upon which the continents "ride" are always in slow motion—until the dramatic slippage that can tumble whole cities.

In the following interview, Mr. Smith talks about the hard work that earned him his job as a geologist and the satisfaction he finds on that job.

On the Job

Q Mr. Smith, can you tell us what you are working on right now?

A I'm on a project that is categorized by the federal government as a Super Fund site. A recycling plant operated there for several years. Recycling solvents, such as dry-cleaning fluids, is a really good idea. Unfortunately, the owner-operator of the plant got careless, and harmful substances were spilled. Because the owner declared bankruptcy, the government will have to pay for the cleanup, which may cost $12 million.

Q What happened as a result of the spills?

A The aquifer that provides water for a town of about 2000 people is in danger. The groundwater contains contaminants, such as trichloroethylene, which are known carcinogens. It seems that the problem was discovered just in time. Pumps are keeping the contamination from reaching the aquifer, which is recharged from precipitation and a nearby creek.

Q What makes your work enjoyable?

A Mostly the fact that I'm always doing something different. For example, earlier this week I was out in the field taking groundwater samples. Tonight I'm looking at several different scenarios to come up with the best way to treat water that may be contaminated in the well field. I set up the "worst-case" scenario and several others of lesser severity.

Early Influences

Q Have you always wanted to be a geologist?

A Actually, I started college with the goal of being a computer programmer. Then I ran up against Calculus 3! So I looked around for other areas that might interest me. My geology class got more and more interesting. I had no desire to be a classical geologist, though. I thought a job in the corporate world would be more likely to help me reach one of my goals, which was financial success.

There are many careers in the field of geology, each with its own skill requirements. Investigate the occupations listed below. Find out what skills and training are needed for each occupation. Write a "Help Wanted" advertisement for one of the careers listed. Include the skills and characteristics of the ideal job candidate.

▶ *physical geologist, historical geologist, economic geologist*

Personal Insights

Q What were you like as a high school student?

A I've always worked hard. I saw all my schooling as being preparation for what I would do in the real world. Peer pressure was present, of course, but I guess I have my own personality and am not very easily swayed. I'm glad things worked out that way for me, because it has really paid off.

Life Without Light

All renewable resources, including plants and animals, get their energy from sunlight. What if Earth no longer received enough sunlight to renew its resources? How could life on Earth continue?

Ring-Rise Ring-Set

A novel by Monica Hughes, *Ring-Rise Ring-Set,* explores this question. In her book, Earth's gravity captures a comet, which falls apart into dust that now encircles the equator like one of Saturn's rings. The ring blocks sunlight from enough of Earth's temperate and polar regions to tip the scales toward a new ice age. Each winter is longer and colder than the last; each summer less vegetation grows, and the glaciers are expanding toward the equator. Life on Earth seems doomed.

In northern Canada, a band of scientists, known as Techs, builds a settlement inside a hill. From there they study the ring to find a way to remove it or render it harmless. Life for the Techs is bleak—there are only synthetic foods, crowded and austere dormitories, and hard work with no labor-saving machinery because fuel is precious.

Fifteen-year-old Liza Monroe runs away from the Techs and finds the Ekoes, descendants of present-day Inuit who still live by hunting caribou in the traditional way. There she finds the warm family life that the Techs have forgotten. She becomes an Ekoe and is happy learning to live close to the land until, one spring day, Tech airplanes dust the snow with a black mold. It is meant to absorb sunlight and drive back the encroaching glacier, but it also kills the caribou upon which the Ekoes depend.

Can Liza convince the Techs to redesign the mold spores in time to save the Ekoe way of life? Will the ring kill Techs and Ekoes alike? Read *Ring-Rise Ring-Set* and find out.

Thinking Critically

1. *Describe* how receiving less sunlight would affect Earth's renewable resources.
2. *Hypothesize* how a ring of comet debris around Earth might be removed or rendered harmless.

Read the statements at the right and below that review major points presented in the chapter. Using the concepts that you have learned, answer each question *in your Journal.*

1 Nonrenewable resources are natural resources that are not recycled or replaced by nature, or they are recycled or replaced so slowly that they are consumed faster than nature can recycle or replace them. *Name two nonrenewable resources.*

2 Renewable resources are natural resources that are recycled or replaced by natural processes in less than 100 years. *Name two renewable resources.*

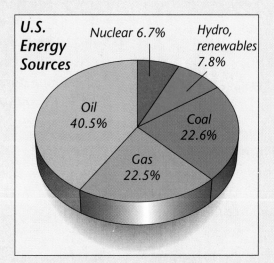

U.S. Energy Sources

Nuclear 6.7%
Hydro, renewables 7.8%
Oil 40.5%
Coal 22.6%
Gas 22.5%

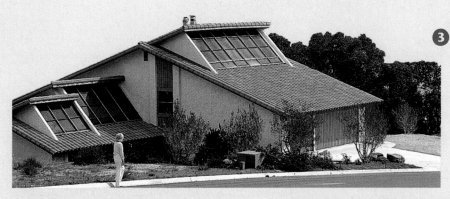

3 Energy resources make up a major part of natural resources and include all materials used to produce energy. *Is solar energy a renewable or a nonrenewable energy resource? Explain.*

4 A reusable resource can be used over and over again in its original form. A recyclable resource can be reprocessed and used over again. *What resources are you reusing and recycling?*

Using Key Science Terms

energy resource

fossil fuel

nonrenewable resource

recyclable resource

renewable resource

reusable resource

solar energy

Answer the following questions about science terms used in this chapter.

1. What is the relationship between solar energy and some renewable resources?
2. Distinguish between renewable and nonrenewable resources.
3. Explain how a reusable resource might also be considered a recyclable resource.

Understanding Ideas

Using complete sentences, answer the following questions in your Journal.

1. How does the law of conservation of matter and energy relate to natural resources?
2. If plants and animals, the basis of fossil fuels, are continuously dying, why are fossil fuels considered nonrenewable?
3. If oxygen is constantly being replenished by plant metabolic activity, why are we concerned about the quality of air?
4. Explain why the use of solar energy could be superior to fossil fuels.
5. Explain some limitations on our use of solar energy.
6. Suggest two reasons why some communities collect grass clippings and leaves for composting rather than allowing citizens to put them in the trash.

Developing Skills

Use your understanding of the concepts developed in this chapter to answer each of the following questions.

1. **Analyzing** In the Investigation on pages 336 and 337, why are meat and dairy products not used in composting?
2. **Concept Mapping** Use the following terms and phrases to complete the concept map about natural resources: *fossil fuels, hydroelectric power plants, oil, natural gas, photovoltaic cells, nonrenewable resources, solar energy.*

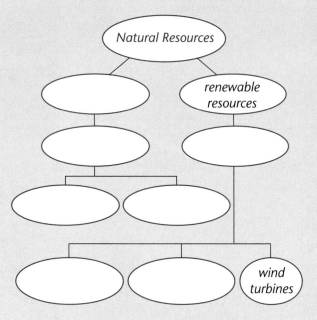

3. **Comparing and Contrasting** In a coal-fired power plant, burning coal heats water to produce steam. In a solar-fueled power plant, water turns the blades of a generator turbine. Compare and contrast these two plants.

4. Analyzing By now you have determined that an automobile uses many of our natural resources. Make a chart that lists the renewable and nonrenewable resources used in your classroom or home. Indicate whether these resources are recyclable or reusable.

Critical Thinking

In your Journal, *answer each of the following questions.*

1. Would an increase in the population of plants and microorganisms help solve possible fossil-fuel shortages? Why or why not?

2. Think about the water cycle. Would the products of desalination, which are fresh water and salt, be considered recycled or reused?

3. How is solar energy linked to wind energy?

Problem Solving

Read the following problem and discuss your answers in a brief paragraph.

Garbage is piling up and the local officials want to enlarge the landfill in your area. With a high water table and a lot of farmland nearby, many people are not happy with this plan. Using what you have learned in this chapter, offer an alternate solution to the problem.

What are the dangers associated with a high water table with regard to landfills? Can the farms benefit from your plan? If so, how? Describe your plan to eliminate the need for a bigger landfill.

CONNECTING IDEAS

1. **Theme—Energy** How can solar energy be used in conjunction with gasoline to power a car?

2. **Theme—Systems and Interactions** Explain how a tree-planting program would enable us to cut down trees and still consider them renewable resources.

3. **In-Depth Look** Based on what you have learned in this chapter, discuss whether rain forests can or cannot be considered renewable natural resources.

4. **Literature Connection** What types of alternative renewable energy sources could not be used in *Ring-Rise Ring-Set?*

5. **Science and Society** Are minerals a renewable resource? How are minerals conserved?

CHAPTER 12

The Formation of Resources
Finding Earth's Treasures

heir remains are stacked neatly in rows forming a canyon of crushed cars. Other rows of uncrushed cars with all usable parts stripped from them await their inevitable flattening. As you walk, you try to avoid the pieces of rusted steel, broken glass, and other miscellaneous parts that are strewn across the ground. This is the end of the road for many cars. But where does that road begin? Does it start in the factory, or even earlier? You might be surprised to find out that many of the resources used to make a car started out millions of years ago, deep within the crust of Earth.

▶ *In the following activity, explore some rocks that may one day end up as part of a car driving past you on the highway!*

356

MiniLab

What parts of cars are made from rocks?

Metal car parts are made from metals that are extracted from ores. In this activity, discover how some metals are extracted from ores.

Procedure

1. Obtain equal amounts of crushed charcoal and hematite (iron oxide) ore. Test each with a magnet and observe the results.

2. Mix the two together and pour into a test tube.

3. Making sure the test tube is pointed away from everyone, heat it over a Bunsen burner until the material glows red. Turn off the flame and allow the tube to cool.

4. Once cool, tap the tube's contents out and crush the contents with a hammer. Test the crushed material with a magnet and record your observations *in your Journal.*

Analysis

1. Compare the results from the magnet tests. What can you infer happened?

Igneous Rocks

12-1

Objectives

■ Describe the origins, features, and types of igneous rocks.

■ Explain how igneous rocks can be a useful resource.

Key Terms

igneous rock

magma

extrusive igneous rock

intrusive igneous rock

Bowen's reaction series

From Liquid to Solid

You may be surprised to learn that much of a car is made from rocks. This doesn't mean that wheels are really stones, and you certainly wouldn't go mining for car bodies. However, both wheels and car bodies are made from iron and other metals that are found in rocks. Metals are used for many things in addition to cars, making rocks an important resource for society. But not every rock is useful in the same way. To find the particular material you need, it helps to find out which kind of rocks contain what you need. It also helps to know how different rocks form.

When looking for rocks that contain iron, geologists often look for igneous rocks. **Igneous rocks** form when hot melted material cools and becomes a solid rock. This melted material is called **magma** when found beneath Earth's surface. There are two kinds of igneous rock, however. The difference is based on where the magma cools. Magma may cool while it's still underneath Earth's surface, or it may break through the surface of Earth at a volcano (in which case the magma is now called *lava*) and then cool. **Figure 12-1** shows how the two different types form.

Figure 12-1

Magma is formed from rock melted deep in Earth.

A Magma comes to the surface at volcanoes and is called *lava.* Lavas cool quickly once on the surface.

B Magmas may also cool and solidify slowly underground.

Figure 12-2

Earth's surface wasn't always as we see it today.

A According to theory, Earth's early surface was a violent place. It was totally molten and without atmosphere as we know it; the formation of solid land came later as Earth cooled.

B As the surface cooled, patches of solid minerals began to form. Like icebergs on the ocean, they floated on the dense iron- and magnesium-rich magma. Drifting together, these patches of lightweight silicon-, oxygen-, and aluminum-based minerals formed the first igneous rocks.

Igneous rocks were Earth's first rocks and made up the early crust. Present scientific understanding is that Earth formed from gas, dust, and ice revolving in space around a newly formed star, the sun. As more gas and dust accumulated, Earth probably developed a liquid interior due to extreme heat and melting. Elements such as iron moved toward Earth's center and began forming a dense core. Hot, less dense material was pushed toward Earth's surface, eventually separating into two layers. The outermost rock cooled to form the crust. The inner rock became the mantle.

None of Earth's present crust is in its original condition. Over geologic time, most of Earth's early crust has been remelted or eroded. Early crust that was not remelted has been under great pressure and heat, changing its original character. **Figure 12-2** shows what Earth may have looked like as the crust formed.

Extrusive Igneous Rocks

Extrusive igneous rocks form when lava cools quickly at Earth's surface. The magma, which forms as heat melts rocks of the lower crust, is less dense than the surrounding rock. The surrounding rock pushes the less dense magma upward until it reaches the surface.

Although interesting, extrusive igneous rocks are rarely sources of minerals used to build automobiles. However, they do get processed into road gravel on which cars travel. They also provide decorative stone and abrasives that clean and polish. Some hand soaps contain pieces of one type of extrusive rock, pumice. What is an advantage of soap that contains rock fragments?

All extrusive igneous rocks share at least one characteristic—a small crystal size. Why? Find out in the next activity.

INVESTIGATION

How does cooling time affect crystal size?

Crystals form as rock material cools from a liquid to a solid. Some rock crystals are large enough to be used as jewelry. Others are so small they can be seen only with the help of a microscope. Why are there such differences in size? In this Investigation, explore how cooling time can affect the size of a crystal.

Preparation

Problem

How can you determine the effect of cooling time on the size of the crystal that forms?

Hypothesis

In your group, brainstorm possible hypotheses and discuss the evidence on which each hypothesis is based. Select the best hypothesis from your list.

Objectives

In this Investigation, you will:

- *Compare* the appearance of crystals that form during rapid cooling and slower cooling.
- *Infer* why cooling time affects the size of the crystal that forms.

Possible Materials

salol (phenyl salicylate)
hot plate
glass petrie dishes or watch glasses
water
ice
stopwatch
thermal mitt

Safety Precautions

Wear safety goggles while handling the salol. When heating the salol, wear a thermal mitt.

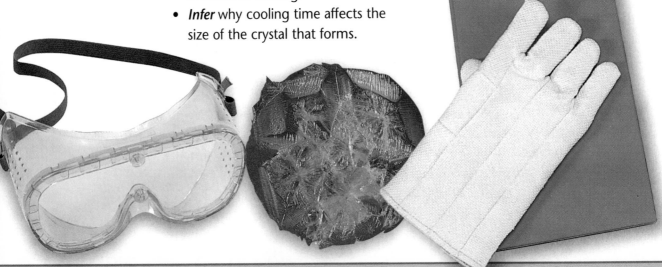

Plan the Experiment

1 Examine the materials provided by your teacher. Salol is a chemical that melts fairly easily and forms crystals as it cools. As a group, make a list of ways you might test your hypothesis. To melt the salol, place it in a watch glass and put it on a hot plate.

2 Agree on one way that your group could investigate your hypothesis. Design an experiment that will allow for quantitative data.

3 Prepare a list of numbered directions. Include a list of materials and the amounts you will need. A small amount of salol is sufficient to observe crystal growth.

4 Design and construct a table for recording your data.

Check the Plan

Discuss the following points with other group members to decide the final procedure for your experiment.

1 Determine how you will measure crystal size. How many crystals should you measure to get an accurate average size?

2 How can you make the crystals cool at different rates? Are there any other variables that may affect crystal size that you should control? Predict how cooling time affects crystal size.

3 *Make sure your teacher has approved your experimental plan before you proceed further.*

4 Carry out your experiment. Make any needed observations, and complete your data table.

Analyze and Conclude

1. **Measuring in SI** How did you measure crystal size?

2. **Comparing and Contrasting** How did temperature affect the size of the crystals that formed? How did this compare with your prediction?

3. **Drawing Conclusions** If you found two rocks, one with large crystals and another with small crystals, what would you conclude about how quickly each of them cooled when they formed?

4. **Designing an Experiment** Can you think of any other things that might affect the size of crystal growth? What other experiments could you do to test the things that affect crystal growth?

As you saw in the activity, the rate of cooling affects the size of crystals. It takes time for crystals to grow. The longer the time they have to grow, the larger the crystals become. Extrusive igneous rocks cool so quickly that crystals have little time to grow. As a result, the crystals are small. In fact, the crystals may be so small that they can be seen only by using a microscope. Some extrusive igneous rocks cool so quickly that they form a glass with few if any crystals. **Figure 12-3** illustrates how some extrusive rocks form, giving them their unique appearance.

Intrusive Igneous Rocks

While extrusive igneous rocks have limited use in making a car, the second kind of igneous rock is a critical resource in automobile manufacturing. These are **intrusive igneous rocks,** which form when magma cools beneath Earth's surface. Places like Yellowstone National Park in Wyoming, Idaho, and Montana are evidence that magma is near Earth's surface, even though there are no volcanoes. The geysers and hot springs in Yellowstone are powered by the heat from the underground magma. Many kinds of valuable metals such as iron, copper, and gold can be found in intrusive igneous rocks.

Just like all igneous rocks, intrusive igneous rocks start out as magma pushed up through Earth's mantle and crust by denser surrounding rock. For intrusive rocks though, the magma starts to cool before it reaches the surface. The surrounding rock acts like a blanket, and causes the magma to cool slowly.

Figure 12-3

When magma reaches Earth's surface, it cools quickly.

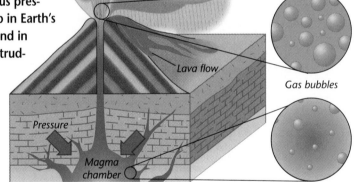

A Relieved of the tremendous pressure they experience deep in Earth's crust, gas and water expand in some magmas and are extruded at Earth's surface, resulting in bubbles.

Lava flow

Gas bubbles

Pressure

Magma chamber

B Rapid cooling of lavas containing little gas leads to formation of the glassy rock called *obsidian*. In Yellowstone National Park, a lava flow tens of meters thick cooled rapidly to form the Obsidian Cliffs.

C Lavas rich in silica and gases such as oxygen, carbon dioxide, and water vapor can foam up when they reach the surface, somewhat like a warm soda pop fizzes when opened. The resulting rock, pumice, has such a low density due to an abundance of gas-formed cavities that it floats on water.

The slow cooling of intrusive igneous rocks allows mineral crystals time to grow. As you saw in the Investigation on pages 360-361, slow cooling means that intrusive rocks usually have large, visible crystals. In **Figure 12-4,** you can see that in some intrusions, crystals can become large, sometimes measuring several meters in length. The difference in crystal size between intrusive and extrusive igneous rocks can be used to classify them. Try this in the next activity.

Figure 12-4

Amethyst is a variety of the mineral quartz. Exotic minerals are often concentrated in intrusive igneous rocks.

MiniLab

Classifying Intrusive and Extrusive Rocks

A close look may be all you need to classify intrusive and extrusive igneous rocks. Test your observation skills in this activity.

Procedure

1. Examine the following rocks: andesite, basalt, diorite, gabbro, granite, obsidian, pumice, rhyolite, and scoria.

2. Based on what you have learned, sort the rocks into intrusive and extrusive categories.

Analysis

1. Fill in the data table below.

2. What are the differences and similarities between the following pairs of rocks?

   a. basalt and gabbro

   b. gabbro and granite

   c. granite and pumice

3. What two characteristics determine the name of an igneous rock?

Data and Observations		
Rock	Rock characteristics	Intrusive/Extrusive
andesite		
basalt		
diorite		
gabbro		
granite		
obsidian		
pumice		
rhyolite		
scoria		

The Formation of Igneous Rocks

Earth's crust is divided into plates that move away from, pass, and collide into each other. As two plates collide, one is pushed downward into Earth's mantle. As the crust plunges into the mantle, the heat and pressure melt the crust to form magma. The chemical composition of a magma depends in part on the crust from which it forms. Magmas that result from the melting of oceanic crust are rich in iron and magnesium. Magmas that result from the melting of continental crust are richer in silicon and aluminum. The composition of the magma determines what kind of rocks a magma will produce when cooled. Hawaii's basalt lavas are rich in iron and magnesium, while the intrusive rocks of California's Sierra Nevada mountains are granites rich in silicon and aluminum.

As early geologists looked at large igneous rock bodies, two problems became clear. How could a well-mixed magma give rise to a granite, which is a rock made up of three or more separate minerals? Shouldn't an igneous rock look uniform throughout?

In addition, some intrusive rock bodies have the same rock all through them while others are layered. For example, an intrusive body might be composed entirely of granite. However, another has different minerals (making up different rocks) in various parts of the intrusion. In some bodies, the minerals even formed layers, as shown in **Figure 12-5.** Called *layered intrusions,* these bodies did not fit ideas then held about magmas. Many scientists thought magmas were well-mixed. Were they? Or were some only partly mixed? Or was there another reason for the layering? See the In-Depth Look on pages 366-367 to learn more about layered igneous intrusions.

■ Bowen's Reaction Series

N.L. Bowen's work in the 1920s showed that cooling magmas produce minerals in a predictable order. As each mineral crystallizes, it removes certain ions from the magma. As cooling continues, the magma's chemistry changes. The change occurs because newly forming minerals remove first one ion, then another, from the magma. This set order of mineral crystallization is called **Bowen's reaction series** and is shown in **Figure 12-6.**

Bowen's reaction series has a branch for the feldspars and a branch that consists of a variety of other minerals. The different feldspar crystals react continuously with the magma, changing their

Figure 12-5

Some intrusive bodies are layered with one or more minerals forming each layer. This is not what early geologists expected to see from cooling of a well-mixed magma.

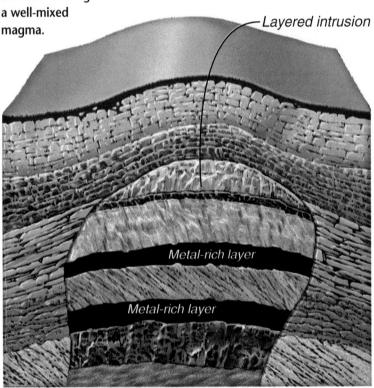

Layered intrusion

Metal-rich layer

Metal-rich layer

composition from calcium-rich feldspar to sodium-rich feldspar. In contrast, the minerals in the left branch have different compositions and all have different crystal structures, as shown in **Figure 12-6.**

All of the minerals of Bowen's reaction series are composed mainly of silicon and oxygen atoms linked together by the common elements of Earth's crust, such as iron, aluminum, sodium, potassium, and calcium. At very low temperatures, as **Figure 12-6** shows, quartz forms when there is little left in the magma except silicon and oxygen. Tetrahedra composed of oxygen and silicon bond together to form three-dimensional crystals, as shown in **Figure 12-7.**

Bowen's reaction series can be used to determine how resistant to weather-

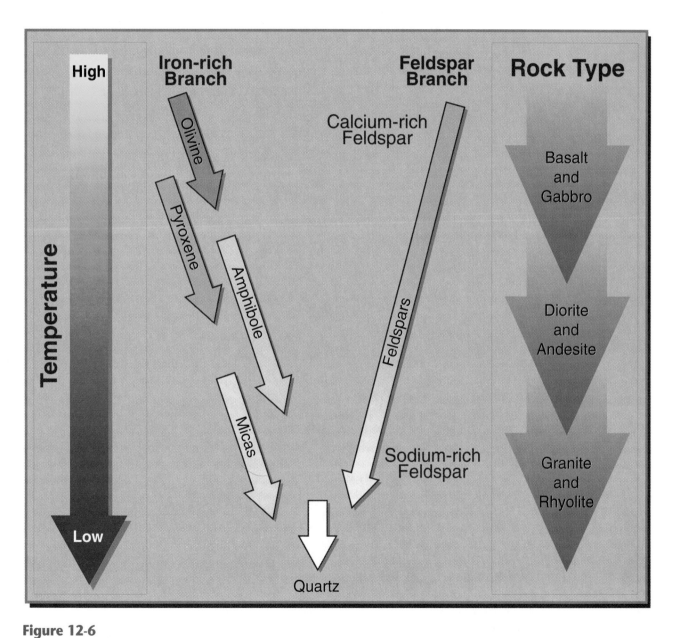

Figure 12-6

The building block for minerals in Bowen's reaction series is the *tetrahedron* (plural: *tetrahedra*). There are two branches to the reaction series—a feldspar branch and a more iron-rich branch. As the temperature of magma lowers, specific types of minerals crystallize out.

Figure 12-7

A feldspar tetrahe-
dron is similar to a
silicon-oxygen
tetrahedron, except
an aluminum atom
is positioned in the
center, rather than
a silicon atom.

Feldspar tetrahedron

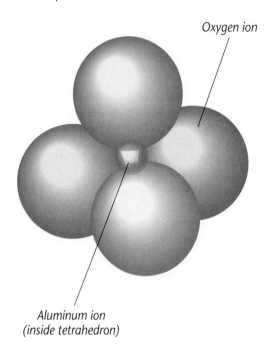

Oxygen ion

*Aluminum ion
(inside tetrahedron)*

ing a mineral should be. Quartz is a mineral that is one of the most resistant to weathering, because its structure is strongly bonded together and it is hard. Minerals at the top of the branches formed at high temperatures, so they are less stable at Earth's surface and more susceptible to weathering.

The tetrahedra in feldspars differ from the iron-rich side of Bowen's reaction series. In feldspar tetrahedra, aluminum can replace the silicon atoms at the centers of the tetrahedra, as shown in **Figure 12-7.** The more aluminum present, the weaker the tetrahedra and the more susceptible the feldspar is to chemical weathering. Although feldspar is the most common mineral group in Earth's crust, under normal surface conditions, it breaks down quickly to form clays.

Buried Treasure

Have you ever dreamed of owning a mine with a rich vein of precious metal? Mines such as this are located in the Bushveld Complex.

Where is the Bushveld Complex?

The Bushveld Complex is located in Central Transvaal, South Africa, and extends into northern Natal, Swaziland, Mozambique, Zimbabwe, and Botswana. It covers an area of close to 66 000 km^2 with a thickness of up to 7 km. The word *bushveld* means "thornbush field." Thornbushes, baobab trees, acacia trees, and tall grasses live on the surface. But far beneath the surface lies the world's largest supply of metal ores.

It is estimated that about 86 percent of the world's

Igneous Resources

Layered igneous intrusions are among the most important sources of metals. Not only valuable in the manufacturing of cars, these metals are used in everything from staplers to jewelry. As iron-rich magmas cool, the first minerals that form sink through the hot liquid and settle to the bottom of the magma body. As cooling continues, other layers form as more minerals crystallize and sink. Each different mineral uses up specific elements from the melt. Minerals can become concentrated in thin layers (1-3 m thick) covering large areas. Some of these layers are eventually mined for their mineral content, as illustrated in **Figure 12-8.**

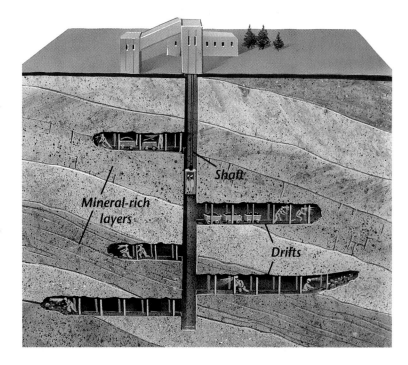

Figure 12-8

To mine an intrusion, a central shaft is dug vertically through the intrusion, then drifts are dug outward along the ore layers.

platinum, 83 percent of the chromium, 64 percent of the vanadium, and about 44 percent of the nickel are in the Bushveld Complex. The platinum ore layer alone is 1 to 5 m thick and hundreds of kilometers long. There is also gold, copper, magnesite, magnetite, fluorite, and tin.

Why is it so rich in metals?

In the 1970s, one hypothesis suggested that the Bushveld Complex was the site of a large meteoroid impact, and that the rich mineral deposits came from space. However, there are no impact structures or other evidence of impacts, so scientists discarded that hypothesis.

In the 1980s, geologists interpreted evidence to conclude that the Bushveld Complex's mineral deposits are an example of a layered igneous intrusion.

Picture a huge underground chamber of molten magma. Streams of magma enter from many directions, each holding a different mix of dissolved minerals. As the streams of magma combine, currents develop and are stirred by convection.

But the chamber is slowly cooling as the heat in the magma warms the surrounding rock. Tiny metal-rich crystals form in the cooling magma and sink. That means the bottom of the chamber rises over the years as the crystallized layers accumulate. The contents of the magma chamber progressively turn crystalline from the floor upward. Mining engineers following veins of precious metal ores have been dissecting the patterns to find where each kind of mineral was laid down.

*inter***NET**
CONNECTION

Visit the Glencoe Homepage, **http://www.glencoe.com/,** for the Chapter 12 link to the Smithsonian Gem & Mineral collection to view a wide range of minerals. Give some examples of how several minerals are used.

■ Vein Deposits: The Leftovers

The order of mineral crystalization explains why veins of rock, rich in metals, are found cutting through surrounding rock. Recall that each mineral incorporates certain elements from the magma as it forms. However, not all types of atoms are used up right away by the crystallizing minerals. Among these leftover elements are gold, silver, and lead. Large amounts of hot water may also be left over from the late stages of magma cooling. The hot water often contains dissolved minerals. These mineral-rich waters fill available cracks in the surrounding rocks. The minerals solidify to form veins of metal-rich quartz, such as those in the Sierra Nevada gold regions of California. In some cases, these waters invade porous rock, like water flowing into a sponge, and cool within cavities in the rock. Gold and copper, shown in **Figure 12-9,** are two of the elements that are concentrated in the cracks and cavities of other rocks.

Igneous rocks are an important source of many materials needed to build cars and numerous other products. The iron used to make the car bodies and engine parts and copper used in wires and circuits are courtesy of magma cooling slowly. Even sandpaper and other abrasives used to polish metals have their origins in intrusive igneous rocks.

Figure 12-9

Copper and gold can be found either concentrated in nuggets or in tiny veins in rocks.

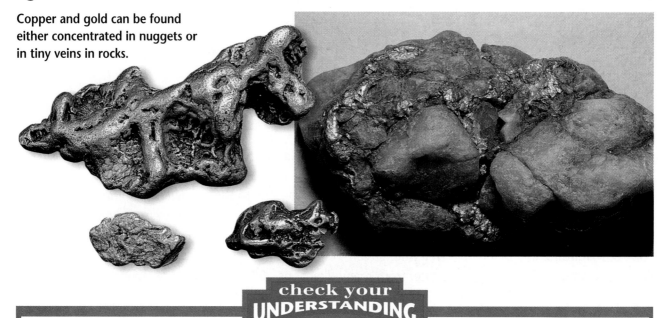

check your UNDERSTANDING

Understanding Concepts

1. Why do intrusive and extrusive igneous rocks have different sized crystals?
2. Why does the composition of magma cooling beneath Earth's surface change as it cools?
3. How are igneous rocks used as resources?

Skill Review

4. **Interpreting Scientific Illustrations** Using Bowen's reaction series as a guide, sketch a vertical section through a layered igneous intrusion, labeling the layers by the major mineral types they might contain. For more help, refer to Interpreting Scientific Illustrations in the *Skill Handbook.*

12-2 Sedimentary Rocks

Sedimentary Origins

Igneous rocks aren't the only important source of mineral resources needed to build a car. For aluminum, glass, fiberglass, and ceramic materials (for spark plugs and other parts), you must look for certain sedimentary rocks. **Sedimentary rocks** are rocks that form when sediments are cemented together. Sediments such as sand, mud, and clay are fragments that result from the weathering of other rocks. In fact, it's the weathering of other rocks that concentrates many of the minerals that are important in manufacturing all sorts of products, including automobiles.

Just as there are different igneous rocks, there are two types of sedimentary rocks as well. And like igneous rocks, only certain sedimentary rocks are valuable resources for manufacturing.

■ Chemical Sedimentary Rocks

As water flows over and through rocks, some minerals in the rocks dissolve in the water and are carried away. **Chemical sedimentary rocks** form directly from minerals dissolved in water. Water, rich in ions, forms deposits when the ions in water combine to form solids. When this happens, minerals come out of solution. This may happen for many reasons, including a change in temperature or evaporation of the water. Chemical sedimentary rocks include rock salt, some limestones, and rock gypsum. **Figure 12-10** shows a typical chemical sedimentary rock.

Materials made from chemical sedimentary rocks are not a major part of a car. Yet, without chemical sedimentary rocks, cars would be different. Limestone, a common chemical sedimentary rock, is used as flux in making steel. Flux is added to molten iron or steel to collect and remove impurities. Without flux, all of the engine parts would have to be made of cast iron and so would be heavy. The added weight would dramatically reduce the acceleration and overall speed of the car. The steel of the car's body would also be unavailable.

Objectives
- Describe the origins and types of sedimentary rocks.
- Identify sources of minerals for automobiles within sedimentary rocks.

Key Terms
sedimentary rock
chemical sedimentary rock
clastic sedimentary rock

Figure 12-10

Chemical sedimentary rocks share a common *texture,* as geologists call it. They look smooth due to intergrown crystals.

Figure 12-11

The rocks shown here were made when pieces, or clasts, of other rocks were cemented together.

■ Clastic Sedimentary Rocks

Clastic comes from a Greek word meaning "to break." Weathering breaks rocks into smaller pieces. Rocks made of broken pieces of other rocks are called **clastic sedimentary rocks.** Clastic rocks include those made from mud and silt (shale), sand (sandstone), and gravel (conglomerate). The rocks in Figure 12-11 are examples of clastic sedimentary rocks.

Clastic sedimentary rocks in their natural form are not found in cars. But useful materials that make the modern automobile possible are often concentrated in clastic sedimentary rocks. These materials are concentrated by processes at Earth's surface.

MiniLab

Identifying Chemical and Clastic Sedimentary Rocks

There are two main types of sedimentary rocks. But how can you tell them apart? Try using your knowledge of how these rocks form to classify them in this activity.

Procedure

1. Examine the rock samples.
2. Using characteristics of chemical and clastic sedimentary rocks, separate the specimens into two groups.
3. Name each specimen.

Analysis

1. What are the outstanding characteristics of clastic rock?
2. Name the fragments observed in the clastic rocks.
3. Place a few drops of acetic acid (white vinegar) on the specimens that you have classified as chemical. Calcite reacts to acids by foaming as it produces carbon dioxide. What mineral was present in one of these specimens?

Lasting Minerals

Many clastic sedimentary rocks are made of quartz sand or clay minerals. Why is this? The effects of temperature, pressure, and water at Earth's surface help answer this question.

Minerals are most stable both chemically and physically under the conditions at which they normally form. Minerals formed at high temperatures and pressures are unstable at Earth's surface and break down quickly. Olivine is a good example.

Olivine contains isolated tetrahedra of silicon and oxygen bound to one another by iron or magnesium atoms. This is a stable arrangement at high temperatures and pressures where there is little free water or oxygen gas. But at Earth's surface, oxygen from the air easily interacts with the iron atoms that connect the tetrahedra that make up olivine. If you have dropped a nail in water or left a tool in the rain, you know how quickly oxygen and water react with iron to form rust. The olivine crystal falls apart as iron is removed. Similar chemical processes can weather the metal-rich minerals amphibole, pyroxene, and feldspar.

Minerals like mica and quartz, which are formed at lower pressures and temperatures, are well-suited to Earth's surface conditions. Their pure silicon and oxygen tetrahedra are strongly linked through shared oxygen atoms. They are not as easily attacked chemically, nor are they as likely to be broken apart as most other minerals in Bowen's reaction series.

Is it any wonder that the most abundant mineral grains in streams and soils are usually quartz and mica? Can you explain why many of Earth's beaches are made of quartz sand? **Figure 12-12** shows how sands resist weathering, while hematite is vulnerable to it.

Connect to...

Biology

Limestones are commonly made of the skeletal remains of corals and algae, as well as shell fragments from other marine animals. Reefs can build up layers of limestone thousands of meters thick such as in the Great Bahama Bank. Investigate how the coral animals build their skeletons from dissolved elements in the seawater.

Figure 12-12

Some minerals are easily weathered, while others are more resistant.

A The grains of sand on this beach have survived the constant action by wind and waves.

B Iron-rich minerals easily weather by interacting with oxygen. The result is hematite.

Science and Society

Issue: Coal: A Hearth-Warming Fossil Fuel

Have you ever seen pictures of what looked like a scenic lake, only to gasp at the sight of floating dead fish? Or have you walked through a once-thriving forest, now reduced to stands of sickly pines?

The Issue

The silent killer responsible for these environmental disasters is acid rain, believed to be caused by exhaust from electric power plants, particularly those that burn coal. Large amounts of sulfur dioxide and nitric oxide can be spewed into the atmosphere from such plants. These pollutants are carried by winds over long distances. Along the way, changes occur, and chemicals such as nitrogen dioxide, nitric acid vapor, sulfuric acid, and nitrate salts fall to Earth in rain, snow, fog, and dew. They even seep into the soil and affect the plants growing there.

In addition to sulfur dioxide and nitric oxide, the improper burning of coal can produce large amounts of carbon dioxide. Carbon dioxide is not a harmful gas, and it plays an important role in regulating the temperature of the atmosphere. The carbon dioxide acts like the glass panes in a greenhouse. It lets solar radiation pass through to be absorbed by Earth's surface. Some of the heat from the surface rises but is blocked by the layer of carbon dioxide. In the past, this *greenhouse effect* has moderated Earth's climate.

Some scientists worry, though, that increased release of carbon dioxide may cause a worldwide rise in temperature, which they call *global warming*. Such a warming could cause the polar ice caps to melt, resulting in a rise in sea level. Coastal cities could be submerged by water.

Strip mines such as this are required to meet the large demand for coal.

The Background

In spite of possible harmful effects of burning coal, it is still used for several reasons. Coal is the world's most abundant fossil fuel. Dependence on coal is growing, especially in the five nations that have 74 percent of the world coal reserves. The United States and the countries that made up the former Soviet Union have 23 percent of the reserves. China has 11 percent; Australia, nine percent; and Germany, eight percent. Until recently, the United States was also the largest consumer of coal. China now holds that position.

Fifty-five percent of the fuel used to generate electricity in the United States is coal. The reason is simple: Coal is the cheapest way to produce electricity. Although it varies in different parts of the country, coal often costs less than half the price of oil and one-third the price of natural gas.

The Question

Because coal is abundant and cheap, new ways have been found to burn it more cleanly and efficiently. One method is called *fluidized-bed combustion*, which sharply reduces emissions of sulfur dioxide and nitrogen oxides. High-pressure air blasts are blown into a boiler, suspending a mixture of burning powdered coal and crushed limestone. The sulfur chemically combines with the limestone. This method removes most of the sulfur dioxide. The tumbling motion of the fuel mixture enables the temperature to be kept at 871°C, which is below the point where nitrogen oxides are formed. This not only sharply reduces emissions of nitrogen oxides, but it also burns coal more efficiently and cheaply than conventional combustion methods. The only drawback is that carbon dioxide emissions are still high. Systems employing this method have been built in the United States and several other countries.

Microbiologist Gregory Olson has a unique idea for reducing carbon dioxide emissions from

Cyanidium caldarium *thrive at high temperatures such as in this hot spring.*

burning coal. He is trying to get microbes to feed on the carbon dioxide in the flue gas. Olson is working with the microbe *Cyanidium caldarium*, which thrives in hot springs and grows best in an acid environment.

Another idea for post-combustion cleanup is to scrub flue gas by injecting ammonia. A reaction occurs that causes the nitrogen oxides to break down to form two harmless products, nitrogen and water. This process reduces nitrogen oxides by more than 90 percent. Injections of a calcium or sodium compound absorb the sulfur compounds in the flue gas. This process reduces sulfur dioxide by more than 85 percent.

GRAPHING CALCULATOR

Use a graphing calculator to graph $Y = 0.55 \times X$, where X is the total amount of electricity produced and Y is the amount of that electricity produced by burning coal. Assume that residents in a town use 2 000 000 kW of electricity each hour. Use the graph to determine how much of that electricity is likely to come from burning coal.

Sedimentary Resources

The same processes that form sedimentary rocks can concentrate minerals that can be used in the manufacture of automobiles. This is especially true for those minerals that are chemically stable at Earth's surface.

Sandstones are made up of grains of sand, which is often made of grains of quartz. Quartz is composed of the elements silicon and oxygen. Because quartz is so stable at the surface of Earth, it remains after most other minerals have chemically or physically weathered. Constant action of waves and wind removes almost everything but quartz sands from beaches. Sandstones formed from such pure beach sands are an excellent source of silicon from which glass is made for car windshields. The glass in windows, lights, and fiberglass insulation all ultimately come from the silicon in such rocks. Silicon is also used for computer chips and sensors now common in cars. Spark plugs, glow plugs, and countless other ceramic parts of a car are the products of clay minerals formed at Earth's surface. **Figure 12-13** shows some ways sedimentary rocks are used by people.

Figure 12-13

Sedimentary rocks have many uses.

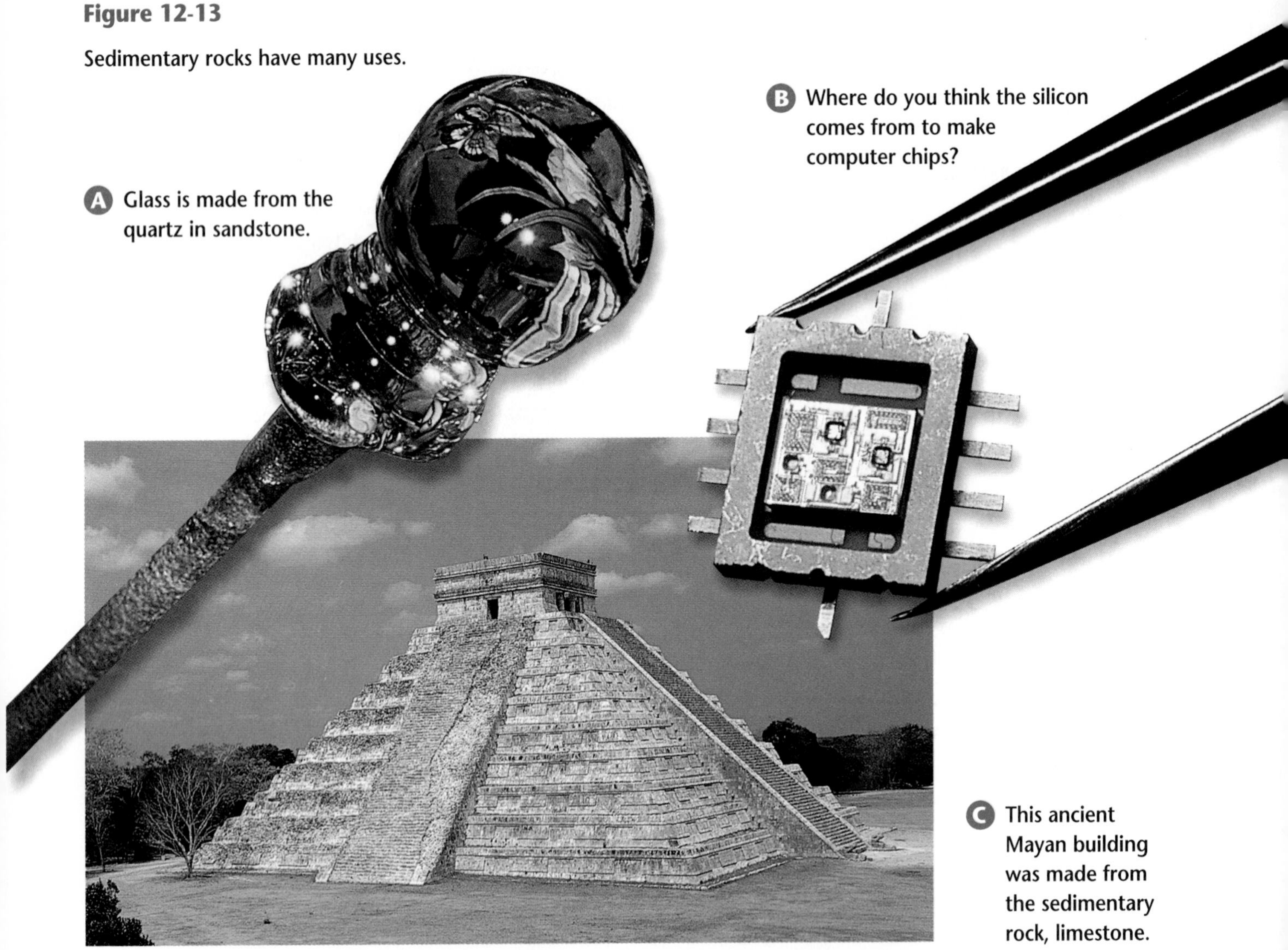

B Where do you think the silicon comes from to make computer chips?

A Glass is made from the quartz in sandstone.

C This ancient Mayan building was made from the sedimentary rock, limestone.

Figure 12-14

Bauxite is a sedimentary rock that is a common source of aluminum.

Even the aluminum in car wheels comes from sedimentary rock. A primary ore of aluminum is bauxite. Bauxite forms when rocks are exposed to large amounts of rain in a warm, humid climate. Silicon, potassium, sodium, and most other elements are chemically removed from the soil, leaving behind undissolved compounds of aluminum. These aluminum oxides make up bauxite. Bauxite often forms nodules the size of peas or slightly larger. **Figure 12-14** shows what bauxite looks like. If aluminum becomes concentrated enough, bauxite can be mined as an ore.

Perhaps most surprising is a possible sedimentary origin for the great iron ore deposits of Michigan, Minnesota, and southern Canada. These deposits formed early in the history of continents. These ancient sedimentary rocks are mined as one of the world's main sources of iron ore.

In all of the above cases, the processes that make sedimentary rocks have served to concentrate useful minerals into economically usable amounts.

check your UNDERSTANDING

Understanding Concepts

1. In general terms, how do the processes that form sedimentary rocks serve to concentrate elements essential to the building of cars?
2. Rank the types of sedimentary rocks in order of importance in the making of an automobile.
3. How does a mineral's position in Bowen's reaction series relate to how easily it breaks down at Earth's surface?

Skill Review

4. **Observing and Inferring** Most of the sand you see is quartz. In Hawaii, there is a beach that is primarily made up of olivine grains. Why do we find olivine in a Hawaiian beach but not near your home? For help, refer to Observing and Inferring in the *Skill Handbook.*

Metamorphic Rocks

Metamorphism

Objectives

- Identify the various types of metamorphism.
- Discuss metamorphic rocks as sources for automotive minerals.
- Compare origins of the classes of rock using the rock cycle.

Key Terms

metamorphic rock
contact
  metamorphism
regional
  metamorphism
rock cycle

You've learned about two types of rock that provide resources in manufacturing a car. There is a third important type of rock, but it contributes only a little to making a car.

When rocks are exposed to high pressure and heat, they change. Even if they don't melt, their structure and properties can change. When this happens, the new material is called **metamorphic rock.** *Metamorphic* comes from the Greek word for "changed shape." These rocks result from two types of metamorphism—contact and regional.

■ Contact Metamorphism

In **contact metamorphism,** hot magma of igneous intrusions heats up the surrounding rock. This heat can cause minerals in the rocks to change or fuse together. **Figure 12-15** shows how contact metamorphism can convert limestone into marble.

■ Regional Metamorphism

Under certain circumstances, an entire region of a continental mass can be exposed to high pressures and temperatures, causing the rocks to undergo changes in mineral composition and

Figure 12-15

When magma is pushed up through a layer of limestone, the heat and pressure change the limestone. The limestone crystals are altered and rearranged to form marble.

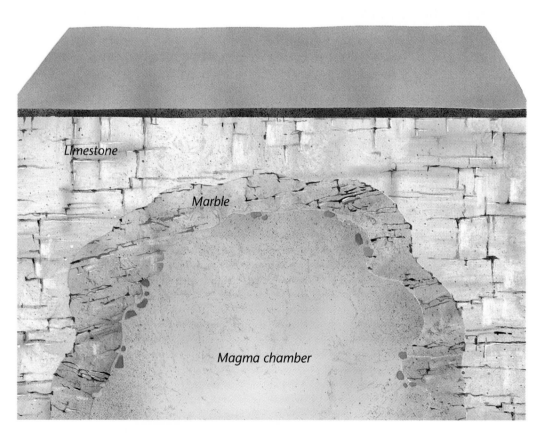

Limestone

Marble

Magma chamber

crystal size. This is known as **regional metamorphism** and most commonly takes place in the middle and lower regions of Earth's crust.

The oldest rocks of Earth's continental crust are dominated by regionally metamorphosed areas. The cores of major continents such as Africa and North America are dominated by slate, schist, and gneiss, typical of regional metamorphism. In the United States, much of New England underwent regional metamorphism early in its history. The famous marble deposits of Vermont were once limestones, and rocks such as shale have been transformed by pressure and heat into slate and schist. **Figure 12-16** on the next page shows rocks that formed by regional metamorphism.

Thinking Lab Inferring and Concluding

Regional or Contact Metamorphism?

When looking at metamorphic rocks in an area, you can use certain clues to determine whether the rocks have formed through regional or contact metamorphism. One clue is the area of metamorphosed rock. Other clues are the degree of metamorphism and the presence of nearby intrusive igneous rocks.

Analysis
Here are two examples in which one of each type of metamorphism has occurred. Keep in mind your knowledge of both types of metamorphism as you read them.

1. During the formation of the Southern Appalachian mountains, many of the shales found in North Carolina underwent extreme pressure and changed into slate.

2. Near Leesburg, Virginia, there is a deposit of red sandstone. In some places, this sandstone falls apart easily. In other places, the sandstone is securely cemented, and in addition, the surface of the sandstone is covered with green nodules of a mineral that is not found in areas with the weakly cemented sandstone. In the areas with the green minerals, an igneous intrusive is found near the sandstones.

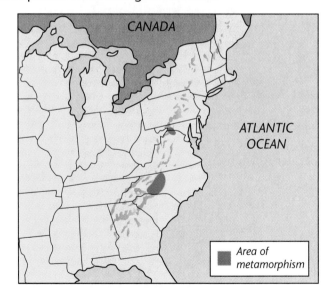

Thinking Critically
From the evidence given, infer which rocks have been regionally metamorphosed and which rocks have been contact metamorphosed. Be certain to outline your evidence. What other evidence would you search for to support your conclusions?

The importance of metamorphic rock products is shrinking as substitutes become available. Until the 1960s, asbestos, a mineral commonly found in metamorphic rocks, was commonly used as a fireproof material in insulation, shingles, and clothing. However, some kinds of asbestos dust, when breathed into the lungs, can increase the possibility of cancer in humans. As a result, most of the asbestos in public buildings has been removed or sealed in place so none can get into the air and be inhaled by people.

Even graphite, a metamorphic form of carbon once used in pencil leads, is used less. New types of pencil leads, which do not smear as easily, substitute clay minerals for graphite. Graphite, however, is still used as a lubricant.

Figure 12-16

Metamorphism often gives rocks a distinctive banding pattern.

A This folded gneiss is a common regionally metamorphosed rock.

B The unique colors and patterns in metamorphosed rocks make them ideal for sculptures.

C The folding that results from regional metamorphism can be seen in this landscape.

The Rock Cycle

The law of conservation of matter states that matter can be neither created nor destroyed. It can, however, simply change form. The natural recycling of the crust illustrates how matter is conserved during processes that reshape the character of Earth. One convenient way to think about crustal recycling is to think of how major groups of rocks can be changed into one another.

Figure 12-17 shows how sedimentary, igneous, and metamorphic rocks are transformed into new rocks. Metamorphic or sedimentary rocks melt and become igneous rocks once they have cooled and solidified. Sedimentary rocks can be buried and placed under pressure and heat without melting and can be changed into metamorphic rocks. Igneous and metamorphic rocks weather, providing the material for sedimentary rocks. These transformations from one rock type to another define the **rock cycle**. With recycling, minerals are redistributed in Earth's crust and can be concentrated into deposits that are economically useful.

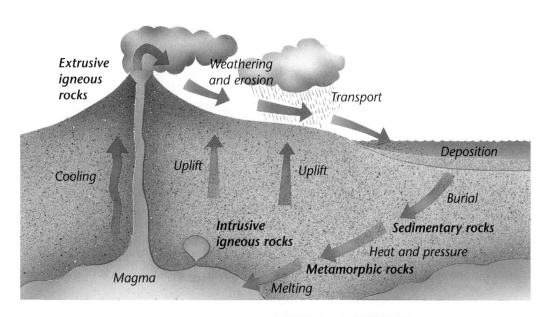

Figure 12-17

The processes that transform rocks from one type to another can be represented by the rock cycle.

check your UNDERSTANDING

Understanding Concepts

1. Most of the states of Maine, Vermont, Massachusetts, and New Hampshire show metamorphic rocks at the surface. What kind of metamorphism is responsible for this?

2. Some of the highest buildings in the world are built on metamorphic rock. Why?

3. Would an automobile manufacturer be interested in buying land with metamorphic rock on it as a source for materials to make cars? Why or why not?

Skill Review

4. **Observing and Inferring** What does the rock cycle tell us about Earth? For help, refer to Observing and Inferring in the *Skill Handbook*.

Reuse, Recycle, re:ART

In this unit about the limited nature of the world's natural resources, you've probably been able to conclude that there are no easy or quick solutions to the problems of pollution and waste. Historically, one solution has been the landfill. Outside many cities and towns around the world, available land is converted into burial mounds for trash.

Recycling and Trash

Now, with acceptable space for landfills becoming harder to find, people are increasingly concerned about finding ways to dispose of trash without compromising Earth's resources. While many cities have mandated recycling programs for materials such as paper, glass, and aluminum in an effort to reduce the amount of these items going into landfills, more creative solutions are being tried.

Art and Trash

In 1993, in Columbus, Ohio, the Solid Waste Authority of Central Ohio introduced a program called re:ART. The program links materials donated by more than 25 businesses and institutions with member schools, nonprofit art organizations, and individual artists. A local artist, school, theater group, or museum, for example, can obtain much-needed materials that might otherwise have ended up in a landfill. Items such as outdated wallpaper, fabrics, paint, scrap metal and wood, drywall, and in one instance, old theater seats, are donated to a "store" where members shop for materials for free. The photo on this page shows how a student at a local visual arts high school has used re:ART materials to create a sculpture. In one year, re:ART saved 100 000 pounds of materials from being buried in local landfills. Such programs encourage responsible and creative use of resources and add to the community.

Thinking Critically

1. Do some *research* to find out what kinds of recycling programs your community has. Are there any unique programs like re:ART? Present the results of your research in an oral presentation or in a short paper.
2. Bring to class items for recycling. *Design* a piece of art made from some of these items.

Read the statements below that review major points presented in the chapter. Using the concepts that you have learned, answer each question *in your Journal.*

1 Igneous rock is still a source of new rock in Earth's crust. Bowen's reaction series explains the structures and minerals we see in igneous intrusions. *What are the two factors that control the makeup of rocks in a cooled igneous intrusion?*

2 Sedimentary rocks are made from the remains of other rocks or from animals and plants. These rocks concentrate many of the materials necessary to our modern technological society. *In what ways does the process of creating sedimentary rock concentrate these important minerals and materials?*

3 Earth is a dynamic system; it is constantly changing. The rock cycle represents the changes rocks can undergo. *What conditions determine how a rock will change in going through the rock cycle?*

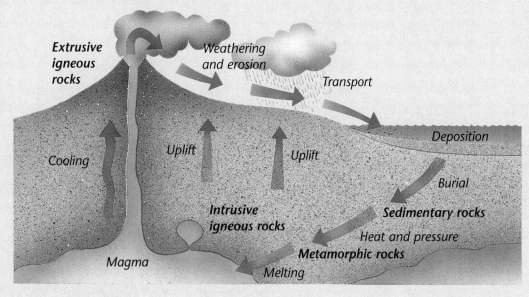

Extrusive igneous rocks

Weathering and erosion

Transport

Deposition

Cooling

Uplift

Uplift

Burial

Intrusive igneous rocks

Sedimentary rocks

Heat and pressure

Magma

Metamorphic rocks

Melting

Using Key Science Terms

Bowen's reaction series
chemical sedimentary rock
clastic sedimentary rock
contact metamorphism
extrusive igneous rock
igneous rock
intrusive igneous rock
magma
metamorphic rock
regional metamorphism
rock cycle
sedimentary rock

Use terms from the list above to answer the following.

1. Overall, how does each type of rock change into different types of rock?
2. Compare regional and contact metamorphism.
3. What do all igneous rocks have in common?

Understanding Ideas

Using complete sentences, answer the following questions in your Journal.

1. Why is the rock in Hawaii different from the rock of the Sierra Nevada mountains?
2. How does our understanding of Bowen's reaction series explain the great abundance of quartz in the streams and fields of Earth?
3. Why are so few metamorphic rocks sources of materials to build cars?

4. Would you agree or disagree with the statement "Sedimentary rocks are as important a source of usable metals as igneous rocks"? Explain.

Developing Skills

Use your understanding of the concepts developed in this chapter to answer each of the following questions.

1. **Sequencing** Briefly describe the history of an automobile windshield, starting with a suitable magma.
2. **Recognizing Cause and Effect** Describe why certain minerals are rarely found in stream deposits while others are common.
3. **Comparing and Contrasting** Compare and contrast the three rock types on the basis of energy needed to form them.
4. **Concept Mapping** Complete the concept map below of the rock cycle.

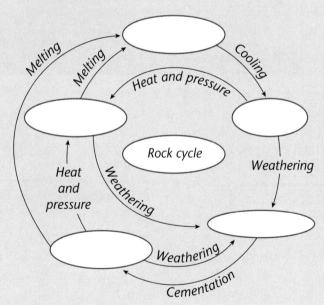

Critical Thinking

In your Journal, *answer each of the following questions.*

1. What would you expect to see as erosion wears away a layered intrusion solidified from iron-rich magma?

2. There is no original crust left anywhere on Earth because it has all undergone some type of change. Why aren't some people worried that buried nuclear waste will someday be brought to the surface by geological processes?

3. You pick up two rocks. Rock A is dark and glassy. When you look at rock B with a hand lens, you notice that it is made up of sand-sized grains. What types of rocks did you find?

Problem Solving

Read the following problem and discuss your answers in a brief paragraph.

As manager of a minerals exploration group, you are faced with a decision. Your company has a chance to lease one of two large ($10\,000\ km^2$) tracts of land in Siberia for mineral exploration. The Russian government says you may explore either area or both areas for 90 days before making your choice. At the end of 60 days, your results in both areas are about equal. Area A is supposed to have numerous intrusions rich in olivine and hornblende, while area B is known to have a number of intrusions that are primarily quartz and mica.

Which area would most likely have more valuable minerals? Explain your answer.

CONNECTING IDEAS

1. **Theme—Energy** Minerals formed in high-energy conditions of great heat and pressure do not survive well in low-energy environments such as normal surface weather. Why?

2. **Theme—Systems and Interactions** How do heat and pressure act together to drive the rock cycle?

3. **Theme—Stability** The phrase "solid as a rock" implies strength and permanence. Yet, we know that all rocks erode into grains of sand destined to be cemented into new, sedimentary rock. Why, then, do we use rocks as symbols of permanence?

4. **Art Connection** How can reusing industrial waste in art conserve resources that come from rocks?

5. **Science and Society** Explain how the sedimentary rock, coal, is a valuable resource despite some of its problems.

CHAPTER 13

Petroleum Chemistry
Petroleum Power

t's a great day for a drive. You decide to go to the beach, but as you cruise along, you notice something disturbing. Crossing a bridge, you see a multicolored slick of oil on the estuary waters. You don't know where it came from—possibly an oil spill, a careless boater, or even someone thoughtless enough to change the oil in the car by letting it drain into a storm sewer. You do know, however, that the same oil that heats our homes and runs the car in which you ride must be used carefully and wisely to avoid damaging the environment we all share.

▶ *In the following activity, explore the source of oil.*

MiniLab

How does petroleum form?

The origin of petroleum involves the recycling of organic materials, which are materials that come from once-living organisms. What part of the organic matter forms petroleum?

Procedure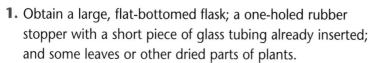

1. Obtain a large, flat-bottomed flask; a one-holed rubber stopper with a short piece of glass tubing already inserted; and some leaves or other dried parts of plants.

2. Place the plant matter in the flask and put the stopper in the neck of the flask.

3. Using a hot plate, gently and evenly heat the flask.

4. Note the color of the organic matter as you continue heating. Have your teacher use a bottle or a test tube to collect some of the gases exiting the glass tube in the top of the flask. Use a match to try to light the gases.

Analysis

1. What happens when you try to light the gas produced?

2. What does this experiment tell you about organic materials and their contents?

Formation and Migration

Objectives

■ Explain what petroleum is and how it forms.

■ Relate properties of rocks to migration and trapping of petroleum.

Key Terms

petroleum
source rock
conodont
migration
porosity
permeability
reservoir

Formation

After more than a century of society's dependence on petroleum, you might think we would know all about it. Yet, there are many unanswered questions concerning how petroleum forms and how it moves underground.

Petroleum is a complex mixture of liquids and gases that forms underground. Because these compounds are composed mainly of hydrogen and carbon, they are called hydrocarbons. The liquid portion is called *oil,* and the gases are called *natural gas.*

■ What is petroleum?

Most scientists studying the formation of oil and gas agree that **petroleum** is the naturally recycled remains of once-living organisms, most of which were microscopic. Most of these microscopic organisms lived in ancient seas in shallow water. As they died, their remains settled to the bottom of the sea. They were covered by more dead organisms and sediments, such as mud. When hardened, these materials became petroleum **source rocks,** which are rocks in which oil and gas are created.

■ The Source

Recycling of once-living organisms into hydrocarbons is the most likely source for the oil that powers your car and the natural gas that heats your home. Sometimes hydrocarbons form rapidly as once-living material (also called organic matter) is recycled. An example of this type of hydrocarbon formation is shown in **Figure 13-1.**

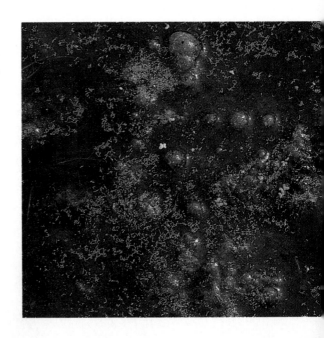

Figure 13-1

Have you ever been close to a foul-smelling swamp and noticed bubbles? If you look at almost any swampy area, especially during the warmer months of the year, you will see an occasional bubble breaking the surface of the standing water. These bubbles may be natural gas, which is a by-product from decaying organic matter in the bottom of the swamp. Other gases are also formed, giving the swamp its foul smell.

However, the presence of organic matter in a rock does not guarantee that oil or gas will form. Some sedimentary rocks that are rich in organic carbon are not source rocks. In other cases, rocks with little organic matter seem to have been the source for huge amounts of oil and gas in major fields. A critical factor for oil and gas formation is heat. Organic matter must be heated to produce the hydrocarbons. Try the following Thinking Lab to help you understand how heat and organic matter are involved in the production of natural gas and oil.

Thinking Lab   Recognizing Cause and Effect

Can color be related to temperature of organic materials?

To determine the relationship between temperature and petroleum production, geologists need to know how hot a source rock has become. An experiment was done to determine whether the color of a sample of organic material would change with a change in temperature. Some light brown, pine sawdust was placed in a one-pint paint can. A hole was punched in the lid, and the lid was fastened tightly onto the can. The can and its contents were heated.

Analysis
After a period of time, the can was removed from the heat and allowed to cool. It was opened, and the sawdust was medium brown. The sawdust was replaced with the same amount of fresh sawdust. The lid was replaced, and the can was heated for the same amount of time at a higher temperature. When cooled and checked again, the material in the can was black.

Thinking Critically
Make a hypothesis about the relationship between temperature and color for heated organic materials. Explain why the sawdust did not burn when it was heated.

■ The Role of Temperature
Geologists disagree on how much heat is needed to create hydrocarbons. One group of geologists cites good evidence that the minimum temperature for oil formation can be very low. Sediments from the Gulf of Mexico, which have never had temperatures much higher than 50°C (the temperature of a warm bowl of soup), contain significant amounts of hydrocarbons. This evidence suggests that oil and gas can form almost immediately after sediments are deposited.

A Examples of conodonts

Figure 13-2

Anita Harris determined the relationship between the colors of toothlike fossils called conodonts and the temperatures to which they have been heated.

B Anita Harris

Connect to...

Biology

When geologists drill into Earth's crust and find fossilized shells of foraminifera, they can reliably date the rocks in which they are drilling. Find out what foraminifera are.

Other geologists are convinced that most hydrocarbons form when somewhat higher temperatures "cook" them out of organic matter in the rock. These experts cite places where rocks that are rich in organic matter have not been heated past 100°C and are not source rocks for any oil or gas.

If a rock has been metamorphosed, you can tell how hot the rock became by looking at how the minerals in the rock have changed. Unfortunately, temperatures that are high enough to change rock sometimes destroy hydrocarbons.

If moderate temperatures generate hydrocarbons but higher temperatures destroy them, we need to know just how hot potential source rocks have been. Then we can hypothesize whether hydrocarbons were generated and whether they may have survived. How do geologists in search of petroleum know how hot potential source rocks have become?

■ Fossil Evidence

One way geologists measure the maximum temperature rocks have reached uses a relationship between the color of certain fossils and the temperatures to which they have been heated. Toothlike fossils called **conodonts,** shown in **Figure 13-2A,** are found in marine sedimentary rocks that were formed between 525 and 225 million years ago. What do the colors of these tiny fossils have to do with the temperature of a rock and the generation of petroleum?

In the late 1960s, a young graduate student, Anita Harris, shown in **Figure 13-2B,** noticed that conodonts in the Appalachian Mountains were of different colors depending on where they were found. Harris continued her work on conodont color while employed by the United States Geological Survey. Soon, she could tell the source of a conodont just by its color. Evidence revealed by her research suggested that color changes in conodonts indicate how deep the conodonts were buried and the highest temperature to which they were exposed.

Harris's findings were supported by those of other geologists. Similar results were found by comparing color changes in other kinds of fossils in younger source rocks. Conodont color does, in fact, reflect the effects of heating on organic materials. Harris's discovery is now used in many areas of study, including oil exploration.

Migration and Concentration

No matter how petroleum is produced, geologists agree that it forms in small amounts at a time throughout large volumes of source rock. To be useful, the small amounts of oil and gas formed must move and be trapped together in large amounts. The following MiniLab will help you understand how oil and gas become trapped.

MiniLab

A Model Hydrocarbon Trap

The trapping and collection of petroleum depend on the basic properties of water, oil, and gas. Hydrocarbons are not trapped in large, open caves or pools underground. Oil traps contain rocks that are saturated with water, oil, and gas. In this experiment, you will trap gas and oil. For simplicity, the rock has been removed, leaving only the water.

Procedure

1. Add water to a large fish tank or the lab sink until it is filled halfway with water. Add just a few drops of blue food coloring to the water to give it a blue tint. Obtain a small, transparent glass bowl or beaker and a length of lab hose.

2. Put the bowl or beaker under water until it fills with water. Once it is full, turn it over without letting it break the surface. You should have an upside-down bowl full of water in the tank.

3. Soak three dry sponges with salad oil.

4. As you hold the inverted bowl near the top of the water, quickly plunge a sponge to the bottom of the tank, hold it under the bowl, and squeeze it out.

5. Repeat step 4 with the other two sponges until there is a visible layer of oil floating in the bowl.

6. Record your observations *in your Journal.*

7. Now put the end of the tube on the bottom of the tank and gently blow air bubbles while moving the end around the tank. What happens when air rises into the bowl? What happens to air that misses the bowl?

Analysis

1. What controls where each material—water, oil, and air (gas)—ends up in the inverted bowl? Why did the oil and air end up in the bowl at all?

2. If the bowl were an oil field and you drilled into the top of it, what material would you expect to hit first? Second? Last?

Ever since the first oil well in the United States was drilled in 1859, most of the world's petroleum has been produced from wells drilled specifically for oil and gas. Simply drilling into source rock will not produce the amount of oil and gas needed. Instead, geologists look for oil in underground places called traps, much like the one you modeled in the MiniLab. Look at **Figure 13-3.** These traps accumulate oil generated over long periods of time and from large areas of source rock. The movement of oil from source rocks to the trap is called **migration.**

■ Migration Theories

Geologists disagree on when petroleum moves from source rocks to the trap and what causes this migration.

Geologists who support the theory of early generation of oil at low temperatures also favor the theory of early migration. These scientists hypothesize that migration takes place as sediments are compressed into rock. As they are being compacted, hydrocarbons and water are squeezed out of the sediments the way water is wrung from a sponge. Escaping water washes the newly released petroleum out of source rocks and causes it to migrate into traps.

Scientists who hypothesize a later origin for oil assume that the petroleum must move through solid rock. This belief is not a problem or major concern because many rocks allow the flow of fluids. In this case, the oil migrates at a much slower rate and gradually fills traps as petroleum accumulates.

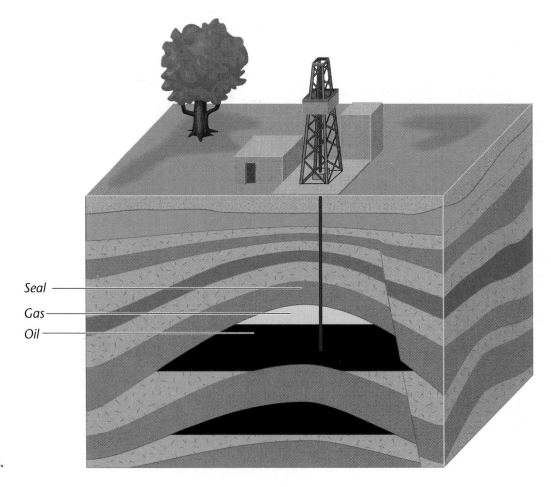

Figure 13-3

Traps must contain a seal through which oil and gas cannot easily pass. Under the seal, oil and gas collect in rocks that allow movement of fluids.

Seal

Gas

Oil

■ How Petroleum Migrates

Oil or gas can move from a source rock to a trap by flowing through sediments or rock. The distance moved may be relatively short, or it may be many miles. For oil or gas to flow through it, there must be space between the grains that make up the rock or sediment. These spaces are called pores. Examine **Figure 13-4A** to see the pores that can be found in soil. Because soil contains pores, water can travel through the soil.

The percentage of open space in a rock or sediment is its **porosity.** The greater the porosity, the more open space there is in the rock to hold or pass oil. A porous rock, sandstone, and a nonporous rock, shale, are shown in **Figures 13-4B** and **13-4C.** Use the following Investigation to find out more about porosity.

Figure 13-4

The porosity of a rock is one factor that determines how easily a fluid passes through the rock.

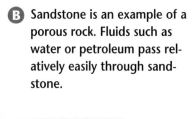

B Sandstone is an example of a porous rock. Fluids such as water or petroleum pass relatively easily through sandstone.

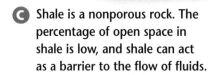

A Most soils are porous. Therefore, water will soak into a porous soil and will fill the spaces between the soil particles and any air trapped in the soil.

C Shale is a nonporous rock. The percentage of open space in shale is low, and shale can act as a barrier to the flow of fluids.

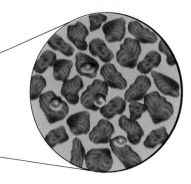

What controls porosity?

Porosity controls how much fluid a rock holds. But what factors control a rock's porosity? In this Investigation, you will predict what physical factors control rock porosity, and then you will evaluate your predictions.

Preparation

Problem
What factors control porosity in rocks?

Hypothesis
In your group, brainstorm possible hypotheses and discuss the evidence on which each hypothesis is based. Select the best hypothesis from your list.

Objectives
In this Investigation, you will:
- *Predict* what factor or factors control porosity in rocks.
- *Determine* an effective way to test each factor and record the data.
- *Make a conclusion* as to which factors most affect porosity.

Possible Materials
400-mL beakers
BBs
marbles
glass beads
small wood cubes
small plastic blocks
100-mL graduated cylinder
water

Safety Precautions
Be careful when handling glass beads.

Plan the Experiment

1 Examine the materials provided by your teacher. As a group, make a list of the possible ways you might test your hypothesis.

2 Agree on one way that your group could investigate your hypothesis. Design an experiment that will allow for the collection of quantitative data.

3 Prepare a list of numbered directions. Include a list of materials.

4 Design and construct a table for recording your data. What will you measure to obtain your data?

Check the Plan
Discuss the following points with other group members to decide the final procedure for your experiment.

1 Determine how you will set up each trial. How many factors can you test in one trial?

2 Have you set up a control? Does your experiment test only one variable?

3 *Make sure your teacher has approved your experimental plan before you proceed further.*

4 Carry out your experiment. Make any needed observations, and complete your data table.

What factors control how well water travels past these rocks?

Analyze and Conclude

1. **Observing and Inferring** From your observations, explain how additional materials or trials might make a difference to your outcome.

2. **Analyzing the Procedure** Did your experiment provide a clear test of your hypothesis? Explain.

3. **Drawing Conclusions** Which of the factors you tested actually affect rock porosity?

4. **Evaluating Predictions** Explain how your results supported or didn't support your hypothesis.

Going Further

Application
Repeat your experiment using actual earth materials such as sand, gravel, soil, and clay. From your results, infer how porosity of the soil might affect performance of a water well drilled into that soil.

You learned in the Investigation what factors affect porosity. But porosity is not the only factor that controls migration of a fluid.

If fluid is to flow through a rock, the pores in the rock must be connected. Think about a sink with a stopper in it. When a small amount of water is added to the sink, the water does not flow down the drain because there is no opening between the sink and the drain. When the stopper is removed, the water flows because there is now a connection between the sections.

A material can be quite porous, but fluids will not pass through it if the pores are not connected. The amount of connection between pores is called **permeability.** Permeability is demonstrated in the following MiniLab.

MiniLab

Permeability: Go with the Flow

The flow of fluid through a solid is controlled by several factors. Porosity, the amount of empty space in a material, is but one factor. In this activity, you will discover another factor that is even more important than porosity.

Procedure

1. Collect several pieces of foam rubber, sponge, and Styrofoam that might have been used in packaging.
2. Cut each type of material into rectangular pieces of equal size and thickness. Weigh each piece of material and record your results in a data table *in your Journal.*
3. Now suspend each sample above a beaker and pour 50 mL of salad oil over it. In your data table, record the time it takes for the oil to drain through each sample.

Analysis

1. Did the oil flow easily through all of the samples? Explain.
2. Did any of the lighter samples not allow oil to flow through? What do you think caused this to be the case?

As was shown in the MiniLab, a great amount of connection between pores means high permeability. Highly permeable materials allow fluids to flow through them easily.

■ Traps

All petroleum traps, or **reservoirs,** share several common features, as shown in **Figure 13-5.** A hydrocarbon reservoir is like a well-designed bottle for a sports drink. There is plenty of space (porosity), a wide neck for easy emptying (permeability), and a leakproof cap (seal).

Because they often have high porosity and permeability, sandstone and limestone are usually the best reservoir rocks. Much of the petroleum from the Gulf of Mexico and northern Alaska comes from porous sandstone such as that shown in **Figure 13-4B** on page 391. The great oil-bearing rocks of the Middle East are mostly limestone.

Figure 13-5

A petroleum trap involves several different types of rocks arranged in certain relationships.

A Traps must be made of porous rock. The greater the porosity, the better the reservoir because there is more space for petroleum in porous rock.

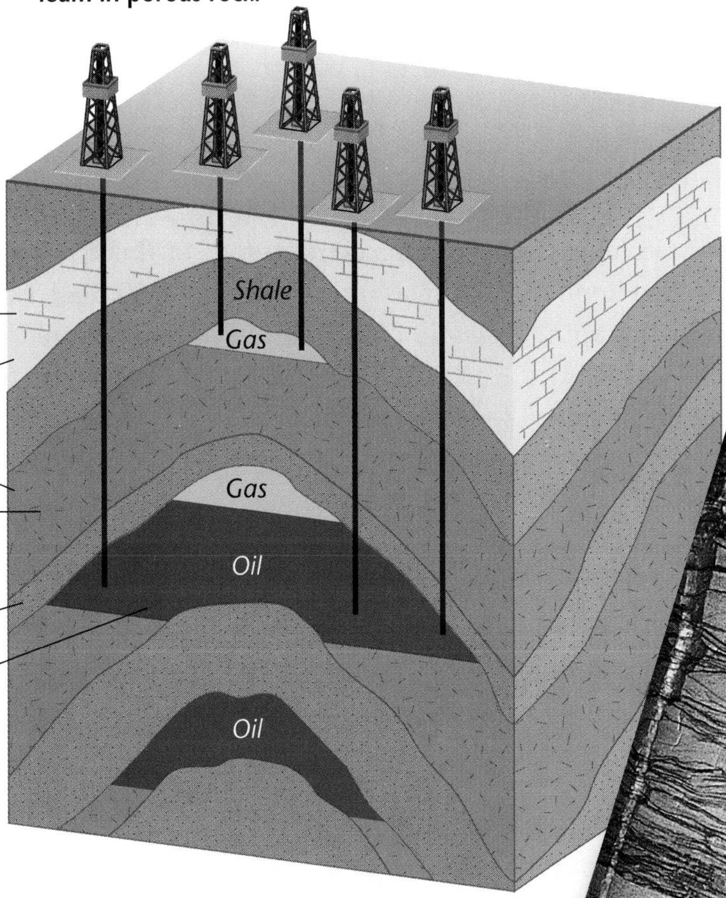

D This core is from a well drilled in porous and permeable limestone. Wells in reservoirs in this type of rock can easily produce hundreds of barrels of oil each day.

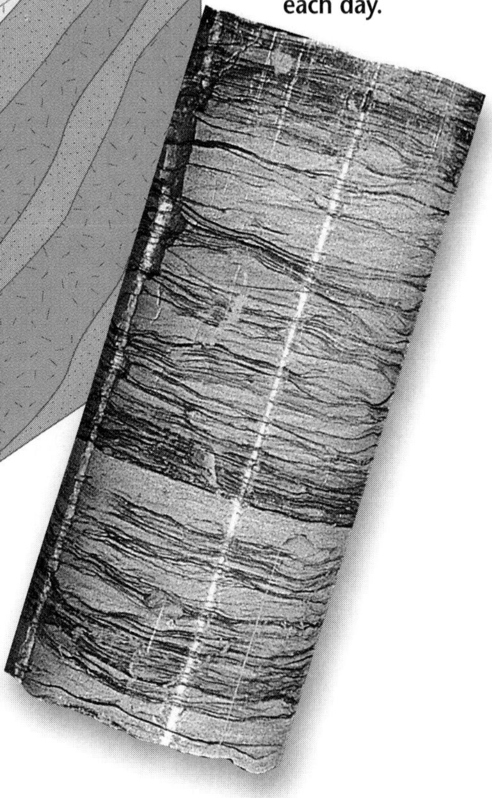

Limestone

Porous rock

Saturated sandstone

Nonporous rock (seal)

Reservoir

Shale

Gas

Gas

Oil

Oil

B Reservoir rocks need to be permeable. Permeable rocks permit oil and gas to flow easily into and through the trap to any wells that are drilled there. Each well then drains hydrocarbons from a large area.

C All reservoirs need a seal. The seal keeps oil in the trap once it arrives. The seal is often a rock that has low permeability, such as shale.

check your UNDERSTANDING

Understanding Concepts

1. Why doesn't drilling wells into source rocks always produce petroleum in usable amounts?
2. Explain how the terms *oil, natural gas,* and *petroleum* are related to each other.
3. Petroleum geologists say that the three things an oil field must have are source, reservoir, and seal. Explain this statement.

Skill Review

4. **Comparing and Contrasting** Compare and contrast the two major theories in the debate about oil generation and migration. What answer might satisfy both sides? For help, refer to Comparing and Contrasting in the *Skill Handbook.*

Exploration and Recovery

Objectives
- Classify and sequence steps in the search for oil.
- Compare and contrast oil-exploration methods.

Key Terms
seismic prospecting
geophone
seismic profile

Figure 13-6

Many types of maps are used to locate oil and gas deposits.

Geologic Mapping

Geologists searching for petroleum depend upon three primary tools: geologic mapping, seismic prospecting, and well logs.

In Chapter 12, we looked briefly at surface geologic mapping. Surface maps created from satellite images are used to map remote areas, as shown in **Figure 13-6A.** However, where there are wells that supply rock samples, maps can be constructed based on rock patterns below Earth's surface. An example of this type of map is shown in **Figure 13-6B.** Based on these maps, geologists can interpret where the best places are to explore for oil and natural gas.

Once an area that is likely to contain oil and gas has been selected, geophysicists join the exploration team. Using an echo-sounding technique called **seismic prospecting,** which is not unlike the fish and depth finders on some sport boats, a picture of the rocks below Earth's surface can be constructed.

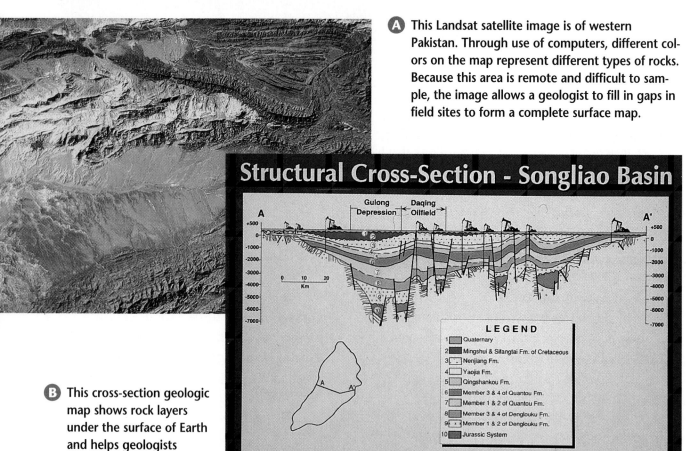

A This Landsat satellite image is of western Pakistan. Through use of computers, different colors on the map represent different types of rocks. Because this area is remote and difficult to sample, the image allows a geologist to fill in gaps in field sites to form a complete surface map.

B This cross-section geologic map shows rock layers under the surface of Earth and helps geologists locate oil and gas deposits.

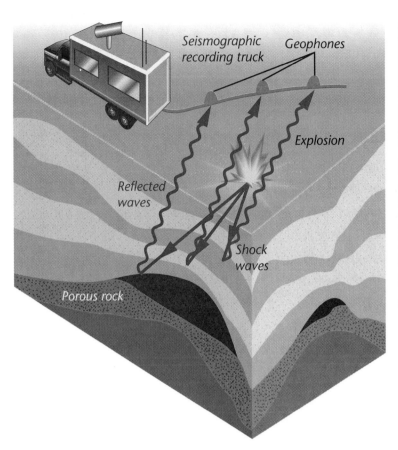

Figure 13-7

Seismic-exploration crews look for oil and gas. Sound waves are generated at the surface and travel down into Earth. The waves hit different rock layers and echo back to the surface. By recording the time it takes for this to happen, a picture of the rocks hidden beneath the surface can be made.

Seismic Prospecting

At noon in a small Oklahoma town, two men and a woman step into a local cafe. Although their muddy coveralls are in the truck bed, everyone knows they are a survey crew prospecting for oil. Trying not to be obvious, the locals strain to hear the newcomers' conversation. If all goes right, an oil company will drill a deep well searching for the energy hidden in the ground. And someone in the cafe might be on the way to being a little less concerned about the price of wheat, corn, or cattle.

The crew is part of a seismic-prospecting team that uses sound waves to show the rock layers beneath Earth's surface. A picture of the inside of Earth, like a sonogram of an unborn child,

tells much about features hidden from everyday sight. Much of the present exploration for oil and natural gas is done using this technique.

■ Creating a Profile

In seismic prospecting, sound waves from a small explosion or vibrating truck travel down into Earth as shown in **Figure 13-7.** As the waves strike different rock layers, some energy is reflected back toward the surface. This reflection of waves is like hearing an echo in a canyon or seeing light reflected back from a mirror.

The following Investigation will help you learn more about waves used in seismic prospecting.

INVESTIGATION

Wave Speed

Two different kinds of waves are used in seismic exploration. One type, a compressional wave, is the same as a sound wave. In a compressional wave, the particles of Earth move back and forth in the direction the wave travels. A second type of wave is a transverse wave. In this wave, the particles of Earth move at right angles to the direction of the wave. You have created a transverse wave if you have ever flicked a rope, sending a snakelike wave down it. Now, model both types of waves and compare some of their properties.

Preparation

Problem

How are compressional and transverse waves alike? How do they differ?

Objectives

In this Investigation, you will:
- *Compare and contrast* types of waves.
- *Measure* length and time.
- *Calculate* the speed of waves.

Materials

meterstick
Slinky or wave spring
stopwatch

Safety Precautions

Do not release either end of a stretched spring. Walk one end of the spring to the other before releasing hold on the spring.

Data and Observations			
Wave Type — Compressional			
Trial	Length of Spring, cm	Time, s	Speed, cm/s
1			
2			
3			
4			

INVESTIGATION

Procedure

1 Work in groups of three students. Decide who will be the timer/data recorder for your group.

2 Make two data tables like the one shown—one for compressional waves and one for transverse waves.

3 On an uncarpeted floor, stretch the Slinky to a length of 1 m. Record that length in your data table.

4 Make a compressional wave by pressing ten coils of spring together and then releasing them. Practice doing this until you can make a wave that travels down the spring. If you need to, you may include more coils in your starting compression.

5 Measure and record the time it takes for the wave to travel down the spring.

6 Extend the spring a meter at a time, and repeat the process of sending a wave and measuring and recording data. Do not extend the spring so far that the spring is damaged.

7 Carefully return the spring to its original length. Repeat the experiment using a transverse wave. A transverse wave can be created by flicking your wrist sharply to the side.

Step 4

Step 7

Analyze and Conclude

1. **Analyzing Data** Using your data for length and time, calculate and record the speed for each trial. Compare the speed and the length for each trial. What relationship is there between length and speed?

2. **Making and Using Graphs** Make a line graph showing length versus speed for both types of waves.

3. **Analyzing Data** Which travels faster: a compressional wave or a transverse wave?

4. **Thinking Critically** If a seismic survey were done with just compressional waves, how would the results compare to a survey done at the same location where only transverse waves were used?

Going Further

Application
All waves lose energy as they travel. Wave types that lose less energy go farther. Which of the two types of waves used in the Investigation needed less energy to travel the spring? Which wave probably goes deeper in a seismic survey?

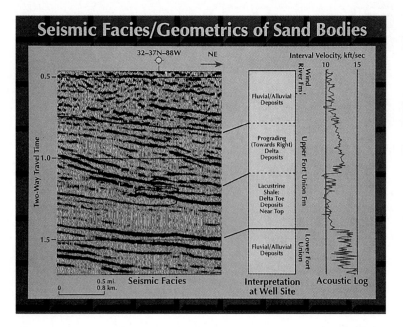

Seismic Facies/Geometrics of Sand Bodies

A A seismic profile helps identify areas likely to contain oil and gas deposits. The key to the right of the profile shows what is indicated by each profile area. The log to the right of the key shows the actual speed of sound in the rocks that is translated into the profile.

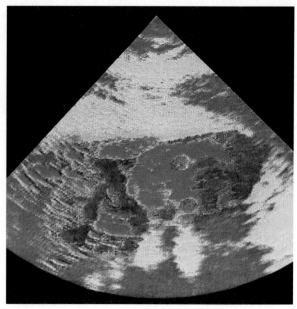

B With no danger to the baby or the mother, sound waves are used to make this picture of an unborn child. Doctors can use such pictures to confirm the position and size of the baby and other important information. The scientific principles used are the same as those used for a seismic profile.

Figure 13-8

Important information can be determined by recording the reflection of sound waves.

You saw in the Investigation how waves can bounce off an object and then return to where the wave started. In seismic prospecting, the reflected sound waves are picked up by special detectors called **geophones** and then recorded. By knowing the time it takes for a sound wave to return and the speed of sound through the rock, the depth of a rock layer is determined. Then a computer generates a picture of the rocks underground.

This picture is called a **seismic profile,** an example of which is shown in **Figure 13-8A.** Seismic profiles help in locating likely places to drill for oil and natural gas.

Well Logging

Once a well is drilled in search of oil and gas, the geologist needs to find out what, if anything, has been found. Different kinds of sensitive instruments that measure properties of the rock and the fluids they contain are lowered down the well hole. This is called *logging the well.* The data these tools recover are called *well logs.*

In most logging, the tools are lowered to the bottom of the well on the end of a cable. The logging tools are then slowly pulled toward the surface, and continuous recordings are made of the rocks at different depths. It is important that the data be continuous. Properties of the rocks will vary when different rock layers are investigated.

Several types of well logs exist. Some well logs record the electrical properties of rocks. Other types measure the level of natural radioactivity. Yet another logging tool actually deter-

Figure 13-9

Drilling an oil well involves many types of equipment.

A Technicians work with devices that measure seismic information and supply detailed images of the borehole.

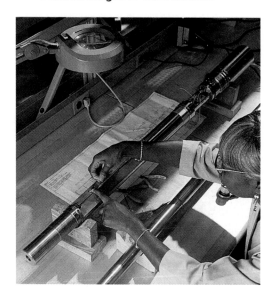

B Workers at the drill site use clamps to add or change a section of pipe.

C All the varied pieces of equipment come together at the site where the platform is constructed and the well is drilled.

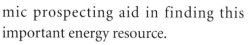

mines whether layers of rock are tilted or horizontal. An example of a well-logging tool is shown in **Figure 13-9A.**

■ Putting It All Together

So far in this chapter, you have learned much about the formation and migration of petroleum. You have learned that well logs, maps, and seismic prospecting aid in finding this important energy resource.

In the next section, we will investigate the chemistry of hydrocarbons. We will also consider how petroleum, as found in the ground, is converted to its many uses.

check your UNDERSTANDING

Understanding Concepts

1. Explain how seismic prospecting is similar to producing a sonogram.
2. Why are surface geologic maps of limited use to those exploring for petroleum?
3. Bats can bounce sound waves off food and locate the food by how long it takes for the sound to return to the bat. Which type of petroleum exploration is similar to this process?

Skill Review

4. **Comparing and Contrasting** In what ways are different well-logging tools alike? For more help, refer to Comparing and Contrasting in the *Skill Handbook.*

13-3 Composition and Use

Objectives

- Determine the composition of petroleum.
- Describe petroleum refining.
- Describe many petroleum products and their uses.

Key Terms

cracking
combustion

Composition

It's well-known that gasoline used to fuel our cars comes from petroleum. Would you be surprised to learn that chemicals from petroleum are used to make the plastics in the dashboard and the fabrics on the seat? What makes petroleum such a versatile resource? To answer this question, examine the chemical makeup of petroleum.

The hydrocarbons that make up petroleum are chains and rings of carbon atoms chemically bonded to each other and to hydrogen. Each different molecule has different properties. The uses of each compound are determined by these properties. Gasoline that fuels our cars is made of hydrocarbons containing chains of five to ten carbon

Fill It Up!

You probably know that the gasoline used in most cars, trucks, and other motor vehicles comes from liquid petroleum. It is a major concern that, like other fossil fuels, the amount of petroleum stored in reservoirs deep below Earth's surface is dwindling. Burning fossil fuels such as oil can also pollute the environment. What are some fuel alternatives to liquid petroleum?

Gasohol

Biomass fuels are plant or animal substances used to provide the energy necessary to do work. Wood, wheat, corn, sugarcane, potatoes, and animal wastes are sources of biomass fuels. Some biomass can be burned directly to produce energy. Other types of biomass must be processed before they can be used as fuels. In some countries, such as Brazil, sugarcane is used to manufacture a fuel for cars,

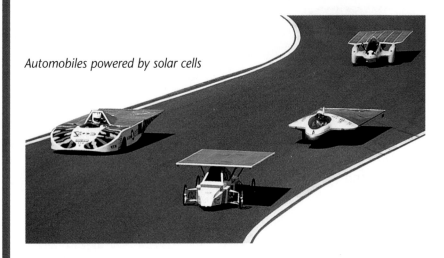

Automobiles powered by solar cells

atoms in length. Natural gas that heats homes contains hydrocarbons with shorter chains of one to three carbon atoms. Plastics, synthetic fabrics, foods, drugs, explosives, and many other products are in part made from hydrocarbon compounds that have a ring structure.

As it comes from the ground, petroleum contains numerous different hydrocarbon compounds. How can this complex mixture be used to make the fuel, motor oil, and tires for a car?

The process of making petroleum into more useful products is called refining. The refining process is done in a petroleum refinery. An example of a petroleum refinery is shown in **Figure 13-10.**

Figure 13-10

A petroleum refinery takes raw petroleum and separates it into numerous different hydrocarbon compounds.

trucks, and other motor vehicles. In the United States, the alcohol that is burned in some vehicles and used in the fuel gasohol, a mixture of gasoline and alcohol, is made from potatoes and corn, wheat, and other grains.

Natural Gas

Like oil, natural gas is a fossil fuel. Unlike the burning of gasoline derived from the liquid petroleum, however, the burning of natural gas emits fewer pollutants into Earth's atmosphere. Currently, a small percentage of vehicles in the United States use this clean-burning fuel. A few natural gas stations exist, and several states and cities power their public-owned vehicles with natural gas.

Fuel Cells

Another alternative to gasoline may someday be the fuel cell. Fuel cells, which are similar to batteries, produce electricity as the result of electrochemical reactions. Some experimental fuel cells containing hydrogen and oxygen have been used to power small trucks and cars.

Solar Cells

Photovoltaic cells, or solar cells, convert light—usually sunlight—into electrical energy. Solar cells consist of layers of semiconducting materials sandwiched between layers of a material that conducts electricity. Automobiles powered by solar cells are currently in the experimental stages.

Thinking Critically

1. Work with the adult members of your family to **determine** how much gasoline your family uses in a typical week. How might this amount be reduced?
2. Some of these alternative fuels are better for the environment, do not deplete petroleum supplies, and are readily available. **Infer** why they are not more widely used.

Refining and Use

If you have seen a refinery, you may have noticed several tall towers. The refining process that separates the different hydrocarbon compounds takes place inside these towers as shown in **Figure 13-11.** Crude oil, which is oil as it comes from the ground, is pumped into the base of the tower and heated until it boils. The crude oil contains different compounds, called fractions, that boil at different temperatures. Materials with the lowest boiling points, such as methane, rise highest in the tower

before condensing and are collected at the top of the tower. Liquid gasoline is also collected near the top of the tower, just a little below methane gas. Other fractions cool and condense lower in the tower and are collected as liquids.

Hydrocarbons with the highest boiling points remain thick liquids and are drained off at the bottom of the tower. These less valuable, longer-chained carbon compounds are often placed in what are known as *cracking towers.* Here, higher temperatures and special chemicals are used to split the long chains into compounds that are mixed to form the more useful gasoline. This splitting process is called **cracking.**

■ Harvesting the Energy

Many refined hydrocarbon compounds can be used as fuels. Look at the illustration of the fractionating tower in **Figure 13-11.** Which of the products do you recognize as types of fuel? For what purposes do you use these fuels in your car or home?

Fueling an automobile with gasoline supplies energy to use when the car is driven. How do we get this energy out of the gasoline and use it to make a car move? In a car's engine, a spark ignites a mixture of gasoline and air and provides the initial energy needed to get the process going. When the hydrocarbons are burned, they react with oxygen to form carbon dioxide and water and the energy that is produced when bonds are broken and re-formed. Carbon monoxide is also produced. Chemists call this burning process **combustion.** Rapid combustion in cars' cylinders heats the gases and releases the energy necessary for cars to go.

Figure 13-11

The towers that separate the different hydrocarbons in petroleum are called fractionating towers.

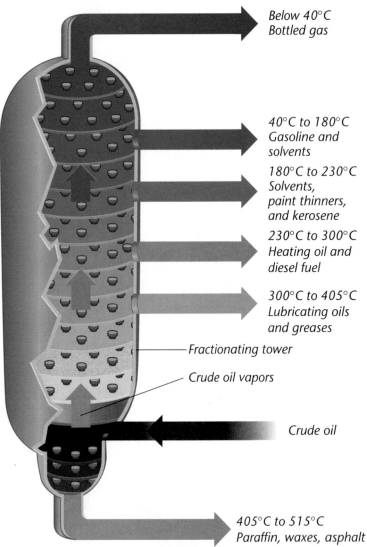

Below 40°C
Bottled gas

40°C to 180°C
Gasoline and solvents

180°C to 230°C
Solvents, paint thinners, and kerosene

230°C to 300°C
Heating oil and diesel fuel

300°C to 405°C
Lubricating oils and greases

Fractionating tower

Crude oil vapors

Crude oil

405°C to 515°C
Paraffin, waxes, asphalt

■ Other Products

What other materials are made from petroleum? Check out the clothes and accessories you are now wearing. From what materials are they made? Some are probably natural, such as cotton, which is harvested from plants. However, it is likely you are also wearing several synthetic materials. The following MiniLab will help you discover a difference between natural and synthetic materials.

MiniLab

A Burning Question

One can easily tell the difference between a natural fiber, such as cotton or wool, and a synthetic fiber, such as nylon or rayon, by holding it in a flame. In this activity, you will discover what that difference is.

Procedure

1. Collect several 2 cm × 2 cm pieces of different types of fabric that have been identified as to what type of fibers they contain. Be sure that you have some samples of natural fibers and some samples of synthetic fibers.

2. Classify each sample as to whether it is synthetic, natural, or a blend of both types.

3. Using tongs, hold the edge of each fabric sample up to the flame of a lit candle. Do not hold the entire piece of fabric in the flame. Dispose of each sample by dropping it in a beaker that has some water in it. Record your observations *in your Journal.*

Analysis

1. What happened to the synthetic materials when they were held to the flame?

2. What happened to the natural materials when they were held to the flame?

3. Explain the behavior of the fabrics that were blends when they were held to the flame.

You saw in the MiniLab that there are differences in natural and synthetic fabrics. **Figure 13-12** shows an example of a blended fabric.

Synthetic fibers are examples of polymers. As you learned in Chapter 7, polymers are huge molecules made of many smaller units that are linked together by chemical bonds. Some polymers, such as your skin, are formed in living organisms.

Figure 13-12

Nylon, polyester, and urethane are made of molecules designed by chemists using methods similar to methods used to improve fuels.

Figure 13-13

Many materials in cars are made from petroleum.

A Most bumpers, dashboards, and even paints are constructed from synthetic plastics.

B Synthetic materials in the upholstery of car seats last longer than fabrics used in years past.

C Puncture-resistant tires are sometimes lined with synthetic fibers that are five times stronger than steel.

Although petroleum is known as a source of fuel, it provides the chemicals used for making many parts of cars. Most of the plastics used in the various parts of a car are synthetic polymers made from chemicals extracted from petroleum. Examples of these polymers are shown in **Figure 13-13.**

Petroleum also is the base for many other materials we use each day as consumers. Think of how your clothing, communications, and other areas of your life would change if petroleum-based products were not available.

check your UNDERSTANDING

Understanding Concepts

1. If refiners did not crack heavier petroleum components, what would probably happen to the amount of gasoline available for sale?
2. List three petroleum products that are used as fuels. Why are these products good fuels?
3. Although many petroleum components are not used frequently as fuels, all will undergo combustion. Explain.

Skill Review

4. **Thinking Critically** Explain why the towers in a refinery are called *fractionating towers.* For more help, refer to Thinking Critically in the *Skill Handbook.*

Science and Society

Issue: Kill the car?

In 1900, horses clip-clopped on streets. This noise got on the nerves of many city dwellers, who wished there were a quieter means of transportation. People even predicted that when automobiles replaced horses, noise would be reduced. They certainly were wrong!

The Issue

Noise is just one of the unwelcome effects produced by automobile traffic. Oxides of carbon, nitrogen, and sulfur—which are produced by burning gasoline—pollute the air we breathe. In addition, stacks of worn-out rubber tires and junkyards containing piles of wrecked and rusting vehicles are common, ugly sights across America. Air pollution, noise pollution, sight pollution, traffic jams, and traffic accidents—it's no wonder that some people say "Kill the car!"

But if we kill the car, how will we get to work, or to shopping malls, grocery stores, sports stadiums, and movie theaters? Buses, subways, and elevated trains produce less pollution per passenger-mile than cars do. However, these mass-transit systems are often slow, inconvenient, and uncomfortable and are not practical for rural areas. Most people would rather ride in cars. Deciding on the best way to move large numbers of people from one place to another is a controversial national issue.

The Background

The gasoline internal combustion engine, invented in about 1860, was found to be more efficient and practical than steam and quickly became the main method for powering vehicles. At that time, no one could foresee the air-pollution problems that the exhaust from gasoline engines would create. The tremendous increase in population, growth of cities, and number of people driving cars and trucks have resulted in many of the environmental problems that we face today.

The Questions

Suggestions about how to solve the environmental problems caused by gasoline-powered vehicles include improved mass-transit systems, cars powered by electricity or sunshine, excluding cars from the center of the city, and even eliminating cars completely. Will politicians and citizens be willing to spend the dollars that are required to resolve this environmental crisis?

Discussing the Issue

1. *Infer* which alternative is the best answer to the environmental problems caused by widespread use of automobiles. Explain.
2. *Discuss* what vehicles other than automobiles can harm the environment.

APPLYING TECHNOLOGY

"Sun-fficient"

To stretch supplies of limited natural resources such as oil, many companies are beginning to use other methods of generating heat and electricity. One such alternative is solar power.

You're the Solar Technician

Many students in your school complain because air circulation is poor. The school can't buy large fans for every classroom, so you are going to produce individual fans for students to use. Because there are not enough electrical outlets available, these fans cannot use the school's electricity to operate. Solar energy will power your invention.

Drawing on Experience

1. Obtain the following materials from your teacher: DC motor, solar-cell module, propeller, wire hanger, wire cutters, glue and tape, and a screwdriver.

2. Cut a 12-inch section of coat hanger and bend the metal as shown. This U shape will cradle the upper part of the motor to hold it off of the desk. The bottom part of the motor, where the wires extend, will rest on the desk. This stand should be self-supporting.

3. You may want to apply tape or glue to the bottom edge of the motor to keep it attached to the wire base.

4. Press the propeller onto the motor shaft.

5. Connect the wires from the motor to the solar-cell module—positive to positive and negative to negative. The solar-cell module should lie flat on the desk and have a source of solar energy or direct classroom lighting.

Testing...Testing

Test the solar-powered fan by placing it in the window of your classroom or on your desk. Test the dependability of your new solar fan under various lighting conditions. You may also want to connect two or more solar-cell modules for improved product performance.

How Did It Work?

Does the solar-powered fan you produced actually improve air circulation in the room and help to cool your skin? How did the fan operate under cloudy conditions with only an artificial light source to power the fan?

interNET CONNECTION

To research other types of solar-powered technology, follow the link for Chapter 13 on the Glencoe Homepage to find information about the University of Michigan's Solar Car Team. How does a solar car work? What elements does it have in common with a solar-powered fan?

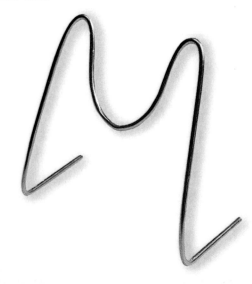

Read the statements at the right and below that review major points presented in the chapter. Using the concepts that you have learned, answer each question *in your Journal.*

1 Geologic mapping, seismic prospecting, and well logging are procedures used in petroleum exploration and recovery. *Is the limestone shown a porous or a nonporous rock?*

Seal

Gas

Oil

2 Petroleum is the naturally recycled remains of living organisms. *Why must petroleum migrate and be trapped in order to be useful?*

3 Petroleum is composed of many different hydrocarbons. After refining, its components are used in many everyday products, such as plastics and fuels. *What petroleum-based products are you wearing today?*

60% COTTON/
40% POLYESTER
RN 48711
MADE IN SINGAPORE
SIZE **M**
SEE REVERSE
FOR CARE

chapter 13
CHAPTER REVIEW

Using Key Science Terms

combustion

conodont

cracking

geophone

migration

permeability

petroleum

porosity

reservoir

seismic profile

seismic prospecting

source rock

Answer the following questions about science terms used in this chapter.

1. What happens in a combustion reaction?
2. What is the purpose of cracking hydrocarbons?
3. Explain why a porous rock may not be permeable.
4. What relationship exists among the terms *natural gas, petroleum,* and *oil?*
5. In what type of petroleum prospecting is a geophone used?
6. What are the requirements of a good source rock?

Understanding Ideas

Using complete sentences, answer the following questions in your Journal.

1. What difference does it make whether hydrocarbons are generated early in sediment deposition or later, after the sediments in the trap have been compressed and cemented into rock?
2. How might we decide which model for hydrocarbon generation, early or late, is more correct?
3. Describe the role migration plays in allowing humans to find and use hydrocarbons.
4. Explain the need for a trap and a seal to intercept and collect migrating hydrocarbons.

Developing Skills

Use your understanding of the concepts developed in this chapter to answer each of the following questions.

1. **Comparing and Contrasting** Compare and contrast the processes that occur when you eat your dinner and when you put gasoline into a car.
2. **Sequencing** Sequence the terms *water, gas,* and *oil* in the order the materials are layered, top to bottom, in a trap. Explain why the materials are layered in this order.
3. **Making and Using Graphs** Make a bar graph that expresses the following information about the uses of petroleum.

Uses	Percentage
Gasoline	46
Other fuels	19
Fuel oils	30
Asphalt	3
Other uses	2

4. **Comparing and Contrasting** An X-ray picture is based on the fact that X rays are absorbed in different amounts by different materials. Explain two ways that an X-ray picture differs from a sonogram, which uses the same principles used in seismic prospecting.
5. **Hypothesizing** Make a hypothesis to explain how the principles used in a petroleum fractionating tower could be used to separate the different gases found in air.

Critical Thinking

In your Journal, *answer each of the following questions.*

1. Hydrocarbon traps in the east end of a producing region are filled with natural gas. At the west end of the area, the traps produce mainly oil. Your geologist says this proves that the east end of the region has not been severely heated. She recommends exploration further east as a good way to find hydrocarbons. Do you agree and spend some money, ask for more proof, or turn down her proposal at once? Why?

2. Examine the definition of *combustion.* How could you prevent a combustion reaction from starting? How could you stop the reaction once it has started? Explain.

3. If natural reservoir pressures are the only means used to move oil to where an oil well is pumping it from the reservoir, the oil well may be able to pump out only 25 percent of the oil the reservoir contains. Infer why the percentage is not greater.

Problem Solving

Read the following problem and discuss your answers in a brief paragraph.

Martin Stone, a petroleum geologist, has done a seismic profile and a geologic map of an area and is certain that a drilled well will produce natural gas and oil. He drills the well, but all that comes out of it is water.

Explain why the results of this well do not necessarily mean that petroleum is not present.

CONNECTING IDEAS

1. **Theme—Systems and Interactions** Assume that a petroleum geologist is to perform the following tests on a possible oil field: *geologic mapping, seismic prospecting, well logging.* Sequence these terms in the order that the tests would be done.

2. **Theme—Energy** Explain how energy from burning gasoline was once energy from the sun.

3. **In-Depth Look** What is one problem that might exist with using electric cars?

4. **Science and Society** Most buses produce more pollution per mile than do cars. How can it be true that buses produce less pollution per passenger-mile than cars do?

5. **Applying Technology** It is known that blue-green light is the best light to power solar cells. Using this fact, how might you modify your fan to improve its performance?

CHAPTER 14

Recycling
Saving Limited Resources

Driving down a highway, you notice a stand of tall evergreen trees. The sight makes you start thinking about things you've learned in this unit—how Earth's natural resources are used as sources of energy and as starting materials to make useful products.

Suddenly, a jarring sight interrupts your thoughts. An auto salvage yard, heaped with acres of rusting car bodies, flashes past your car window. What resources are tied up in those scrap cars? And isn't there any way of reclaiming them instead of just letting them sit there and rust?

Fortunately, there is. Nearly all cars disposed of today are broken into material components to be recycled. The same carbon atoms that made up the rubber in the tires, for example, may be used in asphalt to pave a road.

▶ *In the MiniLab on the next page, find out what kinds of materials you commonly dispose of.*

412

MiniLab

What's in your trash?

The need for recycling large, expensive objects like cars is obvious, but what about the little things such as old notebook paper or a soda can? Small items you throw away could easily fill a number of cars during the course of a year. What do you think happens to the trash you throw away each day?

Procedure

1. Brainstorm a list of general materials you might throw away in a given week (such as plastics or glass).
2. Divide a page *in your Journal* into columns with each type of material as a head. You might want to make an extra column labeled *Other*.
3. Keep track of everything you throw away for a week. List each item in the proper column.

Analysis

1. Total the number of disposed items in each category. Construct a bar graph to show the relative numbers of each type of material.
2. Could any of these materials have been directly reused—either by you or by someone else? Explain.

Why Recycle?

14-1

Objectives

- Evaluate the costs and benefits of the three main final destinations for solid waste.

- Discuss conditions that help determine whether a product is recyclable.

Key Terms

sanitary landfill
incinerator
recycling

Disposing of Resources

Magazine and newspaper headlines remind us that we are running out of natural resources, including fossil fuels, minerals, and trees. Resources from Earth have been removed from their natural deposits and processed to make cars, milk jugs, CD cases, and thousands of other products. What happens to these products when you are done with them? Perhaps you sort cans, newspapers, milk jugs, and other items for recycling. Your community probably also has a trash service to haul away solid waste. Everything you throw away is made of atoms. They can't be destroyed, so they must go somewhere. Try the next activity to see how much space your trash occupies.

MiniLab

How much space does your garbage occupy?

Do you think a landfill operator would be more concerned with the mass or the amount of space occupied by the materials dumped into a landfill? Each person in the United States throws away an average of 1.6 kg of materials each day. The space needed to dispose of this garbage depends on the types of materials in the trash. In this MiniLab, you will compare the volume occupied by 1.6 kg of different kinds of trash.

Procedure

1. Choose three of the following materials and gather a supply of each: glass containers, cardboard, plastic bottles, crushed aluminum cans, uncrushed aluminum cans, or steel cans.

2. Use a balance to measure 1.6 kg of each material.

3. Carefully pack the material that appears to have the largest volume into a box large enough to hold it.

4. Measure and record the length and width of the box in centimeters. Then measure and record the height (depth) in centimeters of the materials packed into the box.

5. Calculate the volume of the material. Repeat this process for the other two materials.

Analysis

1. Create a bar graph to show the volume of each material.

2. How do these volumes compare? Why is this important in the waste-disposal process?

3. Explain why equal masses of different materials don't have equal volumes.

Figure 14-1

When all you see is a few days' worth, it's hard to grasp just how much trash there is.

A A single newspaper seems thin and insignificant, but newspapers make a large stack of trash over time. How tall would a whole year's worth of newspapers be?

B This pie graph shows the average composition of municipal solid waste in the United States. How does this compare with the results of your own trash record in the chapter-opener MiniLab?

What's in the garbage?

On average, every person in the United States throws away 1.6 kg of solid waste, or garbage, every day. **Figure 14-1A** shows how this can add up over one year. It has been predicted that in the year 2000, United States citizens together will produce nearly 216 million metric tons of waste. That's equivalent to the mass of about 154 million cars. What does this waste consist of? **Figure 14-1B** shows a breakdown of municipal solid waste, which comes mostly from homes and businesses such as schools and shopping centers. Even more solid waste is generated by industry, agriculture, and mining. Industries also generate hazardous waste—material that requires special handling or treatment.

Where does our garbage go?

Imagine that you run a company that picks up garbage from hundreds of households. What will you do with it all? You would probably separate it into categories such as things you can burn, things you can bury, and things you can use again. It wouldn't take long for you to run out of space and disposal ideas. Most municipal solid waste is burned in incinerators, buried in landfills, or recycled. Try to keep your own trash tally from the MiniLab on page 413 in mind while we consider these three options.

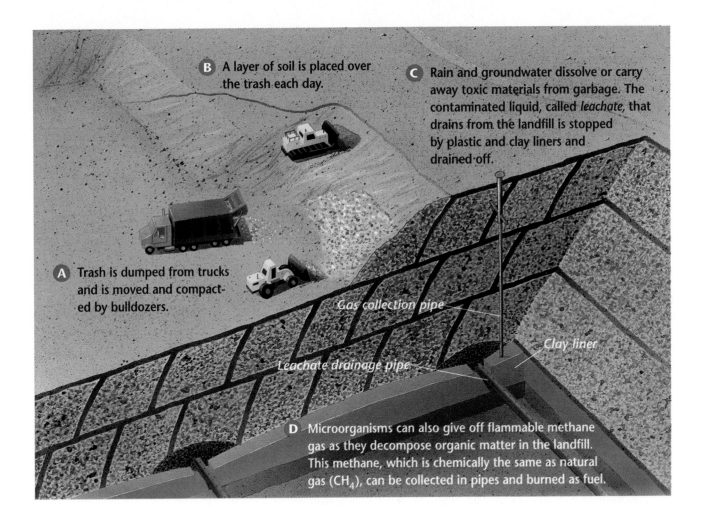

B A layer of soil is placed over the trash each day.

C Rain and groundwater dissolve or carry away toxic materials from garbage. The contaminated liquid, called *leachate*, that drains from the landfill is stopped by plastic and clay liners and drained off.

A Trash is dumped from trucks and is moved and compacted by bulldozers.

Gas collection pipe

Clay liner

Leachate drainage pipe

D Microorganisms can also give off flammable methane gas as they decompose organic matter in the landfill. This methane, which is chemically the same as natural gas (CH_4), can be collected in pipes and burned as fuel.

Figure 14-2

The illustration above shows the creation and structure of a sanitary landfill.

■ Sanitary Landfill: A Stash for Trash

More than 70 percent of municipal solid waste is trucked to sanitary landfills. A **sanitary landfill** is a giant hole in the ground lined with dense clay or plastic, into which trash is dumped, compressed, and then covered with a thin layer of dirt or plastic each day. Do you know where the landfill nearest to your home is located? Sanitary landfills aren't just holes in which to dump garbage. A lot of planning and engineering goes into designing them and deciding where to put them. Study the safety features of the sanitary landfill in **Figure 14-2.** Note that many precautions are taken to prevent pollution to groundwater and soil around the landfill. Even with these precautions, environmental problems can still result from liquid and airborne leakage of toxic materials in a landfill.

Many people think biodegradable materials such as paper and food products will decompose naturally and quickly in landfills. They think of landfills as giant compost heaps, like the one you made in Chapter 11. However, when buried and sheltered from sunlight and plentiful oxygen supplies, these materials do not break down efficiently. Deep inside a landfill, half-eaten hot dogs from the 1960s are still recognizable and undecayed. Like a compost heap, a landfill would have to be constantly turned and mixed with air for materials to decay quickly.

When a sanitary landfill is full, layers of clay and dirt are used to seal it, but production of leachate and methane gas must still be monitored for many years. The covered landfill is replanted with trees and grass and often used for other purposes, such as golf courses and ski slopes. John F. Kennedy airport in New York City is built on an old landfill.

Landfills Filling Up

Some predictions suggest that more than half of the operating landfills will be filled and closed to further use within a few years. Already, many states are closing their landfills to out-of-state waste. It is becoming difficult to find acceptable sites for new landfills for several reasons. The geology of the site is important. It should not be too near to water sources or wetlands. Transporting garbage is costly, so landfills need to be reasonably close to communities that produce the trash. Although everyone wants their trash disposed of, almost no one wants a new landfill built near his or her home. Can you think of some ways to reduce the volume of waste sent to our landfills? With limited remaining landfill space and resistance to building new landfills, other options must be considered.

Trash—A Burning Issue

You know that the ash left after a piece of paper burns is smaller and lighter than the paper was. Burning can reduce the amount of trash to less than half its original size. Nearly 15 percent of municipal solid waste in the United States goes to an incinerator. **Incinerators** are large furnaces in which solid waste is burned at temperatures of nearly 1300°C (2400°F). **Figure 14-3** illustrates the process of incineration.

There are several kinds of incinerators. *Mass-burn incinerators* burn all kinds of solid waste without presorting the garbage except to remove large appliances. Plastics, paper, and rubber all release large amounts of heat as they burn, so this energy can be used to heat buildings or to generate electricity.

Figure 14-3

The image below shows how materials and energy move through a trash-burning power plant.

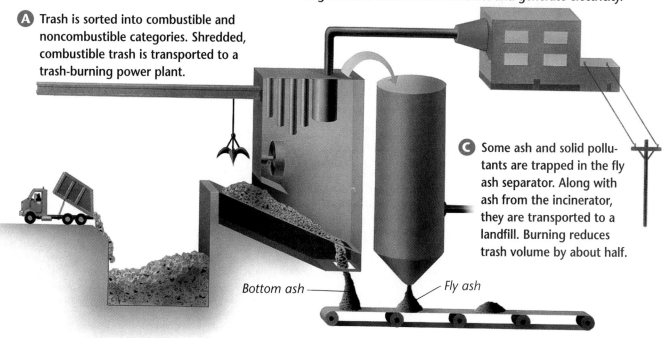

A Trash is sorted into combustible and noncombustible categories. Shredded, combustible trash is transported to a trash-burning power plant.

B As the trash burns, it heats water in the pipes above. The resulting steam is used to drive turbines and generate electricity.

C Some ash and solid pollutants are trapped in the fly ash separator. Along with ash from the incinerator, they are transported to a landfill. Burning reduces trash volume by about half.

Bottom ash

Fly ash

Materials such as glass and high-water-content food waste don't burn efficiently. *Refuse-driven fuel incinerators* remove these materials before burning to achieve better efficiency.

Reducing waste volume and producing heat which can be used to generate electricity are benefits of incineration, but there are some important problems to consider.

■ Incineration Problems

A variety of by-products results when waste is burned in an incinerator. The easily burnable materials produce bottom ash that can be shoveled out and taken to a landfill. Fly ash, which is lighter and rises up a chimney, typically contains toxic materials such as dioxins from burning plastic and heavy metals such as nickel, cadmium, and mercury from household batteries. Gases such as sulfur dioxide and nitrogen oxides, which many think contribute to acid deposition, also may be released.

■ Pollution Control

Federal laws now require that incinerators be equipped with pollution-control devices, as shown in **Figure 14-4,** to clean emissions. However, these devices are expensive and reduce, but do not prevent, air pollution caused by incinerating garbage. For this reason, many people are no more willing to have an incinerator built in their neighborhood than they are to have a landfill located there.

Recycling Cycles

"**W**e're not just putting bikes back in circulation," reports Tom O'Keefe. "We're putting smiles on lots of faces!" Tom and Joe Keating are codirectors of UCAN, the United Community Action Network in Portland, Oregon.

UCAN is helping Portland recycle its bikes and reduce the use of cars.

Bright Idea, Dark Night

Tom got the idea for recycling bikes when he awoke in the middle of the night to hear someone stealing an old bike from his backyard. "That bike wasn't worth $10," he says. "You sure couldn't sell it, so the thief really did want a bike. I figured if people needed transportation that badly, why not *give* them bikes?"

Tom and Joe began their project by asking the local Community Cycling Center to donate ten restored, used

Figure 14-4

Several costly devices are used to reduce air pollution from refuse-driven fuel incinerators. A scrubber uses a chemical spray to neutralize the acidic gases. Some solid pollutants are dissolved in the spray. The contaminated liquid is collected, processed, and reused. The filter removes larger particles and the cleaned gases are vented from the stack. The remaining pollutants are disposed of in a landfill.

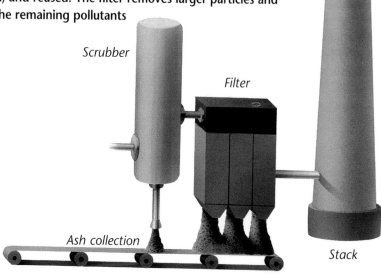

Scrubber

Filter

Ash collection

Stack

Shipped to landfill

Do incinerators or landfills seem like a good waste-disposal option for your community? Even with the best pollution-control devices, sanitary landfills and incinerators are far from perfect solutions to our solid-waste problems. Both present significant environmental hazards and are costly to build and operate. On the next page, consider one option that may reduce our reliance on these methods of waste disposal.

bikes. The center accepts old bikes and teaches young people how to repair them.

When the ten bikes were ready to ride, UCAN painted them very bright yellow and attached small signs reading *Free community bike. Please return to a major street for others to reuse.* Then they left the bikes on the streets.

Putting Portland on Wheels

People of all ages immediately put the bikes to use, and UCAN's phone has been ringing ever since. Callers from across the United States and Canada want to know how to start free bike programs in their communities.

Now the Community Cycling Center is cosponsoring the Portland program. In only six months, they helped put 100 repaired bikes on the streets. The goal was 1000 bikes by the end of the first year. Besides providing free, energy-efficient, nonpolluting transportation, the bikes are helping to increase the sense of community in Portland.

"These bikes send a strong message of honesty and sharing," Tom says. "The yellow paint makes them steal-proof because everyone knows they're part of the program. They belong to everyone. Just having them on the streets is motivating more people to get involved in the community."

One rider called UCAN to ask if he could keep a bike for a while and use it to look for a job. "He didn't just go ahead and keep it, which he could have done," Tom recalls. "He asked for permission. That's pretty special, I think. This project is changing attitudes around here. It just keeps giving and giving and giving."

Thinking Critically

1. *Describe* a time you recall when borrowing a bicycle would have helped you.
2. Would a free bicycle program benefit your community? *Explain* why or why not.

Recycling

What do you think of when you hear the word *recycling*? You may think of sorting recyclable materials in your trash, reusing materials, or buying notebook paper made from recycled fibers. **Recycling** is the process of collecting and sorting waste materials, processing them into new material, and then marketing and using the new material or products made from it. All three of these activities must occur for effective recycling of a product, such as 2-L pop bottles. Less than 20 percent of municipal solid waste is recycled in the United States.

■ Recycling Benefits

Recycling allows valuable natural resources to be used again rather than thrown away. **Figure 14-5** illustrates the flow of resources and energy from man-

ufacturing and use to recycling and disposal. Because these materials already have been taken from Earth and processed once, using recycled materials in manufacturing generally consumes less energy, wasting less fossil fuel. This decrease in our use of fossil fuels reduces related environmental problems such as acid deposition. Acid deposition occurs when by-products of burning fossil fuels are released to the atmosphere. In the atmosphere, sulfur dioxide or nitrogen oxides combine with water. The resulting acidic precipitation falls to Earth. Some sensitive ecosystems are damaged by acid deposition.

Think about the waste generated by all of the households of students in your school. Could you develop a plan that would make it possible to collect most of the recyclable materials that are thrown away? Collecting and sorting recyclable waste from consumers is a big job.

To Find Out More About ...

Acid Rain Control see pages 372-373 in Chapter 12.

Figure 14-5

Resources and energy are used to make products for consumers. When products are reused and recycled, less energy is used. In general, very few additional resources are required to make recycled products for consumers. Would it still make sense to recycle if it took more energy and resources to make recycled products than it took to make new products?

■ Recycling Plans

Some states and communities have developed collection programs. A few states—Michigan, Maine, California, and Oregon, for example—offer cash refunds for returning drink bottles and cans. Many communities have curbside recycling programs as shown in **Figure 14-6.**

When collection, processing, and reuse of recycled materials are all relatively inexpensive, the recycling process is practical. Recycling becomes a promising way to reduce our need for landfills and incinerators while reusing valuable natural resources. In the next section, you'll see how the types of materials found in a car can be recycled. But first, try the following activity to understand the impact of recycling.

B Recycling trucks have compartments to sort and store each type of solid waste. Communities and solid-waste recycling companies differ on how much presorting they require customers to do.

A Many programs give customers small containers like this to sort and store waste.

Figure 14-6

The photos above show two common parts of curbside recycling programs.

Thinking Lab

Predicting

How much can recycling reduce your amount of trash?

Families who participate in typical community recycling programs see a significant reduction in the amount of trash they send to landfills or incinerators. This reduces trash-disposal costs and keeps valuable natural resources in the pool of useful materials.

Analysis

This table shows possible percentages of trash reduction experienced by an average family that recycles. Think about how recycling would affect our waste-disposal system if most households participated. Use this information to help you answer the following questions.

Possible Trash Reduction from Single-family Recycling	
Reduce trash by backyard composting	10–18%
Recycle newspaper	8–10%
Recycle glass containers	6–7%
Recycle plastic bottles	2–5%
Recycle steel cans	1%
Recycle phone books	1%
Precycle	1–4%

Thinking Critically

Based on these estimates, what is the range of trash reduction from household recycling? How would this range be affected if there were not a local market for recycling newspapers?

What can be recycled?

Recycling seems like a good option for dealing with solid waste. Several environmental study groups have estimated that more than 80 percent of municipal solid wastes are recyclable, yet only about 15 percent of waste makes it through the process. Why is there such a difference in what could be and what actually is recycled? Two main factors determine whether something is recyclable: whether we have the technology to process the used materials into new products and whether it is practical to recycle a material in a specific geographic area.

Is recycling possible?

The first requirement for identifying a material as recyclable is to have the technology to recover a material and process it into a marketable product. Not all materials are technically recyclable. For example, small amounts of minerals used in making electronic devices are combined with other materials. At this time, it is not technologically possible to recover enough of these minerals to make new and useful products.

The majority of municipal solid waste is recyclable. Industrial processes have been designed to efficiently recycle

Figure 14-7

Consumers can increase the demand for recycled products by buying products such as these.

Recycled plastic table

Mountain lion sculpture made of discarded bumpers

contains 100% recycled plastics*.

7 Large Trash & Yard Bags

7 BAGS & TIES: 2 FT. 8½ IN. x 3 FT. 4 IN. 1.0 MIL. 33 GAL.

33 GAL.

422

glass, most plastics, aluminum, steel, and paper. Technology and manufacturing are not the largest barriers to recycling a higher percentage of our solid waste. So what is?

■ Is recycling practical?

Have you ever saved up your newspapers or plastic bottles only to find there was no place in your community to take them for recycling? The technology to recycle these products exists, so what's the problem? Think of the three main activities in the recycling process: collection, processing, and consumption. Of these, collection and consumption are the biggest barriers to effective recycling.

Without adequate plans to collect materials from consumers, there will not be enough materials to support recycling plants. Home storage of solid waste can be a barrier. Consumers sometimes aren't willing to give up space in their homes to store waste between collection times. Frequent collection times and easy storage containers can overcome this problem.

Transportation costs also may be extremely high if materials have to be collected and shipped long distances for processing. The consumer enters the picture again in the consumption stage of the process. Consumers must be willing to buy goods made from recycled products. But people don't want to buy them unless they're at least as cheap and of the same quality as the same product made from new raw materials. Some people object to recycled paper products, for example, because they may be coarser than the paper products to which they're accustomed.

Recycled products are often more expensive than their nonrecycled counterparts. This is changing as consumers begin to demand and purchase goods made of recycled materials. **Figure 14-7** shows examples of products made from recycled materials. Collection, transportation, and consumer demand largely determine whether it is practical to recycle a specific material in a community. In the next section, we will investigate how materials that qualify as recyclable are processed.

check your UNDERSTANDING

Understanding Concepts
1. A sanitary landfill is more than just a place to dump trash. What are some of the ways sanitary landfills try to reduce environmental risks?
2. Discuss some of the advantages and disadvantages of using an incinerator to burn municipal solid waste.
3. Describe the three activities that must occur in an effective recycling program.

Skill Review
4. **Observing and Inferring** Although your community drop-off site accepts office paper, glass, aluminum, and steel cans, it refuses to take newspapers. What would you infer about the reason for this? If you need help, refer to Observing and Inferring in the *Skill Handbook.*

Issue:
Recycling: Is It Working?

Have you sorted your trash this week? Citizens of hundreds of cities in the United States have joined the ranks of regular recyclers. They dutifully sort their trash into separate containers marked *Glass, Paper,* and *Metals,* and it makes them feel good. There's satisfaction in knowing that their efforts will ensure that these materials will be available for themselves and others in the future.

The Issue

Recyclers may also be aware that their efforts keep waste disposal from becoming more and more expensive and keep landfills from filling up. Simple calculations favor recycling. It costs $20 to $30 per ton to operate a curbside recycling program. These figures reflect the money made from selling recycled materials. This is a bargain in comparison with $40 to $60 per ton when the disposal company just buries the trash in a landfill. And if that's not convincing, what if the trash is incinerated instead of being buried? That costs $70 to $120 per ton.

The Background

Even though recycling seems to be the wisest thing to do, both for saving resources and saving money, that's not the whole story. The public must get away from the idea that they are recycling when they dump items in containers at curbside. It's not recycled until it's used again. It often costs more for industries to buy recycled goods than to obtain newly mined resources. Less than 20 percent of U.S. trash is recycled, in part because the market for recovered and recycled products is weak.

A large waste-disposal company spent millions of dollars developing a curbside recycling

A tire-burning cement kiln

program. The program was well received by consumers, but it lost money or earned very little during five years of operation because there was no demand for recycled materials.

Forty states have comprehensive recycling programs. However, they collect far more material than they can sell or reuse. This creates the problem of too much supply and too little demand.

Demand for recycled materials is so small and the supply is so great that the average price of a ton of household waste dropped from $100 to $44 between 1988 and 1992. Some states have tried to increase demand for recycled materials by passing laws that ban the use of materials that can't easily be reused or recycled. For example, gable-top milk cartons were banned because they are difficult to recycle. It is hoped that the laws will encourage manufacturers to buy and use recycled and recyclable materials.

The Questions

Although the prospects for recycling glass and plastics look bad for the near future, some creative solutions are being found. A new process was developed at a Seattle company in which plastics are returned to their original material—high-quality oil. A petrochemical company in Houston will reuse the recycled product.

Other recycled products are also beginning to appear. A manufacturer of sportswear is marketing sweaters spun from green plastic soda bottles. Home builders are using wallboard made from recycled paper, wood, and plastic. A new pallet made from recycled plastic outlasts the usual wooden pallet.

A disposal company in Houston uses automation to sort and process paper, glass, plastics, and metal. It grew from 2 to 93 plants in three years, and business is growing at 35 percent a year.

Newspaper recycling

One solution for the waste-disposal problem is to charge consumers for each bag of garbage they discard. Consumers would begin to factor the cost of recycling into their decision to buy a product. However, quotas and fines may force people to separate their trash, but they can't create a demand for the recycled waste. What can be done to increase these markets?

*inter*NET
CONNECTION

Follow the link for Chapter 14 on the Glencoe Homepage, **http://www. glencoe.com/,** for information about the San Francisco Recycling Program. Research how one community deals with recycling. Make a list of recycling tips for home, school, and work. Take the recycling quiz to test your knowledge of this subject.

14-2 Taking the Car Apart

Objectives
- Trace the process of recycling a car.
- Describe the methods used in recycling glass, steel, and plastics.
- Discuss the advantages of recycling glass, steel, plastics, and other materials.

Key Terms
alloy

Separating the Components

Think back to the photo of the auto junkyard at the beginning of this chapter. After looking at our waste-disposal options for everyday materials in the last section, you probably can imagine the need for a way to dispose of the 10 million cars discarded by Americans each year. You might be surprised to know that nearly all of these cars go through a recycling process, making automobiles a large contributor to the recycling industry. About 75 percent of a car is made of commonly recyclable or reusable materials. How are these materials reclaimed and reused?

Today's autos contain more than 600 different materials. Although most of these materials can be recycled, the challenge is recovering these materials from scrapped cars. An average U.S. passenger car built in the early 1990s contains more than 700 kg of steel, 180 kg of iron, 100 kg of plastics, about 70 kg each of fluids and aluminum, 60 kg of rubber, 20 kg of copper, and more than 50 kg of other materials. Because most cars are not built to be recycled easily, taking them apart requires a great deal of labor. **Figure 14-8** illustrates a typical automobile-recycling process.

Figure 14-8

The illustration below shows how a car is reused and recycled. The tires have already been removed and sent to a landfill or used in other products.

A Oil, brake fluid, transmission fluid, and coolant are all drained and properly disposed of.

B Reusable parts such as the radiator, electric motor, and catalytic converter are removed and reconditioned.

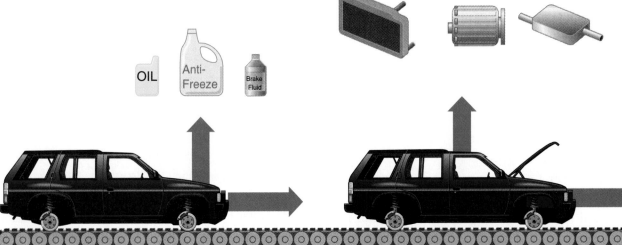

Steel—From Cans to Cars

Each time you open a can of chicken noodle soup or ride in a car, you are probably using recycled steel. Steel is an alloy made of iron and a small amount of carbon. An **alloy** is a mixture of two or more elements in which at least one of the elements is a metal. **Figure 14-9** shows how properties of an alloy can be controlled by the addition of other elements.

Sixty-six percent of steel is recovered, making it the most recycled material in the United States. And because steel is the major component of cars, the automobile-recycling industry is a major contributor of scrap steel. What makes steel so easy to collect and recycle? For one thing, it's easy to separate from other materials. Most recycling programs accept steel and aluminum cans together, for example, although they are recycled separately. It's easy to separate steel and aluminum because

Figure 14-9

Steel is an alloy. The composition of steel is changed to create desired properties for different uses. In addition to iron, the stainless steel in this silverware contains chromium, nickel, and carbon to resist corrosion. Steel also can be coated with materials that resist corrosion, such as the tin coating on this food can.

iron, the main element in steel, is magnetic, while aluminum is not. Therefore, big magnets are used to separate steel from other materials.

The steel headed for recycling is then sorted based on alloy content and sent to a steel scrap-processing plant. Used steel can be reprocessed by melting or by chemical methods. Chemical processing removes unwanted impurities such as other metals. This is useful for steel cans, which are often coated with tin to prevent corrosion. Steel scrap from automobiles is usually remelted. When properly collected and processed to remove impurities, recycled steel can be reprocessed to make any steel product. The soup can you recycle today might show up in a new car.

C The car is fed into a huge shredder. Iron and steel are separated from the shredded remains using large magnets. Other metals such as zinc, aluminum, copper, and chromium are also removed and recycled.

D The remaining 25 percent of the shredded car, commonly called *fluff*, contains a mixture of carpet, fabric, plastics, glass, and dirt. Fluff is difficult to separate and is usually incinerated or placed in a landfill.

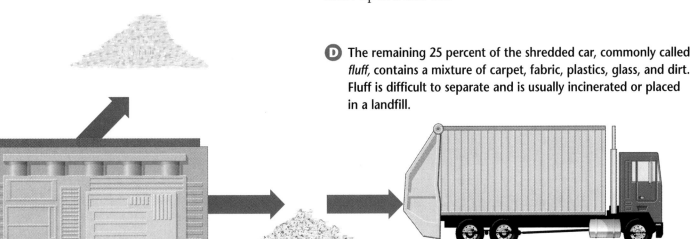

Table 14-1

The Plastics Code System			
Code	Material	% of Containers	Reclaimed For
1 PET	Polyethylene terephthalate (PET)	7%	Carpet, food packaging, fiberfill, fibers, and auto parts
2 HDPE	High-density polyethylene	31%	Drainage pipes, drums, traffic cones, plastic lumber, and combs
3 V	Vinyl chloride	5%	Pipes, hoses, mud flaps, and tile
4 LDPE	Low-density polyethylene	33%	Mixed with HDPE to produce cases, recycling bins, and garbage bags
5 PP	Polypropylene	9%	Household and janitorial products
6 PS	Polystyrene	11%	Insulation and food trays
7 Other	All others and mixed	4%	Storage containers, lumber, and animal pen floors

■ Plastic—Don't Just Bag It

Can you quickly find three examples of plastic around you right now? We use plastic polymers in the clothes we wear and in the containers that store our food. Plastics are also widely used in automobiles. But recall from **Figure 14-8** that most of the plastics in cars are shredded and incinerated or hauled to the landfill. Why aren't they recycled? Many different kinds of plastic—50 or more—are used in a single car. Different plastics can have nearly identical color and density. There's no easy, mechanical way to separate all the different kinds of plastic.

At home, separating plastics is much easier. In the last chapter, you learned that most plastics are polymers composed largely of carbon, hydrogen, and oxygen. Polymers with different structures are used to create plastics with unique properties. To make collecting and recycling of plastics easier, a number within a triangle shape is imprinted on plastic containers to show which type of plastic they are. **Table 14-1** shows the codes for common plastics and some of the uses for each type of recycled plastic.

■ Recycling Plastic

The most common household plastics recycled are clear, 2-L soft drink bottles (made of polyethylene terephthalate, or PET) and translucent milk jugs (made of high-density polyethylene, or HDPE). When a type of plastic is collected and sorted, other materials are removed. For example, opaque lids are usually made of a different plastic and are removed. After plastics are sorted, the recycling process is fairly simple. The plastic bottles are chopped into small pieces and washed. After drying, the material is melted. It is pushed through a screen filter and formed into pellets. The pellets are stored until the material is used to make a new product. PET from 2-L soft drink bottles is often used to make fiberfill for sleeping bags and coats. The plastics-recycling industry promises to grow in the future.

B Sorted glass is ground into pieces of uniform size called *cullet*.

A Consumers must separate glass by color. If different colors of glass are combined and remelted, an unsightly mix results.

D Melted glass is formed into new items.

C Cullet is melted in a glass furnace. Reprocessing glass requires much less energy than making new glass.

Figure 14-10

Glass recycling involves many steps. These photos summarize the four most important steps.

■ Gobs of Glass

Do you know what you're looking through when you gaze out of a car window? Silica (sand) is melted with small amounts of limestone and soda ash to make glass, one of the most versatile and recyclable materials. Most glass in a scrapped car is in the windshield. Windshields—like windows, lightbulbs, and drinking glasses—aren't made of the same kind of glass as bottles and jars, so they can't be recycled with the glass you throw into your recycling bin. Windshields sometimes can be used in other cars or recycled to make fiberglass, but many are crushed and taken to landfills with the fluff.

The glass in jars and bottles, however, is completely recyclable and can be processed to make new containers. **Figure 14-10** shows the glass-recycling process. The raw materials used in making glass are plentiful, but melting recycled ground-up glass, or *cullet*, uses less energy. Recycling also saves landfill space. Glass is nonreactive and will not decay in a landfill. So why isn't more glass recycled? The biggest obstacle is collection of used glass. Bottles and jars take up space while being stored for recycling. Most homes aren't equipped to safely crush glass. Therefore, some people aren't willing to sacrifice the time and space required.

Connect to...

Earth Science

Soil permeability can affect how materials leach from landfills. Find out what factors affect soil permeability.

Figure 14-11

Oil and batteries are recycled separately.

■ Finishing off the Car

Steel, plastic, and glass aren't the only recyclable materials in cars. Motor oil, batteries, and tires are also recyclable.

The United States could save more than 1 million barrels of oil each day if all used motor oil were recycled. Recycling motor oil prevents pollution, too. Car owners who change their own oil can have difficulty recycling oil. Oil is messy and hard to safely transport. Although some automotive service centers, like that in **Figure 14-11,** recycle motor oil, they may not accept used oil from noncustomers. When improperly disposed of, waste oil contaminated with heavy metals, such as lead, nickel, and cadmium, can seep into the groundwater. These can poison plants and ani-

mals. When motor oil is reprocessed for recycling, these impurities are removed. Recycled motor oil is most often used for fuel oil or again as motor oil.

Car batteries also can be effectively recycled to save resources and avoid environmental contamination. Lead is the problem material in car batteries. Prolonged exposure to lead can cause brain and muscular damage. Even low levels of lead can interfere with the normal development and function of the human nervous system. Young children are especially vulnerable to problems caused by lead poisoning. Therefore, it is unsafe to dispose of lead in landfills where it might seep into groundwater. Lead can be removed from batteries, crushed, remelted, and used again to manufacture new batteries.

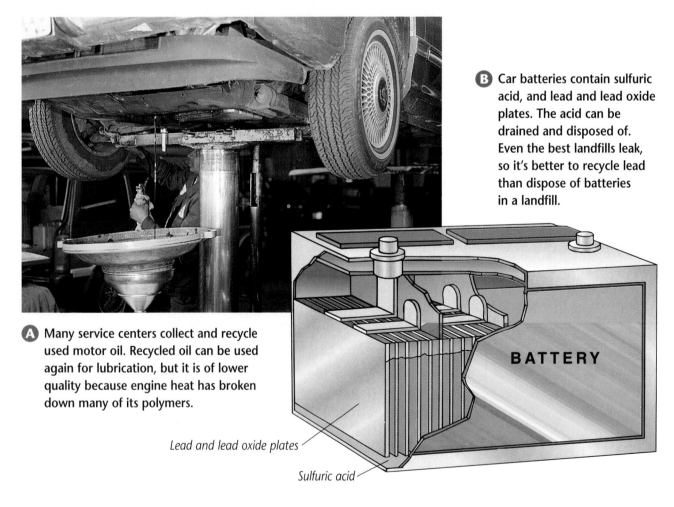

B Car batteries contain sulfuric acid, and lead and lead oxide plates. The acid can be drained and disposed of. Even the best landfills leak, so it's better to recycle lead than dispose of batteries in a landfill.

A Many service centers collect and recycle used motor oil. Recycled oil can be used again for lubrication, but it is of lower quality because engine heat has broken down many of its polymers.

Lead and lead oxide plates

Sulfuric acid

BATTERY

Figure 14-12

These photos show the problem of tire disposal and some solutions.

A Tire piles present a significant fire hazard and provide a breeding ground for rodents and mosquitoes. Old tires can be retreaded and used again or the rubber may be reclaimed for other purposes.

C These rubber hexagons are made from recycled tire rubber. They are attached to pavement and used to separate lanes of traffic.

B Shredded tires can be formed into martial arts and gymnastics mats. Finely shredded tires are sometimes used in place of sand on playgrounds because they absorb impacts better than sand.

Landfill disposal is also not the best option for used tires. There are ways to keep tires out of landfills. The rubber can be separated and chopped or shredded into small pieces. As **Figure 14-12** shows, it can be used to make a variety of products including shoe soles, boat-dock bumpers, and floor mats. Incinerators also can use the energy released when rubber is burned to generate electricity. Health and safety hazards from storing used tires have kept these recycling ideas on a small scale.

Tires also work their way to the top of landfill piles years after they've been buried. As the landfill is compacted by bulldozers, the tires are compressed. When the tires expand, they push aside other waste and move upward.

On the next pages, you can guide an everyday material through a recycling process.

How do you control the quality of recycled paper?

Nearly 80 percent of the solid waste generated by schools is paper. Paper is the largest contributor to landfills, but it doesn't have to be. Recycling most of the car components discussed in this section requires high temperatures, but paper can be recycled through a few simple steps that can be done in your classroom.

Preparation

Problem
How can recycled paper with desired properties be made from scrap paper?

Hypothesis
Read steps 1-4 under Plan the Experiment. Then, within your group, decide what properties you want your recycled paper to have. Write and record a hypothesis that explains how the papermaking process will affect the end product.

Objectives
In this Investigation, you will:
- *Design a plan* for making recycled paper with specific properties.
- *Experiment* with variables that affect the properties of recycled paper.

Possible Materials
a variety of used, clean paper (news-papers, notebook paper, comput-er paper, construction paper, tis-sue paper, greeting cards, etc.)
screen
food coloring
water
hand mixer or electric blender
wire whisk
dishpan
rolling pin
steel can
sponge
decorative items (leaves, small beads, small flowers, fabric, etc.)
600-mL beaker

Safety Precautions

If you use an electric mixer or blender, be careful to turn it on only when mixing the paper, and keep your fingers clear of rotating parts. Materials used to color the recycled paper could stain skin and clothing. Be sure to clean up your area as directed by your teacher.

Plan the Experiment

The general directions to make recycled paper are as follows:

1 Tear used paper into small pieces.

2 Combine a handful of shredded paper with about 2 cups of warm water and blend the mixture to a pulp.

3 Pour the pulp onto a screen over a dishpan.

4 Press out excess water and let the pulp dry.

Check the Plan

Discuss the following points with other group members to decide the final procedure for your experiment.

1 Determine what kind of texture you want your paper to have.

How might the kind of paper you start with affect the final texture? Your method of mixing?

2 How will you end up with the color of paper you want?

3 How will you dry your paper?

4 Prepare a list of numbered directions. Include a list of materials. Keep in mind that you will be sharing mixers or blenders.

5 *Make sure your teacher has approved your experimental plan before you proceed further.*

6 Carry out your experiment. Record your observations *in your Journal* during each step of the procedure.

Analyze and Conclude

1. **Communicating** Write a careful description of your recycled paper product. Comment on its texture, color, and shape. What purpose is it most suitable for?

2. **Recognizing Cause and Effect** Examine the products made by other groups. Find one significant difference between your product and another. Interview the other group about their procedure to find out what caused this difference.

3. **Comparing and Contrasting** Use a microscope or magnifying glass to examine samples of the original paper and your recycled paper. How are they similar? How are they different? What reasons can you infer for any differences?

Going Further

Changing Variables
Choose one improvement you would like to make on your product. Decide how you would change your procedure to make this change. Try it and report on your results.

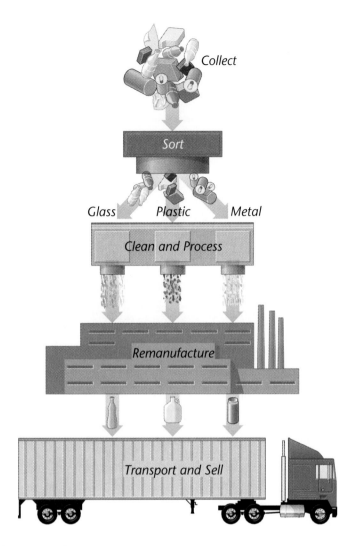

Collect

Sort

Glass   Plastic   Metal

Clean and Process

Remanufacture

Transport and Sell

Figure 14-13

Each recycling process has certain steps in common. Materials must be collected, sorted by type, cleaned, reprocessed, and remanufactured.

As you discovered in the Investigation, many parts of a recycling process can affect the product. The color of the recycled paper depended on the type and color of waste paper you used. How the pulp was shredded and dried affected the texture of the product. During an actual recycling process, waste white copy paper is shredded, bleached, mixed with small amounts of clay, formed into sheets, and dried at high temperatures.

Now you see that recycling involves more than tossing cans into a bin. Whether it's a sheet of notebook paper or an entire automobile that's being recycled, the process takes a number of steps. **Figure 14-13** illustrates the recycling process many materials undergo. Collection, processing, and consumer demand all can present obstacles to efficient reuse and recycling.

Finding efficient ways to recycle materials into products people will buy will become more and more important in the future as we seek to conserve scarce natural resources and to reduce the need for landfills and incinerators. How can you do your part? The next section offers some suggestions.

check your UNDERSTANDING

Understanding Concepts

1. How is a car typically prepared for recycling?
2. Suppose you could follow a 2-L soft drink bottle through the recycling process from the time you throw it into a recycling bin until it is made into something else. Describe the steps you would see.
3. What are some of the benefits of recycling the materials discussed in this section?

Skill Review

4. **Measuring in SI** If the United States produces 175 million metric tons of municipal solid waste in a year and approximately 40 percent of this is paper, determine the mass of paper dumped in one year. If you need help, refer to Measuring in SI in the *Skill Handbook.*

14-3 Cycling Uphill into the Future

What can you do?

In previous chapters, you learned about renewable and nonrenewable resources. Forests, for example, are considered renewable because more trees can be planted when some are cut down. But the fossil fuel and mineral resources used in making cars, plastic beverage bottles, and other products discussed in this chapter are nonrenewable. When they are used up, Earth can't produce any more rapidly. So if we expect to enjoy the conveniences we're accustomed to for years to come, we must find ways to conserve natural resources or replace them with renewable resources.

Think about the personal trash inventory you did in the activity on page 413. Do you now have some other ideas about what can be done with your trash? We discussed advantages and disadvantages of using landfills, incinerators, and recycling. Consumers and their communities must choose the best combination of these methods of waste disposal and conservation of resources.

Other than being an informed citizen, what can you do now to help the situation? Three words—*reduce, reuse, and recycle*—suggest ways you can make a difference in our solid-waste problems today. As you read the three sections that follow, keep a mental list of steps you can take to reduce waste.

■ Reduce

The Environmental Protection Agency recommends a hierarchy of waste-management methods. In order of preference, these methods are source reduction, recycling and composting, waste-to-energy combustion, and landfill disposal for remaining materials. **Source reduction** simply means reducing the amount of waste generated.

Even something as simple as a comb often comes sealed in plastic attached to cardboard backing. Is all this packaging necessary? Maybe not. What kinds of packaging would you prefer if you were grocery shopping with source reduction in mind? See **Figure 14-14** for some suggestions. What suggestions would you give to manufacturers?

Objectives
- Discuss three ways a person can help reduce solid wastes and conserve natural resources.
- Identify methods of source reduction.

Key Terms
source reduction

Figure 14-14

When grocery shopping, buy one large container of a product rather than several smaller ones. Purchase items in containers that can be reused when empty. Look for packaging that is made of recycled materials and can be recycled again. Manufacturers will use more responsible packaging if consumers refuse to buy overpackaged or nonrecyclable products.

How do packing peanuts differ?

Different kinds of materials are used to protect fragile products when they are shipped. After use, they are often discarded and occupy space in landfills.

Procedure

1. Examine polystyrene and starch peanuts. Compare their cushioning abilities. Record your observations *in your Journal.*

2. Equally space nine starch peanuts in a 20-cm × 20-cm square on the floor or a table. Hold a heavy book 15 cm above the peanuts and drop it. Observe any change in the peanuts.

3. Repeat step 2 using the polystyrene peanuts and record your observations *in your Journal.*

4. Place 250 mL of water in a 600-mL beaker. Gently pack another 250-mL beaker with starch peanuts. Add the starch peanuts to the water and stir. What happens? Record the approximate total volume of liquid and peanuts.

5. Repeat step 4 with fresh water and polystyrene peanuts.

Analysis

1. How are these packing materials similar? How are they different?

2. Find out what resources are used to make these two packing materials.

3. Infer the advantages and disadvantages of each type of packing peanut. If your company were shipping fragile goods, which would you use? Use observations to justify your answer.

Figure 14-15

Using disposable paper or plastic cups wastes resources. Plastic bottles are easier to carry and use. Walkers, runners, and hikers often use bottles like this to carry water.

■ Reuse

Do you commonly reuse any products in your home or school? Reusing empty food and drink containers, reusing paper lunch sacks, and using sponges in place of paper towels are all ways to reduce solid waste.

By buying products in reusable packages, you can save money and reduce the amount of solid waste you generate. You can also use a washable cup like those in **Figure 14-15,** rather than a disposable cup, when you buy fountain drinks at a local convenience store. Some products can be reused after simple treatments, for example, rechargeable batteries.

Your purchase choices encourage manufacturers to change their packaging. Manufacturers also have a responsibility to become more resource-efficient. Think of all the materials or products used in your school that could be reused.

■ Recycle

We have already discussed some of the benefits and methods of recycling specific materials. By recycling as many things as possible that you don't plan to reuse, you can decrease solid waste and keep natural resources in circulation. In addition to the car-related materials mentioned in the last section, two other materials deserve specific mention.

One of the most commonly recycled products in the United States is the aluminum beverage can. The recycling process is relatively simple. Cans are crushed, shredded, remelted, and then processed into new cans. Making cans from recycled aluminum requires 95 percent less energy than making cans from bauxite ore, the original source of aluminum. Aluminum can recycling is an excellent illustration of the economic and resource benefits that recycling can provide.

Recall from **Figure 14-1B** that the second largest contributor to landfills by weight is yard waste—raked leaves, cut branches, and grass clippings. Many landfills are now banning yard waste to save space. What else can be done with it? Have you ever left damp grass clip-

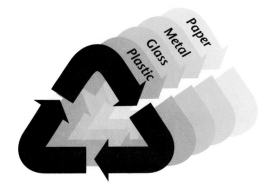

Figure 14-16

Look for this symbol. It indicates products that can be recycled and products made from recycled materials.

pings or leaves in a bag for a week or more? If so, you may have noticed that the waste became a bit warm and mushy. It was on its way to becoming compost. As you saw in Chapter 11, composting occurs when microorganisms decompose organic matter such as grass, leaves, and vegetable scraps. Many people and communities are now handling yard waste with compost piles.

Composting, recycling other materials, landfilling, and incinerating are all tools to manage solid waste ranging from the smallest gum wrapper to scrapped cars. Materials that are thrown away do not just disappear when the trash collector comes on Tuesday morning, so think about your options and **Figure 14-16** before pitching that soda can into the trash.

---

check your UNDERSTANDING

Understanding Concepts
1. How is composting an example of recycling?
2. Apply the concept of reuse to the waste in a school or office. Give examples of how reuse might be helpful.
3. What are some common methods of source reduction that you might consider when grocery shopping?

Skill Review
4. **Concept Mapping** Starting with the heading *Reducing Solid Wastes,* draw a concept map based on the three general ways you can reduce solid wastes and conserve natural resources. Be sure to give examples of each category. If you need help, refer to Concept Mapping in the *Skill Handbook.*

APPLYING TECHNOLOGY

Making Waste Disposal Work

Disposing of waste materials has become a major concern in society. Many landfills are becoming filled to capacity, and the burning of certain toxic materials releases pollutants into the air. Cities are implementing recycling programs to decrease the amount of waste deposited in landfills or burned and to conserve natural resources.

You're the City Recycling Director

You have been asked to analyze the amount and types of waste that are being produced each year by your city and to devise a program for disposing of or recycling the different types of waste.

Drawing on Experience

1. Contact your local solid waste-disposal company. Find out how much waste is produced annually by the city and how much is deposited in landfills or burned. Find the cost per ton for disposal and for incineration.

2. Contact local recycling centers and determine what types of recyclable materials are accepted by each center. Find out how many materials were collected curbside last year by recycling centers. Find the cost per ton for recycling each type of material.

3. Determine the best way to dispose of the following types of materials: newspapers, disposable diapers, magazines, cardboard, plastics, aluminum cans, glass, dead grass

and leaves, and toxic wastes such as oils, paints, solvents, and pesticides.

Testing...Testing

1. Devise a cost-efficient plan that accounts for disposal or recycling of the various types of waste.

2. Make a graph showing the amount of waste produced last year by your city and the amount of the various types of recyclable materials that were picked up.

How Did It Work?

Compare the recycling and waste-disposal programs from last year with your plan for next year. Has there been any improvement in the amount of materials that can be picked up for recycling? Compare the amount of waste your city produces to the volume or mass of a well-known object.

Read the statements below that review major points presented in the chapter. Using the concepts that you have learned, answer each question *in your Journal.*

1 Sanitary landfills are one way of disposing of solid waste. *Why are landfills not an ideal disposal solution?*

2 The majority of a car can be reused or recycled. *What part(s) of a car is/are most difficult to recycle?*

3 Glass, plastic, and steel are three commonly recycled materials. *What are the common parts of the recycling process for each of these materials?*

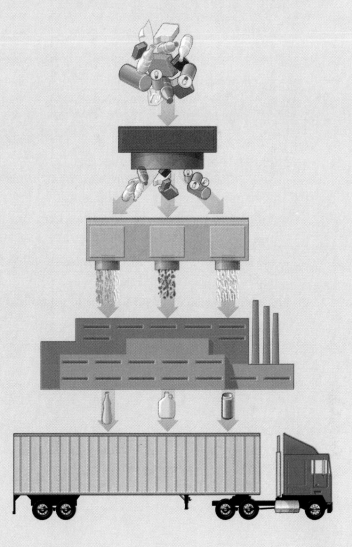

Reviewing Main Ideas **439**

Using Key Science Terms

alloy   sanitary landfill
incinerator   source reduction
recycling

Use terms from the list above in your answers to the following questions.

1. How can waste be used to help generate electricity?
2. Why can steel and aluminum cans be separated with a magnet?
3. How does buying food in bulk quantities help reduce solid waste?
4. What is the best way to dispose of yard waste?

Understanding Ideas

Using complete sentences, answer the following questions in your Journal.

1. Suppose it is scientifically possible to recycle a product. What factors will determine whether it is recycled on a large scale?
2. How does a sanitary landfill differ from an open dump?
3. What are some common methods for collecting recyclable materials?
4. Describe two common sources of metal for the steel-recycling industry.

5. Discuss several reasons why motor oil should be recycled rather than dumped on the ground or in landfills.
6. Explain why the recycling of plastics is a complex issue. What has been done to encourage plastic recycling?
7. Cite several advantages of burning solid waste in incinerators.
8. How are reusable or recyclable materials recovered from scrapped cars?

Developing Skills

Use your understanding of the concepts developed in this chapter to answer each of the following questions.

1. **Making and Using Graphs** The pie graph in **Figure 14-1B** showed the average composition of garbage. Suggest and sketch another type of graph that would illustrate this information.
2. **Interpreting Scientific Illustrations** Use **Figures 14-3** and **14-4** to determine what kinds of products result from the incineration of solid waste. Include both matter and energy products.
3. **Sequencing** You read about the waste-management ideas of the Environmental Protection Agency in Section 14-3. List the sequence of waste-disposal options they recommend.
4. **Measuring in SI** Many environmental information resources describe the energy saved by recycling a product in a unit called the Btu (British thermal unit). What is the SI unit of energy?
5. **Concept Mapping** Pick a resource and create a concept map describing the resource's use, reuse, and recycling process.

Critical Thinking

In your Journal, answer each of the following questions.

1. Although aluminum beverage cans are completely recyclable and recycling is much cheaper than starting with new materials, only about 65 percent of the cans are actually recycled. Suggest why the rate is not closer to 100 percent.

2. Explain how it would be possible for a material to be technologically recyclable but not practical to recycle.

3. Car recycling requires a lot of labor, and 25 percent of the car is still disposed of as fluff. What might auto manufacturers do to make cars more recyclable?

4. Why are communities having trouble locating places to build new landfills and incinerators?

5. Sometimes the terms *rethink* and *reject* are added to *reduce, reuse,* and *recycle* as tools to improve the solid-waste problem. What do you think these terms mean in this context?

Problem Solving

Read the following problem and discuss your answers in a brief paragraph.

Suppose you are superintendent of a large school district in the desert Southwest. Your district is trying to determine the best method of serving school lunches. Because of your location, you are concerned about water conservation because washing reusable dishes demands a lot of hot water. Your other option is to use and recycle polystyrene products.

Identify the advantages and disadvantages of both options. What will your plan be? Defend your answer.

CONNECTING IDEAS

1. **Theme—Energy** How is energy use affected by recycling?

2. **Theme—Systems and Interactions** How does recycling affect the system of consumers and resources?

3. **Theme—Scale and Structure** How does the structure of a car lend itself to recycling?

4. **Eyewitness** How did the UCAN program start?

5. **Science and Society** How has new technology influenced demand for recycled products?

6. **Applying Technology** What are the ways your community deals with solid waste?

UNIT 4
PROJECTS

LET'S ALL GO (RE)CYCLING

Problem
You hear of recycling everywhere you go. Symbols are placed on consumer products to let you know how each piece of waste or product is to be recycled. It would be interesting to find out what people think happens to recycled materials once they are collected. Conduct a survey of students and teachers, and other people you know to reveal ideas people have about what happens to recycled materials. Find out what concerns people have about using products made of reused or recycled products. Then use your data to produce a brochure that could be posted in your school and distributed to the community.

Materials
portable tape player and tape   notebook   pencil or pen

Getting Started
1. Work with three other students from your class to develop a two-part survey consisting, first, of questions about what people believe happens to recycled materials and, second, their concerns about reusing recycled materials.
2. Collect interviews of students, teachers, and people you know (if possible, on tape, so all members of your group can listen to it later).
3. After the interviews, separate the data into opinions and concerns.
4. Produce a brochure containing the opinions and concerns people have about recycling.
5. Post your completed brochure on the school bulletin board and find a way to distribute it to the community, possibly through the local newspaper.

Resources
Almanac of the Environment. Harms, V. New York. G.P. Putnam's Sons, 1994.
Local businesses that indicate they recycle and use recycled materials.

442

AROUND AND AROUND WE GO!

Problem

If you have ever been given the job at home of carrying out the trash, you are aware of the tremendous amount of solid waste produced in your home. In this project, design and build a home recycling station. Make arrangements for storage space for paper, glass, plastic of varied types, metals, and a compost area for organic material. Because organic material decomposes and may give off odors, handle it carefully. Include no meat scraps. Use vegetable wastes only for composting.

Materials

large plastic bags for organic material
can/bottle crusher (optional)
storage containers for each different type of solid waste
guidelines for recycling different plastic products

Getting Started

1. Set up containers in a convenient place in your home to collect each type of solid waste.
2. Ahead of time, determine which solid wastes you could use in another way (this could include plastic bottles, dishes, or other containers that could be used in the home for another purpose).
3. Separate solid waste that you will send to a community recycling station.
4. Separate cans based on metal content, crush them, and store them in separate containers.
5. Separate plastic materials based on the recycling symbol on the product.
6. Safely store glass in a separate container. Contact the local company in charge of collecting recyclable materials and ask whether glass should be crushed.
7. Make arrangements for a local recycling company to pick up materials from your recycling station.

Resources

Local company in charge of collection and recycling of materials.
<u>Almanac of the Environment.</u> Harms, V. New York. G.P. Putnam's Sons, 1994.
<u>Environmental Literacy.</u> Dashefsky, H.S. New York. Random House, 1993.

ALUMINUM CANS

443

Shelter

The house shown below is called Fallingwater. It was designed in the 1930s by Frank Lloyd Wright, a famous American architect. Even such a unique home has many things in common with every other house that is built. Usually the owner picks a location, often with advice from the architect and the builder. Once Wright had designed this house, the engineers had to consider the materials, forces, and energy sources that would allow the design to be carried out. In this unit, learn how all of these things come together to make a shelter.

In the United States, most homes use an outside source for energy or electricity. That's why this electric meter is such a common sight.

These coastal homes were damaged by a hurricane. Making a structure sturdy and choosing a safe place to build are important choices.

Focus On

The Parts of a House

A cross section of a frame house reveals the basic structure of the frame of the house along with all the utilities that supply it with electricity, heat, air-conditioning, water, and sewer. The section also shows how the house is sited.

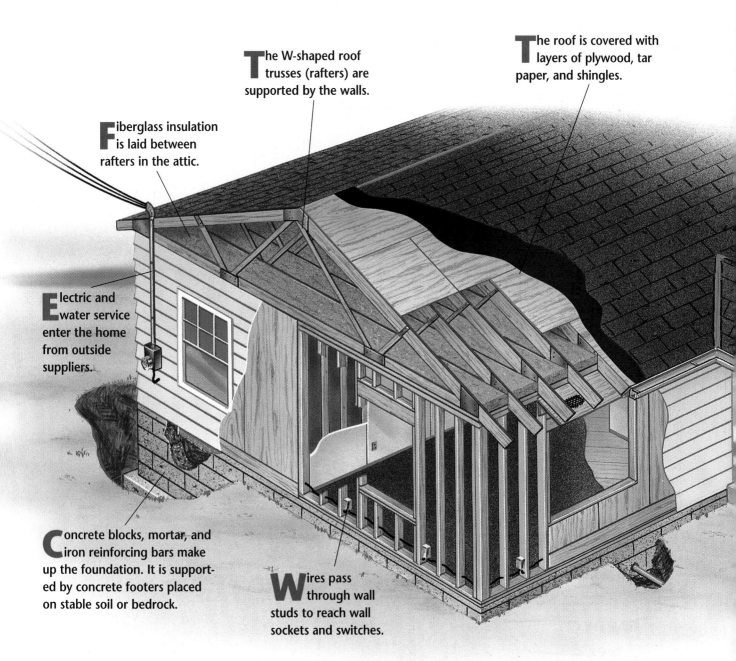

The W-shaped roof trusses (rafters) are supported by the walls.

The roof is covered with layers of plywood, tar paper, and shingles.

Fiberglass insulation is laid between rafters in the attic.

Electric and water service enter the home from outside suppliers.

Concrete blocks, mortar, and iron reinforcing bars make up the foundation. It is supported by concrete footers placed on stable soil or bedrock.

Wires pass through wall studs to reach wall sockets and switches.

Try It!

Houses have been constructed from all sorts of materials, including mud, grass, and felt. Try building a house of cards.

What To Do

1. Obtain a deck of playing cards. Build a small, one-story house with some of the cards. How do you have to support the cards to make the house stable?

2. Build a two-story house of cards. How does its construction differ from that of the one-story house?

3. Try to build a three-story house of cards. Did the three-story house hold up? How was its structure different from the one- and two-story structures? Why was it more difficult to build?

Try It Again

After you have learned about what goes into building a shelter, try this activity again and see whether it is easier with your newfound knowledge of structures.

UNIT 5 PROJECTS

During your exploration of shelters, you may discover new questions or wish to explore related topics. **Flushing Away a Problem?** and **How well are you supported?**, found in the Unit 5 Projects section on pages 592-593, will give you the challenge of working with utilities and structures of buildings. Read through these projects now. By the time you finish this unit, you'll know all you need to know to successfully complete these projects.

CHAPTER 15

Earth's Crust in Motion
Building on Stable Ground

*O*ne of the things your house or apartment is designed to do is keep you out of the weather. It protects you, your family, and your belongings. But how do we know that the building that is protecting us is safe? The first step to putting up a safe building is to select the right site. It's not just a matter of finding a place with a good view or one that's close to schools and places to shop. It must also be a site that can support a building.

▶ *You might think site selection seems easy enough. It may not seem as easy once you look at some of the hazards of building on Earth.*

Does it matter where you build a home?

Look around your community. Are there open spaces without buildings? Why do you think nothing has ever been built on the land?

Procedure

1. Cover a 20 cm × 20 cm piece of stiff cardboard with plastic wrap.
2. Collect a flat rock and 1 cupful each of sand, local soil, and mud.
3. Cover a desk with plastic wrap to protect it and make a separate pile of each item you collected.
4. One at a time, observe what happens as you place the cardboard flat on top of each material, then push down firmly.

Analysis

1. Which materials supported the cardboard? Which materials resisted your pressure on the cardboard best?
2. Which materials would make the best place to build a home? The worst? List them in order, from best to worst.

LAND FOR SALE
2-ACRE LOTS
ZONED RESIDENTIAL

Hazards Caused by Weathering

Hazards of Physical Weathering

Unless it's muddy, you expect the ground you are standing on to hold you up. But even if the ground underfoot looks and feels solid, it may not be firm enough to support buildings. As you noticed in the MiniLab on page 449, some soils move easily under heavy loads. Other soils will move easily under the force of gravity alone. Soils that move easily under loads or under the force of gravity are unstable soils. Building on unstable soils can lead to cracked foundations and slabs, uneven floors, tilted and collapsed buildings, and even leaky roofs. **Figures 15-1** and **15-2** show what can happen when buildings are built on unstable soil.

Objectives

- Classify the types of weathering and how they affect the selection of building sites.
- Compare and contrast types of soil movement caused by gravity.

Key Terms

mass wasting
landslide
creep
mudflow

Figure 15-2

The Leaning Tower of Pisa is supposed to have been the site of Galileo's experiments on falling weights. The tower is a famous example of the problems of building on unstable soil. The tower began to lean soon after it was built on filled-in land, and the lean increases each year. Today, engineers are using a number of methods to keep the historic tower from toppling. How many degrees has the tower tilted away from vertical?

Figure 15-1

Understanding how soil behaves under different conditions can help us avoid building in areas where damage like cracked foundations and twisted walls, shown below, could occur. If we must build on unstable ground, our knowledge of soils can help us engineer buildings to withstand damage that can come from shifting soils.

You learned in Chapter 9 that soils differ depending on the type of rocks from which they form. The geological processes that produce soil also affect its properties. Physical weathering breaks rocks into smaller and smaller pieces through freezing, thawing, rubbing, and striking. When water enters cracks in rocks and then freezes, it expands and forces the cracks wider. Eventually, pieces of rock break away. Many processes cause rocks to strike and rub against one another. Each collision is like a tiny hammer blow that may crack away a bit of rock. Water rolls rocks down streambeds. Waves crash and roll rocks along the seashore. Gravity pulls rocks down slopes. The wind hurls sand against rocks. The sand itself breaks into smaller pieces and the rock gradually wears away.

Some of the soils that result from physical weathering can be a risk to buildings. Although soils formed by physical weathering have rough, angular particles, the grains slide past each other easily, especially when wet. Such soils often move easily, quickly, and for long distances; if you've ever walked up a sand dune, you know *how* easily.

Try the following activity to see one way soils may move.

MiniLab

Can gravity tear down hills and mountains?

A hillside may look as if it is just sitting there, not moving. What happens to sloping ground as a result of gravity?

Procedure

1. Do this activity over a bucket or garbage can to catch any sand that happens to fall.

2. Take a cup of dry, clean sand and pour it onto a piece of cardboard to form a single cone of sand.

3. Once all movement in the pile has stopped, *slowly* tilt the cardboard. Start with a low angle.

4. Carefully observe both the individual grains of sand and the overall shape of the pile. Record your observations.

5. Continue to increase the tilt of the cardboard and observe and record how the shape of the pile changes. Try not to spill any sand.

Analysis

1. What force causes the sand to move?

2. What happens to grains of sand on the sides of the pile?

3. How does this explain the change in shape of the pile as you continue tilting the cardboard?

Mass Wasting

What you just saw in the activity was a model of mass wasting. **Mass wasting** is any downhill movement of soil or rock due to gravity. Types of mass wasting are classified by how the particles of rock or soil move. There are three basic types of mass wasting—falls, slides, and flows. Falls occur through the air. The falling object is not in contact with Earth's surface. Falls such as those warned about on Falling Rock Zone signs often pose serious problems for highways, but not usually for buildings. Slides occur when rock and soil move like blocks down an inclined plane. The blocks of rock and soil are always in contact with Earth's surface. Flows are always in contact with Earth's surface too, but the rock and soil that make up the flow don't move in blocks. The rock and soil move with a tumbling, fluidlike motion.

All hillside soils may move, but their movement isn't always noticeable. The steeper the hillside and the more moisture in the soil, the more obvious the mass wasting.

You've probably heard of landslides. Perhaps you've seen piles of rock and soil where you think a landslide occurred. A **landslide** is the rapid downhill movement of rock and soil. There is often very little water in the material transported in a landslide. The material in a landslide tends to move as one or several pieces of rock and soil along a single plane. Examine **Figure 15-3** to see how a landslide moves down a slope.

Figure 15-3

Landslides occur where there is a large mass of loose rocks and soil on a slope. Weathering can crack and release large pieces of rock upslope. When the rocks fall, they trigger movement among less stable parts of the mass. As the landslide moves down the slope, it spreads out and picks up speed.

■ Creep

Another common kind of mass wasting is slow, flowing movement of soil called **creep.** In creep, soil moves downhill slowly over a long time. Creep is caused by gravity and occurs on almost any slope covered with soils—even the gentlest slopes.

Because creep is slow, its effect on the surface of the land is not always easy to see. However, if you build on land that experiences creep, its gradual effects can become painfully obvious. The foundation of your home may split slowly and send half your home downhill ahead of the rest.

Creep can undermine any construction. As you can see in **Figure 15-5,** railroads yield to creep, making constant repair necessary. Bridges and dams have failed due to creep, and buildings have been brought to the edges of cliffs by its slow and steady movement.

Now you've seen the damage that can be done when soil moves. But what makes the soil start moving in the first place? Does it have to be shaken loose by something like an earthquake? Or can other forces loosen the soil so it can move?

The same natural forces that produce physical weathering set the soil in

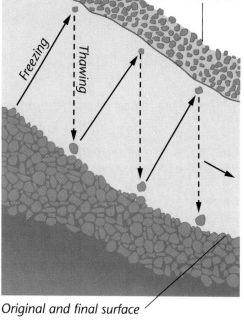

Figure 15-4

When water freezes, it expands slightly. This lifts soil particles up a small distance. When the ice thaws, the soil particles fall downslope. Each lifting and falling movement is tiny, but over time the movements add up. The result is soil creep. Plant roots and burrowing animals also can produce this kind of movement.

Original and final surface

motion—freezing and thawing, wetting and drying, and pushing and lifting. As **Figure 15-4** shows, freezing and melting of water lifts and drops soil grains. Clay swells as it absorbs water and shrinks as it dries. In the process, soil grains are lifted and dropped. Plants push and lift soil as their roots grow. Soil drops into the holes made by rotting roots. Even burrowing animals move the soil. When soil particles move up, even slightly, gravity pulls them downhill.

Do the activity that follows on the next pages to investigate yet another type of mass wasting.

Figure 15-5

This railroad track shows damage from soil creep. Soil underneath has slowly moved downslope and taken part of the railroad with it. What other evidence of soil creep do you see in the picture?

INVESTIGATION

Modeling Soil Flow

Cornstarch and water paste can be used to model soils in one type of mass wasting. In this Investigation, you will find out how the properties of the paste depend on its water content.

Preparation

Problem

How does the water content of soil affect the flow rate of one type of mass wasting?

Objectives

In this Investigation, you will:
- *Measure* mass and volumes in metric units.
- *Infer* behavior of real-world materials from a lab model.
- *Record, communicate,* and *analyze* scientific data.
- *Make, use,* and *interpret* models of natural occurrences.

Materials

balance, stirring rod
cornstarch, 100 g per group
400-mL plastic beaker
plastic wrap, water
graduated cylinder, 10-mL
stopwatch or watch with second
   hand
protractor

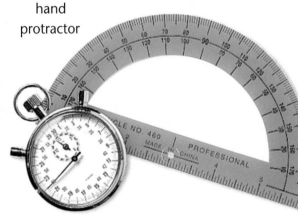

Data and Observations				
Trial	mL of Water	g of Cornstarch	Time to flow (s)	Percent water (Col 3/Col 2)
1	0	100		
2	5	100		
3	10	100		
4	15	100		

INVESTIGATION

Procedure

1 Place the plastic wrap over your table or desk. Place 100 g of cornstarch in a small beaker. Tilt the beaker as if trying to pour the dry cornstarch until the cornstarch just starts to move. Using the protractor, measure and record the angle the side of the beaker makes with the horizontal.

2 Stir 5 mL of water into the cornstarch and mix until a paste forms.

3 Working over the plastic wrap, tilt the beaker to the angle in the first step and record how long it takes the paste to flow to the edge of the beaker. Do not wait more than a minute for it to begin to flow.

4 Add another 5 mL of water to the paste and mix thoroughly. Repeat step 3.

5 Continue adding 5 mL of water at a time and repeating step 3 until the mixture flows like water.

6 *In your Journal,* make a data table like the one shown.

Step 1

Analyze and Conclude

1. **Observing** Describe how the flow of material differed as the amount of water was increased.

2. **Interpreting Observations** At what percentage of water did the paste become thin enough to move to the lip of the beaker in less than a minute? At what percentage of water did it flow as easily as water?

3. **Inferring** If the cornstarch is an accurate model of soils that experience one type of mass wasting, will a small amount of moisture help the soil flow or serve to keep it in place?

Going Further

Thinking Critically
Over what range of soil moisture will the soil you modeled flow at a rate less than water? Is the thinnest mixture a model of creep, a landslide, or some other type of mass movement? Explain.

Figure 15-6

Effects of mudflows

A The town in the top photo was buried by a mudflow in a matter of minutes. Mudflows often travel down existing streambeds, moving as a river of mud. Homes built on the stream bank are especially vulnerable to mudflow damage. Made of volcanic ash, this flow will dry and harden like cement, encasing the town it buried.

B This mudflow was indirectly caused by wildfires higher in the hills. Fire removed vegetation from slopes. Later, heavy rains washed soil down into the valley below. The result was enough to bury cars and clog homes.

■ Mudflows

In the activity you just completed, you made a model of a type of mass movement called a mudflow. A **mudflow** is a movement of earth that occurs on steeper slopes or in areas with wet soil. Mudflows actually move like a fluid in a constantly mixing, liquidlike mass. Flows vary in size, and the same soil may flow again and again.

A mudflow is exactly what it sounds like—a flowing river or sheet of mud. Have you ever seen small mudflows running down bare hillsides during a strong rain? In just minutes, large mudflows have buried entire towns, such as the one shown in **Figure 15-6.**

Areas that are covered with loose volcanic ash can have devastating mudflows because the rain and ash mix and begin to move easily. Mudflows are also caused by melting snow. A volcanic eruption or activity melts the snow high on the volcano's slopes.

Mudflows can travel far and fast. Flows threaten buildings in their path. Homes built in valleys are easily buried and destroyed by mudflows.

If mudflows cut off a stream or river, the flow may act as a dam, and a large lake may form. This poses an additional threat. If the mudflow dam gives way, a flash flood can cause destruction many miles downstream.

Hazards from Chemical Weathering

On a clear, crisp morning in central Pennsylvania, an early commuter flight moves to the end of the runway. Waiting to take off, the pilots feel the plane slowly sink to the left, as if it has a flat tire. The sinking continues until the wing tip almost touches the runway. The effects of chemical weathering have just canceled this morning's flight.

Chemical weathering occurs when water interacts chemically with rock to break down rock or dissolve the rock. For example, limestone can dissolve, leaving large pits known as sinkholes. Examine **Figure 15-7.** Can you see why chemical weathering of underlying rock might pose a hazard to buildings on the surface?

Figure 15-7

This south Florida home has been engulfed by a sinkhole.

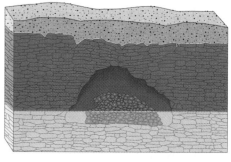

A Sinkholes begin underground when groundwater moving through a rock joint dissolves limestone. As groundwater undercuts the walls, parts of the roof collapse.

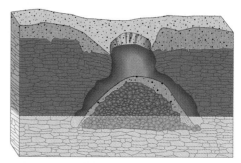

B Eventually, the limestone roof becomes so thin it can't support the weight of the soil above it. What will happen to the sinkhole after it collapses?

■ Sinkholes: The Surprise No One Wants

Sinkholes may form from the surface down or from underground up. How? Mildly acidic (pH~5.8) surface water can run down into cracks and joints in the limestone and dissolve it. As the limestone dissolves, the ground begins to sink. At other times, acidic groundwater forms caves and dissolves rock from below, as shown in **Figure 15-7A** and **B.** When the roof of the cave becomes too thin, it collapses and forms a sinkhole.

Where does the acid in the water come from? A weak, natural acid forms when water mixes with carbon dioxide that is present in the atmosphere.

Figure 15-8

Although this home is built on unstable soil, it is still relatively safe because it is supported by stable bedrock. The builders drilled deep and used concrete pilings to support the foundation. What might happen if the house wasn't supported?

Minimizing Risk

How do you avoid the problems or minimize the risks of hazards presented by weathering? The best way to minimize risk is to avoid it. That's not always as easy as it sounds. "Do not build in dangerous areas" seems like obvious advice, but only if you know where dangerous areas are. How can you find out?

County agricultural agents, the State Geological Surveys, local geologists, and reliable construction contractors are sources of information about possible problems resulting from weathering. Maps that show the type of soil on the surface and its origin may be available.

If you must build on soil that is subject to creep, there are some things you can do. If solid rock is near the surface, you can dig down and build on the bedrock, or sink pilings to bedrock and build on them as shown in **Figure 15-8.** You can remove creeping soils with bulldozers, although this can be expensive if the soil is deep.

Little can be done about earth flows, mudflows, and landslides. Areas that are prone to these problems should never be built on.

In areas with underground limestone, a survey by a trained geologist or geophysicist can help you avoid building over potential sinkholes. The expense of the survey is well worth it when a building could be destroyed.

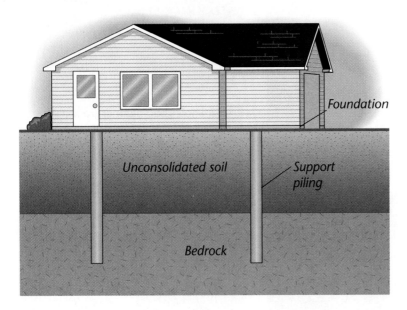

Foundation

Unconsolidated soil

Support piling

Bedrock

check your UNDERSTANDING

Understanding Concepts

1. For both physical and chemical weathering, compare the volume of original rock to the volume of rock left after weathering. Explain any differences in each case.

2. If you found evidence of mass-wasting soil on a hillside, how could you decide whether the type of soil movement was due to a landslide, a mudflow, or creep?

3. You are going to buy land to build on. What sources might you consult before buying and building?

Skill Review

4. **Concept Mapping** Construct a network tree that relates the types of weathering and hazards they present to buildings. Include all types of soil movement covered in this section. If you need help constructing a concept map, refer to the *Skill Handbook.*

The Hazards of Water

Floods

People like to build houses in places that are convenient or scenic, such as a beach or hillside, but they don't always consider safety. Thousands of homes throughout the country are built each year in places that are in serious danger from flooding and erosion.

In this section, explore these threats. You can start by investigating flooding in the following activity.

Objectives
- Classify and investigate factors that lead to flooding.
- Infer how stream erosion can affect the selection of a home site.
- Describe how wave action can make houses collapse.

Key Terms
floodplain

MiniLab

How can a flood occur?

You probably know that floods occur when rivers overflow their banks. You might expect this to happen when winter snows melt and flow into rivers and streams. But how else might flooding occur?

Procedure

1. Take a cutting board or a piece of cardboard covered with plastic wrap and prop it up at about a 30° angle.
2. Take two sponges and put them in water until saturated.
3. Wring out only one sponge. Place both sponges next to each other on the cardboard or cutting board.
4. Slowly drip 100 mL of water onto one sponge. Use a pan to collect and measure the amount of water that runs off.
5. Repeat step 4 for the other sponge.

Analysis

1. In this activity, you made a model that showed how flooding occurs. In your model, what did the sponges represent? What did the dripping water represent?
2. Which sponge retained more water? Why?
3. Infer from your model one way in which floods might occur.

The activity you just completed showed you what happens when soil can't hold any more water. You saw that water ran off the "soil" that was already saturated or full of water. Floods are the result of too much water flowing in a streambed. Have you ever left the water running so fast that the drain in the sink or tub could not handle the flow? Did you end up flooding the

Figure 15-9

Streams usually carry amounts of water that pose no threat to homes nearby. However, even a gentle rain on already-saturated soil can contribute to flooding.

floor? In the same manner, if water flows into rivers and streams too fast to flow out (downstream), water fills the streambed and flows over the banks, flooding the surrounding countryside. The entire area is covered. That's what happened in the second picture in **Figure 15-9.**

How might a stream receive water so quickly? Soil saturation is only one factor that contributes to flooding. When it rains over a large area for a long time, the soil becomes saturated. When the rains continue and the soils cannot absorb any more water, the water runs off the land and into the streams.

Seismograph monitoring station

Shake, Rattle, and Roll

Why do you live where you do? Often, a family chooses its apartment or house because of its location with respect to the schools the children are attending or perhaps the parents' workplaces. Sometimes, a rural home is preferred instead of an urban dwelling.

But how many people do you think consider how the substrate, or soil, might react during an earthquake when selecting their homes?

Earthquake Waves

Earthquakes are more common in some areas of the world than in

others. You may also realize that some earthquakes are more intense than others and can cause more damage and destruction. The material underlying an area struck by an earthquake is often the ultimate factor that determines the damage done by the earthquake.

During an earthquake, seismic waves, or vibrations, are sent in all directions from the source of the quake. These waves then travel at different speeds through Earth and along its surface. In rocks, earthquake waves travel quickly. In unconsolidated materials, like landfill soils, earthquake vibrations trav-

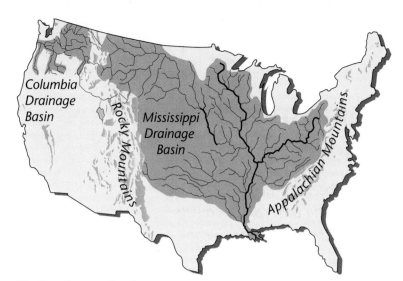

Figure 15-10

The water in a river comes from its drainage basin. The boundaries between drainage basins are called divides. The Continental Divide separates the Mississippi drainage basin from the drainage basins of the western rivers. Where does rain falling in the Mississippi drainage basin eventually go? What about rain that falls in the Columbia drainage basin?

Columbia Drainage Basin

Rocky Mountains

Mississippi Drainage Basin

Appalachian Mountains

Drainage Basins

Streams and rivers receive their water from an area of land known as a drainage basin. **Figure 15-10** shows the drainage basins of two major river systems in the United States. Water enters the drainage basin as rain, snow, discharge from other streams, and from springs and underground streams.

The more water the soil in a drainage basin can hold, the less often its streams or rivers will flood. But what determines how much water soil can hold? You can experiment to find out.

el slowly but are amplified, or magnified, two or three times.

It is best to build on rock for two reasons. First, unlike soil or sand, rock will not usually shift or soften as seismic waves pass through it. Second, seismic energy travels quickly through rocks (up to 7 km/s in rock versus 1100 m/s in soils). The length of an earthquake wave is related to the speed of the wave and the frequency of the wave through the equation $v = f\lambda$, where v is wave speed in meters per second, f the wave frequency in hertz, and λ the length of the wave from crest to crest in meters.

The frequency of seismic waves is fixed at the source, so the faster the speed of the wave, the longer the wavelength must be (at least 12 times longer in rock than in soils). This means waves in rock are long and low-amplitude. Buildings ride these waves like a small boat rides waves on the ocean. Waves in soils are much higher and shorter. The building pitches sharply and may find its ends moving up while the middle tries to move down.

On Shaky Ground

What does this mean for ordinary buildings? The waterfront damage caused by the 1995 earthquake that struck Kobe in Japan occurred because of the unstable subsoils that underlie that area of the city. The spongy, clay-rich soil behaved like jelly as the quake roared through the city. The 1989 San Francisco-area earthquake destroyed hundreds of houses when groundwater made its way upward during the quake, turning the soils in the Marina district into a morass of quicksand.

*inter*NET
CONNECTION

Scientists use seismographs to record an earthquake's waves. To learn more about how they work, visit the Glencoe Homepage for the Chapter 15 link to the University of Berkeley. Once there, follow the directions to construct your own seismograph.

What determines how much water a soil can hold?

You've already seen that runoff from saturated soil helps contribute to filling a riverbed and to the flooding that can be caused as a result. What parts of soils determine how much water it can retain? What determines how quickly a soil will drain?

Preparation

Problem

What factors determine how much water soil can hold, and how does this affect the possibility of flooding in an area?

Hypothesis

Work with your group to develop a hypothesis that suggests an answer to the problem question. Remember, the hypothesis you develop should be something you can test using models in the classroom.

Objectives

In this Investigation, you will:

- *Hypothesize* what soil factors contribute to soil retaining water.
- *Classify* the types of soils by how rapidly they drain.
- *Describe* the relationship between soil type and possible flooding.

Possible Materials

peat moss
sand
clay
potting soil
gravel
funnels
screen
beakers
mixing bowls or containers

Safety Precautions

Wear goggles and aprons as you test your hypotheses. Dispose of all materials as your teacher directs.

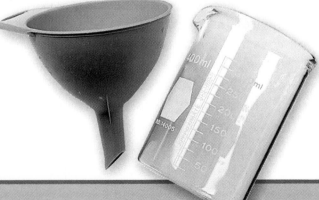

Plan the Experiment

1 Review the definition of *soil* and determine what its chief components are. (Look back at Chapter 9 to find a discussion of soils.)

2 Classify the different components of soil, and figure out which of the available materials will represent each component.

3 Mix up three different kinds of soil. Also be sure to test pure sand and pure clay.

Check the Plan
Discuss the following points with other group members to decide the final procedure for your experiment.

1 How will you test the amount of water each soil will absorb?

2 How will you test how water moves through saturated soil?

3 *Make sure your teacher has approved your experimental plan before you proceed further.*

4 Carry out your experiment. Make any needed observations and complete your data table.

Analyze and Conclude

1. **Interpreting Data** Which soil retained water the best? What was its composition?

2. **Observing and Inferring** How much water did the clay absorb and retain? Why might this also be a problem when it comes to flooding?

3. **Recognizing Cause and Effect** How does the amount of sand in a soil affect how much water is absorbed? How does the amount of sand affect how quickly water moves through the soil?

4. **Making and Using Graphs** If you have not already done so, decide on appropriate graphs to display all of your data. Create the graphs either by hand or by using a computer spreadsheet program. Write a paragraph that explains what the graphs tell you about soils and flooding.

Going Further

Project
Collect soil samples from an area near your home. Test them for water absorption. How will a heavy rain affect soil in your area? Then, contact a city engineer to find out how your community channels away runoff.

To Find Out
More About . . .

***Living on
Floodplains***
Read "Other
People's Money"
on pages 468-469.

Types of Soil

As you discovered in the Investigation, soils with more organic matter, such as peat moss, hold water better than sandy soils. Although sandy soil soaks up water quickly, it can't hold it for long. The water runs through it and into streams. But it is important to remember that no matter how much water a soil type can absorb, if there is enough rain or if there are other sources of water, the soil eventually becomes saturated. When the soil has absorbed as much water as it can, any extra water pools on the surface or runs off into streams, adding to the potential for flooding.

What other factors affect flooding?

What else is important? Think back to the last time you saw rain on bare or packed dirt—on a road or ball field, for instance. There were puddles of standing water, and the ground was muddy. Did you see puddles and mud on nearby grassy areas? Probably not. How would you explain the difference?

Ground without surface plants becomes packed solid and absorbs water slowly. When water hits hard, bare ground, it runs off along the surface and into streams and rivers. This is similar to what happened in the activity when you poured water on the clay. The water did not pass through, but pooled on top.

In contrast, ground that is soft and broken up by plant roots absorbs and holds water well. Thus, occurrences at Earth's surface that damage the plant life also increase the chances that flooding will occur. This is one reason why forest fires are so serious. Not only do we lose trees, but the bare ground left behind no longer absorbs water as well as the ground that had been covered with plant life. As **Figure 15-11** shows, increased surface runoff then leads to mudflows, severe erosion, and possible flooding.

Figure 15-11

A fire removed all the plants from the hillside in the background. The bare ground increases runoff and may increase the likelihood of floods in the area. What evidence of increased runoff do you see?

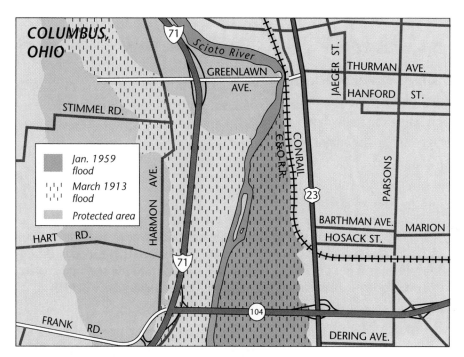

Figure 15-12

Flood maps show the areas affected by floods in the past. The flood in 1913 was higher than that in 1959. Levees and dikes also were built between 1913 and 1959 to protect part of the city. The floodplain shown floods only when rains are unusually heavy. Such heavy floods are expected only once in a hundred years. Other floodplains flood more often and with smaller amounts of rain. Changing climate can make the areas of risk indicated on flood maps unreliable. The Mississippi River, for example, has had several so-called 100-year floods in the last 60 years.

■ Reducing the Risk

Many areas of the country are subject to regular flooding. People living in flood-prone areas must buy federal flood insurance if they are to get any flood insurance at all. Local planning commissions, zoning boards, county supervisors, county agents, insurance agents, and title companies usually keep floodplain maps. A **floodplain** is a flat, low area near a stream that is covered by sediments from the stream. These maps, such as the one shown in **Figure 15-12,** show the risk of flooding in various areas. Try the activity below to model a floodplain.

MiniLab

Is any place on the floodplain safe?

Floodplains are areas in which floods are likely to occur. But do all floods affect the entire floodplain?

Procedure

1. Set up a stream table at an angle of about 5°.

2. Put a row of toothpicks in the sand. The toothpicks should be about 5 cm apart and the line should cross the table.

3. Put the toothpicks in only deep enough for them to stand up.

4. Dig a shallow stream channel down the center of the stream table.

5. Pour enough water for your stream to flow. Then, pour enough for it to flood. Record your observations *in your Journal.*

Analysis

1. How long does it take for the stream to knock down the majority of the toothpicks?

2. Are there any areas in which the toothpicks remain standing? Why?

Connect to...

Physics

Water on the outside of stream bends erodes the land because it is moving quickly. Find out why the water on the outside of the bend moves fastest.

Figure 15-13

Stream erosion and deposition

Erosion by Water

Stream channels wander back and forth over an area known as the floodplain. The floodplain is usually dry but, as the name suggests, it is the area onto which water flows when a stream floods. As you saw in the MiniLab, like a person mopping a floor, a stream will eventually cover every inch of the plain.

Even if you could be sure there would never be a flood, it may not be safe to build on a floodplain near a river or stream. That's because stream channels slowly and constantly change positions, as **Figure 15-13** shows. If you're building a house on a floodplain, it's impossible to find a place that will not eventually be part of the river channel or streambed.

■ Danger at the Seashore

With views of crashing waves and rolling dunes, homes built on beaches or seaside cliffs are romantic and inviting. But both building sites can be dangerous. Try the following activity to find out why.

Figure 15-14

Waves can quickly remove sand that supports the pilings on which many beach homes are built. When that happens, the house will collapse into the sea. Under what conditions do you think sand would be removed most rapidly?

A As a stream flows through a bend, the water on the outside of the bend moves faster than water on the inside of the bend. The more rapidly moving water erodes the bank on the outside of the bend. Sediments are deposited from the slower-moving water on the inside of the bend.

B Over time, the stream erodes the bank on the outer bend of the curve, making the bend sharper. When the bend becomes too sharp, the river takes the shortest route. The curve becomes an oxbow lake. What are some possible hazards of building on the outer bank of a bend in a stream? What might be problems with building on the inner bank?

How do waves cut cliffs down to size?

Oceans are another possible water hazard. Waves can pose as many problems as streams. Why?

Procedure

1. Set up the stream table level and plug the water outlet.

2. Form a large pool to represent the ocean and make a cliff of sand at the shoreline.

3. Using a wave generator or your hand, make waves that hit the shore.

4. Observe the cliff as the waves hit. Record your observations *in your Journal.*

Analysis

1. What happens to the cliff?

2. Why does this occur?

3. What causes cliff erosion?

As you saw with your model, waves erode cliffs and steep slopes on seashores. Waves carry a lot of energy, as anyone who has wiped out while surfing can tell you. They also carry sand and small rocks that act like sandpaper, tearing the land away grain by grain. **Figure 15-15** shows an example of wave action.

The destruction is particularly great when storm waves hit a coast, as shown in **Figure 15-14.** Undercut and without support from below, the cliff slumps, destroying houses and buildings there.

Figure 15-15

This beach in Hawaii shows how the sea moves large amounts of sand. Currents around Hawaii strip all sand from this beach each winter, leaving bare volcanic rock. In spring and summer, the sand is returned.

check your UNDERSTANDING

Understanding Concepts

1. Relate soil type, vegetation, and rainfall in a drainage basin to the risks of a flood.

2. Would you build on land on the outside of a bend in a stream? Why? How about land on the inside?

3. Suggest possible actions one could take to make a seaside cottage or beach home safer from the ravages of erosion.

Skill Review

4. **Designing an Experiment to Test a Hypothesis** Design a short experiment to prove the positive effect of plant roots on the ability of soils to absorb and hold water. If you need help, see Designing an Experiment to Test a Hypothesis in the *Skill Handbook.*

Issue: Other People's Money

"Game called, on account of earthquake." Baseball games are often postponed because of rain. But on October 17, 1989, the third game of the World Series in San Francisco, California, was postponed because of an earthquake. Measuring 7.1 on the Richter scale, this quake caused massive destruction in the San Francisco Bay area, killing more than 60 people and causing $5-10 billion in damage.

The Issue

Every year, thousands of buildings are destroyed and people are killed or injured in natural disasters such as hurricanes, tornadoes, floods, earthquakes, mudslides, and forest fires. Sometimes these disasters are completely unexpected, and no one can be blamed for not being prepared. But often they occur in areas where everybody knew ahead of time that such an event was likely to happen. Homes are built on floodplains, hospitals and skyscrapers are constructed in earthquake zones, and condominiums are built in coastal areas where hurricanes frequently occur.

The costs involved in repairing the damage caused by such disasters are tremendous. Insurance companies pay out large sums of money, and the premiums of all policyholders increase. If the damage is extensive, the region may be declared a disaster area. Then, millions of taxpayer dollars are spent to repair roads and public buildings, to provide medical care for the injured, and to make low-cost loans to help people repair and rebuild.

The Background

Wildfires in California in 1993 roared over 200 000 acres of land and destroyed 700 homes. Hurricane Camille in 1969 caused untold millions of dollars in property damage and left 255 people dead. And the Mississippi River floods in the summer of 1993 caused widespread devastation in the midwest section of the United States, with damage estimates of $10 billion. Whenever such disasters occur, the people who are affected look to the government to help pay for expenses not covered by insurance.

In the five years from 1988 to 1992, the U.S. Federal Emergency Management Agency (FEMA, the main government agency that gives aid to disaster areas) spent an average of more than $1 billion a year in relief to stricken areas. The

Highway collapsed by an earthquake

government, of course, gets its money from taxes, and many taxpaying citizens feel that people who construct buildings in dangerous areas should not receive government aid if their property is destroyed. Some local governments have placed legal restrictions on what can be built in unusually dangerous areas. In 1972, heavy thunderstorms hit Rapid City, South

Flooded and burned downtown in Grand Forks, ND, in 1997

Dakota. A nearby creek overflowed its banks and flooded the town, killing 242 people and causing $128 million in property damage. Because of this terrible event, the town passed a law that says no one can build a private home on the floodplain. This part of town is used for parks and other recreational purposes, but not houses. As the mayor of Rapid City remarked, "Anybody who goes to sleep on a floodplain is crazy."

Each year brings new earthquakes, floods, and hurricanes that destroy property, wreck dreams, and end lives. For humanitarian and financial reasons, it is important that we find ways to reduce the amount of destruction caused by these disasters.

The Question

When a natural disaster strikes, people don't mind helping personally to repair the damage and care for the injured and homeless. And if the event was completely unexpected, most people don't mind if their tax money is spent to help the area recover.

But what if everybody knew the area was dangerous and that such a disaster was likely to occur there? If people build homes, factories, and stores in dangerous areas and then the event happens, should tax money from the rest of society be used to help pay for repairing the damage and rebuilding in the same area?

Tent city set up to house families made homeless by a hurricane

Discussing the Issue

1. Are people more likely to construct buildings in dangerous areas if they know that in case of a disaster, the government will help pay to repair the damage? *Explain.*
2. Should people have the freedom to build a house any place they want to? *Give examples* to defend your answer.

When the Earth Moves

Objectives
- Explain the hazards that earthquakes pose to buildings.
- Describe ways to minimize earthquake hazards.

Key Terms
fault

Faulting

The hazards of landslides, floods, and collapsing cliffs are easy to see. But some building sites have risks hidden from sight.

One type of risk is a fault. A **fault** is a large break in the crust of Earth along which movement has occurred. Some faults, such as those in the San Andreas complex of California, may be hundreds of miles long and reach many thousands of meters into the ground. Other faults can be shallow and relatively small.

In most areas, movement along a fault is one of the least obvious threats to a home. Movement of the crust starts underground. Even when evidence of movement along a fault shows up at Earth's surface, it does not last long because the surface changes so rapidly. Plants grow over gaps and weathering smooths away other evidence. Fault movement may be slow or it may be as swift and dangerous as a quickly opening sinkhole. **Figure 15-16** shows an example of large, quick movement at a fault.

Figure 15-16

In this photograph, you are looking east along a road that shifted in the 1906 San Francisco quake. Notice the car in the background on what used to be the same road. This movement of more than 10 m occurred in several seconds during the quake. What might have happened to a building built over or even near this ground movement?

Earthquakes

When rocks on either side of a fault move quickly, the sliding produces strong waves of energy. These waves move outward at speeds exceeding 5 km per second (18 000 km per hour or 10 000 miles per hour). When the waves hit Earth's surface, they cause the surface to move up and down and/or back and forth, much like the sea, over distances of several meters. This is an earthquake. **Figure 15-17** shows the most damaging forms of earthquake waves.

Large earthquakes devastate large areas, even whole cities as people in California have found out on many occasions. The strongest quakes rearrange the countryside. During the 1811–1812 earthquakes in New Madrid, Missouri, one fault crossing the Mississippi River created a 2-m-high waterfall. Upwards of 50 000 square miles were rearranged so much that many new lakes and swamps formed. **Figure 15-18** shows the location of the New Madrid fault.

Assessing the Risk

Many people live with the risk of earthquakes. But, as we have seen, the amount of damage and risk varies widely depending on where you build. Earthquake risk and damage are studied intensely in areas subjected to quakes. In California, for example, state agencies keep information on risks and past damage. The U.S. Geological Survey has printed numerous reports and maps showing areas of above- and below-average risk. Major city libraries, college libraries, the Government Printing Office, and libraries at many federal centers are sources for these maps and reports.

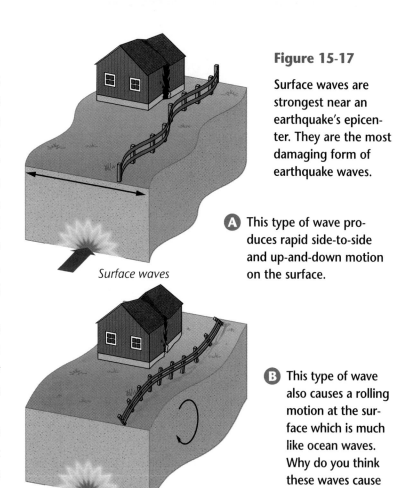

Figure 15-17

Surface waves are strongest near an earthquake's epicenter. They are the most damaging form of earthquake waves.

Surface waves

A This type of wave produces rapid side-to-side and up-and-down motion on the surface.

B This type of wave also causes a rolling motion at the surface which is much like ocean waves. Why do you think these waves cause so much damage?

Figure 15-18

This map shows the location of New Madrid, Missouri, and the New Madrid fault. Although it's been more than a century and a half since the last major earthquake, scientists predict a lot of damage during the next one. Why do you think that is?

Where should you build?

Y ou've already learned that one earthquake can level one part of a city or town and leave another part nearly untouched. How can you choose a safe place to build?

Analysis

The two maps below indicate the areas where damage has occurred during two previous earthquakes. The numbers from I-XII indicate the extent of damage that occurred in the areas. Numbers higher than VIII indicate that extensive damage will probably occur to buildings. Numbers higher than X indicate that even buildings built to earthquake standards are likely to be damaged.

Thinking Critically

Carefully examine the maps. Then select the areas (identified by letters) in which you would build the following structures: hospital, private residence, hotel, city park. Give an explanation for each of your choices. Realize that you can't build everything in the same place. What do you think causes the level of damage to be different in the different areas?

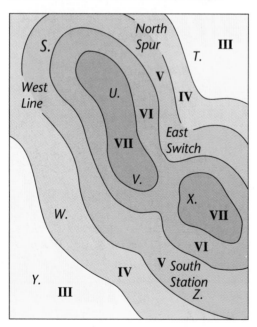

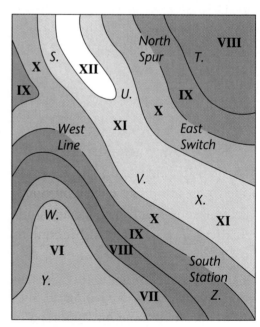

Engineers and architects have devised ways to build structures that can withstand earthquakes. For example, some tall buildings actually rest on steel plates. The entire building moves back and forth during a quake instead of twisting and shaking. Engineers are constantly trying to find new and

different ways to build structures and to alert people to a possible earthquake. One way of making homes more earthquake resistant is shown in **Figure 15-19.**

Now that you've studied and modeled creep, sinkholes, floods, and faults, would you ever build a house without investigating the hazards at the site where you plan to build?

You don't have to be a geologist or soil expert to research the risks. First, just look for signs that other houses in the area have been damaged by unstable soil, water, or movement of earth. Then, head to your local library or geological survey office to dig up maps and reports. A few hours spent there can save you time, money, and headaches later.

Figure 15-19

These crossbraces make the walls more resistant to twisting. This is only one of many earthquake-proofing methods. Strict building codes have also led to much stronger and safer buildings. After a 1995 earthquake in Kobe, Japan, buildings constructed under newer regulations were still standing and older buildings were completely destroyed.

check your UNDERSTANDING

Understanding Concepts

1. Compare the precautions you would take in building in areas where earthquakes are common to the precautions you'd take in building on or near a floodplain.

2. You enter a town after an earthquake. The southern half is leveled but buildings in the northern half, regardless of construction, survived. Explain the probable reason for this and describe how you would use this knowledge in rebuilding the town.

3. Explain how you might identify a fault along which movement has occurred.

Skill Review

4. **Making and Using Graphs** Assume an earthquake wave has a frequency of 2 Hz. Seismic velocities in the rocks of your area range from 1000 m/s to 10 000 m/s. Construct a graph of wavelength versus seismic velocity for your area. To do this, remember:

   velocity = wavelength × frequency

   If a building is safe from earthquake damage *ONLY* if it is shorter than one-fifth of a wavelength, what is the largest building you can build in the area? If you need help making a graph, see the *Skill Handbook*.

Literature Connection

Hobbit Habitats in Our World

"In a hole in the ground there lived a hobbit. Not a nasty, dirty, wet hole . . . it was a hobbit-hole, and that means comfort." J.R.R. Tolkien wrote those words about Bilbo Baggins's home in *The Hobbit.* Hobbit holes are underhill houses with many rooms leading off a long hall that coils around just inside the hill. The outside rooms all have deep, round windows looking out over gardens and meadows.

Bilbo loved his home, and often, while he was away fighting goblins and enduring hardships, he would long for his home's comfortable fireside and steaming teapot.

Today's Underhill Homes

You can, if you choose, live in a hobbit hole today. Modern earth-sheltered homes are being built all over the world. When oriented with windows to the south and thick earth-bermed walls to the north, an underground home almost heats itself. Using earth itself as construction material can make a structure not only warm but also secure, durable, economical, dry, sunny, bright, permanent, easy to maintain, fire-safe, and unobtrusive. *Unobtrusive* means that an underhill or underground home can have a meadow, garden, or forest on every inch of the surface of the land it occupies. A community of earth-sheltered homes could let plant succession occur, offer habitats to wildlife, and beautify the land while enriching and deepening the topsoil. In such a community, all the concrete and asphalt would be underground out of sight.

Keeping Earth Out of Your Home

Of course, underground architecture has its special challenges. Soil can creep out from under a foundation, or it can creep right over a threshold or windowsill. Underground architects have to study the site and plan retaining walls to control the soil's natural inclinations. Also of concern are landslides, mudslides, and sinkholes. Surface houses are hardly more vulnerable than underground homes when it comes to earth movements.

Thinking Critically

1. *List* good qualities that are to be found in a well-built underground home, either that of a hobbit or one built today.
2. *Compare and contrast* living conditions in a standard suburban community with those in a community whose buildings are all underground.

Read the statements below that review major points presented in the chapter. Using the concepts that you have learned, answer each question *in your Journal.*

1 Mass wasting, which is caused by the force of gravity on soils and sediments, can result in many different soil movements. Some such as earth flows are rapid, and some such as creep are slow, but all pose a hazard to buildings. *Why would building in a valley not necessarily avoid the problems associated with mass wasting?*

2 Water can present hazards to houses in many ways. When the soil becomes saturated and rivers are full, floods can occur. The natural course of stream erosion could wear away banks on which there are buildings. Finally, the action of waves can undercut cliffs. *Describe how water also contributes to the hazards involved with chemical weathering.*

3 Faults present hazards in two ways. Rapid movement can occur along faults, resulting in earthquakes. Slow movement also can occur along faults, gradually destroying foundations, pipes, and buildings. *Using the information in this chapter, infer differences between the damage caused by rapid and slow earth movements.*

Using Key Science Terms

creep   landslide

fault   mass wasting

floodplain   mudflow

Choose the word from each list below that does not belong. Explain why it does not belong.
1. fault, mass wasting, earthquake
2. mass wasting, mudflow, floodplain
3. creep, mudflow, landslide, seismic wave

Understanding Ideas

Using complete sentences, answer the following questions in your Journal.
1. What force causes mass wasting?
2. Why is it important to check with several sources including the planning commission or zoning board, and even local contractors, when buying a home or land on which to build?
3. Why is it not always safe to build in a valley instead of on a hill?

4. Other than floods, why is it a poor idea to build on a stream's floodplain?

Developing Skills

Use your understanding of the concepts developed in this chapter to answer each of the following questions.
1. **Concept Mapping** Construct a concept map that helps classify different types of hazards to consider when selecting a housing site. Include the hazards discussed in the chapter and any others you may be aware of.
2. **Interpreting Scientific Illustrations** Look at the mass wasting in **Figure 15-3** on page 452 and **Figure 15-6** on page 456. What differences are there between the shapes of the different movements that make it possible to distinguish one from another without soil samples?
3. **Making Models** If you were to make a model of a landslide, what would you need?
4. **Compare and Contrast** landslides and mudflows.
5. **Designing an Experiment to Test a Hypothesis** Design an experiment to test the hypothesis that larger grains of sand result in steeper slopes. Identify the materials you will need and sketch the setup you plan to use.
6. **Sequencing** List in order the events that occur as a soil particle undergoes creep.
7. **Predicting** Flood plain maps and the earthquake maps on page 472 are used to make predictions about the safety of an area. What factors determine how reliable that safety information is?

8. Hypothesizing You observe that small trees and shrubs on a steep hillside all have unusual curved trunks. What explanation can you suggest for this phenomenon? What further observations would support your explanation?

Critical Thinking

In your Journal, *answer each of the following questions.*

1. Developers bulldoze hillsides into different levels called terraces. They build homes and run streets on the terraces. Homeowner B lives on top of the hill and puts a swimming pool in the backyard overlooking the hillside. In the meantime, Homeowner A, living directly below, decides to enlarge the backyard and digs out the hillside. One rainy night, B's pool and back porch slide downhill, stopping on top of A's game room and garage. Who is responsible for this accident?

2. Why is it unwise to build on earth flows but all right to build on some landslide deposits?

3. Why is there little that can be done to stop mass wasting?

Problem Solving

Read the following problem and discuss your answers in a brief paragraph.

You want to buy a house on a hillside in the mountains outside Denver. Walking around the outside, you notice that the foundation for the house and the foundation for the attached garage are two separate foundations. You also notice that the crack between the two foundations has been patched several times, and each newer patch is bigger than the earlier ones.

1. What do you think is happening?
2. Will there be any problems with the house if you buy it?
3. You would like very much to buy the house; what can you do to be sure it's safe or fix any problems?

CONNECTING IDEAS

1. **Theme—Energy** What change in energy is represented in all forms of mass wasting?

2. **Theme—Systems and Interactions** What changes in the system of a drainage basin make floods more likely?

3. **Theme—Models** Explain how the parts of the mudflow model you made correspond to an actual mudflow.

4. **In-Depth Look** How do soils affect the damage done by earthquakes?

5. **Science and Society** Explain why some people think disaster aid and federal insurance programs can lead to unsafe building locations.

6. **Literature Connection** What are some of the benefits and problems of living in an underground home on a hillside?

CHAPTER 16

Structures and Materials
Choosing the Right Materials

Humans have always needed shelters for protection from high winds and other weather-related elements as well as from predatory animals. While caves provided protection for many early humans, members of the ancient Egyptian and Inca civilizations constructed elaborate buildings of stone. Today's architects use modern materials to design impressive skyscrapers as well as family homes.

Notice the variety of materials used in the construction of the buildings shown on the opposite page. The materials were chosen for use because of their specific properties.

▶ *In the MiniLab on the next page, explore some properties of a material to determine whether it might be useful in building.*

478

What are a material's properties?

Architects can choose from thousands of materials when they design a building. To make the best choice, they need to know the properties of the material.

Procedure

1. In a microwavable bowl, mix 100 mL each of flour, salt, and water. Add one teaspoonful each of cream of tartar and light cooking oil.

2. Heat the material in a microwave oven for 1 minute. Allow it to cool.

3. Break off small samples for testing. Test one sample to see how it reacts to water. Test one with vinegar and one with a lit candle. Observe and record any changes.

4. Shape some of the material into a small column. Observe and record its ability to support various objects.

Analysis

1. Which properties of the material are similar to those of actual building materials?

2. How would this material react to a high level of acid rain?

Built to Withstand Forces

16-1

Objectives

- Identify the forces that buildings must withstand.
- Describe construction techniques that result in sturdy buildings.

Key Terms

tensile stress
compression stress
shear stress

And the Walls Came Tumbling Down

In a familiar story, the wolf was able to blow hard enough to collapse the straw and stick homes of the little pigs, but he couldn't apply enough force to destroy the brick home. All buildings, from the simplest one-room cabin to the largest office building, must be able to withstand certain forces or they will eventually collapse.

Figure 16-1

Different types of foundations are used depending on where the bedrock is located.

A Firm Footing

Have you ever stood on a sandy beach or other soft soil? The weight of your body caused you to sink down and maybe lean to one side. Without a firm foundation, buildings also begin to lean and eventually fall.

Before starting construction, engineers take samples of the soil and rock that lie under the area of the future building. The type of foundation that will be used is determined by the results of their findings. The MiniLab activity on page 481 shows how some foundations work.

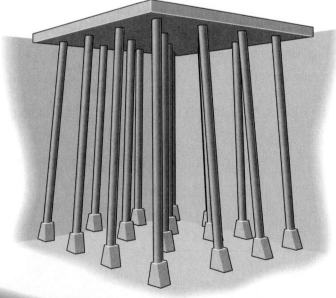

A Pier foundations use piles with shoes or belled bottoms to support buildings in areas that have no solid rock. The wider bottoms spread out the weight of the building much like the weight of a person is spread out when snowshoes are used.

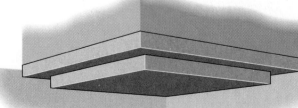

B Raft foundations spread out the weight of a building.

Will it sink?

No matter how well a building is planned and built or what types of materials are used, the quality of a building is no better than the quality of its foundation. Planners and builders must determine the type and location of the soil and rock layers that are below the surface of the proposed building site and plan the foundation accordingly.

Procedure

1. Fill a pie pan with damp sand.

2. Use your finger to press a nickel down into the sand. Observe what happens and record this and all other observations *in your Journal.*

3. Cut out a circle of cardboard that has a diameter twice that of a nickel. Put a nickel at the center of the circle and push it down into the sand.

4. Now push a short pencil point down into the sand until it reaches the bottom of the pie pan. Put a nickel on top of the pencil and push down.

Analysis

1. Why doesn't the second nickel go down as far or as easily as the first nickel?

2. What happens to the nickel placed on top of the pencil? Explain.

To Find Out More About . . .

Building Codes
contact a local architect or contractor to find out what the building restrictions are in your community.

The results of the MiniLab activity can be compared to the types of foundations used to support buildings, as shown in **Figure 16-1.** The bottom of the pie pan represents solid rock. When solid rock is found close to the surface, a raft foundation is built directly on the rock. When the rock layer is deeper, however, the soil between the surface and the rock won't support the weight of a large building. Therefore, large steel or concrete piles are built to reach from the base of the building to the solid rock. These piles are like the pencil in the activity, and they provide support for the weight of the building. A raft foundation spreads out the weight of the building just as the cardboard circle did with the nickel.

Pushing and Pulling

In Chapter 3, you learned that many buildings in Florida were destroyed because they were unable to resist the force of Hurricane Andrew's winds. While most buildings throughout the country don't have to resist such strong winds, they do have to meet specific building codes. They must be strong enough to resist the forces of nature that are found in the area where the building is located. But they cannot be so massive that they collapse under their own weight or cost too much to build. Architects and engineers design buildings that balance these opposing forces when they design and build a building.

■ Stress

In order to prevent buildings from collapsing, every force must have a counter force pushing or pulling in the opposite direction. Have you ever played tug-of-war? In this game, opposing teams apply tension to a rope by pulling it in opposite directions. Tension lengthens or pulls objects apart. You can experience tension if you join hands with another person and both of you pull against one another. A building is subjected to **tensile stress** when opposite forces are applied equally. A building has high tensile strength when it does not break apart because of tension.

A second force works to crush or squash objects. A compression force is the opposite of tension. If you again join hands with another student and this time push against one another, you experience a compression force. **Compression stress** results when two forces are applied through a solid and push toward each other. An example of both tension and compression stresses is shown in **Figure 16-2.**

Sometimes compression and tension stresses are applied to the building at the same time. **Shear stress** occurs when opposite and equal forces work to change the shape of an object because the lines of force are not directly across from each other. The object subjected to shear stress may become twisted or it may break.

■ Natural Shear Stress

A tornado is one example of a natural occurrence that may produce shear stress on a building. Winds from tornadoes are so strong and so unpredictable that it is impossible to build buildings that are tornado-proof. You have probably seen pictures of areas that have been hit by a tornado. Buildings may be totally destroyed or badly damaged. Strong buildings may be able to somewhat resist the shear stress that is produced.

In the next section, learn how certain materials are used to construct buildings that are better able to resist the forces of tension and compression.

Figure 16-2

A beam can be used to illustrate where tension and compression stress occur in a building. As the weight of the building pushes down on the beam, forces may become unbalanced, and its shape may change. The top of the beam is compressed and is shortened or pushed together. The bottom of the beam is under tension and lengthens. As a result, the beam begins to bend.

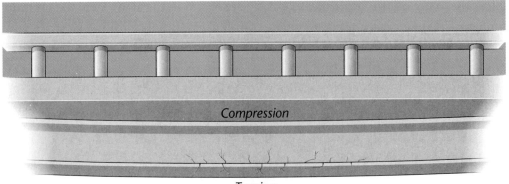

Compression

Tension

Figure 16-3

An American architect, Buckminster Fuller, designed a unique dome-shaped structure out of triangles made from steel rods. The geodesic dome utilizes the strength of the dome and triangle shapes to build a strong, lightweight structure.

A Domes, such as the Epcot Center dome shown in the photo, are excellent for carrying their own weight and withstanding the forces of wind and accumulated snow. The shape of a domed roof spreads out the load so the compression force of gravity is evenly distributed down the sides.

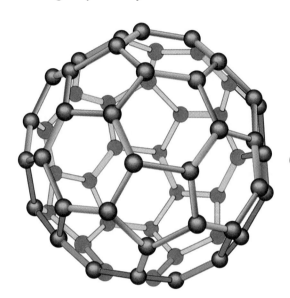

B Recently, a new form of carbon was discovered. Its basic unit is made up of 60 carbon atoms arranged in a shape similar to that of a soccer ball. Its shape and stability are so similar to the geodesic domes designed by Buckminster Fuller that the molecule is named *buckminsterfullerene.*

Connect to...

Biology

Honeybees build storage cells for honey. These cells repeat a stable geometric shape. What shape is used by the bees?

Strength Through Shape

Look at the building shown in **Figure 16-3A.** As people gained experience building structures, they found that certain shapes were more stable and provided better support than other shapes did. A dome is such a shape.

Many cultures have used some type of dome for building. For example, the Inuit people build domes as temporary dwellings on winter hunting trips. Their snow domes, or igloos, are so strong that, once finished, they can easily support the weight of a person.

Why doesn't the top of a dome collapse? Every piece used in the construction of a dome has weight because it is being pulled by Earth's gravity. The pieces around the base of the dome push down. Earth pushes up on the base with an equal and opposite force. At the top of the dome is a piece that is horizontal. It doesn't fall because its weight is pushing outward against each of the pieces it touches. If this one piece were removed, the dome would collapse because the forces no longer would be balanced. Use the MiniLab activity to discover more about the dome and other shapes that make structures strong.

How strong is it?

You have learned how buildings need to be strong to resist the many different forces that act on them. Does the strength of a building depend entirely on the materials that are used to build it? Or is strength affected by how these materials are shaped and put together?

Procedure

1. Use modeling clay to join 10-cm-long pieces of a drinking straw to make a triangle and a square.

2. Press in on the side of the triangle and on the side of the square. Record your observations *in your Journal.*

3. Place half of an empty eggshell under each corner of a piece of cardboard. Make sure the dome shape of each shell is pointing up.

4. Being sure to cover all four shells, carefully place a book on top of the cardboard. Carefully add books until the shells break.

Analysis

1. Which shape—triangle or square—is more easily bent?

2. What does adding books until the eggs break show about the strength of a dome?

In the MiniLab, you discovered that the triangle and dome shapes both are strong and withstand forces well. Triangular shapes spread the force over a wide area and make a structure more rigid. Domes spread the force evenly down the sides to the bottom of the shape.

You have learned that shape and structure can help buildings withstand stress. But shape and structure are not the only things to consider when choosing materials. In the next section, you will learn how the properties of materials themselves help determine how they are used in buildings.

check your UNDERSTANDING

Understanding Concepts

1. What advantage does a shallow layer of solid rock provide for the construction of a skyscraper?

2. What is the difference between tensile and compression stress?

3. Why might an architect review the weather records for the last 50 years before choosing a final design and types of materials for a building?

Skill Review

4. **Inferring** Suppose you built a model bridge using paper. Which form of paper would support more weight—a flat sheet or one that was folded back and forth like a fan? Explain. For more help, refer to Inferring in the *Skill Handbook.*

16-2 Choosing the Right Materials

Thousands of Choices

Have you ever walked down the aisles of a building-supply store? The choices of products used to build a house are staggering. Your final choice is based on several considerations. Do you prefer a natural material, such as wood, or an artificial one made from a plastic fiber? Must the walls be solid stone? Do you prefer large glass windows? Do you want a vinyl or a marble floor? Strength, weight, durability, availability, appearance, and cost all determine your final choices.

■ Wood: A Natural Choice

One of the easiest building materials to use is wood. It can be carved into many shapes. Boards can be nailed, glued, or tied together for building support, and, if proper harvesting procedures are used, wood becomes a renewable resource as new trees are planted to replace those cut down.

Wood's strength comes from the structure of its cells. Woody tissue, made of tubelike xylem cells, is found near the middle of a tree's trunk. **Xylem** cells transport water up through a plant. These cells are strengthened by cellulose fibers that are found in the cell walls. Recall from Chapter 7 that cellulose is a carbohydrate made of glucose molecules. **Figure 16-4** shows why some types of wood are stronger than others.

Figure 16-4

Wood is either hard or soft. Cross sections of the cellular structures of a hardwood and a softwood reveal why hardwoods are stronger than softwoods.

A Hardwood trees, such as oak and maple, grow slowly. Their cells are smaller and have more cellulose fibers in the cell walls, which gives them strength.

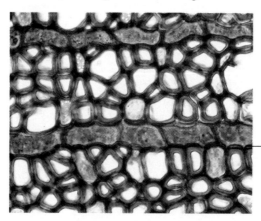

— Cell wall

B Softwood trees, such as pine and fir, grow quickly. Their cells are larger and fewer in number. Lumber made from softwoods is not as resistant to compression forces as that made from hardwoods.

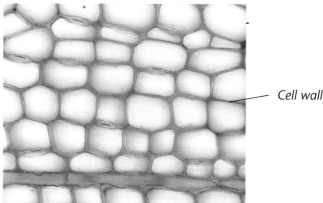

— Cell wall

Objectives
- Classify building materials as natural or artificial.
- Compare building materials based on their properties.
- Explain the electron-sea model for metallic bonding.
- Demonstrate how an alloy is formed.

Key Terms
xylem
reinforced concrete
electron-sea model

Wood does have several properties that make it undesirable as a building material. Unless treated with special chemicals, such as creosote, wood may rot. Wood burns easily, and it is also likely to be attacked by fungi and by termites or other insects. All of these factors may greatly reduce the life span of a wooden building.

Figure 16-5

Stone structures built many years ago are examples of the durability of stone.

■ Stone

Egyptian pyramids, Roman aqueducts, medieval cathedrals, and the Washington Monument, shown in **Figure 16-5,** all have one common feature. They are constructed of stone. As a building material, stone is strong and durable. However, its hardness and weight make it difficult to cut to shape and to move. For example, the pyramids of Egypt were built more than 4000 years ago from huge limestone blocks, each weighing about 2500 kg. These blocks were moved from a quarry, across the Nile, and into position in the pyramid by using levers, wooden sleds, inclined planes, and the muscle power of hundreds of thousands of workers over several decades.

A The pyramids of Egypt, built about 2500 B.C.E.

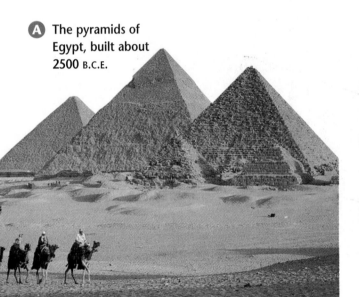

B Cathedral of Notre Dame, built starting in 1163.

C Pont du Gard aqueduct in southern France, built in 19 B.C.E.

D Washington Monument, built starting in 1848.

In addition to walls being built of blocks of stone, stone can be used as an attractive covering for walls made from other materials. This use provides the look of stone but is not as expensive.

Several types of stone make good building materials. Limestone and sandstone, as well as quartzite, are commonly used. Marble and granite are used where harder stone is required.

■ Brick

Another building material that has been used for thousands of years is brick. You may have heard someone remark that a situation was so difficult to overcome that it was like "hitting a brick wall." Indeed, bricks have been used for thousands of years because they are strong. Yet they are easy to manufacture and lightweight enough for an individual person to use.

The first bricks may have been made of sun-dried mud from a riverbank. These bricks were limited in use because they absorbed water too easily and therefore could not be used in wet climates. This type of brick is still used but only in some dry climates.

Today, most bricks are made from moist clay that has been heat-treated to drive off moisture. The color of the brick is determined by what metals are contained in the clay. The resulting material is durable and strong. Bricks can withstand a compression force of several thousand kg/cm^2.

■ Mortar and Cement

In general, cement is any material that joins and holds two surfaces together. When referring specifically to building materials, however, the term *cement* frequently refers to a mixture of

Figure 16-6

Bricklayers can arrange the bricks into many different patterns as they complete a structure. In the pattern shown above, most of the bricks overlap each other. Overlapping provides strength. If bricks are positioned directly on top of each other, the joints, which are the weakest part of a wall, are aligned and may come apart.

limestone and other materials that can be mixed with water and used as an adhesive.

As you study the wall in **Figure 16-6,** notice that the bricks are held together by another material, called *mortar.* Mortar is a mixture of cement, sand, water, and sometimes lime, which is mainly calcium oxide. As the mortar dries, it undergoes several chemical and physical changes. The mortar attaches to the rough sides of the bricks, becomes hard, and fastens the bricks together.

Cement is part of another material, called *concrete,* which is made when water, sand, and small stones are added to the cement. Concrete is useful because it is strong and can be poured into different shapes. Complete the Investigation on the next page to find out how concrete can be made stronger.

Creating a Stronger Material

Concrete is useful in the construction of buildings because it is able to withstand high compression stress. Unfortunately, it does not have a high degree of tensile strength. This is because concrete does not stretch. When placed under tension, it cracks. In this Investigation, you will find out what can be done to increase the tensile strength of a material that has properties that are similar to those of concrete.

Preparation

Problem
What can be done to increase the tensile strength of plaster of paris?

Hypothesis
Have your group agree on a testable hypothesis. Record the hypothesis.

Objectives
In this Investigation, you will:
- *Compare and contrast* the effect on its strength of adding different materials to plaster of paris.
- *Infer* how a similar procedure can be used to strengthen concrete.

Possible Materials
plaster of paris
measuring cup
mixing bowl
aluminum foil
water
spoon
paper towels
goggles
materials to embed in plaster:
   straws
   paper clips
   pipe cleaners
   pencils

Safety Precautions

Comparing the strength of the different plaster of paris materials will involve using force. Only teacher-approved tests may be used.

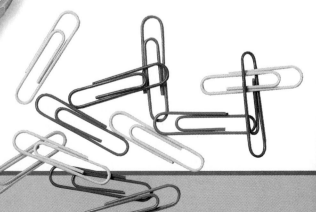

Plan the Experiment

1 Examine the materials provided by your teacher. As a group, decide which materials will be used with the plaster of paris.

2 Agree on how to safely test the effects on its strength of embedding various materials in the plaster of paris.

3 Decide on a control. Prepare a list of numbered directions. Design and construct a table for recording your data.

Check the Plan

Discuss the following points with other group members to decide the final procedure for your experiment.

1 Have you made plans to prepare identical containers and the proper amount of plaster of paris? How will you be sure to use equal amounts of plaster of paris?

2 What size products do you want to produce for testing?

3 How will you position the materials in the plaster of paris?

4 What will be your control? How will you fairly test the strength of the different products?

5 *Make sure your teacher has approved your experimental plan before you proceed further.*

6 Carry out the experiment. Record your observations in the data table.

Analyze and Conclude

1. **Comparing and Contrasting** How does the positioning of the embedded material affect the strength of the plaster of paris?

2. **Interpreting Data** Which embedded material produces the strongest plaster of paris?

3. **Analyzing the Procedure** Why is it important to pour all of the plaster of paris to the same depth in each of the moldings?

4. **Applying** How could you use the data gathered from this experiment to produce a product that is stronger than regular concrete?

Going Further

Application
Fiberglass is a building material used to make products such as boats and bathtubs. Find out how fiberglass is made and how it is similar to the improved material you made in this experiment.

A Reinforced concrete is made when concrete is poured over steel rods that have been laid out in a grid. The rods prevent the concrete from tearing apart. Reinforced concrete is used frequently in foundations.

Figure 16-7

As gravity and the weight of a building push down on its supporting structures, both compression and tension forces are applied. A concrete structure must be able to withstand such forces.

B Sometimes steel cables are stretched tight as concrete is poured over them. After the concrete dries, the cables are released, compressing the concrete. This process results in a stronger type of reinforced concrete known as prestressed concrete, which supports heavier loads than reinforced concrete. Prestressed concrete is used where concrete spans an area, such as in overpasses.

Reinforced for Strength

You learned in the Investigation that plaster of paris can be strengthened by the addition of other materials. Concrete can be strengthened by the addition of long metal rods. A regular concrete beam supports a compression force but cannot withstand the tension force that occurs along its bottom. Extra strength is needed to prevent the beam from breaking. As shown in **Figure 16-7A, reinforced concrete** has steel rods running through it. The rods add strength so that the concrete can withstand the tension force. Prestressed concrete, in **Figure 16-7B,** is an even stronger type of reinforced concrete.

The Strength of Metals

Other materials don't need reinforcement to be strong enough to use in building. If you look at the periodic table in Appendix O on pages 814 and 815, you will notice that most of the elements are classified as metals. Several physical properties of metals, as shown in **Figure 16-8,** allow metals to be used as outside coverings for buildings, for electrical or plumbing services, or for structural support. Metals can be flexible and yet be strong. How can a metal bend easily and be strong at the same time? The answer lies in understanding how the atoms in metals are bonded together.

Figure 16-8

Several physical properties of a metal are illustrated with these copper products.

A Metals provide efficient conductivity of heat and electricity.

C Metals have the property of ductility, or the ability to be pulled into thin wires.

B Metals are malleable, which means they have the ability to be hammered into sheets. This dome is made from copper sheets covered with a thin layer of gold. Metals also have a lustrous appearance.

■ Bonding of Metal Atoms

The strength, flexibility, and durability of most metals indicates that, while it may be difficult to separate metal atoms from each other, it is easy to slide them over and past each other. The **electron-sea model** is a simple way to explain most of these properties. In this model, a regular arrangement of positively charged metal ions is found in a sea of electrons, as shown in **Figure 16-9.** While the electrons are confined to the metal as a whole, outer-level electrons are free to move from ion to ion. It is this mobility of electrons that accounts for a metal being a good conductor of both electricity and heat. It also explains why metals can be pulled or hammered into new shapes.

■ Making Stronger Metals

Understanding the bonding of metal atoms is also important in explaining how metals can be made stronger. Remember that reinforced concrete is made with steel. You learned in Chapter 14 that steel is an alloy, not a pure metal. An alloy is a mixture of a metal with at least one other element that has the properties of a metal. In the following Investigation, find out how alloys can be produced.

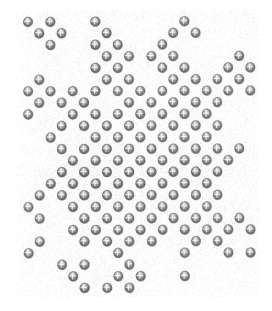

Figure 16-9

According to the electron-sea model, positively charged ions are found in an orderly arrangement with the outer-level electrons uniformly distributed around them. Individual electrons are mobile.

INVESTIGATION

Creating an Alloy

Often, the properties of a material are altered when it is combined with another material. An example of this property change is shown when a base metal is mixed with one or more other elements and an alloy is formed. In this Investigation, you can create an alloy without the extremely high temperatures required to make steel.

Preparation

Problem

How can two metals be combined to form an alloy?

Objectives

In this Investigation, you will:
- *Observe* how an alloy can be made.
- *Recognize the cause and effect* of using heat to mix two metals.
- *Infer* how steel is formed.

Materials

copper penny
zinc, 30-mesh
hot plate
pencil eraser
dilute sodium hydroxide solution
evaporating dishes (2)
goggles
tongs
apron
thermal mitt

Safety Precautions

Perform this Investigation only with a fume hood or other adequate ventilation. Sodium hydroxide is extremely reactive. Do not come in contact with the solution. Do not allow the sodium hydroxide to boil. Follow proper procedures for disposing of materials at the end of the experiment.

This bronze statue of Hans Christian Andersen is made from copper and tin.

INVESTIGATION

Procedure

1 Put on your goggles and apron.

2 The pennies must be clean in order to complete this lab. To do this, rub each side of the penny thoroughly with a pencil eraser.

3 Place a teaspoon of 30-mesh zinc into the other evaporating dish. Carefully pour the dilute sodium hydroxide solution over the zinc to a depth of 2 cm. **CAUTION:** *Sodium hydroxide is caustic and can burn skin. Report any spills immediately.*

4 Using the tongs, place the penny on top of the zinc.

5 Place the evaporating dish on the hot plate, and gently heat the contents until you see a change in the color of the penny.

6 Using tongs, carefully remove the penny and rinse it in tap water. Cool and dry the penny.

7 Set the hot plate control to medium. Using tongs, place the penny on the hot plate. When the penny turns a golden color, use tongs to remove it from the heat.

Step 4

Step 6

Analyze and Conclude

1. Interpreting Observations At what point in the procedure do you think an alloy was produced? What evidence do you have to support your answer?

2. Thinking Critically How does heat help in the formation of an alloy?

3. Interpreting Observations In step 5, the penny turned a silver color. What caused this change?

Going Further

Application
For a new compound to be produced, exact masses of materials react. Were exact amounts used to make the alloy? Explain.

As you saw in the Investigation, high temperatures are required to make alloys. Steel is made when iron is heated to its melting point. At this temperature, the kinetic energy of the iron atoms increases and the bonds between them weaken. Atoms from other elements, such as carbon, can now replace some of the iron atoms or fit in between them, as explained in **Figure 16-10.** As the new mixture cools, a solid with new properties results. In this case, steel is much stronger than iron.

■ Resisting Corrosion

In the Investigation, copper and zinc were mixed together to form the alloy brass. You may be familiar with this alloy because it is used to make candlesticks, fireplace tools, keys, and other items you may see in your home. Bronze, another alloy, is a mixture of copper and tin. Bronze is stronger than brass and is more durable because it resists corrosion. Corrosion is a chemical reaction that may slowly weaken metal and cause it to crumble or break.

Most metals easily combine with oxygen. You may have seen the flaky, orange material on some steel surfaces. This material, called *rust,* is the result of the attraction between iron and oxygen in the air. Why does oxygen combine so easily with metals? You learned that metal atoms have a weak attraction to their outer layer of electrons. Oxygen, on the other hand, has a strong attraction for electrons. When the proper conditions are present, iron will lose its electrons to oxygen. The loss of negative electrons causes iron to become positively charged. When oxygen gains the extra electrons, it takes on an overall charge of 2^-. The attraction of the opposite charges brings iron and oxygen together to form a new compound. A common form of iron oxide, which is rust, has the formula Fe_2O_3.

Figure 16-10

Brass and steel are two examples of alloys.

Ⓐ One type of alloy is formed when atoms of the host metal are the same size as atoms of the additional element. The added atoms can then replace some of the host atoms. Brass is made when zinc atoms replace some of the copper atoms.

Ⓑ Another type of alloy is made when the spaces between the main-metal atoms are occupied by smaller-sized atoms of the additional element. Steel forms when small carbon atoms fit between the larger iron atoms.

Figure 16-11

Corrosion is one of the greatest problems faced when metals are used in buildings.

A The weakening of steel through the oxidation of iron may account for the loss of up to 20 percent of all steel manufactured.

C Vinyl-coated aluminum has a longer life span than does uncoated aluminum because the vinyl protects the aluminum from oxygen in the air.

B Some metal oxides do not weaken a structure. The surface of copper turns to green-colored copper carbonate and several other copper compounds. The Statue of Liberty is covered by this naturally occurring protective coating.

Several methods are used to prevent or slow the corrosion of metals. Stainless steel, also an alloy, is often used in plumbing fixtures because it resists corrosion, just as bronze does. Paint, enamel, or plastic also may be applied to a metal's surface. **Figure 16-11** shows how corrosion may be stopped.

check your UNDERSTANDING

Understanding Concepts

1. Is the oxidation of iron a chemical or physical property? Explain how you determined your answer.
2. How can a metal be both strong and flexible?
3. Explain why an architect might choose to use wood for a building.

Skill Review

4. **Inferring** What do you think might happen to a brick structure if it continuously is allowed to soak up moisture? For more help, refer to Inferring in the *Skill Handbook*.

Science and Society

Technology: "There's no place like home!"

Home is considered to be wherever loved ones are. Scientists warn, however, that the buildings in which people live may be hazardous to their health. People are becoming more aware of the number of potentially harmful chemicals found in materials used in the construction and remodeling of their homes.

The Technology

Walls and floors used to be made from natural lumber. Now, a great deal of plywood is being used. Plywood *is* natural lumber, but with a technological twist. As shown in the photo, to make plywood, thin sheets of wood are glued together so that the grain of the wood in one sheet is perpendicular to the grain in the wood above and below it. This makes the wood stronger and less likely than natural wood to warp. But it also creates problems for people with allergies. The glues used to bond the wood sheets together contain formaldehyde, which helps keep wood from rotting. But formaldehyde causes sore throats and itchy noses. Formaldehyde is also found in particle board, stain-resistant carpets and drapes, insulation, and adhesives used for flooring.

The Background

Although the formaldehyde in a new carpet eventually evaporates and becomes less of a problem to an allergic person, a house has many other potential chemical pitfalls. Unless the house was built with vents for gas stoves and heaters, nitrogen dioxide gas can build up to cause respiratory problems in children. Carbon monoxide released by gas appliances, furnaces, and stoves causes dizziness and flulike symptoms if ventilation in a room is insufficient. In high enough doses, it may result in death.

Plywood manufacturing

Many other materials, especially synthetics, aren't hazardous when in everyday use. But if there is a fire in the home, many seemingly harmless materials produce toxic fumes when they are burned. Most people who die in home fires are killed by smoke inhalation, many times resulting from inhaling toxic fumes.

Organic Solvents

Organic solvents are present in almost all materials used in building or remodeling homes. These solvents easily vaporize. They are used in glues, paints, paint remover, and paint and varnish thinners. Some of these solvents are also used in caulking compounds.

When organic solvents are breathed in or absorbed through the skin over long periods, they can have serious effects. Toluene and n-hexane can affect the nervous system, resulting in changes in mental processes and behavior. Toluene can also affect pregnancy and the growth of a fetus. Methylene chloride forms carbon monoxide and chloride compounds in the body. It affects heart muscle and heartbeat and may also cause cancer. The carbon monoxide formed reduces the amount of oxygen the blood can carry. In animal studies, glycol ethers cause reproductive problems, such as degeneration of the testes and malformations in the young born to female animals exposed to the solvent. Petroleum distillates cause fatty deposits in the liver. High doses also lead to lung problems, anemia, and an irregular heartbeat.

The Question

What is being done to protect people from hazardous chemicals in the home? Organic solvents enter the body by being absorbed through the skin or when fumes are inhaled. Those most at risk are professional painters, varnishers, and do-it-yourselfers who work with these substances over a long period of time. The U.S.

Occupational Safety and Health Administration (OSHA) has established time limits beyond which a worker cannot be exposed to health-threatening solvents. But OSHA has no jurisdiction over a painting contractor with no employees or a person working on his or her own home.

Another U.S. government agency, the Consumer Products Safety Commission (CPSC), requires labels on corrosive or flammable chemicals. It also requires label information about the need for proper ventilation when using products containing such chemicals. Some states have issued laws that have improved the labels on these products. They require that the labels list the possibly harmful ingredients and provide warnings on the dangers to health when using the product. Legislation and public pressure have encouraged manufacturers of items such as mattresses and upholstered furniture to exclude materials that produce toxic fumes when they are burned. These requirements have led some manufacturers to switch to less harmful ingredients in their products.

*inter*NET CONNECTION

For information on chemical safety, follow the link for Chapter 16 on the Glencoe Homepage, **http://www.glencoe.com/**, to the University of Utah's Material Safety Data Sheet Index. Research the ingredients on the labels of paints, paint thinners, varnishes, glues, and caulking compounds on the shelves of home-improvements stores. Search the site for the chemicals you think may be potentially harmful. Make a list of these chemicals and the health hazards associated with each chemical. What precautions should you take when using these products?

16-3 A Revolution in Materials

Objectives

- Identify modern materials that are used in buildings.
- Explain the advantages and disadvantages of using modern materials.

Key Terms

plastic
insulator
ceramic
thin film

Figure 16-12

Plastic is commonly used in insulating materials.

New Materials

Scientists have revolutionized the building industry during the last 50 years. They have introduced new products and developed processes that give natural materials new chemical or physical properties. As a result, modern structures are taller, stronger, and more energy-efficient while using safer, lighter-weight, synthetic materials.

■ Plastics

If you look around you, you will probably find examples of a group of materials called *plastics*. **Plastics** are usually defined as synthetic or natural organic materials that easily can be formed into different shapes through the application of heat and pressure. The properties of some plastics allow them to fulfill a variety of uses.

Most properties of plastics differ from those of metals. You know that metals are good conductors of electricity and heat because of the mobility of their electrons and because their atoms can slide over each other. Because they are good conductors, metal wires are used to transport electricity into a house. Metal pipes and radiators may warm the house by transferring heat from hot water to air inside the house. The chemical bonding of plastics, however, binds electrons to a specific molecule and does not allow them to move freely from atom to atom or allow atoms to slide over each other. As a result, plastics are often used as insulators. An **insulator**, as shown in **Figure 16-12**, is a material through which heat and electricity cannot easily move.

A A necessity, electricity is also a dangerous hazard that can seriously injure or kill a person who comes in contact with it. Plastic insulation covering electrical wires prevents people from contacting the bare metal wires.

B Different forms of plastic insulation act as barriers to the loss of heat. Some prevent heat loss from water heaters or hot-water pipes. Other plastic insulators stop heat from moving through walls to the outside air.

Figure 16-13

Because PVC resists corrosion, it is often used by plumbers to replace metal pipes. PVC is made from the vinyl chloride monomer that contains two carbon atoms, three hydrogen atoms, and one chlorine atom. The units bond to each other in a repeating manner, and the resulting polymer is a strong, rigid material.

Plastics, Plumbing, and Pipes

One type of plastic is used to form the pipes that bring water into a house and remove wastewater and sewage from the house. This polymer is called polyvinyl chloride, or PVC. PVC is also used for siding and floor tile. One common use of this lightweight yet durable material is shown in **Figure 16-13.**

Depending on the manufacturing process, plastics can be made as strong as steel or as flexible as a piece of thread. These two properties are ideal for the new plastic fabrics that are used as roofs over some of the modern tents and domed buildings, an example of which is shown in **Figure 16-14.** One of the biggest drawbacks of plastic fabrics and other plastic building materials is their expense. Chemists and engineers currently are working to develop new,

less expensive, plastic building materials. Study **Table 16-1** to find out about the most commonly used plastics.

Figure 16-14

Some dome roofs, such as the roof on the RCA Dome are made of glass-reinforced plastic fabrics. A plastic coating, also used on nonstick cookware, repels dirt, and coatings of reflective material act to insulate the covered area by reflecting the sun's rays.

Common Plastics and Their Uses		Table 16-1
Name	**Uses**	
Polyethylene	Plastic piping, bottles, electrical insulation, toys	
Polypropylene	Rope, protective clothing, textiles, carpet	
Polystyrene	Containers, boats, coolers, insulation, furniture, models	
Polyvinyl chloride	Rubber substitute, cable covering, tubing, rainwear, gaskets	
Polytetrafluoroethylene	Nonstick cookware surfaces	
Polyvinylidene chloride	Clinging food wraps	

Old Materials, New Uses

Not all the new materials used in buildings are based on new substances. Some types of materials that have been in use for centuries are now being used in new and different ways.

■ Ceramics

The roof in **Figure 16-15** shows roofing tiles made from a dried, claylike material. Dried clay or claylike materials are called **ceramics.** Bricks, pottery, porcelain, cement, glass, and some insulators are all ceramics. You learned that bricks have been used to provide strong, durable structures for thousands of years. They exhibit the properties of most ceramics. Ceramics don't change in size when they are heated or cooled. They are hard, resist corrosion, and are able to withstand high temperatures without cracking.

Brick is an example of a type of ceramic known as a *structural ceramic.* Structural ceramics are used in construction because of their sturdiness and resistance to weather.

Ceramics are used frequently by the defense and space industries instead of metal parts in airplanes, missiles, and spacecraft, as shown in **Figure 16-16** on page 502. They are a lightweight alternative to heavier, more expensive metals.

The Frame Game

About 70 percent of the cost of building a house is labor, not materials. New construction methods and materials reduce labor costs by needing fewer skilled laborers for less total time. What are the choices of materials today?

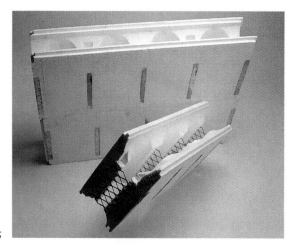

Foam building blocks

Wood

Traditional lumber has many advantages, but it also has many drawbacks. It can have knots; it can split; and it can shrink, twist, and warp over time.

Engineered lumber is made by mixing wood fibers and adhesives. This mixture can be shaped according to what is needed, then dried. It is stable and resists rotting, even in extreme climates. The whole log is used, wasting nothing. It is much stronger and more uniform than lumber that has been cut by a saw, and it can be manufactured to any length desired.

Figure 16-15

The properties of ceramics determine how the ceramics are used. The clay in the tiles on these roofs are resistant to water and help insulate the building.

Metal

Steel can be used instead of wood as a framing material. Steel framing is precut at the factory, which saves construction time. It is noncombustible, termite-resistant, and strong for its weight. A steel-framed house can be built to withstand winds up to 130 miles per hour.

Plastic

Plastics have many advantages: they are lightweight, nontoxic, easy to handle, resistant to moisture and high temperatures, and strong. They will melt but they won't burn.

Plastic lumber doesn't warp, is maintenance-free, needs no paint or stain, and lasts—as far as we know now—forever. Plastics can also be used to replace glass in buildings because they're lightweight, highly soundproof, highly insulating, impact-resistant, and they can be formed by heat and cold into shapes and curves.

Foam

A new technology uses polyurethane foam to make building blocks, as shown in the photo on page 500. Each weighs only eight pounds, compared to 40 pounds for a concrete block. The foam blocks become both the form for the poured-concrete structure and the structure's walls and insulation. Foam-block houses are almost airtight, so forced-air ventilation is needed. Foam blocks are of no interest to termites and rodents, and they won't mildew or rot, even in damp climates.

GRAPHING CALCULATOR

Use a graphing calculator to graph $Y = 5 \times X$, where X is the weight of polyurethane used in blocks, and Y is the weight of the same volume of concrete blocks. Use the graph to determine the difference in weight of a wall containing 240 polyurethane blocks that weigh 4 kg each and the same sized wall made from concrete blocks.

In spite of recent advances, ceramics have two disadvantages that limit their use. One disadvantage is that it is difficult to manufacture ceramic parts that are free of structural defects. These structural defects take the form of microcracks that cause the ceramic to fracture under stress. A second disadvantage is discussed in the following Thinking Lab.

Figure 16-16

Ceramics are found in roofing tiles, grinding wheels, quartz watches, semiconductors, superconductors, and the thermal insulating tiles on the outside surfaces of the space shuttle orbiter.

Thinking Lab

Interpreting Scientific Illustrations

Can car engines be made of ceramics?

Scientists are conducting research to develop a ceramic engine for use in automobiles. Ceramic engines are lighter in weight and more tolerant of high temperatures than are metal engines. They should have greater fuel efficiency and produce less air pollution.

Analysis

The pictures shown here illustrate what happens to a metal and a ceramic when they are dropped or struck by another object. Use the information presented by these pictures to answer the question.

Thinking Critically

What happens to the metal and the ceramic when they are dropped or struck? Explain under what circumstances this property of a ceramic would prove to be a disadvantage for use in a car's engine or as a building material in a house.

■ Thin Films

Glass and metal are two other materials that have been used in various ways for many years. You have seen that metals have new and practical uses, such as new alloys. Glass is now used in safety glass and for other purposes original glass makers could not have envisioned. Glass and metal are now used together in a new and different way.

Have you ever walked by a modern glass building and tried to look inside? Perhaps you could not see the interior of the building but could see only a reflection of the street outside. This reflection is due to what is known as a thin film. A **thin film** is a thin layer of one substance, such as a metal, that is applied and bonded to an underlying material, such as glass. The building shown in **Figure 16-17** has an outer wall of glass panels that are covered with a thin film of metal. Builders and architects use this type of coating to reduce the cost of cooling the building because the thin film reflects a large amount of the sun's light back into the atmosphere. This type of material is especially useful in sunny climates. At the same time, the privacy of the people inside the building is maintained without the need for drapes or blinds.

Figure 16-17

Architects search for new materials that are attractive yet provide strength, and that are energy efficient and cost effective. The thin film on this skyscraper is one example of such a material. Plastic lumber and foam crown moldings can replace wood. A type of steel known as *weathering steel,* which does not rust, is another example of newer materials that are used in construction projects.

Throughout this chapter, you have discovered how common and not-so-common materials are chosen for their properties and that they can be used in buildings. In the next chapter, discover how these materials are actually put together to make a completed structure that is suitable for its environment.

check your UNDERSTANDING

Understanding Concepts

1. How do insulators prevent the conduction of electricity?
2. Explain one reason why a ceramic material would make a good baking pan.
3. Name a natural polymer and a synthetic polymer. Explain each classification.

Skill Review

4. **Inferring** Why would a home owner choose to insulate the metal ducts that carry warm air to different rooms in the house? For more help, refer to Inferring in the *Skill Handbook.*

Come In out of the Rain

Think about all of the clothing you own just for the purpose of keeping you warm or dry. Depending on your geographic location, you may routinely need a heavy coat and gloves or an umbrella. Each of these items could be referred to as human weatherproofing. Just as we protect ourselves when we venture outside, workers on construction projects use materials that will provide weatherproofing for the building itself—to protect the inner structure.

You're the Construction Engineer

Consider your particular geographic location as you encounter your newest construction project. You have been commissioned to build a new building in which teenagers will gather. You want the structure to be secure and protected from the elements of nature.

Drawing on Experience

❶ List all of the elements of nature that strongly affect you and your surroundings throughout the year. Would these factors be extreme cold, extreme heat, rain, or snow? Make a list of the factors you will consider.

❷ Tour a local building-materials store to compile a list of the various materials available for weatherproofing a structure.

❸ Collect samples of as many of the weatherproofing materials that you listed as you can.

❹ Choose the weatherproofing materials you think would be most effective for a structure in your area. Justify each selection.

Testing...Testing

❶ Choose a structure on which you will test your weatherproofing materials. Once this site is chosen, attach the samples you have chosen following the manufacturers' instructions. You may use two or more samples together if you want to.

❷ Allow your chosen materials to be exposed to several elements of nature, either naturally or artificially.

❸ Test each product for success or failure. Record your observations in a written report.

How Did It Work?

❶ Did the weatherproofing materials work as the manufacturers said they would?

❷ Did the material weatherproof as well as you expected it to?

❸ Which materials would you use again and why?

❹ Are certain combinations of materials better than using some products by themselves?

Read the statements below that review major points presented in the chapter. Using the concepts that you have learned, answer each question *in your Journal.*

1 There are many forces, or stresses, that buildings must be able to withstand. These stresses must be considered when constructing a building. *What types of stress would a concrete road experience?*

2 The uses of building materials are determined by the properties of the materials. Wood, stone, brick, and metal are common building materials. *What is one common way to make a metal stronger?*

3 Many new materials, such as plastics and other synthetic materials, are now used in constructing buildings. Older materials, such as ceramics and metals, are used in new ways. *What advantages might plastic lumber have over lumber made from wood?*

Using Key Science Terms

ceramic	reinforced concrete
compression stress	shear stress
electron-sea model	tensile stress
insulator	thin film
plastic	xylem

Answer the following questions about science terms used in this chapter.

1. Which type of applied force causes a solid to lengthen?
2. Which type of applied force causes a solid to twist out of shape?
3. Xylem cells transport what material in trees?
4. Are insulators typically metal, or are they typically nonmetal?
5. In the electron-sea model of metallic bonding, do metals have a weak or strong attraction for electrons? Explain.

Understanding Ideas

Using complete sentences, answer the following questions in your Journal.

1. What is the relationship between the electron-sea model and electrical conductivity?
2. Why is it necessary to melt iron when making steel?
3. Why might a metal object be covered with a plastic coating?
4. How does the bonding of an insulator differ from that of a metal?
5. Why do architects sometimes use triangles and domes when they design buildings?
6. What can be done to help increase the durability of a wooden building?
7. What causes the rusting of steel?

8. What two conditions can change the shape of a plastic?
9. Using glass coated by a thin film of metal is more expensive than using regular glass. Why would an architect choose the more expensive coated glass?

Developing Skills

Use your understanding of the concepts developed in this chapter to answer each of the following questions.

1. **Using Variables** What changes would you expect in the clay you made for the MiniLab at the beginning of this chapter if you doubled the heating time?
2. **Comparing and Contrasting** What are the different effects on a wooden beam when it is under tensile stress compared to when it is under compression stress?
3. **Predicting** If you did not adequately heat the zinc-coated penny in the Investigation, what effect would your actions have on the formation of the alloy? Explain.
4. **Using Variables** Besides varying the type of materials embedded in the plaster of paris in the Investigation on pages 488-489, what else could you do to change the properties of the final product?
5. **Measuring in SI** A bronze trophy has a mass of 952 g. If the bronze is 85 percent copper, how many grams of tin are in the trophy?

Critical Thinking

In your Journal, *answer each of the following questions.*

1. A new apartment building is planned for a city along the east coast of the United States. List three factors that must be considered when materials are chosen for use in the building. Explain how the factors will influence the choices.

2. Some plastics make durable building materials. In what way might these durable plastics be a detriment to the environment?

3. Based on the results of the Investigation with plaster of paris, what could be done to make a ceramic less brittle?

4. What advantage does concrete have compared to stone?

5. Why would a builder use stainless steel rather than regular steel?

Problem Solving

Read the following problem and discuss your answers in a brief paragraph.

Read the children's story about the three little pigs and the wolf. Each pig built his house from a different material: straw, sticks, and bricks. Using what you read in the story and what you learned in this chapter, answer the following questions and tell how the outcome of the story might have changed.

The second pig used wood to build his house. How might a wood house be made strong? The third pig used bricks to build his house. Even though the bricks were strong and durable, the pig could have made a major error when laying the bricks that would have weakened the walls. Explain what error must be avoided when building a brick wall.

CONNECTING IDEAS

1. **Theme—Energy** Why does heating clay change its water content?

2. **Theme—Scale and Structure** Explain how something as tiny as an electron can determine whether a material will be a conductor or a nonconductor.

3. **Theme—Systems and Interactions** Why are metal heating vents usually located near the floor of a room?

4. **Applying Technology** Which would need more weatherproofing, iron or aluminum? Explain.

5. **Science and Society** Compare and contrast the potential hazards involved in laying a new carpet and those involved in painting a room.

6. **In-Depth Look** What advantages do metal-framed houses have over wood-framed houses?

Forces and Machines
Building a House

*W*hat do you notice when you pass a construction site like the one shown below? You might see workers operating large machines that move heavy materials into place. You also might see workers using simple tools such as hammers and screwdrivers like the ones you would use at home. Look closely at the building you are in right now. Can you imagine trying to build it without using tools? In this chapter, investigate how science makes constructing a house a much easier task.

▶ ***In the MiniLab on the next page, experiment with pulleys to find out how they might be used at construction sites.***

MiniLab

How are pulleys used in construction?

Are there pulleys in the large photograph below? Some may not be easily visible because they are concealed in machinery. In this activity, test two different pulley systems to find out how they help in construction.

Procedure

1. Weigh a medium-sized object with a spring scale. Record its weight.

2. Set up pulley system 1 as shown.

3. Measure and record the force that you use to hold the object steady. Record your observations *in your Journal.*

4. Set up pulley system 2 as shown. Repeat step 3.

Analysis

1. For each pulley system, compare the force you used with the object's weight.

2. Give at least one example of how each pulley system might be used at a construction site.

System 1   System 2

509

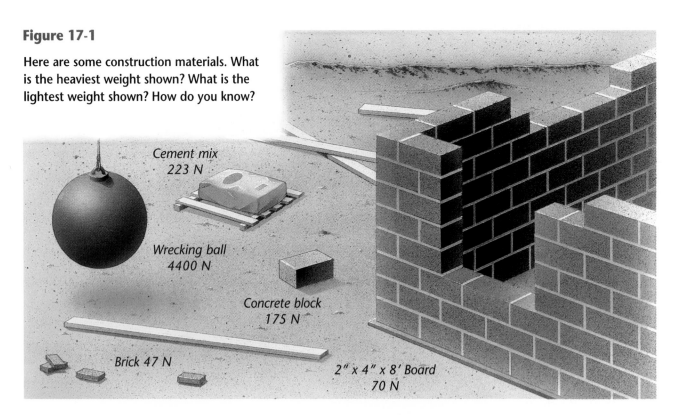

Construction: A Weighty Issue

17-1

Objectives

- Compare and contrast weight and mass.
- Explain why center of gravity is important in moving large objects.

Key Terms

weight, inertia, mass, center of gravity

Measuring Matter

Perhaps you can recall building a model skyscraper out of wooden or plastic blocks when you were younger. You could easily lift the blocks and slide them into place because they weighed so little. Now think about constructing a real building with concrete blocks. You can't easily lift these blocks and slide them into place. You know from experience that real blocks are heavier than model blocks.

Have you ever heard someone gasp, "I can't move that. It must weigh a ton!"? A ton is a big measurement. It's about the weight of 50 concrete blocks. Although you know you can't lift a ton of concrete blocks, you know you can lift a five-pound bag of cement mix. Weight is a common measurement that you use to compare quantities of materials. What are you comparing when you compare weights?

■ Weight a Minute!

Can you lift a portable CD player that weighs 50 newtons? 25 newtons? You can't answer unless you have a sense of how heavy 25 and 50 newtons

Figure 17-1

Here are some construction materials. What is the heaviest weight shown? What is the lightest weight shown? How do you know?

Cement mix
223 N

Wrecking ball
4400 N

Concrete block
175 N

Brick 47 N

2" x 4" x 8' Board
70 N

are. In SI (International System) units, weight is measured in a unit called the newton (N). The weights of some hand tools and building equipment you might see at a construction site are given in **Figure 17-1.** The values may seem unfamiliar. Study the figure to find out whether you could lift a 25-N or 250-N object.

The weight of each of the tools and pieces of equipment depends on the pull of gravity on that particular item. On Earth, **weight** is a measure of the force of gravity between Earth and an object. You might think that if the tools and equipment were located where Earth's gravity was almost zero, you could move a bulldozer as easily as you move a hammer. If you've ever seen videos of the space shuttle crew doing repairs in space, you know that things that are heavy on Earth are also cumbersome in space. In space, these things are neither heavy nor light because there is little gravity. If it isn't their heaviness that makes them difficult to move, what property makes large objects more difficult to move and stop than smaller objects? Do construction workers have to concern themselves with weight *and* this property of matter as they lift, stop, start, and position heavy construction materials?

■ Mass—A Fundamental Measure

Inertia is the tendency for an object to resist a change in its motion. A moving wrecking ball tends to keep moving—right through a brick wall. To build a skyscraper, it's sometimes necessary to do away with some older buildings. One of the more dramatic ways of demolishing a building is with a wrecking ball. As you look at **Figure 17-2,** imagine how the wall shudders as the enormous wrecking ball crashes against it. The demolition crew is making use of the wrecking ball's tremendous inertia.

Figure 17-2

The inertia of the wrecking ball is evident as it crashes through the wall in the left photo. The wall can't stop the ball's motion.

You've experienced inertia if you have ever tried to move a refrigerator. A refrigerator at rest tends to stay at rest because it resists a change in motion.

What else do a swinging wrecking ball and an unyielding refrigerator have in common? Besides great inertia, they each have a lot of mass. **Mass** is a measure of the amount of matter in an object. In the SI system, the unit of mass is the kilogram, kg. The mass of a wrecking ball is about 450 kg, a refrigerator's mass is about 150 kg, and a gallon of milk's mass is about 4 kg.

Mass depends only on the number and kinds of atoms in an object. Weight is different from mass. Weight is a measure of the pull of gravity on the matter in an object.

Weight and mass are directly related. Objects with more mass have more weight. For example, an object with a mass of 1 kg weighs 9.8 N on Earth. A 450-kg wrecking ball weighs about 4400 N. On the moon, where the force of gravity is less, that 450-kg wrecking ball would weigh only about 740 N. Weight depends on two things: the mass of the object and the force of gravity on the object at that location. The inertia of the wrecking ball remains the same everywhere because its mass remains the same. An object's inertia changes only if the object's mass changes.

The Stop and Go of Inertia

If you watch a construction crew, you can see that they lift and move massive objects carefully. Some of the precautions a crew may use are shown in **Figure 17-3.** How do mass, weight, and inertia make these precautions necessary?

Figure 17-3

These photos show how workers take mass, weight, and inertia into account when moving heavy objects.

A The operator of the forklift drives slowly to avoid sudden stops. Why?

B Even though the engine of the crane can easily lift the load of concrete blocks, the crane operator lifts the load slowly. In terms of mass and inertia, why does the operator avoid a sudden upward jerk on the blocks?

Figure 17-4

This mason is carrying a stack of paving bricks. What is it about this arrangement of the bricks that makes them easier to pick up and carry?

Lifting, moving, and positioning heavy construction materials require an understanding of weight and inertia. If you look at a stack of concrete blocks, you may think neatness counts, too. Neatness is important because the load of materials needs to be stable as it is moved from place to place. Crushed and damaged merchandise is bad for business and falling bricks are dangerous. Like the forklift operator, the woman in **Figure 17-4** must safely balance and carry the bricks. Why are they stacked? Do the activity below to find out how weight distribution affects the balance and stability of your body and of loads like the bricks.

MiniLab

What is balance?

The forks of a forklift must support the weight of the material they are hoisting, holding, or hauling. Your feet do the same for you. Let's find out how.

Procedure

1. Stand straight. Without bending your knees, try to touch your toes.

2. Now, stand with your heels and back against a wall and try again.

3. Move away from the wall. Try to stand on your toes for 5 seconds.

4. Now, stand so your toes touch a wall and try to stand on your toes.

Analysis

1. Envision the position of your body at each step. How did the wall affect your body position? Explain.

2. Draw a diagram that shows how your body was affected by gravity as you became unbalanced.

■ Building with Balance

Why did you almost topple over during steps 2 and 4 of the MiniLab activity?

When an object is not supported under its center of gravity, it begins to tip over. If your center of gravity isn't over your feet, you begin to fall. The **center of gravity** of an object is the center of the object's weight distribution. **Figure 17-5** gives some clues to finding the location of an object's center of gravity.

No matter what the shape or make-up of an object, it will balance if its center of gravity is supported. This requirement for balancing applies to humans, too. **Figure 17-6** shows the centers of gravity of two teenagers while touching their toes and on tiptoes. Note how the positions of their bodies change so that their centers of gravity are always supported by their feet or toes. What happens if they can't position their bodies so their centers of gravity are supported? The answer is the same thing that started to happen to you in the MiniLab activity—they will topple over.

Figure 17-5

These figures show how center of gravity affects balance.

A A brick has its center of gravity at its center. A square, rectangle, or sphere made all of the same material has its center of gravity at its geometric center.

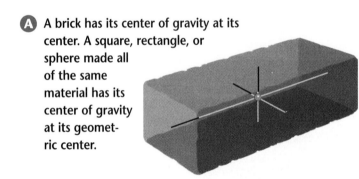

B The center of gravity of each brick is supported by the one beneath. This is also true for groups of bricks. If you picture the top two bricks as a unit, its center of gravity is supported by the third brick, and so on down the pile. Why does the overhang decrease from top to bottom?

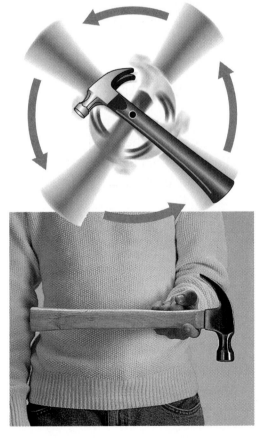

C A hammer isn't of uniform shape or material. However, you can find its center of gravity by giving it a spin. The point it turns around is its center of gravity. The photo shows a hammer supported directly under its center of gravity.

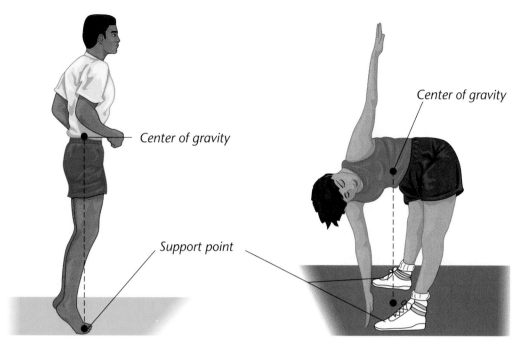

Figure 17-6

These illustrations show how you adjust your body position to stay balanced.

Center of gravity

Center of gravity

Center of gravity

Support point

A When you stand on tiptoes, the area of support provided by your feet decreases. To remain balanced, you must move your center of gravity above that smaller area.

B When you bend forward at the waist, your center of gravity moves to a point above and ahead of your feet. You must move your hips back so that your center of gravity is above your feet.

Center of gravity is an important concept in construction. Proper support is necessary for stability in moving materials. What might happen if a worker attempts to lift a beam without being aware of its center of gravity? You can model what the worker might experience by doing the Try It activity. Proper support is also important for materials in a building. If you look at a brick wall, it's easy to see how the center of gravity of each brick is supported. Materials hidden from view also require this support.

Try It!

Pencil Picker-Upper
Pick up a pencil by using a loop of string. Where does the string support the pencil? Is it easy to lift the pencil quickly? Now, try lifting the pencil again by using two loops of string. Where do the loops support the pencil? Is it easy to lift the pencil quickly?

check your UNDERSTANDING

Understanding Concepts
1. Why is mass considered a more consistent unit for measuring matter than weight?
2. The inertia of heavy building materials makes construction more challenging. How is inertia an advantage after the house is built?
3. Use the center of gravity concept to explain how a steel beam should be safely lifted by a cable.

Skill Review
4. **Comparing and Contrasting** Compare and contrast mass and weight. If you need help, refer to Comparing and Contrasting in the *Skill Handbook*.

people in SCIENCE

Meet Eugene Tsui, Architect

Dragonfly wings, a chambered nautilus, a wasp's nest, even a microscopic insect—these natural designs inspire Eugene Tsui, an innovative architect. He says, "To me, architecture is an artistic expression of an understanding of nature and the world around us."

In the following interview, Dr. Tsui talks about creating buildings that reflect the natural world.

On the Job

Q Dr. Tsui, how is your approach to architectural design different from most architects'?

A Everyone seems to assume that buildings should be made up of squares, rectangles, and cubes. In fact, straight forms and flat planes are structurally weak. If you look to nature, you won't see that straight-angle approach. Everything from ants to seashells to trees have curvilinear forms. Our own bodies are graceful, compound curves, not straight planes and angles. Nature's designs, which have been perfected over billions of years, are more beautiful, sensible, and efficient.

Q Can you give an example of how you use natural forms in your designs?

A My current project, a home for my parents, is based on the structure of the most indestructible organism in the world, the tardigrade. It's an insect-like creature the size of a pin head. It looks like a flea but not as ornery. The tardigrade appears fluid and almost marine-like. It's incredible in its ability to survive extremely high and low temperatures in toxic environments. When you step on it, it doesn't go "crunch." Probably, its elliptical shape accounts for its toughness.

Early Influences

Q Were you interested in architecture when you were in school?

A My very first drawings of houses were just like those of most kids, with the gabled roof, the little square window beside the door, and the curlicue of smoke from the chimney. In high school, I developed interests such as competitive swimming, flamenco dance, and praying-mantis style kung fu. I even designed and made my own clothes and shoes. Then I entered a design competition for high school students and won an honorable mention for most exciting design. There was a lot of peer pressure in high school, but I just went my own way and did what I found interesting.

Q Were there books or people that influenced your thinking when you were young?

A The great artists Leonardo da Vinci and Michelangelo were fascinating to me. Through reading about the work of other philosophers, scientists, artists, and creative minds, I began to see that every great idea and discovery is a minute part of nature's vast knowledge.

Personal Insights

Q How do you feel today about your choice of career?

A If I couldn't design, I would feel as if I were dying. Creativity is like a bubbling, seething, exploding force radiating from within me. People think that I must be overjoyed to see a building completed. However, the real joy was there long ago when I put the idea of the building on paper. The act of creativity is fun, but the realization of an idea is endless hours of grueling labor.

It takes a team to design and build a house. Can you imagine yourself in one of these jobs? Find out something about the job you choose. Then draw a cartoon showing yourself at work.

▶ *general contractor, plumber, roofer, electrician, painter, and interior decorator*

Q What advice do you have for students interested in design and architecture?

A During school years, it's so important to find out who you are and what you are capable of. It's easy to try to be someone else, because you have models to imitate, but originality is vastly superior to imitation. The human mind and spirit are meant to create, to discover new things, to delve into the unknown, to question everything. But instead, we are mainly asked to memorize, to repeat, to confine ourselves to what people think we should be. Dare to be yourself and make it your life's goal to create something original.

The living room of the tardigrade house

517

Pushing Things Around

Objectives

■ Describe the causes and effects of contact forces.

■ Identify situations where work is being done on an object.

■ Explain the difference between work and power.

Key Terms

law of action and reaction

work

power

Contact Forces

If all day long you lifted aluminum panels to a friend putting siding on a house, you would probably be exhausted. Your friend probably would be, too. After all, swinging a hammer all day to attach siding isn't an easy task. You know that both you and your friend have somehow depleted your individual energy supplies. Where did this energy go? What did this energy accomplish? In this section, determine answers to these questions.

Construction is a hands-on and a forces-on activity. The pushes and pulls exerted by workers and equipment have something in common—the forces are exerted by the workers and equipment by contact with hands and shoulders, ropes and cables, and hammers and drills. Forces are always exerted in an interaction between two objects. Do these forces have anything else in common? What forces occur when two materials are in contact?

■ Action and Reaction: A Compatible Couple

At a construction site you hear the clanks of hammers on wood and steel. As a result of these contacts nails are pushed by the hammers into wood. But, does anything happen to the hammer? Did you ever think about the fact that the motion of the hammer is stopped by the nail? In **Figure 17-7,** you can see that the contact results in two equal but opposite forces occurring: one on the nail and one on the hammer. These two forces are an example of an action-reaction force pair.

Figure 17-7

Forces always occur in pairs. The hammer is exerting a force on the nail and the nail is exerting a force on the hammer. The nail is driven into the wood because the hammer-nail force pair is larger than the opposing force pair between the wood and nail.

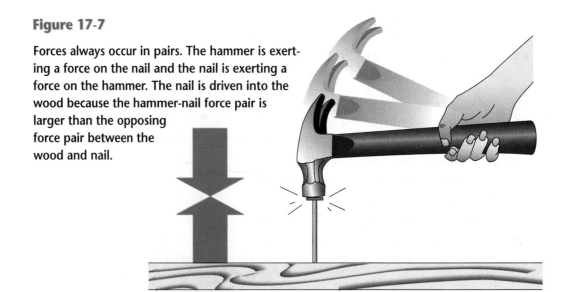

If forces always occur in equal pairs, how do objects ever move? In the case of the hammer and nail, there is more to the picture. To understand what is happening, you must look at all the forces involved. Think of the system of the hammer and nail and the forces affecting it. Tapping the nail gently won't drive it into the board, so you must need to overcome another force pair—friction between the board and nail. Therefore, unbalanced forces are really unbalanced force *pairs*. To experience force pairs, do the MiniLab below.

MiniLab

Do objects exert forces?

Have you ever pushed a stalled car or helped a young relative enjoy a playground swing? Do this activity to explore what's happening during those pushes and pulls.

Procedure

1. Hook two spring scales together, hook-to-hook. Pull gently and steadily on one scale while your partner holds the other scale in place. Record both scale readings *in your Journal.*

2. Now, hold the other spring scale in place while your partner pulls steadily. What do you feel? What are the spring scale readings? Record your observations *in your Journal.*

3. Connect a spring scale to a large desk and pull gently. Don't pull hard enough to move the object. What happens to the object? The spring scale? Record your observations.

Analysis

1. What were the scale readings in step 1? In step 2?

2. Who exerted a force in step 1? In step 2?

3. Who or what exerted forces in step 3?

4. What would you feel if your finger were between the spring scale hook and the desk during step 3?

5. *In your Journal,* make drawings to show what happened in each step. Use arrows to indicate the size and direction of each force.

The MiniLab activity demonstrated that you can't isolate a single force. When you push or pull someone else, you both feel the forces exerted. It's impossible to push something without it pushing back exactly as hard.

Because the two forces in any action-reaction pair are *exactly* equal and opposite, it doesn't matter which force is called the action or which is called the reaction force. Because forces occur only as interactions between two objects, forces always act in pairs. This concept is called the **law of action and reaction,** or Newton's third law of motion. A simple way to state this law is "for every action force there is an equal and opposite reaction force."

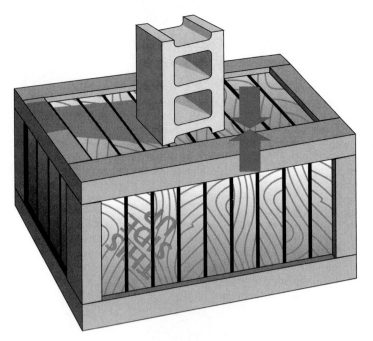

Figure 17-8

One force of the action-reaction pair between the block and crate acts as a support force pushing upward on the block with a force exactly equal in size to the weight of the block.

One force of an action-reaction pair is often responsible for stability. The concrete block sitting on the crate as shown in **Figure 17-8** is stable. The action-reaction pair consists of the weight of the block pushing downward on the crate and an equal but opposite upward force on the block exerted by the crate. The two forces that produce stability are caused by two different interactions—one between the block and Earth, and the other between the block and the crate. The force that the crate exerts on the block is half of an action-reaction pair and is called the support force.

Look back at **Figure 17-5.** The support force of the top brick is the contact force exerted by the next brick down. This support force is an upward force equal to the weight of the top brick. What is the size and direction of the support force the third brick down is exerting? The bottom brick? How do you think the height of the arch might be limited?

Off to Work We Go

Moving bricks by hand isn't an easy task. You have to lift one, carry it, then put it down, over and over. It's tiring because you're transferring some of the energy of your moving muscles to each brick. The transfer of energy through motion defines the concept of work. People use *work* to mean many things—making a bed, raking leaves, or washing dishes. In these examples, work is a task. The scientific meaning of *work* focuses on doing something to one object. **Work** is done when a force moves an object in the direction of the force, for example, a hammer driving a nail. The quantity of work is calculated as the product of the force, F, and the distance, d, that the object moves in the direction of the force. The last statement can be written as an equation.

$$W = F \times d$$
Work = Force × distance

One unit of work is done when a force of 1 N moves an object 1 m in the direction of the force. For example, when you pick up a pair of dropped household scissors and put them on a table, you do work. The scissors weigh about 1 newton and the table is about 1 m high. The work done on the scissors is:

$$W = 1 \text{ newton} \times 1 \text{ meter}$$
$$= 1 \text{ newton-meter}$$
$$= 1 \text{ joule}$$

One newton-meter of work done on an object transfers 1 joule of energy to that object.

Figure 17-9

These images show some examples that seem like work and some that are work.

A Lifting a concrete block seems like hard work and it is. Both the force that a worker exerts on the block and the distance the block moves are in the same direction. Therefore, work is done. A construction worker does 180 J of work each time he or she lifts a 180-N concrete block to a height of 1 m.

When Work Is Done— and Not Done

Do construction workers always do work as they go about moving and lifting construction materials? Look at the examples in **Figure 17-9** of tasks done by workers at a construction site. You might be surprised to see that not all of the workers are doing work. In the activity on the next pages, you can measure your own work.

B Pushing a wheelbarrow loaded with bricks is considered backbreaking work. A worker must do 1200 J of work to roll it just 3 m. How many kilojoules of work are done?

Motion ⟶

Force

C Two boards like this weigh more than 100 N. Yet, no work is done on the lumber to carry it. Why? Look at the direction of the force the construction worker is exerting on the lumber and the direction in which the lumber is moving. Because the distance the lumber is moving is not in the same direction as the force, that force is doing no work on the lumber.

INVESTIGATION

Measuring Work

Physical labor makes your body do work and makes you tired. You get tired because you're transferring energy as you do work. In this activity, you will determine the work you do climbing stairs while carrying a load of building supplies. You might be surprised to learn how much energy you transfer in this task.

Preparation

Problem

How much work do you perform while carrying some materials up a flight of stairs?

Objectives

- *Measure* the total weight moved, the height of stairs climbed, and the time taken to climb the stairs.
- *Calculate* work.
- *Analyze* the conditions required to do work.

Materials

metric tape measure or meterstick
stopwatch
load of material (such as textbooks, bricks, etc.)
bathroom scale

Safety Precautions

Do not carry too heavy of a load. Always lift with your legs, not your back. Climb the stairs at a safe speed.

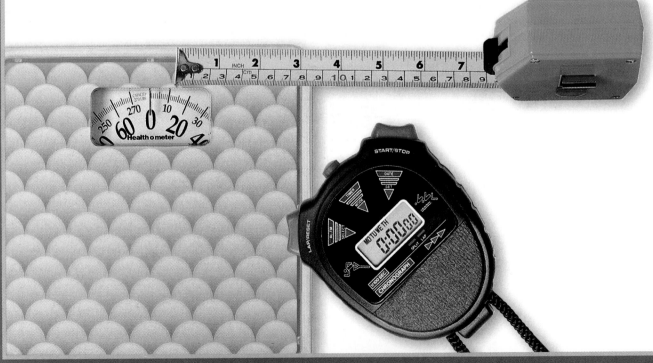

INVESTIGATION

Procedure

1 Do this activity with a partner.

2 Weigh yourself while holding the load. To calculate work in SI units, you must know the weight in newtons. To convert from pounds to newtons, use the following equation:

x pounds $\times$ 4.5 newtons/pound

Record the weight *in your Journal.*

3 Measure and record the height of the stairs. First, measure the height of a single riser. Then, multiply by the number of risers to find the height of the whole flight of stairs.

4 Have your partner measure the time required for you to climb the flight of stairs with the load.

5 Switch roles and have your partner repeat the activity.

6 Calculate the work done climbing the stairs with the load. Remember to express your answer with proper units.

Step 2

Step 3

Analyze and Conclude

1. **Interpreting Data** Describe at least two ways you could have increased the amount of work done.

2. **Observing and Inferring** How would the amount of work change if you performed this task on the moon?

3. **Thinking Critically** Explain whether the amount of work would change if you were to climb a spiral staircase of the same height as in this activity.

Going Further

Application
Car engines are often rated in horse-power. Power is the rate at which work can be done.

$$power = \frac{work}{time}$$

Use your work calculation and time measurement to calculate your power in J/s. How could you make your power rating higher?

205 W

200 W

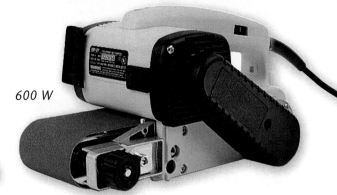
600 W

Figure 17-10

Which sander is the most powerful? Can the most powerful sander do the most work?

To *Find Out More About* ...

Power, read about electric appliances and circuits in Chapter 19.

■ Power to You!

In the Investigation, you explored the two factors that affect work—distance and force. The stair height was the distance and weight was the force you exerted. If you've ever had to run up stairs, you know it's more demanding than walking. That's because you're doing work faster.

When you do the same amount of work in less time, you produce more power. **Power** is the rate at which work is done. To calculate power, the amount of work is divided by the time, in seconds, required to do the work. The equation for calculating power is

$$P = \frac{W}{t}, \quad \text{Power} = \frac{\text{Work}}{\text{time}}$$

The SI unit of power is the watt (W). Look at the sanders shown in **Figure 17-10.** Their power ratings are listed in watts. You may have seen similar ratings on other electrical appliances and tools. How are these power ratings useful?

Power ratings can be used to compare the rate at which appliances, tools, and construction equipment can do work. For example, a bulldozer with twice the power can do the same amount of work as one with half the power. Both can move a mound of dirt, but the more powerful one can do it twice as fast. Machines make modern construction possible because they can produce far greater power than humans.

check your UNDERSTANDING

Understanding Concepts

1. Describe the force pairs involved as you lift a book from the floor to your desk.
2. You carry some roof shingles across a yard and then up a ladder. Which situation involves doing work on the shingles? Explain.
3. You and a friend, who weighs the same as you do, carry equal stacks of books up the same flight of stairs. It takes him 5 seconds longer. Compare the work each of you did. Compare the power each of you developed.

Skill Review

4. **Measuring in SI** What must you measure to calculate work? What SI units should you use? What else should you measure to calculate power? If you need help, refer to Measuring in SI in the *Skill Handbook.*

Tools of the Trade

A Simple Advantage

If you think of machines used in building a house, what examples come to mind? Do you think of electric- or gasoline-powered tools such as drills and saws or human-powered tools such as hammers and screwdrivers? All of these tools are machines—devices that make doing work easier. It's difficult to imagine trying to build a house without using even simple tools.

Ramps, pulleys, screws, and screwdrivers are all simple machines that are handy in building a house. A **simple machine** is a device that does work with only one kind of movement.

Doing work usually involves exerting one force against another, often friction or gravity. Consider using a screwdriver as a lever to pry open a paint can lid held snugly closed by friction, as shown in **Figure 17-11.** You push down on the handle of the screwdriver with an *effort force,* and the tip of the screwdriver pushes up on the can lid with a *resistance force.*

As you can see, the resistance force is greater than the effort force. The size of your effort force has been multiplied, making it possible for you to apply greater force than you could without a machine. The **mechanical advantage** (MA) of a machine is the number of times the machine multiplies the size of the effort force. As shown, the screwdriver used as a lever has an MA of about 20. It takes very little input force to open the lid.

Objectives
- Distinguish between mechanical advantage and efficiency.
- Identify the main purposes of simple machines.
- Give examples and classify some commonly used simple machines.

Key Terms
simple machine
mechanical advantage
efficiency
friction

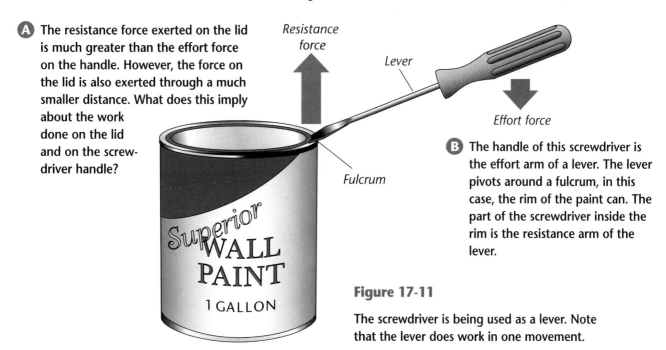

A The resistance force exerted on the lid is much greater than the effort force on the handle. However, the force on the lid is also exerted through a much smaller distance. What does this imply about the work done on the lid and on the screwdriver handle?

Resistance force

Lever

Effort force

Fulcrum

B The handle of this screwdriver is the effort arm of a lever. The lever pivots around a fulcrum, in this case, the rim of the paint can. The part of the screwdriver inside the rim is the resistance arm of the lever.

Figure 17-11

The screwdriver is being used as a lever. Note that the lever does work in one movement.

You can calculate the mechanical advantage of a machine by dividing the resistance force by the effort force.

$$MA = \frac{\text{resistance force}}{\text{effort force}} = \frac{F_r}{F_e}$$

Compare directions of the effort and resistance forces in **Figure 17-11.** When you pushed down on the handle of the screwdriver, the lid was pushed up. Notice that the handle moved through a large distance while the head moved a very short distance. The screwdriver doesn't do more work, it just makes work seem easier. Apply the formula for work. In this case:

$$W = F_r \times d_{head} = F_e \times d_{handle}$$

■ Benefits of Using Simple Machines

Simple machines are used because they give you benefits when doing a task. These benefits are the result of the machine changing the force applied or distance moved by the machines. As you examine **Figure 17-12,** note how the sizes and directions of the effort and resistance forces and the distances they move are affected by simple machines. Some tools magnify speed instead of force. A broom's head moves further and faster than the broom's handle. This enables you to sweep more area faster. The smaller resistance force doesn't matter because you're only moving lightweight dust.

Cantilevering

In the opening pages of this unit, you looked at a photograph of a house designed by Frank Lloyd Wright called Fallingwater. The setting for this home, over a rocky stream and waterfalls, led the architect to a design that seemed to grow from the landscape. Part

of the house juts over the water as if it were another rocky shelf above the stream.

When part of a structure extends balanced but unsupported beyond its foundation, it is called cantilevered construction. Although it seems to project too far to be stable, all

Even though large sections of the bridge extend on either side of its foundation pillars, loads far from the foundation are balanced by support forces.

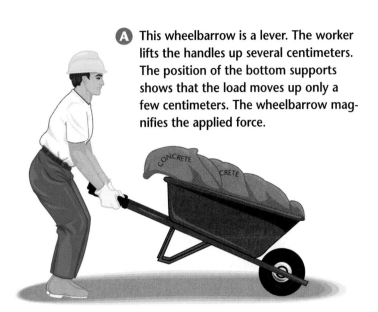

A This wheelbarrow is a lever. The worker lifts the handles up several centimeters. The position of the bottom supports shows that the load moves up only a few centimeters. The wheelbarrow magnifies the applied force.

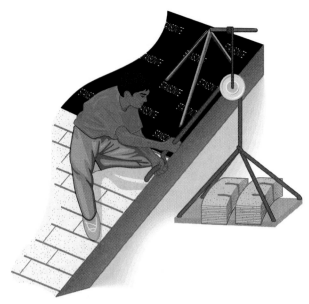

B To raise the shingles, this roofer has to pull as much rope as the roof is tall. The pulley doesn't magnify his lifting force; it only changes the direction of the force.

Figure 17-12

These workers are using two simple machines.

the forces on the building are balanced.

Cantilevered Bridges

Many bridges are built with cantilevered construction. The Firth of Forth bridge in Scotland, with a main span of one-half kilometer, is one of the earliest large-scale examples.

A free arm, or beam, extends far out from a pier or abutment, but the beam is supported and balanced. Most cantilevered bridges have two beams that meet in the middle. Both beams are supported independently. One beam can rise or fall without the other side becoming imbalanced.

As the photograph at the far left illustrates, the Firth of Forth bridge has three large, cantilevered sections. Two smaller spans link the outer main sections to the central section.

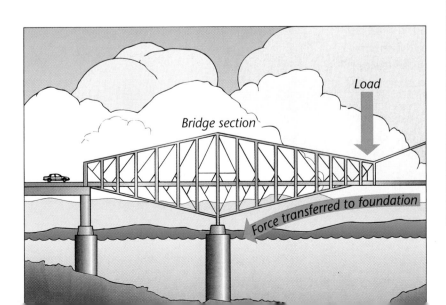

Load

Bridge section

Force transferred to foundation

Thinking Critically

Work with other students to build a cantilever that will support 1 kg using a meterstick and textbooks.

1. *Experiment* to find the maximum length you can construct.
2. *Explain* how the weight of the 1-kg mass is supported.

Efficiency

Many machines can both multiply a force and change its direction. Others can multiply a distance and change the direction of a force. However, no machine can both multiply a force and multiply its distance. This isn't possible because of conservation of energy. Do you see why?

If a machine multiplies the effort force, does it multiply the work that the effort force does? A machine doesn't change the work input, even though the machine multiplies your effort force. This shouldn't be too surprising if you recall that work is a measure of energy transfer. You can't expect the screwdriver to transfer more energy to the lid than the amount you transferred to the handle as you pushed it down. **Efficiency** describes how well a machine converts work input into useful work output. **Figure 17-13** shows an example of energy transfer and finding efficiency.

Figure 17-13

A ramp is an inclined plane. Imagine pushing a box up the ramp. The ramp makes the work a bit easier, but not all the energy you transfer does useful work.

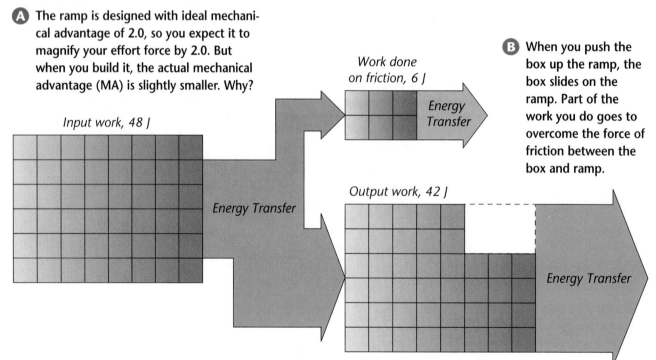

A The ramp is designed with ideal mechanical advantage of 2.0, so you expect it to magnify your effort force by 2.0. But when you build it, the actual mechanical advantage (MA) is slightly smaller. Why?

Input work, 48 J

Energy Transfer

Work done on friction, 6 J

Energy Transfer

B When you push the box up the ramp, the box slides on the ramp. Part of the work you do goes to overcome the force of friction between the box and ramp.

Output work, 42 J

Energy Transfer

C You can find out how much work goes to overcome friction by comparing the work input to the work output. The difference is the energy lost to friction. How much work went to overcome friction in this example? How much useful work was done on the box?

D *Efficiency* is a way to compare the ramp's work input and work output.

Efficiency = $W_{out}/W_{in} \times 100\%$
= 42 J/48 J × 100% = 88%

Lever family

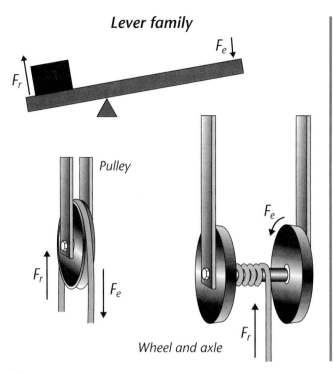

Pulley

F_r

F_e

Wheel and axle

F_e

F_r

Inclined plane family

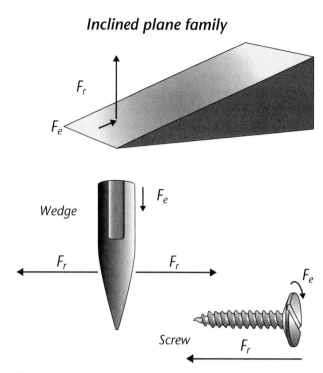

F_r

F_e

Wedge

F_e

F_r F_r

Screw

F_e

F_r

A Levers, pulleys, and wheels and axles all involve turning around a central point, or fulcrum. The MA for a wheel and axle or a lever is calculated by comparing the resistance force and the effort force.

B Inclined planes, wedges, and screws all involve traveling up a slope. The MA for each machine, if there were no friction, could be calculated by dividing the length of the slope by its height.

Figure 17-14

The six types of simple machines can be grouped into two families.

Simple and Compound Machines

There are six simple machines. They are often classified into two families as shown in **Figure 17-14.** Many machines at construction sites are compound machines. A compound machine is a device in which two or more simple machines are linked so that the movement of one machine causes movement in the other. **Figure 17-15** illustrates how two pulleys can be linked so that motion in one pulley causes motion in the other.

What are the benefits of using a compound machine? Look at the two pulleys that make up the compound machine. The top pulley changes the direction of the force. The bottom pul-

ley multiplies the force. The compound machine that they form can do both—it can multiply and change the direction of a force. A compound machine is designed to give you the benefits of each of the simple machines of which it is made.

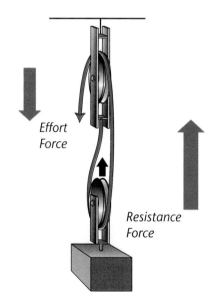

Effort Force

Resistance Force

Figure 17-15

The double pulley is a compound machine. Here the resistance force of the top pulley is supplying the effort force of the lower pulley. To find the approximate MA of a pulley system, count the number of ropes supporting the load, but not the rope supplying the effort force.

How can you make a building accessible?

If you were in a wheelchair or unable to climb stairs, would you be able to get into your home or school and move around? It is now law that public buildings must be accessible to people who use wheelchairs. What are some features you have seen that make this possible? In this experiment, you will use simple machines to design a house, school, or other public building that is accessible to individuals in wheelchairs.

Preparation

Problem
How can you use simple machines to make a building accessible to people in wheelchairs?

Hypothesis
Brainstorm ideas with your group and generate a hypothesis statement that addresses the problem.

Objectives
In this Investigation, you will:
- *Apply* simple machines in the design of the building plan.
- *Explain* the purpose of each simple machine used in the plan, including how it provides a mechanical advantage.

Possible Materials
poster-sized paper
ruler
pencils
markers

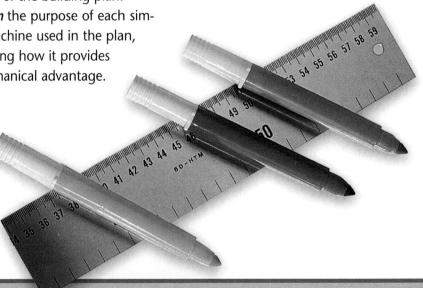

Plan the Experiment

1 Agree on the type of building your group wishes to construct and sketch a diagram of it.

2 Think about a non-accessible building as your control. Determine at least three features that will help make your building accessible and easy to use for people in wheelchairs. At least two must relate directly to simple machines.

3 Review the details about these simple machines on page 529.

4 On your diagram, sketch how and where your features will be used.

Check the Plan
Discuss the following points with other group members before you draw your final design.

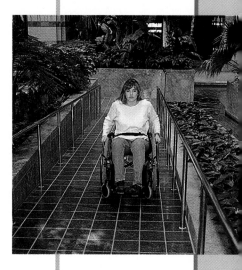

1 Why would your building be difficult to access without these special features?

2 Explain how you can get the most useful mechanical advantage out of each simple machine feature. For example, if you are using an inclined plane for a ramp, would a long, gradual ramp or a short, steep ramp be more effective? Why?

3 *Make sure your group has reached agreement on your features and design.*

4 Clearly draw your final plan on large paper or posterboard. Be sure to label your features. Include a brief description of the function of each simple machine. Prepare to present your plan to the class.

Going Further

Application
Organize and conduct a survey of the number of buildings that are wheelchair-accessible in your neighborhood. You might investigate three categories of buildings: homes, private buildings, and schools and other public buildings. What things should you check for?

Analyze and Conclude

1. **Analyzing** Identify at least two simple machines found in a wheelchair and describe where they are found.

2. **Observing and Inferring** Ramps often have switchbacks to fit into smaller spaces. Why can't they just be shorter?

3. **Thinking Critically** You designed a new wheelchair-accessible building. What changes might be feasible to make an old building wheelchair-accessible?

Issue:
Equal Access

"We hold these truths to be self-evident, that all men are created equal."

When these words were first written, their meaning was defined by the current social context. That is, "all men" actually referred to all free, literate males of European descent who owned land. As the United States has matured, so has the meaning of these words. Today, most Americans would agree that the intent of these words should be to include all *people.*

The Issue

Of course, all persons are not created the same. Some people are good at math, others at art, others at athletics, and still others are good at making social relationships work. We all have different strengths. *Equal* does not mean "the

same." Equality refers to rights and opportunities. Everyone should be given an equal chance to develop his or her strengths and to be a success in life. Sometimes society needs to provide different types of support so that all people can productively pursue their goals. For someone in a wheelchair, a ramp allows access to a building, while steps present a great difficulty. An individual who is blind can read the raised print of Braille without help, but not flat printed text. A hearing-impaired person might need to use a keyboard or relay system such as TTY in order to conduct a telephone call.

The question is, how can society best help all persons, including those with disabilities, participate fully in the opportunities and events of life?

The Background

It is estimated that in the United States today there are about 40 million individuals with some kind of disability. These disabilities vary from mild to severe. Many people do not even realize that they have a disability and simply work around it their entire life. This is particularly true of learning or emotional disabilities. Other disabilities include physical ones, such as impaired vision or hearing.

In 1990, President George Bush signed into law the Americans with Disabilities Act (ADA). It is designed to ensure that disabled persons have the same opportunities for employment, education, and access to buildings and services as other citizens. It requires that buildings be modified, if necessary, so that all people can enter and move through them easily.

Elevator buttons labeled in Braille

A TTY used by hearing-impaired people

The ADA addresses the civil rights of disabled persons; however, it puts the responsibility for providing access on businesses. In order to provide equal access, it may be necessary to install ramps, widen doors, remodel elevators, lower drinking fountains and telephones, and modify rest rooms. This is expensive and may cause financial problems, especially for small businesses with limited budgets. The ADA does take this problem into consideration. The act requires to be made only those changes that are "reasonable" and do not cause "undue hardship." Unfortunately, there are no guidelines to make clear what this means. Until these terms are clarified, business owners remain unsure of their exact responsibilities, and access may remain restricted.

The Question

Some of the changes that the ADA requires may be expensive to accomplish. How much time and money should a business have to spend in its efforts to meet the ADA standards? Should the businesses receive any financial aid in doing so? From whom?

Is there any way other than physically modifying building structures that would guarantee all people access and fair treatment? Can we find a way to balance the rights of disabled persons and the financial realities of those who own and manage businesses? The answers to these questions are still under debate.

Easy-access water fountains

inter*NET* CONNECTION

Accessibility problems for individuals with disabilities are not limited to buildings. Follow the link for Chapter 17 on the Glencoe Homepage, **http://www. glencoe.com**/, to the American's with Disabilities Act Information Center. Use the ADA Information Center to learn how websites can be better structured to allow greater access to persons with disabilities.

■ Machines at Work

In the real world, construction tools and equipment don't carry the labels *Simple Machine* or *Compound Machine*. Most levers don't resemble the planks and fulcrums used to illustrate them. But if you look at the tools doing work in **Figure 17-16,** you just might be surprised to find that a drill also functions as a wheel and axle.

■ Controlling Friction

When a drill like the one in **Figure 17-16** is used several times in a row, the drill bit becomes hot due to friction between the bit and the wood. **Friction**

Figure 17-16

These photos show examples of compound machines.

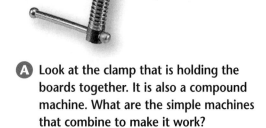

A Look at the clamp that is holding the boards together. It is also a compound machine. What are the simple machines that combine to make it work?

B A head and bit of a drill make up a compound machine. The head and the three teeth that securely hold the shaft of the bit are a wheel and axle. The drill head supplies the effort force and the teeth apply the resistance force to the bit. That resistance force makes the bit rotate. As the bit moves down through the wood, the resistance force lifts the splintered chunks of wood. The bit acts like an inclined plane wrapped around a shaft—in other words, a screw.

C A maul is used to split wood. When it's swung, the handle pivots around the user's hands. The combination of hands and handle acts as a lever. When the maul strikes wood, the wedge-shaped head pushes aside wood fibers. The head acts as a wedge. This combination of machines is easier to use than a separate sledgehammer and wedge.

is a force that opposes motion between two surfaces that are touching. People who build and work with machines need to control friction—either to increase or decrease its effects.

■ Increasing Friction

To remove extra material by sanding or polishing, you need extra friction. As **Figure 17-17** shows, when a board is sanded, friction between the wood and the sand pulls away small pieces of wood. The sand stays put because it is more tightly held to the sandpaper.

To polish metal, you might use a rag and special cleanser. The cleanser makes the rag rougher and more like sandpaper. The friction between the rag and metal is increased and small bits of metal and tarnish are removed as you rub. Of course, the cleanser also has chemicals to help dissolve and remove certain kinds of dirt and tarnish.

■ Reducing Friction

Adding sand to a machine increases the friction inside the machine. As

Figure 17-17

This sander is using friction to remove wood and make the board slightly thinner.

you've learned, increasing friction reduces efficiency.

Coating moving parts with lubricants reduces friction. Lubricants are materials such as motor oil and graphite. Their chemical structure makes them slippery. They fill in holes in surfaces and make the surfaces slide past one another more easily.

The next time you look at a busy construction site, take a good look at the equipment being used. The tools control friction and change work input to make doing the tasks of house construction easier.

Connect to...

Chemistry

A material called graphite can be used as a lubricant to increase the efficiency of some machines. Find out what element graphite is made of and why it improves the efficiency of machines.

check your UNDERSTANDING

Understanding Concepts
1. A lever used to open a window has a mechanical advantage of 8. Does this mean that you get eight times more energy out than you put in? Explain.
2. Many cars have an efficiency of less than 25 percent. What does this say about the energy transferred by the car? Where does the other energy go?

3. A pair of scissors is actually a compound machine. What two simple machines are used to make the scissors effective?

Skill Review
4. **Classifying** List the six types of simple machines. Look around the room. Identify as many simple machines as possible around you and classify each. If you need help, refer to Classifying in the *Skill Handbook*.

HISTORY CONNECTION

The Arch—A Tool and an Art

As early as several thousand years ago, people constructed bridges with arch-shaped spans. In arch bridges, or in any structure that makes use of an arch, the whole mass of the structure is supported from below and the arch spans an opening. The support forces are transmitted outward and downward by compression through the arch and to the ground.

Like many other building features arches probably came about as builders played with ways to distribute and support loads. Arches are found throughout the ancient world constructed from overlapping timbers in bridges, and made of stone, brick, and adobe. In more modern times, they are constructed of steel, laminated wood, concrete, brick, and stone.

Circular arches are probably the best known form. Romans made extensive use of them in aqueducts. Aqueducts were open waterways built high above ground to transport water to cities.

In the diagram below, the parts of a circular stone arch are shown. Each of the blocks, or voussoirs, is wedge-shaped. The center stone at the top is called the keystone. These wedges redirect the weight of the material (above the arch) outward and downward.

In time, arches became a significant tool of architects and builders. The huge, open spaces made possible by arches and domes are not only useful, but evoke a sense of wonder.

Arch structure

Dome of the Rock Mosque

Thinking Critically

1. *Explain* how wedges work in arches.
2. *Describe* how an arch or dome makes large open spaces possible.

536

Read the statements below that review major points presented in the chapter. Using the concepts that you have learned, answer each question *in your Journal.*

1 An object is stable if its center of gravity is supported properly. *Approximately where is the center of gravity of the object this crane is lifting?*

2 Work is done on an object whenever there is movement in the direction of the applied force. *How much work is done on the block when you carry it across a construction site? How do you know?*

3 Simple machines change the size or direction of a force, but don't reduce the work required. *What kinds of simple machines are in this photograph, and how will they affect an applied effort force?*

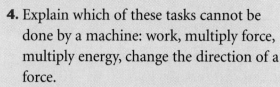

Using Key Science Terms

center of gravity

efficiency

friction

mechanical
   advantage

inertia

law of action and
   reaction

mass

power

simple machine

weight

work

Explain the relationship between the science words in the pairs given below.

1. mass and weight
2. weight and center of gravity
3. friction and efficiency
4. work and power
5. mechanical advantage and simple machine

Understanding Ideas

Using complete sentences, answer the following questions in your Journal.

1. In what ways can inertia affect a large rock used in landscaping the slope of a yard?
2. While fielding a ground ball, a center fielder scoops up the baseball to shoulder height, carries it forward 5 m, then throws the ball to second base. Describe the work done on the ball in these three motions.
3. As you step out of a fishing boat onto an anchored dock, you notice that the boat moves away from you. Explain.

4. Explain which of these tasks cannot be done by a machine: work, multiply force, multiply energy, change the direction of a force.
5. In climbing the same flight of stairs with bookbags of identical weight, why does the person with larger mass always do more work?
6. An umpire tosses an extra baseball bat toward a dugout. Why does it seem to wobble as it rotates through the air?

Developing Skills

Use your understanding of the concepts developed in this chapter to answer each of the following questions.

1. **Observing and Inferring** In a science fiction movie, some characters landed on Planet X, which had the same diameter as Earth. If they now weigh twice as much as they did on Earth, what can you infer about the mass of Planet X?
2. **Comparing and Contrasting** You have studied several types of forces, such as friction and gravity. Compare and contrast these forces by discussing at least two differences between them.
3. **Recognizing Cause and Effect** When using a staple gun to attach insulation, it is recommended that you hold it firmly with two hands. From a physics perspective, why is this good advice?
4. **Measuring in SI** What is the efficiency of a car if it requires an input energy of 200 J to do 40 J of work?

5. Concept Mapping Organize the information about the six types of simple machines in an outline, cluster, or web diagram. For each machine, explain briefly how it works and give at least two examples.

Critical Thinking

In your Journal, *answer each of the following questions.*

1. How does the inertia of a 3-kg pumpkin compare with a 1-kg loaf of bread? How do their weights compare when weighed in the same location? Describe how you could make the pumpkin weigh less than the bread without changing the mass of either.

2. Consider the following tasks done while building a house: (1) carrying a 50-N load of shingles 4 m up a ladder; (2) lifting a 200-N bag of concrete mix 1 m. Compare the work done in these tasks.

3. Can you recall trying to seesaw with a friend who was considerably heavier? Using your knowledge of levers, explain what you would do to make it possible to seesaw with the heavier person.

4. Most mechanics recommend that you change the oil in your car every 5000 km. Why does keeping fresh oil in your car engine improve the efficiency of your car?

Problem Solving

Read the following problem and discuss your answers in a brief paragraph.

One role of health care workers is to help patients stay healthy by eating a reasonable diet. If working in a doctor's office, one of your jobs might be to advise patients about their target calorie intake and food choices. Use your knowledge about the energy needed to perform work and dietary information from the food unit to answer the patient's questions.

1. "I weigh 300 N more than my wife. How should our Calorie (or Joule) intake compare?" Support your answer with a scientific explanation.

2. "What types of foods would be efficient sources of energy?"

CONNECTING IDEAS

1. **Theme—Energy** Where does energy go after you supply it to a machine?

2. **Theme—Systems and Interactions** What must be true of a system consisting of an object and an applied force for work to be done on the object?

3. **Theme—Stability** What makes a supported board stable?

4. **In-Depth Look** What must bridges be designed to support?

5. **Science and Society** What simple machines are used to make buildings more accessible?

6. **History Connection** Why were the arches in aqueducts essential to keeping transportation routes open?

CHAPTER 18

Transfer of Thermal Energy
Heating and Cooling

The wind howls outside as you push the door closed and begin to take off your wet, snowy boots. Even the short walk from the bus stop was hard work because of the bitter cold wind and a frozen ocean of snowdrifts. You immediately notice the warmth inside the house. How is it possible to keep the inside so much warmer than the outside?

How is temperature regulated in the building you live in? Is the air-conditioning or heat on right now? In this chapter, learn about several methods to heat and cool buildings to maintain comfort throughout the year. You will find that insulation is an important part of these methods.

▶ *Try the next activity to begin exploring temperature and comfort.*

MiniLab

How is a home heated?

Your entire home feels warm when the heat is on. Where does energy go when it leaves a heater?

Procedure

1. Put a 100-W light inside a large cardboard box. Make sure the lightbulb won't touch any side of the box. Then, turn it on and close the box.

2. Wait 20 minutes, then feel each side of the box. Record your observations *in your Journal.*

3. Measure the temperature in your classroom. Then, carefully slide a thermometer under the box lid and measure the temperature inside the box. Turn the light off.

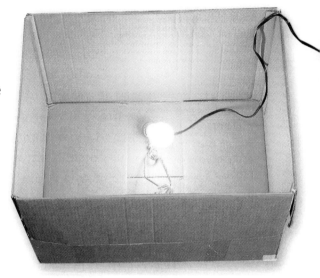

Analysis

1. How were the box sides heated by the bulb?

2. Explain any temperature differences that you observed.

3. What setup changes would alter the observations you made?

numbered **541**

Preventing Energy Loss

18-1

Objectives

- Compare and contrast the transfer of heat by conduction, convection, and radiation.
- Differentiate between thermal conductors and insulators.
- Explain the use of insulators in buildings.

Key Terms

thermal insulator
thermal conductor

How's the weather?

As you observed in the MiniLab on page 541, energy flowed into the light-bulb and, eventually, out through the box. The box and lightbulb are a model of the system of a home and heat source. You want to keep the temperature within a comfortable range inside your home. Controlling that temperature involves controlling the flow of energy.

Have you ever lost electrical power to your home or school during a storm? If power is off for a long time, you may notice several problems. The indoor temperature of your house begins to approach the outside temperature. The contents of your refrigerator and freezer become warmer. Objects and their surroundings eventually tend to reach the same temperature. How does this happen?

Because surroundings affect temperature, homes are built to fit into their surroundings. The two homes shown in **Figure 18-1** are from different parts of the world. Each home is designed to control energy transfer in a way that keeps its residents comfortable. A warm climate requires ways to keep the home and its residents cool. These ways can include many large windows, large porches, and many shade trees. A home in a cool climate has the opposite need. Therefore, it has smaller windows, ways to capture warm sunlight, and thick walls to keep warmth inside.

Climate also influences the machinery needed to control temperature. Homes in the Arctic and Antarctic need only heating systems. Homes in temperate climates, like most of the United States, have heating and cooling systems.

Figure 18-1

The materials and structures of housing depend on climate and the local materials available. How does the dwelling on the near right from New Zealand contrast with the homes in Switzerland on the far right?

Transferring Energy

A heater or air conditioner causes a change in temperature. Such changes in temperature represent a flow of energy. **Figure 18-2** shows another familiar and tasty example of a temperature change. What do these changes have in common? A thermometer shows you that the temperature has changed, but what is a thermometer measuring? Explore a different way to cause a temperature change in the MiniLab below.

MiniLab

What does temperature really mean?

Temperature is a measure of the average kinetic energy of the particles in a material. Can you increase the temperature of an object just by moving it faster?

Procedure

1. Obtain a plastic or foam cup with a tight-fitting lid. Pour enough sand into the cup to just cover the bulb of a thermometer.

2. Measure and record the temperature of the sand to the nearest tenth of a degree. You may have to estimate the final digit.

3. Remove the thermometer and place the lid on the cup. Hold the lid firmly in place and shake the cup vigorously for 3 minutes.

4. Remove the lid and immediately measure the temperature of the sand. Record the temperature *in your Journal.*

Analysis

1. What effect did shaking have on the temperature of the sand?

2. What caused the increase in the average kinetic energy of the atoms that form the granules of sand? Was energy created? Explain.

3. Would the sand become warmer if you shook it longer? Explain.

In the activity, shaking the sand added kinetic energy to the sand. Part of that energy was transferred to increased random motion of the atoms making up the sand by friction between the grains of sand. You measured that increase in energy when you took the sand's temperature.

Temperature doesn't measure the total energy of a mass. A gallon and a quart of water can be at the same temperature, but the gallon has more energy because it's larger. Therefore, you

Figure 18-2

Heat from the oven warms the dough until it becomes the same temperature as the oven. How else does heat affect the cookies?

Bring a pan of water to a boil on an electric hot plate. Measure the air temperature about .5 m directly above the pan. Now, measure the temperature at the same height but about .5 m horizontally away from the pan. Was there any difference between the two temperatures?

have to add more energy to a larger mass to raise its temperature the same amount. In the MiniLab activity, you'd have to shake the container of sand longer to warm a large mass of sand to the same temperature as a small mass.

Temperature and energy transfer are part of your daily life. Suppose you step out of the shower and onto a tile floor. The tile may feel cold to you. What you sense is a transfer of energy from your foot to the colder tile. Heat is the energy that flows naturally from something at a higher temperature to something at a lower temperature. When your feet touch the tile, energy flows from your feet to the tile. Naturally, you want the tile floor and your bathroom to be warm when you step out of the shower. But before you learn how to keep heat where you want it, you need to review how heat moves.

■ Conduction

When you step from the shower onto a cold tile floor, you provide direct contact for heat transfer. All matter is

composed of atoms that are in constant motion. As the motion of these atoms increases, the temperature of the matter increases. When the vibrating atoms in your warm foot bump against the slower vibrating atoms in the cooler tile floor, the motions of the atoms in your foot slow and the motions of the atoms in the tile floor increase. In this process, energy is transferred from your foot to the floor and your foot becomes colder. Your foot loses heat by *conduction*.

Conduction also occurs within matter that is not at the same temperature throughout. Grabbing the metal handle of a hot skillet like the one shown in **Figure 18-3** would be proof that conduction transfers heat from the burner through matter.

■ Convection

In Chapter 2, you learned how an air movement called a convection current drives forms of weather such as thunderstorms. Convection also transfers energy on a much smaller scale. Perhaps you've noticed that rooms in your house are warmer near the ceiling even though heated air comes in through vents near the floor. You can experience something similar in the Try It activity. The temperature difference in the Try It happens because warm air is forced upward by denser, cooler air.

How does convection differ from conduction? In conduction, atoms vibrate about the same position as energy is transferred. In convection, however, the atoms carry energy with them as they move from one location to another. This occurs because atoms of liquids and gases are not in fixed positions, as are the atoms of solids.

Figure 18-3

Conduction transfers heat from the hot burner to the bottom of the skillet and then to the handle. Although not as noticeable as the effects of conduction in a metal skillet, conduction transfers heat through the walls, windows, and ceilings of rooms like this kitchen.

■ Radiation

The heat lamps in **Figure 18-4** don't use conduction or convection to keep food warm. The lamps don't touch the food, and warm air is forced up, not down, by convection. Instead, the lamps use *radiation*. As you learned in Units 1 and 2, some materials absorb and others reflect the sun's radiation. The aluminum foil is reflecting some of the heat lamp's radiation to keep the food from overheating. A dark material would absorb more radiation. Homes use materials to control how radiation is absorbed. Now, apply your knowledge of heat in the Thinking Lab.

Figure 18-4

These heat lamps warm food by radiation. Electromagnetic waves transfer energy to the food and the food's temperature rises. What effect does the foil have on this process?

Thinking Lab   Interpreting Scientific Diagrams

How can you keep soup hot for lunch?

Have you ever used an insulated bottle to keep a food or beverage either hot or cold? Lunch boxes and kits often have containers designed to keep their contents hot or cold. They do this by blocking the three methods of heat transfer.

Analysis

Study the diagram of an insulated bottle. Important features of the bottle are labeled. Use the diagram as well as your knowledge of conduction, convection, and radiation to answer the following questions.

Thinking Critically

Explain how the features of the insulated bottle block conduction, convection, and radiation. How does the process of keeping a drink cold differ from the process of keeping the drink hot?

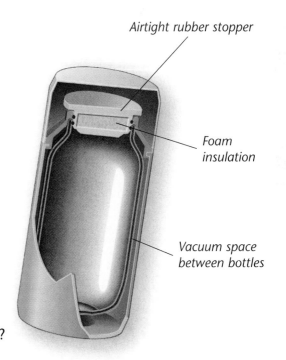

Airtight rubber stopper

Foam insulation

Vacuum space between bottles

Insulation Information

Wearing a heavy coat on a cold day or a white shirt on a hot, sunny day are two ways to reduce unwanted heat transfer. Likewise, when building a comfortable indoor habitat, unwanted heat transfer by conduction, convection, or radiation must be prevented as much as possible. What kinds of materials are most effective at reducing heat transfer? You can find out yourself in the Investigation that follows.

INVESTIGATION

In Hot Water

In the Thinking Lab on page 545, you saw how an insulated beverage container reduced heat transfer. What kinds of containers do you more commonly drink from—aluminum soda cans? Paper, plastic, or foam cups? Glass containers? In this Investigation, compare how well several different containers block heat transfer.

Preparation

Problem

Which types of beverage containers are most effective at blocking heat transfer from a hot drink?

Objectives

In this Investigation, you will:

- *Measure* the temperature change of a hot liquid in several containers over a time interval.
- *Make a graph* showing the temperature change in each container.

Materials

hot plate (or a supply of water at 90°C)
beaker, 600-mL

graduated cylinder, 100-mL
various beverage containers (each about 12 oz, 3 different containers per group)
thermometers (3)
cardboard squares, 15 cm × 15 cm with hole for thermometer (3)
stopwatch (or second hand on watch)
water

Safety Precautions

Use caution when heating water. Be sure to use tongs or thermal gloves when handling containers of hot liquid. Treat thermometers with care and keep them away from the edges of tables.

INVESTIGATION

Procedure

1 With your group, decide on three types of beverage containers to test. Obtain a sample of each type of container. Be sure that the containers are approximately the same size.

2 Heat about 350 mL of water in a beaker to about 70°C.

3 While the water is heating, draw a table *in your Journal* to record your data.

4 Use the graduated cylinder to measure 100 mL of the hot water into each container. **CAUTION:** *Wear a thermal mitt while handling the hot cylinder.*

Step 4

5 Cover each container with a cardboard square. Insert a thermometer into the hole in each piece of cardboard. Don't let the thermometer bulb touch the bottom of the container.

6 Each team member should be responsible for reading the same thermometer every minute at the same time. Take the first reading at time zero minutes.

7 Continue taking readings for all three containers each minute for 15 minutes. Record all measurements in your data table.

8 After you have finished taking the readings, clean all equipment and return it to the proper place.

Step 5

Analyze and Conclude

1. Making and Using Graphs Make a graph to show the cooling patterns of the containers. Plot time on the horizontal axis and temperature on the vertical axis. Show the data points and curve for each container in a different color on the same graph.

2. Interpreting Data What can you learn about cooling by looking at the graphs? Which container was most effective at keeping the water hot? Which was the least effective?

3. Controlling Variables Examine the physical characteristics of the containers. Are there any differences other than the kind of material that might affect their ability to prevent heat transfer? Explain.

Going Further

Application
In addition to preventing heat transfer, what other factors might beverage-packaging companies consider when choosing the best material for their containers? Explain.

■ Halting Heat

On a cold winter day, would you be more comfortable in a flannel shirt or a coat filled with fibers or feathers? Materials that keep us warm by preventing loss of body heat are one type of thermal insulator. Good **thermal insulators** do not transfer heat well. Other materials that do transfer heat well are called **thermal conductors.**

Can you think of some good examples of thermal conductors and insulators? Metals are excellent thermal conductors. That's why they often feel cool. Heat is conducted away from your hand quickly when you touch metal that is cooler than your hand. You might have named insulators such as feathers, fur, wool, or plastic foam. If you look close-

ly at these materials, you will see that they contain many tiny pockets of trapped air. As you can see in **Figure 18-5A,** materials used as thermal insulators are designed with small pockets of trapped air to inhibit convection.

If you've ever gone backpacking or camping, you might have carried a sleeping bag as your overnight insulation. Manufacturers of sleeping bags rate the temperature comfort zones of their bags according to the thickness of a standard insulating material, as shown in **Figure 18-5B.** Just as insulation has an important role in maintaining the comfort of the portable habitat of a sleeping bag, it plays an equally important role in keeping the permanent habitat of your home comfortable.

Landscaping for Shielding and Shade

Do you need to block stiff winter winds from your home? Do you need to funnel cooling summer breezes toward it? In many locations, the winter and summer prevailing winds are different, so you can do both. If not, you can add trees, shrubs, and flowering plants to reduce a high utility bill.

Windbreaks

A windbreak can be a wall, a hedge, a trellised fence, or a group of trees. To block the wind best, a windbreak should cross the prevailing winter winds at right angles. To cool the home in summer, prevailing winds must be guided toward the home. Place two windbreaks approximately parallel to prevailing summer breezes but angled to each other enough to funnel the winds toward the home. What other strategies might work?

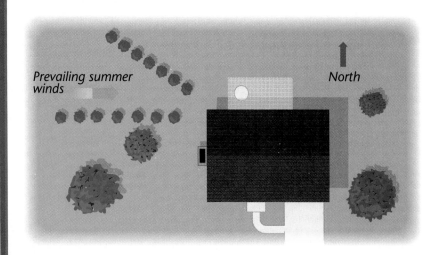

Prevailing summer winds

North

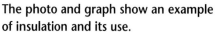

Figure 18-5

The photo and graph show an example of insulation and its use.

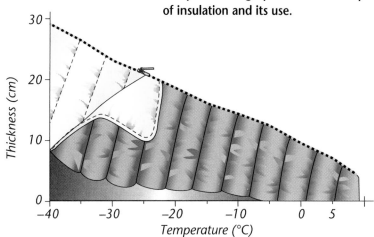

A Conduction by air trapped in the pockets is blocked because the distances between the molecules of the air are relatively large, allowing little heat transfer by contact. Because the volumes of the pockets of air are small, convection currents can't form and heat transfer by convection is blocked.

B The graph shows the recommended thickness of insulation required for maintaining a comfortable environment within the sleeping bag at various minimum outdoor temperatures. What does the graph indicate about the relationship between the insulating properties of this material and its thickness?

Shading Your Home

Most people think planting shade trees near the south side of a home reduces summertime utility bills. In fact, providing shade to the eastern walls of a house is 15 times more effective. Shading the western walls is six times more effective. This is because the eastern and western walls each receive direct sunlight throughout half a day. The southern wall does receive light all day, but the light is not as direct and less energy is transferred.

To reduce solar heating of south-facing walls and windows, a deep roof overhang is more effective than shade trees. A deep roof overhang lets lower-angle winter sunshine in but blocks higher-angle summer sunshine.

If you don't want to wait for shade trees to mature, consider erecting a trellis covered with vines. The vines will grow each year during the spring and the trellis will be covered when hot summer days arrive. Good perennial shade vines include edible fruits such as grapes, chayote, kiwi, and passion fruit and ornamental evergreens such as clematis, honeysuckle, jasmine, trumpet, and hardenbergia. Good annual shade vines are edible vegetables and fruits such as scarlet runner beans, winter squashes, and luffa squashes; and ornamental flowers such as morning glory, hyacinth bean, and moonflower.

Thinking Critically

1. *Describe* one landscaping technique to increase cooling summer breezes.
2. Besides utility bill reduction, *infer* potential benefits of the landscaping techniques discussed.

Figure 18-6

Like blanket layers on a bed, each section of the wall contributes to the insulating properties of the wall. Which section has the least resistance to heat transfer?

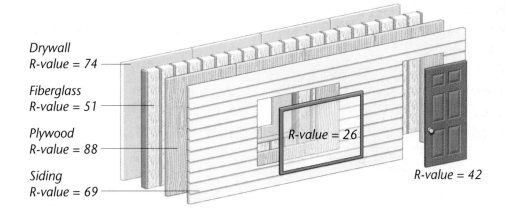

Drywall
R-value = 74

Fiberglass
R-value = 51

Plywood
R-value = 88

Siding
R-value = 69

R-value = 26

R-value = 42

■ Insulating Homes

In the United States, about ten percent of all energy produced is used to heat buildings. This is a substantial part of the country's energy use. To conserve energy and stay comfortable, we must effectively insulate buildings. Insulation reduces the amount of unwanted heat transfer.

To help builders and consumers make decisions about insulation, materials have been assigned an insulation rating. The *R*-value of a material is a measure of the resistance a 1 m × 1 m square slab of the material has to heat flow per centimeter of the material's thickness.

Local building codes often require that newly built houses meet minimum values of insulation in walls and ceilings to maintain economically a comfortable indoor temperature. **Figure 18-6** shows typical *R*-values of sections of a house wall. You can see that some sections of the wall offer much more resistance to heat transfer than others because they have higher *R*-values. The total *R*-value of the wall is 1570, with an average *R*-value of 109 per square meter. In colder climates, average *R*-values for walls are about 250 per square meter and 500 per square meter for ceilings.

In addition to the *R*-value of the insulation, cost, bulk, and safety are important in choosing effective insulation. In the next section, find out how the inside habitat of a building can be controlled by heating and cooling techniques.

check your UNDERSTANDING

Understanding Concepts

1. In what major way does radiation differ from conduction and convection in heat transfer?
2. Give three examples of good insulating materials and list their similarities.
3. If you were building a house, what would you consider in choosing insulation?

Skill Review

4. **Comparing and Contrasting** Compare and contrast heat and temperature. If you need help, refer to Comparing and Contrasting in the *Skill Handbook*.

18-2 Traditional Heating and Cooling

Staying Warm and Keeping Cool

With a little help from technology, humans can live and work in a relatively wide range of temperatures—from the frigid –80°C winters of the Antarctic to intense 54°C heat deep in the gold mines of South Africa. To maintain a comfortable environment, the places where we live and work use a variety of methods to control temperature. During some warm days, using a simple fan to generate a breeze is enough. At other times of the year, you may rely on more sophisticated technology to keep the temperature comfortable. What controls the temperature of the room you're in right now? Are the windows open to cool or warm the building, or is it artificially heated or cooled? Explore the changing temperatures of your classroom in the next MiniLab activity.

Objectives
- Identify several types of conventional heating systems.
- Describe how air conditioners and refrigerators transfer heat.

Key Terms
heat pump

MiniLab

Does the temperature vary in your classroom?

How is the temperature controlled in your science classroom? You may have noticed that some areas of the school, and even areas of a single room, seem warmer than others.

Procedure

1. Find two locations in the room to monitor the temperature. Mark each by placing a small piece of masking tape with your initials on it on the floor.

2. Design a data table to record your temperature measurements. You'll record the outside temperature, and the temperature near the ceiling and near the floor at each indoor location in the morning and afternoon for five days.

3. Use a thermometer accurate to 0.5°C to measure the temperature 15 cm above the floor and 15 cm below the ceiling at each location. Record these measurements and the outside temperature in your data table. Note the time of your measurements.

4. Repeat step 3 at the same times each day for a week.

Analysis

1. Plot your data on a line graph, using a different colored pencil for each area. What does the graph tell you?

2. Calculate the average temperature in each area. Do they differ? Explain.

3. Does the inside temperature seem to be related to changes in the outside temperature? Explain.

18-2 Traditional Heating and Cooling **551**

Figure 18-7

Forced-air and baseboard radiator are two common heating systems.

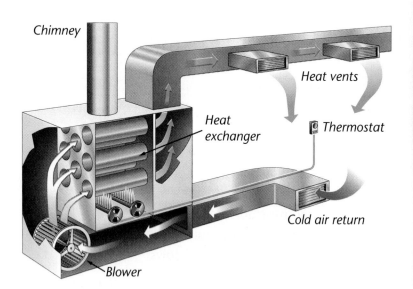

A Fuel such as natural gas or oil is burned in a furnace to warm air. A blower forces the heated air through a system of large pipes, called ducts, to vents in each room. Convection then causes warm air to circulate around the room. Cooler air passes through other vents back to the furnace to be heated.

B Radiator systems are also used to heat buildings. A radiator has a large surface area designed to heat the air near it by conduction. Then convection circulates the heat around the room.

Many climates have hot or cold seasons that are uncomfortable or that produce potentially dangerous temperatures for human health. Even the best-insulated buildings must have methods of heating and cooling for year-round indoor comfort.

■ Turn On the Heat

How do you get heat in your home when you need it? Burning dung, wood, and other plant products such as peat is common in some parts of the world where these materials are more widely available than electrical power. In industrialized countries, electric current produced at a generating plant and natural gas are probably the most common sources of energy used in heating today.

Two common types of heating systems are shown in **Figure 18-7.** As you examine the illustration and photo, notice how the two systems move heat.

■ Be Cool

We have learned that heat is transferred naturally from materials at higher temperatures to materials at lower temperatures. Heating systems depend on this transfer to warm cold rooms. But can the transfer be reversed? If you live in a warm climate, your summer comfort may be improved by air-conditioning. Air conditioners are devices that cool by forcing the transfer of heat from materials at lower temperatures to materials at higher temperatures. In the next MiniLab activity, explore a process that removes unwanted heat.

What does a tire pump do besides inflate tires?

Have you ever used a hand or floor pump to inflate a bicycle tire? If so, you know that it requires a lot of work. What does this work do?

Procedure

1. Obtain a bicycle tire and tube on a wheel, and a pump. Be sure the valve on the pump and the tube are the same type.

2. Deflate the tire.

3. Have each person in the group feel the temperature of the pump shaft. Next, use steady compressions to inflate the tire. Immediately after inflating it, feel the pump's shaft and record how it compares to the original temperature.

4. Observe the temperature of the valve on the tire. Now release the air and deflate the tire. Observe the temperature of the valve again.

Analysis

1. How does compressing air in the pump and tire affect the temperature? Why do you think this occurs?

2. What is the effect of letting air expand as it leaves the tire valve?

In the MiniLab activity, you observed that compressing air raised its temperature, and allowing air to expand lowered its temperature. Air conditioners use both compression and expansion of a gas. They also use two other familiar processes—evaporation and condensation.

Fountains like the one in **Figure 18-8** have been used in hot, dry climates to cool the air in the surrounding courtyards by evaporation. Evaporation is a cooling process that involves a phase change from a liquid to a gas. Because gas is a higher energy state than liquid, molecules take some heat from their environment as they evaporate.

You have felt the effects of your body's main cooling mechanism: sweating. The molecules that make up your sweat transfer heat from your body when they evaporate. This heat transfer has a cooling effect. You also may have noticed that you have trouble cooling down on a hot, humid day. When relative humidity is high, water evaporates much more slowly.

You feel hot and sticky because your sweat doesn't evaporate as quickly. Condensation is the change of a substance from a gas to a liquid. Because this is a change from a higher energy

Connect to...

Biology

Compare how endothermic and ectothermic organisms interact with the temperatures of their surroundings and give an example of each.

Figure 18-8

The transfer of heat from the air to the evaporating water droplets from the fountain cools the air in this outdoor air-conditioning system.

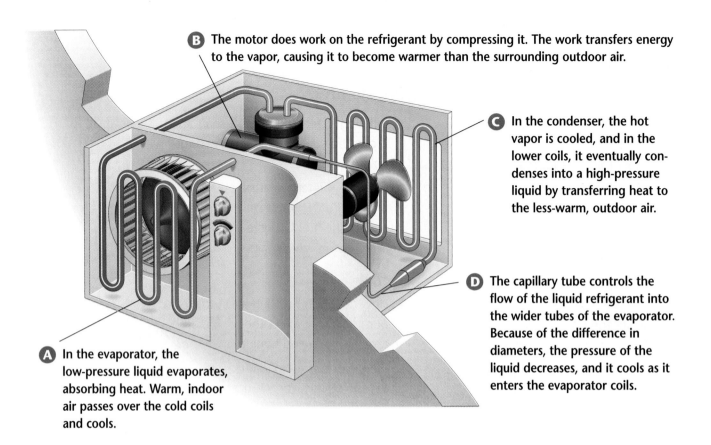

B The motor does work on the refrigerant by compressing it. The work transfers energy to the vapor, causing it to become warmer than the surrounding outdoor air.

C In the condenser, the hot vapor is cooled, and in the lower coils, it eventually condenses into a high-pressure liquid by transferring heat to the less-warm, outdoor air.

D The capillary tube controls the flow of the liquid refrigerant into the wider tubes of the evaporator. Because of the difference in diameters, the pressure of the liquid decreases, and it cools as it enters the evaporator coils.

A In the evaporator, the low-pressure liquid evaporates, absorbing heat. Warm, indoor air passes over the cold coils and cools.

Figure 18-9

This diagram shows how an air conditioner moves heat.

state to a lower energy state, the condensing molecules release energy to their environment.

Air conditioners are sometimes called **heat pumps.** A heat pump is a device that moves heat from one location to another. The transfer of heat from cold to hot materials is not a natural process. Work is done by air conditioners to move heat from cooler to warmer areas.

Figure 18-9 shows how the processes of evaporation, condensation, expansion, and compression make cooling possible in an air conditioner. Some houses accomplish heating and cooling with a heat pump, which is a two-way heat mover. In warm weather, it operates like an air conditioner by transferring heat outside. In cold weather, it transfers heat from the cool outside air to the air inside the house.

check your UNDERSTANDING

Understanding Concepts

1. Compare forced-air and radiator heating systems.
2. Why should heating vents be located near the floor rather than by the ceiling?
3. Why is the evaporation process critical in cooling systems?

Skill Review

4. **Observing and Inferring** Explain whether it is a good idea to cool your kitchen by leaving the refrigerator door open. If you need help, refer to Observing and Inferring in the *Skill Handbook*.

Harnessing the Sun's Energy

Solar Heating

Can you think of any examples of how radiant energy from the sun is converted to another form of energy for some practical purpose? You may have used a solar-powered calculator, seen photos of solar-powered cars, or seen solar panels on houses. In this section, explore how radiant energy from the sun is used to maintain a comfortable indoor habitat.

Getting into a car that has been sitting in a parking lot on a sunny summer day is a reminder that radiant energy from the sun transfers heat. The car may be up to 15°C warmer than the outside air. The sun supplies the energy to drive Earth's weather. Can it also supply energy to help warm homes and heat water? Solar energy is a free source of energy. As **Figure 18-10** shows, some areas have an abundance of solar energy and must paint and design buildings to stay cool. However, all areas don't have so many sunny days. How well does solar heating work in your area? In the Investigation activity on the next pages, design, build, and test a way of collecting and using solar energy.

Objectives
- Distinguish between passive and active solar-heating systems.
- Explain why water is a good material for storing thermal energy.

Key Terms
specific heat

Figure 18-10

The south-Texas blacktop shown above became hot enough under the summer sun to fry an egg. The buildings in the Mediterranean city to the right are painted white to reflect sunlight to help keep them cool.

How can you design a solar heater?

Can you think of other designs for which solar heating might be useful? In this Investigation, use a selection of materials to design and build a solar heater.

Preparation

Problem
How would you design a solar heater to accomplish a specific task?

Hypothesis
Have your group agree on a purpose for which your solar heater will be used. Record a hypothesis.

Objectives
In this Investigation, you will:
- *Design* a solar heater to accomplish a specific purpose.
- *Analyze* the effectiveness of your solar heater and suggest improvements on the design.

Possible Materials
water
a variety of containers
tubing
boxes
aluminum foil
black paint
colored paper
insulating materials (cotton, newspapers, plastic, etc.)
glue, tape, and scissors
thermometers
cardboard
1-gallon plastic milk containers

Safety Precautions

Use caution when cutting materials. If you are dealing with hot water at any time, use tongs or insulated gloves to handle the container. Keep thermometers away from the edge of tables and handle them carefully.

Plan the Experiment

1 Be sure your group has agreed on the purpose of your solar heater.

2 *In your Journal,* sketch a solar heater that would accomplish your purpose. Include a list of the specific materials you would use for this device.

3 Share your idea with the rest of the group. Try to combine the best features of each person's ideas and formulate a group plan.

Check the Plan
Discuss the following points with other group members to decide the final procedure for your experiment.

1 Draw a group model sketch and list the steps in constructing your solar heater.

2 How will you test the effectiveness of your solar heater? Write your testing plan, describing any measurements you might make.

3 *Make sure your teacher has approved your experimental plan before you proceed further.*

4 Build your solar heater. When you are satisfied with its construction, test the effectiveness of your heater. How will you display your results?

Analyze and Conclude

1. **Interpreting Data** Are you satisfied with your design? What could you do to improve the effectiveness of your solar heater?

2. **Measuring in SI** How did you measure the effectiveness of your solar heater? Can you think of any other way the effectiveness of the heater could be measured or described?

3. **Comparing and Contrasting** How does your device compare to the solar-heating systems of your classmates? Describe a way of grouping the heaters by how they function.

Going Further

Thinking Critically
Research the use of solar cells, such as those used in calculators, to generate electricity. Although it is possible, find out why solar cells are not commonly used today to power cars and provide electricity for lighting and heating buildings.

Figure 18-11

Passive solar homes must have features to help them stay warm in winter and cool in summer. In the northern hemisphere, large windows on the south side help collect maximum sunlight. On other sides, the walls are heavily insulated with few windows to prevent heat loss. The radiant energy is absorbed and warms the floors, walls, and even containers of water. These warmed materials continue to warm rooms by convection even after the sun sets.

■ Passive Solar Heating

As already mentioned, the inside of a car sitting in the summer sun warms considerably. This warming is an example of passive solar heating. Buildings can also be heated in a similar manner if designed properly. Passive solar-heating systems absorb radiant energy from the sun for warming without the use of fans or other devices to distribute heat throughout the house. **Figure 18-11** explains some features commonly used in passive solar buildings.

MiniLab

How much heat can it hold?

Campers can use stones heated in a fire to boil water. How many stones would it take to boil a pot of water?

Procedure

1. Measure the mass of three or four rocks provided by your teacher. Place them in an aluminum pan in an oven for 5–10 minutes.

2. Add room-temperature water to a 400-mL glass beaker to equal the mass of the rocks. Measure the water temperature and record it *in your journal.*

3. Using a thermal mitt, carefully remove the pan from the oven. Using tongs, carefully place the heated rocks in the beaker. After one minute, measure the water temperature and and record it *in your journal.*

Analysis

1. How much did the water's temperature change?

2. Assume the rocks and water reached equilibrium each time the rocks were cooled and that the rocks were 500°C. Compare the temperature changes of the rocks and water.

Different materials require different amounts of heat to produce similar changes in their temperatures. As you saw in the MiniLab activity, water can absorb a lot of energy and undergo a relatively small temperature change, so it is said to have a high specific heat.

The **specific heat** of a material is the amount of energy needed to raise the temperature of 1 kg of the material 1 kelvin. Water's high specific heat, its low cost, and its safety make it an ideal material to store and transport heat throughout a solar heating system.

Figure 18-12

Solar heating systems use water to absorb heat.

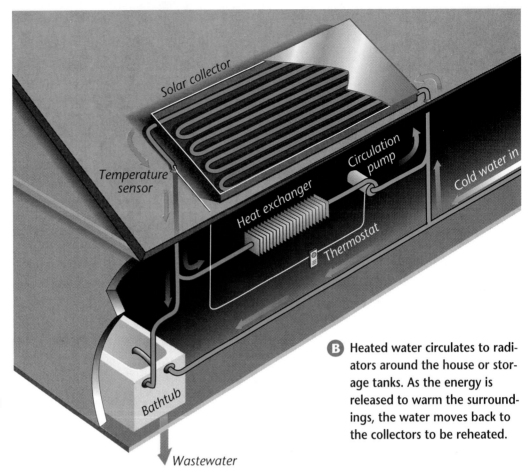

A Solar collectors are mounted on the roof or the south side of a building. They have a black metal plate covered with glass to prevent convection. Water-filled pipes are located just beneath the metal plate. The metal absorbs energy and heats water in the pipes.

Solar collector

Temperature sensor

Circulation pump

Heat exchanger

Cold water in

Thermostat

Bathtub

B Heated water circulates to radiators around the house or storage tanks. As the energy is released to warm the surroundings, the water moves back to the collectors to be reheated.

Wastewater

■ Active Solar Heating

Active solar heating takes the collection and use of the sun's radiant energy one step further than passive solar heating. Most active systems use solar collectors, which are devices that absorb radiant energy from the sun.

Figure 18-12A illustrates one example of a solar collector. Active systems, as diagrammed in **Figure 18-12B,** also pump water warmed by the radiant energy around the house. This allows more effective heating of large spaces than passive systems.

check your UNDERSTANDING

Understanding Concepts

1. Why is passive solar heating referred to as *passive?*
2. Describe the function of a solar collector commonly used in active solar heating.
3. Explain why water is a good material for storing and distributing heat in solar-heating systems. Be sure to use *specific heat* in your explanation.

Skill Review

4. **Comparing and Contrasting** Compare and contrast passive and active solar heating. If you need help, refer to Comparing and Contrasting in the *Skill Handbook.*

Issue:
Oil Prices—A Roller-coaster Ride

One thing you can never be sure of is the price of gasoline at the pump. It's up this week and down the next. You might think that prices are fixed by chance. The price of fuel oil for heating doesn't seem to change as often, but that's because it's not posted on signs at the corner for everyone to see!

The Issue

Why do crude oil prices change? The health of the world economy affects the price of oil, and the price of oil affects the health of the world economy. When oil prices are low, economies usually flourish. When oil prices are high, economies slow down. Because the United States imports 50 percent of the oil it consumes, a $4 drop in the cost of a barrel of oil puts approximately an additional $10 billion per year in American pockets. This adds 0.3 percent to the economic growth of the United States. The reverse is true when oil prices rise.

Oil prices change in response to events around the world. When there is peace in the Middle East, oil prices fall. It's no wonder the United States and other industrialized nations try to foster peace in that sector of the world. Wars, the election of a new president, or the death of a world leader also affect oil prices.

The Background

The greatest changes in oil prices have occurred since the Organization of Petroleum Exporting Countries (OPEC) was founded in 1960. By the late 1990s, OPEC included 11

members: Algeria, Indonesia, Iran, Iraq, Kuwait, Libya, Nigeria, Qatar, Saudi Arabia, United Arab Emirates, and Venezuela. Because approximately 63 percent of the world's proven oil reserves are located in the OPEC countries, their decisions affect oil prices around the world.

By forming OPEC, these less-industrialized countries were able to get higher prices for oil and at the same time ensure the continuation of their oil supplies by reducing the amount they pump. These two factors are closely related; when less oil is pumped, the price of oil rises.

The members of OPEC are not always able to agree among themselves about how much oil should be pumped. For example, OPEC may set a ceiling of 24.5 million barrels per day. If a member nation finds itself in need of money to balance its budget, it may pump more than its quota. Prior to the Gulf War in 1991, Iraq was OPEC's number-two producer. Sanctions on the sale of Iraqi oil were imposed because of Iraq's invasion of Kuwait. When the sanctions are lifted, Iraqi oil will flood the market. This action will cause some producers to charge less in order to compete with the Iraqi oil. This tactic will affect the incomes of all the OPEC nations.

The Question

Although low oil prices help maintain the economy on an even keel, keeping oil prices low and stable raises questions that will have to be answered in the long run. Lower prices per barrel have a triple-bad effect. First, they harm the environment because people use more oil when it is cheaper and send more pollutants into the atmosphere. Second, using more oil makes the United States more dependent on oil from OPEC. It also requires a greater investment in peacekeeping on our part in the Middle East to keep the oil flowing. Finally, greater consumption of oil results in a rapid loss of untapped United States oil. Because oil is a nonrenewable

A barrel is a unit of measure used to measure crude oil. It is equal to 159 L (42.0 gallons).

resource, the more oil that is pumped, the less there will be for the future.

Experts do not agree on how long the world's oil reserves will last. Some of them warn that if oil continues to be consumed at present rates, it won't last for more than 35 years. Some optimists disagree. They claim that higher oil prices will stimulate oil companies to search for new oil reserves. They hypothesize that Earth's crust may contain 100 times more oil than has been projected.

If new oil reserves are found, should that be an invitation to industrialized nations to continue using oil at the present rate of consumption? Why or why not? What should the United States do to prepare for a time when oil supplies will be depleted?

*inter*NET CONNECTION

Follow the link for Chapter 18 on the Glencoe Homepage, http://www. glencoe.com/, to learn more about the global demand for oil and other fossil fuels. Make a graph showing how the price of oil has fluctuated over the past several years. Compare the world's current oil supply with oil demand. How is global use of oil and other fossil fuels predicted to change in the future?

Heating and Cooling Decisions

With the help of heating and air-conditioning, we can stay comfortable all year long, regardless of the temperature outside. But is a heating system for a large office building the same as one in a small home? To keep heating and cooling costs down, it's important to pick the most efficient heating and cooling systems for the size and type of building you have.

You're the Heating and Cooling Technician

You are planning to install a heating and cooling system in a small 1500-sq.-ft. new home. The builder has asked you to recommend the best system for the job. You will need to suggest what type of system would be best for your local climate, whether it should be electric or gas-powered, and how large of a system you might need.

Drawing on Experience

1. As a group, discuss what demands you would need for heating and cooling in your local climate. Is air conditioning more important than heating? Do you need both?

2. As a group, contact the local utility companies to find out the rates for natural gas and electricity.

3. From a building-supply store or heating and cooling company, get information such as brochures that describe various heating and cooling systems. A heating and cooling technician may be able to help you find the information you need.

Testing...Testing

1. Make a table that compares the features of the various systems you investigated. Be sure to consider factors like overall comfort.

2. Find out how large of a system you would need to efficiently heat a 1500-sq.-ft. house. Put this information in your table.

3. Using the information you got from the utility companies, calculate about how much it would cost to operate each of the systems. Include this information in your table.

4. As a group, discuss the features of the systems and decide which would be your recommendation for the house.

How Did It Work?

1. Prepare a report that summarizes the information you discovered. Include your table in your report and describe the reasons for your recommendation.

2. What are some suggestions you could give the builder for things to keep in mind while building the house to help lower the heating and cooling costs?

Read the statements below that review major points presented in the chapter. Using the concepts that you have learned, answer each question *in your Journal.*

1 Thermal insulators block the three ways of heat transfer—conduction, convection, and radiation. *Why are metals poor thermal insulators?*

2 Air conditioners and heat pumps move energy by using compression, expansion, condensation, and evaporation. *What is the purpose of the heat exchanger on an air conditioner?*

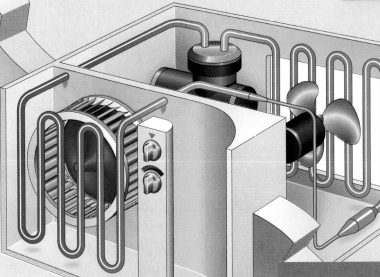

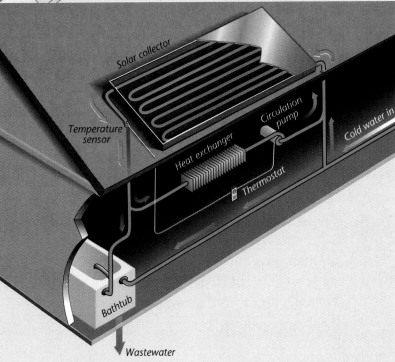

Solar collector

Temperature sensor

Circulation pump

Heat exchanger

Thermostat

Cold water in

Bathtub

Wastewater

3 Active and passive solar heating can help reduce the use of other energy resources. *Why is water often used in active solar heating systems?*

Using Key Science Terms

heat pump   thermal conductor

specific heat   thermal insulator

Answer the following questions using what you know about the science terms listed above.

1. What is the purpose of a heat pump?
2. Explain the relationship between the specific heat of a material and the amount of heat required to produce a large temperature change.
3. What is the purpose of an insulator?
4. Why would materials such as iron and copper be ideal for constructing the bottom of a frying pan?

Understanding Ideas

Using complete sentences, answer the following questions in your Journal.

1. How does convection occur? Explain using a specific example.
2. How is energy transferred from the sun to Earth? Explain why this energy transfer differs from conduction and convection.
3. Why do good thermal insulators often contain pockets of trapped air?
4. Why is water used to store and transport thermal energy in solar-heated homes?
5. Describe how a solar collector works.
6. On what basis are insulating materials compared and rated?
7. Why is sweating an effective method of cooling your body, and why is it harder to stay cool on a humid day?
8. Why does the back of a refrigerator feel warm, but the air and materials inside feel cool?

Developing Skills

Use your understanding of the concepts developed in this chapter to answer each of the following questions.

1. **Sequencing** Order the events that occur in the removal of heat from an object by a refrigerator. Start with the placing of a warm piece of pie in the refrigerator and end with the change of the coolant from a gas to a liquid.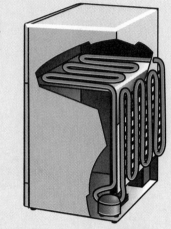

2. **Interpreting Data** Water has a specific heat of 4190 J/kg K and sand has a specific heat of 800 J/kg K. Suppose you were going to heat an equivalent mass of both from room temperature to 80°C. How would the amounts of heat required to do this compare?

3. **Formulating Models** Conduction is a process that takes place at the particle level of matter. Although you can observe its effects, the transfer of energy cannot be seen directly. Develop a model or analogy using visible objects to demonstrate conduction.

4. **Hypothesizing** Propose a hypothesis to explain why a person with a fever often feels chills, even in a warm room.

5. **Concept Mapping** Complete a concept map to illustrate the three methods of heat transfer.

Critical Thinking

In your Journal, *answer each of the following questions.*

1. What types of information might be useful in selecting proper insulation for different parts of your house?

2. Loose vermiculite—a fluffy, granular insulator—has an *R*-value of 1.09/cm, and loose cellulose has an *R*-value of 1.46/cm. If only vermiculite were available, how could you achieve the same insulating effects as with cellulose?

3. A few buildings are heated entirely by electricity. Hidden heating coils are warmed by electrical energy. These coils heat air by conduction, and other materials are somewhat warmed by radiation. Where would you place these heating coils so they are out of sight and still effective?

4. Many houses with passive or active solar systems supplement their heating capabilities with gas or electric sources. Why do you think this is necessary?

Problem Solving

Read the following problem and discuss your answers in a brief paragraph.

Suppose you are a design engineer for a company that sells outdoor clothing in a cold climate. Think about the kinds of clothing you have seen for cold climates. Using what you know about insulating materials and the effect of color on absorption of radiation, suggest some reasonable coat designs and materials for extremely cold temperatures.

How will the activities done while wearing the coat affect your design? Would you choose one layer of a certain material or several layers? Explain.

CONNECTING IDEAS

1. **Theme—Energy** Heat is a measure of thermal energy. Why are home builders interested in controlling the movement of thermal energy?

2. **Theme—Systems and Interactions** How does air interact with the system of fibers and pockets in some thermal insulators?

3. **Theme—Models** If receiving a moving basketball represents getting some heat, how would you model two different methods of heat transfer using two people and some basketballs?

4. **In-Depth Look** What are two ways landscaping could reduce a home's utility bills?

5. **Science and Society** Why might it be beneficial to encourage higher prices for oil now, before dwindling supplies force up prices?

6. **Applying Technology** What are two factors to consider when buying a heating or cooling system?

CHAPTER 19

Electrical Energy
More Power to You

H*ave you ever spent a night in your home when the electricity was off? Of course it was dark, but did you also notice how quiet it was without the stereo, television, or humming motors? Did you begin to feel the loss of heat or air-conditioning?*

Did you notice what ties together all the things you sensed when the electricity was off? Just as oil, propane, or natural gas bring energy into our homes for our use, electricity does, too. What do you need to know about electricity? Certainly you need to know how to use it wisely and safely, and how to deal with minor emergencies such as a blown fuse or a tripped circuit breaker. And perhaps you need to know enough so that you can remodel your home or design a new one.

▶ **To start learning more about what goes on in the circuits behind the walls, do the activity on the next page.**

MiniLab

How is electricity used in your home or school?

You've just read about some of the different uses of electricity that you missed when it was off. Now, you can think critically about what those uses have in common.

Procedure

1. Make a list of the uses of electricity in your home or school.

2. Compare your list with that of a classmate to find any uses you may have overlooked.

3. Group the uses into categories such as heating, cooling, moving things, providing light, and powering devices that produce sound or other forms of information.

4. Gather at least three months of electric bills and find the average cost for a month's electricity.

Analysis

1. Many of the categories in step 3 involve energy. How many different forms of energy are included in these categories?

2. Do some research to find the source of the electricity used in your community. What forms of energy were used to produce this electricity?

Electricity: A Convenient Energy Carrier

19-1

Objectives

■ Contrast direct current and alternating current.

■ Calculate the power and energy use of appliances in the home or school.

Key Terms

potential difference
volt
current
kilowatt-hour
ampere

Electric Current: Carrying Charges

You can probably tell from the survey in the MiniLab that electricity is used in many ways and many times, and that the devices using the electricity are providing energy. Electricity must bring these devices their energy.

At home, you can often sense some of the effects of electricity in the glowing warmth of lightbulbs. How does a lightbulb produce light and heat? You can start learning how by examining electric circuit models.

■ Circuit Models

Trying to see what actually goes on inside an electric wire is impossible. Using some familiar systems that you can see and understand to model an electric circuit makes the invisible easier to grasp. **Figure 19-1** shows some circuit models.

Figure 19-1

These illustrations show different ways of visualizing an electric circuit.

A A pump drives the water through a pipe to the waterwheel. Falling water turns the wheel. Water falls further into the pipe, where it is carried back to the pump.

B Water is heated in the furnace. Hot water flows to a radiator, where the room air is heated. Cooler water flows back to the furnace for reheating. What is the source of the energy?

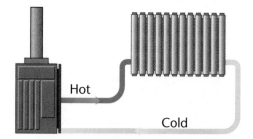

Hot

Cold

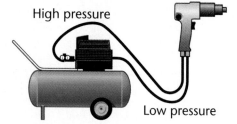

High pressure

Low pressure

C A person loads the balls on the top ramp. They roll to the end and fall, then roll back to the person to be lifted again. What carries the energy?

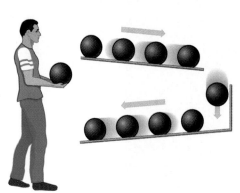

D An air compressor increases the pressure of air. Compressed air flows to the tool, where it drills holes. Air loses pressure in the tool and returns to the compressor.

The models are different, but they share some striking similarities. In each model, there is a source of energy, something that carries energy, and something that uses energy either to do work or to convert it to another form. How is a circuit like the hot-water heating system shown in **Figure 19-1B?**

Energy Sources: Batteries and Generators

In a circuit, the battery is like a home furnace. A furnace burns fuel to add energy to the water passing through it. The battery uses chemical potential energy to add to the energy of the charges passing through the circuit.

A furnace uses the added thermal energy of the water to warm a home. The energy of electrical charges in a circuit is used to provide light and heat, and to do work. In neither system is energy used up; it is transferred to a less concentrated form such as light or heat.

Water in a furnace circulates continuously. It isn't used up, but carries energy again and again. Charges also move through a circuit again and again. When a battery "dies," it still contains an equal number of positive and negative charges. However, its supply of useful chemical potential energy is exhausted.

The change in energy of the water is found by measuring its temperature change. A battery increases the potential energy of electrical charges. The energy change for each unit of charge is called electric potential difference, or just **potential difference.** Potential difference is measured in **volts,** abbrevi-

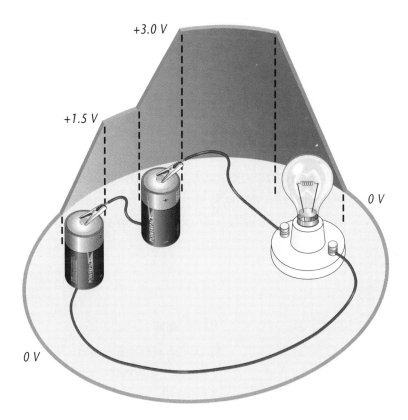

Figure 19-2

Each battery has a potential difference across it of 1.5 volts. So together, the two batteries raise the potential by 3.0 V. The charges have a 3.0-V potential drop going through the bulb. The net change in potential during a complete trip is zero.

ated *V.* Thus, in a circuit, a flashlight battery creates a potential difference of 1.5 V across its terminals. No matter how many charges flow through it, it increases the electric potential of each charge by 1.5 V. As the charges flow through a bulb in the circuit, each of their potentials is reduced by 1.5 V. Therefore, the potential difference across the lamp is also 1.5 V. The total change in potential of each charge as it moves through the complete circuit is zero. You can see how the batteries and lamp affect the potential in a circuit in **Figure 19-2.**

In the Investigation activity on the next pages, you can observe and measure the effects of changing potential.

INVESTIGATION

Batteries and Lightbulbs

Electricity and magnetism are closely tied to each other. In this activity, you'll use that relationship to observe some effects of electricity in simple circuits.

Preparation

Problem

How can you tell that charges are flowing through the wires of an electric circuit?

Objectives

In this Investigation, you will:

- *Measure* relative current size using a compass.
- *Compare* the currents in two different circuits.

Materials

2 D-cells
battery holder
bulbs (1 round, 1 long)
bulb sockets (2)
connecting leads (5)
compass

INVESTIGATION

Procedure

1 On a flat surface, make a circuit with the round bulb in a socket, a battery, and clip leads. The glowing bulb shows you that there is a flow of electric charge, called an *electric current,* through the bulb. Sketch the circuit in your Journal. **CAUTION:** *If a clip lead starts to become hot, immediately disconnect it and try another connection.*

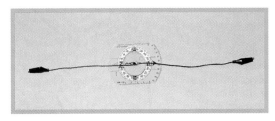

Step 2

2 Disconnect one of the clip leads and place the compass beneath the other clip lead. Hold the wire of the clip lead above or below the compass so that it is horizontal and aligns with the compass needle as shown. Connect the other clip lead. Slowly lower the wire onto the compass. Observe the effect on the compass needle.

3 Raise the wire and turn it in the opposite direction. Lower the wire onto the compass and observe and record the effect on the needle.

4 Repeat steps 2 and 3 for the wire connected to the ⊕ end of the battery.

5 Repeat step 4 for the wire connected to the ⊖ end of the battery. Compare the compass angle and the current direction in each wire.

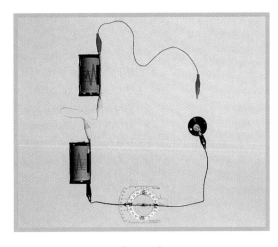

Step 6

6 Connect two batteries as shown. How did the brightness of the bulb change?

7 *In your Journal,* predict how much the compass needle will rotate with two batteries rather than with one. Explain. Now try it, and record your results.

8 Does the brightness depend on the kind of bulb used? Quickly connect first one bulb, then the other. Describe the brightness of each bulb.

Analyze and Conclude

1. Interpreting Scientific Illustrations Sketch and label the parts of a bulb and socket that are electrical conductors and those that are insulators. Show the path the current takes through the socket and bulb.

2. Observing and Inferring To compare the brightness of the two bulbs, you constructed two similar circuits—each containing one of the bulbs. In which circuit would you expect a larger angle between a wire and the compass needle beneath it? Why?

Going Further

Application
Use a magnifying glass to inspect the thin wire in each bulb. Compare the length and thickness of the wires. Recalling the difference in brightness of the bulbs, did a difference in the length or thickness of the wire in the bulbs affect the current through them? How?

Figure 19-3

This diagram shows the parts and function of a simple electric circuit.

A A circuit that lights a bulb is a complete loop through which electric charges can move.

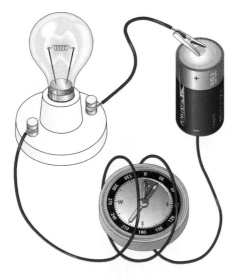

B When there is current through the bulb, it releases energy that you see and feel. Energy can't be created or destroyed; therefore, the bulb must be converting some form of energy into light and heat.

C You can detect current through a bulb by observing that it is lit. You also can detect a current and its direction with a compass.

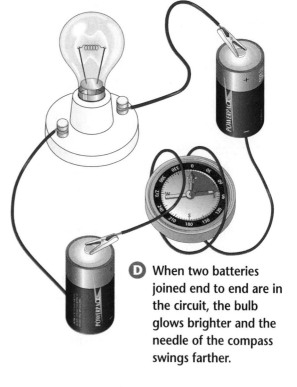

D When two batteries joined end to end are in the circuit, the bulb glows brighter and the needle of the compass swings farther.

■ The Current Connection

In the Investigation, you used a compass to make qualitative measurements of current. **Current** is a measure of the amount of charge per second that moves through any location along a circuit. You have just seen that you can make current flow in a circuit that lights a bulb with a battery. Other important properties of circuits are summarized in **Figure 19-3.**

In a closed circuit containing a battery, the current direction in the circuit is always from the positive terminal of the battery through the circuit to the negative terminal of the battery, and then through the battery itself. A current that has only one direction in a circuit is called a direct current, or DC.

A battery maintains a constant potential difference across its terminals. A flashlight battery, for example, always creates a 1.5-V potential difference across its two terminals. Charges leave the more positive terminal, move through the circuit, and return to the other terminal. They gain 1.5 V inside the battery and lose 1.5 V in the circuit. A battery is like a hot-water furnace that raises the temperature of the water a fixed amount, no matter what the temperature of the incoming water is.

An oscilloscope plot of the potential difference maintained by a 140 V battery during several seconds of use is shown in **Figure 19-4A.** The straight line indicates that the current in the circuit is DC.

■ AC and the Power Grid

Unlike battery circuits, the electrical energy used in our homes and schools is not produced directly from chemical energy, but from energy of motion. A device that converts mechanical energy to electrical energy is called a *generator.*

Rather than DC, most generators produce alternating current, or AC. The potential difference, or voltage, across a generator's terminals varies continuously. The voltage increases from zero as one terminal becomes more positive than the other. Then, the voltage decreases, passes through zero, and the terminal becomes more negative. Finally, the voltage returns to zero and the cycle repeats. In North America, the cycle repeats 60 times each second. One cycle per second is called a hertz (Hz); therefore, household electricity is called 60-Hz AC. A graph of the potential difference across the terminals of a 120-V AC generator or across the two slots of a home wall outlet is shown in **Figure 19-4B.** Because the potential difference is repeatedly changing from positive to negative and then back, the direction of the current through the circuit is constantly being reversed. Because charges can transfer electrical energy in whichever direction they move, AC can be used to operate most household appliances.

Do you recognize a circuit model in **Figure 19-1** on page 568 that you can use to visualize an AC circuit? Perhaps the best model is the compressed air drill. The top hose is at a higher pressure and air flows through it to the drill and back through the lower hose. Then the lower hose can be pressurized so that the air flows back through the drill.

Alternating current is used to distribute electrical energy because its potential can be increased or decreased efficiently by transformers. Alternating current can be carried long distances at tens or hundreds of thousands of volts with little energy loss. A transformer then reduces its potential difference for use in our homes. In most homes, 240-V AC is used to operate electric ranges, while wall outlets supply 120-V AC.

Now that you have investigated how a circuit carries electrical energy, next consider how electrical energy is used.

Figure 19-4

These oscilloscope plots show voltage changes over time.

Ⓐ The straight white line indicates the unchanging voltage of DC.

Ⓑ The white line shows the variation of the potential difference between the two slots in a wall outlet. Why do you think it is called 120 V, when the peak potential difference is actually 170 V?

Ⓒ These are the international symbols for AC and DC. Which is which?

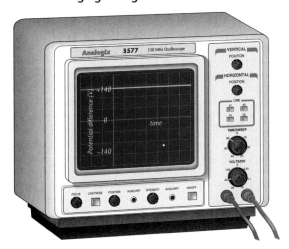

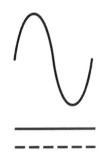

Electrical Energy and Power in Use

You've already made a list of the ways electrical energy is used in your home. It's now time to find out how much is used. Maybe someone has said to you, "It's too dark to read there; you'll ruin your eyes! Turn on the light." You may have turned a lamp with a three-way bulb up another notch. Or, you may have switched on one with a 75-W bulb and switched off another with a 40-W bulb. You probably know that the higher a bulb is rated in watts, the brighter the bulb is. A brighter light implies more energy. Based on that, what do you think a watt is?

■ Watts, Kilowatts, and Kilowatt-hours

Do you recall the difference between power and energy? Power is the rate at which energy is used, transferred, or converted. Suppose you drink a can of diet soda that has 2 Calories (8360 J) of energy. If you drink it in 10 seconds, then you are putting food energy into your body at a rate of 8360 J/10 s or 836 J/s. So, the power provided by drinking soda at that rate is 836 J/s. One joule per second is a watt (abbreviated W), so the power is 836 watts. The symbol used for power is P. **Figure 19-5** shows some additional energy equivalents. It can help you compare the energy used by everyday objects and activities.

Building More Than Houses

"**I** asked what I would be doing that first morning," Nutan Khosla remembers. "They said I would go up on top of the house and roof it. I almost turned around and went home. I was thinking 'There's no way I can do this!'" But the Habitat for Humanity worksite coordinator guided her through the steps, such as using chalk lines to keep the shingle rows straight. "It turned out to be a lot of fun. And the very next workday, someone asked for help with roofing. I volunteered because I knew how to do it!"

Nutan is in her third year at Case Western Reserve University in Cleveland, Ohio, but she started working with Habitat for Humanity while she was in high school in Port Clinton, Ohio.

What is Habitat for Humanity?

Habitat for Humanity is a nonprofit group that builds houses for low-income families. It began in 1976 in Americus, Georgia, and now builds homes in nations around the world. Habitat for Humanity has more than 300 campus

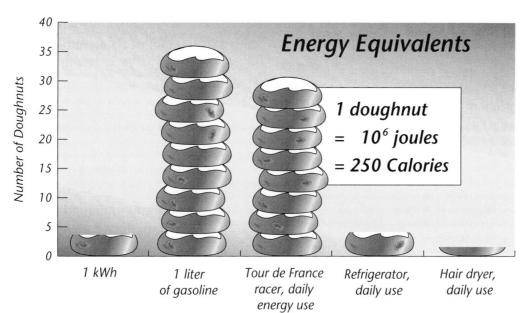

Figure 19-5

It's easier to understand new energy units when they are compared to familiar items.

Energy Equivalents

1 doughnut
= 10⁶ joules
= 250 Calories

Number of Doughnuts

1 kWh | 1 liter of gasoline | Tour de France racer, daily energy use | Refrigerator, daily use | Hair dryer, daily use

A This bar graph uses the Calories in jelly doughnuts to compare amounts of energy.

B Where do the appliances get their energy? The cyclist? Where does the energy go?

chapters and more than 1000 affiliates (nonstudent groups).

"At Habitat, you get to meet so many people," Nutan says. "Working on the houses requires a lot of cooperation. You need to be willing to give and accept responsibility, but it makes you feel good that you know how to do things."

Nutan remembers the first time she hammered a nail. "It took me about 15 minutes to get it in. When I look back, I laugh! But at Habitat, you learn the proper techniques."

As cochair of Habitat for Humanity's Outreach Committee at Case Western Reserve, Nutan helps organize two groups of about ten students for the Saturday work-

days. She takes the workers to the site, assigns jobs, answers questions, and keeps track of tools.

What's so good about Habitat for Humanity?

Nutan says other students often ask if Habitat for Humanity is worth their time and effort. "I tell them it's not just a charity where you give money and never know how the money is used. When you work on a house, you see progress right before your eyes. You tell yourself, 'Wow! I helped do this!'"

"I personally wish there was some kind of requirement for students to go on a workday somewhere at least twice

before they graduate," Nutan says. "It doesn't have to be a Habitat for Humanity work-day—just someplace where they can volunteer. People should volunteer whenever they can. Volunteering helps make you what you are."

*inter*NET
CONNECTION

Visit the Glencoe Homepage, **http://www.glencoe.com/**, for the Chapter 19 link to the Habitat for Humanity site on the World Wide Web. What other types of projects does the organization sponsor? Why do you think working on such projects is a learning experience for Nutan and other volunteers?

Figure 19-6

This illustration shows the relationship between joules and kilowatt-hours.

What if you drank the soda slowly over 1000 seconds (about 20 minutes) instead of gulping it? Then the power is only 8.36 watts. When a fixed amount of energy is transferred, the faster it is transferred, the greater the power.

Electrical energy is usually measured in the unit of a kilowatt-hour, as shown in **Figure 19-6**. A kilowatt is 1000 watts, so one **kilowatt-hour** is the electrical energy used by a device if energy is delivered to it at a rate of 1000 W for one hour.

You know from experience that the brighter the bulb, the greater its power. In the Investigation, you found that the brightness of a bulb was increased by using two batteries instead of one. This is because power used by a device depends on the potential difference across it. You also found that there was less current in the circuit with the dimmer, long bulb. That is because power also depends on current. The power used by a device is the product of the current through it and the potential difference across it:

$$\text{Power} = \text{Current} \times \text{Voltage}$$
$$P = IV$$

The quantity used to measure current is the **ampere,** abbreviated A, and often called *amp.* Now, find out how the energy is used in your home or school.

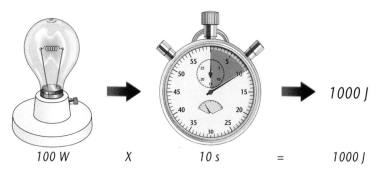

100 W   X   10 s   =   1000 J

A A 100-W bulb uses 1000 J in 10 s. For many purposes, joules are too small an energy unit to use.

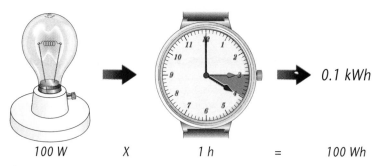

100 W   X   1 h   =   100 Wh

B A 100-W lightbulb lit for one hour uses (100 W)(1 hour) = 100 Wh or 1/10 kWh. An entire day's use would be 2.4 kWh.

MiniLab

Who's got the power?

Now that you know how to find out how much power is delivered to an appliance, it's time to apply this knowledge to your survey results.

Procedure

1. Make a table similar to the one below. It should include at least ten different appliances.

Data and Observations					
Appliance	Potential difference (V)	Current (A)	Power (W)	Time used per day (h)	Energy used per day (kWh)
Refrigerator	120		612		

2. Most appliances have a label that lists the voltage and power for which they are designed. A few may list the current. Find these labels on the appliances. **CAUTION:** *Be sure to unplug the appliance before you look for the label.* **NEVER** *remove any part of the case or covering.*

3. Estimate the amount of time the appliance is run each day. You will need to average values for seldom-used appliances.

4. Complete the table by filling in the potential difference and either current or power.

5. From the power and the estimated time it is used each day, find the energy used in kWh.

Analysis

1. Which appliance has the highest power rating?

2. Which appliance uses the most energy? Does it have the highest power?

Electric heating elements in ovens and hair dryers have large power ratings. However, they aren't usually on all the time. Appliances that run almost all the time such as refrigerators usually use more energy.

Knowing the energy use of tools and appliances is important. Because appliances are used for many years, investing in the most energy-efficient ones possible can save money.

You've constructed a simple circuit and you've seen how electrical energy is used in your home or school. In the next section, you'll explore more complicated circuits.

---

check your UNDERSTANDING

Understanding Concepts

1. What evidence did you find in the Investigation that current is not used up in the lamp?

2. What in the bowling-ball model in **Figure 19-1** on page 568 corresponds to current? To potential difference? Source of energy?

3. Which uses more energy: a 100-W lamp that is on for 10 hours per day or a 1000-W hair dryer used for 30 minutes a day?

Skill Review

4. Making and Using Graphs On the graph, when is the potential difference most positive? Most negative? Zero? What is the difference in time between successive times when it is most positive? For more help, refer to Making and Using Graphs in the *Skill Handbook.*

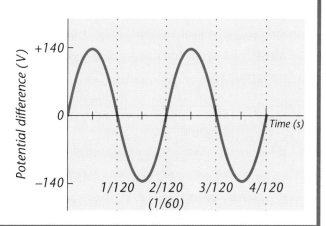

Issue:
Global Concern Over Acid Rain

Twenty years ago, scientists began observing a strange change in the ancient ruins of Mexico and Central America. The brightly colored murals that decorated the temples of the Mayan civilization were fading to white. Corrosive holes appeared in the walls of the temples and pyramids, as if something were eating away at the stone. These historic monuments, which had stood for more than a thousand years, were being destroyed by an unknown agent. What was causing the damage?

The Culprit

Through scientific investigations and hard work, the answer to the pyramid dilemma was solved. Toxic chemicals from oil refineries many kilometers away were drifting into the region and falling as acid rain. The problem was worsened by fumes from the numerous buses that transported tourists to the historic sites.

Sulfur and nitric oxides (sometimes called SO_x and NO_x) are two of the major components of acid rain. Coal-burning electric power plants are responsible for 60 to 70 percent of SO_x and NO_x released in the air. However, the burning of other fossil fuels, such as oil, also contributes to the problem.

When fossil fuels are burned, SO_x and NO_x rise into Earth's atmosphere. These substances react with sunlight and moisture and are carried by the wind for great distances. The resulting sulfuric acid and nitric acid particles fall as acid rain, snow, or fog.

As archaeologists were studying the destruction of the Mayan ruins, much research was being conducted elsewhere on the adverse effects of acid rain. Scientists knew that acid rain could kill fish, destroy trees, leach minerals from the soil, and damage buildings. For many years, though, they believed that acid rain was only a problem of the industrial countries of North America and Europe. The plight of the ancient Mayan ruins helped provide scientists with evidence that acid rain affected the world at large.

The Present

As more and more countries move toward industrialization, scientists are concerned that the acid rain problems experienced by Europe and North America will be repeated. East Asia, for instance, now produces more than a third of

Mayan temple in Central America

the world's SO_x. China in particular is undergoing rapid industrialization, and depends on coal-burning power plants to meet its energy needs. Given its growing rate of coal consumption, scientists estimate that by the year 2005, China could surpass the United States as the world's largest producer of air pollution.

Environmental problems have already surfaced throughout China, where approximately 40 percent of the country is thought to have been affected by acid rain. Japanese scientists believe that the problem has extended beyond China's borders. They say that the southern forests of Japan are being damaged by acid rain that drifts across the sea from China.

The Response

Scientists from around the world are combining their resources and expertise to ensure that acid rain problems are dealt with effectively. In Sweden, where the causes and effects of acid rain were first identified, researchers are attempting to map acid rain patterns on a global scale. They already know that portions of North America and Europe are vulnerable to acid rain. By examining soil types and vegetation, they hope to pinpoint areas that may have been ignored in previous studies. Already, portions of southern China, southeast Asia, equatorial Africa, and the Amazon Basin have been identified as being potentially susceptible to acid rain problems.

The Issue

Methods to reduce acid rain problems, such as installing scrubbers on the smokestacks of coal-burning power plants, have already been developed. However, the technology can be too expensive for many developing countries. These countries cannot stop their efforts to industrialize without causing great hardship to their

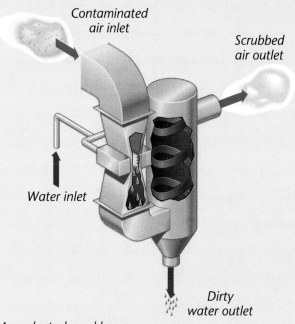

Contaminated air inlet

Scrubbed air outlet

Water inlet

Dirty water outlet

A smokestack scrubber

citizens. But their pollution is affecting other countries that have already taken steps to control acid rain output.

Who do you think should pay for the damage caused by acid rain—the countries that produce pollution, or the countries that are affected by the pollution? Or is some combination of cost-sharing the best and fairest way to tackle the problem?

Discussing the Issue

1. Research Japan's Green Aid Plan. What is Japan doing to help other countries reduce pollution problems?
2. On a map or globe, locate the areas recently identified by Swedish scientists as being susceptible to acid rain problems. What do these regions have in common? Why do you think it's important to reduce pollution in these areas?

19-2 Series and Parallel Circuits

Objectives

- Explain the function of resistance in an electrical circuit.
- Demonstrate that the currents in the paths of a parallel circuit are independent.

Key Terms

series circuit
resistance
parallel circuit

Series Circuits

Now that you can construct a circuit and light a lamp, what more do you need to know to wire a house? For example, how do you put a switch in the circuit? A circuit breaker or fuse? A dimmer? How do you connect two lamps so you can turn one off without affecting the other? Finally, how can you control one lamp from two or more different locations? After exploring these questions with batteries and bulbs, you'll get a chance to plan the electricity in a new home.

First, you will need to explore some basic circuits. In the Investigation on pages 570-571, when you put two batteries in the circuit, you put one after the other. The only path the current could follow was from one battery to the next and around the circuit. A circuit that has only one path through which charges can flow is called a **series circuit**. **Figure 19-7** shows an example of a series circuit. What are the properties of such a circuit?

Figure 19-7 is the circuit you investigated at the beginning of the chapter. As you discovered, the current was the same everywhere in the series circuit. That result agrees with what we know about charges: They can't be created or destroyed. So, if the current had changed, then some charges must have left or entered. There were no conductors that could allow them to do that.

You also saw that replacing the round bulb with the long one changed the current. Are there other ways to change current in a series circuit? Do the Minilab on the next page and find out.

Figure 19-7

In this flashlight, the current has only one path through the two batteries and the bulb. The circuit is called a *series circuit*.

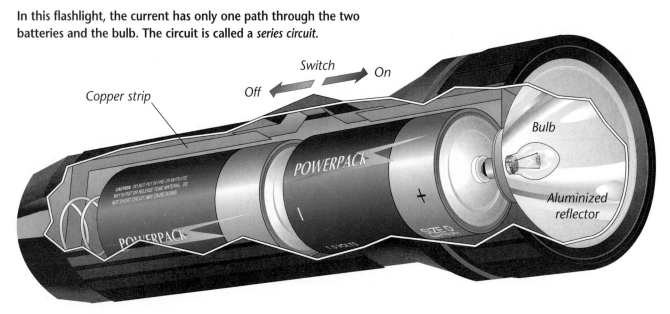

How do fuses work?

When some of the lights go out in an older home, excess current may cause a blown fuse. What physical properties make a fuse work?

Procedure

1. Pull a long, single strand from a pad of steel wool. **CAUTION:** *Steel wool is fine and strong enough to cut skin. Be careful while handling it.*

2. Using a piece of tape at each end of the strand, attach it lengthwise to a 3" × 5" card.

3. Attach one clip lead to the positive terminal of a battery and one clip lead to the negative terminal.

4. Gently attach a clip lead to one end of the steel wool strand.

5. Touch the second clip lead to the opposite end of the strand. Mark the clip's position with a pencil dot. **CAUTION:** *Don't touch the strand with your fingers. It may become hot enough to burn you.*

6. Move the clip forward a few millimeters. Mark its position again.

7. Repeat step 6 until there is an observable change in the strand. Record what you observe *in your Journal.*

8. Measure and record the distance between the last pencil dot and the stationary clip lead.

Analysis

1. What happened to the strand as you moved the clip lead closer to the stationary clip lead?

2. What would happen if the strand were part of a working circuit?

Figure 19-8

This photo shows a view from a theater light booth down onto the stage. Theater lighting uses different colors and intensities of light to set scenes and evoke moods. The switches and controls dim and brighten banks of large stage lights at a touch. What mechanism makes the lights dim?

■ Controlling the Current— Switches, Dimmers, Fuses

In the MiniLab activity, when too much current passed through the wire, it melted and broke the circuit. Any lamps that were part of the circuit would have gone out. This is how fuses protect other parts of a circuit from excess current. Without this sort of protection, excess current could damage appliances and start wiring fires.

Breaking a circuit is a drastic way of controlling brightness by changing current. Adding and removing batteries is a time-consuming method. Is there another way to dim or brighten a lamp? **Figure 19-8** shows there must be some practical way to accomplish this. Do the Investigation activity on the following pages to discover the solution.

Current Changes

In the MiniLab, the thin steel wire conducted current differently depending on its length. How does changing the wire affect the brightness of bulbs?

Preparation

Problem
How do the length and thickness of Nichrome wire change the current in a circuit?

Hypothesis
In your group, brainstorm possible hypotheses and discuss the evidence on which each is based. Select the best hypothesis from your list.

Objectives
In this Investigation, you will:
- *Observe* how the current in a series circuit depends on the thickness and length of Nichrome wire in that circuit.

Possible Materials
2-battery holder
D-cells (2)
round bulb and socket
clip leads
compass
thin Nichrome wire
thick Nichrome wire

Safety Precautions

Resistors can become very hot. Use care when manipulating sharp wire ends.

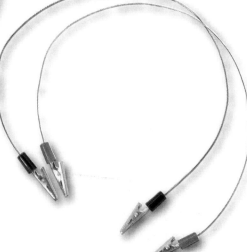

Plan the Experiment

1 Set up the circuit shown on page 571 using two D-cells and a round bulb. Put the compass in place to measure the current. Make sure the bulb lights and the compass needle deflects. Disconnect one of the clip leads.

2 Find the thicker of the two pieces of Nichrome wire.

3 Construct a data table to record wire thickness and length, compass deflection, and bulb brightness.

Check the Plan

Discuss the following points with other group members to decide the final procedure for your experiment.

1 Determine how you will put the Nichrome wire in series with the bulb so that you can see the effects of varying its length. Don't connect the clip lead to the battery until the plan is checked. **CAUTION:** *Nichrome wire can get hot.*

2 Plan an experiment to find out if it matters whether the current goes through the bulb or Nichrome wire first.

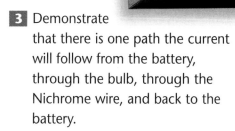

3 Demonstrate that there is one path the current will follow from the battery, through the bulb, through the Nichrome wire, and back to the battery.

4 *Make sure your teacher has approved your experimental plan before you proceed further.*

5 Carry out your experiment.

Analyze and Conclude

1. **Observing** Did the Nichrome wire get hot? Which wire got hotter: the thick or thin? Long or short lengths?

2. **Recognizing Cause and Effect** If a friend in another class were to ask whether the Nichrome wire should go before or after the bulb, what would you say, and what evidence would you give to support your statement?

3. **Interpreting Data** Which thickness of Nichrome wire reduces the current more?

4. **Predicting** If you were to design a dimmer that could change the bulb brightness from full to not visible, what length and thickness of wire would you use?

Going Further

Changing Variables
Replace the Nichrome wire with a second bulb— either the round or long bulb. Try first one, then the other, and decide which one acts like the thin wire and which like the thicker one. Is your conclusion in agreement with the inspection of the wire in the bulbs you made in the last Investigation?

■ Electrical Resistance

Did you notice in the Investigation that the Nichrome wire controlled the amount of current in the circuit? It did so because it somehow opposed the flow of charges.

Resistance is the property of a conductor that causes electrical energy to be converted to thermal energy as current passes through it. Some conductors such as clip leads have almost no resistance. However, both the bulb and the Nichrome wire you used have much greater resistances. They both became warm when they were placed in the circuit. You can think of resistance as the charges experiencing friction as they pass through Nichrome wire and a bulb. As a result, some of the energy they carry is converted into thermal energy.

The resistance of wire depends on several things. A wire's resistance increases with length. So the longer of two similar wires will have a greater resistance. The resistance of wire also increases as its diameter decreases.

Therefore, the thicker of two wires of equal length will have less resistance.

An increase in the resistance in a series circuit decreases current in the circuit. That was obvious when you observed the deflection of the compass needle and the brightness of the bulb as you increased or decreased the length of the Nichrome wire in the circuit.

In your home, you have switches that turn lights and appliances off and on. In the Investigations, you haven't used a switch, but you were able to turn the bulb off and on just by touching a clip lead to another conductor. As you can see in **Figure 19-9,** a switch is just a safe and more convenient way of opening and closing a circuit.

When a switch is on, or closed, it is just like a clip lead. It has almost no resistance. When it is off, or open, no current passes. You could say that an open switch has an infinite resistance. It is like a dimmer that uses an infinitely long wire. The resistance is so large that no current passes at all.

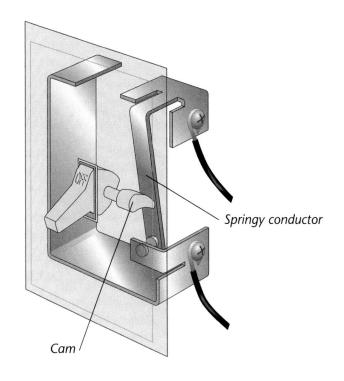

Figure 19-9

When the lever arm on this switch is moved up, the cam allows the springy conductor to move down, touching the contact and closing the circuit. Current passes through the switch. When the switch is open, no current flows because air is a nonconductor at usual household voltages.

Springy conductor

Cam

Parallel Circuits and Their Uses in the Home

What would happen if lights in your home were wired in series circuits? First, as you added more lights, the current through them would go down. The lights would become dimmer and dimmer. Second, if you unscrewed one lamp, or if the wire filament in it broke, no current could go through it. Because in a series circuit there is only one path for current, there would be no current anywhere in the circuit and all the other lights would go out, too.

There is a circuit that solves these problems. A **parallel circuit** provides multiple paths for the current, and each path uses current independently. You can learn more about parallel circuits in the following MiniLab.

To Find Out More About ...

Home wiring see Designing Electrical Circuits on page 588.

MiniLab

How can two lamps be lit independently?

You'll now explore the parallel circuit. You should have two D-cells in their holder, two lamp sockets, two round and two long lamps, a compass, and about six clip leads.

Procedure

1. Assemble the single-bulb circuit, using two clip leads between the battery and lamp and placing the compass as shown.

2. Watch both the brightness of the bulb and the compass as you add a second round bulb.

3. Unscrew the first bulb from its socket. What happens to the compass and the second bulb?

4. Replace the first bulb with a long bulb. Record the results.

5. Which clip leads carry only the current through a single bulb? Put the compass under those leads to find the currents through each of the two bulbs. Try unscrewing the bulbs, one at a time, while you watch the compass. Does turning off the current through one bulb affect the current through the other?

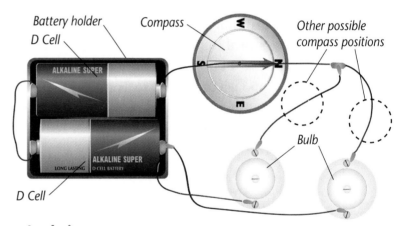

Battery holder
D Cell
Compass
Other possible compass positions
Bulb
D Cell

Analysis

1. In steps 1-4, the compass shows the current supplied by the batteries. From your experiments, report whether or not a battery always supplies the same current. Give an example from your data to support your answer.

2. If two bulbs are in parallel and you change the current through one, does the current through the other change? What observations support your statement?

From the MiniLab, you can conclude that the currents in a parallel circuit are independent and they add. Suppose you turn on a 60-W lamp in one 120-V circuit in your home. There will be a current of 0.5 ampere in the circuit. If you plug a 1200-W hair dryer into another circuit, there will be a current of 10 A in that circuit. The current in the first lamp won't change. The two circuits require a total current of 10.5 amperes in your home's circuit.

Suppose your sister plugs in a second hair dryer. It also needs 10 A, so the total current into the home would be 10 A + 10 A + 0.5 A, or 20.5 A.

■ Uses of Circuit Breakers

If both hair dryers were plugged into the same bathroom outlet there could be a problem. All conductors have some resistance. With a 20-A current through them, the wires going to the bathroom could become hot enough to start a fire. For this reason, a fuse or circuit breaker is put in series with wires leading to a number of outlets.

A circuit breaker uses a strip made of two metals. When an unsafe current heats the strip, it bends and opens the circuit. A spring holds the breaker open until it is reset.

Most household circuits are protected by a 15-A circuit breaker. When the current through the breaker is more than 15 amps, the breaker trips. A breaker can only be reset after unplugging the appliance that caused it to trip. One 10-A hair dryer in a circuit won't trip a 15-A breaker, but two will.

Throughout your home, you often run appliances whose currents total 15 amps or more. Why don't they trip a breaker? The wires bringing electricity into the home are thicker and have lower resistance than those in the walls. Therefore, they can safely carry more current—usually 100 or 200 A.

Special-purpose Circuits

Can any lights in your home or school be turned on and off from two different places? You can't tell by looking at the switch whether the light is on or off. You just know that if you flip the switch and the light was off, it'll go on; if it was on, it'll go off. How does this happen? You can find out by doing the Thinking Lab using a double-throw, or three-way, switch like the one shown in **Figure 19-10.**

You've now covered the basics of electrical circuits, so it is finally time to put these ideas to work in a home or school.

Figure 19-10

With the lever arm as shown, contacts 1 and 3 are connected. When the lever arm is moved up, contacts 1 and 2 are connected.

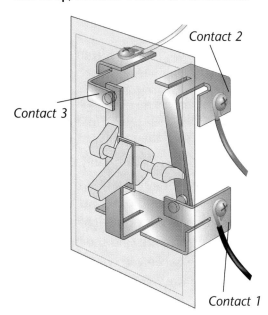

Contact 2

Contact 3

Contact 1

How can you control one light from two switches?

Lights in staircases often are in circuits in which they can be turned on and off by two three-way switches—one at the bottom of the stairs and one at the top. Can you design a circuit that models this type of house circuit?

Analysis
Sketch your circuit first on paper, using this drawing as a start. You can add as many clip leads as you need.

Thinking Critically
Without constructing a circuit using batteries, bulbs, and switches, how could you demonstrate that your plan will work?

Silently moving through the circuitry of your home, electricity is transporting energy to the appliances and devices you use every day.

As you discovered in the Science and Society feature on pages 578 and 579, the ways electricity is generated can affect regional economies and the global environment. Even though electricity seems commonplace, the actions you take in your home when you flip on a switch may, when joined by the choices of thousands of others, have an effect in and beyond your community.

check your UNDERSTANDING

Understanding Concepts
1. When a round bulb and a long bulb are connected in parallel across two D-cells, the current through the round bulb is larger. Which bulb has a higher resistance? Explain.
2. You have one dimmer, one switch, and two bulbs. You want the dimmer to control one bulb. You want the switch to control the other. What series and parallel circuits would you use? Sketch your circuit.
3. A circuit with two identical bulbs in parallel has equal currents through each bulb. If one bulb is removed, does the current through that bulb now go through the remaining bulb, making it twice as bright? Explain.

Skill Review
4. **Observing and Inferring** Jack, who lives in Maine, told his cousin Bob, who lives in Florida, that the electrical wires running through his neighborhood were thicker than those inside the house because they had to hold ice and snow without breaking. Bob said that the wires in his neighborhood were also thicker, but they never had ice problems. Can you suggest another reason they might be so thick? For more help, refer to Observing and Inferring in the *Skill Handbook*.

Designing Electrical Circuits

Have you ever been frustrated by the location of electric outlets and lights in your home or school? Here's your chance to design the wiring for a room the way you want it.

You're the Electrical Engineer

Your task is to make a plan for wiring a kitchen or other room of your home or school. You will need to show the position of outlets to service the necessary appliances and lights, and connect them to appropriate circuit breakers.

Drawing on Experience

① Draw a floor plan of the room you are going to wire. It can be an existing room or one you create.

② Make a list of all of the appliances that will be in the room and indicate their approximate locations. Decide how many outlets you will need and their locations.

③ Identify where you will want ceiling lights and fans. Indicate on the plan where switches should go.

④ Label each outlet, light, and fan with a letter.

Testing...Testing

① Make a table of all of the appliances like the one shown below.

② Find the power and current for each appliance, rounding up to the nearest ampere.

③ Arrange the outlets, ceiling lights, and fans into circuits. Group nearby outlets and ceiling features together so they can be wired to the same 15-A circuit breaker. Don't overload any of the circuits. You should leave excess capacity.

④ Electric ranges, water heaters, and clothes dryers use 240 V instead of 120 V. Each should have its own circuit breaker.

⑤ Number the circuit breakers and draw the circuit box. Draw the wires from each circuit to the item they service.

How Did It Work?

① Present your design to the rest of the class. Discuss the convenience features you added.

② After discussing the design, what changes would you make?

Label	Appliance	Power (W)	Current (A)	Circuit number
A	Lamp	100	1	

ead the statements below
that review major points
presented in the chapter. Using
the concepts that you have
learned, answer each question
in your Journal.

1 Alternating cur-
rent (AC) is con-
stantly changing
direction. *What
is the advantage
of AC over DC?*

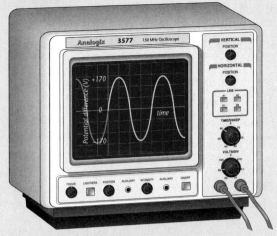

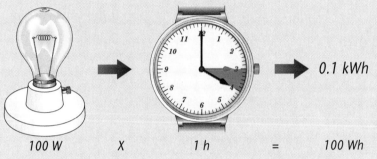

100 W   X   1 h   =   100 Wh

0.1 kWh

2 Appliances are rated by the power they dissipate, measured in watts. The energy they
use is equal to their power multiplied by
the time they are used. *How many times as
long would a 5-W appliance have to be
turned on in order to use as much energy
as a 20-W appliance?*

3 In a series circuit, the current is the same in all circuit components. In a
parallel circuit, the currents add. *Are the electrical outlets in your home on
parallel or series circuits?*

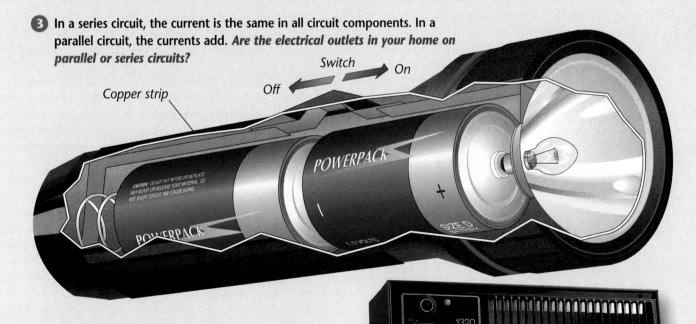

4 Fuses and circuit breakers are designed
to protect circuits from excess current.
*How many 100-W appliances could
safely use the same 20-A circuit?*

Using Key Science Terms

ampere   potential difference
current   resistance
kilowatt-hour   series circuit
parallel circuit volt

Answer the following questions using what you know about the science terms.

1. Distinguish between a series and a parallel circuit.
2. Which of the terms above is a unit that measures energy?
3. A battery produces a constant _____.
4. When Nichrome wire is put in series with a lamp, the lamp gets dimmer because of the wire's _____.
5. The number of charges per second that pass a point is proportional to the _____.

Understanding Ideas

Using complete sentences, answer the following questions in your Journal.

1. What is needed to have a complete circuit?
2. What is a source of energy in an electric circuit?
3. If you want to control the brightness of a bulb with a dimmer, should you put the dimmer before the bulb, after the bulb, or in either place? Explain.
4. In some holiday light strings, if one bulb burns out, all bulbs go out. Are these wired in series or parallel, or can't you tell?
5. The 15-A breaker for your bathroom is always tripping because you and your sister use hair dryers at the same time. Should you replace it with a 30-A breaker? Explain.
6. A vacuum cleaner is advertised as having a 10.5-A motor. What is its power in watts?
7. A large flashlight has three 1.5-V D-cells connected in series. What is the potential difference across the series of cells?
8. Three hundred amps pass through a car's starter motor when it is connected to the 12-V battery. What power does it develop?

Developing Skills

Use your understanding of the concepts developed in this chapter to answer each of the following questions.

1. **Concept Mapping** Complete a concept map of electric energy in circuits.
2. **Predicting** If you replace a 40-W lamp with a 60-W lamp, does the current decrease, increase, or remain the same?
3. **Predicting** An ordinary lamp rated at 60 W and a compact fluorescent lamp rated at 13 W produce the same amount of light. Which uses more current? More energy? Explain.

4. Recognizing Cause and Effect A bulb has 0.5-A current through it when put into one flashlight, but only 0.3 A when put into another. Which flashlight has more batteries connected in series?

Critical Thinking

In your Journal, *answer each of the following questions.*

1. The electric bill shows that your house has used 534 kWh during the past 31 days. Find the average power used in kilowatts and watts, and the average current assuming that the house uses 240 V.

2. Soda straws can model electrical resistance. Cut narrow and wide ones to the same length and blow through them. What does the amount of air coming through represent? The pressure you feel in your cheeks? Which straw has a higher resistance?

Problem Solving

Read the following problem and discuss your answers in a brief paragraph.

Pat, Chris, and Robin were asked to predict what would happen to the current in a circuit containing a battery and a bulb. Pat said that the current is used up in the bulb, so none would come out. Chris said that some of the current was converted into light and heat, but what was left over would come out. Robin said that there would be the same current everywhere in the circuit.

Based on the results of your Investigation, write a comment to each of the three students, explaining what happens, why, and what does make the light we see.

CONNECTING IDEAS

1. **Theme—Models** Refer to the bowling-ball circuit model on page 568. The lifter must put a ball on the upper track as soon as there is room. If the model is changed to represent a parallel circuit with two bulbs, would the lifter expend more energy? Explain.

2. **Theme—Scale and Structure** Electrical power can vary over a large range. A hearing aid might use 2 mW, a lamp 25 W, a stove 8 kW. A typical power plant produces 1000 MW. How many stoves can one power plant run? How many 25-W lamps?

3. **Theme—Energy** Some people prefer to think of electricity as an *energy carrier* because it can never be used directly— only converted. Give three examples supporting that viewpoint.

4. **Science and Society** What was causing damage to the Mayan temples?

5. **Eyewitness Accounts** What wiring and building skills do you think you might learn as a Habitat for Humanity volunteer?

6. **Applying Technology** What other details might an electrician need to use the circuit plan you created and drew?

FLUSHING AWAY A PROBLEM?

Problem

Is water a problem in your area? In many parts of the United States, obtaining clean, safe water is becoming a problem—one that is likely to become more serious in the future. In the average home, two-thirds of the water is used by the shower and toilet. Other water usage stems from watering gardens and lawns, and washing dishes and clothes. Only low-flow showerheads and low-consumption toilets can be used in new homes, according to the National Energy Policy and Conservation Act of 1992. Could your home save money by replacing showerheads and toilets?

Getting Started

1. Find the cost for water and sewerage in your area.
2. Keep track of the number of times the toilets are flushed and the total time the showers are turned on in one week.
3. Holding a bucket under a showerhead, measure the time taken for one gallon of water to be collected. To find the number of gallons used by showerers in one week, divide the number of minutes the shower is on by the number of minutes needed to collect one gallon of water.
4. With the help of your parent or guardian, turn off the water to a toilet and remove the tank lid. Flush twice to empty the tank. Now, use a bucket to measure the amount of water needed to fill the tank. Because some water is needed to fill the bowl, the actual amount used is somewhat more than your measurement. Calculate the number of gallons used by toilets in the house in one week.
5. New showerheads use only 2.5 gallons/minute, and new toilets use 1.6 gallons per flush. How much less water would have been used if your home had met these standards? How much money could have been saved?
6. Find the price of water-saving toilets and showerheads. If the cost of water doesn't rise, in how many years would the money saved from using less water pay for the new devices?

Resources

"Water-saving showerheads" and "Water-saving toilets," <u>Consumer Reports</u>, Volume 60, No. 2, February, 1995, pp. 118-124.

HOW WELL ARE YOU SUPPORTED?

Problem

Does the floor in your home sag or bounce when you walk across it? What supports a floor? The wooden beams under a floor are called *joists*. But wood is becoming expensive, and home builders are replacing solid wood joists with wooden "I"-shaped beams. In this project, make and test models of floors to compare the old and new kinds of joists.

Materials

cardboard

2 books for support

balsa wood strips

modeling knife

ruler

glue for wood models

three 1/2-lb weights

coat hanger

Getting Started

1. Build a scale model of part of a floor supported by two joists. First decide on the scale. In the model, 1/8" equals 1" is one suggestion. Typical solid joists are 1.5" wide; 5.5", 7.5", or 9.5" deep; and 12' to 14' long. Purchase two strips of wood to represent these joists. Weigh each joist.

2. An "I" beam is made of three pieces of 3/4"-thick wood glued together into a beam the same size as a solid joist. Purchase the wood and glue it together to make two scale "I" beams. Weigh each "I" beam.

3. Floor joists are spaced 16" apart. Glue your model joists to cardboard the correct distance apart. Support ends of the joists on the edges of books. Gently push down on the center. If the joists twist, use toothpicks to make X-shaped braces between the two joists.

4. Design a method to measure the sag of the model when weights are put in the center. You could tape one end of a straightened clothes hanger to the "floor." Motion of the free end will be much larger than that of the floor. Does deflection depend on the spacing of the joists?

5. Compare the deflections of the models when you put weights on them.

6. Summarize your results. How does the sag depend on weight? On length of floor? On type of joist? What are the advantages and disadvantages of the new kind of joist?

Resources

Timber Frame Houses, New York: Taunton Books, 1992, pp. 26-30.

CARPENTER'S
WOOD GLUE

FOR
DARKER
WOOD

SAFE! NO HARMFUL FUMES*

Disease

Jeninne is feverish. Kwon has been feeling tired for days. Isaac notices that his knuckles are larger than normal. Each of these people is experiencing a symptom of a disease. In this unit, discover different types of diseases and their causes. Find out that the body is not defenseless in its battle to maintain or regain health. Learn how diseases are identified and what you can do to maintain health.

× 1700

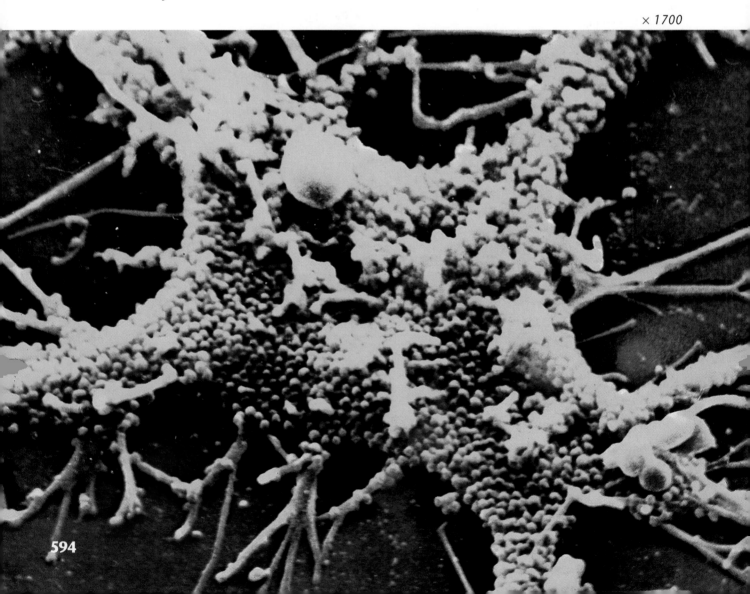

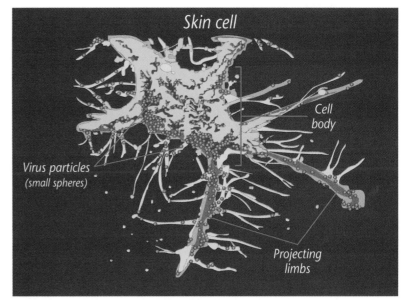

Cell attacked by viruses

Oral cold sores are caused by Herpes Simplex Type 1 virus particles covering the surface of a cell.

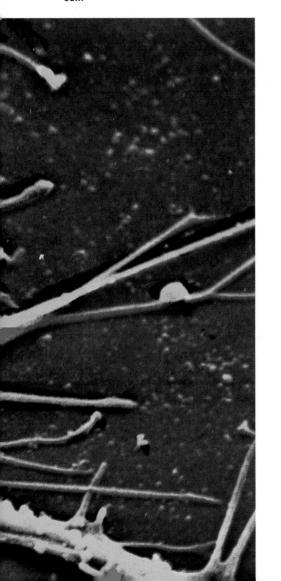

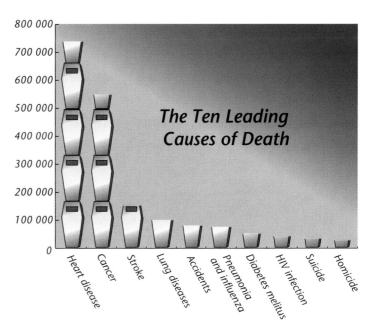

The Ten Leading Causes of Death

Source: National Center for Health Statistics, U.S. Department of Health and Human Services, 1993

Diseases make up six of the ten most common causes of death in the United States. The threat of these diseases may often be lessened through lifestyle choices.

Focus On

Human Body Defenses

Getting a cold? Cut your finger? Maybe you are waiting for the results of a test that tells you whether or not you have a life-threatening condition. Before you became aware of the symptoms associated with any of these conditions, your body had started to work to combat them. You'll find out more in this unit about what your body's defenses are.

Your body has many physical barriers against the invasion of unwanted organisms, such as disease-causing bacteria. Before causing damage inside your body, these organisms must get past your first line of defense: skin, saliva, and mucus.

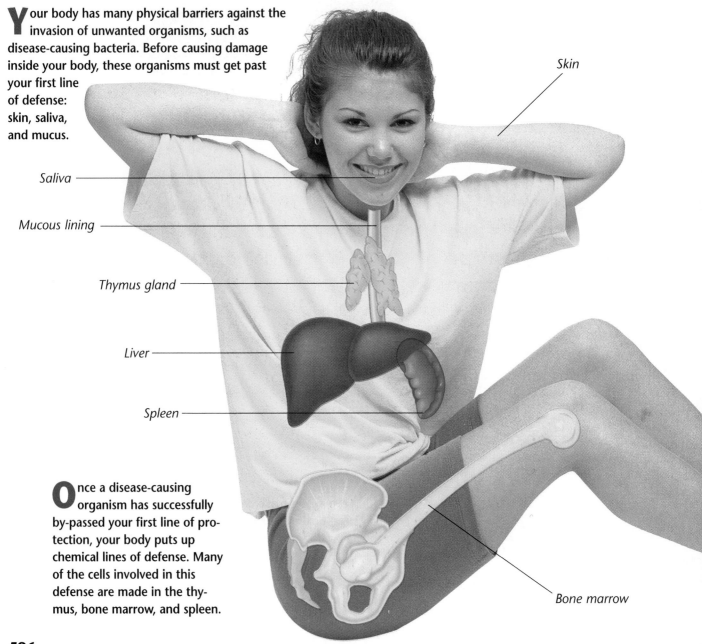

Skin

Saliva

Mucous lining

Thymus gland

Liver

Spleen

Bone marrow

Once a disease-causing organism has successfully by-passed your first line of protection, your body puts up chemical lines of defense. Many of the cells involved in this defense are made in the thymus, bone marrow, and spleen.

Vaccination is an important part of keeping the body prepared for disease. It is generally thought that most people understand the value of vaccination and that they have had all their shots. Find out whether this is true.

What To Do

1. Survey 50 students in your school to find out if they know what a vaccination is.

2. Ask students to list what they think they have been vaccinated against.

3. Construct a graph showing the numbers of students in the sample who think they have been vaccinated against smallpox, chicken pox, diphtheria, whooping cough, and polio.

Try It Again

After your class has learned more about disease and the way in which the body is defended against it, try this activity again to see whether your schoolmates' awareness has improved.

Organs within your body, such as the liver and spleen, maintain your body's health by removing toxins and dead cells from the body.

UNIT 6 PROJECTS

During your exploration of disease, you may discover new questions or wish to explore related topics. **Tracking Disease Trends** and **Analysis of Disease Articles**, found in the Unit 6 Projects section on pages 694-695, will give you the challenge of becoming more aware of what your body faces each day. Read through these projects now. By the time you finish this unit, you'll know all you need to know to successfully complete these projects.

Types of Disease
Getting Sick

D*iseases that affect humans range from the minor inconvenience of a head cold to life-threatening ailments such as cystic fibrosis or AIDS. What causes disease? The common cold results from a viral infection that is easily spread from one person to another. But viruses don't cause malaria or tuberculosis. What causes those diseases, and how are they spread? Why do cancer and heart disease occur? In this chapter, you'll investigate the causes of disease and begin exploring the reasons why some people contract an illness when others don't.*

▶ *In the following activity, compare how healthy and not-so-healthy yeast organisms respond to changes in their environment.*

MiniLab

How can internal balance be maintained?

Your body is made up of trillions of cells, which all have to maintain stable internal environments. How do healthy yeast cells maintain a balanced internal environment?

Procedure

1. Label one microscope slide A and the other slide B. Using the dropper provided, make a wet mount of a healthy yeast *culture A* on slide A. Place a small drop of congo red dye to one side of the drop of yeast culture.

2. Repeat step 1 using the unhealthy yeast *culture B* on slide B.

3. Using a microscope, observe each slide, first under low power, then high power. Draw and label your observations *in your Journal*.

Analysis

1. Describe the different ways the two yeast cultures responded to the presence of the dye.

2. Name one way healthy cells can help maintain a balanced internal environment. Explain.

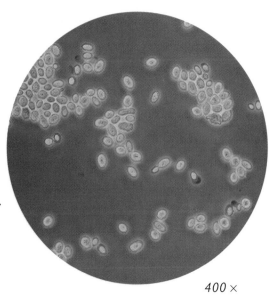

400 ×

Yeast

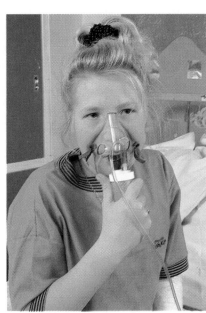

20-1 Health and Disease

Objectives
- Relate the concept of homeostasis to the causes of disease.
- Review the functions of major organs and systems of the human body.

Key Terms
homeostasis
disease

Homeostasis

A healthy yeast cell is capable of maintaining an internal balance of water, nutrients, and other substances inside the cell. In the same way, a healthy human body maintains a balanced, stable internal environment in spite of changes in its surroundings.

How does maintaining internal stability affect your health? Even with your best efforts, you sometimes become ill. Illness occurs when the body's systems become unbalanced and are unable to function properly.

A cell maintains a stable internal environment by controlling the substances that enter and leave it. Similarly, as shown in **Figure 20-1,** a healthy human body remains at a stable temperature of about 98.6°F (37°C) even when activity and room temperatures change. The ability of living organisms to maintain a stable internal environment despite changes in their surroundings is called **homeostasis.** In the human body, there are certain organ systems whose main job is to maintain homeostasis.

Figure 20-1

The human body has temperature-regulating mechanisms that keep our internal temperature nearly constant.

Ⓐ Intense exercise causes increased metabolism that adds much heat to your body, but it is normally released through evaporation almost as fast as it is added.

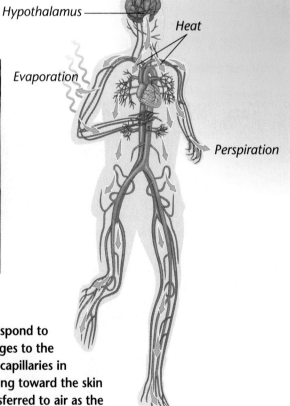

Hypothalamus

Heat

Evaporation

Perspiration

Ⓑ Heat-sensitive nerve cells of the hypothalamus respond to the blood becoming too warm. They send messages to the rest of the body to increase the flow of blood to capillaries in the skin and to increase perspiration. Blood moving toward the skin carries excess body heat with it. This heat is transferred to air as the water in perspiration evaporates from the skin over the entire body.

The hypothalamus responds to the body becoming cold by increasing body heat. One of the first ways the body responds to low temperatures is shivering. Shivering is work done by muscles and it can raise heat production considerably. As the body metabolizes food to shiver, energy of movement transforms into heat energy. Small blood vessels in feet, hands, arms, and legs also contract, thus reducing heat loss through the skin.

If blood becomes too cold, the hypothalamus begins a process that speeds up the body's metabolism. Metabolic processes release heat, so an increase in metabolism increases the body's temperature. This is essential because when the temperature of the human body falls below 90°F (32°C), the brain cannot function properly and unconsciousness results. Below 80°F (27°C), the heart begins to beat abnormally and death may result.

■ **Body Systems Help**

As shown in **Table 20-1,** the organs of the body work together in systems that have specific functions, many of which are involved in maintaining homeostasis. In the Investigation on the next page, you'll uncover some clues about how your body's internal temperature responds to changes in your activity level as well as to changes in its external conditions.

Connect to...

Chemistry

In Chapter 4, you learned that pH is an important factor in any environment. Our internal environments must also be kept at a stable pH, between 7.2 and 7.6, to maintain homeostasis. Find out which organs are responsible for maintaining this constant pH.

Table 20-1

Maintaining Homeostasis		
System	Major Components	Function
Circulatory system	heart, blood vessels	As blood circulates through the body, it helps cells and tissues maintain a balance of oxygen, water, and nutrients. It delivers needed substances and removes wastes.
Digestive system	mouth, esophagus, stomach, intestines, liver	Breaks down food substances into building blocks and energy-rich molecules used to maintain the body. The liver stores and releases these molecules as needed.
Respiratory system	nasal passages, lungs, trachea	Lungs enable the body to deliver oxygen and remove carbon dioxide via the circulatory system.
Urinary system	kidneys, bladder	The kidneys remove wastes from the blood and help maintain the proper balance of water and salts in the body.
Nervous system	brain, spinal cord, nerves, sense organs	Brain regulates most body activities, receives and responds to nerve information, and causes muscle movement.
Muscular system	muscles	Muscles allow the body to move, move materials throughout the body, and produce body heat.

What's Your Temperature?

The metabolic activities that give life to your body—digestion, respiration, circulation, muscle movement, and so on—release energy in the form of heat. What is the temperature of your body? Does your temperature change when your level of activity increases or decreases? Does your temperature change when the temperature of your environment changes?

Preparation

Problem

Determine how environmental temperature and activity levels affect your body temperature.

Hypothesis

In your group, brainstorm possible hypotheses and discuss the evidence on which each hypothesis is based. Select the best hypothesis from your list.

Objectives

In this Investigation, you will:
- *Observe* how body temperature responds to change in activity level or changes in external temperature.

Possible Materials

thermometer suitable for measuring body temperature (with disposable covers)

thermometer suitable for measuring air temperature

jump rope

Safety Precautions

Students with medical conditions may not be able to exercise. Handle thermometers carefully. Report breakage immediately.

DESIGN YOUR OWN
INVESTIGATION

Plan the Experiment

1 Examine the materials provided by your teacher. As a group, make a list of the possible ways you might test your hypothesis.

2 Agree on one way that your group could investigate your hypothesis. Design a series of experiments that will allow for the collection of quantitative data.

3 Prepare a list of numbered directions. Design and construct a table for recording your data.

Check the Plan
Discuss the following points with other group members to decide the final procedure for your experiment.

1 What is your independent variable?

2 What control will be used?

3 What data will you collect?

4 *Make sure your teacher has approved your experimental plan before you proceed further.*

5 Carry out your experiment. Make any needed observations and complete your data table.

Analyze and Conclude

1. **Checking Your Hypothesis** Was your hypothesis supported by your data? Use specific experimental data to explain why or why not.

2. **Interpreting Observations** Did different students have different body temperatures under the same conditions? Did body temperatures vary with changing conditions? If so, by how much? Did activity level influence body temperature? Did the temperature of the surroundings influence body temperature?

3. **Analyzing Data** Use the data collected during your experiment to calculate your average body temperature. Compare it with the average body temperature of all other students in your class. What is the normal temperature range for you and your classmates?

4. **Thinking Critically** Explain why body temperature is used by physicians in evaluating a person's health.

Going Further

Project
Find the normal body temperature range of other warm-blooded species, such as mice, bats, birds, elephants, or cats. How do these body temperatures compare with your body temperature?

Disease Disturbs Homeostasis

As you saw in the Investigation, your body maintains homeostasis even when the surroundings change. You contract a cold as a result of cold viruses invading the cells lining your nasal passages. These cells respond by becoming inflamed and swollen. Fluid leaks from them, your eyes water, and you begin to sniffle and sneeze. These responses are attempts by your body to maintain homeostasis while getting rid of the invaders. A **disease** is a change in the body that disrupts homeostasis and impairs one or more of the body's essential functions. The common cold is a disease, but not a serious one. Other diseases such as diabetes are of greater concern.

One type of diabetes, *diabetes mellitus,* illustrated in **Figure 20-2,** affects the level of sugar in the blood of about four percent of all people in the United States. This form of diabetes upsets the homeostasis of several body systems. Normally, carbohydrates broken down by the digestive system are converted into glucose, a type of sugar used to fuel cellular processes. The pancreas, a small organ beneath the stomach, produces the hormone insulin. Insulin assists in moving glucose from the blood into cells, where it can be used to provide energy and stores glucose to be used later. When this process is disrupted by diabetes, victims must compensate with the medications or dietary modifications shown in **Figure 20-3.**

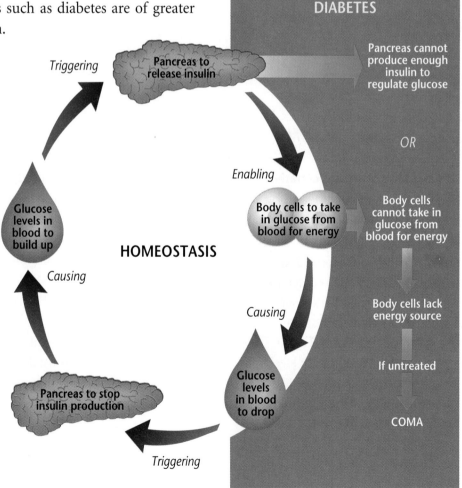

Figure 20-2

Diabetes mellitus is a disease that affects the level of sugar in the blood, which in turn affects the digestive, urinary, and circulatory systems. Excess sugar in the blood draws water from body cells. This sugar and water greatly increase urine production. The result is dehydration and excessive thirst. In the absence of sugar, most body cells can burn fat as an energy source. Use of such fat causes an acid waste that is harmful in large amounts and may lead to coma.

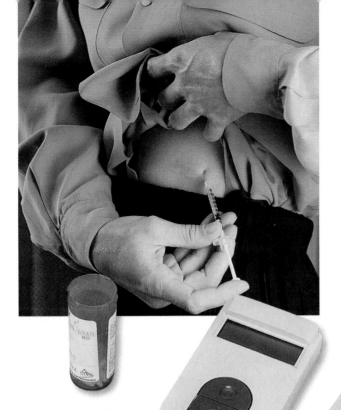

Figure 20-3

Some diabetics can take pills that stimulate the pancreas to produce more insulin. Others must take regular injections of insulin. All diabetics must carefully match their diet to their energy needs and insulin availability, as instructed by their physician.

Glucose meter for monitoring blood

Islet for taking blood samples

Your body is like a finely tuned machine, with many systems working together to make it run well. Each system has a specific function that is determined by the organs in the system, the type of tissues that make up the organs, and the unique type of cells that make up the tissues. Disease can alter the ability of cells, tissues, or organs to function properly. When this happens, the balance—or homeostasis—of the systems working together is affected. In the next section, see how foreign particles and organisms can cause disease by challenging the homeostasis of a victim.

check your UNDERSTANDING

Understanding Concepts

1. Using human body temperature as an example, explain the meaning of the term *homeostasis.*

2. How does disease affect homeostasis? Give an example.

3. Explain how body organs maintain homeostasis within an organ system.

Skill Review

4. **Making Graphs** Create a graph of the data obtained in the Investigation. For more help, refer to Making and Using Graphs in the *Skill Handbook.*

Communicable Diseases

20-2

Objectives

- Describe how organisms cause communicable diseases.
- Compare and contrast the primary characteristics of bacteria, protists, fungi, and viruses.

Key Terms

communicable disease
pathogen
vector

Diseases You Can Catch

What are the most common diseases that affect you and the people around you? For most people, that answer would probably be the common cold, influenza (a respiratory disease known as the flu), strep throat, or a childhood disease such as chicken pox.

You may also know about more serious diseases such as tuberculosis, malaria, and AIDS. These particular diseases all have one characteristic in common. The following activity will give you an opportunity to discover what that characteristic is.

MiniLab

How does disease spread?

How do you catch a cold or the flu? Do these diseases spread the same way as tuberculosis or athlete's foot?

Procedure

1. Your teacher will provide you with a cup partly filled with a clear liquid and an empty cup. **CAUTION:** *Do not drink the liquid or get it on your skin.* Label the empty cup CONTROL and pour half of the liquid into it. Put it aside for the moment. A percentage of the class has received a "diseased" liquid containing a chemical that irritates skin.

2. Exchange part of the liquid in your cup with a classmate by pouring half of the liquid in your cup into your classmate's cup, then taking half of it back. Write down the name of the first classmate with whom you exchange the liquid.

3. Repeat, exchanging the liquid in the same way with two more classmates. Write down the names of the second and third classmates with whom you exchanged.

4. Back at your desk, add two drops of phenolphthalein solution to both of your cups. If the liquid turns pink, it is diseased.

Analysis

1. At the end of the activity, determine how many of the control cups were "diseased." How many of the exchange cups became diseased?

2. Using the records you made, trace the source of the disease you or a classmate contracted.

3. What do you think the diseased liquid used in the activity represents?

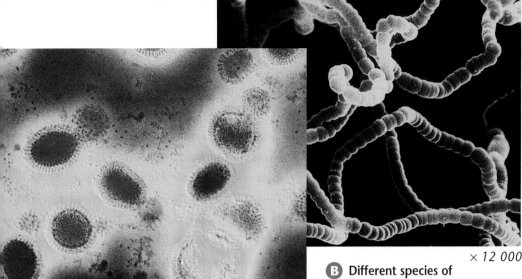

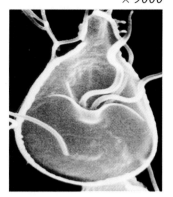

A This is one of many viruses that cause influenza, which is commonly called the flu.

× 68 063

B Different species of *Streptococcus* bacteria cause sore throats and tooth decay in humans.

× 12 000

C *Giardia*, a protist, infects the human digestive system and causes weight loss, extreme fatigue, cramps, nausea, and diarrhea.

× 9000

Figure 20-4

Pathogens are viruses or living organisms that cause disease.

When you talk about getting sick, you often say you've caught a cold, or the flu, or a sore throat. Any disease that can be spread from one person to another like this is called a **communicable disease.** The diseased liquid used in the MiniLab represents a pathogen. A **pathogen** is a disease-causing virus or microscopic organism. Some common pathogens are shown in **Figure 20-4.**

Where do pathogens come from? They are always with us—living in people or other animals, or sometimes in the air or growing in soil or water. People who are infected with a pathogenic microorganism can spread it to others, even if they show no symptoms of illness. Animals—such as dogs, cats, and wild animals—carry rabies and can transmit it to humans.

Abiotic sources of pathogens include soil, air, and water. Soil contains the bacteria that cause tetanus and many other pathogens that can cause cuts and scratches to become swollen and infected. Soil also contains bacteria that cause a form of food poisoning called *botulism.* Water that has been contaminated by animal wastes may contain a variety of pathogens that cause intestinal diseases such as typhoid fever.

Types of Pathogens

Organisms living on Earth are grouped into six kingdoms. Two of these kingdoms—the animal and plant kingdoms—contain the organisms with which you are most familiar. But you also will encounter organisms from the other four kingdoms—Archaebacteria, Eubacteria, Protista, and Fungi. Most of these organisms are too small to see without the help of a microscope. Archaebacteria are found in environments such as hot springs, so they do not usually cause disease in humans.

Few plants and animals cause human disease; most of the pathogens that cause problems for humans belong to the Eubacteria, Protista, or Fungi kingdoms. Another type of pathogen, viruses, are not considered to be forms of life and so are not classified as living organisms.

■ Eubacteria

Think about the times in your life when you have had a cut that became infected, a bout of food poisoning, or a case of strep throat. Now you have an idea of what a bacterial infection is like. Bacteria, the organisms that make up the Kingdom Eubacteria, are unicellular organisms that live virtually everywhere on Earth. Even though most bacteria are about 100 times larger than viruses, they are still too small to be seen without the aid of a microscope. But on nutrient agar, bacteria multiply, often forming colonies that are large enough to see with the unaided eye.

Not all bacteria are pathogens. In fact, most bacteria have probably

A *Escherichia coli* **are found in intestines but may sometimes cause intestinal ailments.**

B *Treponema pallidum* **causes syphilis, a sexually transmitted disease.**

Figure 20-5

The Kingdom Eubacteria includes thousands of species of bacteria.

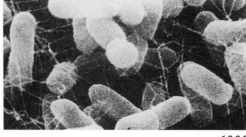

× 6000

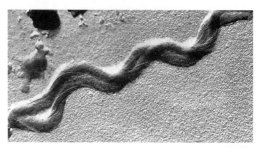

× 7075

Lyme Disease

IN-DEPTH LOOK

Lyme disease is a bacterial disease named after a town in Connecticut where the first cases of the illness were observed. Since its recognition nearly a quarter of a century ago in the United States, the disease has also been diagnosed in Europe, Asia, Africa, and Australia. What is Lyme disease, what are its symptoms, and why is it dangerous?

Transmission

Lyme disease is transmitted to humans and other mammals by several different kinds of ticks—small, black arachnids that live on deer, mice, birds, and dogs. The ticks themselves, however, do not cause the disease. Rather, they inject a bacterium into their victims when they bite. Often, the victim doesn't feel the bite because an anesthetic is released when the tick's mouthparts puncture the skin.

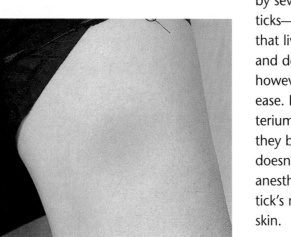

Bull's-eye rash indicates tick bite

formed extremely helpful relationships with humans. For example, there are probably billions of bacteria in a spoonful of soil, and most of these are decomposers that help break down dead plants and animals and animal wastes. Bacteria that live in your digestive tract help break down the food you eat and produce vitamins you need. Bacteria are used to make milk into yogurt and cheese and cabbage into sauerkraut. Diseases caused by bacteria get more publicity. They include tetanus, tuberculosis, pneumonia, meningitis, typhoid fever, cholera, strep throat, leprosy, and the sexually transmitted diseases syphilis and gonorrhea. Four species of bacteria are illustrated in **Figure 20-5.**

C Species of *Staphylococcus* cause boils and other skin infections.

× 34 000

D Some *Lactobacillus* help break down food in the digestive tract.

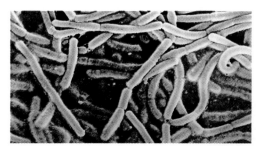

× 2200

Lyme disease can be transmitted during any stage in the life cycle of the tick. Humans, however, are generally infected when the animal is either in the larval or the adult stage.

Symptoms

Symptoms of the disease, which can appear anywhere from three to 32 days after being bitten, vary widely from victim to victim, making diagnosis difficult. Many people with Lyme disease, however, experience fatigue, headaches, fever, chills, and nausea. These early signs are often accompanied by a bull's-eye rash around the bite site. Though small at first, this rash can grow to the size of a football.

Secondary symptoms of Lyme disease occur weeks, months, or even a few years after the person has been bitten. These more severe symptoms include episodes of arthritis, dizziness, and shortness of breath, as well as other disorders of the cardiovascular, muscular, and skeletal systems.

Treatment

Even in its latest stages, Lyme disease is treatable. Antibiotics such as amoxicillin, tetracycline, and doxycycline are prescribed and taken for as few as ten and as many as 30 days. Many victims of Lyme disease take the medication orally; others are given the dosages intravenously.

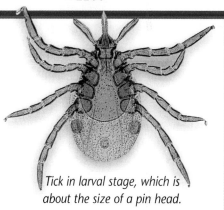

Tick in larval stage, which is about the size of a pin head.

Thinking Critically

1. *Infer* how you would dress if you were going to hike through a wooded area that could harbor ticks.
2. If a tick were to attach itself to your skin, *determine* whether it would be wise to kill it upon removal from your body? Why or why not?

Figure 20-6

Kingdom Protista can be divided into three groups: plantlike, animal-like, and funguslike protists.

A Plantlike protists include algae such as these diatoms as well as giant seaweeds. Most contain chlorophyll or other pigments that enable them to perform photosynthesis.

× 200

× 48 273

B Animal-like protists, known as protozoa, include amoebas at left and the fast-moving species of *Paramecium* below. They feed by capturing and consuming other organisms or are parasites.

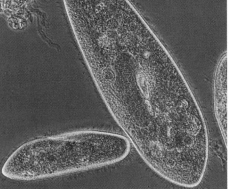

C Funguslike protists include slime molds, shown below, and water molds, which are important decomposers.

× 100

× 4

Ever since you were a child, you've heard "wash your hands before eating." People who prepare and serve food in restaurants are required by law to wash their hands frequently. Does it really help? Experiments show that antibacterial soaps inhibit or reduce the number of bacteria that are able to reproduce and multiply.

■ Protista

Imagine a group of hikers walking beside a beautiful mountain stream. The sun is hot. The stream is cool. One of the hikers dips a hand in the water and takes a drink. Two weeks later, that hiker is home in bed, feeling awful with cramps, nausea, and diarrhea. This person may have come down with a disease called giardiasis. This intestinal infection was caused by *Giardia*, shown on page 607, a member of the Kingdom Protista that was consumed along with the drink of stream water. These microscopic protists are also known as *protozoa*.

The Kingdom Protista is an extremely diverse group of organisms. Protists are plantlike, animal-like, or funguslike organisms that do not appear to be very complex and require a moist environment in which to live. As **Figure 20-6** shows, protists range from unicellular amoebas to giant seaweeds and creeping, gelatinous slime molds. And many of the smallest, such as *Giardia* and *Paramecium*, have complex, internal structures. Although only a few protists cause disease, those diseases can be serious. They include malaria, African sleeping sickness, and amebic dysentery, all of which can be life-threatening.

Malaria is caused by protists. One form is fatal. The pathogen is a unicellular protist called a *Plasmodium*. The female *Anopheles* mosquito is the carrier in malaria. The mosquito bites an infected person or animal, picks up the pathogen, and transfers it to another animal or human.

Figure 20-7 diagrams the life cycle of *Plasmodium*. What is the relationship between the *Plasmodium's* life cycle and the symptoms of malaria present in infected individuals? Use the Thinking Lab located on page 612 and the diagram below to identify what causes the fevers and chills of malaria.

Figure 20-7

Plasmodium, the pathogen that causes malaria, spends part of its life in mosquitoes and part of its life in humans.

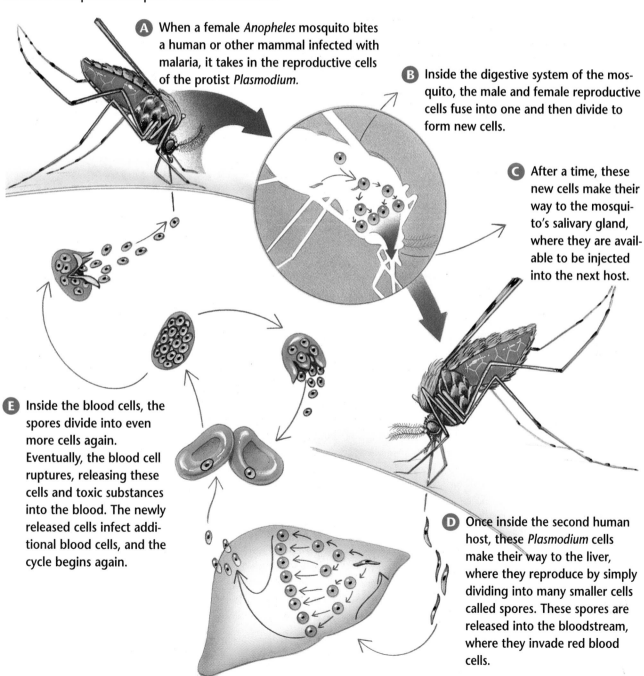

A When a female *Anopheles* mosquito bites a human or other mammal infected with malaria, it takes in the reproductive cells of the protist *Plasmodium*.

B Inside the digestive system of the mosquito, the male and female reproductive cells fuse into one and then divide to form new cells.

C After a time, these new cells make their way to the mosquito's salivary gland, where they are available to be injected into the next host.

E Inside the blood cells, the spores divide into even more cells again. Eventually, the blood cell ruptures, releasing these cells and toxic substances into the blood. The newly released cells infect additional blood cells, and the cycle begins again.

D Once inside the second human host, these *Plasmodium* cells make their way to the liver, where they reproduce by simply dividing into many smaller cells called spores. These spores are released into the bloodstream, where they invade red blood cells.

What causes the fever and chills of malaria?

You may never have encountered anyone who suffers from malaria. However, in the tropical and subtropical regions of the world where the *Anopheles* mosquito lives, malaria is a frequent cause of illness and death. The symptoms of malaria are caused in part by the human body's response to the waste products given off by the pathogen. In many cases, these substances are poisonous to the human body. Fever, nausea, and vomiting are signs that the body is trying its best to get rid of the pathogen and its toxic wastes.

Analysis
The symptoms of malaria include chills, fever, headache, and nausea. The disease is unusual because the symptoms occur in cycles. The chills come first during the "cold stage" and last for up to an hour. The infected person feels cold, nauseous, and usually has a headache. Next comes a high fever during the "hot stage," accompanied by temperatures up to 106°F, increased nausea, vomiting, and an even more severe headache. Then comes the "wet stage," accompanied by profuse sweating. Then the symptoms disappear completely for two or three days before a new cycle begins.

Thinking Critically
Compare the above information with the life cycle of *Plasmodium* shown in **Figure 20-7** on the previous page. Suggest a reason for the cyclic pattern of malaria symptoms.

■ Fungi

In addition to diseases such as strep throat and malaria, caused by bacteria and protists, still others are caused by fungi. How are mushrooms and athlete's foot related? A mushroom is a fungus and athlete's foot is a disease caused by fungi. Members of the Kingdom Fungi include yeasts, mushrooms, and molds. Most fungi are decomposers, absorbing nutrients as they break down dead plant and animal bodies and other organic matter. As you learned in Chapter 5, decomposers are essential to all ecosystems.

Fungi are responsible for a low percentage of human diseases. Many are caused by fungi that normally live in the soil. For example, coccidioidomycosis, or San Joaquin Valley Fever, is a lung infection caused by a fungus that lives in desert soils. A rise in the number of cases of this disease followed a severe windstorm in the San Joaquin Valley of central California. Only a small minori-

Figure 20-8

The most common fungal diseases that exist among humans are those in which the infection is limited to the skin.

A Ringworm, shown below, is caused by a fungus species and can occur on different parts of the body. It is most commonly seen in young children. The disease got its name from the ring-shaped growth pattern of the infection, common to many fungal infections. It was once thought that the disease was caused by worms coiled up under the skin.

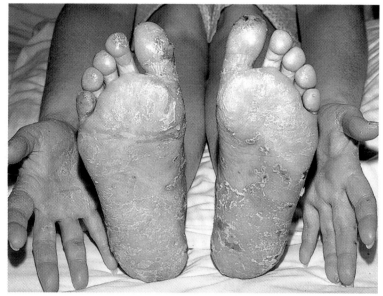

B Athlete's foot fungus, shown above, commonly grows in warm, moist areas on the feet. The infection causes itching and burning and is spread by contact with contaminated surfaces such as swimming pools, shower floors, or wet towels.

ty of those who inhaled the dusty air, including travelers just passing through the area, contracted this serious disease. The fungus grows in the tissues of the lungs, causing fever, coughing, and chest pain. In rare cases, the fungal growth spreads to other organs.

Other types of soil fungi can cause skin infections in gardeners, farmers, and others who come into close contact with the soil. Athlete's foot and ringworm, shown in **Figure 20-8,** are the two most common fungal diseases that occur in humans.

■ Viruses

Human diseases caused by viruses include colds, influenza, rabies, smallpox, herpes, chicken pox, measles, mumps, hepatitis, infectious mononucleosis, warts, and acquired immune deficiency syndrome (AIDS). However, if a virus isn't alive, how can it cause a disease? Viruses cannot perform all the functions that are characteristic of living cells. Viruses can't grow or move. They are not capable of cellular respiration. They lack the membranes and other structures found in cells. The only lifelike function that viruses can perform is reproduction, and they don't accomplish that by themselves. A virus can reproduce only inside a living cell.

Viruses contain an inner core of genetic material. These genetic materials—either DNA (deoxyribonucleic acid) or RNA—contain instructions for reproducing all parts of the viruses. To carry out those instructions, the virus must invade and take over a living cell. **Figure 20-9** on page 614 shows how a virus reproduces itself.

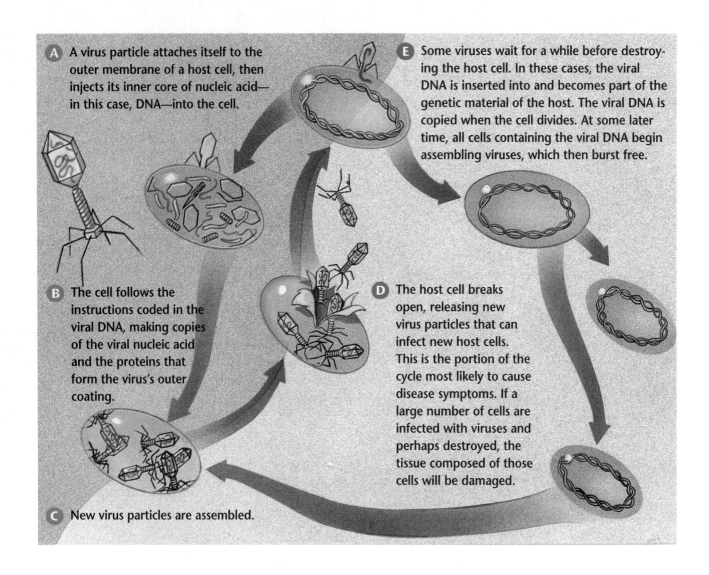

A A virus particle attaches itself to the outer membrane of a host cell, then injects its inner core of nucleic acid—in this case, DNA—into the cell.

E Some viruses wait for a while before destroying the host cell. In these cases, the viral DNA is inserted into and becomes part of the genetic material of the host. The viral DNA is copied when the cell divides. At some later time, all cells containing the viral DNA begin assembling viruses, which then burst free.

B The cell follows the instructions coded in the viral DNA, making copies of the viral nucleic acid and the proteins that form the virus's outer coating.

D The host cell breaks open, releasing new virus particles that can infect new host cells. This is the portion of the cycle most likely to cause disease symptoms. If a large number of cells are infected with viruses and perhaps destroyed, the tissue composed of those cells will be damaged.

C New virus particles are assembled.

Figure 20-9

A virus is made up of an inner core of genetic material surrounded by an outer coating of protein. Viruses reproduce by taking over the workings of a living cell.

Host cell damage results during the life cycle of many viruses. The appearance of an open sore—or groups of damaged cells as in herpes and chicken pox—is a major symptom of some viral infections. However, cells and tissues can be damaged by microscopic living organisms, too.

How Diseases Spread

How do pathogens get from one person to another? One way to catch a cold is by inhaling microscopic droplets of fluid exhaled by someone already infected with a cold virus. That's why

it's recommended that you cover your mouth and nose when you sneeze. When you do sneeze, fluid droplets spread far and wide. They may also fall on another object, so if you touch the object and then touch your nose or mouth, the pathogen may infect your body. Other ways to catch a cold are by kissing or by sharing food or eating utensils with someone who has a cold.

Some bacterial diseases, such as Lyme disease or malaria, are spread by insects or other nonhuman animals. An organism that carries a disease from one host to another is called a **vector**. **Figure 20-10** shows how communicable diseases can be spread.

Figure 20-10

Communicable diseases can be spread in several ways.

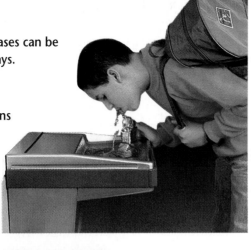

A *Water* Pathogens may be picked up by drinking or swimming in polluted water.

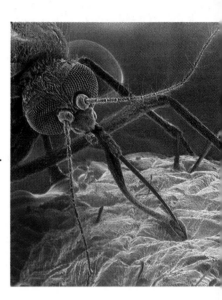

B *Vectors* The most common vectors are insects or other arthropods that feed on human blood. Mosquitoes spread diseases such as malaria and yellow fever.

C *Contaminated inanimate objects* Pathogens may be picked up from contaminated items such as door-knobs, toys, food, blood, and intra-venous needles.

D *Direct contact* Pathogens can be spread by touching, biting, kissing, and sexual contact.

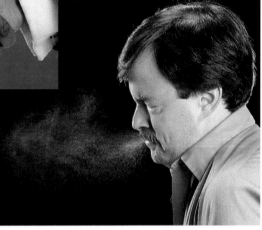

E *Air* Pathogens may be spread through the air in droplets of water or dust.

Communicable diseases are caused by pathogens. Most pathogens are either viruses, bacteria, protists, or fungi and can be spread from one vic-tim to another by vectors. In the next section, you'll examine lifestyle, heredi-tary, and environmental factors related to noncommunicable diseases.

check your UNDERSTANDING

Understanding Concepts
1. How are communicable diseases caused?
2. Why aren't viruses living organisms?
3. How is the way a *Plasmodium* treats its host similar to the way a virus treats its host?

Skill Review
4. **Making and Using Tables** Using a table, compare the characteristics of bacteria, pro-tists, fungi, and viruses. For more help, refer to Making and Using Tables in the *Skill Handbook.*

20-3 Noncommunicable Diseases

Objectives

■ Explain how heart disease and skin cancer develop.

■ Determine how a genetic disease is passed from parent to offspring.

Key Terms

noncommunicable disease
allele
homozygous
heterozygous

Diseases You Can't Catch

In the year 1900, the most common causes of death were tuberculosis and pneumonia—communicable diseases caused by bacterial infection. Since then, medical researchers have developed antibiotics, vaccines, and other methods for effectively preventing and curing many communicable diseases. You'll learn more about these cures and treatments in Chapter 21. Today, death from communicable diseases is not nearly as common as it was 100 years ago, particularly in developed parts of the world. Many people are living longer, healthier lives.

Noncommunicable diseases, particularly heart disease and cancer, have become major causes of death. A **noncommunicable disease** is an illness that is not caused by a pathogen and is not spread from person to person. The longer an individual lives, the more likely it is that he or she will develop a noncommunicable disease such as cancer, heart disease, emphysema, arthritis, or diabetes. If pathogens aren't responsible, then what causes noncommunicable diseases? They can result from lifestyle choices, environment, heredity, or a combination of these factors.

Figure 20-11

Choices you make daily can affect your state of health.

Lifestyle Diseases

How many times a week are you given advice about how to stay healthy? You've probably been told more times than you can remember that it's a good idea to eat lots of grains, fresh fruits, and vegetables and to limit salty and fatty foods. You've also heard that you should get plenty of rest and exercise and not use tobacco. Think seriously for a minute about what will happen if you don't follow this advice. In addition to other health problems, your circulatory system will probably suffer. As **Figure 20-12** shows, becoming a "couch potato" can affect your circulatory system in several ways, including the promotion of heart disease.

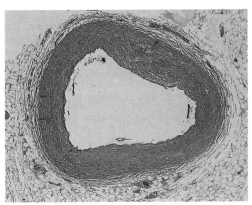
Healthy artery

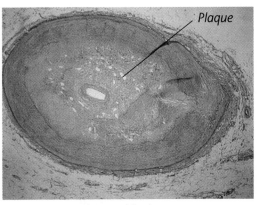
Plaque

Artery with plaque

A Fatty deposits in the walls of arteries are known as plaques; they cause the inside of the arteries to become narrower. Less blood can pass through, resulting in higher blood pressure. In addition, the arteries become less flexible. If plaques give way, they can block vessels and blood flow as they move. As a result, they contribute to strokes and heart attacks.

Figure 20-12

When you consume fatty foods such as animal fats, meats, dairy products, and fried foods, the fat content of your blood rises and you increase the chance of heart disease. Over time, these fats and cholesterol interact with the inner linings of your arteries to form thickened but weakened areas on the walls.

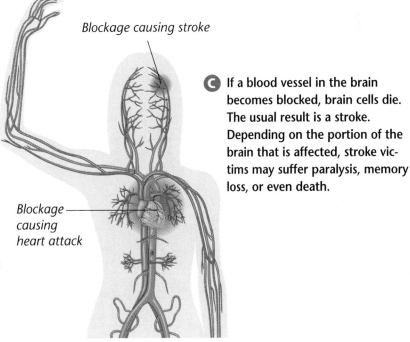
Blockage causing stroke

Blockage causing heart attack

B Or, eventually an artery becomes completely blocked. When this happens, cells in the organs to which this blood is being carried die because their blood supply, and therefore their oxygen supply, is cut off. For example, if the blockage occurs in arteries that feed the heart muscle itself, some of the heart cells begin to die from lack of oxygen. Eventually, this results in a heart attack.

C If a blood vessel in the brain becomes blocked, brain cells die. The usual result is a stroke. Depending on the portion of the brain that is affected, stroke victims may suffer paralysis, memory loss, or even death.

Most doctors recommend limiting the amount of fat you eat as well as getting plenty of exercise to help keep your circulatory system in good shape. Lifestyle choices like these are extremely important, but they aren't the only factors that determine whether or not you become a victim of heart disease. It's possible to inherit a tendency toward circulatory problems from your parents. As a result, it can be especially important for people with a family history of heart and artery disease to make healthy lifestyle choices.

Hereditary Diseases

Do you have the same eye color as your dad? Is your hair color the same as your grandmother's? Are you tall like your mom, or short like your aunt? The

Figure 20-13

Inherited genes are responsible for strong family resemblances.

information coded in your genes instructs the cells of your body to form the features that make you recognizable as an individual. Children inherit many harmless characteristics such as eye color, skin tone, or height, illustrated in **Figure 20-13.**

■ Hemophilia and Sickle-Cell Anemia

Other inherited characteristics are not as harmless. Do you know anyone who suffers from hemophilia or sickle-cell anemia? If you do, you know someone who has an inherited disease. Both hemophilia and sickle-cell anemia are genetic defects that cause blood abnormalities. Sickle-cell anemia occurs among African Americans and, to a lesser extent, among Greeks, Italians, and Latin Americans.

In hemophilia, the blood does not clot normally, so simple injuries such as bruises or small cuts can result in excessive blood loss, requiring transfusions and medications that promote clotting. In sickle-cell anemia, some red blood cells become crescent-shaped instead of round. These cells carry less oxygen than normal cells. They get caught in tiny blood vessels, causing pain by clogging the blood flow. They also damage cells and tissues by cutting them off from oxygen and nutrients. Sickle-cell treatment includes blood transfusions and drugs.

■ Cystic Fibrosis

Another type of inherited disease is cystic fibrosis, or CF, described in **Figure 20-14.** CF causes the membranes that line the digestive tract and lungs to produce a mucus that is thick. The buildup of this mucus in lungs makes

Figure 20-14

Cystic fibrosis results from a defect in a gene that controls the chloride content of cells. As a result, tremendous amounts of salt are excreted in sweat. Chloride is an ion that combines with sodium to form sodium chloride, or salt.

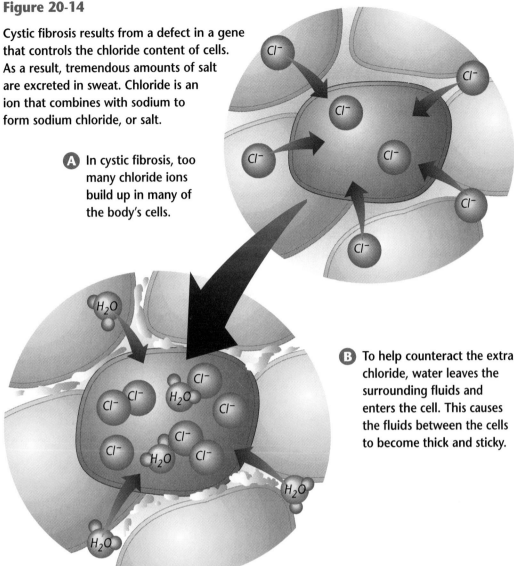

A In cystic fibrosis, too many chloride ions build up in many of the body's cells.

B To help counteract the extra chloride, water leaves the surrounding fluids and enters the cell. This causes the fluids between the cells to become thick and sticky.

breathing difficult. It provides an environment that encourages the growth of bacteria that cause pneumonia and other respiratory infections.

The presence of thick mucus in the digestive tract keeps enzymes from reaching food to be digested. As a result, victims may become nutrient-deficient. Enzyme supplements and special diets enable them to absorb more nutrients. Daily physical therapy helps loosen mucus in their lungs, which they then cough up. Though the disease is fatal, new therapies have

increased life expectancy dramatically.

What determines whether a child will inherit a disease? Human chromosomes, which contain the genetic material, come in pairs. There are 23 pairs, and you inherit one chromosome of each pair from your mother and one from your father. Each chromosome consists of thousands of genes. Genes that control a specific trait have different forms. For example, in the case of cystic fibrosis, the gene that regulates the chloride content of cells has two forms: normal and abnormal.

To Find Out More About ...

Cystic Fibrosis, contact your local chapter of the Cystic Fibrosis Foundation.

The different forms of a gene are called **alleles.** A child inherits one chloride-regulating allele from the mother and one from the father. If the child inherits two alleles that have the same form, he or she is **homozygous** for that characteristic. In the cystic fibrosis example, a homozygous individual expresses the characteristic in question. A child who inherits two different alleles is **heterozygous** and is a carrier of the characteristic. A carrier does not experience the symptoms of the disease-causing allele but has a 50 percent chance of passing it on to an offspring.

A Punnett square is used to show the possible combinations of the parents' alleles. The letters representing alleles of the gene of one parent are placed along the top of a two-by-two cell square. The letters representing alleles of the other parent's gene are listed along the left side. To find the possible combinations of offspring, each cell of the square is filled with the allele above and on the left side.

The Punnett square in **Figure 20-15** shows all the combinations of alleles that could be present in any children this couple might have. Only children who are homozygous for the CF allele have the disease cystic fibrosis. Therefore, each mating between the parents described in this Punnett square has a 50 percent chance of producing a homozygous child who will never have CF and doesn't have a CF allele to pass on. There is also a 50 percent chance of producing a heterozygous CF carrier.

What portion of the potential children shown in the Punnett square are heterozygous carriers of the CF allele? What might happen if one of these children marries a CF carrier? The MiniLab on page 621 will help you determine the outcome.

Figure 20-15

In this family, the mother is homozygous for the normal form of the cystic fibrosis gene. Both of her alleles are normal. The father is heterozygous for the gene. One of his alleles is normal, the other carries the gene for CF.

B If we call the allele for CF *f,* the father's heterozygous alleles can be symbolized *Ff.*

A If we call the normal allele *F,* the mother's homozygous alleles can be symbolized *FF.*

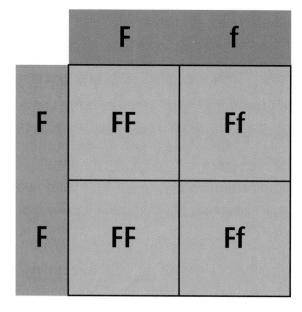

C It is not possible for this couple to give birth to a child with CF because only the father carries the gene for CF.

Key: *FF* = normal cells
  Ff = carrier of cystic fibrosis gene

What are the chances?

Because cystic fibrosis occurs only in individuals who are homozygous for the CF allele, healthy individuals can carry the CF gene without knowing it. What happens if two CF carriers have children? What are the chances that those children will have the disease?

Procedure

1. *In your Journal,* draw a blank Punnett square. Across the top, write the two alleles of the father, who is heterozygous for CF.

2. Down the left side of the square, write in the two alleles of the mother, who is also heterozygous for CF.

3. Fill in the possible allele combinations of the offspring.

Analysis

1. Is there a chance that any of this couple's children will be carriers of the CF allele? If so, what percentage?

2. Is there a chance that any of this couple's children will have CF? If so, what percentage?

3. Is there a chance that any of this couple's children will be free of the CF allele? If so, what percentage?

The MiniLab shows that the likelihood of genetic diseases is passed from one generation to another. In diseases such as cystic fibrosis, it is even possible for someone to get a disease when his or her parents do not show any sign of it. The parents are carriers of the cystic fibrosis gene. This begins to explain why some people experience a disease—in this case, an inherited disease—and others do not.

Environmental Diseases

Many substances in our environment have the potential to cause disease. For example, you may have heard about air-quality alerts. Days when air-pollution levels are high, particularly during hot summer months, present problems to people suffering from res-

piratory diseases. People with asthma and emphysema are advised to avoid strenuous activity and to stay indoors to prevent severe breathing problems. Pollutants released into the air from industries and automobile exhaust include nitrogen oxides, sulfur oxides, and hydrocarbons. These react with water vapor and sunlight to form strong acids, ozone, and other irritants. Constant exposure to polluted air can cause serious lung disease, as well as other related diseases including cancer.

Cancer is also linked to other substances in the environment. Research shows that many substances, when administered in high doses, cause cancer in laboratory animals. Whether or not all these substances pose a danger to human health has not yet been determined. The amounts of materials used in research may be significantly

Figure 20-16

Visible light represents only a portion of the energy that radiates from the sun. The electromagnetic spectrum shows all of the wavelengths included in the sun's rays.

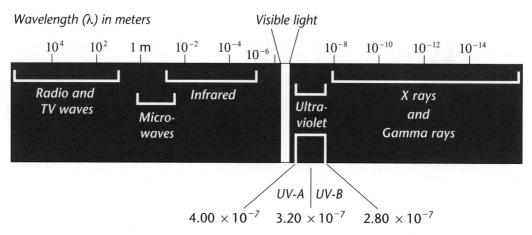

A Ultraviolet, or UV, is the name given to the part of the electromagnetic spectrum with wavelengths ranging from 280 nm to 400 nm.

B UV-B rays penetrate the skin, causing sunburn and potentially causing cancer in people who have been sunburned many times during their lives.

C UV-A rays penetrate the skin even more deeply than UV-B rays. UV-A rays cause the skin to wrinkle and age. They also increase the chance that UV-B rays will cause cancer. Although sunscreens block UV-B rays, most do not protect the skin from UV-A rays.

higher than an individual would encounter in a lifetime. However, there is at least one environmental hazard with an undisputed link to cancer—sunlight.

■ Skin Cancer

As **Figure 20-16** shows, the sun gives off many wavelengths of light, including ultraviolet, also called UV, radiation. These UV rays are responsible for sunburn and skin cancer. Skin cancer makes up one-third of all cancers diagnosed in the United States, and its incidence is increasing.

The energy from UV rays that penetrates the skin can damage the genetic material contained in skin cells. Damaged cells may become cancerous and begin reproducing abnormally through the process of mitosis (see Appendix I), forming masses known as tumors. Cancer cells gradually take over and

destroy neighboring tissues by reproducing much more quickly than normal cells, and by preventing normal cells from receiving the nutrients they need.

Skin cancer is one of the most common types of cancer, especially among light-skinned people who spend a lot of time in the sun. It usually, though not always, develops on the parts of the body most often exposed to the sun, especially the face and neck. Some forms of skin cancer, called carcinomas, are relatively harmless if diagnosed and treated during the early stages of the disease. Carcinomas develop in the upper portions of the skin, forming rapidly growing red or pink tumors. **Figure 20-17** shows an example of another, more deadly form of skin cancer called malignant melanoma.

Cancer is the second leading cause of death in the United States, with heart

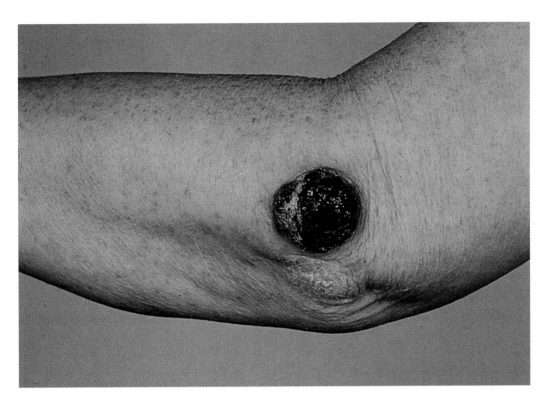

Figure 20-17

Malignant melanoma makes up only three percent of all skin cancers. This rate of occurrence, however, is growing faster than that of any other kind of skin cancer. Melanoma tumors develop in deeper layers of the skin and are more difficult to treat.

Try It!

Making Changes?
Sometimes, knowledge about disease can cause people to change their behavior. Interview friends and relatives to find out whether information about the causes of heart disease and skin cancer motivates them to reduce their fat consumption or give up trying to get that perfect suntan.

disease being the number-one killer. While some cancers are caused by environmental conditions, other types, such as breast cancer, are believed to have an inherited or genetic factor as well. Cancer may also be caused by infection with particular viruses.

In this chapter, you found that disease often occurs when the body's normal functions are altered. Communicable diseases are caused by pathogens and spread from one host to another through the air, on inanimate objects, or by vectors. Noncommunicable diseases arise as a result of an unhealthy lifestyle, something in our surroundings that is harmful, genetic abnormalities inherited from our parents, or some combination of these reasons. In all of these cases, disease affects the systems in the body so that homeostasis is disturbed.

Understanding the cause of a disease is the first step in learning how to prevent and cure it. In the next chapter, learn how your body fights disease.

check your UNDERSTANDING

Understanding Concepts
1. Explain how heart disease develops.
2. Explain the relationship between sunlight and skin cancer.
3. Explain why it is possible for healthy, normal parents to give birth to a child with a genetic disease such as cystic fibrosis.

Skill Review
4. **Comparing and Contrasting** Explain the difference between communicable and noncommunicable diseases. For more help, refer to Comparing and Contrasting in the *Skill Handbook.*

Issue:
Is health-care reform needed?

Jed's father quit his job in 1992 after the company he worked for moved to another state. As a result, his family lost their medical insurance. Then to top it off, the 40-year-old man suffered a heart attack. His condition required angioplasty to clear the plaque from a blocked coronary artery and a five-day stay in intensive care. His medical bills reached almost $40 000.

To address problems like this, the Health Insurance Portability Act was passed to help people keep insurance coverage if they change jobs. The law took effect July 1, 1997.

The Issue

In 1995, the United States spent an estimated $988.5 billion on health care. Health care already consumes 20 percent of the federal budget, or about $375 billion a year. Experts estimate that if health-care spending continues to increase, in ten years it will be 33 percent of the federal budget.

Many people claim that in the United States, we have the best medical care in terms of hospitals and physicians but the worst system for financing it. Based on fee for service, the system may encourage some physicians and hospitals to treat patients in the most expensive way, thereby increasing their fees.

Another cause of high costs is the mounting number of malpractice suits filed each year. One physician in five is sued per year.

Premiums for malpractice insurance range from $2000 for family physicians in rural areas to $100 000 for some specialists in major cities. To avoid being sued for negligence, a physician may prescribe additional tests and X rays. A patient with a headache may be whisked to an MRI to provide a record in case a malpractice suit is filed.

In 1965, the federal government established a health-insurance program known as Medicare for people over 65 years of age. At that time, it was projected that Medicare insurance would cost the government $9 billion by 1990. Instead, by 1990, its actual cost was $67 billion. Unless some dramatic changes are made, the Medicare system may suffer a financial collapse by 2012.

The Background

Medical technology has added a great deal to the cost of medical care. The computerized axial tomographic (CAT) scanner is an X-ray machine that makes cross-sectional views of the

brain and other parts of the body. The magnetic resonance imager (MRI) uses a magnetic field instead of X rays to make cross-sectional views of the body. Although they greatly enhance the diagnosis and treatment of disease, such machines are expensive to buy and to operate. In order to compete for patients, every hospital tries to purchase one or the other of these high-tech machines.

Not every new medical breakthrough adds to the cost. Many new drugs are extremely cost-effective. Antibiotics, which kill off pathogens for just a few dollars, are a great bargain. Vaccines and analgesics are similarly cost-effective. Surgery that requires little or no cutting is another technological advance. Patients spend less time in the hospital and need less time to heal. Even something so small as surgical staples has helped keep medical costs down. Staples cost four times as much as sutures and thread, but the stapled patient leaves the hospital 3.5 days sooner than the sutured patient.

The Questions

What can the health-care industry do to reduce costs? A *Health Maintenance Organization (HMO)* is a medical-care group that provides services to members, who pay a monthly or yearly fee. When ill, a member goes to an HMO-approved clinic where the staff and the physicians work for a salary and not on a fee-for-service basis. These health-care providers perform 50 percent fewer electrocardiograms and chest X rays. Using only HMO services, a member spends little more than an annual fee.

One reason HMOs cost less is that no forms have to be filled out. Paperwork is usually 22 percent of medical costs. A family may pay as little as half as much for health-care expenses

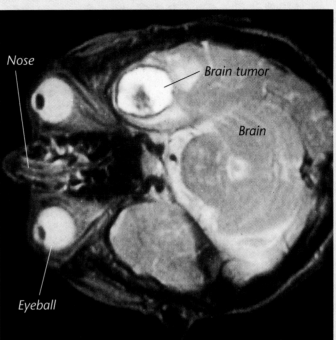

CAT scan of a cross section of a human head

Labels on image: Nose, Brain tumor, Brain, Eyeball

using an HMO as it would with a regular health-care insurer.

Some health-insurance companies encourage customers to use *preferred providers*. The providers are a group of hospitals and doctors who agree to offer service at discount fees. In return, the preferred providers are assured of a large pool of patients. The patients may have fewer choices of physicians and hospitals, but their savings are considerable. The quest goes on. How else can health-care costs be reduced?

Discussing the Issue

1. *Explain* what an *HMO* is. What is a *preferred provider*?
2. Some insurers refuse to insure people with preexisting conditions, which are illnesses contracted before an applicant is covered by the insurer. If insurers are forced to insure people with preexisting conditions, *infer* how that might drive up the cost of health insurance for everyone.

Plagues and Viruses

Before the 20th century, many diseases like tuberculosis, smallpox, and malaria were greatly feared because medical science had little knowledge about how to treat or cure them. Given the right conditions, bacterial infections, viral infections, or parasitical infections could spread rapidly through communities, causing illness and death of epidemic proportion. Scientists searched feverishly to locate cures for these dreaded diseases, and, in the mid-20th century, science began to discover some answers.

Weekly Death Census in London newspaper, 1665

The Eradication of Disease

In the 1950s and 1960s, scientists all over the world were beginning to proclaim the end of the time when viruses, bacteria, and plagues would be a threat. The development of penicillin at the end of World War II led to the introduction of a variety of other antibiotic drugs that could be used to treat and eliminate certain diseases, and in 1955, Jonas Salk discovered an experimental polio vaccination. In 1966, the U.S. Centers for Disease Control classified bubonic plague, malaria, and smallpox as diseases eradicated within the United States, while typhoid, polio, and diphtheria were classified as almost-eradicated within the United States. It appeared that by the end of the 1960s, the United States was safe from any major bacterial or viral outbreaks.

The Coming Plague

In the early 1970s, such optimism began to vanish. A virus that attacked the human immune system (HIV) soon turned up in the United States and began to invade certain sectors of the population in near-epidemic proportions. Tuberculosis, caused by airborne bacteria, has begun to make a comeback, killing almost 3 million people annually. What is causing the rise of diseases once thought to be eliminated? Many blame the overcrowded conditions of cities for the rapid spread of airborne bacterial diseases, while others point to the introduction of new strains of viruses brought by travelers from other countries. To make matters even worse, many bacteria and viruses have developed drug-resistant strains that are now infecting humans. Because these diseases cannot be treated with conventional drugs, scientists must search quickly to come up with a vaccine or antibiotic that treats the new strain. As optimistic about eradicating disease as researchers were in the 1960s, researchers in the late 20th century have reasons to be pessimistic about disease outbreaks.

*inter*NET CONNECTION

Follow the link for Chapter 20 on the Glencoe Homepage for an interview with the first scientist to view the newly emerging and deadly Ebola virus in an electron microscope. Infer what might happen if an Ebola outbreak occurred in the United States.

Read the statements below that review major points presented in the chapter. Using the concepts that you have learned, answer each question *in your Journal.*

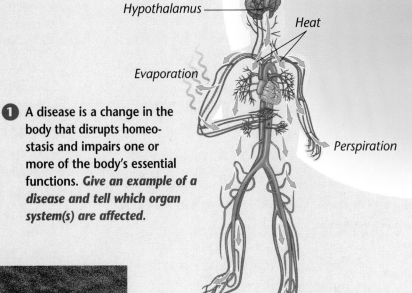

Hypothalamus

Heat

Evaporation

Perspiration

1 A disease is a change in the body that disrupts homeostasis and impairs one or more of the body's essential functions. *Give an example of a disease and tell which organ system(s) are affected.*

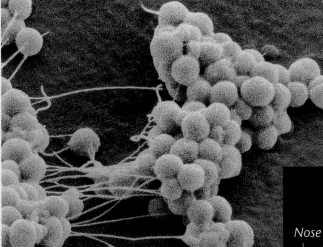

2 Communicable diseases are caused by pathogens and can be spread from one person to another. *Name the four most common pathogens.*

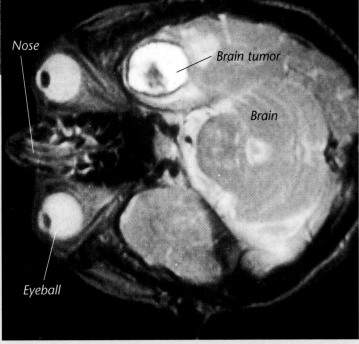

Nose

Brain tumor

Brain

Eyeball

3 Noncommunicable diseases are illnesses that are not caused by pathogens, nor are they spread from person to person. *Name three different possible causes of noncommunicable diseases and give an example of each.*

Using Key Science Terms

allele
communicable
   disease
disease
heterozygous
homeostasis

homozygous
noncommunicable
   disease
pathogen
vector

For each set of terms below, choose the one term that does not belong and explain why it does not belong.

1. disease, homeostasis, pathogen, vector
2. communicable disease, pathogen, non-communicable disease, vector
3. allele, heterozygous, vector, homozygous

Understanding Ideas

Using complete sentences, answer the following questions in your Journal.

1. How does sweating help the human body maintain homeostasis?
2. What hormone is affected by diabetes?

3. Give examples of five ways in which pathogens are spread.
4. What causes cystic fibrosis and how is it transmitted?
5. Why must hikers and campers be careful about drinking water from streams?

Developing Skills

Use your understanding of the concepts developed in this chapter to answer each of the following questions.

1. **Concept Mapping** Use the following terms and phrases to complete the concept map about diseases at the bottom of the page: *bacteria, cancer, communicable, environmental, fungi, hereditary, malaria, noncommunicable, protists, stroke, viruses*

2. **Recognizing Cause and Effect** This winter, far more students than usual are coming down with the flu. Explain the steps the school administration might recommend to slow the spread of the disease.

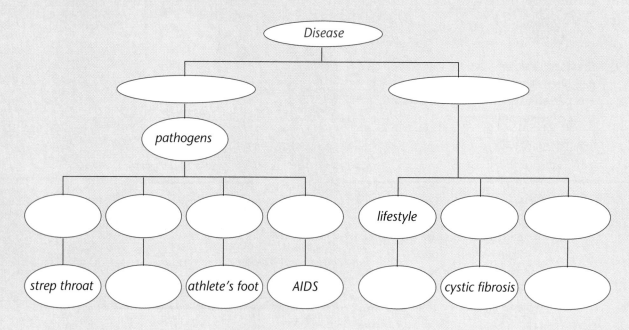

Critical Thinking

In your Journal, *answer each of the following questions.*

1. One of the most important ways cells maintain homeostasis is by regulating fluid content. Relate the need for cells to maintain the proper internal fluid balance to the causes and symptoms of diabetes and cystic fibrosis.

2. Frostbite is the formation of ice crystals in the cells of skin. If severe, it can result in the loss of fingers and toes. When exposed to cold temperatures, one of the body's responses is to reduce circulation in the hands and feet—areas where the blood is cooled. As a result, cooling of the blood is slowed, which helps preserve the heat of internal organs. Explain how this response helps maintain homeostasis even if the result is severe frostbite in the fingers and toes.

3. The chance of getting skin cancer is greater in individuals who have had many sun-burns over their lifetimes than in individuals who have not. Suggest a hypothesis that would explain why this is so.

Problem Solving

Read the following problem and discuss your answers in a brief paragraph.

Use Punnett squares as needed to answer the following questions. A couple is interested in predicting the chances that they might have children with sickle-cell anemia. The man's father is homozygous for the normal allele, and his mother is heterozygous. Calculate the percentage chance that the father carries the allele for sickle-cell anemia.

The woman's parents are both homozygous for the normal allele. What is the likelihood that the mother carries the allele for sickle-cell anemia?

What is the likelihood that this couple will have a child with sickle-cell anemia?

CONNECTING IDEAS

1. **Theme—Stability and Change** Describe how the invasion of a flower garden by a fast-growing weed is like the invasion of human tissues by a pathogen.

2. **Theme—Systems and Interactions** Compare and contrast the feeding relationships of a colony of bacteria living in a human throat with a clump of grass living in the soil.

3. **Theme—Energy** The evaporation of sweat cools the body. The evaporation of water from a lake cools the nearby land. Compare and contrast the result of sweat evaporating from the body and water evaporating from the surface of a lake.

4. **History Connection** What diseases are receiving a lot of news coverage today?

5. **Science and Society** What preventive measures can people take to reduce the cost of expensive health care?

CHAPTER 21

Preventing and Treating Disease
Maintaining Your Health

Millions of infectious viruses, bacteria, and other organisms are in the air you breathe, on every object you touch, and even on your skin. Why don't these pathogens make you sick all the time? To maintain homeostasis, the human body has a number of defenses against attack by pathogens. In this chapter, learn about those defenses. You'll also find out about some of the techniques of modern medicine used to boost those defenses and, in the event you do become sick, to treat disease.

▶ ***In the following activity, examine the characteristics of one of the first lines of defense you have against disease.***

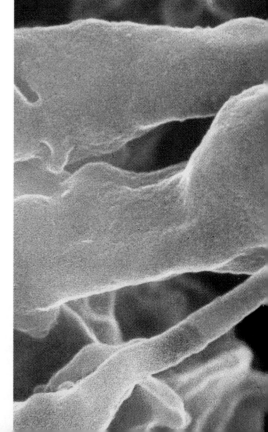

White blood cell attacking bacteria

What's getting under your skin?

Humans are not the only organisms with skin. Most multi-cellular organisms have some kind of outer covering. What is the skin's function?

Procedure

1. Obtain two apples similar in type, size, and ripeness. Completely peel one of the apples.

2. Leave the two apples overnight in an open container in a warm, moist place. Predict what will happen to the two apples overnight.

3. Two days later, peel away part of the skin of the second apple and compare it with the one peeled earlier.

Analysis

1. *In your Journal,* compare the color and texture of the flesh of both apples.

2. What is responsible for the difference in the two apples?

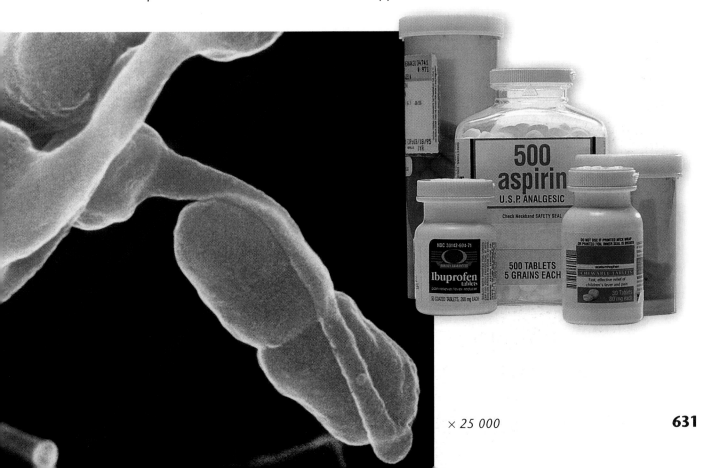

$\times 25\ 000$

21-1 Lines of Defense

Objectives
- Identify the body's defenses against infection.
- Explain how the inflammatory response helps rid the body of pathogens.

Key Terms
inflammatory response
phagocyte
macrophage

First Line of Defense: Physical Barriers

Even though billions of bacteria and fungi can be found in a handful of soil, you probably don't worry about getting an infection every time you get your hands dirty. But you do have to be careful to keep open cuts and scratches clean. Like the skin of an apple, the skin of your body acts as a barrier that prevents pathogenic organisms from entering and upsetting your body's homeostasis. Unlike the apple, your body has large openings to the outside. But don't worry—membranes lining your mouth, throat, nasal passages, and other internal surfaces help to fend off pathogens. What happens if an unwanted invader does manage to penetrate these physical barriers, as demonstrated in **Figure 21-1?** Your body has still more ways to protect itself.

■ Skin

Like the outer wall of a castle, your skin protects your body from enemies that lurk outside it. Human skin is a system composed of organs that help maintain the body's homeostasis. It both covers and protects body organs. In addition to preventing harmful microorganisms and most harmful materials from entering the body, it also prevents loss of body fluids. Skin is made up of two layers. The thinner, outer layer is composed of both dead and living cells and is called the *epidermis.* The outermost portion of the epidermal layer is made up of layers of dead cells and forms a protective and waterproof shield over the rest of the skin and the body. It is bathed in sweat and oil that are produced by glands in deeper layers. It is also covered with bacteria.

Beneath the epidermis layer lies the *dermis,* which is a thicker layer containing nerve fibers, blood vessels, sweat glands, oil glands, and other structures embedded in connective tissue. **Figure 21-2** gives a detailed view of the skin.

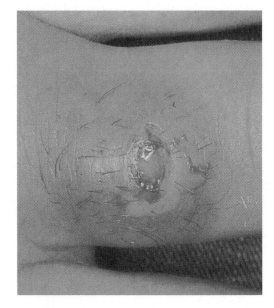

Figure 21-1

Breaks in skin allow unwanted pathogens to enter the body. The injured area often becomes red and swollen.

Figure 21-2

The skin is an organ made up of several tissues, each with a function that helps maintain the body's homeostasis.

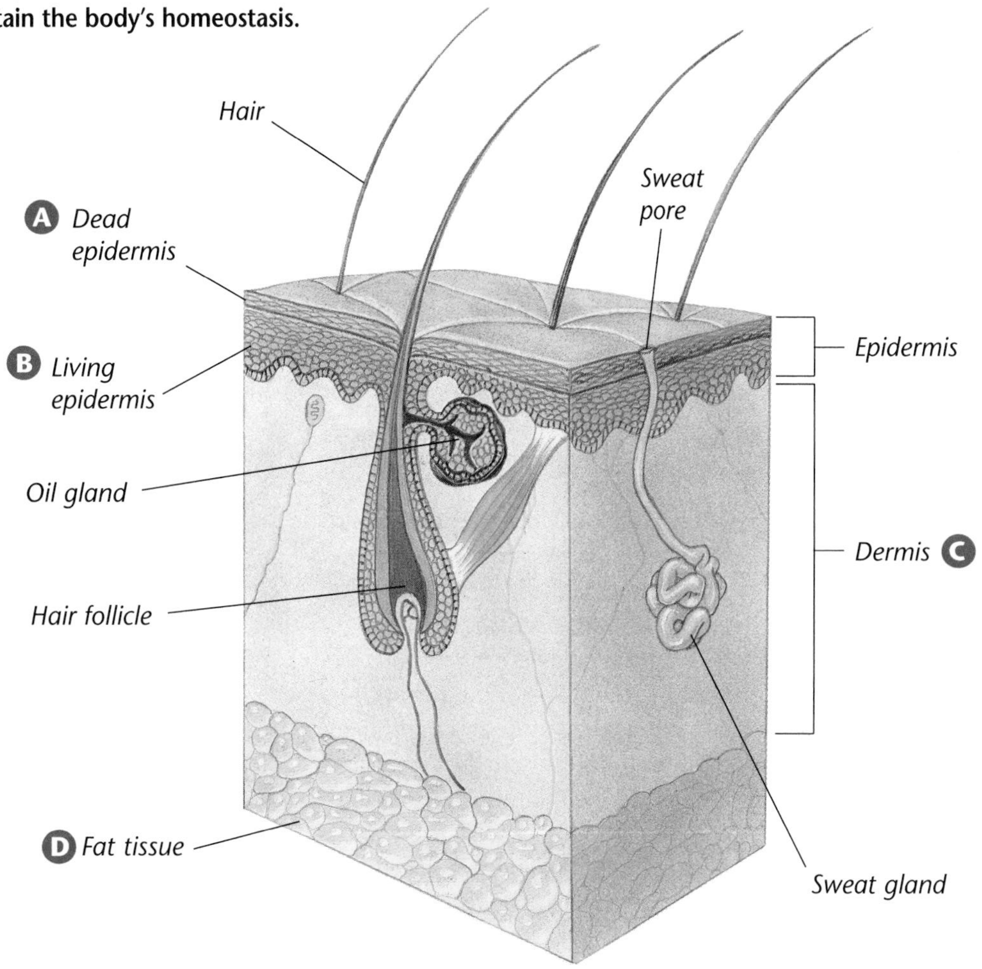

A *Dead Epidermis* When you look at your own skin, what you see is the top layer of the epidermis, which is made of dead cells. Dead cells are constantly being shed and, as they fall or are rubbed off the body, they take along any pathogens that happen to be resting on them.

Hair

Sweat pore

A *Dead epidermis*

B *Living epidermis*

Oil gland

Hair follicle

Epidermis

Dermis **C**

D *Fat tissue*

Sweat gland

B *Living Epidermis* The living epidermis includes basal cells, which form the bottom layer of the epidermis, and melanin-producing cells. Melanin is the pigment that gives skin its color and helps protect skin cells from being damaged by exposure to sunlight.

C *Dermis* Sweat moves from sweat glands present in the dermis layer to the surface of the skin. Oil moves up along the hair follicles. The chemical characteristics of both sweat and skin oil inhibit the growth of some kinds of bacteria. Skin oil also keeps hair from drying and becoming brittle and helps keep skin soft.

D *Fat Tissue* A layer of fat tissue separates the skin from other tissues and organs. This fat layer helps cushion the body against blows, insulates the body against heat loss, and stores food.

While skin protects the outer portions of our body, an inner skin called the *mucous membrane* lines and protects the internal surfaces of hollow organs of your body.

■ Body Secretions

The air you breathe in a single day contains billions of particles, including dust and dirt as well as bacteria, viruses, and other pathogens. These particles can cause trouble if they reach your lungs. Your skin can't prevent them from entering your body. But the tissues lining your nasal passages, throat, and other internal surfaces have another way of protecting your body from invasion.

The throat and nasal passages, stomach and intestines, and all other surfaces inside the body are covered with mucous membranes. A mucous membrane is one or more layers of cells that produce a thick, sticky fluid known as mucus. Foreign particles that make their way in through the body's openings are trapped in this coating of mucus. In addition to being sticky, mucus produced by some parts of the body is important because it contains an enzyme called lysozyme that destroys the outer wall of bacterial cells and kills the invading particles. Other body secretions—including sweat, tears, and saliva—also contain lysozyme.

Lining the trachea tissue are cilia. Cilia are tiny, hairlike structures that move in waves. They carry dirt-filled mucus from the respiratory tract. As **Figure 21-3** shows, ciliary motion works with mucus to help rid the body of foreign particles.

Figure 21-3

The cilia that line the trachea and all air passages are covered with mucus that helps trap dust, bacteria, smoke, and other particles that come into your body along with the air you breathe. The wavelike motion of the cilia moves the mucus and the trapped particles to the part of the throat that lies behind the mouth. There, the foreign matter is either swallowed and destroyed by the digestive system or coughed out of the body.

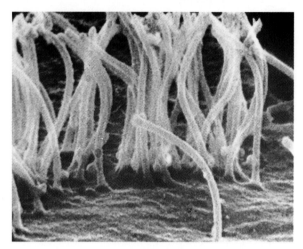

× 10 000

Second Line of Defense: Inflammatory Response

Figure 21-4

Bacteria are always living on your skin, even if you've just taken a shower. Most of these bacteria are harmless. While competing for available living space on your skin, their presence helps prevent the growth of more troublesome organisms.

What happens when you get a splinter stuck in your skin? The area around the injury becomes red, warm, and swollen. If the wound becomes infected, pus forms and the swelling increases. These events mean that bacteria have made it past your body's first lines of defense and started an infection. When pathogens manage to penetrate the skin or find a way through protective mucous membranes, your body calls its second line of defense into action.

Figure 21-4 shows bacteria that live on your skin. There are even colonies of bacteria living on the mucous membranes inside your body. Under ordinary circumstances, these organisms are harmless. However, when a splinter

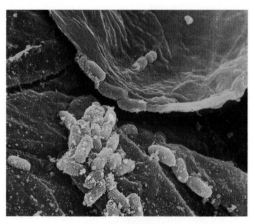

× 8000

Figure 21-5

The inflammatory response is the body's defense against foreign particles that manage to make their way past the skin or mucous membranes.

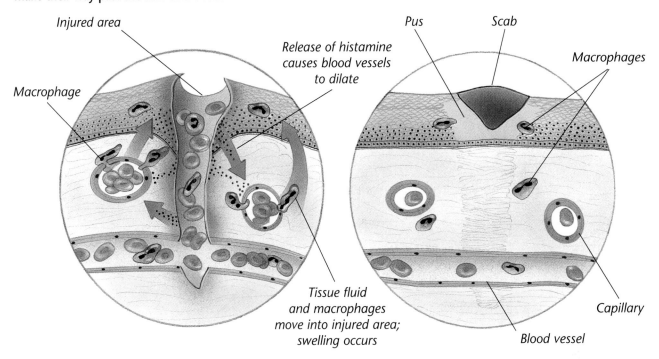

Injured area

Macrophage

Release of histamine causes blood vessels to dilate

Pus   Scab

Macrophages

Tissue fluid and macrophages move into injured area; swelling occurs

Blood vessel

Capillary

A Damaged tissue releases a substance called *histamine,* which causes blood vessels to expand and become porous. Blood flow to the area increases, increasing the pressure in the vessels and pushing fluids and white blood cells into the surrounding tissue. The increase in fluids in the injured area causes redness, swelling, and heat.

B As blood moves into the opening in the skin, it clots and forms a scab to close the wound and reestablish the body's front line of defense. Macrophages and other phagocytes surround and engulf foreign particles in a process known as *phagocytosis,* which means "eating cells." Once ingested, the pathogens are chemically broken down and destroyed. If the wound becomes infected, pus may form. Pus is a combination of tissue fluid, dead phagocytes, and dead or living pathogens.

pushes through your skin, it brings along with it not only any organisms that happen to be on its surface, but also some of the bacteria that have been living on your skin. Once they penetrate the epidermis, even harmless bacteria may cause an infection. Your body takes action to get rid of all foreign particles by initiating a sequence of events known as the inflammatory response.

The **inflammatory response** is the body's initial local healing reaction to infection or injury. The term *inflammatory* comes from the word *inflame,* which means "to set on fire." The body's

inflammatory response is demonstrated in **Figure 21-5.** Damaged skin tissue produces chemicals that cause nearby blood vessels to swell, delivering more blood to the area. This blood carries many types of blood cells, including several types of white blood cells known as phagocytes. **Phagocytes** are white blood cells that surround, engulf, and consume foreign particles. **Macrophages,** the largest of the phagocytes, engulf damaged cells as well as large numbers of invading pathogens. **Figure 21-6** on the next page shows macrophages in the process of consuming a group of bacteria.

Figure 21-6

Macrophages engulf invading pathogens as well as damaged cells.

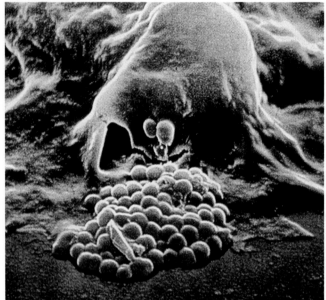

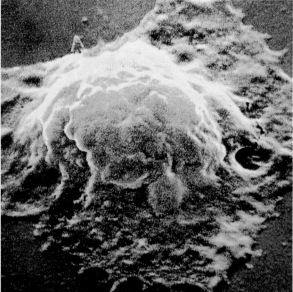

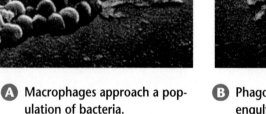

A Macrophages approach a population of bacteria.

B Phagocytosis takes place as the macrophages engulf the bacteria.

Connect to...

Chemistry

When the inflammatory response is widespread enough, the body develops a fever to fight the infection better. How does an increase in temperature help phagocytosis more effectively fight pathogens?

Skin and body secretions including mucous membranes, sweat, tears, and saliva make up your body's first line of defense while the inflammatory response is called the second line of defense. Together, these two defensive lines are useful against almost any kind of pathogen. They are known as non-specific defenses because your body only has to recognize that the invading particle is foreign. Nonspecific defenses can't always protect you from infection, but the body's defenses have not yet been exhausted. The body is also capable of recognizing a specific pathogenic organism and developing defenses to target that pathogen if it ever invades your body again.

In the next section, the immune system (the third line of defense) will be examined. The immune system is known as a specific defense.

check your UNDERSTANDING

Understanding Concepts

1. Describe how the skin protects the body from infection.
2. Describe how the mucous membranes protect the body from infection.
3. When is the inflammatory response initiated?

Skill Review

4. **Concept Mapping** Sequence the events that take place during the inflammatory response. For more help, refer to Concept Mapping in the *Skill Handbook.*

636 Chapter 21 Preventing and Treating Disease

The Immune System

Third Line of Defense: The Immune System

Objectives
- Compare and contrast active and passive immunity.
- Sequence the steps involved in developing antibody immunity.
- Differentiate between antibody immunity and cellular immunity.
- Explain how autoimmune disorders affect the body.

Key Terms
active immunity
passive immunity
antigen
antibody
B cell
T cell
antibody immunity
cellular immunity
autoimmune disease

If you had chicken pox or German measles when you were younger, you probably remember being sick in bed with an itchy rash. Your doctor may have tried to console you by letting you know that you would never have this uncomfortable disease again because your body was building up an immunity to it. Immunity is the body's ability to recognize and resist infection by specific pathogens or toxins. The immune response is the process by which the body develops immunity to a particular disease.

The body can have two general types of immunity, active and passive immunity. **Active immunity** occurs when your body on its own produces substances, called antibodies, that destroy particular pathogens to which you have been exposed. In contrast, **passive immunity** occurs when these antibodies are produced by another source, human or an animal, and then transferred into your body. Active and passive immunity are further described in **Figure 21-7** and **Figure 21-8** on the next page.

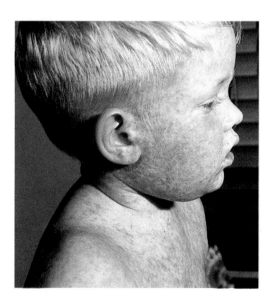

Figure 21-7

Antibodies are produced within your own body during active immunity.

A While this child is suffering from measles, his body is busy developing active immunity to the measles virus. If he is ever again invaded by that virus, his body will chemically recognize and destroy it quickly enough to prevent him from becoming ill. Although such natural active immunity takes time to develop, it may last a long time or even a lifetime.

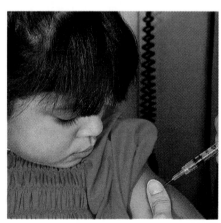

B Artificial active immunity requires a vaccination. Booster shots containing dead or weakened pathogens are injected into your body. Your body, in turn, produces antibodies against these pathogens. Some vaccinations are long-lasting and often permanent.

Figure 21-8

Passive immunity is a method of receiving antibodies produced in another human or an animal.

A An immune mother transfers her antibodies to the fetus through the placenta and to her baby through her breast milk. This gives the baby natural passive immunity for several months against all the pathogens to which the mother is actively immune.

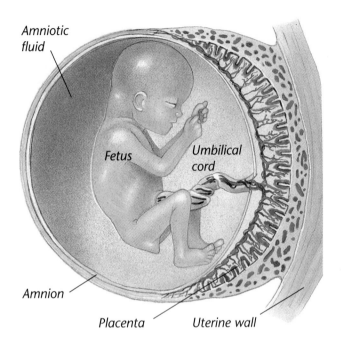

Amniotic fluid

Fetus

Umbilical cord

Amnion

Placenta   Uterine wall

B Some diseases, such as tetanus, develop so rapidly that if you have not been immunized previously, the body cannot build up active immunity quickly enough to fight them. In these cases, another animal such as a horse or pig is used to develop an immunity to the disease. That temporary immunity is transferred by injecting blood serum containing antibodies from the animal into a human.

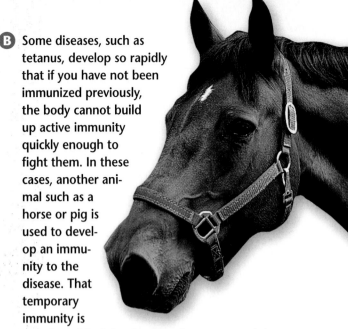

How is immunity developed? The process begins with macrophages, which are the giant white blood cells that engulf and destroy pathogens. The next activity will give you an opportunity to watch a cell engulf and destroy a foreign particle.

MiniLab

What is phagocytosis?

Amoebas, unicellular protists, and macrophages may seem worlds apart, but they share an important similarity. Using phagocytosis, amoebas consume food and macrophages destroy foreign particles in the body. By watching phagocytosis in an amoeba, you can get an idea of how phagocytosis occurs in a macrophage.

Procedure

1. Make a wet mount slide of an amoeba culture.

2. Observe the slide under low power of the microscope. The unicellular amoebas will look grainy and irregularly shaped. Record how they move.

3. Place a drop of food culture on the slide. Watch carefully to see whether you can catch an amoeba in the act of engulfing its meal.

4. Add a coverslip to your slide and observe it under high power. Record your observations.

Analysis

1. Describe the phagocytosis process.

2. List two differences between an amoeba and a human macrophage.

Building Immunity with Antibodies

By observing how a cell can surround and consume a particle in the previous MiniLab, you have seen what happens in an inflammatory response as well as what occurs during the first step in developing immunity. Your immune system begins recognizing a specific pathogen when a macrophage engulfs it. How can a macrophage tell the difference between a particle that belongs in your body and one that doesn't? One of the ways a macrophage does this is by chemically recognizing the presence of antigens.

■ Antigens

An **antigen** is any foreign substance that can cause an immune response. An antigen might be one of the proteins making up the outer coating of a virus particle or the cell wall of a bacterium. A waste product given off by a pathogen, or a toxin it secretes, might also be an antigen. Antigens are markers that can be used to identify specific pathogens. For example, strep throat bacteria have antigens that are different from those of any other pathogen as well as different from your own body tissues. The same is true of the measles virus, the chicken pox virus, or the virus that causes AIDS.

■ Antibodies

Your immune system is capable of recognizing an antigen and forming chemicals called antibodies that can be used to fight it. **Antibodies** are molecules produced by certain kinds of white blood cells to chemically neutralize or destroy antigens. Antibodies, as illustrated in **Figure 21-9,** are made of proteins with shapes that match those of different antigens. The name *antigen* refers to the fact that it is an *anti*body-*gen*erating molecule. Antibodies do not destroy pathogens on their own, but they help start the process.

Figure 21-9

Antibody molecules are made up of protein chains organized into a Y shape. The shape of the two ends at the top of the Y is variable. When an antibody is created, these two ends are shaped so that the antibody binds only to the antigen it is programmed to destroy. When an antibody binds to an antigen, it marks the antigen for quick destruction by nearby macrophages or neutralizes the antigen by preventing it from attaching to a host cell.

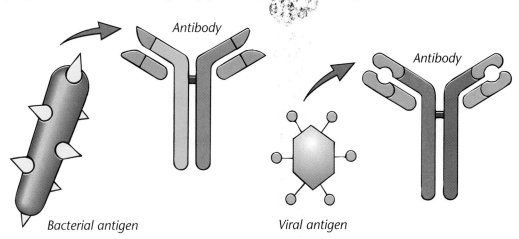

Antibody

Antibody

Bacterial antigen

Viral antigen

Figure 21-10

Antibody immunity uses B cells and antibodies to help destroy pathogens, including bacteria, viruses, and toxins.

Figure 21-10 illustrates how antibodies are formed. One method in which the immune system destroys specific pathogens is called **antibody immunity**, a form of chemical warfare involving several types of cells. Follow their activity in **Figure 21-10.** The white blood cells directly involved in defending the body against infection and disease are B cells and T cells. **B cells** are white blood cells that are produced in *bone marrow*. **T cells** are white blood cells that are produced in bone marrow as well, but they undergo development in the *thymus*, which is a small organ located just above your heart.

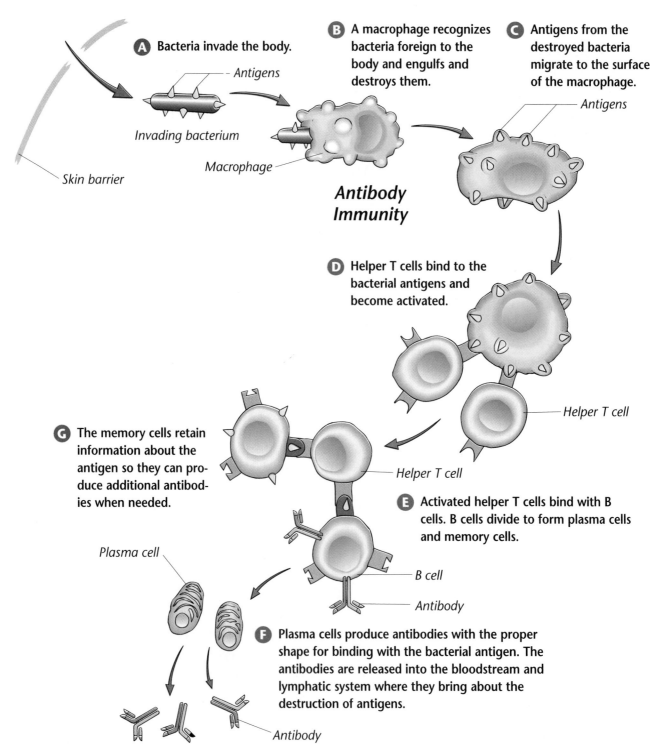

A Bacteria invade the body.

Antigens

Invading bacterium

Skin barrier

B A macrophage recognizes bacteria foreign to the body and engulfs and destroys them.

Macrophage

Antibody Immunity

C Antigens from the destroyed bacteria migrate to the surface of the macrophage.

Antigens

D Helper T cells bind to the bacterial antigens and become activated.

Helper T cell

Helper T cell

G The memory cells retain information about the antigen so they can produce additional antibodies when needed.

E Activated helper T cells bind with B cells. B cells divide to form plasma cells and memory cells.

Plasma cell

B cell

Antibody

F Plasma cells produce antibodies with the proper shape for binding with the bacterial antigen. The antibodies are released into the bloodstream and lymphatic system where they bring about the destruction of antigens.

Antibody

■ Antigen-Antibody Reactions

Antigens and antibodies play important roles other than just fighting disease. Y-shaped antibodies have two sites that can bind to antigens. As shown in **Figure 21-10G,** if an antibody comes into contact with its corresponding antigen, it binds to the antigen, marking it for quick destruction by nearby macrophages or other phagocytes. This antigen-antibody complex is sometimes referred to as a clump.

Differences in blood type are due to the presence or absence of antigens on the membranes of red blood cells. The following activity will also give you a closer look at what happens when antibodies and antigens contact one another in blood and will show the importance of known blood types.

MiniLab

What if you needed a blood transfusion?

Do you know what your blood type is? One of the characteristics you inherited from your parents is your blood type, which is either A, B, AB, or O. These blood types are identified by antigens carried on the surface of the red blood cells and antibodies carried in the blood plasma. For example, if your blood type is A, your red blood cells carry the antigen A and your blood serum contains antibodies against B antigens. Type B blood is the opposite—the cells carry the antigen B and the serum contains the antibody against A. If a person with type A blood receives a transfusion of type B, blood cells will clump together.

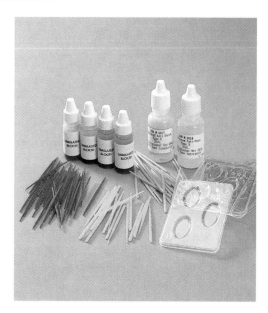

Procedure

1. Obtain four blood-testing plates from your teacher. Place a drop of simulated type A blood inside the circles marked on one of the cards, as indicated.

2. Add a drop of anti-A serum to one of the circles and a drop of anti-B serum to the other. Observe the results and record your observations.

3. Repeat steps 1 and 2 for each of the other simulated blood types.

Analysis

1. What happened when type A blood was mixed with anti-B blood serum? Explain why an antigen-antibody reaction results in clumping.

2. Discuss how clumping of blood cells could lead to death in a person who receives a transfusion of an incompatible blood type.

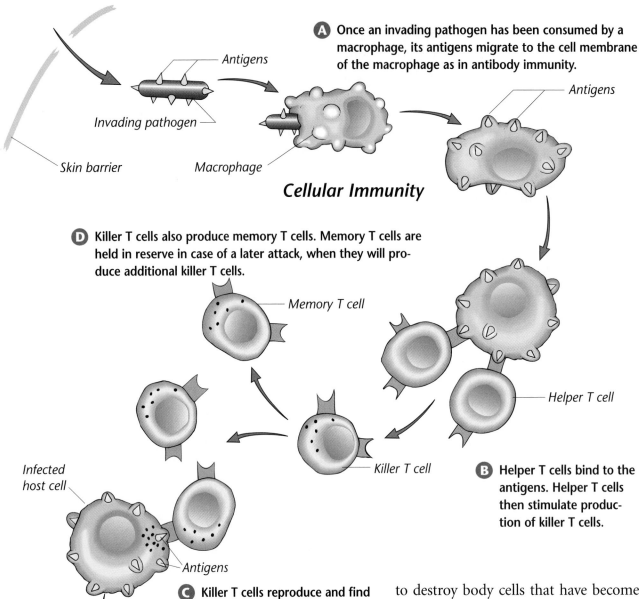

A Once an invading pathogen has been consumed by a macrophage, its antigens migrate to the cell membrane of the macrophage as in antibody immunity.

Antigens

Invading pathogen

Skin barrier

Macrophage

Antigens

Cellular Immunity

D Killer T cells also produce memory T cells. Memory T cells are held in reserve in case of a later attack, when they will produce additional killer T cells.

Memory T cell

Helper T cell

Killer T cell

B Helper T cells bind to the antigens. Helper T cells then stimulate production of killer T cells.

Infected host cell

Antigens

C Killer T cells reproduce and find already infected host cells. The killer T cell binds to foreign antigens that have become part of the infected host cell's surface membrane and kill the host cell.

Destroyed infected cell

Figure 21-11

In cellular immunity, host cells that have already been infected by the pathogen are destroyed, thus depriving the pathogen of a place to live and reproduce.

Cellular Immunity

As demonstrated in the previous activity, antigen-antibody reactions can have serious health effects. Your body is also capable of developing a second type of immunity, called cellular immunity,

to destroy body cells that have become cancerous or infected with a virus. **Cellular immunity** is an immune response that involves macrophages, antigens, and T cells, but not B cells or antibodies that are dissolved in blood. Cellular immunity destroys infected cells before they can spread to the rest of the body. Because the pathogens have infected body cells, antibodies on the surface of B cells cannot get to the antigen. As **Figure 21-11** shows, cellular immunity involves three kinds of T cells—helper T cells, memory T cells, and killer T cells. Killer T cells defend the body against viruses, multicellular parasites, fungi, some cancer cells, and foreign tissue transplants.

Autoimmune Diseases

Do you have an older friend or relative who suffers from rheumatoid arthritis? Rheumatoid arthritis is classified as an autoimmune disease. Sometimes the body's immune system cannot tell the difference between its own cells and the cells of invading pathogens or other foreign particles. When this happens, the body may begin to battle itself. An **autoimmune disease** is a condition in which the body's immune system attacks its own cells. In rheumatoid arthritis, for example, antibodies and T cells attack the membranes that protect the joints, causing pain or crippling in the hands, knees, and other joints. Medical researchers are not yet certain whether this arthritis is caused by a genetic abnormality that is inherited, or whether it results from defects in the immune system brought on by the aging process. Another autoimmune disease, often called Type I or juvenile onset diabetes, is a form of diabetes mellitus and develops in people under 20 years of age. It may be inherited. In this disease, the body's immune system attacks the pancreas cells that secrete insulin. Other autoimmune diseases include those that attack the nervous system, as described in **Figure 21-12.**

Figure 21-12

Myasthenia gravis is an autoimmune disease in which nerve cells that control muscle movement are destroyed, resulting in weak muscles. In multiple sclerosis, T cells and macrophages attack the outer covering that protects the body's own nerve cells. Symptoms are diverse depending on what nerve cells are attacked and include reduced sensory perception and motor coordination.

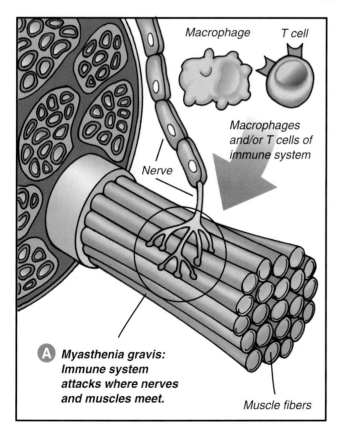

Macrophage   T cell

Macrophages and/or T cells of immune system

Nerve

A **Myasthenia gravis: Immune system attacks where nerves and muscles meet.**

Muscle fibers

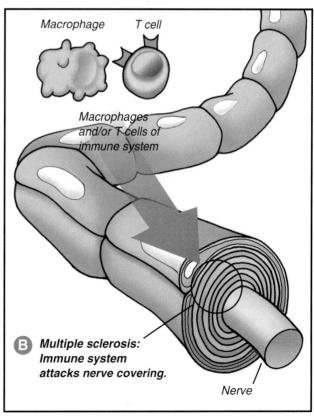

Macrophage   T cell

Macrophages and/or T cells of immune system

B **Multiple sclerosis: Immune system attacks nerve covering.**

Nerve

AIDS

Autoimmunity is only one form of disease that results from breakdowns within the immune system. Some diseases result from an inability of the immune system to respond adequately to an attack. At the present time, the most well-known—and probably the most dangerous—immune system disease is AIDS, or Acquired Immune Deficiency Syndrome. AIDS is caused by HIV, a virus that destroys helper T cells. As **Figure 21-13** shows, AIDS slowly destroys the immune system, leaving the body weakened and unable to resist infections.

Figure 21-13

The virus that causes AIDS is called the human immunodeficiency virus, or HIV. It destroys the human immune system by attacking and destroying helper T cells.

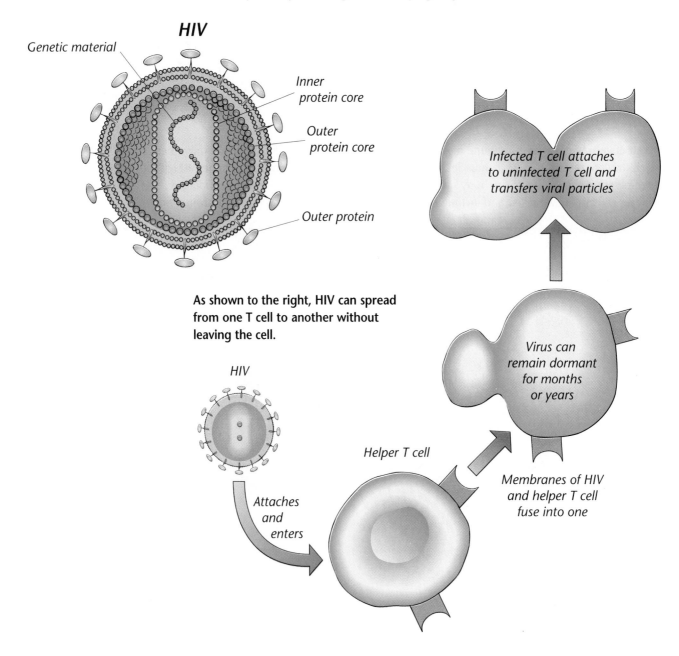

HIV

Genetic material

Inner protein core

Outer protein core

Outer protein

Infected T cell attaches to uninfected T cell and transfers viral particles

As shown to the right, HIV can spread from one T cell to another without leaving the cell.

HIV

Attaches and enters

Helper T cell

Virus can remain dormant for months or years

Membranes of HIV and helper T cell fuse into one

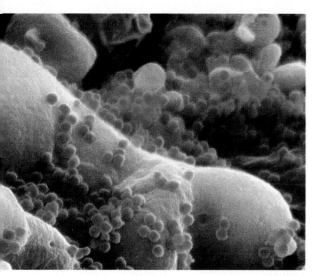

Figure 21-14

× 80 000

HIV particles (blue spheres) covering body cells.

■ Transmitting AIDS

The AIDS virus, shown in **Figure 21-14,** does not survive long outside the human body. It can be transmitted from one person to another in only four ways: (1) by contact with semen and vaginal secretions during sexual activity, (2) by injection with infected blood when intravenous drug users share AIDS-infected hypodermic needles, (3) by receiving transfusions of infected blood or by contact with infected blood during medical or dental procedures, and (4) from mother to child during pregnancy. Knowledge of these transmission methods is important because a person can be infected with HIV for many years before he or she develops symptoms of AIDS. This means people could infect others with the disease before finding out they are infected themselves, as illustrated in the Chapter 20 MiniLab on page 606 using diseased liquids.

In this section, you learned how your body attacks specific types of invaders using two levels of protection. The antibody immunity uses B cells with antibodies on their surface to stop pathogens that are in the circulatory system. If a pathogen gets inside one of your own cells without being discovered and destroyed by antibodies, then your cellular immunity uses T cells to destroy the infected cell. In the next section, you will see how knowledge of the immune system helps prevent disease and what kinds of preventive treatments can be given when the immune system does not provide enough protection.

Try It!

AIDS Awareness Many people are afraid to have any contact with AIDS sufferers because they don't understand that HIV is not spread by ordinary social contact. For example, you cannot become infected simply by sharing classrooms, homes, or bathrooms with people who have the AIDS virus. Do some research on your own to find out more about how HIV is spread and how AIDS can be prevented.

check your UNDERSTANDING

Understanding Concepts

1. Compare and contrast active and passive immunity.
2. How does cellular immunity differ from antibody immunity?
3. HIV itself does not cause the life-threatening symptoms associated with AIDS. Infected individuals become ill because they cannot fight off infections. How could this occur?

Skill Review

4. **Concept Mapping** Construct an events chain showing how antibody immunity comes about. For more help, refer to Concept Mapping in the *Skill Handbook.*

Science and Society

Issue: Getting Your Shots

In March of 1976, a three-year-old girl named Rahima Banu, in the country of Bangladesh, came down with smallpox. Why is this worth mentioning? Because she was one of the last people in the world ever to be infected with the disease. The smallpox virus was making a last stand in Rahima's body, and when she recovered, smallpox was defeated.

Just ten years before, in the mid 1960s, 2 million people contracted smallpox and died every year. Today, the only place in the world where the smallpox virus can be found is in some carefully guarded test tubes in a few bacteriology laboratories—one in Russia and one in Atlanta, Georgia. In 1979, the World Health Organization said that children did not need to be given vaccinations against smallpox anymore.

New vaccinations developed during the 1980s have significantly reduced the number of childhood disease cases. However, the number of outbreaks is increasing in the 1990s, a fact which has been linked to fewer children receiving vaccinations.

Childhood Diseases

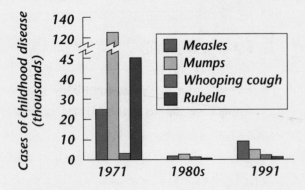

Source: Centers for Disease Control

The Issue

Since 1796, when Edward Jenner introduced the idea of vaccination, scientists have been fighting—and winning—the war against diseases like smallpox, polio, measles, and diphtheria. But there is still much work that needs to be done in this area of medicine. Smallpox may be gone but the other old, deadly plagues, and newer ones such as AIDS, still threaten the lives of millions of people worldwide. The goal of public health organizations is to see that every child in the world is vaccinated against the major killer diseases. Figuring out what the best ways are to accomplish this goal, and deciding how much the federal government should be involved, are important issues in modern preventive medicine.

The Background

Every year, 14 million children in the world die, more than 500 000 of them in the United States. Many of these deaths could be prevented if all children were immunized to protect them against deadly diseases. In the United States, less than half the children who are eight months old have had the recommended vaccinations. Why is this?

One reason some children don't get their shots is because their families cannot afford health insurance or medical treatment. That's why some cities and states provide free vaccinations, paid for by tax money, for people who can't afford to pay a doctor.

Sometimes it's just because parents don't realize how important it is that their children be

Increasing Costs

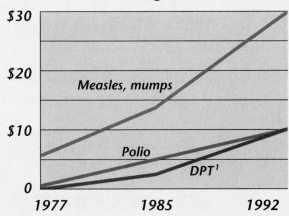

¹ Diptheria, tetanus, pertussis
Source: Centers for Disease Control

The cost of vaccinations has increased greatly over the past 15 years.

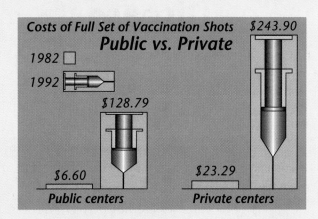

Vaccinations given in a private doctor's office are twice the cost of those given in public centers. The cost of a full set of vaccination shots multiplied 10 to 20 times in 10 years.

given the life-saving vaccines. Therefore, health organizations, as well as government agencies, sponsor educational programs through radio, television, and newspapers to remind parents to have their children immunized.

To be able to immunize everyone who is at risk requires several steps. First, scientists must discover vaccines for yet-unconquered diseases. The vaccines must then be tested, manufactured, distributed, and made available to the public. And citizens should be educated to realize the importance of immunization so that they go to the doctor's office, hospital, or clinic to receive treatment. The research, production, and education campaigns require funding.

Although most people would agree that universal immunization is a good thing, there is much debate about how to achieve it, how to pay for it, and especially, what the role of the federal government should be.

The Questions

Today, we have laws that dictate that children must have certain immunization shots before they enter school. But each year a few

people who get vaccinated have serious side effects and some have even died from the vaccines. As a result, some parents don't want their children to be immunized.

Should the government have the power to enforce vaccinations even if the parents don't want it? Should tax money be spent to provide free shots for families who can't afford to pay? Or should the role of the government be restricted to providing information to the public and letting the individual decide whether or not to be immunized? Just how far should the government be required to go to protect the health of its citizens?

Discussing the Issue

1. **Identify** two reasons why children do not receive vaccinations against known diseases.
2. Design a survey to **collect data** from your relatives to identify who has had all of the recommended vaccinations.

21-3 Preventing and Treating Disease

Objectives

- Explain how vaccines stimulate the development of active immunity.
- Compare the effects on disease of chemical drugs, radiation, and other therapies.

Key Terms

vaccine
antibiotic
analgesic

Medical Help

You've learned about the many ways the human body has of fighting off disease. But it's obvious that the body's defenses are not perfect. Modern medical research has developed a variety of ways to help prevent disease and to help people get well if they do become ill. These methods range from vaccines and drugs to more dramatic treatments such as surgery and radiation therapy.

Vaccines

Worldwide, infectious disease causes more deaths than accidents or any other kind of illness. The most effective way to prevent many communicable diseases is to vaccinate people against them. Do you remember receiving a series of vaccinations before and during your first few years of school? A **vaccine** is a substance formed from weakened, dead, or parts of pathogens or antigens that stimulates the body to develop active immunity to a disease. A vaccine is too weak to cause disease, but it stimulates the immune system to react as if it had been infected. Memory B cells and T cells are formed. If the body is later attacked by the pathogen, the immune system responds before illness occurs.

The first vaccine ever developed was a weakened version of the smallpox virus, as shown in **Figure 21-15.** Smallpox was an extremely serious, contagious disease that killed thousands of

Figure 21-15

In the year 1796, an English country doctor named Edward Jenner demonstrated the vaccine he had developed against the smallpox virus, shown at right. The demonstration was successful, and since then the vaccine has been used to immunize millions of people.

× 68 498

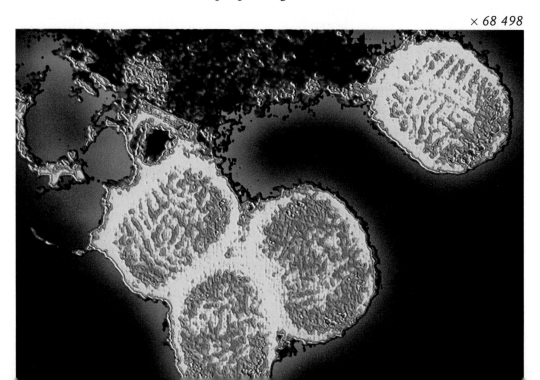

648

Childhood Immunization Schedule						Table 21-1
	Immunization					Childhood Immunization Schedule, suggested by the Committee on Infectious Diseases.
Age	Diphtheria Pertussis Tetanus	Polio	Measles Mumps Rubella	Hepatitis B (liver infection)	Influenza B	
Birth – 2 weeks				x		
2 months	x	x		x	x	
4 months	x	x			x	
6 months	x			x	x	
15 – 18 months	x	x	x		x	
4 – 6 years	x	x	x			
14 – 16 years	x[1]					

[1]tetanus diphtheria booster; also recommended for adults every ten years

Source: *The Report of the Committee on Infectious Diseases*

people every year. But a worldwide vaccination program has completely eliminated it. The last known naturally occurring case of smallpox occurred in Somalia in 1977. Because the disease no longer exists, there is no longer any need to vaccinate people against it. Other serious diseases, such as polio and tuberculosis, were also once considered to no longer be serious threats due to comprehensive vaccination programs. However, skipped vaccinations and other issues have led to recent outbreaks.

■ Immunization Schedule

Table 21-1 lists the schedule of immunizations recommended for children in the United States. Some of these diseases, such as diphtheria, may be unfamiliar to you. At one time, they were serious causes of illness and death in infants and young children. They are no longer serious threats because the vaccines against them have been so successful.

The challenge facing medicine today is to develop vaccines quickly for a new disease or a new strain of an old disease. Ways need to be found to immunize children in countries that do not yet have easy access to vaccinations and to get people to take advantage of immunization programs that are available in many countries.

Chemical Medicines

In addition to vaccines, which are usually made from the pathogens they are intended to resist, there is also a variety of chemical medicines, or drugs, available for fighting disease. Many of these medicines are substances originally derived from plants or fungi. Modern chemists and pharmacists have studied these substances and learned how to synthesize many of them. They include antibiotics to fight bacterial infections, drugs used in cancer chemotherapy, and pain-relieving drugs. In the following Investigation, you will observe the response of bacteria to different antibiotics.

How do antibiotics affect the growth of bacteria?

The effectiveness of an antibiotic against a particular strain of bacteria can be tested in the laboratory. Medical researchers and physicians use this information to determine which antibiotics to prescribe to someone with an infection. You can do the same kind of testing using sterile petri dishes containing nutrient agar and paper disks that have been soaked with antibiotics. When one of these disks is placed on the culture dish, the antibiotic diffuses into the agar. If the antibiotic is effective against the bacteria growing in that part of the dish, a clear ring called a zone of inhibition will form around the disk. The zone of inhibition shows that the bacteria in this region have been killed.

Preparation

Problem

How can you determine which antibiotic is most effective against a particular strain of bacteria?

Hypothesis

In your group, brainstorm possible hypotheses and discuss the evidence on which each hypothesis is based. Select the hypothesis you would like to test.

Objectives

In this Investigation, you will:
- *Compare* the effectiveness of different antibiotics against a particular strain of bacteria.
- *Determine* which antibiotic would be most effective in treating an infection caused by this strain of bacteria.

Possible Materials

commercially available bacteria cultures
sterile nutrient agar petri dishes
antibiotic disks
sterile disks of blank filter paper
marking pen
cotton swabs
forceps
37°C incubator
metric ruler
laboratory burner

Safety Precautions

Always wash your hands after handling materials that contain live bacteria. Properly dispose of cotton swabs, antibiotic disks, and culture dishes.

DESIGN YOUR OWN
INVESTIGATION

Plan the Experiment

1 Decide on a way to test your group's hypothesis. Keep the possible materials in mind as you plan your procedure. Be sure to include a control.

2 Prepare a list of numbered steps to follow as you conduct your experiment. Make a list of the materials you will need.

3 Design a table for recording your data. What will you measure? How will you measure it?

Check the Plan
Discuss the following points with other group members to decide the final procedure for your experiment.

1 What is your one independent variable?

2 What is your control?

3 How will you safely handle the bacteria? How will you safely handle the antibiotic disks?

4 What data will you collect, and how will you record them?

5 *Make sure your teacher has approved your experimental plan before you proceed further.*

6 Carry out your experiment and make any needed observations.

Analyze and Conclude

1. **Measuring in SI** How did you measure the zones of inhibition? How did you make sure each test section was measured in the same way?

2. **Comparing and Contrasting** Did one antibiotic cause a larger zone of inhibition than the others? What would be the significance of this result?

3. **Analyzing** Did your data support your hypothesis? Explain why or why not.

4. **Drawing Conclusions** If you were a physician treating a patient with an infection caused by this strain of bacteria, what antibiotic would you prescribe? Why?

Going Further

Analyze
Think of ways to improve your procedures if you were to do this experiment again. Explain your reasons for the changes.

Figure 21-16

Bacterial colonies are destroyed by *Penicillium* mold, growing in the same agar plate.

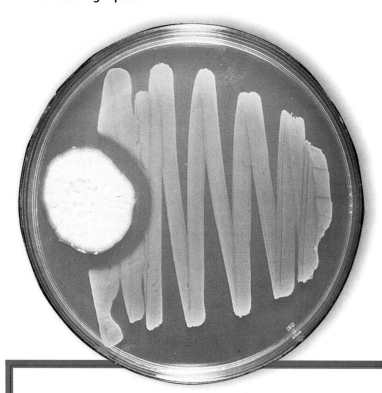

■ Antibiotics

Vaccines have been developed to protect against some of the most serious pathogens, but not all. Medical science has also developed chemicals that slow or stop the progress of disease, such as the antibiotics you tested in the previous Investigation. **Antibiotics** are substances produced by microorganisms, usually bacteria or fungi, that kill or slow the growth of other microorganisms. If you've ever taken penicillin, streptomycin, or tetracycline, you've used antibiotics to cure an infection.

The discovery of antibiotics happened by accident. The antibiotic penicillin is produced by mold called *Penicillium*. In 1928, the English scientist Sir

Kelly (left) and sister, Jenny

A Close Call

Everything seemed fine until Kelly's freshman year in high school. She had been running track and playing field hockey, but then she began tiring easily. When she developed a rash and nose bleeds, her mother took her to the doctor, who gave her a blood test.

The Unexpected

The next day, the doctor sent Kelly for more tests. After being diagnosed with leukemia, she started chemotherapy

that same night. Kelly had acute lymphoblastic leukemia, which affects the blood-forming tissues. She would have to undergo chemotherapy for two years, along with radiation treatments. In October of her sophomore year, while still undergoing chemotherapy once a month, Kelly was able to return to school. She went gladly, wearing a wig to cover her baldness.

By her junior year, despite the continued treatments, Kelly's hair had grown back and she had rejoined her field hockey team. She counted the days until May 13, when she

Alexander Fleming was growing some cultures of staphylococcus bacteria in his laboratory. He noticed that a mold had contaminated some of his cultures and was growing along with the bacterial colonies in a few of the culture dishes, as shown in **Figure 21-16.**

In the areas where the mold was growing, the bacteria were being destroyed. Further experimentation indicated that the *Penicillium* mold produced a substance that destroyed the cell walls of the bacteria.

Antibiotics can be extremely effective in curing diseases caused by pathogenic organisms, including bacteria, fungi, and protists. However, antibiotics have no effect on diseases caused by viruses.

■ Chemotherapy

Antibiotics are not the only drugs that have been developed to fight disease. You may have heard about cancer patients undergoing chemotherapy, which is the use of drugs to treat cancer. The drugs now developed for chemotherapy are tested for their ability to kill or stop the growth of cancer cells. Many of these drugs work by destroying cells that are in the process of dividing. Because cancer is a condition in which cells divide abnormally, chemotherapeutic drugs have more of an effect on the cells of a rapidly growing tumor than they do on normal cells. However, some of the normal cells in the body reproduce fairly often, including hair follicles, the lining of the

would have her last chemotherapy treatment and a final blood test.

The Unthinkable

But after she returned home on the 13th, the hospital called. "They found some leukemic cells in my blood. I had a relapse," Kelly says. "That was really hard. The next step was more chemo and a bone marrow transplant. I knew what was coming this time. I would lose my hair again and my coordination. I would get acne and my face would puff up. It was hard."

That weekend, more than 300 friends and family threw a party for Kelly to show their support. On Monday, tests showed that Kelly's older sister, Jenny, had bone marrow that was a perfect match for Kelly and suitable for the transplant.

The transplant took place July 1, 1994. Kelly spent most of the summer in the hospital and in isolation. Undergoing extensive chemotherapy, Kelly's immune system was weakened. Now a tutor comes to her home to help her keep up with her senior-year classes. Kelly plans to graduate with her class.

The Unstoppable

"Before this happened," Kelly says, "I took my life for granted. Now I cherish life so much—the smiles and hugs, even trees, just being able to walk. I used to hate the word *cancer,* but now I know it doesn't always mean death. I want to be a doctor—so I can help find out what's causing cancer." With Kelly's excellent prognosis, in a few years she may even be called "Dr. Gabelman."

Thinking Critically

1. *Infer* why Kelly had to have a tutor at home to keep up with her senior-year classes.
2. *Explain* how chemotherapy affects cells.

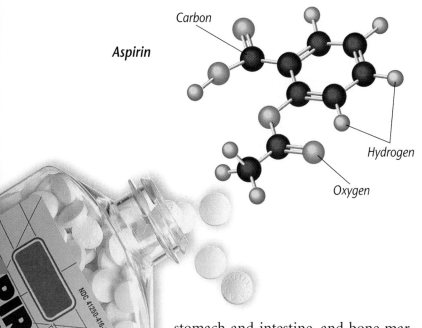

Aspirin

Carbon

Hydrogen

Oxygen

Figure 21-17

Aspirin relieves head and muscle pain and reduces fever. Like many drugs in use today, it originally came from a plant—the bark of the willow tree. As an extract of willow bark, aspirin has been in use for more than 2000 years.

Physicians warn children and teenagers not to take aspirin because it has been associated with a potentially fatal disease called Reye's syndrome. Also, some adults cannot use aspirin because it can cause digestive upsets and other problems. Fortunately, a number of alternative analgesics are available, labeled under numerous trademark names including acetaminophen, ibuprofen, and phenacetin.

Other Treatments

Radiation, in the form of X rays, can help diagnose some illnesses. Radiation can also help treat disease. Like chemotherapy, radiation therapy is most often used to treat cancer. High-energy X rays, radioactive isotopes, or electron beams are used to bombard cancer tumors with high-energy particles. The energy of the particles may destroy the cancer cells directly, or they may knock electrons from DNA molecules, causing the cell to die when it tries to divide.

stomach and intestine, and bone marrow. Therefore, cancer patients who are being treated with chemotherapy sometimes experience side effects that include hair loss, digestive system upsets, and fatigue.

■ Pain Relievers

One of the most frequently used drugs in the world today is simple aspirin, shown in **Figure 21-17.** It is one of a group of drugs called **analgesics,** which relieve pain without affecting consciousness. Unlike stronger pain-relieving drugs, such as morphine or codeine, analgesics are not addictive. You may have used aspirin to relieve headaches, muscle aches, or to help reduce fever. How aspirin acts to relieve pain and reduce fever is not completely understood. It is thought that aspirin blocks the action of one of the substances involved in sending pain messages from the muscles to the brain. Because the hypothalamus is the part of the brain that controls body temperature, it is also believed that aspirin probably reduces fever by influencing the hypothalamus.

■ The Search Continues

Medical scientists are always looking for new substances that can be used to cure or treat disease. Some researchers test plant materials to see whether they have antibiotic properties, relieve pain, or have other desirable effects on the body. Other researchers use computers and complex laboratory equipment to design entirely new molecules that might make useful drugs. Once a promising substance is identified, it must be thoroughly tested. These new drugs are considered experimental until they have been proven safe and effective.

One of the most well-known experimental drugs developed in recent years is zidovudine, or AZT. AZT is given to HIV-infected individuals to help delay the progression to AIDS. The AZT is a molecule that is normally found in the body. It is used by the cell to form an altered thymine, one of the nucleic acids that make up DNA. HIV mistakenly uses the AZT molecule instead of thymine when making copies of itself, as shown in **Figure 21-18.** Viruses that have the incorrect DNA cannot duplicate properly, which slows the spread of the virus within the body. Unfortunately, AZT causes some serious side effects including liver and bone marrow damage as well as nausea and cannot be used by all AIDS patients. The search continues for more and better drugs to fight AIDS. There is also hope that a vaccine against HIV will someday be developed.

■ Final Diagnosis

Although exposed to a great variety of disease-bearing pathogens every day, not everyone is sick. Obviously, the lines of defense in the human body are working effectively to maintain homeostasis. However, you will occasionally come down with a disease of some type, and it is important that you be examined by a doctor who can diagnose the disease. Without a correct diagnosis, effective medical treatment is delayed, sometimes leading to a more serious illness.

Diagnosing disease is a science. Scientific methods are employed in which medical doctors and scientists work together to identify the causes of and cures for disease. In the next chapter, you'll learn about laboratory techniques and medical technologies that are being used by hospitals and labs in an effort to identify various diseases.

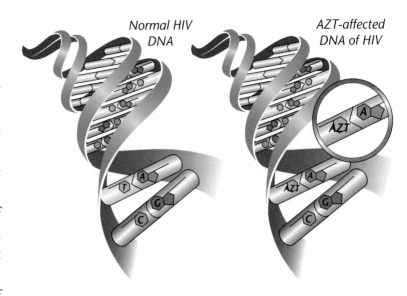

Normal HIV DNA   *AZT-affected DNA of HIV*

Figure 21-18

When AZT is used to make HIV DNA instead of thymine, incorrect duplication occurs and the spread of the AIDS virus slows down.

---

check your UNDERSTANDING

Understanding Concepts
1. How does a vaccine affect the immune system?
2. Explain the difference between a vaccine and an antibiotic.
3. Compare the effects of chemotherapy and radiation therapy on cancer cells.

Skill Review
4. **Making and Using Tables** Construct and complete a table listing the various types of medical help available. Indicate whether they are preventive methods or treatment. Include the diseases for which they are used. For more help, refer to Making and Using Tables in the *Skill Handbook*.

people in SCIENCE

Meet Crystal Terry, Anesthesiologist

Some TV shows make the role of a doctor seem grand and glamorous, but that's not real life in the operating room, explains Dr. Crystal Terry. "Sometimes patients can be very hostile when they are in pain and scared. I can be friendly and helpful when all of a sudden—pow!—they're yelling at me. Doctors have to be able to tolerate the imperfections that accompany a science that involves people."

In the following interview, Dr. Terry describes how she became an anesthesiologist and why she feels her job is important.

On the Job

Q What is your typical working day like?

A I get into the operating room early to check over my anesthesia machine. With all the dials that measure the flow of gases and monitor the patient's heart rate and blood pressure, it reminds me of the cockpit of a plane. Then I check my utilities cart. Its drawers contain things such as drugs to correct abnormalities in heart rate and tubes for giving medication intravenously. I plan for the worst that can happen. It never does, and that's fine with me! When all the mechanical things are prepared, I'm ready to meet the day's patients.

Q How do you deal with that?

A I see two parts to my patient responsibilities. One, I thoroughly evaluate a patient's health and identify any potential problems that might interfere with the anesthetics or surgery. Two, I make a patient feel comfortable with the idea that I'll be taking care of him or her after inducing a state of sleep. To me, the most challenging aspect of my job is to convey a sense of competence and compassion to a person who is usually at a very critical point in his or her life. I always make a point of touching a patient, nonverbally conveying the feeling that there is a human contact.

Early Influences

Q How did you first become interested in the medical field?

A My father was a general practitioner and took me with him on his rounds, starting when I was eight or nine years old. One of my earliest memories is of watching my dad sew up a man's badly lacerated finger in the emergency room. As Dad described the steps to me, I remember thinking how amazing it was that the man didn't seem to be feeling pain. I didn't realize at the time that Dad had given him anesthesia.

Q Were your career plans evident to you while you were in high school?

A For a long time, I wanted to be a veterinarian because I loved animals, especially horses. Then I had a brief period in which I wanted to be an actress and a dancer. I think it's healthy to have those kinds of dreams. But a young person needs to figure out that work is just as much a part of living as breathing, eating, and sleeping and that learning how to do something well is enjoyable as well as necessary. Just about everything I've learned has turned out to be valuable. For instance, my training on stage has taught me how to be attentive and focused with patients, even when I've dealt with seven surgeries in a single day. That takes a lot of energy.

There are many careers in the field of medicine, each with its own skill requirements. Write a Help Wanted advertisement for one of the careers listed. Include the skills, training, and characteristics of the ideal job candidate.

▶ *doctor, medical records technician, X-ray technician, phlebotomist, physician's assistant, paramedic*

Personal Insights

Q Has your interest in the arts continued?

A I'm learning to play jazz piano and I do fund-raising for an African-American dance troupe. I also own and run a flower shop with my mother. Another interest is mentoring students in premed and medical school. Medicine is a tough field and students need encouragement.

Art and Healing

Art Connection

Medical research points in many directions. One direction involves the patient's own mind and nervous system. Medical researchers are discovering that patients can improve their own healing rates if they become artists.

The Mind-Body Connection

Stress and anxiety seem to predispose the body to illness. Depressed patients develop post-operative infections and complications more easily and heal more slowly than nondepressed patients. Sometimes, they don't heal at all. When doctors prescribe creative activities, many patients' health improves.

Patients with quadraplegic injuries, patients with multiple sclerosis, patients with inoperable cancers, and abused children are just a few of the categories of people who can be helped by art therapy. Becoming an artist gives the patient, who may feel like a victim, a sense of being in control. More concretely, creative activity affects the immune system by increasing the endorphin levels in the brain.

Endorphins are naturally occurring chemicals found in many regions of the brain and spinal cord. They interfere with normal nerve activity that causes people to experience pain. When endorphins chemically break down within the body, the smaller chemicals formed react against mental depression by producing a temporary state of joy and excitement. Cell chemistry, body temperature, blood pressure, and many other body systems are also changed for the better when the patient concentrates on creating art or completing a craft.

In many cases, not only the process of creating but also the product—the painting, sculpture, quilt, or other artwork—is valuable to the medical team. Abused children, for instance, may be so traumatized that they can't talk about their problems. If they can express their pain and rage nonverbally on canvas, they can begin to resolve it.

The *Healing Quilt* shown on this page was made by a woman who was going through a difficult physical and emotional time in her life. The butterflies coming out of a dark tunnel into the light of day represent her healing process and anticipation of a hope-filled future.

interNET CONNECTION

Art can help people who have experienced the loss of a loved one. Follow the link for Chapter 21 on the Glencoe Homepage to find information on the AIDS Memorial Quilt. What is the quilt's purpose? How do you think the quilt helps people deal with grief and stress following the death of a loved one?

Read the statements below that review major points presented in the chapter. Using the concepts that you have learned, answer each question *in your Journal.*

1 Your body has three different lines of defense against disease. The first line of defense is the physical barriers formed by your skin and body secretions. *How are these first lines of defense effective in preventing some diseases?*

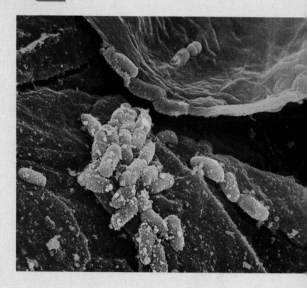

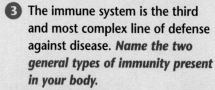

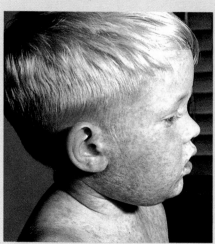

2 The second line of defense, the inflammatory response, is the body's initial reaction to infection or injury. *What types of white blood cells are involved in the inflammatory response?*

3 The immune system is the third and most complex line of defense against disease. *Name the two general types of immunity present in your body.*

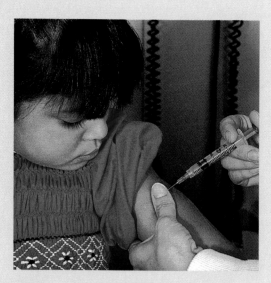

4 Many diseases can be prevented using vaccines or treated using various medications and procedures. *What is the difference between active and passive immunity?*

Using Key Science Terms

active immunity

analgesic

antibiotic

antibody

antibody immunity

antigen

autoimmune disease

B cell

cellular immunity

inflammatory
  response

macrophage

passive immunity

phagocyte

T cell

vaccine

For each set of terms below, choose the one term that does not belong. Provide an explanation for why it does not belong.

1. vaccine, T cell, antibiotic, B cell
2. active immunity, vaccine, passive immunity
3. cellular immunity, B cell, T cell

Understanding Ideas

Using complete sentences, answer the following questions in your Journal.

1. What role do phagocytes play in defending the body against disease?

2. What is the difference between active and passive immunity?
3. How does a person become infected with HIV?
4. How does immunity differ from non-specific defenses against pathogens?
5. Once you have had a disease such as mumps, why don't you usually get it a second time?
6. How does AZT affect HIV?

Developing Skills

Use your understanding of the concepts developed in this chapter to answer each of the following questions.

1. **Concept Mapping** Use the following terms and phrases to complete the concept map about disease: *active immunity, body secretions, dermis, immune response, inflammatory response, mucous membranes, passive immunity, pus, second line of defense, specific defense, tetanus shot, third line of defense*

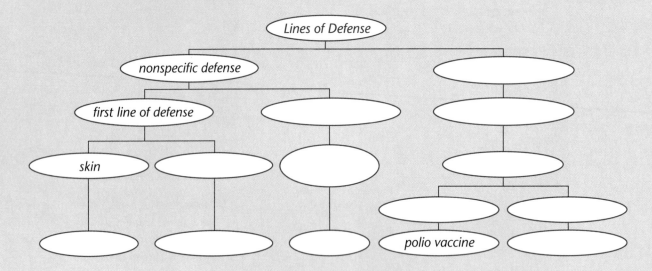

2. Predicting A virus particle in the air enters the nasal passages of a human. What happens to the virus? Describe three possible outcomes.

Critical Thinking

In your Journal, *answer each of the following questions.*

1. Antibiotics destroy pathogens by causing their cell walls to rupture. Why don't antibiotics have an effect on viruses?

2. Why do chemotherapy and radiation have a greater effect on cancer cells than on normal cells?

3. Explain how radiation therapy could cause cancer as well as help cure it.

4. Why does the combination of cilia and mucus make a better defense than mucus alone?

5. Third-degree burns destroy both the epidermis and dermis of the skin. Explain why burn victims must be kept in an environment as free of pathogens as possible.

Problem Solving

Read the following problem and discuss your answers in a brief paragraph.

A third-grade student in school has never been vaccinated against the measles virus. Suppose the virus successfully invades her body for the first time.

What is likely to happen to her? Describe what will happen to some of the white blood cells in her body. Suppose the virus again invades her body four months later. What is likely to happen to her white blood cells? What might this mean for the rest of the students in her class and their families?

CONNECTING IDEAS

1. **Theme—Stability and Change** How does AIDS upset the homeostasis in the body?

2. **Theme—Systems and Interactions** Describe the interaction of skin bacteria with the body. What happens when this interaction is upset?

3. **Theme—Energy** Explain how radiation can be used to destroy cancer cells.

4. **Science and Society** Discuss what type of immunity vaccinations represent.

5. **Art Connection** How can art be interpreted as a form of preventive or healing medicine?

CHAPTER 22

Detecting Disease
Examining the Causes of Disease

H ow does a physician determine what is wrong with someone who is ill? Physicians are a bit like detectives who hunt for clues and use them to find out why a person is ill. In this chapter, explore some of the scientific methods used to diagnose diseases. These methods range from simple observation of a patient's symptoms to laboratory tests and the use of complex technological devices.

▶ *In the following activity, examine blood samples and discover one method of detecting whether infection is present.*

MiniLab

Can infection be detected?

Red blood cells carry oxygen to body tissues, and white blood cells fight infection.

Procedure

1. Observe a prepared slide of human blood cells under low power and then high power. Without moving the slide, count and record the number of red blood cells and the number of white blood cells in your field of view.

2. Move the slide to two different positions and again count red blood cells and white blood cells.

Analysis

1. Which type of blood cell occurs in the greater number?

2. Calculate the percentage of white blood cells observed.

3. Suppose you are a physician examining a blood sample with ten times more white cells than normal. What conclusion might you draw about the health of the individual?

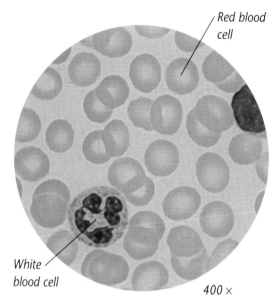

Red blood cell

White blood cell

400 ×

Field of blood cells

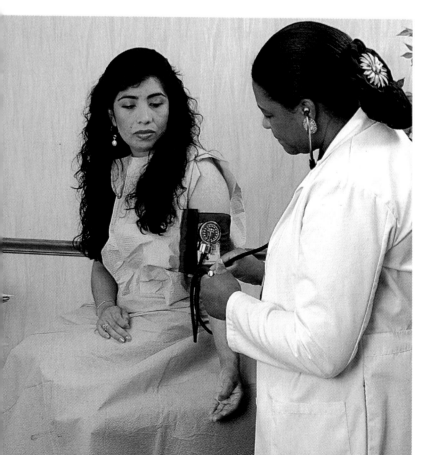

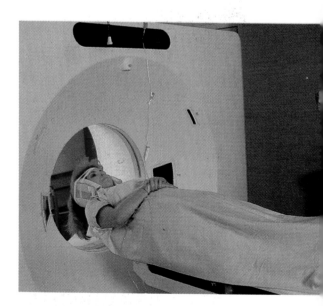

Patient undergoing a CAT scan

Observing Diseases

22-1

Objectives

- Name some common symptoms of disease.
- Explain how external examination is used to diagnose disease.
- Explain how the pathogen responsible for a disease is identified.
- Distinguish between epidemic and endemic disease.

Key Terms

disease cluster
Koch's postulates
endemic disease
epidemic

Examining the Evidence

When you are sick, a physician is able to examine different pieces of evidence, called symptoms, to see how the homeostasis of your body has been upset. The doctor will take your temperature, look at your ears and throat for signs of infection, and listen to your lungs to see whether excess mucus is present. Perhaps the doctor will take a blood test to see if your body has mounted an immune response. If it has, you will experience a number of similar symptoms regardless of what disease is present, as the previous MiniLab and **Figure 22-1** suggest. For example, an elevated number of white blood cells in the blood may suggest that an infection is present, but doesn't reveal the identity of the pathogen. Perhaps it is a bacterial infection. The Applying Math on page 665 illustrates how rapidly pathogenic bacteria can reproduce in the body.

Do you remember the last time you went to the doctor for a general checkup? Your height and weight were recorded and your pulse and blood pressure were measured. Your doctor probably also tested your reflexes, checked your eyes and ears, and listened to your heart and lungs. Many of these checks are done to detect disease

Figure 22-1

Why does infection by a cold or flu virus cause many of the same symptoms as infection by a bacteria such as *Streptococcus?* The answer lies in the body's immune response, in which the body responds to both types of infection in the same manner.

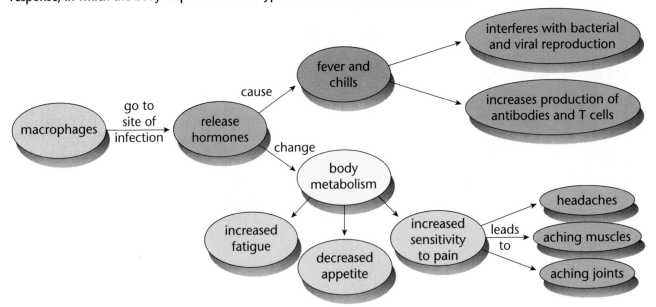

early, even before any symptoms appear. In many diseases, including cancer and heart disease, early detection and treatment can sometimes avoid or postpone serious illness.

■ Blood Pressure

Blood pressure is one of the first signs used to evaluate a person's cardiovascular health. Blood pressure is the force exerted by blood pressing against artery walls. When someone's blood pressure is higher than normal, there is too much pressure on the artery walls. The walls could break open, which may lead to a stroke or kidney failure.

High blood pressure could result from a number of factors including heredity, obesity, heart problems, plaque deposits in the arteries, and chemical imbalances. Additional tests may indicate that changes in diet, exercise habits, prescription drugs, or other actions to lower blood pressure are required. Measuring blood pressure, illustrated in **Figure 22-2**, like taking a temperature, is one way to see if the homeostasis of the circulatory system is slowly changing.

Applying Math | **Calculating Reproduction Rates**

A few species of bacteria are disease-causing pathogens that can cause us to seek medical help. How fast do they multiply inside your body? Assume that each bacterium cell divides every 20 minutes. If you started with a single bacterium cell, how many cells would there be after eight hours? Make a table or graph that covers eight hours.

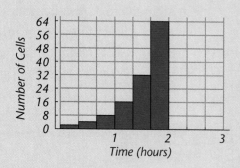

Practice Problem

1. If you started with two bacterium cells, how many cells would there be after six hours?

Figure 22-2

Blood pressure rises and falls as the heart contracts and then relaxes and is measured in mm mercury. When the ventricles contract, blood pressure rises sharply to a maximum called systolic pressure. The lowest pressure occurs just before the ventricles contract and is called diastolic. The dashed line represents the cuff pressure of the apparatus used to measure blood pressure, which is being slowly released. When the cuff pressure equals the systolic pressure, the first sound of blood flow is heard and the sound stops when it equals the diastolic pressure.

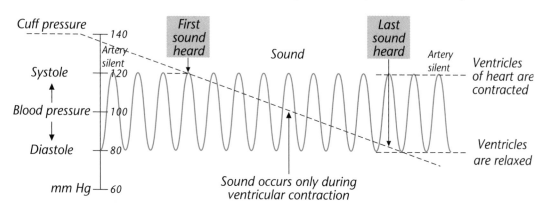

The Spreading Sickness

High blood pressure is a problem for many people, but what happens if a less common disease begins to affect a population? Disease detectives work at two different levels. One, a family physician, looks for the cause of disease in an individual. Another kind of detective, an epidemiologist, monitors disease outbreaks and looks for patterns of illness occurring in whole populations.

It isn't likely that only one person in your entire school or town will get the flu this winter. A communicable disease like the flu usually infects many members of a population before it runs its course. Epidemiologists work to identify the pathogen, environmental pollutant, or other factor that causes a particular disease. In the following activity, model outbreaks of disease.

MiniLab

Where do disease outbreaks occur?

Epidemiologists look for patterns in disease outbreaks. This activity uses iron filings to model disease distribution.

Procedure

1. Drop a handful of iron filings into a wide, flat cardboard lid. Observe the random pattern in which the filings are distributed over the cardboard.

2. Remove the iron filings and place a magnet or two underneath the box.

3. Toss the filings into the box again.

Analysis

1. How do the magnets affect the distribution of the iron filings?

2. How does the second distribution pattern model the occurrence of a communicable disease?

■ Finding Disease Clusters

In the MiniLab, you compared a random distribution of iron filings with a clumped, or clustered, distribution that was caused by the presence of a magnet. A similar thing happens in a population when something is causing people to become ill. When disease occurs with a clumped, nonrandom distribution in a population, epidemiologists call it a **disease cluster.** For example, suppose the flu is going around your neighborhood, but most of the people who are sick go to your school. If the sick students are still attending school, then your school represents a disease cluster within the population of humans in your town. Disease clusters usually occur in a specific geographic region. The presence of a disease cluster suggests that something in the area is causing the disease, just like a magnet caused the clumped distribution of iron filings.

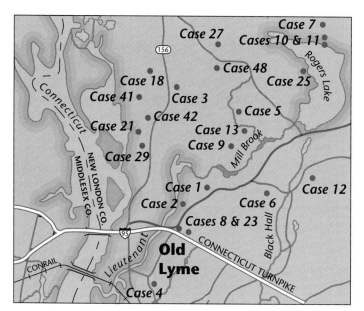

Figure 22-3

This map shows the number of Lyme disease cases observed and recorded around Old Lyme, Connecticut, in the mid 1970s.

A disease cluster indicates that there is something unique to the population, or unique in the area where they live, that is causing or spreading the disease. Lyme disease, as discussed in Chapter 20, is one example of an illness that was first noticed as a disease cluster. In the mid 1970s, when Lyme disease was first identified, it seemed to affect only people living near Lyme, Connecticut, as shown in **Figure 22-3.** Scientists from the Centers for Disease Control had reason to suspect that a tick might be the vector for this disease. The symptoms of swollen joints and a red, bull's-eye rash on the skin resembled the symptoms of another disease spread by ticks in Europe.

To test their hypothesis, researchers collected ticks in the area around Lyme by dragging light-colored cloths through the underbrush. As a result, they collected a species of tick that is similar to the European vector. They isolated a bacterium, as shown in **Figure 22-4,** from the tick and found that it caused symptoms of Lyme disease in deer and other mammals.

To understand what was causing Lyme disease, researchers started by recognizing that the disease occurred primarily in people living near Lyme, Connecticut. But the vector they suspected could have been carrying any number of disease-causing viruses, bacteria, or protists. How did they identify the pathogen responsible for the disease? How did the researchers prove that this bacterium caused these Lyme disease symptoms in humans?

Figure 22-4

Borrelia burgdorferi, a bacterium, is the pathogen that causes Lyme disease. These bacteria can be found in certain ticks.

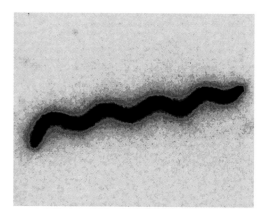

Koch's Postulates

It is possible to isolate specific pathogens that cause a disease in humans. In 1876, Robert Koch, a German doctor, was studying a disease called anthrax. The disease causes skin and lung problems in cattle, sheep, and other livestock, but can also be transmitted to humans. While working on anthrax, he established a set of experimental steps, now called **Koch's postulates,** for determining which pathogen causes a particular disease. Koch's postulates, summarized in **Figure 22-5,** are based on the premise that a pathogen taken from a diseased organism will cause the identical disease in a second organism. In the next Investigation, design an experiment to identify a pathogen.

Figure 22-5

If all four of Koch's postulates are met, a specific pathogen is confirmed as the cause of a specific disease. Once a specific pathogen has been identified and can be cultured in the laboratory, the search for a treatment or cure can begin.

A *Postulate #1* The pathogen must always be present in the host organism that has the disease.

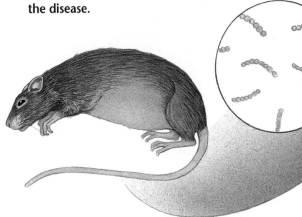

Aaaa Choo!

Sneezing; runny nose; itchy, watery eyes; dry, scratchy throat—sound like a cold? Yes. These same symptoms, however, are a part of many people's daily lives. Allergies to dust, foods, pollen, insect venom, medications, and mold spores are thought to affect as many as 40 to 50 million people in the United States. Just what is an allergy?

Allergies

An allergy is a sensitivity to a substance, called an *allergen,* to which most people have no reaction. Some allergens—like mold spores, dust, and pollen—are inhaled. Other allergens are applied to the skin or injected under the skin. Still others, like foods, are ingested.

When allergens are taken into the body of a person who is allergic to these substances, the body's immune system mistakes these substances for bacteria or viruses. This, in turn, causes the body to produce an antibody known as immunoglobulin E, or IgE, which attaches itself to cells in the nose and throat. These IgE antibodies can cause reactions that lead to runny noses, congested nasal passages, watery eyes, and so on.

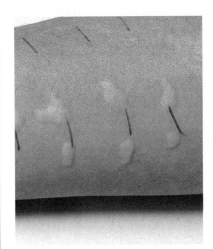

Scratch tests used to identify allergens

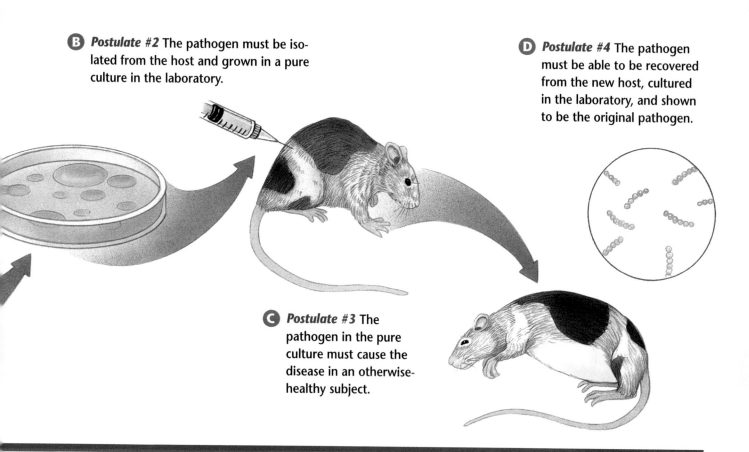

B *Postulate #2* The pathogen must be isolated from the host and grown in a pure culture in the laboratory.

D *Postulate #4* The pathogen must be able to be recovered from the new host, cultured in the laboratory, and shown to be the original pathogen.

C *Postulate #3* The pathogen in the pure culture must cause the disease in an otherwise-healthy subject.

Testing for an Allergy

Skin tests are conducted to determine whether or not a person has allergies. Generally, a doctor will do scratch or prick tests to measure a person's reaction to suspected allergens. During such tests, pictured in the photo at left, the skin is scratched or pricked and an oil containing dilute concentrations of one or more allergens is placed on the area. The reaction is monitored over time.

In some cases, more sensitive tests are performed. Intradermal tests involve injecting the allergen under the person's skin. The degree of the reaction is determined by observing the redness of the area tested as well as the size of any welts, which are bumps, that appear.

Treatment

The most obvious treatment for an allergy is, of course, avoiding the allergen. Unfortunately, many allergens are virtually everywhere. Some allergic symptoms are relieved through medications. Severe allergies are often treated by immunotherapy, or allergy shots. These injections contain dilute amounts of the allergens to which a person has reacted. The shots are often given once or twice a week for several years until the person has built up an immunity to the allergen.

*inter*NET
CONNECTION

To learn more about allergies, visit the Glencoe Homepage, **http://www. glencoe.com/**, for the Chapter 22 link to the Allerdays website. How does weather influence certain allergies? What climate conditions tend to worsen the problems?

Identifying the Pathogen

Many diseases can cause the same symptoms. How have researchers determined what species of bacteria causes strep throat or which virus causes AIDS? In this Investigation, use a laboratory model to demonstrate how scientific methods are used to determine which of many possible pathogens causes a particular disease. The fresh bread represents a potential disease victim.

Preparation

Problem

How do you identify the pathogen that causes a specific disease?

Hypothesis

In your group, brainstorm possible hypotheses and discuss the evidence on which each hypothesis is based. Select the best hypothesis from your list for your experiment.

Objectives

In this Investigation, you will:
- *Analyze* how scientific methods are used to identify the pathogen responsible for a disease.

Possible Materials

slice of moldy bread (label as slice A)
2 slices of fresh bread (label as slice B and slice C)
sterile petri dish with agar
sterile cotton swabs

Safety Precautions

Always wash your hands after handling materials that contain bacteria, fungi, or other live organisms. Keep organisms covered at all times. Dispose of contaminated objects as directed.

Plan the Experiment

1 Decide on a way to test your group's hypothesis. Keep the available materials in mind as you plan your procedure. In a laboratory analysis, the disease pathogen is not transferred directly from one organism to another. The pathogen is taken from a diseased organism, cultured, and then transferred to a healthy organism.

2 Be sure your procedure includes a control.

3 Decide how long you will observe your laboratory culture before transferring it to a healthy test "organism," and how long you will observe this test organism after you have inoculated it with the suspected pathogen.

Check the Plan

Discuss the following points with other group members to decide the final procedure for your experiment.

1 What is your one independent variable?

2 What control will be used?

3 What data will you collect? How will it be recorded?

4 *Make sure your teacher has approved your experimental plan before you proceed further.*

5 Carry out your experiment and make any needed observations *in your Journal.*

6 Give all contaminated objects to your teacher for proper disposal.

Slice A

Analyze and Conclude

1. **Evaluating Your Hypothesis** Explain how your results either support or do not support your hypothesis.

2. **Interpreting Observations** Did slices A and B exhibit the same disease symptoms?

3. **Analyzing Data** According to your results, were you able to identify the pathogen that caused slice A to become moldy?

4. **Thinking Critically** What was the purpose of slice C? Did it become diseased? Why or why not?

5. **Thinking Critically** What scientific methods were used in this Investigation?

Going Further

Project
This activity used a model to demonstrate how pathogens are identified. Describe a laboratory procedure that could be used to identify the pathogen causing a sore throat in a person.

Endemic and Epidemic Diseases

Some diseases occur only occasionally in a population. For example, malaria is rare in the United States except in people who have returned from traveling in tropical climates. However, malaria is always present in regions of Earth near the equator. A disease that is always present in a population is called an **endemic disease.** Malaria is endemic in the tropics, but not in temperate regions. The common cold is an example of an endemic disease in temperate regions.

In addition to endemic diseases, communicable diseases can spread rapidly. They can even spread all over the world fairly quickly because people travel. Suppose a businessperson from Iowa goes to a meeting in New York City. While there, she is exposed to a new strain of influenza carried by someone who came to the meeting from London. Within a month, several dozen people in Iowa have come down with this new flu.

Sometimes, so many people come down with the same illness in a short time span that it causes concern for the general health of the population. An **epidemic** occurs when large numbers of people living in the same area become ill with the same disease. In 1918–1919, an epidemic of influenza caused about 20 million deaths including more than 500 000 Americans. The bubonic plague caused the deaths of about 60 million people during the Middle Ages in Europe and Asia.

To Find Out More About ...

Air Travel and Disease read the Science and Society article *Diseases: Frequent Fliers?* on pages 726–727 in Chapter 23.

Figure 22-6

In the early 1950s, children with polio were placed in iron lungs to assist them in their breathing.

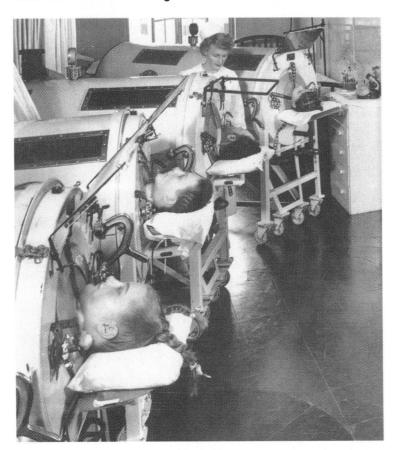

Polio and AIDS Epidemics

An epidemic of the disease poliomyelitis affected children and adults all over the world during the first half of the 20th century. When someone first becomes ill with polio, he or she has similar symptoms to someone with the flu—headache, fever, and nausea. The polio virus may further attack nerve cells in the spine, the base of the brain, or both. If it invades nerves that control swallowing and breathing, as shown in **Figure 22-6,** death may result. Many polio victims were crippled because the virus destroyed the nerves controlling their leg muscles. At the peak of the epidemic in 1953, 133 344 cases of the disease were reported in the United States. Since the 1950s, when a vaccine was developed, polio has become rare. Another important epi-

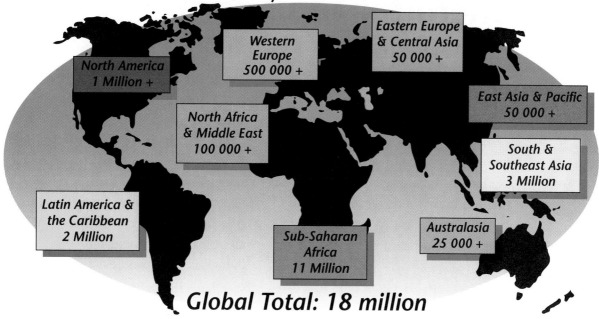

Estimated distribution of total adult HIV infections from late 1970s/early 1980s until late 1994

North America
1 Million +

Western Europe
500 000 +

Eastern Europe
& Central Asia
50 000 +

East Asia & Pacific
50 000 +

North Africa
& Middle East
100 000 +

South &
Southeast Asia
3 Million

Latin America &
the Caribbean
2 Million

Sub-Saharan
Africa
11 Million

Australasia
25 000 +

Global Total: 18 million

Figure 22-7

HIV is responsible for an epidemic that is affecting people all over the world. Just 15 years after the disease was first reported, AIDS surpassed accidents, heart disease, and cancer to become the primary cause of death in Americans ages 25 to 44. Between 1981 and 1995, more than 441 000 people became ill with AIDS and more than 225 000 died from the disease.

demic that has affected large portions of the human population is the AIDS epidemic, as demonstrated in **Figure 22-7.**

The process of detecting disease can focus on looking at the symptoms of an individual and isolating specific pathogens, or finding reasons for various diseases found within the whole population. In the next two sections, you will see how chemical and technical tools are used to detect disease in individuals.

check your UNDERSTANDING

Understanding Concepts

1. How are external examinations used to diagnose disease?
2. Using your knowledge of the human immune system, why can different diseases have similar symptoms?
3. How are Koch's postulates used to confirm the relationship between a pathogen and a disease?

Skill Review

4. **Comparing and Contrasting** Distinguish between endemic and epidemic diseases. For more help, refer to Comparing and Contrasting in the *Skill Handbook.*

22-2 Chemical Tools for Detection

Objectives

- Explain how body fluids are used to diagnose disease.
- Distinguish between passive transport and active transport.
- Explain how electrophoresis is used to identify microorganisms and biological molecules.

Key Terms

passive transport
active transport
electrophoresis

Detecting Salts and Biological Molecules

You've seen how observing external symptoms and culturing tissues can be used to diagnose disease. Physicians can also use body fluids—including blood, urine, breath, and perspiration—to detect imbalances in the body's chemistry.

The kinds of chemicals found in and around the cells of the body include salts, carbohydrates, proteins, and lipids. In a healthy body, biological processes keep these substances in balance—homeostasis is maintained. In disease, the concentrations of some of these substances may be out of balance. Measurements of their concentrations can be used to determine what is out of balance. Sometimes these chemical imbalances may be caused by pathogens, but they also occur in noncommunicable diseases like diabetes or cystic fibrosis.

In Chapter 4, you learned that because water molecules are polar, many salts will dissolve to form a solution of negative and positive ions. This attraction between water and ions can draw either of them through a membrane in a living cell. This process, in which ions or other particles move from an area of higher concentration to an area of lower concentration, is called diffusion. The result of diffusion is an equal concentration of particles throughout a fluid and on either side of a cell membrane.

■ Passive Transport

When diffusion occurs through a cell membrane in your body, as illustrated in **Figure 22-8,** it is called **passive transport.** The word *passive* refers to the fact that it does not require energy to occur.

A Lipids and particles that do not dissolve in water but dissolve in lipids easily pass through the two-molecule lipid layer that makes up most of the cell membrane.

B Channel proteins embedded in the cell membrane provide water-filled tunnels through which water molecules and dissolved particles can pass.

Figure 22-8

All particles of matter are in constant motion. In many instances, to maintain homeostasis, particles move from areas of greater concentration to areas of lesser concentration.

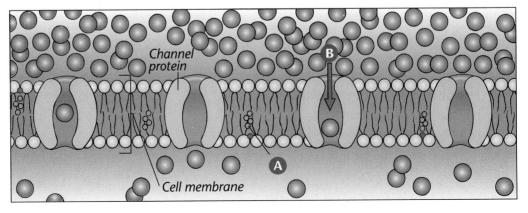

Channel protein

Cell membrane

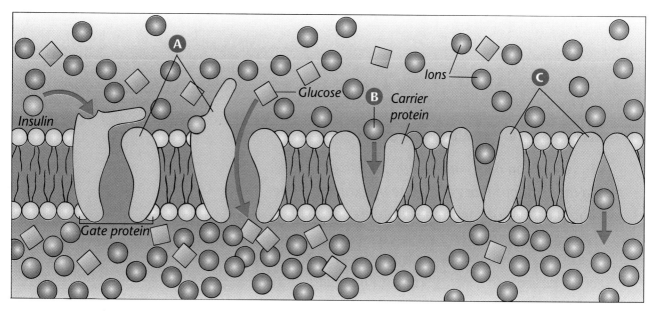

A A gate protein is a type of carrier protein. When a signal molecule combines with the gate protein, the gate opens and allows the passage of particles. In this diagram, the hormone insulin is the signal molecule that enables glucose to pass into the cell.

B A carrier protein attaches to an ion outside the cell.

C Energy from the cell causes the carrier protein to change shape and release the ion into the interior of the cell.

■ Active Transport

Sometimes, the biological activities that take place within your body result in some cells needing more or fewer particles inside them than are found in the surrounding environment. In order to maintain homeostasis, particles, such as sodium ions or protein molecules, need to be pumped either into or out of the cell, as demonstrated in **Figure 22-9.** The process of pumping particles from an area of low concentration to an area of higher concentration is called **active transport.** *Active* refers to the fact that the cell uses energy to move these particles.

Imagine dropping a deck of cards on the floor. It doesn't take energy for the cards to distribute themselves randomly on the floor—which is analogous to passive transport—while you do use energy to collect the cards together into separate, organized piles

as in the process of active transport. Both types of transport are useful in maintaining the body's homeostasis.

In some diseases, such as diabetes and cystic fibrosis, some of the proteins involved in active transport are defective. As a result, the cells are not able to maintain the proper balance of substances inside and outside of the cells. In Chapter 20, you learned that diabetics either do not produce enough insulin or the cells are unable to take in glucose from the blood. As a result, too much sugar builds up in the blood after a diabetic eats a meal. Excess glucose, not allowed in the cells by insulin, is eliminated from the body in urine. In the following Investigation, you'll examine simulated body fluids in a way similar to how a medical doctor detects diseases such as diabetes and cystic fibrosis (CF).

Figure 22-9

Carrier proteins embedded in the membrane of a cell can regulate the passage of certain ions and molecules in the process known as active transport. There is a higher concentration of chloride ions inside this cell than outside it. Processes going on inside the cell require that more chloride ions be moved into it.

INVESTIGATION

Testing Body Fluids to Detect Disease

Physicians can determine whether a person is suffering from various types of disease by examining the concentrations of important substances in body fluids such as urine and sweat. A urine test for excess glucose is commonly used to screen for diabetes. To screen patients for cystic fibrosis (CF), sweat is tested for excess sodium or chloride ions.

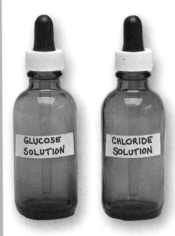

GLUCOSE SOLUTION

CHLORIDE SOLUTION

Preparation

Problem

Does the imaginary patient who is being screened for diabetes and CF have abnormal levels of glucose or chloride ions in his or her body?

Objectives

In this Investigation, you will:

- *Analyze* the composition of a solution using chemical tests.

Materials

simulated urine
simulated sweat
beaker, 600-mL
hot plate
distilled water
silver nitrate solution
Benedict's solution
glucose solution in dropper bottle
chloride solution in dropper bottle
marking pencil
test tubes (6)
test-tube holder
test-tube rack

Safety Precautions

Use care when handling hot objects. Wear eye protection at all times. Wash your hands after the activity is completed. Be sure to follow your teacher's instructions for disposing of your solutions.

INVESTIGATION

Procedure

1 Make a data table like the one shown and record all observations.

2 Label one test tube *Urine* and a second test tube *Sweat*. Pour 3 mL simulated urine into one test tube. Pour 3 mL simulated sweat into the other test tube.

3 Label four other test tubes as follows: *G, no G, Cl,* and *no Cl,* as shown in the photograph. Pour 3 mL distilled water into each of the four test tubes. Two of these test tubes will serve as controls for the glucose analysis and two for the chloride analysis.

4 Add five drops of chloride solution to the *Cl* test tube and five drops of glucose solution to the *G* test tube.

5 Add five drops silver nitrate solution to the *sweat, Cl,* and *no Cl* test tubes. Observe any color change. **CAUTION:** *Silver nitrate reacts with skin and clothing. Notify your teacher immediately if any is spilled.*

6 Place 250 mL water in the beaker and heat it on the hot plate.

7 Add 3 mL Benedict's solution to the three test tubes marked *urine, G,* and *no G*. Place these test tubes in a hot-water bath. **CAUTION:** *Benedict's solution can cause burns. Immediately flush skin and clothes with water if spilled.*

8 Leave all test tubes in the water bath for five minutes. Do not allow to boil. Record the colors of the solutions in the data table.

Step 4

Data and Observations	
Test tube	
Sweat	
Chloride ions	
No chloride ions	
Urine	
Glucose	
No glucose	

Analyze and Conclude

1. Interpreting Data Assuming that the chloride ion and glucose levels are abnormally high, should this patient undergo further tests for diabetes or cystic fibrosis? Why or why not?

2. Experimenting Why did you perform the tests on samples of distilled water?

3. Comparing and Contrasting How do the reactions that identify chloride ions and glucose molecules differ?

Going Further

Project
Interview a medical technician to find out about other kinds of medical tests that analyze urine or other body fluids. For example, find out how home pregnancy tests work.

Electrophoresis

One method used to identify microorganisms and body molecules is a process called electrophoresis. **Electrophoresis** is a method of identifying biological substances by analyzing their electrical and chemical, or electrochemical, properties. An electric current is used to drag substances through a gel. Each type of molecule in the substance moves through the gel at a different rate, creating layers, or bands, that can be used to identify it.

How does this work? Imagine tying an object to a string and dragging it through a dense forest. If the object is small and smooth, such as a round rubber ball, it will follow right along without getting caught in bushes or tree branches. But if the object is large or oddly shaped, such as a chair or bicycle, it will get stuck frequently and your movement through the forest will be slowed. Similarly, small molecules move through the electrophoresis gel more quickly than large molecules. Electrophoresis is a technique that uses an electrical field to separate molecules or charged particles. When an electrical current is applied to the gel, the molecules begin moving to the other end. The size of a molecule and the difference in electrical charge

Figure 22-10

Electrophoresis apparatus can be used to compare the DNA of a virus isolated from a flu patient with the DNA of several known strains of flu viruses. The samples to be tested are placed in small depressions at one end of the electrophoresis gel.

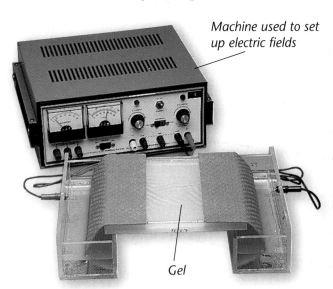

Machine used to set up electric fields

Gel

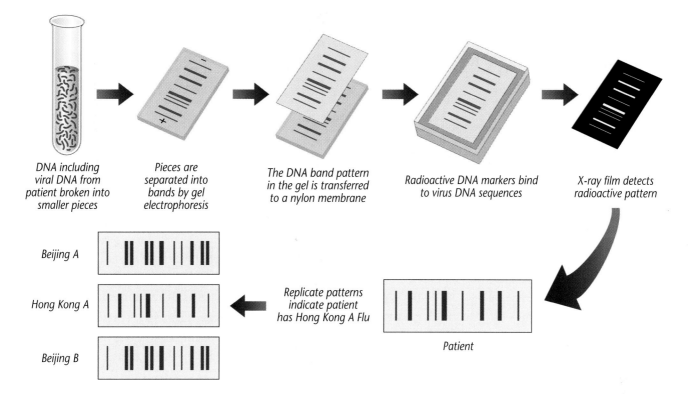

DNA including viral DNA from patient broken into smaller pieces

Pieces are separated into bands by gel electrophoresis

The DNA band pattern in the gel is transferred to a nylon membrane

Radioactive DNA markers bind to virus DNA sequences

X-ray film detects radioactive pattern

Beijing A

Hong Kong A

Beijing B

Replicate patterns indicate patient has Hong Kong A Flu

Patient

Figure 22-11

In the electrophoresis process, after 40 to 60 minutes, the electricity is turned off and the gel is examined. By comparing the banding pattern of the DNA of the unknown virus with the banding patterns of known viruses, the unknown substance can be identified. In this example, the patient is diagnosed as having Hong Kong A flu.

between the two sides of the chamber determine the speed of its progress. As **Figure 22-10** and **Figure 22-11** show, electrophoresis could be used to distinguish among different viruses by analyzing the composition of their viral DNA.

Chemical and physical tests can be used as tools to find out whether disease has affected the homeostasis of the body. In the next section, you will see how technological tools are also used by doctors and scientists to detect disease within an individual.

check your UNDERSTANDING

Understanding Concepts

1. Describe three ways in which proteins regulate the movement of molecules and ions into and out of the cell.
2. Explain why the chemical analysis of body fluids can be used to detect disease.
3. What is the purpose of electrophoresis?

Skill Review

4. **Comparing and Contrasting** Explain the difference between active transport and passive transport. For more help, refer to Comparing and Contrasting in the *Skill Handbook*.

22-3 Technical Tools for Detection

Objectives

- Describe how a light microscope enlarges an image.
- Explain how X rays, ultrasound, and magnetic resonance imaging are used to diagnose disease.

Key Terms

light microscope
X ray
magnetic resonance imaging (MRI)

Seeing the Problem

You've seen how physical observations and the analysis of body fluids can be used to diagnose diseases, but how do physicians detect diseases that are analyzable by such methods? Modern medical science also has available a variety of technologies to help pinpoint the cause of an illness or the location of a tumor or bone fracture. You are already familiar with some of these. You may have used a light microscope to observe some types of pathogens. If you've ever broken a bone, you know something about X rays. Both the microscope and the X-ray machine help the physician see objects that are small or that are located deep inside the body.

Light Microscope

Body cells and pathogens are too small to see without some kind of magnification. Ranging in size from 5×16^{-6} m and smaller, as shown in **Figure 22-12,** bacteria and viruses cannot be seen even with a hand lens. One of the most important technological tools used to diagnose disease caused by such small pathogens is the light microscope. The **light microscope** is an instrument that uses light rays and lenses to make an enlarged image of an

Figure 22-12

Pathogens, such as these viruses, require the aid of optical technologies to be seen.

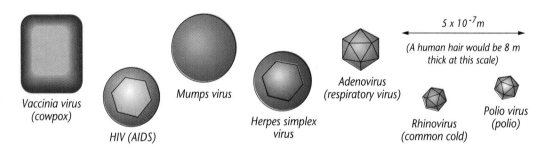

Vaccinia virus (cowpox)

HIV (AIDS)

Mumps virus

Herpes simplex virus

Adenovirus (respiratory virus)

$5 \times 10^{-7} m$

(A human hair would be 8 m thick at this scale)

Rhinovirus (common cold)

Polio virus (polio)

Figure 22-13

A magnifying glass makes an object appear larger than it is by bending, also called refracting, the rays of light coming from the object. When you hold a magnifying glass close to an object, light rays from the object travel to and through the lens. The lens changes the direction of the rays. As a result, even though the object is close to the lens, the light rays appear to be coming from a larger object placed farther away. Your eye sees the larger image.

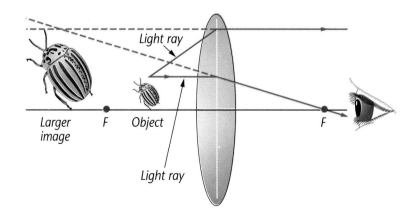

Larger image

F

Object

Light ray

Light ray

F

Figure 22-14

As light rays travel from the object on a microscope stage to the eye, they are refracted and reflected by a series of lenses and mirrors.

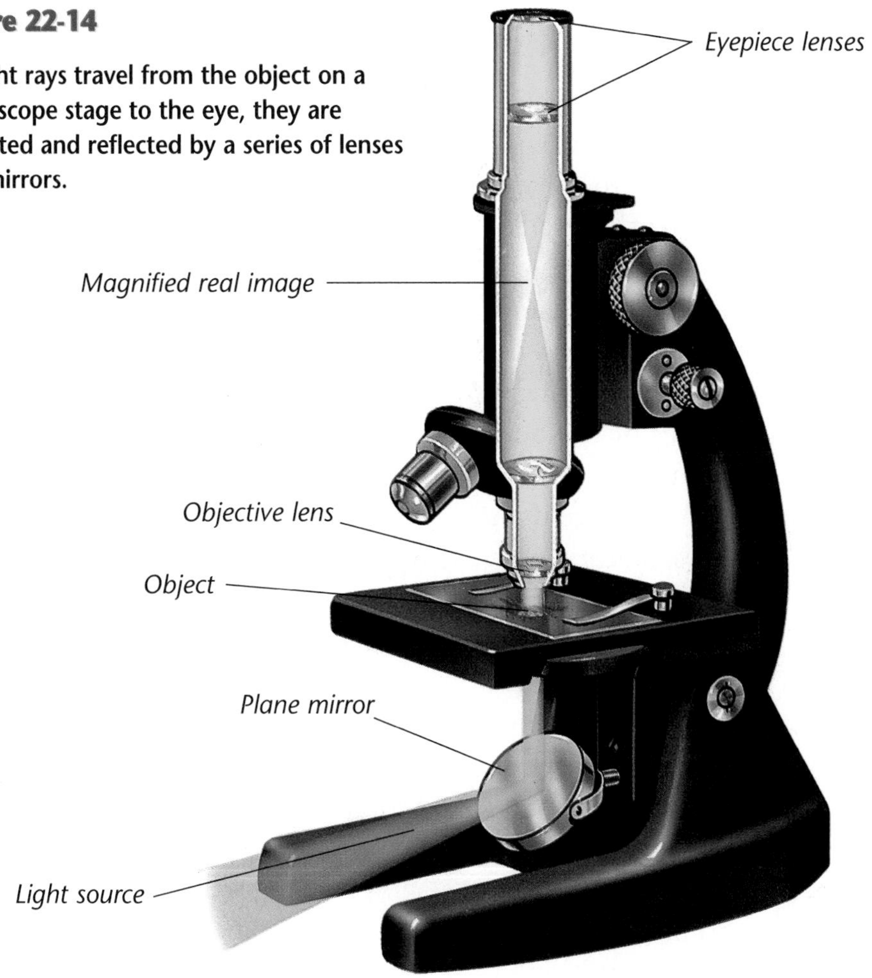

object. Do you know how the microscope works? To find out, you first need to understand how a magnifying glass makes an enlarged image, as described in **Figure 22-13.**

A magnifying glass is made of a curved piece of transparent glass called a lens. A single lens cannot bend light rays far enough to enable you to see a bacterium or a body cell. The magnification of tiny objects requires using several lenses at once. The microscope you use in the classroom is called a compound microscope because it contains several lenses. These lenses are combined to increase the magnification of an object. **Figure 22-14** shows the pathway of light rays as they travel through the lenses of a compound microscope.

Although compound microscopes can be used to observe tissues or pathogens removed from your body, it is often safer and more convenient to be able to see inside the body without invading it surgically. Images of body organs are common ways used by doctors to observe internal conditions.

■ X Rays

Up to the discovery of X rays in 1895, the only way physicians could examine the inside of the human body was by direct inspection. They could either dissect dead bodies to study human anatomy or they could perform surgery to determine the cause of a disease by observing internal evidence. X rays provided the first imaging technology to observe the body's interior without opening it up.

You saw how the compound microscope uses one form of electromagnetic radiation—visible light—to form an image. **X rays** are a form of electromagnetic radiation, but of higher frequency and energy than visible light, that can be used to form an image. X rays pass directly through low-density materials such as the soft tissues of the body, paper, cloth, and aluminum. But they will not be absorbed by more dense materials such as bones, cancer tumors, and heavy metals such as lead. This is illustrated in **Figures 22-15A, 22-15B,** and **22-15C.** Therefore, X-ray images, or radiographs, can be used by physicians to observe the living skeletal system and organ placements, and specific medical concerns such as broken bones, enlarged organs, and many tumors without surgery or pain.

There are serious limitations to using X rays, however. X rays are two-dimensional pictures. Therefore, some problems cannot be diagnosed because different body organs and other structures involved may be hidden deep within tissues or behind a more dense object. More importantly, X rays carry enough energy to damage the DNA in living cells. As you have already learned, damaged DNA can lead to cancer, or, if the damage occurs in egg or sperm cells, genetic abnormalities can be inherited. Because of this risk, X rays are used only when necessary and only in combination with lead aprons or screens to protect surrounding tissues not being examined.

■ CAT Scans

While a single X ray provides a two-dimensional image, such as **Figure 22-15C,** imagine being able to take many X rays of the same hand from several different directions at the same time. As shown in **Figure 22-15D,** technology called CAT scanning, discovered in the 1950s, does just that. A CAT scan, also known as a CT scan, is a computerized three-dimensional image of a slice of an object.

A If you hold your hand in front of a window, what you see is a silhouette. Visible light cannot penetrate your tissues, so your hand blocks the light from the window.

B If you hold your hand in front of a high-intensity lamp, you can see a glow through the thinnest skin between your fingers. The slightly more intense light waves from the lamp can barely penetrate thin tissues.

Figure 22-15

Visible light has only enough energy to penetrate the thinnest materials. Higher-energy X rays can penetrate soft tissue.

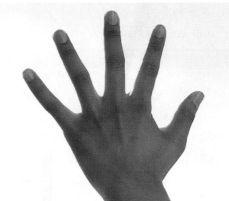

CAT stands for *computerized axial tomography* or, more simply, *computerized tomography (CT)*. Tomography is the use of X rays from many different directions to get a combination of pictures. As illustrated in **Figure 22-16,** a computer is used to combine the information from the different X rays to create a three-dimensional image that has greater contrast from surrounding tissues or bones. The resulting image is more clear and provides more precise information to a physician who is trying to diagnose a problem. In addition to producing cross-section images, the computer can store information, manipulate it, and show it as sequential images, producing moving pictures of the working body.

CAT scans can be used to identify size and location of cancerous tumors that are surrounded by less dense tissues, particularly in the brain and breast. Cir-

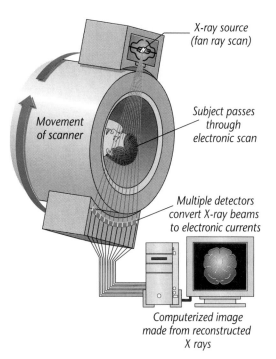

X-ray source (fan ray scan)

Movement of scanner

Subject passes through electronic scan

Multiple detectors convert X-ray beams to electronic currents

Computerized image made from reconstructed X rays

Figure 22-16

CAT scans involve both acquiring data using X rays and the reconstruction of the X rays to form computerized images.

culatory diseases that are caused by heart abnormalities and blood vessel blockage can be visualized using this technology. CAT scans are also useful in the reconstruction of damaged or deformed bones. While the CAT scan is a refinement of the use of X-ray imaging technology, other technologies have been developed that can create images without using harmful X rays.

C X rays are more energetic than visible light. If you hold your hand in front of an X-ray source, the waves will penetrate your soft tissues but not your bones. Because the eye cannot perceive X rays (and would be damaged by exposure to X rays), photographic film is used instead. The film is developed to produce a photographic image of the bones in your hand.

D A CAT scan is a method of taking several X-ray photographs of the same part of the body. A computer pieces the photographs together to create three-dimensional images and cross-sectional views of internal body structures.

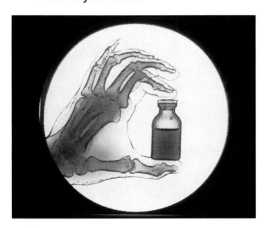

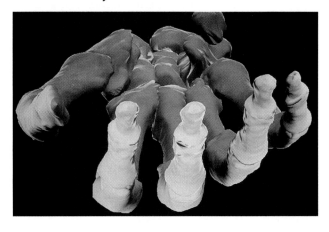

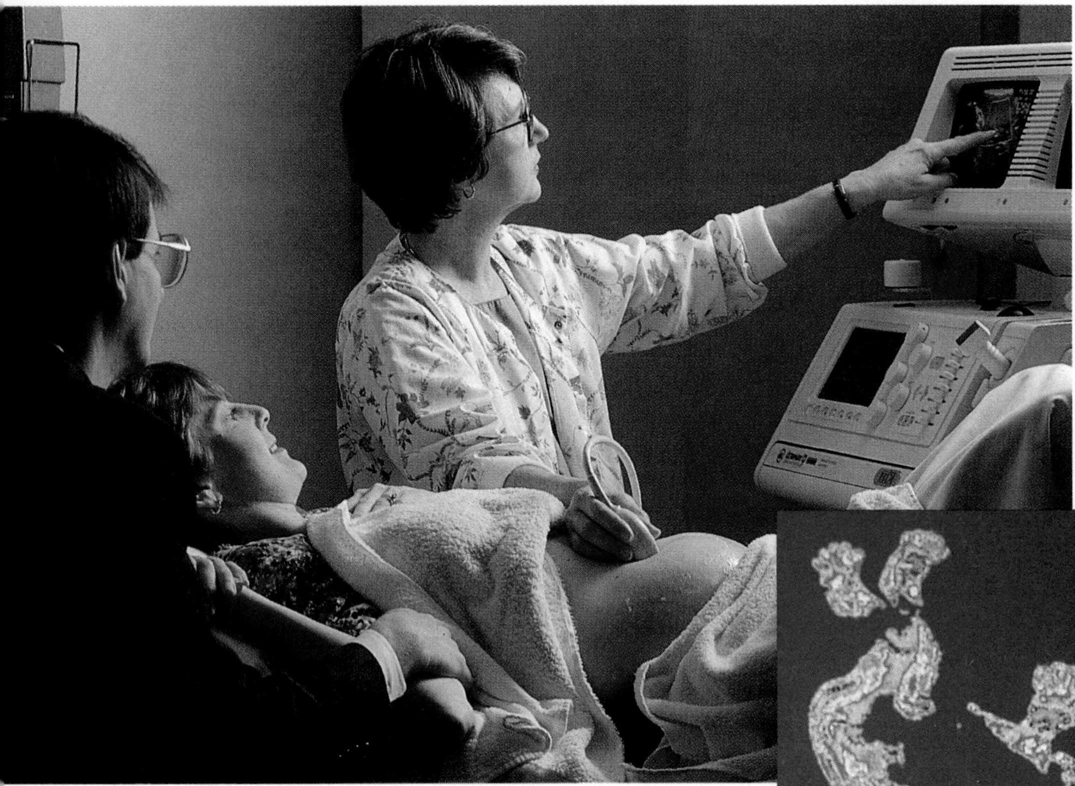

Figure 22-17

Ultrasounds are used for many different purposes.

A During an ultrasound examination, expectant parents are able to observe the fetus inside the womb.

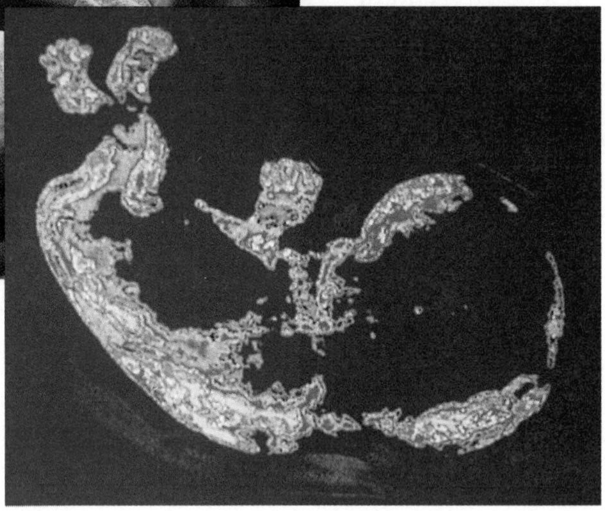

B By analyzing the ultrasound images, called sonograms, the physician can evaluate the fetus's health and development and begin early treatment if any problems are evident.

Connect to...

Chemistry

In addition to medical and biological uses, manufacturers of household and personal products also use ultrasound technology. How do these manufacturers use this technology?

■ Ultrasound

To allow physicians to examine a patient's internal organs without having to resort to surgery, sound waves are used to create an image called a sonogram. Sound waves, like light waves, also can reflect off parts of the body to create an image. Ultrasound is based on the same principles of sonar that are used by bats to locate flying insects. Ultrasound uses higher pitches, which give more precise locations because sound waves become shorter as the pitch rises. Different tissues inside the body have different densities. Therefore, they can be distinguished from one another in the sonogram. During an ultrasound examination, a probe that emits ultrahigh-frequency sound waves is passed back and forth over a specific part of the body. These waves echo back to a sensitive receiver that transforms the sound waves into an image. The video image, called a sonogram, of the scanned tissue depends on the shape and the density of the tissue. **Figure 22-17** shows what a sonogram looks like.

In addition to evaluating the health of the developing fetus, ultrasound images can also assist a physician during fetal surgery. Early cancer detection is also possible through the use of sonograms. The following activity will give you an idea of how ultrasound imaging works.

How is an echogram made?

An echo is a reflection of sound off the surface of an object. Bats and dolphins use echoes to navigate through air and water. Scientists use sound waves to map features on the ocean floor. Physicians can also use sound waves to view tissues inside the body. Using marbles in place of sound waves and objects of different densities in place of body tissues, you can make an echogram that shares some similarities with a sonogram.

Procedure

1. Set up a cardboard barrier like the one shown in the photograph.

2. Have your partner arrange the objects on the other side of the barrier. You should not be able to see the objects.

3. After the items have been arranged, roll a series of marbles through the opening at the bottom of the barrier.

4. Closely observe the manner in which the marbles roll back to you. Use your observations to make a rough sketch of what you think is on the other side of the barrier.

Analysis

1. How close did your sketch come to the actual arrangement of objects on the other side of the barrier?

2. What happened when one of your marbles hit the low-density (soft) object? The high-density (hard) object? Describe how this activity models ultrasound imaging.

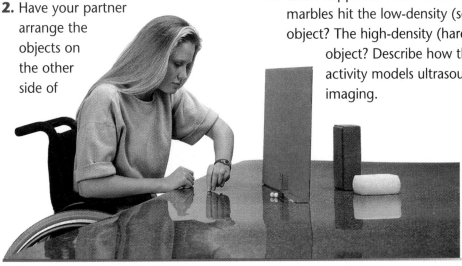

■ Magnetic Resonance Imaging

Magnetic resonance imaging is another method of viewing the structures inside the body that produces images more clear than a CAT scan or ultrasound. **Magnetic resonance imaging,** or **MRI,** uses electricity and magnetism rather than X rays or sound waves to create exceptionally clear images of organs and tissues.

The following activity allows you to model the principle behind magnetic resonance imaging. You will explore how magnets in different materials placed inside coiled wire will respond when an electric current is passed through the coil. The different responses of magnetized atoms in our body to a similar, artificial electromagnetic field form the basis of magnetic resonance imaging.

How does electricity move magnets?

In this activity, explore what happens to magnets placed inside a coil of wire when an electric current is passed through the coil.

Procedure

1. Place a compass, a cup of water, and a cup of oil inside a coil of wire. Float a cork on the surface of each liquid. Place a needle on each cork on the surface of each liquid.

2. Turn on the switch that allows electric current to flow from the battery through the coil. *In your Journal,* record what happens to the two needles and to the compass.

Analysis

1. How did the compass needle respond to the flow of electricity through the coil?

2. What force moved the floating needles? Compare the response of the floating needles to the response of the compass needle.

■ How MRI Works

The nuclei of the atoms in the body act like tiny magnets in the MiniLab. Ordinarily, these nuclear magnets point in random directions. However, if the body is placed in a strong magnetic field, the magnetic fields within the nuclei all line up in the same direction, parallel to the magnetic field's lines of force. It takes a different amount of time for the nuclei of different kinds of atoms to respond to the magnetic field and to return to their original positions when the magnetic field is removed. For an MRI scan, the patient is placed inside a giant version of the wire coil you used in the MiniLab activity above. When an electric current flows through the coil, a magnetic field is produced. As the atoms of the body align themselves along the magnetic field, a sensitive receiver detects the differences in their responses. A computer uses the signals from the receiver to create an image like the one shown in **Figure 22-18B.**

Magnetic resonance imaging uses the water molecules of the body as the basis for the images it produces. Because different body tissues contain different amounts of water, MRI images show clear differences between these tissues, which allows for analysis and diagnosis. Unlike X-ray pictures, in which bones can hide other tissues, MRI images clearly identify these tissues because bones have very little water content. Therefore, MRI is effective in studying the brain and other soft tissues.

MRI images can clearly show the difference between healthy and diseased tissues. It has often been used to make early diagnoses of such diseases as multiple sclerosis, atherosclerosis, and brain tumors. Unlike X rays, magnetic resonance imaging does not destroy cells or interfere with their function.

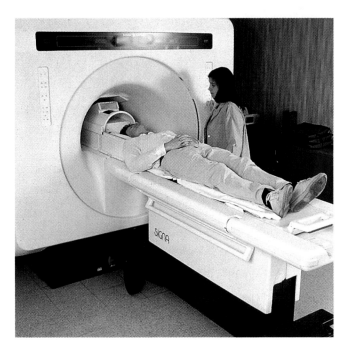

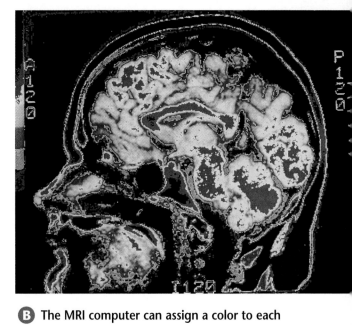

B The MRI computer can assign a color to each type of tissue; the colors respond differently to the magnetic field, forming a color-enhanced image that is much more detailed than the black-and-white images produced by X rays and CAT scans.

A The patient is slid into the center of a giant coil of wire. A strong magnetic field is induced as an electric current is passed through the coil.

Figure 22-18

Because MRI does not use ionizing radiation, it enables physicians to examine the inside of the body in great detail without the potential hazards associated with an X ray or CAT scan.

■ Technology Summary

All of these technologies have unique strengths and limitations. When used together, many diseases that were previously difficult to detect are now being diagnosed and treated. In addition to detecting diseases associated with the heart, brain, bones, and nerves, as well as cancer, it is also possible to detect silent diseases—diseases that do not produce identifiable symptoms. X rays, CAT scans, ultrasounds, and MRI make surgeries safer and prevent some unnecessary surgery.

In this chapter, you have seen how the progression of a disease, such as strep throat, heart disease, or diabetes, can be monitored using physical or chemical tests. Whether it is your next bout of strep throat or the next epidemic, using all the sciences to detect and identify disease is a critical, first step toward finding appropriate treatments.

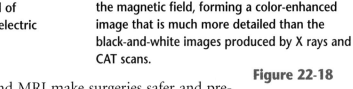

check your UNDERSTANDING

Understanding Concepts

1. List two medical technologies that use electromagnetic waves to produce medical images. How do these technologies work?
2. How is a sonogram produced?
3. How does magnetic resonance imaging work?

Skill Review

4. **Comparing and Contrasting** Examine the different types of images produced by X rays and CAT scans. For more help, refer to Comparing and Contrasting in the *Skill Handbook*.

Technology:
The Cost of MRI

An athlete limps into the doctor's office with a sprained ankle. In the past, the doctor would feel the ankle with fingers trained to determine the extent of the injury and would probably order an X ray before bandaging the sprain. But that was before high technology took over the medical field. Today, a doctor is faced with more choices. The doctor could bypass the less expensive X ray (from $80 to $120). Instead, the patient could be signed up for magnetic resonance imaging (MRI) at a cost of $1000 or more. Although MRI can detect soft-tissue injury better than an X ray can, it is not always necessary. An X ray can reveal fractures and bone fragments.

The Technology

Some patients pressure their doctors to prescribe using MRI, even for routine diagnosis. The threats of malpractice suits and losing their patients to other doctors put additional pressure on doctors. Because MRI isn't foolproof and costs so much, many nonspecialists and specialists, such as orthopedists and sports medicine doctors, are questioning whether it is being used too much, particularly for common sports injuries. They point out that often a doctor's fingers plus the patient's history can effectively reveal what's wrong.

Of course, it's different when the structure to be scanned is an inaccessible organ consisting of soft tissue. An MRI has a good chance of revealing such problems as brain tumors. It can also show how well the heart is functioning after a heart attack. But the decision to order an MRI is often not clear; sometimes physicians order one to relieve worried patients. Doctors and patients should discuss whether the MRI would change the way the illness would be treated. If not, there may be no need for an expensive MRI.

The Background

What is MRI? How does it work? Matter has many physical properties, including magnetic properties. Although some materials are not magnetic themselves, they develop a type of magnetization when placed in a magnetic field. In the presence of low-frequency radio waves, magnetic properties allow extremely detailed cross sections of normal and diseased tissues of the body to be produced. In contrast to X rays and gamma rays, radio waves are considered to be biologically safe.

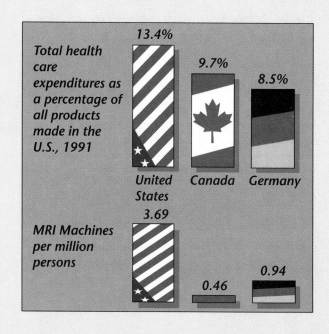

Total health care expenditures as a percentage of all products made in the U.S., 1991

13.4% United States
9.7% Canada
8.5% Germany

MRI Machines per million persons

3.69 United States
0.46 Canada
0.94 Germany

The magnetic field produced by the powerful magnet of the MRI machine forces the hydrogen nuclei of the body's water molecules to line up in parallel. A radio pulse tips the magnetic axes to one side. When the pulse stops, the magnetic axes relax and emit a radio signal that can be used by a computer to construct an image of a part of the body.

Not all nuclei have magnetic properties. Carbon-12 and oxygen-16 have no magnetic properties. Hydrogen-1, carbon-13, sodium-23, and phosphorus-31 all have nuclei with magnetic properties. When any of these isotopes are placed in a magnetic field produced by an MRI machine, they absorb radio waves of characteristic frequencies.

The Questions

The United States has 3.69 MRI machines per million persons—four times as many machines per million persons as Germany and eight times as many per million as Canada. This reliance on expensive technology worries some people, such as Richard D. Lamm, the Governor of Colorado between 1975 and 1987. He wrote in *Science,* December 3, 1993, "The United States spends 50 percent more on health care than its leading competitors. In spite of this, statistics do not show that we are as healthy as the people in Europe, Canada, or Japan."

Still, dependence on technology continues to increase. Those concerned with the high cost of health care complain about the relentless creation of ever-more-expensive treatments for an ever-increasing array of illnesses. They wonder if most people would pay $1000 for an MRI brain scan if, judging from their symptoms, the chances were 99.9 percent that it wouldn't reveal anything worth treating. Only in one in 1000 MRIs of the brain does a brain tumor show up. If doctors know that there is almost no chance that a patient has a brain tumor,

wouldn't it make sense for them not to recommend an MRI? Or, is the cost of an MRI worth the patient's peace of mind? What about the rights of that one patient in 1000 in whose brain a tumor is discovered?

This raises the question of whether imaging equipment is available to everyone equally. Suppose a person on Medicare or Medicaid has a medical problem. Unless there is an excellent chance that only MRI will provide the information needed for an accurate diagnosis, the doctor may not order one. The reason for this is that Medicare and Medicaid will not pay for what they consider to be unreasonable or unnecessary treatment. The hospital would then have to bear the expense unless the patient could manage to pay. Many hospitals are finding it more and more difficult to accept the cost. With health care expenses spiraling, the decision about ordering an MRI is becoming more and more critical.

GRAPHING CALCULATOR

The equation $Y = 3.69 \times X$, where X is the number of millions of persons and Y is the total number of MRI machines available for that many people, relates the number of MRI machines available and the population in the United States. Write a similar equation to relate MRI machines available and population in Germany. Use a graphing calculator to graph this equation. Use the graph to determine the number of MRI machines available to a German city with a population of 3 260 000.

APPLYING TECHNOLOGY

To Your Health

The public's need for information about health issues has created a great demand for editors and writers with an interest in medicine. They are employed, for example, by newspapers, magazines, and hospitals to explain medical issues in terms that everyone can understand.

You're the Health Editor for the Local Newspaper

You have been assigned the task of producing a brochure about the career of an ultrasound technician. Ultrasound is a technique used to obtain video images of internal organs using sound waves. Ultrasound allows for fetal monitoring and early cancer detection. Your goal is to explain what an ultrasound technician does. Your materials will be a research library and writing and interviewing tools.

Drawing on Experience

1 In the library, find background information on the basics of ultrasound imaging. Prepare a list of questions to ask an ultrasound technician about the education requirements, the training process, and the job responsibilities.

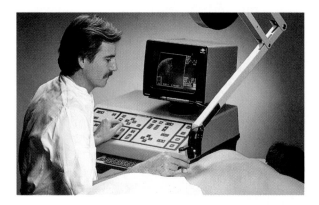

2 Contact a local hospital or health care clinic and obtain the name of an ultrasound technician.

3 Telephone the technician to schedule a time and place for the interview.

4 Arrive at the interview on time. Ask the technician the questions on your list. In addition to recording the answers on paper, you may want to record the interview on an audiocassette.

5 Listen carefully to the technician's answers and you'll probably think of follow-up questions to ask.

Testing...Testing

1 Combine the information obtained from your library research and the interview to write a brochure describing the career.

2 Send the brochure to the technician you interviewed and ask if the information is accurate. Exchange your brochures with your classmates and proofread each other's work. Check that spelling, grammar, and punctuation are correct.

3 Incorporate the necessary changes, proofread again, and give the brochure to your teacher for copying.

How Did It Work?

What changes were necessary to improve the brochure? How much initial research did you need to do to prepare for the interview? Distribute the brochure to other students with an interest in medical technology to determine if they find the brochure to be informative.

Read the statements below that review major points presented in the chapter. Using the concepts that you have learned, answer each question *in your Journal.*

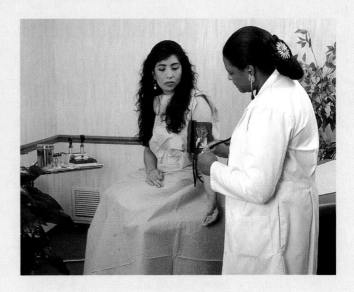

1 Diseases can be monitored using physical or chemical tests. *What are two standard tests used by physicians during a checkup?*

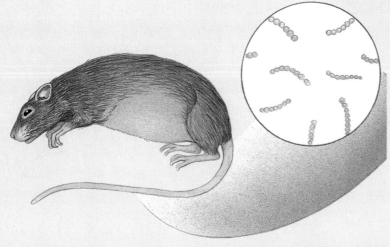

2 New diseases can be identified within populations. *How do epidemiologists isolate pathogens responsible for new diseases?*

3 Medical scientists' understanding of light, electricity, and magnetism have created technologies that can identify disease within the body. *Name two such technologies.*

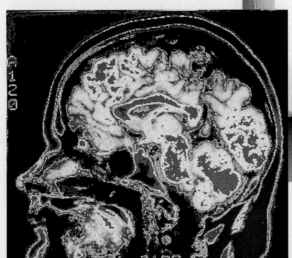

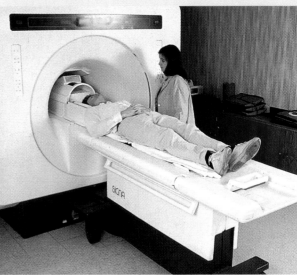

Using Key Science Terms

active transport

disease cluster

electrophoresis

endemic disease

epidemic

Koch's postulates

light microscope

magnetic resonance
imaging (MRI)

passive transport

X ray

For each set of terms below, choose the one term that does not belong. Provide an explanation for why it does not belong with the other terms.

1. disease cluster, endemic disease, Koch's postulates
2. electrophoresis, magnetic resonance imaging, ultrasound, CAT scan
3. active transport, passive transport, gate protein, carrier protein

Understanding Ideas

Using complete sentences, answer the following questions in your Journal.

1. Could Koch's postulates be used to determine the cause of a noncommunicable disease? Why or why not?
2. What is the difference between a disease cluster and an epidemic?

3. Why does electrophoresis better identify viruses than light microscopes?
4. In what direction do molecules of a substance flow during passive transport?
5. Compare sonograms and X rays.

Developing Skills

Use your understanding of the concepts developed in this chapter to answer each of the following questions.

1. **Concept Mapping** Use the following terms and phrases to complete the concept map about detecting disease in an individual: *biological molecules, body fluids, blood pressure, heart, light microscope, magnetic resonance imaging, salts, technology, temperature, ultrasound, X ray.*

2. **Recognizing Cause and Effect** A bacterium isolated from the blood of a diseased pet bird has been cultured in the laboratory. When a healthy bird is exposed to the bacterium, it becomes ill. None of the bacteria found in the second bird's bloodstream match the cultured bacterium. Do these results follow Koch's postulates? Why or why not? What might be the next step in determining what caused the disease in the first bird?

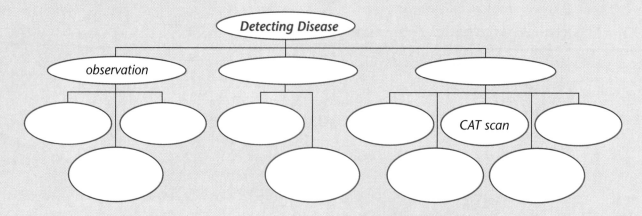

3. Observing and Inferring A doctor examines a patient who is complaining of sneezes, sniffles, fever, and a sore throat. A sample of throat tissues is sent to the laboratory, but the culture does not reveal the presence of any disease-causing bacteria. What kind of pathogen is likely to be causing this illness? If you were the physician, would you prescribe an antibiotic to cure the illness?

4. Critical Thinking Why can an X ray be used to determine the location of a cancerous tumor?

Critical Thinking

In your Journal, *answer each of the following questions.*

1. A health screening is a type of general examination used to evaluate the overall health of an individual who is not experiencing any symptoms of disease. Most health screenings include measurement of pulse, blood pressure, and temperature and chemical tests of urine and blood. Why?

2. If you were given the choice of undergoing a CAT scan or an MRI scan, which would you choose? Why?

3. Explain how you could use two lenses to project an image onto a wall or screen so that several people could observe it at the same time.

Problem Solving

Read the following paragraph and discuss your answers in a brief paragraph.

A disease first appears as a disease cluster around a particular town in rural Illinois. Over a period of months, the disease appears in several neighboring areas, but not more than 100 miles from the location of the first reported case. It is known that people who have the disease have traveled to cities farther away, but no one has reported the disease in any of these distant locations.

How would you begin looking for the cause of this disease? Do these facts provide enough information to determine whether the disease is communicable or noncommunicable? Why or why not?

CONNECTING IDEAS

1. **Theme—Stability and Change** What does the presence of glucose in a urine sample indicate about the homeostasis of the patient's body?

2. **Theme—Energy** Use the concept of energy to explain the difference between the operation of a light microscope and an X-ray machine.

3. **In-Depth Look** How do allergies affect the body's homeostasis?

4. **Science and Society** How are energy sources used in MRIs?

5. **Applying Technology** Why are medical technicians necessary for the treatment of disease?

TRACKING DISEASE TRENDS

Problem
When comparing numbers of sick individuals over the past several years, diseases in the United States may appear to occur in patterns—either increasing, decreasing, or remaining about the same. How do these trends compare in different regions?

Materials
blank outline of the United States
colored pencils or markers

Getting Started
1. Obtain copies of the pamphlet <u>Morbidity and Mortality Weekly Report</u> for the last week of both last year and the previous year.
2. Locate a table in each issue titled <u>Cases of Selected Notifiable Disease, United States</u> for the last week of each year.
3. Using a blank map of the United States, color code and label the nine regions listed in the table. Pick four diseases from the table. Record the total number of reported cases by region for these diseases on your map for this past year and the year before last. Also, indicate the change that has occurred.
4. Prepare a report of your findings. Include the report and map. Also answer the following questions in *your Journal:*
   A. Why may there be a different trend for the same disease when compared in different regions?
   B. Why may there be a different trend for different diseases within the same region?

Reference
<u>Morbidity and Mortality Weekly Report</u>, U.S. Department of Health and Human Services.

ANALYSIS OF DISEASE ARTICLES

Problem

Newspapers and magazines usually contain current articles that discuss, describe, and deal with a variety of medical topics related to disease. These articles could range in content from research on AIDS to progress toward a cure for cancer.

Materials

tape

newspapers

magazines

scissors

unlined paper

Getting Started

1. Collect at least five disease-related articles from current magazines or newspapers. Mount each article onto a sheet(s) of unlined paper.

2. Prepare a table for each article to include the following information.

   A. Source of article

   B. Title of article

   C. Disease described

   D. Communicable or noncommunicable disease? Explain.

   E. Organism responsible (if applicable)

   F. Organ(s) affected by disease

   G. Symptoms

   H. How disease is spread (if applicable)

   I. How disease is detected

   J. Prevention or treatment

3. Complete each chart and include it with the appropriate article. Use the resource provided below for any additional help as needed.

Resources

The Cambridge World History of Human Disease. Kiple, Kenneth. Cambridge University Press, 1993.

Flight

The engines of the huge airplane sputter a few times, then one by one, they roar to life, drowning out the sounds of the birds in the nearby woods. The plane rolls down the runway, accelerating until it lifts off into the air. Within minutes the plane becomes a speck against the clear blue sky. How can such huge machines get off the ground and fly through the air with the grace of a bird? In this unit, you'll explore the world of flight, and discover the forces that make it possible.

Watching birds inspired many early inventors to build wings for humans. While most of these early flight attempts ended in failure, or even death, people kept trying.

As people learned more about the forces involved in flight, they began to invent balloons, gliders, and powered aircraft that succeeded in lifting them off the ground.

Today, air travel is a routine part of many lives. Do you think someday space travel will be just as routine?

Unit Contents

Focus On

A Jumbo Jet

To get a jumbo jet off the ground takes a lot of parts, power, and controls. But flight isn't always so complicated. As you'll find out in the next activity, an airplane can be as simple as a piece of scrap paper.

A fully loaded 747 passenger airliner can weigh as much as 3 580 000 N (805 000 lb). Its wings spread over 59 meters (195 feet). Yet it can fly almost 1000 kilometers per hour and is capable of traveling 9600 km (almost 6000 miles) without stopping. How can something so huge even get off the ground?

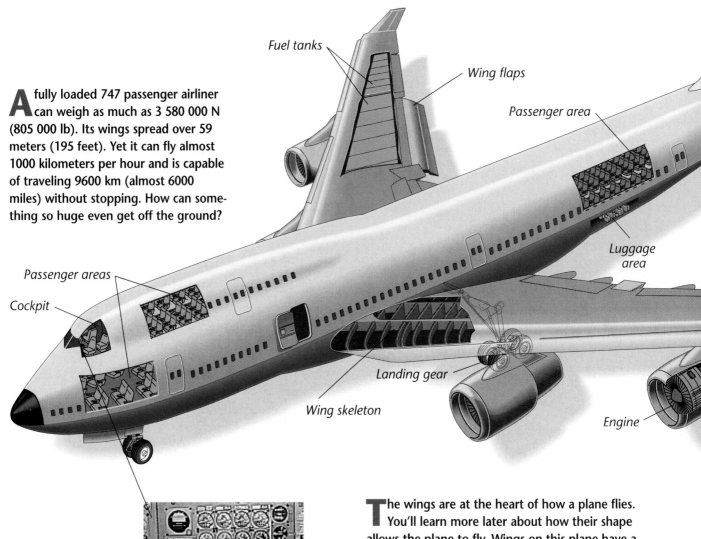

Fuel tanks

Wing flaps

Passenger area

Luggage area

Passenger areas

Cockpit

Landing gear

Wing skeleton

Engine

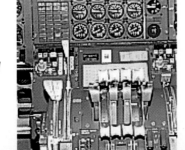

Instrument panel

The wings are at the heart of how a plane flies. You'll learn more later about how their shape allows the plane to fly. Wings on this plane have a surface area of over 500 square meters (about 5500 square feet). Compare that area to the amount of living area you have at home.

Rudder

Tail flaps

Try It!

Have you ever folded a single piece of paper into a paper airplane? Why is it that some of them fly fairly straight, while others perform turns and loops as they fly across the room? In this activity, you'll explore this question.

What To Do

1. Make a paper airplane using a single sheet of notebook paper.

2. Throw the airplane. *In your Journal,* describe how it flies. **CAUTION:** *Don't throw the airplane toward any of your classmates.*

3. Find how to control the flight path of the airplane. See if you can make the plane travel farther, turn, or loop. What changes did you make to the plane? Are real airplanes controlled in similar ways?

Try It Again

After you've learned more about flight and the forces that affect an airplane, try this activity again and see if it's easier to design your airplane.

The plane is steered and controlled by moving large flaps on the back edges of the wings and tail. In this unit, you'll discover how these surfaces change the characteristics of the wing to make the plane ascend, descend, or turn.

UNIT 7 PROJECTS

During your exploration of flight, you may discover new questions or wish to explore the structures of flight further. **Design an Airplane Wing** and **Bird Wings,** found in the Unit 7 Projects section on pages 794-795, will give you the challenge of designing, building, and testing a model airplane wing and investigating the wings of different birds. Read through these projects. By the time you finish this unit, you'll know all you need to know to successfully complete both of these projects.

CHAPTER 23

Physics of Flight
Getting Off the Ground

*L*ooking up at the sky you see a flock of geese flapping their wings and staying in a perfect V-formation. Off in the distance, you notice the silvery glint of a jet airliner. From another direction, you hear the chop-chop-chop sound of a traffic helicopter. And although you've seen jet planes and watched the space shuttle take off, you've always wondered how all these things manage to get off the ground.

▶ *Before a plane can take off, it must first accelerate. In the next activity, you'll investigate what's involved in acceleration.*

MiniLab

What does acceleration feel like?

In this lab, you will experience constant and changing speed firsthand.

Procedure

1. Go with your class to the first course your teacher has laid out for you. Note the paper markers along the wall.

2. At each clap of the hand, move forward to the next marker. Repeat until you complete the course.

3. Repeat step 2 for the second course.

Analysis

1. To calculate how fast you went, make a chart of the data for each course. It should include the distance moved, time, and speed for each interval along the course. Calculate speed by dividing the distance moved by the time it took to move that distance.

2. Draw a graph for each course showing your speed during each of the five intervals. Draw a smooth line through the five points and compare the graphs.

23-1 What accelerates a plane forward?

Objectives

- Experiment with balanced forces resulting in constant speed.
- Describe how an unbalanced force produces acceleration.
- Explain the concept of momentum.

Key Terms

acceleration
thrust
Newton's second law of motion
momentum

Acceleration

The pilot sits in the plane at the end of the runway. The control tower radios to the pilot, saying all is clear and she may now take off. The pilot revs up the engine, releases the brakes, and the plane speeds off down the runway. As the plane moves faster and faster, the pilot is pushed back into her seat. Eventually, the plane lifts off into the air and flies away. **Figure 23-1** shows a plane rapidly accelerating for takeoff from an aircraft carrier.

Even if you've never flown in an airplane, you've probably experienced a similar situation. A car or bus starting from a stoplight, or roller coaster speeding down a long hill share something in common with the airplane speeding down the runway. All of these are exam-ples of acceleration. **Acceleration** is the rate at which velocity changes. The term *velocity* includes both speed and direction. This means an object can acceler-ate not only when its speed changes, but also if its direction changes.

In the MiniLab on the previous page, you walked the first course at a constant speed. You moved the same distance at each hand clap. In the sec-ond course, however, your speed increased from one interval to the next. You had to go a greater distance during the same amount of time. As an air-plane takes off, it must also accelerate, traveling a greater distance during each time interval. **Figure 23-2** shows a graph of the acceleration of a plane during takeoff.

Figure 23-1

When a jet takes off from an aircraft car-rier, it must acceler-ate rapidly. To help it, a catapult beneath the deck flings the aircraft forward.

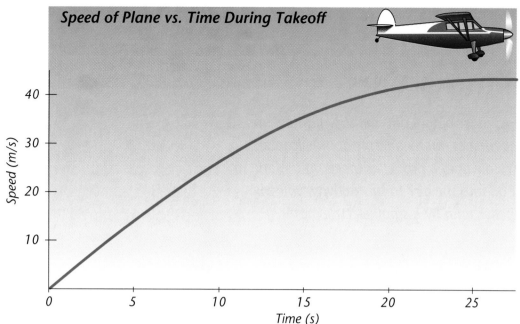

Figure 23-2

For an object moving in a straight line, the acceleration is the change in the speed divided by the time interval over which the speed changed.

Speed of Plane vs. Time During Takeoff

Speed (m/s) vs *Time (s)*

■ Calculating Acceleration

Acceleration is calculated by dividing the change in speed by the time over which the change happened. In the walking and clapping lab, for example, your speed on the second course increased from 1 tile per clap to 3 tiles per clap over a time interval of 1 clap. Your change in speed was 3 tiles/clap – 1 tile/clap = 2 tiles/clap. So your acceleration was

$$\frac{2\text{ tiles/clap}}{1\text{ clap}} = 2\text{ tiles/clap/clap.}$$

When speed is graphed versus time, acceleration is indicated by the slope of the line as in **Figure 23-2.**

■ The Causes of Acceleration

Now you understand what acceleration is. But what causes acceleration? To stand up, you need to push your feet against the floor. In turn, the floor pushes on your feet. You've discussed forces in Chapter 16, so you know that forces are pushes or pulls that occur when two things—in this case, your feet and the floor—interact. Now that you

know how to accelerate yourself, we're going to explore how to accelerate a small cart using a propeller like those used on many airplanes. Unlike a plane, however, this cart will stay on the ground.

Applying Math | **Calculating Average Acceleration**

The velocity of a runner changes from 0 m/s at the starting line to 5 m/s when she crosses the finish line 10 seconds later. Calculate the runner's average acceleration.

Known Information: Beginning velocity (v_i) = 0 m/s
Ending velocity (v_f) = 5 m/s
Time interval (t) = 10 seconds

Unknown Information: Acceleration (a)

Equation to Use: $a = \frac{v_f - v_i}{t}$

Solution: $a = \frac{v_f - v_i}{t} = \frac{5\text{ m/s} - 0\text{ m/s}}{10\text{s}} = 0.5$ m/s/s

Practice Problem

1. At the top of the hill, a roller coaster's velocity is 10 m/s. Just before it reaches the bottom of the hill three seconds later, its velocity is 32 m/s. What is the roller coaster's average acceleration?

INVESTIGATION

Propelling a Cart

While large passenger planes and military fighters are powered by jet engines, many aircraft and helicopters use propellers. How does a propeller speed up a plane so that it can lift off into the air? In this activity, you will explore a propeller spun by a small electric motor.

Preparation

Problem

What is the relationship between force and acceleration?

Objectives

In this Investigation, you will:
- *Measure* the force resulting from a spinning propeller.
- *Calculate* the acceleration of a propeller-driven cart.
- *Identify* the relationship between the force and acceleration.

Materials

flat, level surface at least 1.5 m long
shelf paper, pencils, and stopwatches or distance-measuring probeware for computer or calculator
low-friction cart with added masses
fan cart
string
pulley
several 5 g, 10 g, and 20 g masses

Safety Precautions

Keep your hands and head away from the propeller.

INVESTIGATION

Procedure

Part A How does the cart move with the motor off?

1 Lay the shelf paper along the length of the table. Station several students along the table and give one student the stopwatch. That student will count the seconds out loud.

2 At 0 seconds a student will give the cart a soft push. Don't turn the motor on.

3 As each second is called, a student will put a mark on the paper opposite the propeller. The marks on the paper are a record of the location of the cart each second.

Step 1

4 Before pushing the cart, predict whether the cart will accelerate, decelerate, or stay at a constant speed as it moves across the table. Record your prediction *in your Journal*.

5 Create a table *in your Journal* (like that in the opening MiniLab) of the time and distance of the cart from its starting point.

Analyze and Conclude

1. Describe Describe *in your Journal* the pattern of marks on the paper.

2. Calculate Calculate the speed, *v,* in each interval just as you did in the MiniLab.

3. Make a Graph Make a graph of the speed versus the time. Describe how the speed changes over time. Does it increase? Decrease? Is it constant?

4. Compare How did the cart's motion compare with your prediction?

INVESTIGATION

Part B Measuring the Force Produced When the Propeller Spins

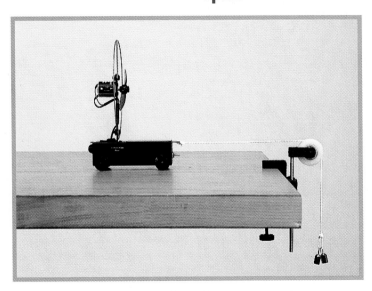

Step 2

1 Attach string to the back of the cart. Turn on the motor. Hold the string and feel the force. The force of your hand balances that created by the propeller. What is the speed of the cart? Does it accelerate? Turn off the motor.

2 You will now find the force created by the propeller by balancing it with the weight of a small mass. Put the string over the pulley and attach two 10 g masses to the end of the string. Turn on the motor. If the mass is pulled up, add a 5 g mass; if down, replace the 10 g mass with a 5 g mass. Add or subtract masses until the cart doesn't move. The force of the propeller is now balanced by the pull of the string. The two forces are equal in size and opposite in direction. There is no acceleration.

3 Give the cart a gentle push. Notice its speed as it moves along. Does it accelerate? Turn off the motor.

4 Record the value of the mass that balanced the force of the propeller.

Analyze and Conclude

1. **Calculate** Use a graphing calculator to graph the equation $Y = 9.8 \times X$, where X is mass, Y is weight, and 9.8 is the force of gravity on Earth in N/kg. Use this graph to convert the mass that balanced the force of the propeller to weight.

2. **Compare and Contrast** What are the two horizontal forces on the cart? Are they balanced? How can you tell? What is the size of each force?

INVESTIGATION

Procedure

Part C Measuring the Acceleration of the Cart

1 Put a piece of clean shelf paper on the table and station students to record the location of the cart.

2 Predict the motion of the cart if you remove the string and turn on the motor. Record your prediction *in your Journal.*

3 Remove the string from the cart. Turn the motor on and let the cart go.

4 Measure the location of the cart every second as you did in Part A.

5 Record the data in a new table.

Analyze and Conclude

1. **Calculate** Calculate the speed of the cart at each second.

2. **Make a Graph** Graph the speed versus the time using a computer spreadsheet program.

3. **Communicate** Describe how the speed depends on the time. Does it increase? Decrease? Is it constant?

4. **Calculate** Find the acceleration of the cart by calculating the slope of the graph. Slope is the change along the *y*-axis divided by the change along the *x*-axis. First, find the change in speed. Then find the change in time. Divide the change in speed by the change in time to obtain the acceleration.

5. Were the forces on the cart balanced? How could you tell?

Going Further

Changing Variables
To gain a greater understanding of the propeller and cart, change either the number of batteries powering the motor (force) or the mass of the cart. Repeat Part C. If you used a different number of batteries, you must also measure the new force by repeating steps 1 and 2 of Part B. What happened to the acceleration of the cart when the force was the same but the mass was different? When the mass was the same but the force was different?

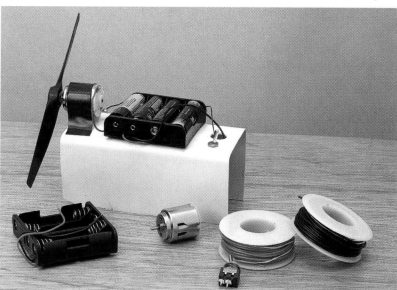

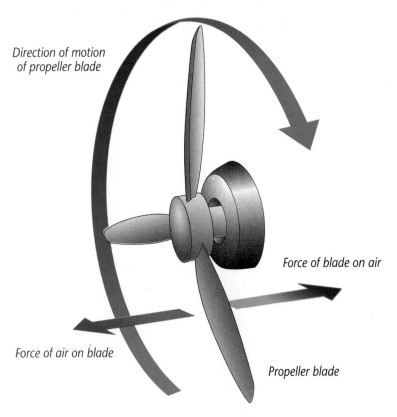

Direction of motion
of propeller blade

Force of blade on air

Force of air on blade

Propeller blade

Figure 23-3

The moving propeller blade exerts a force on the air. According to Newton's third law, the air exerts a force on the propeller that is equal in size, but opposite in direction.

Balanced and Unbalanced Forces

Now you've seen that a propeller produces a force on a cart. Can you figure out how it happens? Hint: Remember Newton's third law from Chapter 17. Apply that law to the propeller-air system, as shown in **Figure 23-3.** The forward force on the propeller is called **thrust.**

The key to understanding Newton's laws is considering the forces on an object. When the thrust was balanced by an equal force on the cart in the opposite direction, then the cart either remained at rest or moved at a constant speed, as shown in **Figure 23-4.**

When the forces were unbalanced, as they were when you removed the string and masses, then the cart's speed changed. If there is only one force on an object, it is unbalanced. If there are two

unequal forces acting in opposite directions, then there is an unbalanced force.

■ Newton's Second Law

An acceleration means that something speeds up more in the same time. The cart's acceleration can be increased if its mass is decreased or the thrust acting on the cart is increased.

This relationship between force (F), mass (m), and acceleration (a) is called **Newton's second law of motion.** It is often written in equation form as

$$a = \frac{F}{m} \text{ or } F = ma.$$

These equations are just two ways of writing the same thing, Newton's second law of motion. However, each equation can give you a different way of looking at motion. The first suggests how mass has the property of inertia. If a bowling ball and a soccer ball are pushed with the same force, which would accelerate more? The second equation lets you see that if there is no unbalanced force, then the acceleration will be zero.

Figure 23-4

The cart remains at rest when the thrust is balanced by an equal force in the opposite direction.

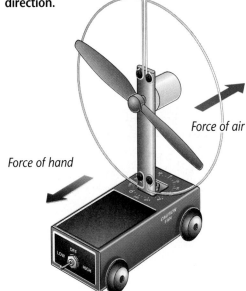

Force of air

Force of hand

Momentum

Have you heard a sportscaster say that a team has momentum? What does that mean? It usually means that it's hard to stop a winning team. Scientifically we say that a moving object has momentum and a force must be exerted on it either to increase or decrease its velocity.

The **momentum** of an object is the product of its mass and velocity, or *mv*. That is, two objects with different masses traveling at the same speed will have different momentums. For example, if a bowling ball and a soccer ball were rolling at the same speed, the bowling ball would have more momentum because it has more mass. You would experience this difference if you tried to stop the two balls. Which would be easier to stop? However, a soccer ball moving at a high velocity can have the same momentum as a slow-moving bowling ball. **Figure 23-5** shows how momentum can apply to roller skaters.

Applying Math **Force and Momentum**

To understand more about how a force changes an object's momentum, you can rewrite Newton's second law. You know acceleration is:

$$\frac{\text{change in velocity}}{\text{change in time}}$$

Scientists and mathematicians use the Greek letter *delta* (Δ) to stand for *change in*. So, acceleration becomes:

$$\frac{\Delta v}{\Delta t}$$

Then, Newton's second law, $F = ma$, is:

$$F = m\frac{\Delta v}{\Delta t}$$

Multiplying both sides by Δt gives:

$$F\Delta t = m\Delta v$$

This shows that applying the same force (F) for the same time (Δt) to two different masses causes an equal change in momentum ($m\Delta v$) for each mass. What does this imply about the velocities if one mass is larger than the other?

How can an object's momentum change? Look again at what Newton's second law says about the relationship between force and momentum. If an unbalanced force acts on an object for some time, the object's momentum changes.

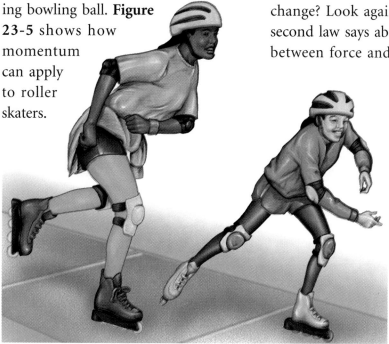

Mass × *Velocity* = *momentum*
50 kg × 3 m/s = 150 kg · m/s

Mass × *Velocity* = *momentum*
30 kg × 5 m/s = 150 kg · m/s

— Equal —

Figure 23-5

The roller skater with lower mass can have more momentum than a heavier roller skater if she skates faster.

Table 23-1

		Force ×		Speed	Momentum
Force (N)	Time (s)	Time (N·s)	Mass (kg)	Change (m/s)	Change (kg m/s)
0.194	1.0	0.19	0.5	0.367	0.18
0.205	1.0	0.21	1.0	0.192	0.19
0.187	1.0	0.19	1.5	0.121	0.18

Force and Momentum Change

Now, use what you know about force, time, and momentum to compare the data above, taken with a propeller-driven cart.

This is experimental data, and the agreement between the momentum change and the product of force and time isn't perfect. Still, you can see that although the 0.5 kg mass is moving three times faster, its momentum change is identical to that of the 1.5 kg mass. If the unbalanced force were zero, the momentum would not change.

Think about how to get an airplane moving on a taxiway. You can rev up the motor to get the propeller spinning and use its thrust to accelerate the air-plane. But you're still on the ground. In the next sections, you'll find out more about forces and learn how to get into the air and stay there.

Figure 23-6

The propeller pushes backward on the air, and the air provides the forward thrust that accelerates the airplane.

check your UNDERSTANDING

Understanding Concepts
1. In the Investigation, when were the forces on the cart balanced?
2. A 1.0 kg cart and a 0.5 kg cart have the same momentum. What can you conclude about their speeds?
3. A student finds that the cart speeds up for one second, then goes at a constant speed. Does the propeller create the only force on the cart? Explain.

Skill Review
4. **Predicting** A propeller cart sped up from 0 to 0.5 m/s in 2.0 seconds. Mass was added to the cart. Would it now take more or less time for it to speed up from 0 to 0.5 m/s? For more help, refer to Forming a Hypothesis in the *Skill Handbook*.

The Force of Gravity

Contact and Noncontact Forces

When you roll a ball, lift a book, or push a cart, you exert forces. As you remember from Chapter 17, these are all contact forces. These are forces that are exerted directly on an object. What forces were put on the cart in the Investigation activity on pages 704-707? **Figure 23-7** shows the contact forces that were on the cart.

Are there any forces acting on the cart other than those shown in the illustration? What would happen if the cart rolled off the end of the table? You would quickly realize there is a downward force acting on the cart—gravity.

Gravity is the force toward Earth that every object with mass experiences. When you kick a soccer ball in the air, it eventually comes back down to the ground. Your foot exerted the force that initially made it rise into the air, but gravity is the force that pulled it back down.

When an airplane flies, it exerts a force on the air that acts in the opposite direction of gravity. You'll learn more about the force that allows a plane to fly later. For now, let's focus on gravity.

Objectives
- Compare gravity and contact forces.
- Explore the acceleration of a falling object.
- Define weight.
- Describe how an object reaches terminal speed.

Key Terms
gravity
terminal speed

Figure 23-7

There were several forces acting on the cart used in the last Investigation.

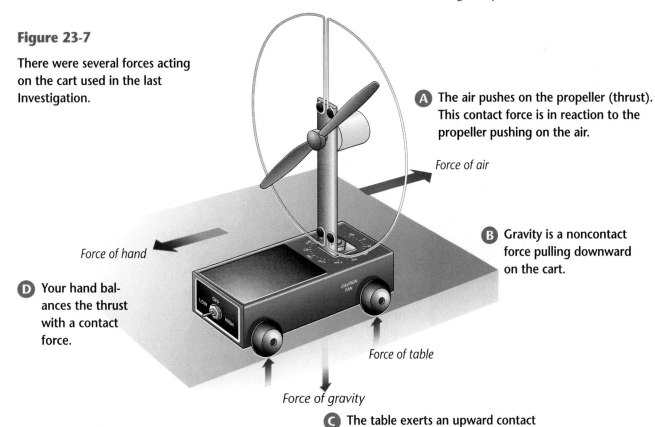

A The air pushes on the propeller (thrust). This contact force is in reaction to the propeller pushing on the air.

Force of air

B Gravity is a noncontact force pulling downward on the cart.

Force of hand

D Your hand balances the thrust with a contact force.

Force of table

Force of gravity

C The table exerts an upward contact force on the wheels of the cart.

Acceleration Under Gravity

As you learned from previous activities, a constant, unbalanced force on an object will cause it to accelerate. The propeller on an airplane accelerates the plane down the runway. Do falling objects experience constant acceleration? As you found in previous activities, you can tell if an object is accelerating by marking its position at certain time intervals and calculating its average velocity over each interval. If the velocity increases, the object is accelerating.

Things fall too fast, however, to record their position accurately using a pencil and paper. Can you think of any way to study the speed of a falling object? The photograph in **Figure 23-8** shows one way. In the next activity, you will use this photograph to find out if a falling ball accelerates.

Figure 23-8

The many images of the tennis ball in this single picture were made by leaving the camera's shutter open. Each time the strobe light flashed, a new image was made of the ball during its drop.

Thinking Lab | Interpreting Illustrations

How fast does a ball fall?

How does a ball fall? You will use strobe photos of a falling ball to explore its speed as it falls.

Analysis
The photo shows a falling ball. The photo was made using a strobe light that flashed 10 times each second. As a result, you see an image of the ball each 1/10 second. You can find the speed of the ball in the time between two flashes by dividing the distance between the images by the time interval, 1/10 s.

Thinking Critically
Where in its fall is the ball when its speed is smallest? Where is it when its speed is greatest? Does the speed of the ball ever become constant? How do you know?

Gravity may act to accelerate a falling object, but how does gravity affect something that's sitting on the ground? Do you think gravity affects a plane sitting on a runway, for example? It might help to think about it in terms of forces. The plane isn't accelerating, so the forces acting on it must be balanced. If gravity is a force that acts on all objects with mass, then it must be balanced by another force. What do you think that force is? The balancing force is provided by the ground pushing up on the plane.

■ Weight and the Parachutist

Fruit can be hung from a spring scale to measure the upward force needed to balance the force of gravity.

Suppose you were parachuting and measured the upward force of the parachute on you. Would it be the same if you were hanging from a motionless scale? If you weigh something with a scale, does the force exerted by the scale depend on whether the object is at rest or moving at a constant speed? Find out in the next activity.

Connect to...

Earth Science

Air drag slows raindrops until they reach a constant speed. The speed depends on the size of the drop. Investigate the size of drops and their speed.

MiniLab

What's the weight?

Does a parachutist weigh the same while falling as on the ground? You can use a model on a desk top to answer that question. You will need a balance and a 1-L or 2-L plastic soda bottle (with cap) with the top cut off as shown.

Procedure

1. Remove the screw cap. Hold the top, upside down, at the top of the bottle, and let it fall into the bottle. Note how fast it falls.

2. Replace the screw cap and let it fall into the bottle again. Record *in your Journal* how fast it falls.

3. Place the entire bottle (with the top and screw cap) on the balance and record its weight. Remember, the balance measures the upward force it exerts on the bottle, which is equal to the downward force of gravity on the bottle.

4. Repeat step 2 with the bottle on the balance. Before you do, predict in writing whether the scale will show a larger, equal, or smaller value while the top is falling.

Analysis

1. What was your prediction? What did the balance show?

2. Explain the result based on what you have learned about forces on an object when it is moving at a constant speed.

Air

Weight

Figure 23-9

With the parachute open, the parachutist falls at a terminal speed. At this speed, the force of weight is balanced by the air pushing upward on the parachute.

■ Terminal Speed

Although parachutists don't fall in a bottle, they do reach a constant speed, called their **terminal speed.** The air, and Earth under it, exert an upward force equal to the downward force of gravity on the person. **Figure 23-9** shows the forces that are balanced as a parachutist falls at terminal speed.

You've seen that forces can affect an object by direct contact and at a distance. Gravity causes weight. Objects held in place on Earth or above it experience contact forces. When all the forces on an object are balanced, there is no change in its velocity. If there is an unbalanced force, the object's velocity changes. In the next section, you will learn more details about the forces affecting a plane.

check your UNDERSTANDING

Understanding Concepts

1. When you hold a book on your hand, what are the contact and the noncontact forces on the book?

2. Suppose you saw a strobe photo of a falling ball in which the vertical distances between the images were all the same. What would be the acceleration of the ball?

3. What could you conclude about the forces on the ball in question 2?

Skill Review

4. **Interpreting a Graph** The graph shows the speed versus time for four different carts. Which lines show data taken using a

cart with balanced forces? Which with unbalanced forces? For more help, refer to Interpreting a Graph in the *Skill Handbook*.

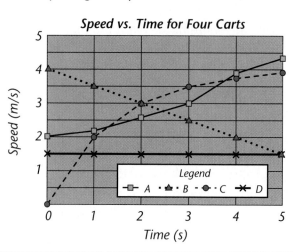

Speed vs. Time for Four Carts

Legend
- ■ A · ▲ · B · ● · C ✳ D

Flying Through Air

23-3

Moving Through the Air

How have you noticed the force of moving air? You've probably felt it when you've ridden a bike. On a blustery day, the wind can almost push you over. When you feel the wind in your face or see it stir a pile of leaves, you know it is another contact force.

The force of air on a moving object is called *air drag* or simply **drag.** Drag opposes an airplane's forward movement. To keep the plane moving forward, thrust must be increased or drag must be reduced. Increasing thrust takes more engine power and that takes more fuel. That is why aircraft designers look for ways to reduce drag.

■ How Drag Depends on the Falling Object

On what does drag depend? Make a list of the properties that you think could affect the amount of drag on a moving object. What properties of the object did your list include? Its size? Its shape? How about the properties of the air? Perhaps at high altitudes where the air is thin, meaning it has low density, the force is less. Would you expect the drag on a dandelion seed to be the same as that on a bowling ball? In the following activity, explore how air drag depends on the size and shape of a falling object.

Objectives
■ Relate air drag to an object's shape.
■ Explore lift.

Key Terms
drag
lift
Bernoulli effect

Figure 23-10

The parachute on this dragster causes enough drag to slow the car down.

INVESTIGATION

How does air drag depend on the falling object?

Parachutes and gliders fall very differently. How does air drag depend on an object's size and shape?

Preparation

Problem

How does the air drag force depend on the properties of the falling object?

Hypothesis

Have your group agree on the properties to be examined and the hypothesis to be tested. Record your hypothesis.

Objectives

In this Investigation you will:

- *Compare* the terminal speed of objects of different size, shape, or other properties.
- *Relate* the terminal speeds to the drag force on the objects.

Possible Materials

coffee filters of various sizes (at least 5 of each size)

thread

balloons (different shapes and sizes)

paper clips or coins

tissue paper or toy parachutes

Plan the Experiment

1 Examine the materials available and plan which properties you will examine.

2 To compare speeds, drop two objects from the same height. Keeping the slower object at the same height, drop the other object from a greater height at the same time until both objects land at the same time. Then compare the ratio of heights.

3 Prepare and construct a table for recording your data.

Check the Plan
Discuss the following points with other group members to decide the final procedure for your experiments.

1 What properties will you be testing?

2 How will you vary only one property at a time?

3 If you examine the effect of size, will you test the width, area, or volume?

4 *Make sure your teacher has approved your experimental plan before you proceed further.*

5 Carry out your experiment. Make any needed measurements and complete your data table.

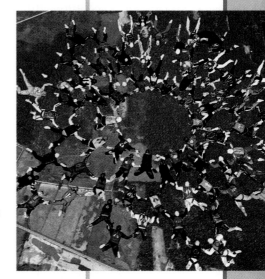

Analyze and Conclude

1. **Comparing and Contrasting** Did the drag force depend on width (or height), on area, or on volume? How could you tell?

2. **Drawing Conclusions** How would you design part of a plane to give the least drag? What shape would you use to give the largest drag?

3. **Analyzing the Procedure** Were your results affected by any object not reaching terminal speed quickly? What equipment might you use to improve your experiment?

Going Further

Application
What are the benefits of reducing drag in an automobile? What shapes would you think have the least amount of drag? Investigate car shapes. Design an automobile that is functional, yet has a shape to reduce drag. How could you test your design to see how drag affects it?

Air drag on airplanes has been studied since the time of the Wright brothers. Now that you've seen how an object's size and shape affect air drag, you can understand why today's airplanes are designed with sleek, streamlined shapes. These shapes keep drag to a minimum.

Experiments show that the drag not only depends on the shape and area of the object that the air hits, but also on the density of the air and the square of the object's speed. That is, the drag on

an airplane going 40 m/s is four times the drag on the same plane going 20 m/s.

Getting a Lift

Drag and thrust affect how an airplane moves through the air. But how does it get up in the first place? It needs a method of getting an upward force larger than the force of gravity. Try some methods yourself in the MiniLab.

MiniLab

How can you get a lift?

Try this activity to find out if paper airplanes get lift.

Procedure

Fold your own favorite model of paper airplane or follow the directions and illustrations here. Start with a piece of 8½″ × 11″ paper.

1. Fold the paper in half the long way and open it again.

2. Fold two corners (A) to the center. Then fold the new corner (B) into the center (along fold C).

3. Fold the plane in half. Make pencil marks at the end of the wing to divide it into fourths.

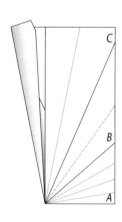

4. Fold one wing at the pencil mark closest to the center as shown. Repeat with the other wing.

5. Create winglets by folding the wing up at the pencil mark farthest from

the center. Straighten the wings and put a paper clip on the bottom, near the center of the plane.

6. Test-fly the plane. If it dives, move the paper clip back. If it rises and then falls, move it forward.

Analysis

1. If the thrown plane flies horizontally or rises, there is no downward drag on it, but there is an upward force to balance its weight. Explain where it came from. Hint: Would you get the same result if you held the plane horizontally and dropped it?

Figure 23-11

Aircraft, like gliders, can fly because of the way their wings affect the air that moves across them.

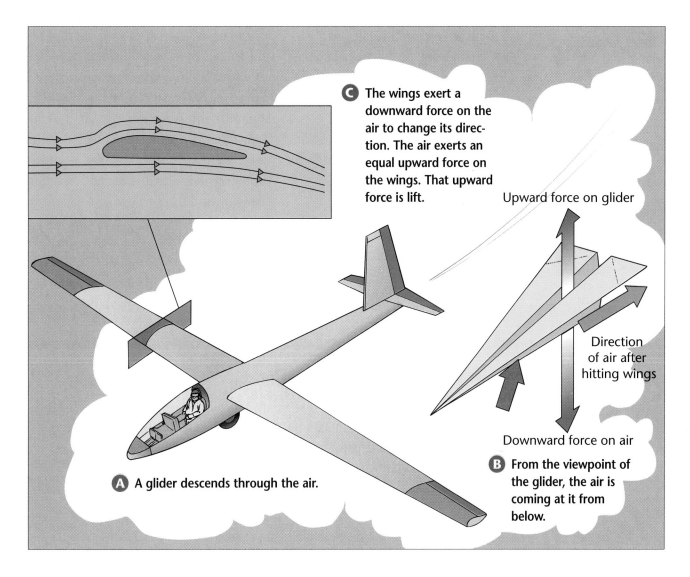

C The wings exert a downward force on the air to change its direction. The air exerts an equal upward force on the wings. That upward force is lift.

Upward force on glider

Direction of air after hitting wings

Downward force on air

A A glider descends through the air.

B From the viewpoint of the glider, the air is coming at it from below.

A paper airplane stays in the air longer because of an upward force exerted by air on its wings, called **lift.** When a plane flies, the lift force acts in the opposite direction of gravity, allowing it to stay in the air. Animals that fly, such as birds, bats, and insects, have wings that are able to lift them through the air. There are even some squirrels, frogs, and lemurs that can glide from trees using flaps of skin extended to act as wings.

As you will soon discover, lift has several causes. The shape of the wing can affect air in a couple of ways to cause lift. The angle of the wing to the oncoming air also has an effect on lift. **Figure 23-11** discusses how lift is able to keep a glider in the air. Like a paper airplane, gliders don't use engines to produce thrust. They simply glide through the air, using air currents to stay aloft for hours.

■ What increases lift?

Wings can get more lift if they are shaped with a nearly flat bottom and a curved top. That shape is called an airfoil. **Figure 23-12** shows what happens when an airfoil moves through air.

Notice that the air leaving the wing is deflected downward. The wing must exert a force on the air to change the direction of the air. And, as you saw with the glider, the air must exert an upward force on the wing.

Just as drag is related to air density and to an object's area and speed, lift is influenced by certain properties of the air and the wing. The lift generated by a wing depends on the wing area, the square of the speed of the air moving past it, and a number called the lift coefficient, which takes into account the wing shape and the angle between the wing and the air flowing past it.

Figure 23-12

An airfoil like the one below changes the direction of air flow as air moves across it. By doing this, the wing produces lift.

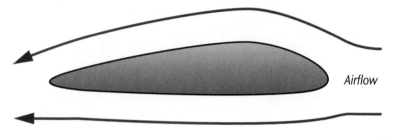

Airflow

■ Stall Speed

Because the lift depends on the square of the speed of the air moving over the wing, an airplane's speed

Flying Back in Time

"Back when I started flying planes, the greatest hazard in aviation was starvation," David Binns recalls with a smile. "I lived from hamburger to hamburger!"

In the early 1930s, Binns made his living by flying open biplanes. He would land in farmers' fields to pick up one or two brave passengers. After they piled into the seat in front of him, Binns took them wherever they wanted to go. Often they asked for a windy sight-seeing trip to get a bird's-eye view of their town and maybe wave at friends below. After the trip, Binns flew back to the field where, he hoped, more passengers would be waiting.

makes a big difference in the amount of lift produced. For lift to balance the force of gravity, there is a minimum speed at which the plane must be moving. This is the speed where lift equals the plane's weight. Below that speed, the plane will start to drop out of the air. This is called the *stall speed*. For a plane to get off the ground, it must accelerate past the stall speed.

When a plane lands, the plane's stall speed is also very important. Jets like the one shown in **Figure 23-13** have flaps that increase the wing area and lift. This allows the plane to fly slower before landing without dropping below the stall speed. A pilot slows the plane down until the stall speed is reached as the wheels touch the ground.

Figure 23-13

As a plane slows down before landing, flaps on the wings are extended to increase the wing area. This allows the plane to fly slower without dropping below the stall speed.

A Flying Circus

Binns loved flying so much that in 1937 he joined the National Air Show and traveled around the nation performing for crowds. In the shows, he flew a lightweight airplane specially built for aerobatics (airplane acrobatics).

He and the other pilots were called barnstormers, and they thrilled audiences by sending their planes into loops and rolls in the sky. During his part of the show, Binns pretended to be an inexperienced pilot who couldn't control his plane. The crowd loved it.

Sharing a Chute

The ride Binns will never forget was not part of an air show. In 1937, he and his co-pilot were flying a small open plane 6,000 feet up when the parachute Binns was wearing opened unexpectedly—inside the plane! The parachute pulled him outside the plane, where he and the chute became tangled in the wires that supported the plane's tail.

Binns yelled for his copilot to shut off the plane's motor and jump, using his own parachute. By the time his friend jumped free of the plane, Binns' parachute was supporting Binns—and the entire small plane! Luckily, the chute cushioned the crash that followed. It was a rough landing, but the plane was able to be repaired, and Binns had to spend only

one night in the hospital.

At the age of 80, David Binns still loves to fly in small planes. "I'll fly in anything I can," he says. "I just like the freedom of flying."

Find Out More About It

Find out how the air show planes were modified so they could do aerobatics.

Thinking Critically

1. What were early stunt pilots called? *Describe* some of the aerobatic tricks they did.
2. Suggest a *hypothesis* that explains why people enjoy watching air shows.

■ Bernoulli Effect

There are a couple of ways wing shape can generate lift. Do the Try It activity to better understand one way.

Air moving over the top of a wing has to go a longer distance than that moving over the bottom. But because it takes the same time to cross the wing, it moves faster. The **Bernoulli effect** states that when air moves faster, the pressure it exerts is less. Therefore, the pressure above the wing is less than that below the wing. Recall that pressure is related to force—pressure is force divided by area. If pressures above and below the wing are unbalanced, so are forces above and below the wing. The result is an upward force on the wing. This is also the reason the cups swung together. Unbalanced forces resulted in a net force on each cup toward the other. **Figure 23-14** shows how air moving across a wing can vary in air pressure.

The Bernoulli effect can affect things other than airplanes, too. If you've ever walked through a city on a

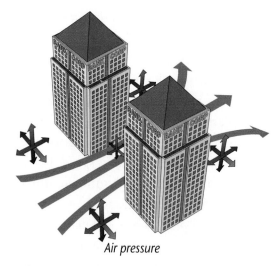

Air pressure

Figure 23-15

When wind blows into the gap between two buildings, the air moves faster. Because the air moves faster, the pressure it exerts is less, according to the Bernoulli effect.

windy day, you may have noticed how fast the wind was between two buildings. As the air squeezed into the gap between the buildings, it moved faster. If you walk out of a building into a strong wind like this, you may even have a hard time catching your breath because of the low pressure caused by the fast-moving air. **Figure 23-15** illustrates how air pressure changes as wind blows between buildings.

The Bernoulli effect also works with fluids other than air. Gases and liquids are considered fluids because they can flow. The Bernoulli effect can be observed in a river. If the stream narrows, the water moves faster as it flows through the narrow section. If you were to have water running through a pipe that has a narrow section, the water pressure in the narrower pipe would be lower as the water speeds up through it.

Figure 23-14

Even though the distance between A and B is greater for air flowing on top of the wing than it is for air flowing below it, the air travels the distance in the same time.

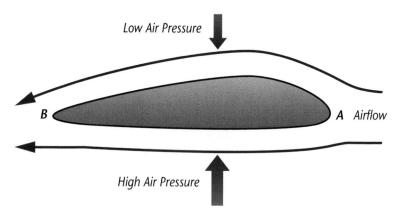

Low Air Pressure

B

A *Airflow*

High Air Pressure

■ Coanda Effect

The Bernoulli effect only accounts for a portion of the lift generated as air moves across an airplane wing, however. You can explore another effect that generates lift in the next Try It activity.

Fluids such as water and air tend to follow the curve of a smooth surface as shown in **Figure 23-16.** This happens because molecules in air and water are weakly attracted to the surface. It is known as the *Coanda effect.* In the Try It activity, the water from the faucet was flowing straight down. When you put the curved spoon into the water stream, the water changed direction as it followed the curve. On an airplane wing, air is attracted to the wing's upper surface. An equal and opposite force pulls the wing up. Air also follows the wing's curve and is deflected downward as it

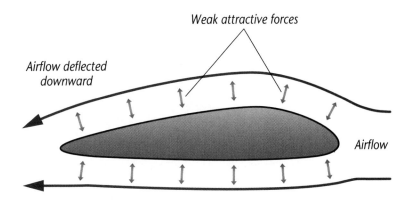

Figure 23-17

Just as running water follows the curve of a spoon, flowing air follows the curve of an airplane wing to create lift.

leaves the wing, producing more lift by another action/reaction pair. This is shown in **Figure 23-17.**

The same forces between molecules that pulled the spoon into the water can create a force opposing forward motion on a wing. In addition, the wing, just like any other object that moves through the air, causes a drag force. Some of the drag comes when the air has to change direction to get around the wing. More drag comes from friction between the wing and the moving gas molecules.

For the Coanda effect to work, the flow of air must remain attached to the surface of the wing. This is why wing shape is important. If the wing's curve isn't smooth, or if it curves too sharply, the weak force attracting the air to the wing surface won't be enough to keep the flow along the surface, and lift will be lost. This will also increase the drag, slowing the plane and the movement of air across the wing surface. Both airplane and bird wings share this smooth curve of their wings. In Chapter 24, you'll discover how the shape and movement of bird wings allow for flight.

Try It!

The Coanda Effect
Hold the back of a spoon under a faucet out of which a thin stream of water comes. Hold it loosely so it can swing. How does the water flow around the spoon? How does the spoon move?

Figure 23-16

Water or any fluid, such as air, follows a curved surface because of forces between the molecules of the fluid and those of the surface.

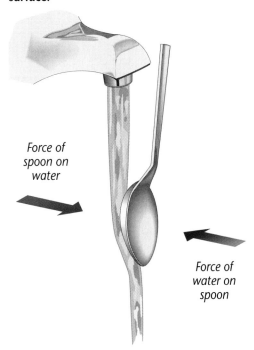

Force of spoon on water

Force of water on spoon

Figure 23-18

Angle of attack allows planes to fly upside down and still get lift.

amazing inverted maneuvers routinely done by skilled aviators hint that there might be something else to lift.

This missing link is the angle of the wing as it moves through the air. When a plane flies, it almost always flies with the front edge of the wing slightly higher than the trailing edge. The angle of the wing with respect to the oncoming air is called the *angle of attack.* This means the oncoming air hits the bottom edge of the wing. This increases the pressure of the air underneath the wing compared to the air pressure above the wing. The result is an upward force, or lift.

You can feel this force if you hold a piece of cardboard or other flat object in a strong wind, or in front of a powerful fan. As you hold the cardboard flat and parallel to the airflow, it stays where it is. If you angle the front edge slightly, you will feel the lift force.

The angle of attack is critical, however. If the angle is too steep, the air won't follow the curvature of the wing, and the wing loses lift and gains drag. This is shown in **Figure 23-19.**

■ Angle of Attack

The Bernoulli and Coanda effects may explain a large part of lift, but they don't give you the entire picture. If those were the only effects causing lift, planes would never be able to fly upside down as shown in **Figure 23-18.** This is because the lift force would then be in the same direction as gravity. They also don't explain why a paper airplane with a flat wing is able to soar as long as it can. The success of flat wings and the

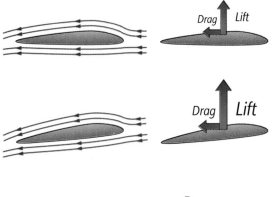

Ⓐ Angle of attack is zero. Lift and drag are small.

Ⓑ As the wing is tilted up, the lift and drag increase. Planes have a large angle of attack just after taking off. Why do you think that is?

Figure 23-19

The amount of lift generated by a wing is affected by its angle of attack.

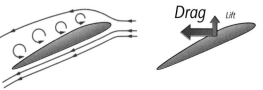

Ⓒ If the attack angle is too large, the air above the wing can't follow the wing's curved shape, and lift is greatly reduced.

The Four Forces

As you have seen, there are four forces on a plane. The forward force of the air on the propeller is called the *thrust;* the rearward force of the air on the plane is the *drag.* The downward force is that of gravity, or *weight,* and the upward force of the air on the wings is the *lift.* **Figure 23-20** shows how the four forces are balanced during an airliner's flight.

If the four forces are balanced, then both the horizontal and the vertical velocities are constant. The plane can be climbing or descending, but only at a constant speed. For the plane to accelerate upward, lift must be greater than gravity.

The four forces change during the course of a flight. When a plane is sitting on the runway, there is no lift, thrust, or drag. There is only the balance of weight and the upward push from the ground. Adding thrust from the propeller sets the plane in motion, accelerating it down the runway. As it moves, air flows

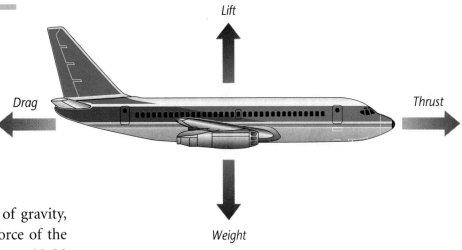

Figure 23-20

The forces of weight, lift, thrust, and drag are balanced during level flight.

over the plane's wing. Thanks to the wing's shape, the moving air creates lift. The faster the plane goes, the greater the lift becomes. But, the force of drag also increases. Eventually, the lift force becomes greater than the force of gravity, and the plane takes off. While it's in level flight, the four forces are balanced. When landing, the plane slows down, reducing lift. The lift force is eventually reduced as the plane slows to stall speed, just as the wheels touch the runway, and the plane slows to a stop.

check your UNDERSTANDING

Understanding Concepts

1. To design a bike with the least air drag, what two properties should you carefully consider?

2. What are the causes of lift?

3. The paper clip on your paper glider is too far back; the glider climbs steeply, then falls. Describe what happened to lift.

Skill Review

4. **Categorizing** On which of these shapes could the Bernoulli effect and/or the Coanda effect create lift?

Technology: Diseases: Frequent Fliers?

The frequent flier, armed with a bulging briefcase, boarded a plane in Hong Kong. She felt on top of the world, even before takeoff. Three whirlwind days of meetings ended with a contract to take back to the home office in San Francisco.

The next morning, not only the frequent flier, but several of her fellow passengers awakened to the aching body symptoms of the flu. The other passengers were spread throughout the city. Within a week, San Francisco was in the throes of a flu epidemic.

The flier did not realize that she was harboring a stowaway on her flight home. Lodged in the flier's respiratory tract was a hitchhiking virus that eventually made her homecoming less than happy.

The Technology

How often does it happen that microbes travel halfway around the world? More often than you might suspect. Traveling viruses are not new. Bubonic plague caused the death of one-quarter of the population of Europe during the Middle Ages. Before the twentieth century, the disease was responsible for several other epidemics that killed millions of people. Outbreaks still occur in parts of Asia, South America, and Africa.

Spanish soldiers and missionaries in the sixteenth century wrote about the smallpox epidemics, which struck down the people who lived in the Caribbean, Mexico, Peru, and Brazil. These viruses came by ship from ports in Spain and Portugal. The Europeans who carried the virus had already developed an immunity to the disease it caused. In another instance, the British fleet brought convicts and soldiers to Australia in 1788. By 1789, a smallpox epidemic had killed many Aborigines, the people already living in Australia before the fleet arrived. Today microbes still travel by ship but, just like their human hosts, go faster by plane.

The news media keep people on alert during outbreaks of diseases around the world. On September 29, 1994, the news of an outbreak of plague was reported in India.

News reports were sketchy at first about the early cases of pneumonic plague in Surat, a city in western India. But people around the world became alarmed when they learned that the disease had spread to the capital of India, New Delhi. Soon Bombay, Calcutta, and Madras also reported cases. People worried about where else it would spread.

The Background

The bacteria that cause the plague, *Yersinia pestis,* are related to *Escherichia coli*—those usually harmless bacteria found in great numbers in human intestines. *Yersinia* are transmitted from one animal to another by fleabite. Where people live close to rodents, fleas may transmit the bacteria from an infected rodent to a person. Fleas rarely transmit the organism directly from one person to another. However, in some cases in humans, the bacteria become established in the lungs, causing pneumonic plague. It is highly contagious.

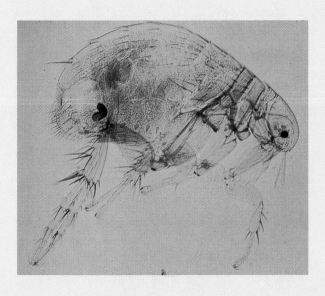

The Question

When word of plague in India was broadcast throughout the world, people were on edge. From some areas came a public outcry to close the airports in India and restrict immigration from there. History shows that plague is deadly dangerous. However, if it is treated early enough with antibiotics, recovery is almost guaranteed. Fortunately, there is also a vaccine against the microorganism that causes pneumonic plague.

The plague isn't the only deadly, contagious disease in the world. New viral diseases are constantly developing and spreading, and they are much more difficult to treat. A highly contagious, untreatable, and nearly 100 percent fatal virus called *ebola zaire* has appeared in tropical Africa. The virus failed to spread to a larger population mainly because the village where it first appeared had no access to high-speed transportation.

What should this country do to safeguard its citizens against serious diseases that are carried by planes and other methods of travel from other countries? Would the same restrictions apply to less serious diseases, such as flu? Why might there be a difference in the restrictions?

*inter*NET CONNECTION

The Centers for Disease Control and Prevention track the global spread of serious diseases and offer advice to travelers who may be visiting a disease-infected area. Follow the link for Chapter 23 on the Glencoe Homepage, **http://www.glencoe.com/,** for information about the Centers for Disease Control and Prevention. If you were planning to visit a disease-infected area, what strategy would you use to avoid contracting the disease?

APPLYING TECHNOLOGY

Planning an Airport

As with any large project, planning is the key to success. Good planning involves anticipating problems and considering as many factors as possible. These elements are vital for projects such as choosing a site for an airport. The benefits and problems associated with airports can cause a lot of controversy in a community.

You're the...City Planner

Imagine your community is planning a new airport and you're on the commission assigned to the task of finding the best site for it. You will need to use your knowledge of your community, airplanes, and the effects an airport can have on an area to make your decision.

Drawing on Experience

1 With a group, make a list of all the things you can think of that an airport would need to operate efficiently.

2 Do some research about airports and how they run. How much space do they need? What are some negative effects of an airport? If available, call or visit a city planner for your community. Make a final list of things to consider when choosing a site for an airport.

3 Using a local map, find two or three locations that would be reasonable sites for an airport.

4 Choose the best site and write a proposal that outlines your reasons for choosing that site.

Testing...Testing

1 Present your proposal to the rest of the class and listen to their proposals.

2 As a class, discuss the proposals and predict who might object to each.

3 Decide which of the proposals is the best and prepare a public announcement of the proposed site. Include a map of the site and reasons why this is the best choice.

How Did It Work?

What was the most difficult part of preparing your proposal? Was everybody completely satisfied with the final site? What were some objections? What controversy might you expect from residents near the site chosen for the airport?

Read the statements below that review major points presented in the chapter. Using the concepts that you have learned, answer each question *in your Journal.*

Air

Weight

① Lift, drag, gravity, and thrust are the four forces that affect how a plane flies. *If a plane's speed doubles, how would the force of drag be affected?*

Lift

Drag

Thrust

Weight

② If all the forces on an object are balanced, there is no change in its velocity. *Which two forces on a plane must be unbalanced for the plane to begin to climb?*

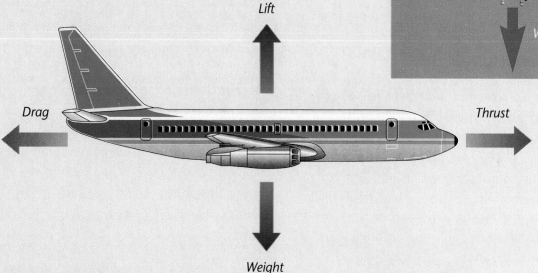

Drag   Lift

Drag   Lift

③ A plane gets lift from the angle of attack, the Coanda effect, and the Bernoulli effect. *Why is lift greatly reduced if the angle of attack is too great?*

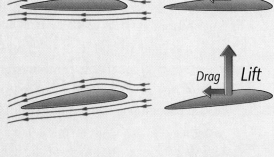

Drag   Lift

Using Key Science Terms

acceleration

Bernoulli effect

drag

gravity

lift

momentum

Newton's second
law of motion

terminal speed

thrust

For each set of terms below, choose the one term that does not belong and explain why it does not.

1. weight, drag, lift, terminal speed
2. Bernoulli effect, Newton's third law, lift, terminal speed
3. lift, drag, weight, momentum

Understanding Ideas

Using complete sentences, answer the following questions in your Journal.

1. Explain how you can be accelerating but your speed is not increasing.
2. If you are running alongside your friend who is smaller than you are, which of you has the greater momentum?
3. If a parachutist is falling straight down at her terminal speed, what is her acceleration?
4. What are the forces acting on a plane that is climbing?
5. How do the lift and force of gravity compare on a plane that is climbing at a constant rate of 10 m/s?
6. What are the contact and noncontact forces on a parachute while it is falling?
7. If you increase the speed of the airplane, which of the forces on it change? How?

Developing Skills

Use your understanding of the concepts developed in this chapter to answer the following questions.

1. **Concept Mapping** Make a concept map of force and acceleration.
2. **Predicting** If two parachutists use identical parachutes, but one parachutist is twice as heavy as the other, how will their terminal speeds compare?
3. **Controlling Variables** Suppose you wanted to see how the terminal velocity of parachutes depends on their area. Could you make the parachutes out of different sizes of cloth and keep all other parts the same? Explain.
4. **Recognizing Cause and Effect** What is the effect of the motion of the propeller? What accelerates the plane forward?
5. **Making and Using Graphs** The table below gives the altitude of a small plane versus time. Draw a graph of the vertical speed of the plane in meters/second versus time.

Altitude of Plane Versus Time	
Time (s)	Altitude above sea level (m)
0	225
30	226
60	230
90	235
120	240
150	245
180	245
210	240

Critical Thinking

In your Journal, answer each of the following questions.

1. If the engine of an airplane suddenly failed, would you expect the plane to fall straight down? Explain.
2. If a large airliner and a smaller private jet have the same acceleration when taking off, which jet's engines produce the most thrust?
3. You saw two airplanes at a local airport. They looked the same, but one had much larger wings than the other. Which plane would you expect to have the lower stall speed? Why?

Problem Solving

Read the following problem and discuss your answers in a brief paragraph.

You are starting a company to manufacture propeller-driven carts to sell to schools that are using this textbook. You want the carts to reach high speeds. Using what you have learned since you used the cart, describe in words and pictures the features of your cart design.

1. Discuss the influence of the cart's mass on its performance.
2. Would drag or lift be important? Why?

CONNECTING IDEAS

1. **Theme—Models** Would the drag on a hardball with a 9-inch circumference be larger or smaller than that on a softball with a 12-inch circumference?
2. **Theme—Systems and Interactions** How does the interaction of air and an airfoil produce lift?
3. **Theme—Systems and Interactions** If nothing else changes, how will a change in speed affect an object's momentum?
4. **Applying Technology** How could an airport with a sloped runway reduce noise?
5. **Science and Society** How has air travel affected the spread of disease?

CHAPTER 24

Structures of Flight
Soaring Birds and Planes

As the sailplane glides over the lake, carving perfect arcs across the cobalt sky, a hawk circles slowly below it. Both are images of grace and balance. Both the pilot and the bird seem to have the freedom to go anywhere they desire. And they can, as long as they continue to balance the forces that make flight possible. The bird reacts instinctively, using subtle wing movements to guide it through the air. The pilot must rely on experience, the aircraft, and a knowledge of aerodynamics.

▶ *In the following activity, you'll compare different birds to find out what characteristics they have that allow them to fly.*

MiniLab

What are some adaptations of birds?

In this activity, watch birds in a natural setting to examine their similarities and differences.

Procedure

1. Find an area, such as a park or your backyard, where you can watch at least three different kinds of birds.

2. Using binoculars, focus on each bird. Examine its appearance—its color; the size and shape of its wings, tail, beak, and other parts; and anything else you notice. Notice how it flies. Record your observations *in your Journal.*

Analysis

1. Compare the appearances of the birds you studied.

2. Compare the flying methods of the birds you observed.

The Structure of Birds and Planes

24-1

Objectives

- Compare which bird flight structures are equivalent to the parts of an airplane.
- Explain how the shapes of bird and plane wings vary with the fliers' sizes and the type of flying to be done.
- Model how birds and planes change direction in flight.

Key Terms

wing loading
aspect ratio
wingspan

Form and Function

In the MiniLab on the previous page, did you notice any differences in the way birds fly? Maybe you saw that some birds, such as crows and gulls, seem to fly with hardly any wing movements, while ducks and hummingbirds beat their wings rapidly. What did you notice about the shapes of these birds' wings? In this section, we'll study the structures of airplanes and birds such as those shown in **Figure 24-1.** We'll explore how their body structures and flight are related.

Do you see similarities between the shapes of airplanes and birds? How are shapes related to the jobs for which different types of planes and birds are suited? Could you use some of the things you learned about airplane flight in Chapter 23 to understand bird flight?

Figure 24-1

Airplanes and birds come in many sizes and shapes.

A Aircraft can carry anything, from just one person on a short trip to several tons of cargo across oceans. Why do you think their shapes are so different?

B Birds also come in many shapes and sizes like this woodpecker (top) and condor (bottom).

Figure 24-2

Birds possess a number of structural features related to flight.

A Covering the wings are light, smooth feathers.

Hollow bone

Beak

B Having beaks instead of bony jaws and teeth reduces weight.

Sternum

C All birds that fly have an enlarged breastbone, called the sternum, to which huge flight muscles are attached.

D The bodies of flying birds are streamlined and compact, allowing birds to move through air with little drag.

Wing

E Unlike the flexible skeletons of humans, bird skeletons are rigid. A number of bones, such as those in the spinal column and rib cage, have fused together, forming rigid structures that provide firm surfaces for the attachment of the powerful flight muscles.

Feather

F Bird bones are much lighter than the bones of most other vertebrates. They are extremely thin, hollow, and filled with many air spaces. Tiny crosspieces within the bone provide strength and rigidity.

Lung

Air sacs

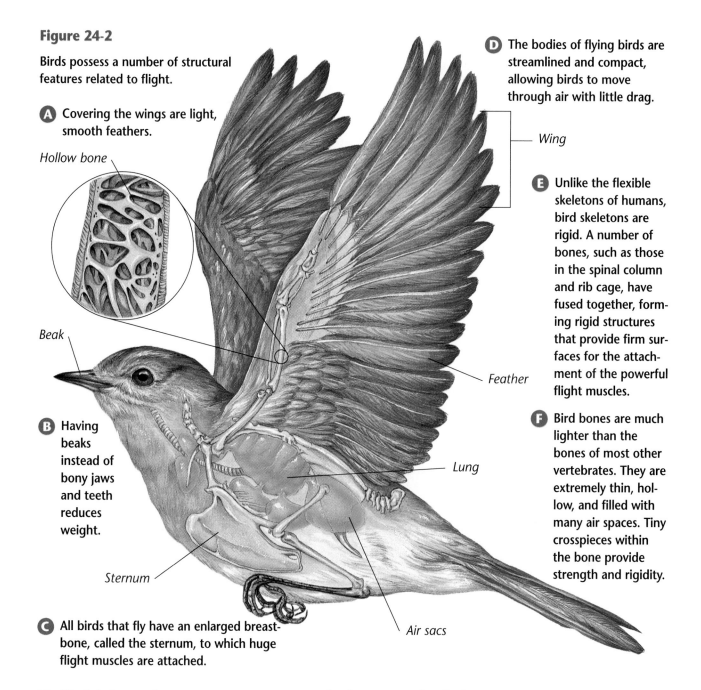

■ Bird Adaptations

What is needed for flight? It's more than just flapping a pair of wings. As you saw in Chapter 23, lift is needed to balance weight, and thrust to balance drag. Lift is provided by the wings, so adaptations that reduce weight also lower the load placed on the wings. As you will see in the next section, wings also produce thrust, so any reduction in air drag also takes a load off the wings. **Figure 24-2** shows some of the struc-

tural adaptations for flight in a common bird, a bluebird. As you study the illustration, consider how each of these adaptations meets one or more of the requirements of flight.

Airplane designers use similar strategies. Strong, lightweight metal alloys made of aluminum, magnesium, and titanium have been developed for the aircraft industry. Internal supports, like the bones in birds, have holes to reduce weight further and to maintain strength.

Swing and Drag
Why do airplanes and birds tend to be longer than they are wide? Find out by getting a piece of stiff cardboard that's about 30 cm square. In an area clear of obstacles, swing the cardboard, holding it in different positions. In which position did the cardboard have the least resistance as you swung it through the air? Why do you think there's a difference in the amount of drag on the cardboard as you hold it in different positions?

Reducing Drag

How do the size and shape of a bird or plane affect its flight? You saw in Chapter 23 that air drag depends on the shape and size of the object. Streamlined objects—ones that are rounded in the front and pointed in the back—allow air to flow around the object with less drag than other shapes. Skin surfaces are smooth, and projections—such as feet and wheels—are retracted during flight to further reduce drag.

As you discovered in the Try It activity, an important factor in determining air drag is the frontal area. This is the area that faces the oncoming air. When the edge of the cardboard faced the oncoming air, you noticed there was little drag because the edge of the cardboard had little area. **Figure 24-3** shows how the shape of airplanes reduces frontal area. Many birds also have this general body shape. With long, narrow heads and bodies, even large birds have little frontal area compared to their overall surface area.

Figure 24-3

Compare these two views of the same airplane. How does its shape reduce frontal area?

Producing Lift

What's the most obvious feature of a bird or airplane? Right, its wings. You already know that wings provide the upward force, or lift, that keeps the bird or plane in the air.

Recall from Chapter 23 that air is forced down partly by the tilt of the wing and partly by the tendency of the air to follow the curved upper surface

(the Coanda effect). The longer path taken by air moving over the upper surface also reduces the pressure there (the Bernoulli effect), causing an upward force.

The amount of lift depends on the wing area, the speed of the air across the wing, and the shape and angle of the wing. That is, for a plane to fly, the lift must be at least as large as the weight of the plane. Because lift depends on speed and wing area, larger wings can produce greater lift than smaller wings at slow speeds. So a bird or plane only needs to fly fast enough for its wings to produce a lift as large as its weight. For example, a light glider with large wings can fly slowly, while a heavier jet fighter with smaller wings must fly faster.

There's an easy way to tell how fast a bird or plane must fly. By dividing the weight by the wing area, you get a number that indicates how effectively a wing produces lift. This number is called **wing loading.** A light bird with large wings has a small wing loading and can fly slowly. If an airplane carries too much weight, its wing loading increases. Its engines may not be able to give it enough speed to allow it to take off.

Science AND MATH

If you don't know the surface area of an irregular shape such as a bird wing, you can estimate it by using graph paper. From a picture of a wing, trace the outline onto the graph paper and count the number of squares covered by the wing. This is your estimate of surface area. To determine the size of each square, you will need to find the scale of the drawing you used.

Thinking Lab

Recognizing Cause and Effect

How is the shape of a bird's wings related to its style of flight?

Birds, like airplanes, have different types of wings, making them better suited for certain types of flying. The kind of flying a bird does is largely dependent on its wing loading and shape.

Analysis

Study the characteristics of the birds listed in the table. Calculate the wing loading of each bird by dividing its weight by its wing area. List the birds in order of their wing loading. Using the dimensions given, make a scale drawing of each bird's general wing shape. Compare and contrast their flight characteristics with their wing shape.

Bird Characteristics					
Bird	Wing length (m)	Wing width (m)	Wing area (m^2)	Weight (N)	Flight characteristics
Wren	0.17	0.025	0.0042	0.10	flies in wooded areas
Brown pelican	2.10	0.214	0.45	26	flies straight, carries loads
Andean condor	3.00	0.38	1.14	115	glides long distances

Thinking Critically

Based on the table, what wing shapes are best for what kind of flying? What airplanes can you think of that share these basic wing shapes and flight characteristics?

Figure 24-4

The aspect ratio is the span divided by the average width. A long, narrow wing has a high aspect ratio.

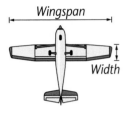

Wingspan

Width

■ Wing Shapes

If you've ever been to an airport or looked through a book about airplanes, you've probably noticed that there are many kinds of airplanes. Each kind is designed for a specific use. Some are made for doing quick turns, rolls, and other aerobatic stunts, while others are made for speed. If you look at the wings of these planes, you'll notice some differences. There are short, wide wings; long, slender wings; and everything in between. Some wings sweep back so much that they form triangles. Others stick straight out from the plane's body. How does wing shape affect how a plane flies?

As you saw in the activity, long thin wings are seen on birds that fly long distances. Birds with shorter, wider wings are more maneuverable. When comparing birds that are different sizes, it's easier to look at the ratio of length to width than at the actual dimensions. This quantity is called **aspect ratio.** The aspect ratio is found by dividing the length by the average width of the wing. The length, or **wingspan,** is the distance between both wing tips as shown in **Figure 24-4.** A wren, for example, has an aspect ratio of about 6.9. This is lower than the aspect ratio of the pelican, which is 9.8. Wings with higher aspect ratios have greater lift and less drag than lower-aspect ratio wings. Low-aspect ratio wings, however, can turn more quickly and, therefore, are more maneuverable. The wren, for example, dashes in and out of dense brush, while the pelican flies fairly straight through open sky.

Birds hold their wings in different positions to adjust for different conditions, and airplanes have been developed that mimic this adaptation. When the pigeon in **Figure 24-5** increases its flying speed from 8 to 22 m/s, it reduces its wing area by 40 percent and its wingspan by 37 percent by holding its wings closer to its body.

Figure 24-5

By shifting its wings back, some planes and birds can reduce both wing area and wingspan. While this increases its wing loading, the higher speed that results creates sufficient lift for flight.

Figure 24-6

Look at the structure of this barn owl's wing to see how the feathers overlap, covering the wing.

■ Feathered Wings as Airfoils

Birds are the only animals that have feathers. These lightweight structures provide insulation and play an important role in flight. As you can see in **Figure 24-6,** feathers cover birds' wings.

Flight feathers are extremely flexible and resilient structures. The weblike system of barbs, barbules, and tiny hooks helps to maintain the surface of the feather, allowing for a smooth flow of air over the entire wing. The structure of a typical flight feather is shown in **Figure 24-7.** Smooth airflow is important for generating lift without too much drag.

Compared to the wing of an airplane, a bird's wing appears to be an incredibly complicated structure of muscles, tendons, bone, blood vessels, and skin. Bird wings, like the wings of aircraft, are also shaped like airfoils.

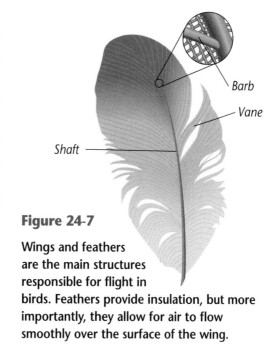

Barb

Vane

Shaft

Figure 24-7

Wings and feathers are the main structures responsible for flight in birds. Feathers provide insulation, but more importantly, they allow for air to flow smoothly over the surface of the wing.

Controlling Flight

Have you ever watched a flock of birds diving, swooping, and turning above a field? Or, maybe you've been at an air show where a stunt pilot did aerobatics. How do birds and planes control their direction?

On a plane, movable flaps called control surfaces are adjusted to make the plane tilt up or down, roll from side to side, or turn right or left. As **Figure 24-8** shows, special terms are used for these movements. *Pitch* is the motion of the plane as its nose points up or down. *Yaw* is the motion made as the nose turns left or right. *Roll* describes the tilting motion made as one wing dips lower than the other. You can explore how to control pitch, yaw, and roll on a paper airplane in the MiniLab activity on the next page.

Figure 24-8

Pitch, yaw, and roll describe changes in the orientation of an airplane.

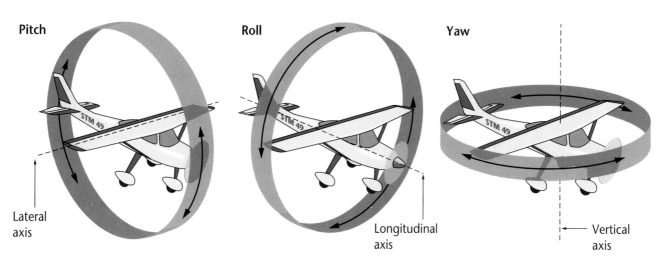

Pitch

Roll

Yaw

Lateral axis

Longitudinal axis

Vertical axis

How can you control the flight of a paper airplane?

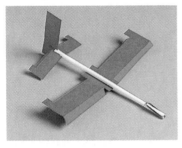

Follow the instructions below to construct a controllable plane.

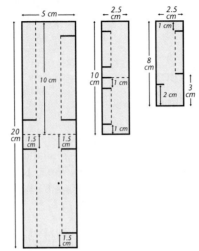

Procedure

1. Mark and cut out 3 pieces of stiff paper (such as a manila folder) matching the dimensions shown.

2. Make cuts along the solid lines. Use a ruler to help bend the paper along the dashed lines.

3. Make a 1-cm cut in one end of a plastic straw.

4. Join the two smaller pieces at the slots as shown. Glue this into the slot in the straw so the horizontal wing is on top of the straw.

5. Glue the wing under the straw so that the leading edge of the wing is 8.5 cm from the front end of the straw. Stick two paper clips in the nose end of the straw as shown.

6. Launch the plane and see how it flies. Record your observations *in your Journal.*

Analysis

1. What happens when you launch the plane after bending the tail flaps up slightly? Down slightly?

2. Try slightly raising first one wing flap and then lowering the other. How do they affect the flight?

3. Try bending the rudder slightly to one side. Do this first alone, then after slightly raising the wing flap on the side to which the rudder was bent.

How does a plane change the direction it is moving? As you found out in the activity, flaps on the wings and tail can change a plane's direction. Remember that a change in either speed or direction results in an acceleration, and acceleration can occur only if opposing forces are unbalanced.

Three basic types of control surfaces on an airplane, shown in **Figure 24-9,** direct the motions just described. The movable flap on the vertical tail fin is called the *rudder;* those on the horizontal tail surface are called the *elevators.* The flaps on the wings are called *ailerons.* All three types of flaps are connected to controls in the cockpit.

Birds don't have rudders, elevators, and ailerons to control yaw, pitch, and roll. What do birds have that helps them achieve the same effects? Birds change their pitch by moving their wings forward and back or by adjusting their tail feathers. They usually turn left or right by rolling, which is done by adjusting their primary wing feathers

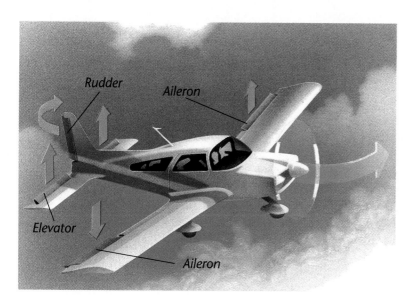

Figure 24-9

When a plane makes a horizontal turn, all three types of control surfaces must be used. Direction of motion of the flaps needed for a left turn is shown.

Rudder

Aileron

Elevator

Aileron

or their tails. Without a vertical tail, birds control yaw by raising their wings higher above their bodies.

■ **Landing**

Have you ever watched a plane or large bird land? Speed must be reduced, but not too much. At the stall speed, lift equals weight, so below stall speed, the flyer will fall out of the sky. Both birds and planes have several ways to increase the lift of wings, and thus lower stall speed. Planes extend flaps and other parts of the wing to increase lift at landing speeds.

Birds, as shown in **Figure 24-10,** spread their feathers to increase their wing area and produce the same effect. These methods also increase drag, so they are used only when landing.

Figure 24-10

Some birds can separate their primary feathers, and many spread their feathers and tails to increase lift while landing. Webbed feet also help slow some birds down.

check your UNDERSTANDING

Understanding Concepts

1. What are some flight adaptations of birds?
2. An albatross is a heavy bird with long but thin wings. Would you expect this bird to excel at soaring or at quick changes in direction and speed? Explain.
3. Why are the wing flaps on an airplane extended during landing?

Skill Review

4. **Comparing and Contrasting** An airplane wing has the following control features to control its flight: ailerons and flaps. How does a bird control its flight? For more help, refer to Comparing and Contrasting in the *Skill Handbook.*

people in SCIENCE

Meet Fernando Arenas, Airline Pilot

"A pilot sees things that only the angels get to see," says airline pilot Fernando Arenas. "It's an immense and beautiful world beneath our wings. Americans don't realize how enormous our own country is. West of the Mississippi River, the U.S. looks pretty empty from 33 000 feet."

In the following interview, Mr. Arenas candidly shares his thoughts about both the romance of flight and the down-to-earth practicalities of his career.

On the Job

Q Mr. Arenas, you're responsible for the safety of hundreds of passengers on each of your flights. Does it feel like a heavy burden?

A The way I handle it is to fly the cockpit. I figure if I get myself up and down safely, everything else follows me. I also have more mundane responsibilities to take care of: Do the flight attendants have enough meals? Does a passenger seat fail to incline? Is someone insisting on bringing aboard a monster suitcase? Ultimately, the captain is responsible for it all.

Q What's it like to fly a Boeing 767?

A The aircraft is almost too much whiz-bang for me. I like doing the hands-on flying. I don't use the buttons and gadgets of the autopilot until I have to, because I love flying and "kicking the rudder." Takeoff and landing are pretty much in my hands. Then I level off the plane and slap on the autopilot. If there's a weather problem, I'm involved all the way. But in clear weather, I can enjoy the gorgeous view, like the Greenland ice caps sparkling in the sun.

Early Influences

Q Do you remember your first airplane ride?

A It happened when I was about 12 years old. I had minor surgery, and the doctor promised me that if I toughed it out, he'd take me up in a single-engine plane. He treated me to some steep maneuvers that felt like a roller coaster ride. I loved it! But I never dreamed at the time that I'd one day be a pilot. I lived in the Chicago inner city, and that seemed way beyond my reach.

Q How did it happen that you realized that dream?

A I left school as soon as I could, at 16, like most of my friends. In the 1950s, a guy had to figure out what to do about his military obligations, so I enlisted in the Air Force. I learned aircraft maintenance because being a pilot required a high school diploma. Later I got my GED and went to college on the G.I. bill. That's when I got to go up in an open cockpit bi-wing plane. In that setting, you really feel one with nature, like Saint-Exupery and other pilots have written. The instructor rolled the plane and pulled a loop. When we straightened out, I said "Wow! This is all right!" I took lessons to get my pilot's license and just happened to be in the right place at the right time when airlines really started to grow in the early 1960s.

There are many careers in the field of aviation, each with its own skill requirements. Investigate the jobs listed below. Find out what skills and training are needed for each occupation. Write a "Help Wanted" advertisement for one of the careers listed. Include the skills and characteristics of the ideal job candidate.

▶ *airline pilot, air-traffic controller, airplane mechanic, travel agent*

Personal Insights

Q What advice do you have for a young person thinking of a career in aviation?

A Flying is fun, but the romance of flight is just a small part of it. In fact, for every hour a pilot spends in the air, he or she puts in an hour of ground time. Education should involve some math and science, which is important in this business. However, I've done career counseling in high schools and sometimes surprise even the teachers by saying that good English is the most important skill.

24-2 Getting Up To Speed

Objectives

- Explain the various flight styles birds use to obtain thrust.
- Describe how birds obtain the energy needed for flight.
- Compare methods different aircraft use for providing thrust.

Obtaining Thrust

As you remember from Chapter 23, wings generate lift as a result of air passing rapidly over them. To get the needed airspeed, birds use their wings to generate the forward force, called thrust. Most airplanes use their engine-driven propellers or jet engines. But a few birds spend most of their time soaring—flying with motionless wings. And some planes, called gliders, remain in the air without engines.

Gliding and Soaring

Watching a glider or a soaring bird in the sky is fascinating. They seem to remain in the air effortlessly. How do they do it?

Gliding is like roller-skating down a ramp. You accelerate down a ramp because of the force of gravity on you. But as you move down the ramp, you also move forward. In the case of gliding or soaring, **Figure 24-11,** part of the force of gravity again gives a forward thrust.

Figure 24-11

A bird gliding steadily through still air uses gravity to provide thrust.

A The lift force is always at right angles to the bird, while the drag force is parallel to the bird.

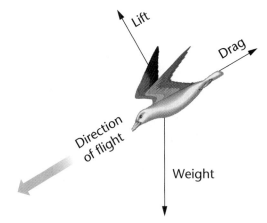

B The force of weight, pointed toward Earth, points somewhat in the direction of flight. This forward component provides the thrust.

Figure 24-12

A bald eagle is one species of bird that nests at the top of tall trees and can begin its flight in a glide. The swift, which nests high in the rocks, can do the same thing.

To stay in the air for a long time, the glider should make the angle between its flight path and the horizontal as small as possible. But reducing this angle also reduces the forward component of gravity, and thus, the thrust. Therefore, to keep the glider from stalling, the drag force must also be small.

Both birds and planes must reach a high altitude before beginning their glide. Gliding planes are towed by a powered plane. Birds can flap their wings to get high enough to soar.

Once in the air, gliders can regain altitude by finding upward-flowing wind. As you learned in Chapter 1, the air over an area of warmer land is heated and pushed upward by denser, cooler air. Both gliding birds and planes seek such a thermal air current and make circles in it as they rise higher and higher, as shown in **Figure 24-13.**

Figure 24-14

Gliders must be towed to a certain altitude before they can glide.

Figure 24-13

Gliding birds and planes can reach higher altitudes using rising air currents. Those currents produced when the sun warms one part of Earth more than others are called thermals. Those produced when winds are driven upward by the land are called updrafts.

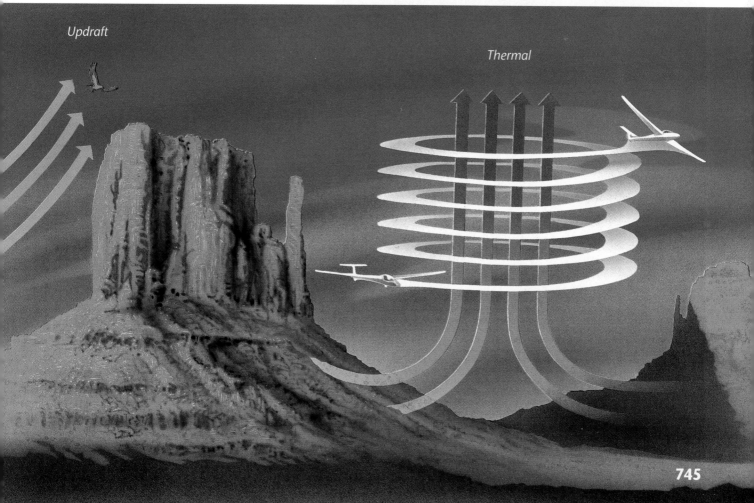

Updraft

Thermal

Figure 24-15

Notice how the wings of this eagle in fast forward flight flap almost straight up and down.

■ Fast Forward Flight

Have you ever watched a pigeon, gull, or duck fly? If so, you may have noticed its wings flapping almost straight up and down. Birds flying at high speed can obtain as much lift as they need from their speed. They flap their wings for thrust. The wing movements are mostly vertical, as shown in **Figure 24-15.**

The movement of the wings requires powerful muscles. Most of the force is needed to pull the wing down. This force is supplied by the pectoralis muscles, which are connected between the upper wing bone and the sternum. The sternum is enlarged, providing the muscle with a large area for connection.

The flight muscles take up more than 15 percent of the mass of the bird. Mallard ducks have exceptionally large muscles because their high wing loading means they have to fly fast and beat their wings rapidly.

Figure 24-16

This is a diagram of a simplified bird wing viewed from the side. When the wing moves down, it tilts, pushing air backwards. What direction do the feathers push the air when the wing moves upward?

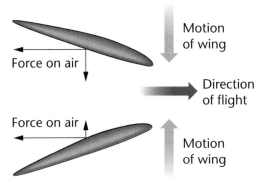

Figure 24-17

Sequence of motion of a dove's wings in slow flight. Follow one point on the bird's wing through the flapping motion. What pattern does it follow?

■ Slow Forward Flight

Birds flap their wings in a different way when moving slowly. Have you watched a bird maneuver onto a tree branch or come to rest on a window ledge?

Recall that a bird or plane moving below the stall speed no longer has enough lift to balance its weight. For this reason, birds flap their wings to produce lift in addition to thrust.

Flapping can produce lift in two ways. The downstroke of the wings pushes air down, which creates an upward force on the wing. The second source of lift comes when birds move their wings horizontally. The forward speed of the wings is large enough to be greater than stall speed, and so lift is generated. The wing movements of a bird in slow flight are shown in **Figure 24-17.**

MiniLab

What are some flying styles of birds?

You've learned about three flying styles: gliding, and fast and slow forward flight. In this activity, watch birds in a natural setting to find out which birds use which styles.

Procedure

1. Return to the area you used in the chapter opening MiniLab.

2. Locate some birds, then sit quietly in an area far enough away from the birds so that they are not disturbed.

3. Using binoculars, focus on a single bird. Examine again the way it flies. Does it use only one style? If not, when does it use each style? Record your observations *in your Journal.*

4. Locate and study different types of birds. Try to find at least three different species.

Analysis

1. Did the flying style used depend on the size of the bird? If so, which style or styles were used by the largest birds? By the smallest?

2. If you observed one species using different styles, when was each used?

Fueling Flight

The pectoralis muscle provides the thrust for a bird. Those muscles do work using stored energy. Just as with humans, that energy comes from food.

People often use the expression "eating like a bird" to mean that a person eats very little. However, birds consume from four percent to 30 percent of their body weight in food each day. How much would you have to eat if you really ate like a bird?

■ Fueling Bird Muscles

If you were about to run a 100-m dash, you would want a fuel that could get to your leg muscles rapidly. Would you choose carbohydrates or fats for your fuel? As shown in **Figure 24-18**, some birds fly only in short bursts. In these species, carbohydrates, in the form of glycogen, are the best fuels. Carbohydrates, as you learned in Chapter 8, can be used directly in the process of cellular respiration.

Birds that don't sprint, but rather cruise, such as ducks and geese, require a lot of energy for their long trips. But they also need to conserve weight. These birds need a higher-energy fuel. In long-distance fliers, fat is the better fuel because fats contain more than twice as much energy per unit mass as carbohydrates.

Hovering Flight

Have you ever watched a hummingbird getting nectar from a flower? If so, you've seen the ultimate in slow-speed flight. The wings of a hummingbird move too quickly for you to see the pattern. For the most part, the wings move horizontally, with a figure-eight pattern. When the wing is moving backwards, it rotates so that lift is created during all parts of the wing motion.

The smallest hummingbirds flap their wings 70 times per second, while larger species have a rate of only 12 beats per second. This rapid motion puts large strains on the wings. But the birds are adapted to deal with these stresses. The wrist and elbow joints are fused so that the upper wing is rigid and short. The shoulder joint rotates, allowing the wing to rotate. The part of the wing that corresponds to a hand is very long. The combined result of these features is a large,

Figure 24-18

Like the engines of modern aircraft, birds use different fuels for different kinds of flying.

Ⓐ Migratory birds, such as ducks and geese, travel long distances and use fat for an energy source.

Ⓑ Quick-moving, short-distance fliers—such as this prairie chicken, and pheasants, finches, and starlings—need short bursts of power from their breast muscles. These species use carbohydrates as a source of fuel because carbohydrates can be used in cellular respiration without first being converted like fat must be.

lightweight wing composed mostly of primary feathers.

Helicopters as Models

A helicopter mimics the hummingbird in its ability to hover. A large, rotating blade provides lift. But, unlike the hummingbird, the rotation of the blade tends to make the helicopter body rotate in an opposite direction. A smaller vertical propeller on the tail of some helicopters operates to eliminate the rotation. On large helicopters, two blades rotate in opposite directions to provide lift.

Helicopters obtain thrust to move forward or side to side by changing the angle of the blade. Just as a bird changes the angle of its wing on different parts of its stroke, helicopter blades can be swiveled during the rotation to provide thrust in any desired direction. For example, if the blade is swiveled to a slightly larger angle while moving toward the rear, the air will exert a larger forward thrust on the blade.

Thinking Critically

1. *Describe* the adaptations of hummingbird wings that enable them to beat so rapidly.
2. *Compare* how lift is accomplished in hummingbirds and helicopters.

When hovering, hummingbirds move their wings in a sideways figure-eight pattern.

To Find Out
More About ...

Migrating Birds
consult a field
guide that identifies
birds and describes
their migration
patterns.

When the platter of chicken or turkey comes your way, do you reach for white meat or dark meat? Have you ever stopped to wonder why there are two meat colors in poultry? The variation is related to the different energy demands of muscles in birds.

For example, chickens seldom fly, but they use their leg muscles often. Chicken legs are dark meat because the muscle cells contain large amounts of a dark-colored chemical, called myoglobin. Myoglobin helps supply muscles using fat with plenty of oxygen.

A chicken's breast, on the other hand, is white meat. These muscles generate the flapping power for the wings.

Chickens fly only for short bursts, so their flight muscles use carbohydrates, which can be used without myoglobin. Thus, these muscles appear lighter in color.

■ The Need for Oxygen

In Chapter 8, you learned that oxygen combined with food releases energy in the process of cellular respiration. Because of the high energy demands of flight, birds also have a high demand for oxygen. As shown in **Figure 24-19,** a bird's respiratory system is equipped with nine air sacs in addition to a pair of lungs. When a bird inhales, about 75 percent of the air passes directly into the air sacs rather than to the lungs. When birds exhale, oxygenated air from the air sacs passes into the lungs before it leaves the body. In this way, birds receive oxygen when they inhale and when they exhale.

■ Keeping Cool

Muscles, like other engines that convert stored energy to work, are inefficient. About 80 percent of the energy is turned into thermal energy instead of work. The feathers covering a bird are great at keeping out cold, but they also prevent heat loss. So how does a bird keep cool? The respiratory system in birds not only allows efficient use of oxygen, but also helps transfer wasted thermal energy to the air.

The large surface area of lungs and air sacs brings blood vessels into close contact with the colder air the bird inhales. Heat transfers thermal energy from the warm blood to the cooler air. Thus, the bird is able to get rid of waste energy and cool itself.

Figure 24-19

The system of air sacs in a bird's respiratory system allows it to receive oxygen-rich air while both inhaling and exhaling. Two full breaths are required to move air through the system.

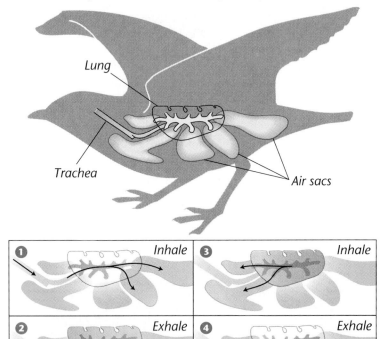

In the first breath, air moves into the posterior air sacs (step 1), then into the lungs (step 2). The second breath moves air from the lungs into the front sacs (step 3), then out through the trachea (step 4).

Airplane Thrust

From the time of the Wright brothers' first flight in 1903 until almost 1945, the propeller was used to provide thrust for airplanes. The propeller was turned by the same type of engine used in automobiles.

One problem with using propellers to provide thrust is speed. Engineers found that these planes are limited to a top speed of about 450 miles per hour. In 1939, a revolutionary plane was flown in Germany. It had no propeller. Instead, the hot gases produced by burning fuel were expelled in a jet out the back of the engine. As a result, the plane was given forward momentum. The plane could fly 100 miles per hour faster and much higher than any other fighter plane. If it weren't for the lack of fuel in wartime Germany, this new weapon could have changed the course of World War II.

Today's turbofan jet engine, **Figure 24-20,** is used in many of the larger, faster airplanes.

Figure 24-20

Jet engines are commonly used on airliners.

Ⓐ In the combustion chamber, kerosene burns, which produces extremely hot gases that leave the rear of the chamber through fanlike turbines.

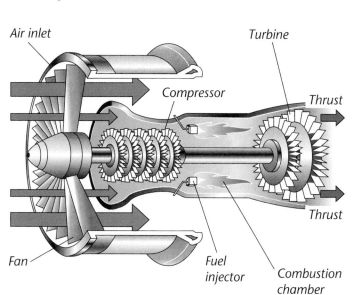

Air inlet

Turbine

Compressor

Thrust

Thrust

Fan

Fuel injector

Combustion chamber

Ⓒ The rotating shaft turns yet another turbine at the front of the engine. This fan directs air to the outside of the engine, cooling and quieting it, and generating more thrust.

Ⓑ The rotation of the turbine blades turns a shaft to which a turbine located in front of the combustion chambers is connected. These turbines increase the density of the air to be burned 15 times. The compression heats the air and pushes more air into the chambers.

Figure 24-21

The burst of power needed for this jet to take off is provided by burning kerosene.

Connect to...

Chemistry

Look up the chemical properties of gasoline and kerosene and make a chart comparing them as fuels. Find the number of joules of energy in 100 L of each fuel.

■ Airplane Fuel

While the engines of propeller-driven airplanes use gasoline as a fuel, jet engines use kerosene. Both liquids are distilled from petroleum, known as crude oil. Kerosene is composed of larger hydrocarbon molecules. As a result, it is denser and needs a higher temperature to be ignited, making it safer. But the energy released per kilogram is the same as that of gasoline. The greater density means that more stored energy can be put in a tank.

In this section, you have looked at both birds and airplanes. By closely examining some of the important characteristics of birds, you've seen that, like modern aircraft, birds also possess the important features of lightness, strength, rigidity, and a powerful energy source.

Did you know that the principles of flight are used not only in the animal kingdom, but in the plant kingdom as well? In the next section, you'll see how adaptations in flowering plants improve their ability to disperse.

check your UNDERSTANDING

Understanding Concepts

1. Describe the features of bird bones that make them ideal structures for flight.
2. Why do birds have to flap their wings differently when flying slowly?
3. Why do chicken breasts contain white meat whereas chicken legs contain dark meat? Explain your answer in terms of energy requirements of sprint and cruise muscles.

Skill Review

4. **Making and Using Tables** Make a table of the important flight characteristics of birds. Next to each feature, identify the modern aircraft feature that would correspond with the bird adaptation. For more help, refer to Making and Using Tables in the *Skill Handbook*.

Science and Society

Issue: City Birds— Perks or Pests?

In the big city, surrounded by structures of steel, glass, and concrete, many people regard birds as welcomed guests. Feeding pigeons in the park is a popular, relaxing pastime.

The Issue

City birds can also be real pests. They congregate on the ledges of buildings, build their nests in air conditioners, and deposit their droppings on windowsills, statues, and sidewalks. It costs the city lots of money to clean up the mess. What is worse, these birds may carry dangerous diseases such as parrot fever, tuberculosis, encephalitis, and meningitis.

The Background

With at least three million pigeons residing in New York City, plus all of the sparrows, starlings, and other species, there are probably as many birds as there are people in New York.

Officials have tried many ways to get rid of unwanted city birds. They've tried shooting them, poisoning them, scaring them with explosives, shocking them with electricity, and putting barbed wire or sticky jelly with "hot" chemicals on places where they roost. Some cities have brought in peregrine falcons, which are birds of prey that dive down and snatch a pigeon in midair for lunch.

Sometimes these measures work. Often they don't. In addition, many people object to the more drastic methods, saying that they are too cruel. More humane ways to control city birds have been tried. For example, instead of poisoned corn, grain that contains a chemical that sterilizes the birds so they cannot produce offspring is scattered. Another technique is to place plastic owls or falcons on the roofs and ledges of buildings to scare away unwanted birds.

The Questions

Some difficult questions have to be answered. Can we coexist with the urban birds? Should we attempt to get rid of city birds completely? Is there an optimum number of birds that will maintain a population, but cause the least amount of trouble? And after we've answered these questions, another remains: What methods should we use to achieve our goals?

interNET CONNECTION

Urban birds are not the only ones who have trouble coexisting with humans. Follow the link for Chapter 24 on the Glencoe Homepage to visit the Raptor Center. Why weren't the educational birds re-released into the wild? How were their problems associated with humans?

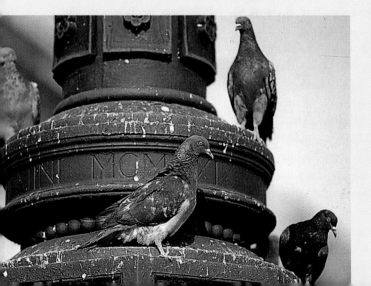

Flight in Plants

24-3

Objectives

- Describe some adaptations that allow seeds to be spread as widely as possible.
- Distinguish between winged seeds and those that use parachutes.

Key Terms

dispersal

Winged Seeds

Have you ever watched a maple seed falling? It looks like a tiny helicopter, doesn't it? Why would trees have seeds like these? For an answer, look for maple seeds in early autumn or spring. How far are they spread from the parent tree?

Why does a spinning seed fall so slowly? As you learned in Chapter 23, the upward force of air on the seed itself, called the air drag, results in a constant falling speed, called the terminal speed. But when it is spinning, a maple seed falls six times more slowly than when it is not spinning. That

means there must be some extra upward force—some extra lift acting on the spinning seed. Where does it come from?

Look at a drawing of the winged seed, **Figure 24-22.** The seed itself, located at one end, is lower than the rotating blade. From the point of view of the blade, the air is coming at it from slightly below. Thus, it acts just like the airfoil of a plane or bird. A maple seed about 5 cm long has a mass of 0.13 g and spins at 13 revolutions per second. The terminal speed is 1 m/s—about the speed of a falling coffee filter.

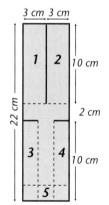

MiniLab

Make Your Own Maple Seed

You'll need a piece of paper 6 cm x 22 cm, scissors, pencil, paper clip, and ruler.

Procedure

1. With the pencil, draw all lines shown. Cut on the solid lines.

2. Folding along the dotted lines, fold pieces 1 and 2 in opposite directions. Fold pieces 3 and 4 toward the center so that they overlap.

3. Finally, fold up the bottom tab 5 and place a paper clip on it.

4. Hold your paper seed by the clip high above your head and let it go. Try flying it indoors and outside in a gentle breeze.

Analysis

1. How much farther does your model seed go from you than it would if you folded it up flat and dropped it?

2. What can you conclude about winged seeds?

Figure 24-22

The spinning fall of a maple seed moves air across the wing, creating lift.

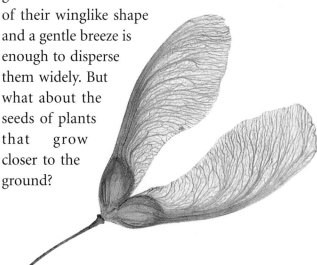

Applying Math   Calculating Seed Dispersal

A maple seed falls straight down from a branch, taking 5 seconds to hit the ground. If there is a 4 m/s breeze, how far will the seed be carried from the tree?

Known Information:	time, $t = 5$ s
	wind speed, $V = 4$ m/s
Unknown Information:	Distance, d
Equation to Use:	$d = V \times t$
Solution:	$d = V \times t = 4$ m/s $\times 5$ s
	$= 20$ m

Practice Problem

1. A seed from a cottonwood tree falls from a branch 20 m off of the ground. The seed falls at a rate of 0.5 m/s. If there is a 4 m/s breeze, how far will the seed be carried from the tree?

Several other trees—especially the sycamore, spruce, ash, and tulip—have developed winged seeds that slow their descent. What is the advantage of seeds that fall slowly and travel far? Trees and many other plants have sexual reproduction systems that result in the formation of seeds. A mature seed contains an embryo from which the next generation plant will grow. If all seeds fell directly under the parent, they would crowd each other and never grow into mature plants. When the parent tree died, it would leave no descendants.

Figure 24-23

When these maple seeds mature, they will break off of the stem and begin their flight to the ground.

The spreading of seeds over a wide area is called **dispersal.** How effective do you think wind is in dispersing seeds? Suppose the wind gives a seed a horizontal speed V, equal to the wind speed. Then the distance the seed is carried is given by $d = Vt$, where t is the time in the air. If a seed falls rapidly to the ground, t is small and so is the distance it is carried.

Maple seeds fall from treetops, so they have a long distance to travel to the ground. The combination of their winglike shape and a gentle breeze is enough to disperse them widely. But what about the seeds of plants that grow closer to the ground?

How can seeds use flight to disperse?

You've learned that some seeds fall at slower speeds, allowing them to be carried farther by the wind. In this Investigation, you will explore which seeds are most effective at dispersing.

Preparation

Problem

What kinds of seeds disperse the farthest from where they start to fall?

Hypothesis

In your group, brainstorm possible hypotheses and discuss the evidence on which each hypothesis is based. Select the best hypothesis from your list.

Objectives

In this Investigation, you will:
- *Analyze* plant seeds to determine which types disperse the farthest.
- *Infer* how some seeds are adapted for sufficient dispersal to avoid competition.

Possible Materials

one or more spinning seeds from each of a variety of trees like the sycamore, ash, maple, tulip, lime, or spruce

one or more plumed seeds like those from milkweed, dandelion, cottonwood tree, or cotton plant

meterstick

stopwatch

large box fan

Plan the Experiment

1 Examine the materials provided by your teacher. Make a list of the possible ways you could test your hypothesis.

2 Agree on one way that your group could investigate the hypothesis. Design an experiment that will allow for the collection of quantitative data.

3 Prepare a list of numbered directions. Include a list of the materials and the amounts you will need.

4 Design and construct a table for recording your data. How long do you think the seeds will remain in the air? How will you measure this?

Check the Plan
Discuss the following points with other group members to decide the final procedure for your experiment.

1 Determine how you will test the dispersal distance of different seeds. How can you control the conditions so they are the same for each seed?

2 Should you test more than one example of each type of seed? How will you compare the data from more than one seed? What observations will allow you to calculate the terminal speed of each seed?

3 *Make sure your teacher has approved your experimental plan before you proceed further.*

4 Carry out your experiment. Make any necessary observations and complete your data table. Display your results graphically.

Analyze and Conclude

1. **Measuring in SI** How did you calculate the terminal speed of each seed? What were the results?

2. **Comparing and Contrasting** Compare the terminal speeds of the different types of seeds.

3. **Inferring** What plant adaptations allow seeds to disperse the farthest?

4. **Drawing Conclusions** Using your results, how could you summarize the relationship between a seed's terminal speed and its dispersal distance?

Going Further

Extension
With a group, design and test a seed that can disperse without the help of a breeze. What are the characteristics of a plant that would benefit the most from such a seed?

Plumes and Parachutes

As a child, did you ever blow on the white puff of a dandelion that had gone to seed? The tiny white plumes seemed to float forever in the breeze. Unlike a maple seed, a dandelion seed doesn't have meters to fall before hitting the ground. If it is to be dispersed in a gentle breeze, it must have an even slower terminal speed.

The dandelion seed, shown in **Figure 24-24,** looks like a tiny parachute. With the seed well below the plume, the parachute falls in a straight line without twisting or fluttering. The terminal speed of such a seed is about 0.2 m/s, which gives it plenty of time to be carried by a breeze, even if the seed is released just a few centimeters above the ground. Dandelion seeds typically

Figure 24-25

A gentle breeze is all that's needed to blow dandelion seeds from the flower head.

are blown from the plant in early afternoon when it is most likely to be dry and breezy with gentle thermals—the ideal conditions for best dispersal. Milkweeds and the cottonwood tree also produce seeds with parachutes.

Figure 24-24

The seed of a dandelion looks and acts like a parachute. Gravity exerts a downward force, mainly on the seed, while the air drag is up, mainly on the plume of fibers.

Floating Cells

If you get hay fever, then you probably have a good idea when fungi and ferns are spreading their spores and when trees and other plants are spreading their pollen. *Hay fever* is the common term for the allergic reaction many people have to spores and pollen in the air.

Have you ever seen the spores and pollen grains that cause your misery? Probably not, unless you've looked at them under a microscope.

Spores

Fungus

Figure 24-26

These fungus spores are so small they can be seen only under a microscope. About 200 fungus spores, placed side-by-side, will fit across the head of a pin. They are carried a long distance by the slightest breeze.

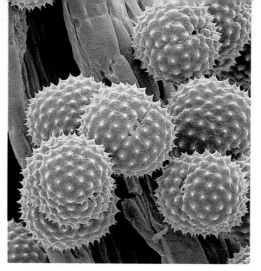

Figure 24-27

These are pollen grains as seen under a microscope.

Fungus spores, like those shown in **Figure 24-26,** are about 0.005 mm in diameter. Pollen, **Figure 24-27,** ranges from 0.015 to 0.2 mm in diameter. Their terminal speeds are small—about 0.06 cm/s for a small fungus spore and 0.5 to 3 cm/s for tree pollen. As a result, these particles can hardly be said to fall. They are carried by the slightest breeze or current.

The science and engineering of flight has come a long way since the primitive flapping machines of the early 19th century. It can go even further. What do you imagine air and space travel will be like when you are old enough to be a great-grandparent?

In the next chapter, you'll take a flight into space to discover some of the important questions people are asking about Earth and the universe. Some of these questions may be answered if humans design spacecraft that can travel to the outer planets and beyond. Will humans engaged in this new quest be able to learn from nature again?

check your UNDERSTANDING

Understanding Concepts
1. How do wings affect the dispersal of a seed?
2. Why does a plume increase the distance a milkweed seed is likely to be found from the plant?
3. Would you expect a plant that grows close to the ground to have winged seeds? Explain.

Skill Review
4. **Making and Using Tables** Create a table listing various types of seeds, the adaptations that increase dispersal, and an application of the same aerodynamic principle in a bird or airplane. For more help, refer to Making and Using Tables in the *Skill Handbook.*

Twist and Fly

Aviation technology has revolutionized the way people travel. Planes today are lighter, faster, and more efficient than they were even ten years ago. Engineers constantly improve airplanes, incorporating new materials and designs.

You're the Aeronautical Engineer

You have been asked to design the lightest and fastest airplane possible for a local aeronautical company. Your main concern is the placement of the parts of the plane to actually fine-tune the aerodynamics of the plane. Your materials will be either a balsa airplane kit or pieces of balsa wood, a propeller, glue, a straight pin, a thumbtack, and a rubber band.

Drawing on Experience

1. Obtain pieces of balsa wood, a propeller, and a rubber band from your teacher.

2. Sketch the airplane parts and transfer the outline of the body, wings, and tail to a piece of balsa wood.

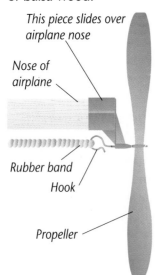

This piece slides over airplane nose

Nose of airplane

Rubber band

Hook

Propeller

3. Cut out the pieces of the plane and assemble the plane.

4. Attach the propeller to the front of the plane with a thumbtack. Make sure the propeller is attached so that it is free to turn.

5. Push a straight pin into the wood of the rear of your plane.

6. If you use an airplane kit, hook a rubber band from the hook on the back of the propeller to the hook on the rear of the plane as shown in the figure to the left.

Testing...Testing

1. Turn the propeller counterclockwise to twist the rubber band 30 to 40 times. Hold the propeller in place until you are ready to fly your aircraft.

2. Standing in a clear, open area, release the propeller to allow the plane to fly.

3. Depending on the success of the flight of the plane, readjust the wing position and weight of the plane to improve its flight.

4. Continue to fly your plane and make adjustments until you have a smooth, successful flight.

How Did It Work?

What adjustments were necessary to improve the flight of the plane? Why was it important to wind the propeller counterclockwise? What does the rubber band take the place of? Try making the plane from different materials to determine any changes necessary due to the construction material.

Read the statements below that review major points presented in the chapter. Using the concepts that you have learned, answer each question *in your Journal.*

1 The wing area and shape determine the amount of lifting force the wing produces. The lift increases with the speed of the plane or bird. *Would a heavy but fast-flying bird or plane require a wing with a small or large area? Large or small aspect ratio?*

2 Airplanes extend flaps and slats during both takeoff and landing in order to increase wing lift at low speeds. *How do birds increase their lift when flying slowly?*

3 Birds obtain energy from both carbohydrates and fat that the animal has stored. *Which energy source do migrating geese use? Hummingbirds?*

4 Milkweed, dandelion, and maple seeds are adapted so that even gentle breezes spread them over large distances. *Which of the forces that act on airplanes also act on each of these seeds?*

Using Key Science Terms

aspect ratio   wing loading
dispersal   wingspan

Use the terms from the list to answer the following questions.

1. What is wingspan divided by average width of a wing?
2. Why do some plant seeds have wings?
3. What determines the stall speed of a bird or plane?

Understanding Ideas

Using complete sentences, answer the following questions in your Journal.

1. Why is the body of a bird covered with smooth contour feathers?
2. Why is kerosene used rather than gasoline in a jet engine?
3. What is the purpose of the wing on a maple seed?
4. An albatross has a wingspan of 2.5 m and an aspect ratio of 18. What is the average width of its wing?
5. How can a plane change its pitch from level flight to a dive?
6. Why do some birds run when taking off?
7. Why is it an advantage for a dandelion seed to have a plume?

Developing Skills

Use your understanding of the concepts developed in this chapter to answer each of the following questions.

1. **Concept Mapping** Make a concept map of bird flight adaptations.
2. **Recognizing Cause and Effect** What can you tell about the use of a muscle in a bird from the amount of myoglobin in it?
3. **Predicting** Two birds have the same weight, but one has a much larger wingspan than the other. Which would be more likely to spend much of the time soaring?
4. **Predicting** When an airplane was being considered for use on an aircraft carrier, the Navy asked the designer to reduce the wingspan. What effect would this have on the landing speed?

Critical Thinking

In your Journal, *answer each of the following questions.*

1. Two birds have the same wing loading. One has a weight of 20 N, the other 30 N. If the wing area of the first is 0.25 m², what is the wing area of the second?

2. You are shown two snapshots of a bird taken from below. In one, the feathers are spread to increase the wing area, while in the other they are smoothly together and the wing area is smaller. In which picture do you think the bird is flying faster? Why?

3. Would you expect a bird to breathe more rapidly in cold or hot weather? Explain.

4. Would seedlings from a tall or short maple tree be more likely to grow far from the tree? Explain.

5. A developer wants to build homes on land used as a rest stop by migrating geese. Will this cause the geese any harm?

Problem Solving

Read the following problem and discuss your answers in a brief paragraph.

Imagine archaeologists have just uncovered a partial fossil of a pterosaur, which is an extinct flying reptile. While the entire body was recovered, only part of the wings were fossilized. From the size of the body, the scientists estimated the pterosaur weighed about 0.625 kN.

1. If the wing loading for this animal were 0.05 kPa, what would the wing area be?

2. Other fossilized pterosaurs have had an aspect ratio of about 8 and an average wing width of about 1.25 m. What might be this pterosaur's wingspan?

CONNECTING IDEAS

1. **Theme—Models** In what ways do airplanes model bird flight? How are they different?

2. **Theme—Scale** A science fiction film shows a 200-pound bird flying slowly with a human in its claws. How could you use what you have learned in this chapter to argue why this could not happen?

3. **Theme—Energy** What do carbohydrates and fats have in common? How are they different?

4. **In-Depth Look** Compare hovering flight with other types of bird flight you learned about.

5. **People in Science** Why would it be helpful for a pilot to have good math skills?

6. **Applying Technology** Describe how you solved problems of wing shape, weight, drag, and thrust in your airplane designs.

CHAPTER 25

Physics of Space Flight

Flying Beyond Earth's Atmosphere

*A*s the spacecraft approaches the broken satellite, the astronaut skillfully maneuvers her craft into position using bursts from tiny rockets to control the ship's movements. Once in position, her crewmates go to work repairing the damaged satellite. Not long ago, this would have sounded like science fiction. Today, it's becoming a routine mission. How do spacecraft like the shuttle get into space? Why do we want to go into space anyway? In this chapter, explore some of the reasons why we want to travel into space and how we can get there.

▶ *In the next activity, you'll explore how satellites are used every day in your community.*

What information can you get from space?

Today, a surprising number of our activities depend on artificial satellites in space. Explore the commercial use of satellites in your community.

Procedure

1. With your class, brainstorm organizations in your community that might make use of satellites. Include those that might be using communication, weather and environment, natural resources, and navigation satellites.

2. Organize groups to call selected government offices, businesses, universities, or other organizations. Decide on the questions you will ask to find out such information as how they use satellites, which satellites they use, and how much it costs.

Analysis

1. Present a report, oral or written, that answers the questions above and others you have selected.

Venus

25-1 Why go into space?

Objectives

■ Describe the uses of space-based observations of Earth.

■ Explain the uses of space-based observations of the planets and stars.

Key Terms

electromagnetic wave

electromagnetic spectrum

Looking Inward Toward Earth

When you flip on a local television station to find out what tomorrow's weather will be, you'll probably see photos of clouds taken from satellites in orbit around Earth. Other kinds of satellites make it possible to make overseas phone calls or send TV programs to remote parts of the world.

These examples illustrate two ways satellites are used—to relay information between two points on Earth, or as distant eyes to watch what's happening on our planet.

■ The Electromagnetic Spectrum

Satellites are like artificial moons that circle Earth, collecting and sending information using electromagnetic waves. An **electromagnetic wave** is a disturbance in electric and magnetic fields that carries energy through space at the speed of light.

Just as the wavelengths, or distances between peaks, of ocean waves vary between tiny ripples and huge swells, electromagnetic waves come in many wavelengths. When you turn on a car radio, you are hearing signals transmitted by radio waves—electromagnetic waves with the longest wavelengths. The microwave oven you use to heat up food uses shorter electromagnetic waves. Visible light, ultraviolet radiation, and X rays are even shorter forms of electromagnetic waves. The collection of wavelengths is called the **electromagnetic spectrum**. Look at **Figure 25-1** to see ways electromagnetic waves from all parts of the spectrum are used in everyday life.

A Shortwave radio is used for long-distance communication.

B The VHF (very high frequency) and UHF (ultrahigh frequency) bands carry FM radio and television, among other communication services.

C Microwaves are used both for short-range communications and for cooking.

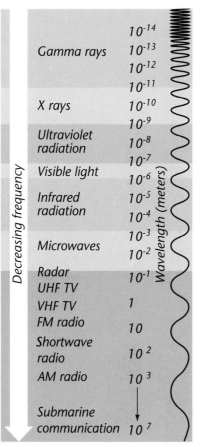

D Heated objects emit mostly in the infrared.

E Our eyes can detect the visible part of the spectrum that we call light.

F Ultraviolet rays cause chemical reactions, such as those involved in suntanning.

Figure 25-1

Part of the electromagnetic spectrum

■ Communications Satellites

Communications satellites—the ones used to send TV and telephone signals around the world—relay electromagnetic waves. As shown in **Figure 25-2,** a sending station at one place on Earth beams waves to a satellite. The satellite receives them, strengthens them, and sends them to a receiving station that may be thousands of miles from the sending station. Your school or home may have a "dish" to receive signals directly from a satellite.

■ Weather Satellites

Satellites are not only used for communication, but as you learned in Chapter 1, they are also valuable tools for predicting weather. And just as in communication, electromagnetic radiation is involved in weather satellites, too.

Can you tell how quickly a storm will reach you by looking at one photo? It would be much easier if you had an identical photo taken a short time later so you could see how fast the storm is moving. Weather changes are observed from geostationary satellites, which are satellites that stay above the same point

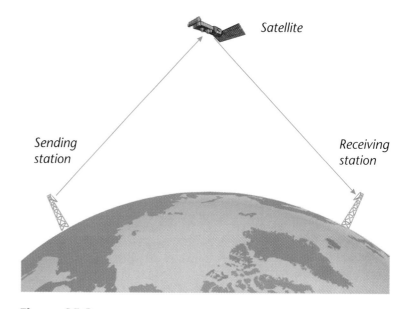

Figure 25-2

Satellites allow signals to be transmitted between distant locations that cannot easily be connected by cables.

on Earth at all times. They do this by orbiting Earth 36 000 km above the equator, at the same rate at which Earth spins. They are sometimes called geosynchronous because their orbit is synchronized with Earth's rotation.

Geostationary satellites are so far above Earth that they can't show details, so other weather satellites have been put into a polar orbit around Earth, **Figure 25-3.** These satellites, only 850 km above the surface, can look in detail at storms. While they can see only a narrow strip of Earth on each pass, Earth turns underneath them as they orbit. As a result, on each pass the satellite photographs a strip of land to the west of the previous one.

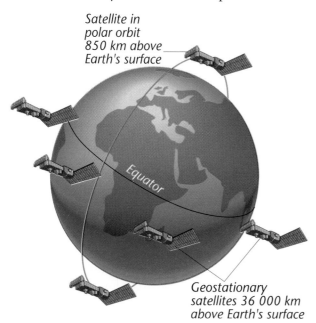

Satellite in polar orbit 850 km above Earth's surface

Equator

Geostationary satellites 36 000 km above Earth's surface

Figure 25-3

Earth's weather is observed by a network of satellites. Geostationary satellites are stationed above a certain part of the globe, taking photos continuously. Polar satellites take close-up photos as Earth turns under them.

Figure 25-4

This is a composite of green, red, and infrared images from a Landsat satellite. It shows part of the Mississippi River during a flood. Healthy crops and other plants are shown in bright red. Cities are seen as green or dark gray, and water is blue.

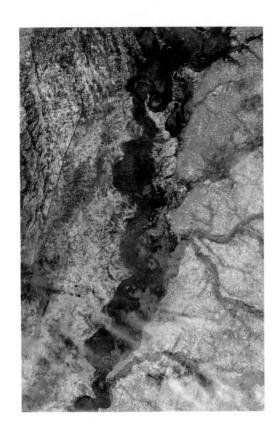

■ Finding Resources from Space

Think what it would have been like if you were an explorer walking across the American continent about 200 years ago. You would notice its natural resources such as wood and stones for building, fertile soils for farming, rivers and lakes for water and transportation, and abundant animals for food and fur. You could cover only a small part of the continent, so you and other explorers would have to compare notes to assemble a complete picture.

If you lived about 80 years ago, you might have been one of the first people to photograph these resources from an airplane. Even though you can see a larger area than you can on the ground, you need to combine your photos with

Navigating by Satellite

A GPS receiver

Have you ever been lost? How did you find your way? Did you look at a map? Did you use familiar landmarks to help you? Did you use a compass to lead you in the right direction? If you were lost at night, you might have relied on the stars for guidance. What are some other ways that you might navigate in unfamiliar territory? Maybe in the future, you'll use the GPS.

What is the GPS?

The Global Positioning Satellite (GPS) system is a group of 24 navigation satellite tracking and ranging (NAVSTAR) devices that orbit high (20 200 km) above our

planet every 12 hours. With the help of complex navigational equipment and atomic clocks, each satellite knows its exact location at any time of the day. Pocket-sized GPS units used by Earthbound hikers, geologists, aviators, and boaters receive signals from three different satellites. Computers calculate the time it takes for the signal to travel from the satellite. It is then possible to determine the user's exact position by the triangulation method, as in the illustration on page 769. This system can pinpoint a person's position on Earth to within about 30 m. It's hard to be lost with GPS above you.

hundreds of thousands of photos taken of every part of the country to produce a composite photo.

Photos taken by astronauts circling the globe showed the value of replacing aerial photography with satellite-based systems. One of the most successful series of satellites designed to look at natural resources is the Landsat series. Landsat detects reflected radiation in six wavelength bands and infrared emitted by Earth in a seventh band. Look at **Table 25-1** for a list of the bands and their uses. You can get Landsat photos of almost anyplace in the world either by computer or by mail. **Figure 25-4** is an example of a Landsat satellite image that is a combination of different wavelength bands.

Table 25-1

Landsat Wavelength Bands	
Wavelength μm	**Color and use**
0.45 - 0.52	Blue green: shows bottom of lakes, distinguishes soil from plants and deciduous from coniferous trees
0.52 - 0.60	Green: assesses plant vigor
0.63 - 0.69	Red: matches chlorophyll absorption to discriminate vegetation types
0.76 - 0.90	Reflected IR: determines biomass content, helps map shorelines
1.55 - 1.75	Reflected IR: indicates moisture content and penetrates thin clouds
2.08 - 2.35	Reflected IR: distinguishes rock types
10.4 - 12.5	Thermal IR: provides maps at night, finds heated water, soil moisture

How is it used?

While originally developed for use by the U.S. government's defense department, GPS technology has many practical applications. Wilderness hikers and mountaineers can tread along unbeaten paths without the fear of getting lost. Field geologists can produce extremely accurate maps using the GPS. Pilots—both commercial and those who fly for pleasure—can depend on the system to prevent collisions both in the air and on runways. Sailors, who are often surrounded by nothing but water, can also rely on this extremely precise navigational system. Getting lost while driving may become a thing of the past, thanks to GPS.

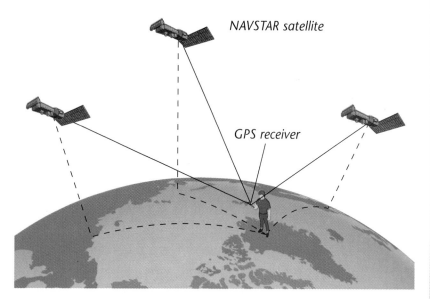

NAVSTAR satellite

GPS receiver

The computers aboard the NAVSTAR satellites know their exact position above Earth. By comparing the distances from the receiver to three satellites, the position of the receiver can be determined.

*inter*NET
CONNECTION

Visit the Glencoe Homepage for the Chapter 25 link to the U.S. Coast Guard Navigation Center to learn more about GPS applications. How does the GPS help sailors navigate?

Looking Outward into Space

Most of what we know about space has been discovered through the use of telescopes. We have found distant galaxies, exploding stars, and other interesting phenomena. Early astronomers observed moons circling Jupiter and they also tracked the movements of the objects they observed.

From watching the planets and their moons, we have learned more about the motion of Earth and its moon around the sun. By observing other stars, we have learned more about our sun.

Observations of the universe have also given us clues about its origin. Observations, such as the movements of galaxies, have led astronomers to hypothesize that there was a giant explosion somewhere between 13 and 22 billion years ago that gave birth to the matter of the universe.

■ The Size of the Universe

As we look farther and farther into space, we begin to get a sense of just how vast our universe is. For most of us, imagining distances that large is difficult. To describe these huge distances, astronomers have to use a bigger measuring stick than a meter or a kilometer. Instead, they use light-years and astronomical units (AU). An AU is the distance from the sun to Earth—about 150 million km. A light-year is the distance light can travel in one year, or about 10 trillion km. To understand these units, and to get a better feel for our place in space, take the tour of the universe in **Figure 25-5.**

Figure 25-5

On the imaginary journey on this page and the next, every step we take is further away than the last. Start with something familiar—a meterstick. Move your eye close to it so that it totally fills your view.

A Now, pretend you step back, way back, until you can see an area one kilometer wide. You're now looking at a city block.

B Step back until you're looking at an area 1000 km across. It takes you about 11 hours to drive across this view. You can see cities, rivers, mountains, and lakes.

C In the next step, even Earth itself looks small. It is only about 12 500 km in diameter, and the field of view is now 1 million km across.

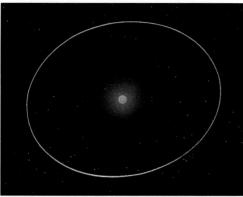

D Now we're looking at 1 billion km. The inner solar system is now within view, but even the sun looks like a tiny dot. Our view is about 7 AU.

E Now we're looking at thousands of stars. Our sun is too faint to see. Our view is about 100 light-years across. There are about 63 000 AU in one light-year (ly).

F With a view of 100 000 ly, we're looking at billions of stars in a part of the Milky Way galaxy.

G Now the view is 100 million ly across, and the galaxy itself is reduced to a dot. The Milky Way is one of several galaxies called the Local Group.

H At 20 billion light-years, we're looking at what astronomers hypothesize is the entire universe. However, by observing distant galaxies, we have evidence that the universe is expanding.

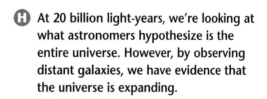

To Find Out More About ...

Planets, Stars, and Constellations
look for *Astronomy Sky Almanac,* a monthly calendar of celestial events found in *Astronomy* magazine.

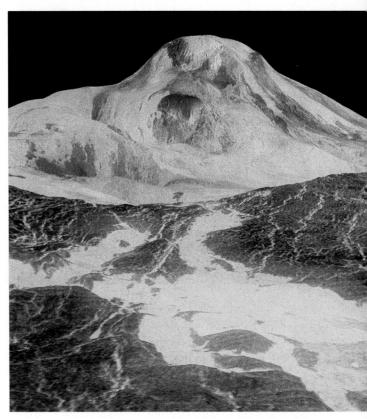

Figure 25-6

This robot space probe, *Magellan,* explored Venus. It sent back the image on the right, of Maat Mons, a volcano on Venus.

■ Why should we study the planets?

Humans have long wondered about the moon and planets—how they are similar to and different from Earth and whether life could exist on them. Although Earth's best telescopes have been used to study them, our atmosphere causes problems that not even the best telescope can overcome. You've probably seen one of the problems yourself if you've noticed how stars twinkle. As light passes through the atmosphere, slight variations in the amount and kind of gas shift the image right and left and up and down, making it appear to twinkle.

Planets don't twinkle when viewed through a telescope on Earth, but their images are blurred. In addition, astronomers need to observe planets in the IR and UV to learn exactly which atoms are in their atmospheres. But Earth's atmosphere blocks most IR and UV wavelengths. This means Earth-based telescopes cannot be used.

One solution to the problems caused by Earth's atmosphere is to observe the planets from space. In the 1970s and 1980s, a series of crewless spacecraft, such as the one in **Figure 25-6,** were sent to Venus, Mercury, Mars, Jupiter, Saturn, Uranus, and Neptune. Sometimes traveling for years, these spacecraft—called probes—have orbited Mercury, Venus, and Mars, sending back images in the visible and infrared parts of the spectrum. Because the atmosphere of Venus is opaque to the visible part of the spectrum, the Magellan probe used microwave radar to map its surface. The probes also measured magnetic fields and looked for charged particles near the planets.

■ Detecting Life on Other Planets

Could there be life on other planets? Mars is the only one that could possibly support life, but the robot probe shown in **Figure 25-7** found no sign of life there. Some scientists hypothesize, however, that Mars might have been warmer and wetter 500 million years ago, making conditions tolerable for life.

If we hope to detect life on other planets, we should ask whether a spacecraft could detect evidence of life on Earth from orbit. We know that objects such as the Great Wall of China and the Great Barrier Reef off Australia can be seen from space. At night, the lights of major cities are evident. These observations are evidence of life on Earth.

But there are other ways of detecting life, such as using infrared instruments to detect oxygen and methane in the atmosphere. Oxygen is so reactive that it can exist in the atmosphere only if plants are continuously producing it. Methane gas is destroyed by UV from the sun, so it is usually found in the atmosphere only if it is replenished by biological processes. It wasn't until 1990 that a satellite found these signs of life in our own atmosphere!

While the instruments on space probes are sensitive, they are not as good as telescopes in space would be. But telescopes are much too massive to send on interplanetary journeys. New possibilities opened up for long-term studies of the planets and stars from above the atmosphere when the Hubble Space Telescope was placed in orbit in 1990. A flawed mirror made the telescope nearsighted at first, but after being repaired, the Hubble can take excellent photos, as **Figure 25-8** shows.

Figure 25-7

In 1976, the American spacecraft *Viking 1* landed on Mars and sent back this picture.

Figure 25-8

On the left is Saturn, as seen from the Hubble Space Telescope in orbit. Notice how much detail can be seen in the rings. On the right is Saturn, as seen by a large telescope on Earth.

Figure 25-9

This is the Horsehead Nebula in the Orion constellation. This may be a stage in the birth of a new star.

Connect to...

Biology

Find out about the prolonged effects of weightlessness on bone and muscle mass and what measures astronauts take to counteract these conditions.

■ Why should we study the stars and galaxies?

Planets are not the only heavenly bodies that have fascinated people for ages. At least 6000 stars can be seen without a telescope.

For hundreds of years, astronomers have looked to the stars for clues to the mysteries of our star, the sun. How was it created? How and when will it die? There are no answers yet, but there are clues, many of which come from observations made from space.

Astronomers believe that the sun was born about 5 billion years ago from a giant cloud of gas—mostly hydrogen—and dust. The atoms and molecules slowly came closer and closer together, attracted by the gravitational force. When the atoms at the center of the cloud were close together, they had enough energy that collisions between them produced fusion reactions. Energy was released as electromagnetic radiation, including light.

How can these ideas be tested? Astronomers have found that large clouds of gas still exist, and so have searched for evidence of stars being formed. Because the process is likely to take millions of years, astronomers don't expect to see a star born while they are watching. Instead, they look for different objects at different stages in the process. What would a newly born star look like? It would be dim, and the leftover gas and dust surrounding it would make it even more dim. The cloud should also make the light more red, just as dust in our atmosphere creates red sunsets. So astronomers search for gas clouds containing dim stars with more than the normal amount of red and infrared radiation. One candidate is a glowing cloud of gas, called a *nebula,* such as the one shown in **Figure 25-9.** As you know, infrared is blocked by Earth's atmosphere, so the search for new stars is an excellent job for telescopes in space.

Uses of a Space Station in Orbit

If you had the chance to spend a few months on a space station orbiting Earth, would you go? How would everyday life be different there?

The biggest difference would be weightlessness. Remember that the reason astronauts and objects are weightless in space is not that there is no gravity—it's because the astronauts and their ships are accelerating together toward Earth.

Another difference would be the lack of atmosphere. The space station would need to have an artificial atmosphere inside, and to work outside the station, you'd have to wear a space suit.

American and Russian astronauts have remained in space for extended periods, and the Russian space station Mir has been resupplied several times with fuel, food, and people. The International Space Station has been proposed as a combined effort between the United States, Europe, Canada, Russia, and Japan. As shown in **Figure 25-10,** it will be a permanent station so large that it would have to be built in orbit. Why go to so much effort and expense?

People in favor of building a space station argue that it could be used for manufacturing processes that are best done in a weightless, vacuum environment, but opponents say that robots can do the job just as well. Proponents

also say that a space telescope would be easier to maintain than the Hubble, which requires visits from space-shuttle crews every few years. But others argue that vibrations would make a telescope on the space station less usable.

If humans are to make trips to other planets or stars, a space station will be necessary. How can we get there? You'll explore this question in the next section.

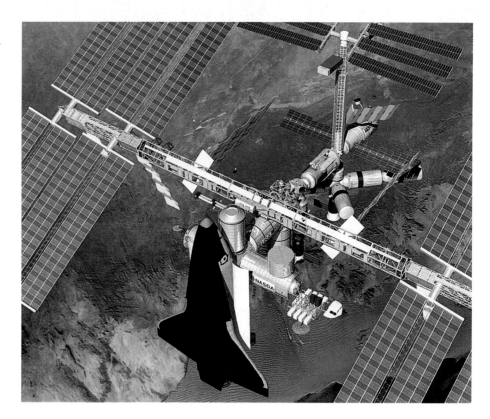

Figure 25-10

The International Space Station is a proposed orbiting laboratory. What problems would you want to research in a space laboratory?

---

check your UNDERSTANDING

Understanding Concepts
1. Suppose you are an astronaut approaching a planet around a distant star. You want to know whether the planet has plants on its surface. How could you find out?
2. Why are two sets of weather satellites used?
3. What evidence do we have that stars are still being formed?

Skill Review
4. **Making and Using Graphs** Draw a graph of the visible and infrared parts of the electromagnetic spectrum similar to **Figure 25-1.** Look at the seven wavelength bands used by Landsat, **Table 25-1,** and mark their locations on your graph. For help, refer to Making and Using Graphs in the *Skill Handbook.*

Issue:
What is Science Fiction?

"Use the force, Luke!" Do you recognize that phrase? Probably. Science fiction movies such as *Star Wars* are extremely popular. But what does it mean to say that fiction is about science? Are the two related?

Isaac Asimov, a famous scientist and science fiction writer, once noted that science fiction is a means of exploring the effects of rapid technological change—and, by association, rapid societal change. In the past century, science and technology have advanced at an astounding rate. Science fiction writers from the early 1900s observed steady developments in many areas. In transportation, for example, first there were cars, then airplanes. What next? Spaceships? Years

This spaceship, from the movie When Worlds Collide, *vaguely resembles the space shuttle, but do you think it could ever reach orbit?*

before the first satellite was launched, many of these writers predicted the event.

In effect, they were looking at known scientific developments and taking them one step further in their minds. They were trying to predict the future based on the present. To do this well, the writer must have some scientific background. Here are some examples of predictions—good and bad—made by science fiction writers.

Science Fiction and Science

In 1908, several years before army tanks were used in World War I, H.G. Wells wrote "The Land Ironclads." In his story, he accurately predicted the development of tanks. Wells used his knowledge of armor, automobiles, and ironclad warships to make this prediction.

In 1921, long before the energy crisis of the 1970s or today's global warming concerns, H.G. Wells wrote a novel, *Secret Places of the Heart*. In the book, a character worries about coming problems due to human exploitation of natural resources. Wells knew that Earth's resources were finite. He observed the wasteful practices in his time and, in his writing, predicted their long-term effects.

H.G. Wells was not the only science fiction writer to make accurate predictions. Four years before the first atomic bomb was set off in 1945, Robert Heinlein, using the pen name of Anson McDonald, wrote "Solution Unsatisfactory." In it, he described the death of all humanity caused by military use of radio-active dust similar to fallout. He had studied radioactivity and its dangers, and thus was able to describe its potential effects accurately.

Arthur C. Clarke wrote *2001: A Space Odyssey* in 1969, predicting hotels orbiting Earth and a permanent moon colony by the year 2001. At the time, NASA's *Apollo* program was well underway and Clarke foresaw a bright future for it. Although some of his predictions did not come true, his descriptions of space flight were accurate.

The authors mentioned above all worked from what they knew of current science and technology. Sometimes, however, a new technology takes an unexpected turn. The computer revolution caught science fiction writers by surprise. No one predicted the big changes that came from computers. The technology was new and the change from room-sized computers to desktop PCs happened quickly.

The Value of Science Fiction

Science fiction can be a vehicle to explore problems, as well as a means to look into the future of technology. Science fiction also allows writers to look at food shortages, war, the rights

of individuals, and the clash of different cultures. In a way, writers have used science fiction as a "safe" laboratory to think about the effects of new knowledge and technology on society.

What's next?

Writers are still asking, "What if..." Current science fiction novels explore the dangers and wonders of cyberspace, global warming, shrinking biodiversity, and a host of other topics. Reading them is one way to explore how science and technology may shape the world.

Investigating the Issue

1. *Analyze* a favorite science fiction book, movie, or TV show for its science content. What scientific knowlege did the writer seem to have? What changes in technology and/or society would be required for the story to become a reality?
2. Pick a current science or technology topic and *write* a short story projecting how it will affect your life 25 years from now.

How can we go?

25-2

Objectives

- Explain how a rocket accelerates a spaceship.
- Compare the kinds of propellants used in liquid- and solid-fuel rockets.
- Describe the speeds required for travel in space and means of attaining those speeds.

Key Terms

propellant
specific impulse
stage

Rocket Power

Now that you've seen why we might go into space, how can we get there? Because there's no atmosphere, the propeller and jet engines that power airplanes will be of no use. We'll need a rocket.

The first recorded use of a rocket was in China in the early thirteenth century. It is recorded that "arrows of flying fire" were used in the defense against the attacks of Genghis Khan. The rockets consisted of gunpowder packed in a bamboo tube, with the hot gases escaping through a small hole at the rear. About 50 years later, the Arabs made improvements, and by the year 1400, rockets were introduced into Italy. In the War of 1812, the

British used rockets against the Americans, as immortalized in the words of *The Star Spangled Banner*, "...the rockets' red glare..."

◼ Robert Goddard

Most of the credit for developing the modern rocket goes to a man who dreamed of space travel when he was a high school student. Robert H.

Figure 25-11

Here is Robert Goddard with one of his early rockets, ready for a test flight.

Goddard couldn't confine his dreams to the diary where he wrote about them. He had to try them out. In college, he was almost expelled for an experiment that filled a building with smoke. Starting in 1909, when he was 27, he worked on solid-fueled rockets using his own money, but in 1916 the Smithsonian Institution funded his experiments. At the time, some people believed that a rocket engine could not work in a vacuum such as in space. But Goddard showed that a rocket would produce thrust in a vacuum chamber. In 1919, the Smithsonian published Goddard's "A Method of Reaching Extreme Altitudes." Few paid attention to the physics, theory, or experiments in the paper, but Goddard created a stir with his suggestion that one could reach the moon and set off a flash to announce the arrival. Newspapers called him the "moon man," and the *New York Times* poked fun at him, saying he "seems to lack the knowledge ladled out daily in high schools."

It took until March of 1926 for Goddard to be able to test his first liquid-propellant rocket similar to **Figure 25-11.** It was powered by gasoline and liquid oxygen and was 10 feet long. By 1941, his rockets had reached altitudes of 9000 feet. Although his experiments paved the way for the use of rockets in space flight, he died in 1945—too early to see that happen.

■ **Parts of a Rocket**

What makes up a rocket? There are three basic parts—the payload, propellant, and body. **Figure 25-12** shows the basic parts of the space shuttle. The *payload* is the item to be delivered, perhaps a satellite to be put into orbit or the

Figure 25-12

The space shuttle has certain basic parts in common with all rockets: an engine, propellant, body, and payload.

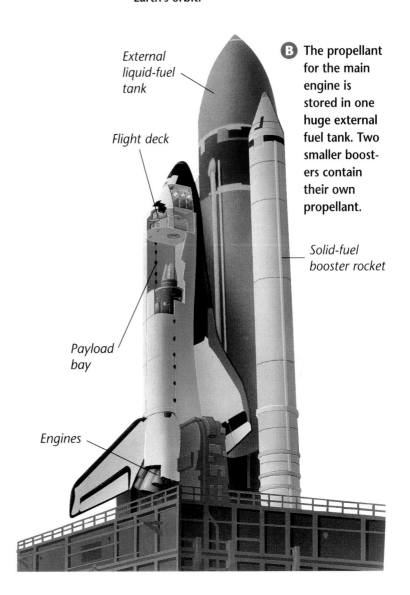

Ⓐ The body of the shuttle consists of the orbiter, external fuel tank, and booster rockets. The orbiter carries the payload and crew into Earth's orbit.

Ⓑ The propellant for the main engine is stored in one huge external fuel tank. Two smaller boosters contain their own propellant.

External liquid-fuel tank

Flight deck

Solid-fuel booster rocket

Payload bay

Engines

astronauts and their equipment in the shuttle. The **propellant** is the fuel and oxidizer that will be used in firing the rocket. The *body* is everything else: the rocket engines, fuel tanks, computers, shell, etc. In some rockets, part or all of the body is discarded during the flight.

Figure 25-13

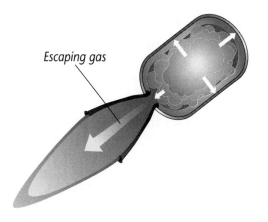

Escaping gas

The expanding gases would push outward on all sides of the rocket with equal force but because of the nozzle, the rearward force is very small. Therefore, they exert an unbalanced forward force on the rocket.

The Rocket Engine

How does a rocket work? Remember that a jet engine produces the forward force, called thrust, by expelling hot gases backward at high speed. How does pushing gases in one direction exert a thrust in the other? Find a balloon and feel the force!

MiniLab

The Balloon Rocket

While few people get to experience the force of a rocket like the space shuttle, you can model the idea of the force with a simple balloon rocket.

Procedure

1. Blow up a large balloon and hold the end opposite the neck of the balloon against the palm of your hand.

2. Let go of the neck. Did you feel the force? If you didn't, try it with your palm facing down and the balloon nozzle facing the ground. What happens to the balloon when all of the air is gone?

Analysis

1. Make a diagram of the deflating balloon. Draw arrows showing the forces exerted on the balloon by the air inside it.

2. Explain, based on Newton's second law of motion, why the balloon accelerates forward.

■ Propelling a Rocket

Of course, rockets aren't balloons. Rockets carry an oxidizer such as oxygen or some other chemical to combine with the fuel. Perhaps the simplest reaction is between the fuel hydrogen and the oxidizer oxygen. While these elements are gases at normal temperatures, they can both be turned into liquids for use in rockets by cooling them to close to absolute zero ($-273°C$). Whatever their physical state, the chemical reaction is the same:

$$2H_2 + O_2 \rightarrow 2H_2O.$$

That is, two molecules of hydrogen combine with one molecule of oxygen to produce two molecules of water. This reaction produces a large amount of energy. Where does the energy come from? The energy stored in the hydrogen and oxygen bonds is much greater than that stored in the water bonds. During the combustion, it is this excess stored, or potential, energy that is released in the form of kinetic energy. Kinetic energy is released as molecules of the combustion products escape through the rocket nozzle at high speeds.

Figure 25-14

Rocket propulsion is a matter of expelling mass at high speed.

■ Impulse and Exhaust Speed

To understand rocket propulsion, Newton's second law of motion can help. Newton wrote it as *Impulse = change in momentum*. Remember that the impulse, *I*, is the product of the force times the time it was exerted, or *Ft*, and that momentum is the product of mass and speed, or *mv*. Now use a thought model of a rocket moving in space as shown in **Figure 25-14** to see how to increase the speed of a rocket.

While the engine is firing, the gas and rocket exert forces on each other. According to Newton's third law, the force exerted on the rocket by the gas is equal to the force exerted on the gas by the rocket, but they are in opposite directions. That means that the impulse exerted on the gas is equal to the impulse exerted on the rocket, but, again, they are in opposite directions.

Newton's second law says that the impulse equals the change in momentum. For the rocket, the new momentum is $M(V + v)$. The old momentum was MV so the change is Mv. For the expelled gas, the new momentum is $m(V - v_{exhaust})$. The old momentum was mV, so the change is $-mv_{exhaust}$. The change in momentum of the rocket is the same as the change in momentum of the gas, but again they are in opposite directions; that is, $Mv = -mv_{exhaust}$. From this equation, we find that the rocket gains a speed $v = -(m/M)v_{exhaust}$. Thus, the faster the gas can be expelled, the greater the gain in speed of the rocket.

A Before firing its engine, the rocket, mass *M*, and its propellant, mass *m*, are moving at speed *V*.

B The engine fires briefly. The fuel and oxidizer react, expelling the mass of gas, *m*, from the engine at a speed $v_{exhaust}$. The ship's speed increases from *V* to *V* + *v*.

Applying Math **Calculating Change in Speed**

A skateboarder is coasting down the street at a constant speed of 5 m/s. She's carrying a 6-kg bowling ball and she has a mass of 50 kg. What will her new speed be if she throws the ball behind her at a rate of 2 m/s?

Known Information: mass of skateboarder,
$$M = 50 \text{ kg}$$
mass of bowling ball, $m = 6$ kg
velocity of thrown bowling ball,
$$v_{exhaust} = -2 \text{ m/s}$$

Unknown Information: change in skateboarder's speed (*v*)

Equation to Use: momentum = mass × speed

Solution: Change in skateboarder's momentum =
    –Change in ball's momentum
$$Mv = -mv_{exhaust}$$
or: $v = -(m/M)v_{exhaust}$
$$= -(6 \text{ kg}/50 \text{ kg}) \times (-2 \text{ m/s})$$
$$= -0.12 \times (-2 \text{ m/s}) = 0.24 \text{ m/s}$$
New speed = 5 m/s + 0.24 m/s = 5.24 m/s

Practice Problem

1. How would the skateboarder's speed change if she threw a bowling ball, with a mass of 10 kg, behind her at 20 m/s?

Figure 25-15

Just before launching, the shuttle's external fuel tank is filled with liquid oxygen. The oxygen is so cold that frost often forms on the outside of the tank.

From these results, you can see that it's important that the exhaust speed be as high as possible. How can that be achieved?

If two particles are given the same kinetic energy, the less massive one will have the higher speed. Thus, the lighter the gas, the more speed the rocket will gain. Studies of rocket engines show that the final speed of the rocket is faster if the ratio of hydrogen to oxygen is 4:1. But only two molecules of hydrogen react with each molecule of oxygen to form water. The extra two hydrogen molecules don't take part in the reaction, so why are they needed? The hydrogen is less massive than the water, so expelling the excess hydrogen with the water decreases the average mass, giving the rocket a greater speed.

The equation $v = -(m/M)v_{exhaust}$ shows what happens when the rocket first fires. What happens in the next firing? As the fuel burns and is expelled, the total rocket mass, M, is reduced even more, so the speed increases even more.

■ Propellants and Specific Impulse

Propellants are rated by a measure called the **specific impulse,** which is the ratio of impulse to weight: $I_{sp} = I/W$. Because impulse is measured in newton-seconds and weight in newtons, specific impulse is measured in seconds. Specific impulse is related to the exhaust speed in a simple way. Exhaust speed equals the specific impulse times g (9.8 m/s^2). That is, $v_{exhaust} = I_{sp} g$. **Table 25-2** shows the specific impulse of some liquid fuels.

Not all rocket fuels are liquid, however. The space shuttle uses solid-fuel boosters during its launch. Missiles also commonly use solid fuel because it can be stored in the rocket for long periods, while liquid fuels can only be added shortly before launch time.

Table 25-2

Specific Impulse of Liquid Fuels		
Fuel	Oxidizer	Specific impulse I_{sp} (s)
ethyl alcohol	liquid oxygen	248
hydrazine	nitrogen tetroxide	265
kerosene	liquid oxygen	265
liquid hydrogen	liquid oxygen	364
liquid hydrogen	liquid fluorine	373

Using Specific Impulse of Fuels

Make a table for the two most common fuels, kerosene/liquid oxygen and liquid hydrogen/liquid oxygen, in which you include their specific impulses with another column for the exhaust speeds, $v_{exhaust}$. Calculate the two exhaust speeds using the formula $v_{exhaust} = I_{sp} \, g$, where $g = 9.8 \text{ m/s}^2$.

Analysis

1. The first stage of the Saturn V booster, **Figure 25-16**, sent men to the moon in the 1970s. You can find the thrust of this giant rocket. You need to know that it burned 2.1 million kg of kerosene and liquid oxygen in 150 seconds. The thrust is given by the exhaust speed times the rate at which the fuel was burned (mass of fuel divided by the time taken). First find the rate at which fuel was burned, and then find the thrust.

2. The second stage burned liquid hydrogen and liquid oxygen, which generated a thrust of 1 million newtons. From the thrust and exhaust speed, you can find the rate at which fuel was burned. The rocket fired for 7 minutes and 25 seconds. Find the total amount of fuel burned.

3. Suppose hydrogen and fluorine had been used in this second stage. For the same thrust, would a larger or smaller amount of fuel have been needed?

Thinking Critically

Compare the thrust provided by each stage and the rate at which fuel was burned in each stage. How could you use graphics to visually compare the data?

Figure 25-16

The Saturn V rocket ready to launch astronauts to the moon stood 132 m high and weighed more than 28 million N.

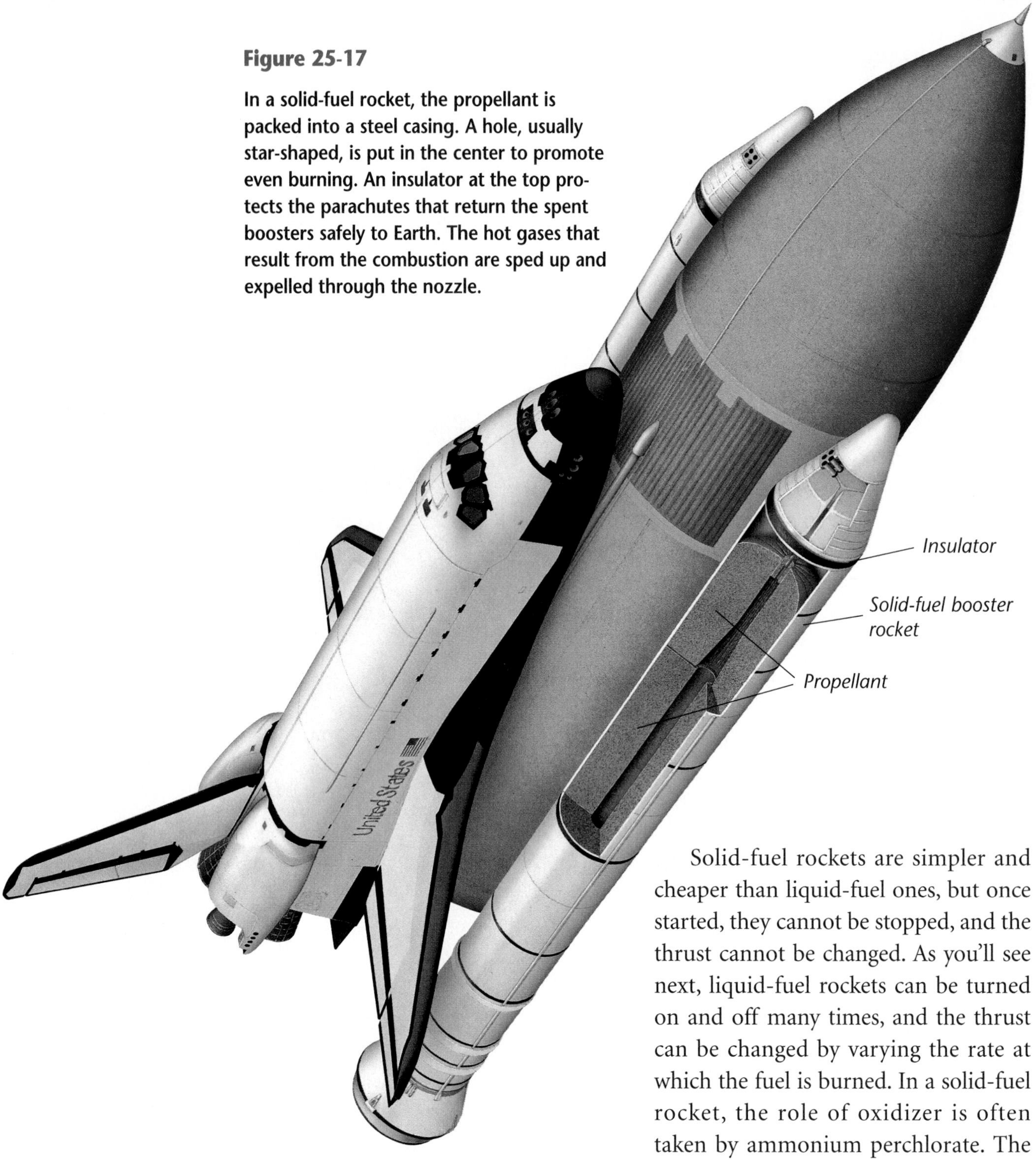

Figure 25-17

In a solid-fuel rocket, the propellant is packed into a steel casing. A hole, usually star-shaped, is put in the center to promote even burning. An insulator at the top protects the parachutes that return the spent boosters safely to Earth. The hot gases that result from the combustion are sped up and expelled through the nozzle.

Insulator

Solid-fuel booster rocket

Propellant

■ Solid-fueled Rockets

Compared to a liquid-fueled rocket, a rocket that uses solid fuels is simple. The propellant consists of the fuel and the oxidizer, both solid chemicals, mixed together with a binder, usually a rubbery polymer. It is packed in a metal casing and a nozzle is attached, as shown in **Figure 25-17.**

Solid-fuel rockets are simpler and cheaper than liquid-fuel ones, but once started, they cannot be stopped, and the thrust cannot be changed. As you'll see next, liquid-fuel rockets can be turned on and off many times, and the thrust can be changed by varying the rate at which the fuel is burned. In a solid-fuel rocket, the role of oxidizer is often taken by ammonium perchlorate. The fuel is usually flakes of aluminum, iron oxide, or copper chromite bound in a hydrocarbon such as epoxy or polyurethane. The specific impulse of such a propellant is 175 to 250 seconds. The space shuttle uses solid-fuel booster rockets that together burn 1.1 million kg of fuel in 100 seconds to provide a thrust of almost 26 million N.

■ Liquid-fueled Rockets

Figure 25-18 shows the parts of a simple rocket that are powered by liquid fuels. The fuel is liquid hydrogen; the oxidizer is liquid oxygen.

Figure 25-18

A liquid-fueled rocket needs tanks to hold the fuel and the oxidizer. Valves control the flow of these liquids. When the valves are opened, a turbine pump pushes the liquids into the combustion chamber where they react.

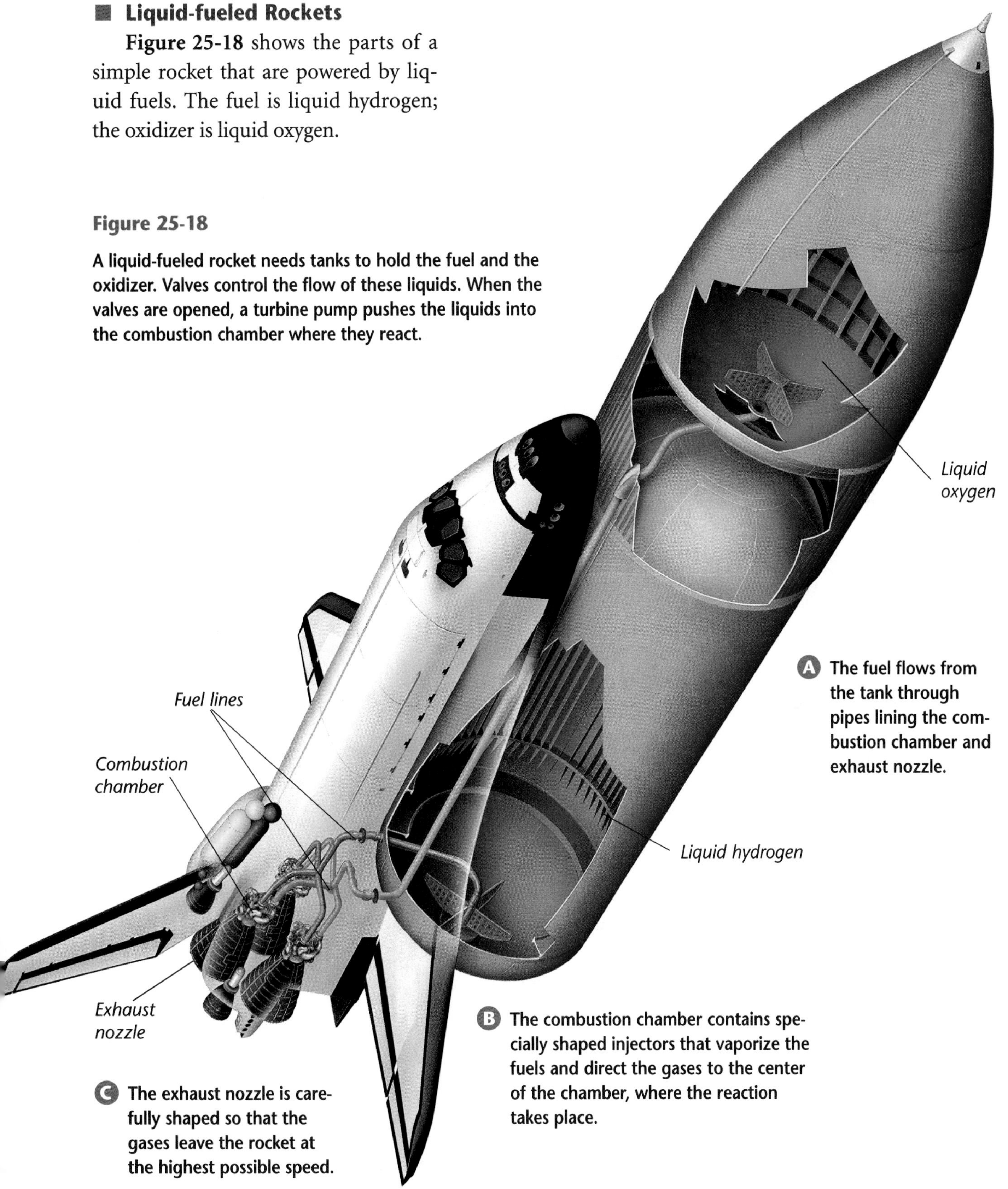

Liquid oxygen

Fuel lines

Combustion chamber

Liquid hydrogen

Ⓐ The fuel flows from the tank through pipes lining the combustion chamber and exhaust nozzle.

Exhaust nozzle

Ⓑ The combustion chamber contains specially shaped injectors that vaporize the fuels and direct the gases to the center of the chamber, where the reaction takes place.

Ⓒ The exhaust nozzle is carefully shaped so that the gases leave the rocket at the highest possible speed.

INVESTIGATION

How does the rocket nozzle affect its performance?

You've probably launched a balloon rocket many times. Blow it up, let it go, and off it flies. The energy you store in it when you blow it up is changed into kinetic energy as it moves. In this Investigation, you'll try to maximize the distance the balloon moves along a guiding line.

Preparation

Problem
What length and diameter of nozzle will allow the balloon to go the greatest distance?

Hypothesis
In your group, brainstorm possible hypotheses and discuss the evidence on which each hypothesis is based. Select the best hypothesis from your list.

Objectives
In this Investigation, you will:
- *Compare* the distances traveled by a tethered balloon as the size and shape of the nozzle are changed.
- *Infer* which rocket nozzle shapes make the rocket go farthest.

Possible Materials
large balloons (25-30 cm diameter round or 10 × 40 cm long balloons)
rubber tubing of assorted diameters
scissors
plastic drinking straws
cellophane or packing tape
15 m nylon fishing line
measuring tape
stopwatch
string

Safety Precautions

Use caution when tools are being used to shape nozzles.

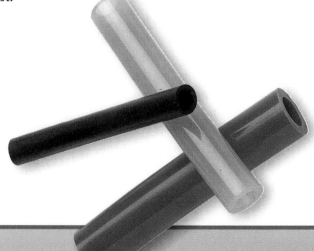

Plan the Experiment

1 You may wish to test your rocket nozzles on a length of fishing line stretched tightly and level to the ground. Thread the line through a straw that is taped to your balloon, as in the photograph on this page. Insert different nozzles into the end of the balloon to test them.

2 Examine the materials provided by your teacher. As a group, make a list of the possible ways you might test your hypothesis.

3 Agree on a way that your group could investigate your hypothesis. Design an experiment that will allow for the collection of quantitative data.

4 Prepare a list of numbered directions. Include a list of materials and the amounts you will need.

5 Design and construct a table for recording your data *in your Journal.* How will you measure the performance of each nozzle?

Check the Plan

Discuss the following points with other group members to decide the final procedure for your experiment.

1 Determine how you will make the balloon nozzles. What factors will you vary? What elements will you control?

2 How can you control the variables when testing the nozzles? How can you make sure the same amount of air is in the balloon for each test?

3 *Make sure your teacher has approved your experimental plan before you proceed further.*

4 Carry out your experiment. Make any needed observations, and complete your data table.

Going Further

Changing Variables

Try balloons of the other shape (round or long). Try tilting the line upward, or completely vertical. Which nozzle gets the balloon highest? If you have probeware, measure the distance as a function of time for the balloons and find their speed and acceleration versus time. When is their acceleration greatest? Their speed?

Analyze and Conclude

1. **Measuring in SI** Find the average speed of your fastest balloon over the course.

2. **Making and Using Graphs** Make two plots: one of distance traveled versus the hole diameter, the other of distance versus nozzle length.

3. **Drawing Conclusions** Find the nozzle that made the balloon go farthest. Which nozzle gave the balloon the fastest speed?

4. **Analyzing the Procedure** Because the air drag depends on both the speed and the cross-sectional area of the balloon, it varies throughout the race. When is it smallest? When is it greatest?

A The space shuttle includes two solid-fuel booster rockets that fall back into the ocean after their propellant is exhausted and an external tank, which holds liquid oxygen and hydrogen that is also released when the fuel is all burned.

Figure 25-19

The mission may vary, but every shuttle flight follows certain basic steps.

■ Rocket Stages

A spaceship in orbit around Earth is traveling at more than 7 km/s. To reach this speed, a rocket needs a high fuel-mass to rocket-body-mass ratio, such as 22 to 1. Could a rocket holding this much propellant be built? Even with the most sophisticated and expensive materials, the largest possible ratio of propellant to rocket body mass is about ten to one.

The solution to this problem is to build a rocket in stages. A rocket built in **stages** is really one rocket built on top of another. After one rocket burns all of its propellant, the empty rocket shell—including fuel tank and engine—is discarded. The mass of the remaining rocket is now much less, so it requires a smaller mass of propellant to accelerate.

Figure 25-19 shows how the space shuttle uses stages to accelerate it to orbital speed.

Reaching for the Stars

For decades, humans have dreamed of visiting other solar systems. What would be needed for such a trip? Let's see what it would take to travel to the nearest star, Proxima Centauri.

The distance to Proxima Centauri is 4.2 light-years, or about 40 trillion km (4×10^{13} km). Let's plan a journey of 5000 years. If we were to go at constant speed, we would need a speed of 260 km/s. Could we reach this speed with a rocket using chemical propellants? As you found earlier in this section, the best of today's propellants, liquid fluorine and

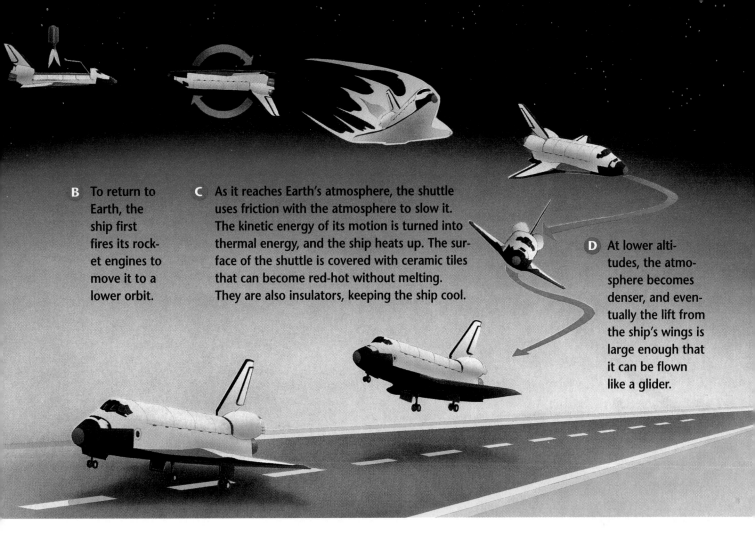

B To return to Earth, the ship first fires its rocket engines to move it to a lower orbit.

C As it reaches Earth's atmosphere, the shuttle uses friction with the atmosphere to slow it. The kinetic energy of its motion is turned into thermal energy, and the ship heats up. The surface of the shuttle is covered with ceramic tiles that can become red-hot without melting. They are also insulators, keeping the ship cool.

D At lower altitudes, the atmosphere becomes denser, and eventually the lift from the ship's wings is large enough that it can be flown like a glider.

liquid hydrogen, have an exhaust speed of 3650 m/s. Suppose that scientists are able to increase this to 5000 m/s. If we were to send a robot spacecraft with a mass of about 1000 kg, we would need to use 10^{25} kg of fuel. But the mass of Earth is only 6×10^{24} kg. The trip is impossible using chemical fuels.

Is there any hope for future space travelers? Perhaps a distant descendant of yours will invent a rocket fuel yet unthought of and fulfill the dream.

check your UNDERSTANDING

Understanding Concepts
1. How does firing gas from a rocket backward accelerate the rocket forward?
2. Why are two- or three-stage rockets used to launch satellites?
3. If you burn two units of hydrogen with one unit of oxygen, you get the highest temperature. Why is this mixture not used in rockets?

Skill Review
4. **Sequencing** Write a detailed description of the steps involved in getting a satellite in orbit. Include fuels, forces, rocket description, and other factors. For help, refer to Sequencing in the *Skill Handbook.*

Imaginary Images

How do you paint a picture of something no one has ever seen before? Ask Michael Whelan; he knows. His images of far away planets, fictional characters, and imaginary landscapes have graced the covers of many science fiction and fantasy books. The image at the right, *Trantorian Dream,* appeared on the cover of Isaac Asimov's novel, *Foundation's Edge.* Whelan's imagination and skill have led to multiple international awards.

Making Art

Book publishers arrange for cover art in different ways. Usually, the author, editor, or publisher suggests an idea. How the idea becomes art is mostly up to the artist. She or he may complete several detailed sketches, called studies, before painting a final version. Better-known artists may go directly from idea to finished art.

Although Whelan's art springs from his imagination, the images are rooted in reality. Those who buy the books behind his cover art expect things they are familiar with to be portrayed accurately. Consequently, he must sometimes refer to science books. Without thousands of hours of astronomical observations, no one on Earth would know that galaxies like the one shown really are spiral-shaped. Of course, other artistic details such as color, perspective, and lighting must also be true to reality.

Thinking Critically

1. *Identify* what is based in reality and what is imaginary within the painting *Trantorian Dream.*
2. *Describe* an idea for new cover art for a book that you have read. Then, sketch the idea.

Read the statements below that review major points presented in the chapter. Using the concepts that you have learned, answer each question *in your Journal.*

① Satellites in space can be used for communications or to observe Earth. *How can satellites be used to explore for resources on Earth?*

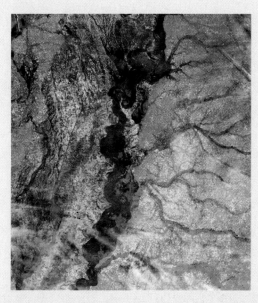

② Exploring space from in space, such as on a space station, can give us much more information about space. Robot probes can be used to explore other planets without risking human lives. *What can we learn from exploring the universe?*

③ Accelerating a rocket is a matter of expelling a propellant through a nozzle, creating a reaction force that pushes the rocket forward. By using certain propellants and rocket stages, rockets can reach an orbit around Earth and beyond, but propellant mass ratios limit how fast they can travel. *How does using stages allow a rocket to accelerate using less propellant?*

Using Key Science Terms

electromagnetic spectrum
electromagnetic wave
propellant
specific impulse
stage

Answer the following questions about science terms used in this chapter.

1. Distinguish between electromagnetic waves and the electromagnetic spectrum.
2. Which is larger: the light-year or astronomical unit?
3. Define the term *specific impulse*.
4. Describe how a propellant propels a rocket.

Understanding Ideas

Using complete sentences, answer the following questions in your Journal.

1. Why doesn't a rocket need air to push against?
2. Explain why rockets that launch satellites are two- or three-stage rockets.
3. Which Landsat wavelength bands would help to find out if a power plant was discharging heated water? To find out if plants were growing in a dry region?
4. How is infrared radiation used by satellites orbiting Earth?
5. How are satellites used in communications on Earth?
6. Where does the energy come from to accelerate a rocket?

Developing Skills

Use your understanding of the concepts developed in this chapter to answer each of the following questions.

1. **Concept Mapping** Create a concept map of Newton's third law applied to a rocket. Use as many concepts from this chapter as you need.
2. **Predicting** If the weight of a toy rocket were 2.5 N, what would be the smallest thrust of a rocket motor needed to accelerate it upward?
3. **Interpreting Scientific Illustrations** The graphs show the thrust of two small rocket motors versus time. Which engine has the larger impulse? Explain.

Rocket Thrust versus Time

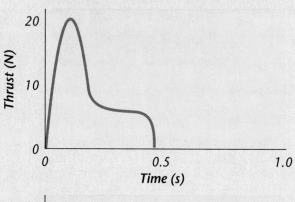

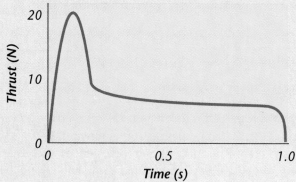

Critical Thinking

In your Journal, *answer each of the following questions.*

1. Astronomers have built telescopes on Earth that have flexible mirrors that can eliminate the distortions due to the atmosphere. What advantages would an ordinary telescope in orbit still have?

2. What would be the advantage of a geostationary satellite in watching a hurricane in the Atlantic? Of a polar satellite?

3. A fortune-teller predicts that in 2005, the space shuttle will be sent on a mission to a nearby star. Do you think the prediction is likely to come true? Explain.

4. You and some of your friends go to see a new science fiction movie in which a space probe from a distant galaxy orbits Earth collecting information. The information is relayed and weeks later, an invasion force arrives from the distant galaxy. Your friends think the movie is realistic. How would you respond?

Problem Solving

Read the following problem and discuss your answers in a brief paragraph.

Engineers tested a rocket engine powered by a nuclear reactor in 1972 and found it had a specific impulse of 825 s. They plan a new design that has a specific impulse of 5000 s. It is proposed that these engines power a spaceship that sends astronauts to Mars. One of the engines would be fired only when it is already orbiting Earth.

1. What is the exhaust speed of the two engines?

2. For a mission to Mars, the speed of the rocket must be increased by 4.0 km/s. Find the ratio of speed increase to exhaust speed.

3. What is the mass ratio for these two rockets?

4. What would be the advantages and disadvantages of using such an engine?

CONNECTING IDEAS

1. **Theme—Energy** What are the energy conversions when a rocket engine burns propellant?

2. **Theme—Scale and Structure** Considering the size of the universe, to what extent can we use space travel to explore space?

3. **Science and Society** Many people find science fiction very entertaining. What is it about space travel and future worlds that is so fascinating?

4. **In-Depth Look** How can satellites in space make navigation on Earth easier?

5. **Art Connection** How can observations of stars and galaxies help an artist draw an imaginary world that has never before been seen?

DESIGN AN AIRPLANE WING

Problem

The lift and drag of an airplane wing depend on its size, shape, and the speed of the plane. Calculations, even done with the help of computers, cannot perfectly predict performance. For that reason, aeronautical engineers build and test smaller models before building full-scale planes. Imagine you're an engineer whose job it is to design and test an airplane wing to be used on a large cargo plane.

Materials

heavy posterboard or balsa wood	modeling knife	spring scale	glue
	scissors	small weights	fan
thin paper	tape	string	

Getting Started

1. Consider first the characteristics of a cargo plane and the requirements for its wing. Will the plane have to fly very fast? Remain in the air at very slow speeds? Does it have to be very maneuverable? Must the wing produce a lot of lift? Will drag be important? *In your Journal* make a list of the plane and wing characteristics that will be needed.

2. Use the material in Unit 7 and the references below to design a wing that will do the job. Make scale drawings of the wing from both the top and side.

3. Build the wing you designed. Devise a way to measure the lift produced by the wing.

4. Test the wing. Make any needed improvements and retest it. Would a full-scale version be suitable for a cargo plane?

Resources

McEntee, Howard G. The Model Aircraft Handbook. New York: Funk and Wagnalls, 1975.

Stensbol, Ottar. Model Flying Handbook. New York: Sterling Press, 1979.

Winter, William J. The World of Model Airplanes. New York: Charles Scribners, 1983.

UNIT 7 PROJECTS

BIRD WINGS

Problem

The lifestyle of a bird depends on the nature of its flight. Some make fast, long, migratory flights, others hover above a flower; some soar lazily on thermal currents, others flit and dart with amazing maneuverability. The way a bird flies depends mainly on its wings, but can wing shape and size alone predict its flight?

Getting Started

1. With the aid of references, investigate several birds that fly in a variety of ways. Create a table of relevant facts including their weight, flying style and speed, and food consumed. Video clips of the flight might be included.
2. Make scale drawings from a bird guide to calculate the wingspan, area, aspect ratio, and wing loading (weight divided by wing area).
3. Explore the conclusions you can draw regarding the relationship between wing characteristics and flying style.
4. Test your conclusions by selecting a bird whose wing characteristics are known, and predict its flying style. Does your prediction agree with what is known?

Resources

Kaufmann, John. <u>Birds in Flight.</u> New York: William Morrow, 1970.

Peterson, Roger T. <u>Field Guide to the Birds.</u> Boston: Houghton Mifflin, 1980.

Terris, John K. <u>How Birds Fly.</u> Mechanicsville, PA: Stackpole Books, 1994.

A GUIDE TO FIELD IDENTIFICATION

BIRDS OF NORTH AMERICA

EXPANDED, REVISED EDITION

APPENDICES

Table of Contents

APPENDIX A

International System of Units

The International System (SI) of Measurement is accepted as the standard for measurement throughout most of the world.

Three base units in SI are the meter, kilogram, and second. Frequently used SI units are listed below.

Table A-1: Frequently Used SI Units	
Length	1 millimeter (mm) = 1000 micrometers (μm)
	1 centimeter (cm) = 10 millimeters (mm)
	1 meter (m) = 100 centimeters (cm)
	1 kilometer (km) = 1000 meters (m)
	1 light-year = 9 460 000 000 000 kilometers (km)
Area	1 square meter (m^2) = 10 000 square centimeters (cm^2)
	1 square kilometer (km^2) = 1 000 000 square meters (m^2)
Volume	1 milliliter (mL) = 1 cubic centimeter (cm^3)
	1 liter (L) = 1000 milliliters (mL)
Mass	1 gram (g) = 1000 milligrams (mg)
	1 kilogram (kg) = 1000 grams (g)
	1 metric ton (t) = 1000 kilograms (kg)
Time	1 s = 1 second

Temperature measurements in SI are often made in degrees Celsius. Celsius temperature is a supplementary unit derived from the base unit kelvin. The Celsius scale (°C) has 100 equal graduations between the freezing temperature (0°C) and the boiling temperature of water (100°C).

Several other supplementary SI units are listed below. These units are commonly used in discussions of energy, force, and pressure.

Table A-2: Supplementary SI Units			
Measurement	Unit	Symbol	Expressed in Base Units
Energy	Joule	J	$kg \cdot m^2/s^2$ or $N \cdot m$
Force	Newton	N	$kg \cdot m/s^2$
Power	Watt	W	$kg \cdot m^2/s^3$ or J/s
Pressure	Pascal	Pa	$kg/(m \cdot s^2)$ or N/m^2

APPENDIX B

°F   °C

210 —   — 100
200 —   — 90
190 —
180 —   — 80
170 —
160 —   — 70
150 —
140 —   — 60
130 —
120 —   — 50
110 —
100 —   — 40
90 —
80 —   — 30
70 —   — 20
60 —
50 —   — 10
40 —
30 —   — 0
20 —
10 —   — -10
0 —
-10 —   — -20

Table B-1: SI/Metric to English Conversions

	When You Want to Convert:	To:	Multiply By:
Length	inches	centimeters	2.54
	centimeters	inches	0.39
	feet	meters	0.30
	meters	feet	3.28
	yards	meters	0.91
	meters	yards	1.09
	miles	kilometers	1.61
	kilometers	miles	0.62
Mass and Weight	ounces	grams	28.35
	grams	ounces	0.04
	pounds	kilograms	0.45
	kilograms	pounds	2.2
	tons	tonnes (metric tons)	0.91
	tonnes (metric tons)	tons	1.10
	pounds	newtons	4.45
	newtons	pounds	0.23
Volume	cubic inches	cubic centimeters	16.39
	cubic centimeters	cubic inches	0.06
	cubic feet	cubic meters	0.03
	cubic meters	cubic feet	35.30
	liters	quarts	1.06
	liters	gallons	0.26
	gallons	liters	3.78
Area	square inches	square centimeters	6.45
	square centimeters	square inches	0.16
	square feet	square meters	0.09
	square meters	square feet	10.76
	square miles	square kilometers	2.59
	square kilometers	miles	0.39
	hectares	acres	2.47
	acres	hectares	0.40
Temperature	Fahrenheit	Celsius	$5/9 \ (°F - 32)$
	Celsius	Fahrenheit	$9/5 \ °C + 32$

Safety in the Science Classroom

1. Always obtain your teacher's permission to begin an investigation.

2. Study the procedure. If you have questions, ask your teacher. Understand any safety symbols shown on the page.

3. Use the safety equipment provided for you. Goggles and a safety apron should be worn when any investigation calls for using chemicals.

4. Always slant test tubes away from yourself and others when heating them.

5. Never eat or drink in the lab, and never use lab glassware as food or drink containers. Never inhale chemicals. Do not taste any substances or draw any material into a tube with your mouth.

6. If you spill any chemical, wash it off immediately with water. Report the spill immediately to your teacher.

7. Know the location and proper use of the fire extinguisher, safety shower, fire blanket, first aid kit, and fire alarm.

8. Keep materials away from flames. Tie back hair and loose clothing.

9. If a fire should break out in the classroom, or if your clothing should catch fire, smother it with the fire blanket or a coat, or get under a safety shower. NEVER RUN.

10. Report any accident or injury, no matter how small, to your teacher.

Follow these procedures as you clean up your work area.

1. Turn off the water and gas. Disconnect electrical devices.

2. Return all materials to their proper places.

3. Dispose of chemicals and other materials as directed by your teacher. Place broken glass and solid substances in the proper containers. Never discard materials in the sink.

4. Clean your work area.

5. Wash your hands thoroughly after working in the laboratory.

Table C-1: First Aid	
Injury	Safe Response
Burns	Apply cold water. Call your teacher immediately.
Cuts and bruises	Stop any bleeding by applying direct pressure. Cover cuts with a clean dressing. Apply cold compresses to bruises. Call your teacher immediately.
Fainting	Leave the person lying down. Loosen any tight clothing and keep crowds away. Call your teacher immediately.
Foreign matter in eye	Flush with plenty of water. Use eyewash bottle or fountain. Call your teacher immediately.
Poisoning	Note the suspected poisoning agent and call your teacher immediately.
Any spills on skin	Flush with large amounts of water or use safety shower. Call your teacher immediately.

Table D-1: Safety Symbols

Disposal Alert
This symbol appears when care must be taken to dispose of materials properly.

Animal Safety
This symbol appears whenever live animals are studied and the safety of the animals and the students must be ensured.

Biological Hazard
This symbol appears when there is danger involving bacteria, fungi, or protists.

Radioactive Safety
This symbol appears when radioactive materials are used.

Open Flame Alert
This symbol appears when use of an open flame could cause a fire or an explosion.

Clothing Protection Safety
This symbol appears when substances used could stain or burn clothing.

Thermal Safety
This symbol appears as a reminder to use caution when handling hot objects.

Fire Safety
This symbol appears when care should be taken around open flames.

Sharp Object Safety
This symbol appears when a danger of cuts or punctures caused by the use of sharp objects exists.

Explosion Safety
This symbol appears when the misuse of chemicals could cause an explosion.

Fume Safety
This symbol appears when chemicals or chemical reactions could cause dangerous fumes.

Eye Safety
This symbol appears when a danger to the eyes exists. Safety goggles should be worn when this symbol appears.

Electrical Safety
This symbol appears when care should be taken while using electrical equipment.

Poison Safety
This symbol appears when poisonous substances are used.

Skin Protection Safety
This symbol appears when use of caustic chemicals might irritate the skin or when microorganism contact might transmit infection.

Chemical Safety
This symbol appears when chemicals used can cause burns or are poisonous if absorbed through the skin.

Solar System Information

Planet	Mercury	Venus	Earth	Mars	Jupiter	Saturn	Uranus	Neptune	Pluto
Table E-1: Solar System Information									
Diameter (km)	4878	12 104	12 756	6794	142 796	120 660	51 118	49 528	2290
Diameter (E = 1.0)*	0.38	0.95	1.00	0.53	11.19	9.46	4.01	3.88	0.18
Mass (E = 1.0)*	0.06	0.82	1.00	0.11	317.83	95.15	14.54	17.23	0.002
Density (g/cm^3)	5.42	5.24	5.50	3.94	1.31	0.70	1.30	1.66	2.03
Period of rotation									
days	58	243	00	00	00	00	00	00	06
hours	15	00	23	24	09	10	17	16	09
minutes	28	14$_R$	56	37	55	39	14$_R$	03	17
R = retrograde									
Surface gravity (E = 1.0)*	0.38	0.90	1.00	0.38	2.53	1.07	0.92	1.12	0.06
Average distance to sun (AU)	0.387	0.723	1.000	1.524	5.203	9.529	19.191	30.061	39.529
Period of revolution	87.97d	224.70d	365.26d	686.98d	11.86y	29.46y	84.04y	164.79y	248.53y
Eccentricity of orbit	0.206	0.007	0.017	0.093	0.048	0.056	0.046	0.010	0.248
Average orbital speed (km/s)	47.89	35.03	29.79	24.13	13.06	9.64	6.81	5.43	4.74
Number of known satellites	0	0	1	2	16	18	15	8	1
Known rings	0	0	0	0	1	thou-sands	11	4	0

* Earth = 1.0

Care and Use of a Microscope

Coarse Adjustment Focuses the image under low power

Fine Adjustment Sharpens the image under high and low magnification

Arm Supports the body tube

Low-power objective Contains the lens with low-power magnification

Stage clips Hold the microscope slide in place

Base Provides support for the microscope

Eyepiece Contains a magnifying lens you look through

Body tube Connects the eyepiece to the revolving nosepiece

Revolving nosepiece Holds and turns the objectives into viewing position

High-power objective Contains the lens with the highest magnification

Stage Supports the microscope slide

Diaphragm Regulates the amount of light entering the body tube

Light source Allows light to reflect upward through the diaphragm, the specimen, and the lenses

Care of a Microscope

1. Always carry the microscope holding the arm with one hand and supporting the base with the other hand.
2. Don't touch the lenses with your fingers.
3. Never lower the coarse adjustment knob when looking through the eyepiece lens.
4. Always focus first with the low-power objective.
5. Don't use the coarse adjustment knob when the high-power objective is in place.
6. Store the microscope covered.

Using a Microscope

1. Place the microscope on a flat surface that is clear of objects. The arm should be toward you.
2. Look through the eyepiece. Adjust the diaphragm so that light comes through the opening in the stage.
3. Place a slide on the stage so that the specimen is in the field of view. Hold it firmly in place by using the stage clips.

4. Always focus first with the coarse adjustment and the low-power objective lens. Once the object is in focus on low power, turn the nosepiece until the high-power objective is in place. Use ONLY the fine adjustment to focus with the high-power objective lens.

Making a Wet Mount Slide

1. Carefully place the item you want to look at in the center of a clean glass slide. Make sure the sample is thin enough for light to pass through.
2. Use a dropper to place one or two drops of water on the sample.
3. Hold a clean coverslip by the edges and place it at one edge of the drop of water. Slowly lower the coverslip onto the drop of water until it lies flat.
4. If you have too much water or a lot of air bubbles, touch the edge of a paper towel to the edge of the coverslip to draw off extra water and force air out.

Making Scale Drawings

When you draw objects seen through the microscope, the size that you make your drawing is important. Your drawing should be in proportion to the size the object appears to be when viewed through the microscope. This is called drawing to scale. Drawing to scale allows you to compare the sizes of different objects. It also allows you to form an idea of the actual size of the object being viewed, Figure 1.

Learning the Skill

1. Draw a circle on your paper. The circle may be any size.
2. Imagine the circle divided into four equal sections, as in Figure 2.

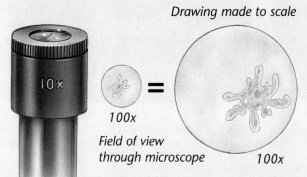

Drawing made to scale

100x

Field of view
through microscope   100x

Figure 1

3. Locate an object under low or high power of the microscope. Imagine the field of view also divided into four equal sections.
4. Note how much of the field of view is taken up by the object. Also note what part of the field of view the object is in.
5. Draw the object in the circle. Position the object in about the same part of the cir-

cle as it appears in the field of view. Also, draw the object so that it takes up about the same amount of space within the circle as it actually takes up in the field of view, Figure 2.

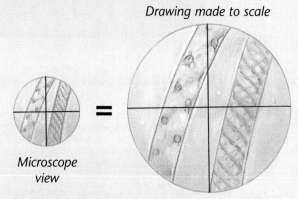

Drawing made to scale

Microscope
view

Figure 2

Troubleshooting

Figure 3 shows objects that haven't been drawn to scale correctly. One object has been drawn too small. One object has been drawn too large. The object in Figure 2 is drawn to the correct size and in the correct position.

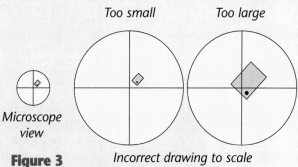

Too small   Too large

Microscope
view

Figure 3   Incorrect drawing to scale

Diversity of Life: Classification of Living Organisms

Scientists use a six-kingdom system for the classification of organisms. In this system, there are two kingdoms of organisms, Kingdoms Archaebacteria and Eubacteria, which contain organisms that do not have a nucleus and lack membrane-bound structures in the cytoplasm of their cells. The members of the other four kingdoms have cells which contain a nucleus and structures in the cytoplasm that are surrounded by membranes. These kingdoms are Kingdom Protista, Kingdom Fungi, the Plant Kingdom, and the Animal Kingdom.

Kingdom Archaebacteria

One-celled prokaryotes; absorb food from surroundings or make their own food by chemosynthesis; found in extremely harsh environments including salt ponds, hot springs, swamps, and deep sea hydrothermal vents.

Kingdom Eubacteria

Cyanobacteria one-celled prokaryotes; make their own food, contain chlorophyll, some species form colonies, most are blue-green

Bacteria one-celled prokaryotes; most absorb food from their surroundings, some are photosynthetic; many are parasites; round, spiral, or rod-shaped

Kingdom Protista

Phylum Euglenophyta one-celled; can photosynthesize or take in food; most have one flagellum; euglenoids

Phylum Bacillariophyta one-celled; make their own food through photosynthesis; have unique double shells made of silica; diatoms

Phylum Dinoflagellata one-celled; make their own food through photosynthesis; contain red pigments and have two flagella; dinoflagellates

Phylum Chlorophyta one-celled, many-celled, or colonies; contain chlorophyll and make their own food; live on land, in fresh water or salt water; green algae

Phylum Rhodophyta most are many-celled and photosynthetic; contain red pigments; most live in deep saltwater environments; red algae

Phylum Phaeophyta most are many-celled and photosynthetic; contain brown pigments; most live in saltwater environments; brown algae

Phylum Myxomycota
Slime Mold × 5

Phylum Chlorophyta
Desmids × 50

Phylum Foraminifera many-celled; take in food; primarily marine; shells constructed of calcium carbonate, or made from grains of sand; forams

Phylum Rhizopoda one-celled; take in food; move by means of pseudopods; free-living or parasitic; amoebas

Phylum Zoomastigina one-celled; take in food; have one or more flagella; free-living or parasitic; zoomastigotes

Phylum Ciliophora one-celled; take in food; have large numbers of cilia; ciliates

Phylum Sporozoa one-celled; take in food; no means of movement; parasites in animals; sporozoans

Phyla Myxomycota and Acrasiomycota one- or many-celled; absorb food; change form during life cycle; cellular and plasmodial slime molds

Phylum Oomycota many-celled; live in fresh or salt water; are either parasites or decomposers; water molds, rusts, and downy mildews

Kingdom Fungi

Phylum Zygomycota many-celled; absorb food; spores are produced in sporangia; zygote fungi; bread mold

Phylum Ascomycota one- and many-celled; absorb food; spores produced in asci; sac fungi; yeast

Phylum Basidiomycota many-celled; absorb food; spores produced in basidia; club fungi; mushrooms

Phylum Deuteromycota members with unknown reproductive structures; imperfect fungi; penicillin

Lichens organisms formed by symbiotic relationship between an ascomycote or a basidiomycote and green alga or cyanobacterium

Plant Kingdom
Non-seed Plants

Division Bryophyta nonvascular plants that reproduce by spores produced in capsules; many-celled; green; grow in moist land environments; mosses and liverworts

Division Lycophyta many-celled vascular plants; spores produced in cones; live on land; are photosynthetic; club mosses

Division Sphenophyta vascular plants with ribbed and jointed stems; scalelike leaves; spores produced in cones; horsetails

Division Pterophyta vascular plants with feathery leaves called fronds; spores produced in clusters of sporangia called sori; live on land or in water; ferns

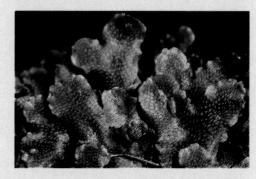

Division Bryophyta
Liverwort

Lichens
British soldier lichen × 3

APPENDIX H

Seed Plants

Division Ginkgophyta deciduous gymnosperms; only one living species called the maidenhair tree; fan-shaped leaves with branching veins; reproduces with seeds; ginkgos

Division Cycadophyta palmlike gymnosperms; large compound leaves; produce seeds in cones; cycads

Division Coniferophyta deciduous or evergreen gymnosperms; trees or shrubs; needlelike or scalelike leaves; seeds produced in cones; conifers

Division Gnetophyta shrubs or woody vines; seeds produced in cones; division contains only three genera; gnetum

Division Anthophyta dominant group of plants; ovules protected at fertilization by an ovary; sperm carried to ovules by pollen tube; produce flowers and seeds in fruits; flowering plants

Division Coniferophyta
Pinecones

Division Anthophyta
Strawberry Blossoms

Division Anthophyta
Strawberries

Animal Kingdom

Phylum Porifera aquatic organisms that lack true tissues and organs; they are asymmetrical and sessile; sponges

Phylum Cnidaria radially symmetrical organisms with a digestive cavity with one opening; most have tentacles armed with stinging cells; live in aquatic environments singly or in colonies; includes jellyfish, corals, hydra, and sea anemones

Phylum Platyhelminthes bilaterally symmetrical worms with flattened bodies; digestive system has one opening; parasitic and free-living species; flatworms

Phylum Arthropoda
Orb Weaver Spider

Phylum Cnidaria
Jellyfish

Phylum Arthropoda
Hermit Crab

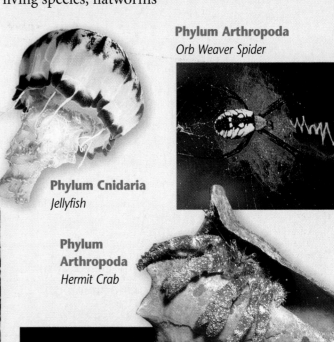

Phylum Mollusca
Florida Fighting Conch

Phylum Annelida
Sabellid Worms Feather Duster

Phylum Nematoda round, bilaterally symmetrical body; digestive system with two openings; some free-living forms but mostly parasitic; roundworms

Phylum Mollusca soft-bodied animals, many with a hard shell; a mantle covers the soft body; aquatic and terrestrial species; includes clams, snails, squid, and octopuses

Phylum Annelida bilaterally symmetrical worms with round segmented bodies; terrestrial and aquatic species; includes earthworms, leeches, and marine polychaetes

Phylum Arthropoda large phylum of organisms that have segmented bodies with pairs of jointed appendages and a hard exoskeleton; terrestrial and aquatic species; includes insects, crustaceans, spiders, and horseshoe crabs

Phylum Echinodermata saltwater organisms with spiny or leathery skin; water-vascular system with tube feet; radial symmetry; includes sea stars, sand dollars, and sea urchins

Phylum Chordata organisms with internal skeletons, specialized body systems, and paired appendages; all at some time have a notochord, dorsal nerve cord, gill slits, and a tail; includes fish, amphibians, reptiles, birds, and mammals

Phylum Arthropoda
Giant Swallowtail Butterfly

Phylum Echinodermata
Blood Sea Star and Red Sea Urchin

Phylum Chordata
Eastern Box Turtle

Phylum Chordata
Great Horned Owl

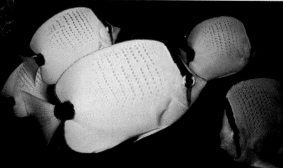

Phylum Chordata
Lemon Butterflyfish

Mitosis

Mitosis is the process by which a nucleus divides into two nuclei, each containing the same number of chromosomes that the original cell had. Usually, the cytoplasm then also divides.

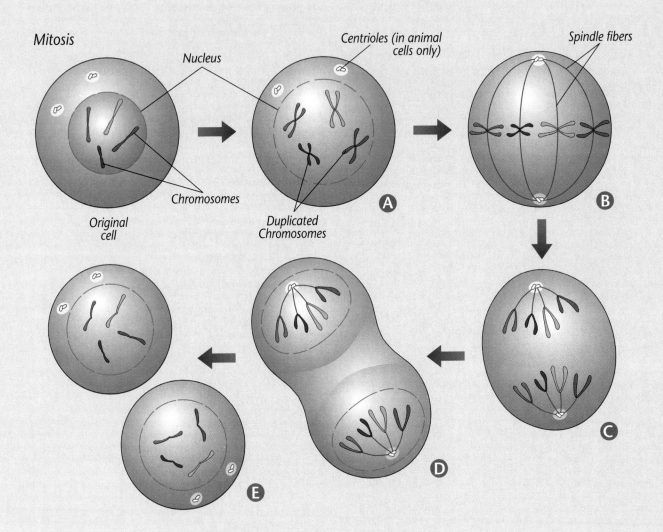

Mitosis

Nucleus

Centrioles (in animal cells only)

Spindle fibers

Chromosomes

Original cell

Duplicated Chromosomes

A

B

C

D

E

KEY:

A Chromosomes duplicate

B Duplicated chromosomes line up

C Duplicated chromosomes separate

D Cytoplasm separates

E Two new cells contain same number of chromosomes as original cell

Meiosis

Meiosis is the process whereby the nucleus of a cell (usually limited to cells in reproductive organs) undergoes two divisions to produce four nuclei, each containing half the number of chromosomes as the original cell. Meiosis in many organisms results in the production of eggs and sperm.

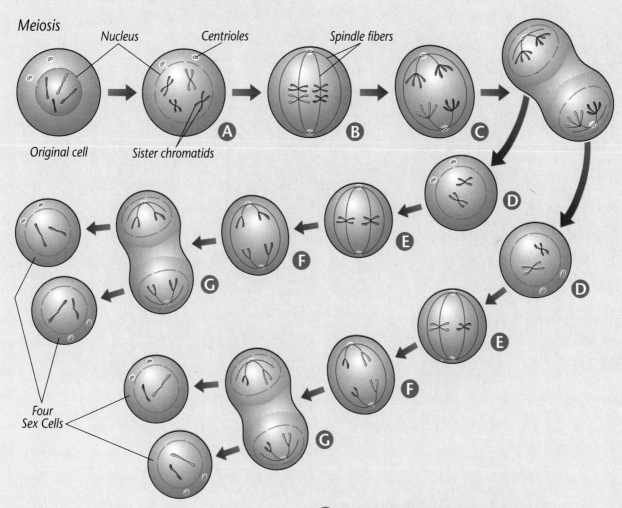

Meiosis

Nucleus   Centrioles   Spindle fibers

Original cell   Sister chromatids

Four Sex Cells

KEY:

D The first division in meiosis has occurred as the cell divides, forming two new cells.

A Each chromosome doubles itself, forming a sister chromatid.

B The doubled chromosomes come together in matching pairs.

C The chromosomes separate.

E The chromosomes again line up along the center of each new cell.

F The sister chromatids separate and move to opposite ends of the cell.

G The cells divide. Four new cells are formed.

Animal Cell

Refer to this diagram of an animal cell as you read about cell parts and their jobs.

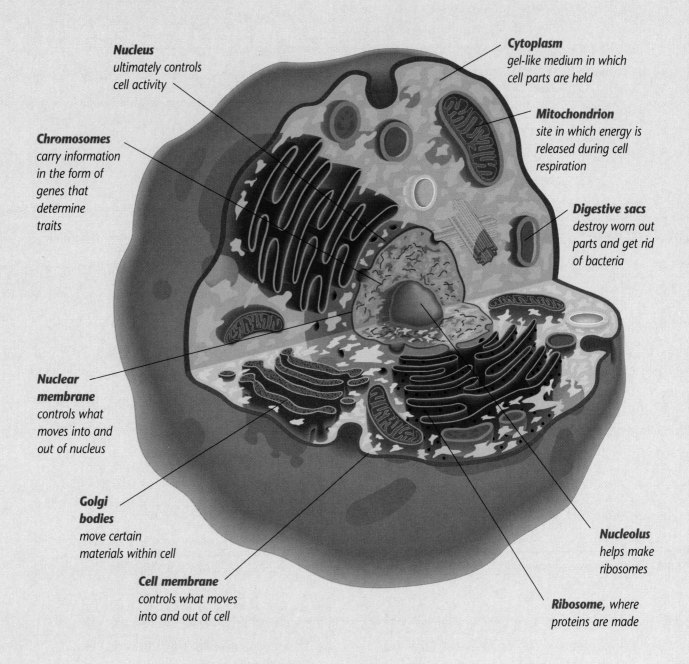

Nucleus
ultimately controls
cell activity

Chromosomes
carry information
in the form of
genes that
determine
traits

**Nuclear
membrane**
controls what
moves into and
out of nucleus

**Golgi
bodies**
move certain
materials within cell

Cell membrane
controls what moves
into and out of cell

Cytoplasm
gel-like medium in which
cell parts are held

Mitochondrion
site in which energy is
released during cell
respiration

Digestive sacs
destroy worn out
parts and get rid
of bacteria

Nucleolus
helps make
ribosomes

Ribosome, where
proteins are made

Plant Cell

Refer to this diagram of a plant cell as you read about cell parts and their jobs.

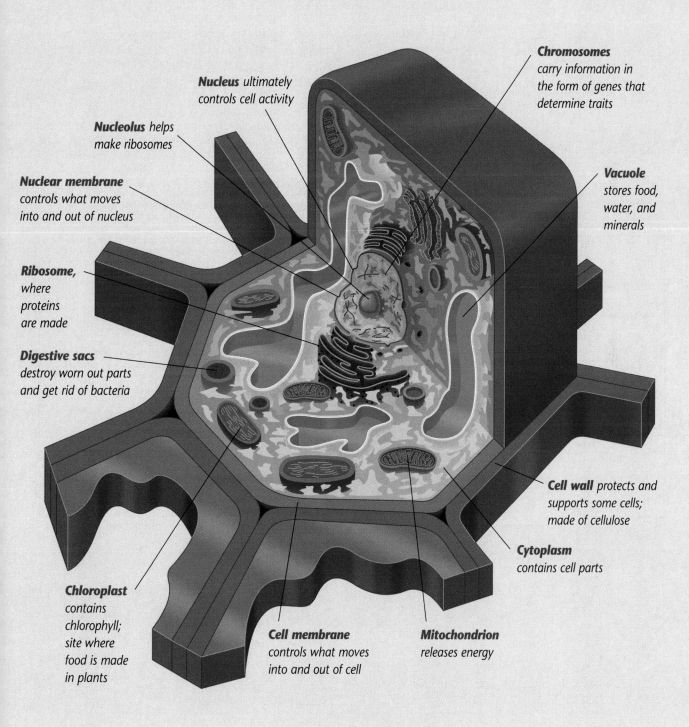

Nucleus *ultimately controls cell activity*

Nucleolus *helps make ribosomes*

Nuclear membrane *controls what moves into and out of nucleus*

Ribosome, *where proteins are made*

Digestive sacs *destroy worn out parts and get rid of bacteria*

Chromosomes *carry information in the form of genes that determine traits*

Vacuole *stores food, water, and minerals*

Cell wall *protects and supports some cells; made of cellulose*

Cytoplasm *contains cell parts*

Chloroplast *contains chlorophyll; site where food is made in plants*

Cell membrane *controls what moves into and out of cell*

Mitochondrion *releases energy*

APPENDIX M

Weather Map Symbols

SAMPLE PLOTTED REPORT AT EACH STATION

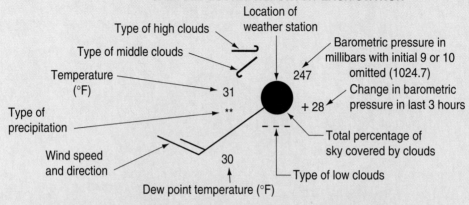

Location of weather station

Type of high clouds

Type of middle clouds

Temperature (°F) → 31

Type of precipitation → ✳✳

Wind speed and direction

Dew point temperature (°F) → 30

247

+ 28

Barometric pressure in millibars with initial 9 or 10 omitted (1024.7)

Change in barometric pressure in last 3 hours

Total percentage of sky covered by clouds

Type of low clouds

SYMBOLS USED IN PLOTTING REPORT

Precipitation	Wind speed and direction	Sky coverage	Pressure Tendency	
≡ Fog	◯ 0 calm	◯ No cover	⌒ Rising, then falling	
✳ Snow	1–2 knots	◍ 1/10 or less	Rising then steady; or rising, then rising more slowly	Barometer now higher than 3 hours ago
● Rain	⊱ 3–7 knots	◖ 2/10 to 3/10	╱ Rising steadily or unsteadily	
Thunderstorm	⊻ 8–12 knots	◑ 4/10	✓ Falling or steady, then rising; or rising, then rising more quickly	
, Drizzle	⟱ 13–17 knots	◐ 1/2	— Steady, same as 3 hours ago	
▽ Showers	⟱ 18–22 knots	⊖ 6/10	⋁ Falling, then rising, same or lower than 3 hours ago	
	23–27 knots	◕ 7/10	Falling, then steady; or falling, then falling more slowly	Barometer now lower than 3 hours ago
	➤ 48–52 knots	◍ Overcast with openings	⟍ Falling steadily, or unsteadily	
	1 knot = 1.852 km/h	● Complete overcast	⟋ Steady or rising, then falling; or falling, then falling more quickly	

Some types of high clouds		Some types of middle clouds		Some types of low clouds		Fronts and pressure systems	
⌐⌐	Scattered cirrus	∠	Thin altostratus layer	⌒	Cumulus of fair weather	(H) or High (L) or Low	Center of high or low pressure system
⌐⌐	Dense cirrus in patches	⫽	Thick altostratus layer	⊔	Stratocumulus	▲▲▲▲	Cold front
⌐	Veil of cirrus covering entire sky	⌐	Thin altostratus in patches	- - -	Fractocumulus of bad weather	●●●	Warm front
—	Cirrus not covering entire sky	⌐	Thin altostratus in bands	—	Stratus of fair weather	▲●▲●	Occluded front
						▲▽●▽	Stationary front

Relative Humidity

	Table N-1: Relative Humidity									
Dry Bulb Temperature	**Dry Bulb Temperature Minus Wet Bulb Temperature, °C**									
	1	2	3	4	5	6	7	8	9	10
10°C	88	77	66	55	44	34	24	15	6	
11°C	89	78	67	56	46	36	27	18	9	
12°C	89	78	68	58	48	39	29	21	12	
13°C	89	79	69	59	50	41	32	22	15	7
14°C	90	79	70	60	51	42	34	26	18	10
15°C	90	80	71	61	53	44	36	27	20	13
16°C	90	81	71	63	54	46	38	30	23	15
17°C	90	81	72	64	55	47	40	32	25	18
18°C	91	82	73	65	57	49	41	34	27	20
19°C	91	82	74	65	58	50	43	36	29	22
20°C	91	83	74	66	59	51	44	37	31	24
21°C	91	83	75	67	60	53	46	39	32	26
22°C	92	83	76	68	61	54	47	40	34	28
23°C	92	84	76	69	62	55	48	42	36	30
24°C	92	84	77	69	62	56	49	43	37	31
25°C	92	84	77	70	63	57	50	44	39	33
26°C	92	85	78	71	64	58	51	46	40	34
27°C	92	85	78	71	65	58	52	47	41	36
28°C	93	85	78	72	65	59	53	48	42	37
29°C	93	86	79	72	66	60	54	49	43	38
30°C	93	86	79	73	67	61	55	50	44	39

Periodic Table

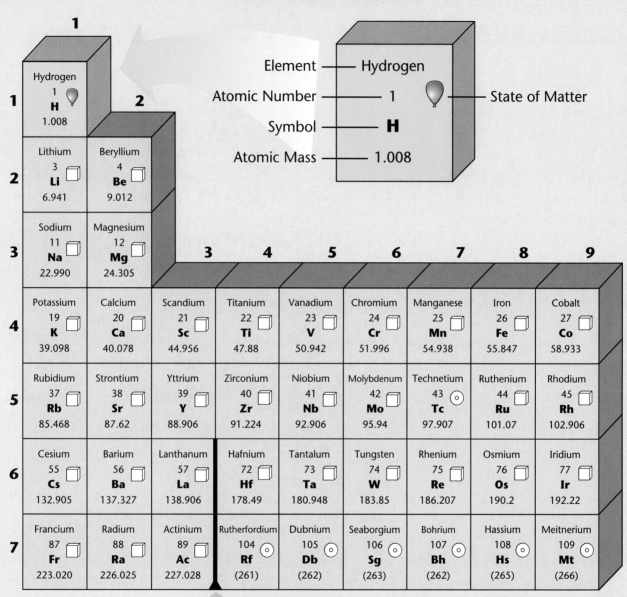

Lanthanide Series

Actinide Series

Gas

Liquid

Solid

Synthetic Elements

Metal

Metalloid

Nonmetal

			13	**14**	**15**	**16**	**17**	**18**
								Helium 2 He 4.003
			Boron 5 B 10.811	Carbon 6 C 12.011	Nitrogen 7 N 14.007	Oxygen 8 O 15.999	Fluorine 9 F 18.998	Neon 10 Ne 20.180
10	**11**	**12**	Aluminum 13 Al 26.982	Silicon 14 Si 28.086	Phosphorus 15 P 30.974	Sulfur 16 S 32.066	Chlorine 17 Cl 35.453	Argon 18 Ar 39.948
Nickel 28 Ni 58.693	Copper 29 Cu 63.546	Zinc 30 Zn 65.39	Gallium 31 Ga 69.723	Germanium 32 Ge 72.61	Arsenic 33 As 74.922	Selenium 34 Se 78.96	Bromine 35 Br 79.904	Krypton 36 Kr 83.80
Palladium 46 Pd 106.42	Silver 47 Ag 107.868	Cadmium 48 Cd 112.411	Indium 49 In 114.82	Tin 50 Sn 118.710	Antimony 51 Sb 121.757	Tellurium 52 Te 127.60	Iodine 53 I 126.904	Xenon 54 Xe 131.290
Platinum 78 Pt 195.08	Gold 79 Au 196.967	Mercury 80 Hg 200.59	Thallium 81 Tl 204.383	Lead 82 Pb 207.2	Bismuth 83 Bi 208.980	Polonium 84 Po 208.982	Astatine 85 At 209.987	Radon 86 Rn 222.018
(unnamed) 110 Uun	(unnamed) 111 Uuu	(unnamed) 112 Uub						

Gadolinium 64 Gd 157.25	Terbium 65 Tb 158.925	Dysprosium 66 Dy 162.50	Holmium 67 Ho 164.930	Erbium 68 Er 167.26	Thulium 69 Tm 168.934	Ytterbium 70 Yb 173.04	Lutetium 71 Lu 174.967
Curium 96 Cm 247.070	Berkelium 97 Bk 247.070	Californium 98 Cf 251.080	Einsteinium 99 Es 252.083	Fermium 100 Fm 257.095	Mendelevium 101 Md 258.099	Nobelium 102 No 259.101	Lawrencium 103 Lr 260.105

Table of Contents

Organizing Information

▶ Classifying

You may not realize it, but you make things orderly in the world around you. If you hang your shirts together in the closet, if your socks take up a particular corner of a dresser drawer, or if your favorite CDs are stacked together, you have used the skill of classifying.

Classifying is the process of sorting objects or events into groups based on common features. When classifying, first observe the objects or events to be classified. Then, select one feature that is shared by some members in the group but not by all. Place those members that share the feature into a subgroup. You can classify members into smaller and smaller subgroups based on characteristics.

How would you classify a collection of CDs? You might classify those you like to dance to in one subgroup and CDs you like to listen to in the next column, as in the diagram. The CDs you like to dance to could be subdivided into a rap subgroup and a rock subgroup. Note that for each feature selected, each CD only fits into one subgroup. Keep selecting features until all the CDs are classified. The diagram above shows one possible classification. Remember, when

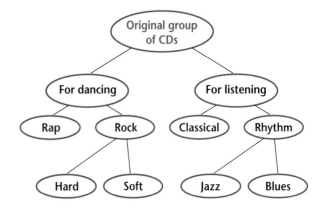

you classify, you are grouping objects or events for a purpose. Keep your purpose in mind as you select the features to form groups and subgroups.

▶ Sequencing

A sequence is an arrangement of things or events in a particular order. A sequence with which you are most familiar is the use of alphabetical order. Another example of sequence would be the steps in a recipe. Think about baking chocolate chip cookies. Steps in the recipe have to be followed in order for the cookies to turn out right.

When you are asked to sequence objects or events within a group, figure out what comes first, then think about what should come second. Continue to choose objects or events until all of the objects you started out with are in order. Then, go back over the sequence to make sure each thing or event in your sequence logically leads to the next.

▶ Concept Mapping

If you were taking an automobile trip, you would probably take along a road map. The road map shows your location, your destination, and other places along the way. By looking at the map and finding where you are, you can begin to understand where you are in relation to other locations on the map.

A concept map is similar to a road map. But, a concept map shows relationships among ideas (or concepts) rather than places. A concept map is a diagram that visually shows how concepts are related. Because the concept map shows relationships among ideas, it can make the meanings of ideas and terms clear, and help you understand better what you are studying.

Network Tree Look at the concept map about Protists. This is called a network tree. Notice how some words are circled while others are written across connecting lines. The circled words are science concepts. The lines in the map show related concepts. The words written on the lines describe the relationships between concepts.

Network Tree

```
                 (  Protists  )
                       |
                    include
          /            |            \
 (animal-like)  ( plantlike )  ( funguslike )
 (  protists )  (  protists )  (  protists  )
       |              |              |
    known as       known as       known as
       |              |              |
 ( protozoans )   (  algae  )       /  \
                          (water molds)(slime molds)
```

When you are asked to construct a network tree, write down the topic and list the major concepts related to that topic on a piece of paper. Then look at your list and begin to put them in order from general to specific. Branch the related concepts from the major concept and describe the relationships on the lines. Continue to write the more specific concepts. Write the relationships between the concepts on the lines until all concepts are mapped. Examine the concept map for relationships that cross branches, and add them to the concept map.

Events Chain An events chain is another type of concept map. An events chain map, such as the one on the effects of gravity, is

Events Chain

Sound wave enters ear.

↓

Eardrum vibrates.

↓

Bones in middle ear vibrate.

↓

Optic nerves in cochlea stimulated.

↓

Impulse transmitted to brain.

↓

Brain interprets sound.

used to describe ideas in order. In science, an events chain can be used to describe a sequence of events, the steps in a procedure, or the stages of a process.

When making an events chain, first find the one event that starts the chain. This event

is called the initiating event. Then, find the next event in the chain and continue until you reach an outcome. Suppose you are asked to describe what happens when a sound wave enters your ear. An events chain map describing the steps might look like the one on page 818. Notice that connecting words are not necessary in an events chain.

Cycle Map   A cycle concept map is a special type of events chain map. In a cycle concept

Cycle Map

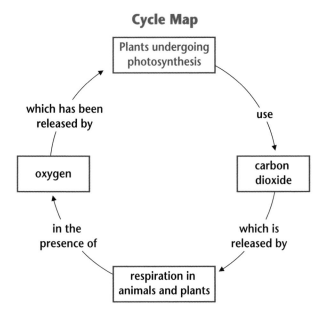

map, the series of events does not produce a final outcome. Instead, the last event in the chain relates back to the initiating event.

As in the events chain map, you first decide on an initiating event and then list each event in order. Because there is no outcome and the last event relates back to the initiating event, the cycle repeats itself. Look at the cycle map for photosynthesis and respiration shown above.

Spider Map   A fourth type of concept map is the spider map. This is a map that you can use for brainstorming. Once you have a central idea, you may find you have a jumble of ideas that relate to it, but are not necessarily clearly related to each other. By writing these

Spider Map

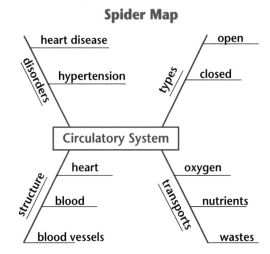

ideas outside the main concept, you may begin to separate and group unrelated terms so that they become more useful.

There is usually not one correct way to create a concept map. As you construct one type of map, you may discover other ways to construct the map that show the relationships between concepts in a better way. If you do discover what you think is a better way to create a concept map, go ahead and use the new way. Overall, concept maps are useful for breaking a big concept down into smaller parts, making learning easier.

▶ Making and Using Tables

Browse through your textbook and you will notice tables in the text and in the activities. In a table, data or information is arranged in a way that makes it easier for you to understand. Activity tables help organize the data you collect during an activity so that results can be interpreted more easily.

Parts of a Table Most tables have a title. At a glance, the title tells you what the table is about. A table is divided into columns and rows. The first column lists items to be compared. In the table shown to the right, different magnitudes of force are being compared. The row across the top lists the specific characteristics being compared. Within the grid of the table, the collected data is recorded. Look at the features of the table in the next column.

What is the title of this table? The title is "Earthquake Magnitude." What is being compared? The distance away from the epicenter that tremors are felt and the average number of earthquakes expected per year are being compared for different magnitudes on the Richter scale.

Using Tables What is the average number of earthquakes expected per year with a magnitude of 5.5 at the focus? Locate the column labeled "Average number expected per year" and the row "5.0 to 5.9." The data in the box where the column and row intersect are the answer. Did you answer "800"? What is the distance away from the epicenter for an earthquake with a magnitude of 8.1? If you

Earthquake Magnitude		
Magnitude at Focus	Distance from Epicenter that Tremors Are Felt	Average Number Expected Per Year
1.0 to 3.9	24 km	>100 000
4.0 to 4.9	48 km	6200
5.0 to 5.9	112 km	800
6.0 to 6.9	200 km	120
7.0 to 7.9	400 km	20
8.0 to 8.9	720 km	<1

answered "720 km," you understand how to use the parts of a table.

Making Tables To make a table, list the items to be compared down in columns and the characteristics to be compared across in rows. Make a table and record the data comparing the mass of recycled materials collected by a class. On Monday, students turned in 4 kg of paper, 2 kg of aluminum, and 0.5 kg of plastic. On Wednesday, they turned in 3.5 kg of paper, 1.5 kg of aluminum, and 0.5 kg of plastic. On Friday, the totals were 3 kg of paper, 1 kg of aluminum, and 1.5 kg of plastic. If your table looks like the one shown below, you are able to make tables to organize data.

Recycled Materials			
Day of Week	Paper (kg)	Aluminum (kg)	Plastic (kg)
Mon.	4	2	0.5
Wed.	3.5	1.5	0.5
Fri.	3	1	1.5

▶ Making and Using Graphs

After scientists organize data in tables, they may display the data in a graph. A graph is a diagram that shows the relationship of one variable to another. A graph makes interpretation and analysis of data easier. There are three basic types of graphs used in science—the line graph, the bar graph, and the pie graph.

Line Graphs A line graph is used to show the relationship between two variables. The variables being compared go on two axes of the graph. The independent variable always goes on the horizontal axis, called the *x*-axis. The dependent variable always goes on the vertical axis, called the *y*-axis.

Suppose a school started a peer-study program with a class of students to see how science grades were affected.

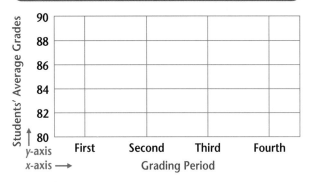

Average Grades of Students in Study Program

Grading Period	Average Science Grade
First	81
Second	85
Third	86
Fourth	89

You could make a graph of the grades of students in the program over the four grading periods of the school year. The grading period is the independent variable and is placed on the *x*-axis of your graph. The average grade of the students in the program is the dependent variable and would go on the *y*-axis.

After drawing your axes, label each with a scale. The *x*-axis lists the grading periods. To make a scale of grades on the *y*-axis, look at the data values. Because the lowest grade was 81 and the highest was 89, you will have to start numbering at least at 81 and go through 89. You decide to start numbering at 80 and number by twos through 90.

Next, plot the data points. The first pair of data you want to plot is the first grading period and 81. Locate "First" on the *x*-axis and locate "81" on the *y*-axis. Where an imaginary vertical line from the *x*-axis and an imaginary horizontal line from the *y*-axis would meet, place the first data point. Place the other data points the same way. After all the points are plotted, connect them with the best smooth curve. In this instance, the best smooth curve is a straight line.

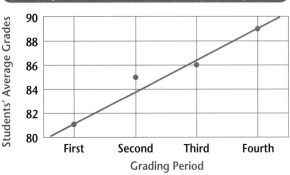

Bar Graphs Bar graphs are similar to line graphs. They compare data that do not continuously change. In a bar graph, vertical bars show the relationships among data.

To make a bar graph, set up the *x*-axis and *y*-axis as you did for the line graph. The data is plotted by drawing vertical bars from the *x*-axis up to a point where the *y*-axis would meet the bar if it were extended.

Look at the bar graph comparing the masses lifted by an electromagnet with different numbers of dry-cell batteries. The *x*-axis is the number of dry-cell batteries, and the *y*-axis is the mass lifted.

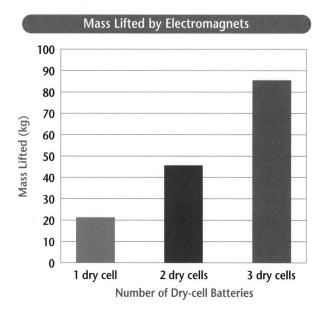

Pie Graphs A pie graph uses a circle divided into sections to display data. Each section represents part of the whole. All the sections together equal 100 percent.

Suppose you wanted to make a pie graph to show the number of seeds that germinated in a package. You would count the total number of seeds. You find that there are 143 seeds in the package. This represents 100 percent, the whole pie.

You plant the seeds, and 129 seeds germinate. The seeds that germinated will make up one section of the pie graph, and the seeds that did not germinate will make up the remaining section.

To find out how much of the pie each section should take, divide the number of seeds in each section by the total number

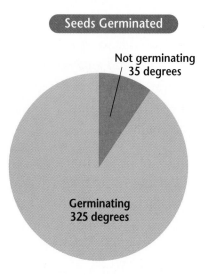

of seeds. Then multiply your answer by 360, the number of degrees in a circle, and round to the nearest whole number. The section of the pie graph in degrees that represents the seeds germinated is figured below.

$$\frac{129}{143} \times 360 = 324.75 \text{ or } 325 \text{ degrees (or } 325°)$$

Plot this group on the pie graph using a compass and a protractor. Use the compass to draw a circle. It will be easier to measure the part of the circle representing the nongerminating seeds, so subtract 325° from 360° to get 35°. Draw a straight line from the center to the edge of the circle. Place your protractor on this line and use it to mark a point at 325°. Use this point to draw a straight line from the center of the circle to the edge. This is the section for the group of seeds that did not germinate. The other section represents the group of 129 seeds that did germinate. Label the sections of your graph and title the graph.

Thinking Critically

▶ Observing and Inferring

Imagine that you have just finished a volleyball game. At home, you open the refrigerator and see a jug of orange juice on the back of the top shelf. The jug feels cold as you grasp it. Then you drink the juice, smell the oranges, and enjoy the tart taste in your mouth.

As you imagined yourself in the story, you used your senses to make observations. You used your sense of sight to find the jug in the refrigerator, your sense of touch when you felt the coldness of the jug, your sense of hearing to listen as the liquid filled the glass, and your senses of smell and taste to enjoy the odor and tartness of the juice. The basis of all scientific investigation is observation.

Scientists try to make careful and accurate observations. When possible, they use instruments such as microscopes and thermometers or balances to make observations. Measurements with a balance or thermometer provide numerical data that can be checked and repeated.

When you make observations in science, you'll find it helpful to examine the entire object or situation first. Then, look carefully for details. Write down everything you observe.

Scientists often make inferences based on their observations. An inference is an attempt to explain or interpret observations or to say what caused what you observed. For example, if you observed a CLOSED sign in a store window around noon, you might infer the owner is taking a lunch break. But, it's also possible that the owner has a doctor's appointment or has taken the day off to go fishing. The only way to be sure your inference is correct is to investigate further.

When making an inference, be certain to use accurate data and observations. Analyze all of the data that you've collected. Then, based on everything you know, explain or interpret what you've observed.

▶ Comparing and Contrasting

Observations can be analyzed by noting the similarities and differences between two or more objects or events that you observe. When you look at objects or events to see how they are similar, you are comparing them. Contrasting is looking for differences in similar objects or events.

Suppose you were asked to compare and contrast the planets Venus and Earth. You would start by looking at what is known about these planets. Arrange this information in a table, like the one on page 824.

Comparison of Venus and Earth		
Properties	**Earth**	**Venus**
Diameter (km)	12 756	12 104
Average density (g/cm³)	5.5	5.3
Percentage of sunlight reflected	39	76
Daytime surface temperature (degrees)	300	750
Number of satellites	1	0

Similarities you might point out are that both planets are similar in size, shape, and mass. Differences include Venus having a hotter surface temperature that reflects more sunlight than Earth reflects. Also, Venus lacks a moon.

▶ Recognizing Cause and Effect

Have you ever watched something happen and then made suggestions as to why it happened? If so, you have observed an effect and inferred a cause. The event is an effect, and the reason for the event is the cause.

Suppose that every time your teacher fed the fish in a classroom aquarium, she or he tapped the food container on the edge of the aquarium. Then, one day your teacher just happened to tap the edge of the aquarium with a pencil while making a point about an ecology lesson. You observed the fish swim to the surface of the aquarium to feed. What is the effect, and what would you infer to be the cause? The effect is the fish swimming to the surface of the aquarium. You might infer the cause to be the teacher tapping on the edge of the aquarium. In determining cause and effect, you have made a logical inference based on your observations.

Perhaps the fish swam to the surface because they reacted to the teacher's waving hand or for some other reason. When scientists are unsure of the cause of a certain event, they design controlled experiments to determine what causes the event. Although you have made a logical conclusion about the behavior of the fish, you would have to perform an experiment to be certain that it was the tapping that caused the effect you observed.

▶ Measuring in SI

The metric system is a system of measurement developed by a group of scientists in 1795. It helps scientists avoid problems by providing standard measurements that all scientists around the world can understand. A modern form of the metric system, called the International System, or SI, was adopted for worldwide use in 1960.

Metric Prefixes			
Prefix	Symbol	Meaning	
kilo-	k	1000	thousand
hecto-	h	100	hundred
deka-	da	10	ten
deci-	d	0.1	tenth
centi-	c	0.01	hundredth
milli-	m	0.001	thousandth

The metric system is convenient because unit sizes vary by multiples of 10. When changing from smaller units to larger units, divide by 10. When changing from larger units to smaller, you multiply by 10. For example, to convert millimeters to centimeters, divide the millimeters by 10. To convert 30 millimeters to centimeters, divide 30 by 10 (30 millimeters equals 3 centimeters).

Prefixes are used to name units. Look at the table for some common metric prefixes and their meanings. Do you see how the prefix *kilo-* attached to the unit *gram* is *kilogram*, or 1000 grams? The prefix *deci-* attached to the unit *meter* is *decimeter*, or one-tenth (0.1) of a meter.

Length You have probably measured lengths or distances many times. The meter is the SI unit used to measure length. A baseball bat is about one meter long. When measuring smaller lengths, the meter is divided into smaller units called centimeters and millimeters. A centimeter is one-hundredth (0.01) of a meter, which is about the size of the width of the fingernail on your ring finger. A millimeter is one-thousandth of a meter (0.001), about the thickness of a dime.

Most metric rulers have lines indicating centimeters and millimeters. The centimeter lines are the longer, numbered lines, and the shorter lines are millimeter lines. When using a metric ruler, line up the 0-centimeter mark with the end of the object being measured, and read the number of the unit where the object ends, in this instance 7.5 cm.

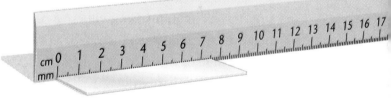

Surface Area Units of length are also used to measure surface area. The standard unit of area is the square meter (m^2). A square that's one meter long on each side has a surface area of one square meter. Similarly, a square centimeter (cm^2) is one centimeter long on each side. The surface area of an object is determined by multiplying the length times the width.

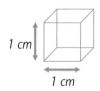

Volume The volume of a rectangular solid is also calculated using units of length. The cubic meter (m^3) is the standard SI unit of volume. A cubic meter is a cube one meter on each side. You can determine the volume of rectangular solids by multiplying length times width times height.

Liquid Volume During science activities, you will measure liquids using beakers and graduated cylinders marked in milliliters. A graduated cylinder is a cylindrical container marked with lines from bottom to top.

Liquid volume is measured using a unit called a liter. A liter has the volume of 1000 cubic centimeters. Because the prefix *milli-* means thousandth (0.001), a milliliter equals one cubic centimeter. One milliliter of liquid would completely fill a cube measuring one centimeter on each side.

Mass Scientists use balances to find the mass of objects in grams. You will use a beam balance similar to the one illustrated. Notice that on one side of the balance is a pan and on the other side is a set of beams. Each beam has an object of a known mass called a *rider* that slides on the beam.

Before you find the mass of an object, set the balance to zero by sliding all the riders back to the zero point. Check the pointer on the right to make sure it swings an equal distance above and below the zero point on the scale. If the swing is unequal, find and turn the adjusting screw until you have an equal swing.

Place an object on the pan. Slide the rider with the largest mass along its beam until the pointer drops below zero. Then move it back one notch. Repeat the process on each beam until the pointer swings an equal distance above and below the zero point. Add the masses on each beam to find the mass of the object.

You should never place a hot object or pour chemicals directly onto the pan. Instead, find the mass of a clean beaker or a glass jar. Place the dry or liquid chemicals in the container. Then find the combined mass of the container and the chemicals. Calculate the mass of the chemicals by subtracting the mass of the empty container from the combined mass.

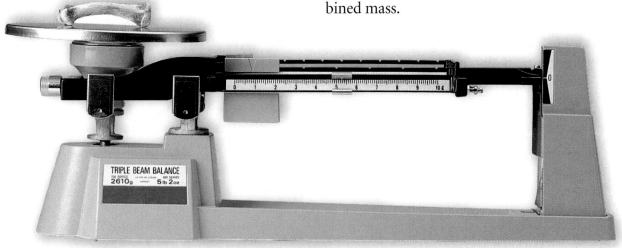

Practicing Scientific Processes

You might say that the work of a scientist is to solve problems. But when you decide how to dress on a particular day, you are doing problem solving, too. You may observe what the weather looks like through a window. You may go outside and see whether what you are wearing is warm or cool enough.

Scientists use an orderly approach to learn new information and to solve problems. The methods scientists may use include observing to form a hypothesis, testing a hypothesis, separating and controlling variables, and interpreting data.

▶ Using Observations to Form a Hypothesis

You observe all the time. Scientists try to observe as much as possible about the things and events they study so they know that what they say about their observations is reliable.

Some observations describe something using only words. These observations are called qualitative observations. If you were making qualitative observations of a dog, you might use words such as *furry, brown, short-haired,* or *short-eared.*

Other observations describe how much of something there is. These are quantitative observations and use numbers, as well as words, in the description. Tools or equipment are used to measure the characteristic being described. Quantitative observations of a dog might include a mass of 45 kg, a height of 76 cm, ear length of 14 cm, and an age of 283 days.

Suppose you want to make a perfect score on a spelling test. Begin by thinking of several ways to accomplish this. Base these possibilities on past observations. If you put each of these possibilities into sentence form, using the words *if* and *then,* you can form a hypothesis. All of the following are hypotheses you might consider to explain how you could score 100 percent on your test:

> If the test is easy, then I will get a perfect score.
>
> If I am intelligent, then I will get a perfect score.
>
> If I study hard, then I will get a perfect score.

Scientists make hypotheses that they can test to explain the observations they have made. Perhaps a scientist has observed that plants that receive fertilizer grow taller than plants that do not. A scientist may form a hypothesis that says: If plants are fertilized, then their growth will increase.

▶ Designing an Experiment to Test a Hypothesis

Once you state a hypothesis, you probably want to find out whether or not it explains an event or an observation. This requires a test. A hypothesis must be something you can test. To test a hypothesis, you design and carry out an experiment. Experiments involve planning and materials. Let's figure out how to conduct an experiment to test the hypothesis

stated before about the effects of fertilizer on plants.

First, you need to write out a procedure. A procedure is the plan that you follow in your experiment. A procedure tells you what materials to use and how to use them. In this experiment, your plan may involve using ten bean plants that are each 15 cm tall (to begin with) in two groups, Groups A and B. You will water the five bean plants in Group A with 200 mL of plain water and no fertilizer twice a week for three weeks. You will treat the five bean plants in Group B with 200 mL of fertilizer solution twice a week for three weeks.

You will need to measure all the plants in both groups at the beginning of the experiment and again at the end of the three-week period. These measurements will be the data that you record in a table. A sample table has been done for you. Look at the data in the table for this experiment. From the data, you can draw a conclusion and make a statement about your results. If the conclusion you draw from the data supports your hypothesis, then you can say that your hypothesis is

Growing Bean Plants		
Plants	**Treatment**	**Height 3 Weeks Later**
Group A	no fertilizer added to soil	17 cm
Group B	3 g fertilizer added to soil	31 cm

reliable. *Reliable* means that you can trust your conclusion. If it did not support your hypothesis, then you would have to make new observations and state a new hypothesis—one that you could also test.

▶ Separating and Controlling Variables

In the experiment with the bean plants, you made everything the same except for treating one group (Group B) with fertilizer. In any experiment, it is important to keep everything the same except for the item you are testing. In the experiment, you kept the type of plants, their beginning heights, the soil, the frequency with which you watered

them, and the amount of water or fertilizer all the same, or constant. By doing so, you made sure that at the end of three weeks, any change you saw was the result of whether or not the plants had been fertilized. The only thing that you changed, or varied, was the use of fertilizer. In an experiment, the one factor that you change (in this case, the fertilizer) is called the *independent variable.* The factor that changes (in this case, growth) as a result of the independent variable is called the *dependent variable.* Always make sure that there is only one independent variable. If you allow more than one, you will not know what causes the changes you observe in the dependent variable.

Many experiments also have a control—a treatment that you can compare with the results of your test groups. In this case, Group A was the control because it was not treated with fertilizer. Group B was the test group. At the end of three weeks, you were able to compare Group A with Group B and draw a conclusion.

▶ Interpreting Data

The word *interpret* means "to explain the meaning of something." Information, or data, needs to mean something. Look at the problem originally being explored and find out what the data show. Perhaps you are looking at a table from an experiment designed to test the hypothesis: If plants are fertilized, then their growth will increase. Look back to the table showing the results of the bean plant experiment.

Identify the control group and the test group so you can see whether or not the variable has had an effect. In this example, Group A was the control and Group B was the test group. Now you need to check differences between the control and test groups. These differences may be qualitative or quantitative. A qualitative difference would be if the leaf colors of plants in Groups A and B were different. A quantitative difference would be the difference in numbers of centimeters of height among the plants in each group. Group B was in fact taller than Group A after three weeks.

If there are differences, the variable being tested may have had an effect. If there is no difference between the control and the test groups, the variable being tested apparently had no effect. From the data table in this experiment on page 828, it appears that fertilizer does have an effect on plant growth.

What is data? In the experiment described on these pages, measurements were taken so that at the end of the experiment, you had something concrete to interpret. You had numbers to work with. Not every experiment that you do will give you data in the form of numbers. Sometimes, data will be in the form of a description. At the end of a chemistry experiment, you might have noted that one solution turned yellow when treated with a particular chemical, and another remained clear, like water, when treated with the same chemical. Data, therefore, are stated in different forms for different types of scientific experiments.

Are all experiments alike? Keep in mind as you perform experiments in science that not every experiment makes use of all of the parts that have been described on these pages. For some, it may be difficult to design an experiment that will always have a control. Other experiments are complex enough that it may be hard to have only one dependent variable. Real scientists encounter many variations in the methods that they use when they perform experiments. The skills in this handbook are here for you to use and practice. In real situations, their uses will vary.

Representing and Applying Data

▶ Interpreting Scientific Illustrations

As you read this textbook, you will see many drawings, diagrams, and photographs. Illustrations help you to understand what you read. Some illustrations are included to help you understand an idea that you can't see easily by yourself. For instance, we can't

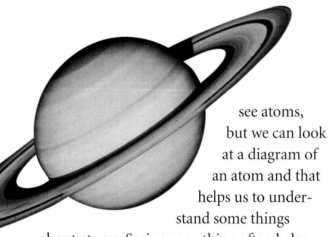

see atoms, but we can look at a diagram of an atom and that helps us to understand some things about atoms. Seeing something often helps you remember more easily. The text may describe the surface of *Jupiter* in detail, but seeing a photograph of Jupiter may help you to remember that it has cloud bands. Illustrations also provide examples that clarify difficult concepts or give additional information about the topic you are studying. Maps, for example, help you to locate places that may be described in the text.

Captions and Labels Most illustrations have captions. A caption is a comment that identifies or explains the illustration. Diagrams, such as the one of the feather, often have labels that identify parts of the item shown or the order of steps in a process.

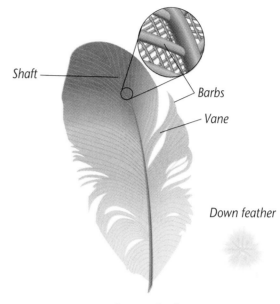

Shaft

Barbs

Vane

Down feather

Contour feather

Learning with Illustrations An illustration of an organism shows that organism from a particular view or orientation. In order to understand the illustration, you may need to identify the front (anterior) end, tail (posterior) end, the underside (ventral), and the back (dorsal) side of the organism shown.

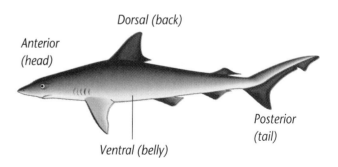

Dorsal (back)

Anterior (head)

Posterior (tail)

Ventral (belly)

You might also check for symmetry. Look at the illustration on the following page. A shark has bilateral symmetry. This means that drawing an imaginary line through the center of the animal from the anterior to posterior end forms two mirror images.

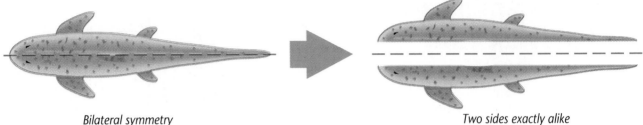

Bilateral symmetry

Two sides exactly alike

Radial symmetry is the arrangement of similar parts around a central point. An object or organism such as a hydra can be divided anywhere through the center into similar parts.

Some organisms and objects cannot be divided into two similar parts. If an organism or object cannot be divided, it is asymmetrical. Regardless of how you try to divide a natural sponge, you cannot divide it into two parts that look alike.

Some illustrations enable you to see the inside of an organism or object. These illustrations are called sections.

Look at all illustrations carefully. Read captions and labels so that you understand exactly what the illustration is showing you.

▶ Making Models

Have you ever worked on a model car or plane or rocket? These models look, and sometimes work, much like the real thing, but they are often on a different scale than the real thing. In science, models are used to help simplify large or small processes or structures that otherwise would be difficult to see and understand. Your understanding of a structure or process is enhanced when you work with materials to make a model that shows the basic features of the structure or process.

In order to make a model, you first have to get a basic idea about the structure or process involved. You decide to make a model to show the differences in size of arteries, veins, and capillaries. First, read about these structures. All three are hollow tubes. Arteries are round and thick. Veins are flat and have thinner walls than arteries. Capillaries are small.

Now, decide what you can use for your model. Common materials are often best and cheapest to work with when making

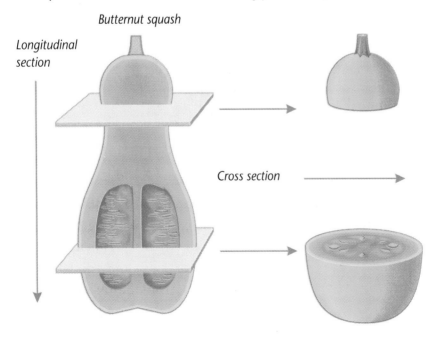

Butternut squash

Longitudinal section

Cross section

▶ Predicting

When you apply a hypothesis, or general explanation, to a specific situation, you predict something about that situation. First, you must identify which hypothesis fits the situation you are considering. People use prediction to make everyday decisions. Based on previous observations and experiences, you may form a hypothesis that if it is wintertime, then temperatures will be lower. From past experience in your area, temperatures are lowest in February. You may then use this hypothesis to predict specific temperatures and weather for the month of February in advance. Someone could use these predictions to plan to set aside more money for heating bills during that month.

▶ Sampling and Estimating

When working with large populations of organisms, scientists usually cannot observe or study every organism in the population. Instead, they use a sample or a portion of the population. To sample is to take a small representative portion of organisms of a population for research. By making careful observations or manipulating variables within a portion of a group, information is discovered and conclusions are drawn that might then be applied to the whole population.

Scientific work also involves estimating. To estimate is to make a judgment about the size of something or the number of something without actually measuring or counting every member of a population.

Suppose you are trying to determine the effect of a specific nutrient on the growth of black-eyed Susans. It would be impossible to

models. Different kinds and sizes of pasta might work for these models. Different sizes of rubber tubing might do just as well. Cut and glue the different noodles or tubing onto thick paper so the openings can be seen. Then label each. Now you have a simple, easy-to-understand model showing the differences in size of arteries, veins, and capillaries.

What other scientific ideas might a model help you to understand? A model of a molecule can be made from gumdrops (using different colors for the different elements present) and toothpicks (to show different chemical bonds). A working model of a volcano can be made from clay, a small amount of baking soda, vinegar, and a bottle cap. Other models can be devised on a computer. Some models are mathematical and are represented by equations.

test the entire population of black-eyed Susans, so you would select part of the population for your experiment. Through careful experimentation and observation on a sample of the population, you could generalize the effect of the chemical on the entire population.

Here is a more familiar example. Have you ever tried to guess how many beans were in a sealed jar? If you did, you were estimating. What if you knew the jar of beans held one liter (1000 mL)? If you knew that 30 beans would fit in a 100-milliliter jar, how many beans would you estimate to be in the one-liter jar? If you said about 300 beans, your estimate would be close to the actual number of beans.

Scientists use a similar process to estimate populations of organisms from bacteria to buffalo. Scientists count the actual number of organisms in a small sample and then estimate the number of organisms in a larger area. For example, if a scientist wanted to count the number of bacterial colonies in a petri dish, a microscope could be used to

count the number of organisms in a one-square-centimeter sample. To determine the total population of the culture, the number of organisms in the square-centimeter sample is multiplied by the total number of square centimeters in the culture.

Glossaries and Index

GLOSSARY

This glossary defines each key term that appears in bold type in the text. It also indicates the chapter number and page number where you will find the word used.

A

abiotic factors: all the nonliving, or physical, features in an ecosystem—such as light, temperature, oxygen, and water—which can directly affect whether an organism can survive in an environment. (Chap. 4, p. 126)

acceleration: rate of change in velocity, which occurs only if opposing forces are unbalanced. (Chap. 23, p. 702)

acid: solution containing more hydrogen ions than hydroxide ions; on the numerical pH scale, solutions with a pH under 7 are acidic—for example, vinegar, with a pH of 3.0, is acidic. (Chap. 4, p. 136)

acid precipitation: precipitation high in sulfur and nitric oxides, which damages trees and crops, kills fish in lakes and rivers, damages buildings, and causes illness. (Chap. 6, p. 189)

active immunity: occurs when your body forms antibodies to a pathogen to which you've been exposed, either by having the disease or by being vaccinated against it. (Chap. 21, p. 637)

active transport: pumping of particles in or out of a cell from areas of lower concentration to areas of higher concentration—which, if defective, disrupts homeostasis. (Chap. 22, p. 675)

air mass: body of air that is consistent in temperature, amount of moisture, and air pressure, and whose degree of moisture and level of temperature are the same as the area below it. (Chap. 2, p. 69)

alleles: different forms of a gene; abnormal alleles can result in the inheritance of such diseases as sickle-cell disease or cystic fibrosis. (Chap. 20, p. 620)

alloy: mixture of two or more elements, with at least one element being a metal, and whose composition can be changed by the addition of other elements; steel is an alloy of iron and carbon. (Chap. 14, p. 427)

amino acids: the building blocks of proteins; the body makes 12 amino acids, and the remaining eight amino acids needed by the body, called essential amino acids, must be obtained from protein in food. (Chap. 7, p. 216)

ampere: unit that measures electrical current; often called amp or A. (Chap. 19, p. 576)

anabolic reactions: energy-requiring reactions that take place during metabolism and that build up complex molecules. (Chap. 8, p. 256)

analgesics: nonaddictive, pain-relieving drugs such as aspirin, ibuprofen, and acetaminophen. (Chap. 21, p. 654)

antibiotics: substances, such as penicillin and tetracycline, that are produced by microorganisms and that fight infections, but have no effect on diseases caused by viruses. (Chap. 21, p. 652)

antibodies: Y-shaped protein chains that bind to antigens, marking them for destruction by phagocytes, or that neutralize antigens by preventing them from attaching to host cells. (Chap. 21, p. 639)

antibody immunity: immune response in which the body uses B cells with antibodies on their surface to destroy specific pathogens in the circulatory system. (Chap. 21, p. 640)

antigens: foreign molecules in the body, such as the cell wall of a bacterium, that are markers for specific pathogens. (Chap. 21, p. 639)

antioxidants: food additives, such as BHA and vitamin E, that prevent or slow the chemical changes that can occur when certain foods come in contact with oxygen. (Chap. 10, p. 302)

aspect ratio: in planes and birds, the quantity determined by dividing the wingspan by the average width of the wing, which can affect lift, drag, and maneuverability. (Chap. 24, p. 738)

autoimmune disease: disease, such as myasthenia gravis or rheumatoid arthritis, that occurs when the body's immune system attacks its own cells. (Chap. 21, p. 643)

autotrophs: organisms that manufacture their own food using sunlight (photoautotrophs) or energy stored in chemical compounds (chemoautotrophs); also called producers. (Chap. 5, p. 148)

B

barometric pressure: measure of the air pressure of the atmosphere; helps us predict the possibility of blue skies and sunshine or gray skies and rain. (Chap. 1, p. 27)

base: solution containing more hydroxide ions than hydrogen ions; on the numerical pH scale, solutions with a pH over 7 are basic—for example, lye, with a pH of 14, is basic. (Chap. 4, p. 136)

B cell: type of white blood cell, produced in the bone marrow, that is involved in antibody immunity but not in cellular immunity. (Chap. 21, p. 640)

GLOSSARY

Bernoulli effect: states that when a fluid moves faster, it exerts less pressure; in birds and planes, explains why pressure below the wing is greater than above the wing. (Chap. 23, p. 722)

biological controls: alternatives to pesticides that include planting genetically resistant crops and introducing natural predators such as frogs. (Chap. 10, p. 299)

biotic factors: all the living organisms that populate an ecosystem—for example, the biotic factors of an urban ecosystem include humans, cats, dogs, trees, spiders, pigeons, squirrels, and roaches. (Chap. 4, p. 116)

biotic potential: a population's highest rate of reproduction under ideal conditions—which is never reached—because of such limiting factors as predator-prey relationships. (Chap. 6, p. 174)

blocking highs: high-pressure air masses that cause a hurricane to change its direction. (Chap. 2, p. 74)

Bowen's reaction series: describes the predictable order of mineral crystallization in cooling magma. (Chap. 12, p. 364)

C

calorie: amount of heat required to raise the temperature of 1 gram of water by 1°C; energy equivalent based on food is measured in Calories, written with a capital "C"; 1 Calorie equals 1000 calories. (Chap. 7, p. 211)

Calvin cycle: set of chemical reactions that takes place during photosynthesis, in which simple, three-carbon sugars are formed using energy from the light reactions and CO_2 from the air. (Chap. 8, p. 255)

carbohydrates: food category consisting of sugars, which can be classified by the length of their carbon skeletons, and starches, which are polymers composed of glucose molecules. (Chap. 7, p. 212)

carrying capacity: largest population of organisms that an environment can support over time and under certain conditions, such as the availability of food and water. (Chap. 6, p. 175)

catabolic reactions: energy-releasing reactions that take place during metabolism, in which complex molecules are broken down into smaller molecules. (Chap. 8, p. 256)

cellular immunity: immune response in which the body uses T cells to destroy cells infected with a specific pathogen. (Chap. 21, p. 642)

cellular respiration: catabolic process in which stored energy in glucose is released a little at a time through a series of chemical reactions. (Chap. 8, p. 256)

cellulose: carbohydrate made of glucose chains arranged in side-by-side rows connected by bonds, and which form rigid, fiberlike plant cell walls that give plants structural support. (Chap. 8, p. 241)

center of gravity: center of an object's or person's weight distribution that must be supported for stability. (Chap. 17, p. 514)

ceramics: dried clay or claylike materials that are hard, heat and weather resistant, and brittle; found in such items as roofing tiles and semiconductors. (Chap. 16, p. 500)

chemical sedimentary rocks: type of rocks, such as limestone and rock salt, that is formed when minerals dissolved in water come out of solution for such reasons as temperature change or evaporation. (Chap. 12, p. 369)

chemical weathering: in soil formation, the process that occurs when the minerals in rocks react with water or other substances, causing the chemical makeup of the rock to change. (Chap. 9, p. 269)

chlorophyll: green pigment in the chloroplasts of plant cells that absorbs energy from the sun and reflects green wavelengths of light, giving plants their green color. (Chap. 8, p. 254)

chloroplasts: structures in green plant cells that contain chlorophyll and convert light energy into chemical energy, which is stored in glucose molecules. (Chap. 8, p. 254)

clastic sedimentary rock: type of rock, such as sandstone and shale, which is formed from fragments of other rocks that are concentrated by temperature, water, and pressure at Earth's surface. (Chap. 12, p. 370)

climax community: occurs when primary succession slows, resulting in a stable, mature, ecological community. (Chap. 6, p. 186)

combustion: in car engines, the burning process that begins with ignition of a mixture of gasoline and air, and produces energy to power the car by breaking and reforming chemical bonds. (Chap. 13, p. 404)

communicable disease: disease, such as syphilis or influenza, that you can catch from another person, and that is caused by a pathogen. (Chap. 20, p. 607)

community: interacting populations of organisms in an area that rely on one another for such survival needs as food and shelter. (Chap. 4, p. 123)

compression stress: results when two forces push toward one another through a solid material, causing it to compress, or shorten. (Chap. 16, p. 482)

conduction: transfers heat from a higher-temperature material to a lower-temperature material by the vibration of particles as the two materials are in contact. (Chap. 2, p. 52)

conodonts: fossils whose color changes help geologists determine how hot potential source rocks became and whether petroleum may be present. (Chap. 13, p. 388)

contact metamorphism: occurs when magma of igneous intrusions heats surrounding rock, causing the minerals to change or fuse—for example, as occurs when limestone crystals are changed to marble. (Chap. 12, p. 376)

convection: transfers heat by the flow within a heated fluid, which reduces its density, and which is forced upward by denser, cooler fluid. (Chap. 2, p. 56)

convection cell: variably sized region caused by rising and falling currents of air, which are heating, cooling, and changing in density; giant convection cells produce Earth's global winds. (Chap. 2, p. 57)

Coriolis effect: describes the apparent deflection of global winds in the northern hemisphere to the right and in the southern hemisphere to the left. (Chap. 2, p. 60)

cracking: refining process in which heavy, longer-chained hydrocarbons are broken, or split, by heat and chemicals into compounds that are then combined to form gasoline. (Chap. 13, p. 404)

creep: slow downhill movement of soil, due to gravity, whose gradual effects can be highly damaging; creep is set in motion by natural forces on the soil such as wetting and drying. (Chap. 15, p. 453)

current: number of charges per second that move through a circuit—which applies to both alternating current, where current is constantly reversed, and direct current, where current moves in only one direction. (Chap. 19, p. 572)

decomposers: heterotrophs, such as fungi and bacteria, that obtain energy by breaking down dead or decaying plants and animals, whose nutrients can then be absorbed and recycled. (Chap. 5, p. 150)

Delaney Clause: federal law that regulates which chemicals can be used in foods processed in the United States, and that does not permit the use of cancer-causing chemicals in foods. (Chap. 10, p. 303)

denaturation: process of chemical change, caused by cooking, in which amino acid chains uncoil and attach to each other, resulting in changes in the appearance and texture of food. (Chap. 10, p. 312)

dew point: reached when air cools to the temperature at which it cannot hold more moisture, which then condenses and can form dew or frost or clouds. (Chap. 1, p. 27)

digestion: process of breaking down of lipids, carbohydrates, and proteins, by specific chemical changes, into smaller molecules that can be absorbed by the cells of the body. (Chap. 7, p. 224)

disease: change in the ability of the body's cells, tissues, or organs to function properly, disturbing homeostasis; examples include chicken pox, cystic fibrosis, and AIDS. (Chap. 20, p. 604)

disease cluster: pattern of disease occurrence that is clumped, nonrandom, usually occurs in a geographic region, and indicates something is unique to the population or area. (Chap. 22, p. 666)

dispersal: spread of seeds away from parent plants by wind; adaptations such as winglike shape or parachutes allow seeds to be spread as far as possible. (Chap. 24, p. 755)

diversity: important biotic factor that is the measure of the number of species populating an ecosystem; high species diversity helps an ecosystem recover after such disasters as famine or flood. (Chap. 4, p. 117)

Doppler radar: uses radio signals to detect the location, direction, and speed of winds in a storm, and whether precipitation is moving toward or away from the radar station. (Chap. 1, p. 35)

drag: rearward force of air on a plane, which depends on such factors as its size and shape, and square of its speed. (Chap. 23, p. 715)

ecosystem: interactions of all the biotic and abiotic factors of a specific area, powered by a flow of energy; the greater the diversity of an ecosystem, the more complex its interactions. (Chap. 4, p. 116)

efficiency: in machines, a way to compare work input and work output; efficiency is never 100% because of energy lost to heat produced by friction. (Chap. 17, p. 528)

electromagnetic spectrum: entire range of electromagnetic waves—from the shortest to the longest wavelengths—including microwaves, radio waves, visible light, and X rays. (Chap. 25, p. 766)

electromagnetic wave: energy-carrying wave—produced by a disturbance in electric and magnetic fields—that travels at the speed of light through space. (Chap. 25, p. 766)

electron-sea model: model that explains the conductivity, malleability, and ductility of metals based on the mobility of their electrons and ability of their atoms to slide over each other. (Chap. 16, p. 491)

electrophoresis: process that produces DNA banding patterns for identification of specific pathogens, including viruses, based on electrochemical analysis of biological molecules and microorganisms. (Chap. 22, p. 678)

endemic disease: disease, such as the common cold, that is always present in a specific population. (Chap. 22, p. 672)

energy resources: sum total of all renewable and nonrenewable materials used to produce energy, including fossil fuels, solar energy, and nuclear power. (Chap. 11, p. 332)

enzymes: proteins that speed up chemical reactions in the body by reducing the amount of energy needed to break chemical bonds; enzymes can be used over and over again and are unchanged at the end of a chemical reaction. (Chap. 7, p. 219)

epidemic: disease occurrence that affects large numbers of people in a specific location; some epidemics, such as AIDS, affect people all over the world. (Chap. 22, p. 672)

erosion: movement of soils by the forces of wind and water; erosion-control methods include contour farming, terracing, and minimum tillage. (Chap. 9, p. 285)

evacuate: to leave an area threatened by disasters, such as hurricanes or floods, in order to save lives. (Chap. 3, p. 85)

evaporation: cooling process that occurs when air changes from a liquid into water vapor. (Chap. 2, p. 58)

exponential growth: increase in a population of living organisms that occurs at a fixed rate, and has the potential for skyrocketing growth if the organisms reproduce rapidly under ideal conditions. (Chap. 6, p. 173)

extrusive igneous rocks: rocks, such as pumice and obsidian, that are formed from quickly cooling lava at Earth's surface and have small or few if any crystals. (Chap. 12, p. 359)

fault: break in Earth's crust along which rapid rock movement can occur, producing earthquakes, or slow rock movement can occur, gradually destroying foundations and buildings. (Chap. 15, p. 470)

floodplain: low-lying, flat land area that is usually dry, but which is likely to become flooded when a nearby stream overflows. (Chap. 15, p. 465)

food chain: model to illustrate energy flow through an ecosystem, and which represents only one of many possible routes for the transfer of energy and matter from producers to consumers to decomposers. (Chap. 5, p. 156)

food web: model showing the complex network of interconnected food chains, indicating all possible feeding relationships within an ecosystem. (Chap. 5, p. 158)

fossil fuels: oil, natural gas, and coal—formed from the buried remains of marine organisms—which provide over 85 percent of the energy used in the United States. (Chap. 11, p. 332)

friction: force that resists motion between two touching surfaces; in machines, lubricants may reduce friction and increase efficiency. (Chap. 17, p. 534)

geophones: in seismic prospecting, the specialized detectors that pick up reflected sound waves passing through rock layers, and whose information is used to determine the rock layer's depth. (Chap. 13, p. 400)

geostationary satellite: weather satellite that stays above a certain point on Earth, and takes photographs continuously to help meteorologists predict weather system movement and speed. (Chap. 1, p. 33)

gravity: force toward Earth that acts on all objects with mass, and which is balanced by the force of the ground pushing back. (Chap. 23, p. 711)

gusts: hazardous winds formed when the speed of wind suddenly increases, resulting in an even larger increase in force; gusts can severely damage buildings and uproot trees. (Chap. 3, p. 87)

Haber process: manufacturing process that uses high pressures and temperatures to change hydrogen and nitrogen to liquid ammonia, which is used in fertilizer to enrich nitrogen-poor soils. (Chap. 8, p. 248)

habitat: the "home address" of an organism—for example, a freshwater pond can be home to many species of plants, fishes, frogs, snails, algae, and bacteria. (Chap. 5, p. 145)

heat: measure of thermal energy, which flows naturally from an object at a higher temperature to an object at a lower temperature. (Chap. 2, p. 52)

heat pumps: two-way energy movers that do work by transferring heat in the air either inside or outside a building in order to cool or heat the structure. (Chap. 18, p. 554)

heterotrophs: organisms that cannot manufacture their own food and feed on other organisms; herbivores, carnivores, and omnivores are heterotrophs; also called consumers. (Chap. 5, p. 149)

heterozygous: having one normal allele and one abnormal allele for a specific characteristic; individuals heterozygous for a characteristic are carriers. (Chap. 20, p. 620)

homeostasis: maintenance of an organism's stable internal environment by the healthy functioning of organ systems, in spite of changes in the organism's surroundings. (Chap. 20, p. 600)

homozygous: having two alleles with the same form—either normal or abnormal—for a specific characteristic; individuals homozygous for the abnormal allele express that particular characteristic. (Chap. 20, p. 620)

humus: soil layer composed of partially decayed animals and plants, including large amounts of dead leaves and branches; the high content of organic matter in humus gives it a dark color. (Chap. 9, p. 273)

hydrolysis: chemical process during digestion in which enzymatic action splits a polymer into its smaller units, and H^+ and OH^- ions from water reattach to the molecules. (Chap. 7, p. 225)

ice wedging: type of physical weathering in which water freezes and thaws within the cracks of rocks, eventually causing the rocks to loosen and split apart. (Chap. 9, p. 268)

igneous rocks: rocks formed underground from slowly cooling magma or formed on the surface of Earth from quickly cooling lava. (Chap. 12, p. 358)

incinerators: large furnaces that reduce municipal waste volume by burning materials at high temperatures, releasing energy that can be used to drive turbines and generate electricity. (Chap. 14, p. 417)

inertia: tendency of an object at rest to remain at rest and of an object in motion to continue moving at the same speed and in the same direction. (Chap. 17, p. 511)

inflammatory response: the body's second line of defense, which produces a local healing reaction, and is initiated when foreign particles, such as pathogens, get past the skin or mucous membranes. (Chap. 21, p. 635)

inhibitors: food additives, such as calcium propionate and BHT, that slow spoilage in foods, such as breads and cheeses, but may not entirely prevent spoilage from occurring. (Chap. 10, p. 303)

insulator: material, such as polyethylene or polyvinyl chloride, that electricity or heat cannot move through easily. (Chap. 16, p. 498)

interspecific competition: competition between different species—for food, shelter, and other limited resources; helps control population size. (Chap. 6, p. 179)

intrusive igneous rocks: rocks formed below ground from slowly cooling magma; may contain valuable metals such as copper and gold, and usually have large, visible crystals. (Chap. 12, p. 362)

isobars: lines drawn on a weather map that connect areas having the same atmospheric pressure; meteorologists can use high-pressure and low-pressure areas shown by isobars to help locate fronts. (Chap. 1, p. 40)

kilowatt-hour: unit that measures electrical energy, and can be determined by multiplying the number of kilowatts used by a device times the number of hours used. (Chap. 19, p. 576)

Koch's postulates: set of four experimental steps—all of which must be met—to identify a specific pathogen causing a specific disease. (Chap. 22, p. 668)

landslide: hazardous, rapid movement of a mass of loose weathered rocks and soil down a slope, due to the action of gravity. (Chap. 15, p. 452)

law of action and reaction: describes that every action force has an exactly equal and opposite reaction force; because single forces cannot be isolated, action-reaction forces always occur in pairs. (Chap. 17, p. 519)

law of conservation of energy: energy is continuously cycled (transformed), but cannot be destroyed or created by ordinary chemical means. (Chap. 8, p. 251)

law of conservation of matter: matter cannot be destroyed or created, but atoms are continually recycled and reorganized through chemical reactions. (Chap. 8, p. 238)

lift: upward force of air on a plane's wings that depends on wing area, air speed across the wing, and shape and angle of the wing. (Chap. 23, p. 719)

light microscope: uses light rays and lenses to enlarge body cells and pathogens so they can be seen. (Chap. 22, p. 680)

light reactions: series of reactions that convert light energy to chemical energy during photosynthesis, result in the splitting of water molecules and release of oxygen, and provide energy to drive the Calvin cycle. (Chap. 8, p. 255)

lipids: food category consisting of fats and oils, which are either saturated and solid at room temperature, or are unsaturated and liquid at room temperature. (Chap. 7, p. 214)

lock-and-key model: model of how an enzyme works, describing the temporary formation of an enzyme-substrate complex, production of a new substance, and freeing of the unchanged enzyme. (Chap. 7, p. 220)

macrophages: giant phagocytes that destroy invading pathogens through the process of phagocytosis, and also engulf and destroy damaged cells. (Chap. 21, p. 635)

magma: molten material formed when rock of the lower crust is melted deep inside Earth's surface. (Chap. 12, p. 358)

magnetic resonance imaging (MRI): diagnostic tool that uses an artificial magnetic field to produce detailed images of the inside of the body, without the use of ionizing radiation. (Chap. 22, p. 685)

mass: measure of the amount of matter in an object, which depends on its number and types of atoms; more mass in an object will result in more weight. (Chap. 17, p. 512)

mass wasting: downhill movement of soils and rocks, which can move rapidly (landslides, mudflows) or slowly (creep), and can pose serious threats to living organisms and structures such as buildings and bridges. (Chap. 15, p. 452)

mechanical advantage: number of times a machine multiplies the effort force, which can help determine how to get the best mechanical advantage from simple machine features. (Chap. 17, p. 525)

metabolism: sum total of the body's anabolic and catabolic reactions, which is influenced by temperature, and whose rate can vary in individuals. (Chap. 8, p. 256)

metamorphic rock: type of rock formed when rocks are exposed to heat and high pressure, causing the material's properties and structure to change. (Chap. 12, p. 376)

migration: movement of petroleum from source rocks, through permeable rocks or sediments, and into a porous trap. (Chap. 13, p. 390)

momentum: product of the mass of an object times its velocity, which can change if an unbalanced force acts on it for some time. (Chap. 23, p. 709)

mudflow: swift movement of earth in a liquidlike flow that can destroy buildings, threaten living organisms, and cause flash floods. (Chap. 15, p. 456)

Newton's second law of motion: acceleration equals force divided by mass, or force equals mass times acceleration. (Chap. 23, p. 708)

niche: role of a species in a community and the way it uses the resources of its habitat to survive and reproduce; a single habitat can support many different species, but no two species can occupy the same niche. (Chap. 5, p. 146)

nitrogen fixation: process that changes atmospheric nitrogen into a form plants can use to begin synthesizing proteins; occurs naturally by nitrogen-fixing bacteria in plant roots and by lightning storms. (Chap. 8, p. 245)

noncommunicable disease: disease you can't catch from another person, but which can be inherited, result from an unhealthy lifestyle, or occur in reaction to something harmful in the environment. (Chap. 20, p. 616)

nonrenewable resources: natural resources, such as fossil fuels, gold, and topsoil, that cannot be replaced by nature or are consumed faster than they can be replaced or recycled by natural means. (Chap. 11, p. 331)

parallel circuit: has multiple paths for a current to flow through; its currents are independent and they add. (Chap. 19, p. 585)

GLOSSARY

parent material: type of rock—for example, granite or sandstone—that soils evolve from over time, and whose properties influence the composition of the soil. (Chap. 9, p. 272)

particulates: tiny, solid particles of soot, which are released by the inefficient burning of fossil fuels; particulates pollute the air and can cause lung damage. (Chap. 6, p. 188)

passive immunity: occurs when antibodies are transferred through the placenta or breast milk, or by injection of antibodies produced in an animal. (Chap. 21, p. 637)

passive transport: diffusion through a cell membrane by the movement of particles from areas of greater concentration to areas of lesser concentration—which, if defective, disrupts homeostasis. (Chap. 22, p. 674)

pasteurized: term used to describe milk heated to a certain temperature for a specific amount of time to kill bacteria and slow spoilage. (Chap. 10, p. 307)

pathogen: virus or living organism that causes disease, and that can spread from one person to another by direct contact, contaminated inanimate objects, water, air, and vectors. (Chap. 20, p. 607)

permeability: degree to which the open spaces, or pores, in rocks or sediments are connected; fluids flow easily through highly permeable materials. (Chap. 13, p. 394)

pesticide: chemical agent, such as an herbicide or insecticide, used to control or kill pests and protect hosts. (Chap. 10, p. 294)

petroleum: oil and natural gas gradually formed underground from the remains of living organisms. (Chap. 13, p. 386)

pH: unit of measure that shows how acidic or basic a solution is; acids have a pH below 7, bases have a pH above 7, and neutral solutions have a pH of 7. (Chap. 4, p. 136)

phagocyte: type of white blood cell that surrounds, engulfs, and destroys pathogens by chemically breaking them down, thus protecting the body against disease. (Chap. 21, p. 635)

photosynthesis: process by which organisms such as green plants produce food by a series of chemical reactions and release oxygen as waste. (Chap. 8, p. 254)

physical weathering: in soil formation, the process that breaks down rocks into smaller and smaller pieces—without affecting their chemical makeup—by freezing, thawing, striking, and rubbing. (Chap. 9, p. 268)

plastics: group of natural organic or synthetic materials that can be processed with heat and pressure into a variety of shapes and strengths, and used as insulators, textiles, and siding. (Chap. 16, p. 498)

polar molecule: a molecule with a positively charged end and a negatively charged end. (Chap. 4, p. 134)

pollution: harmful environmental contamination from natural sources, such as volcanos, and from human activities, such as the inefficient burning of fossil fuels. (Chap. 6, p. 187)

population: group of individuals of the same species adapted to the living conditions of a specific area. (Chap. 4, p. 116)

porosity: amount of open space, or pores, between the grains of rocks or sediments, which controls how much fluid they can hold. (Chap. 13, p. 391)

potential difference: energy change, measured in volts, for each unit of electrical charge; power used by an electrical device is calculated by multiplying the potential difference across it by the current passing through it. (Chap. 19, p. 569)

power: rate at which work can be done, which can be calculated by the following equation: Power = Work/Time. (Chap. 17, p. 524)

primary succession: establishment of a new community whose gradual growth causes changes in the environment—which can then support new species—and that begins with colonization of a bare, rocky area by hardy pioneer organisms, such as lichens. (Chap. 6, p. 186)

propellant: solid or liquid chemical fuel used to fire a rocket. (Chap. 25, p. 779)

proteins: food category consisting of amino acid polymers; proteins help maintain a healthy body and are found in such foods as dried beans, fish, meat, and cheese. (Chap. 7, p. 216)

R

radiation: transfer of energy from the sun to Earth's surface by electromagnetic waves. (Chap. 2, p. 53)

recyclable resource: material, such as glass, plastic, and steel, that can be reprocessed and remanufactured into new items. (Chap. 11, p. 345)

recycling: process in which natural resources are reused, involving the collection, sorting, and cleaning of waste materials, which are then remanufactured and marketed. (Chap. 14, p. 420)

regional metamorphism: occurs when an entire region is exposed to high pressures and heat, and rocks change in crystal size and composition. (Chap. 12, p. 377)

reinforced concrete: concrete strengthened with steel rods so it can withstand tension forces in addition to compression stress. (Chap. 16, p. 490)

relative humidity: amount of moisture in the air compared with the amount of moisture the air could hold at that specific temperature; percentage of relative humidity increases in cooling, low-pressure air masses and decreases in warming, high-pressure air masses. (Chap. 1, p. 26)

renewable resource: natural resource, such as trees and nitrogen, that can be recycled or replaced by nature in 100 years or less. (Chap. 11, p. 335)

reservoirs: porous traps with permeable reservoir rocks, such as limestone, and a seal, such as shale, that keeps migrating petroleum in the trap. (Chap. 13, p. 394)

resistance: property of a conductor, such as copper or Nichrome wire, to convert electricity to thermal energy as charges passing through it experience friction. (Chap. 19, p. 584)

reusable resources: resources—for example, water and glass jars—that can be used over and over again in their original form. (Chap. 11, p. 345)

rock cycle: crustal recycling in which one type of rock is transformed into another type of rock by forces, such as heat, pressure, or weathering. (Chap. 12, p. 379)

S

salinity: salt concentration in bodies of water; changes in salinity can harm an ecosystem and destroy living organisms. (Chap. 3, p. 98)

sanitary landfill: giant hole in the ground into which most municipal solid waste is dumped, and whose organic material is decomposed by microorganisms and whose leachate is drained off. (Chap. 14, p. 416)

secondary succession: process through which an ecosystem recovers from disasters, such as floods or fires, and which occurs more quickly than primary succession because seeds and fertile soil are already present. (Chap. 6, p. 186)

sedimentary rocks: type of rock that is formed from the weathered remains of other rocks, decayed plants, and animals, which are cemented together, concentrating important materials. (Chap. 12, p. 369)

seismic profile: computer-generated picture of rocks below Earth's surface, which helps to identify areas likely to contain petroleum deposits. (Chap. 13, p. 400)

seismic prospecting: echo-sounding technique, used by geologists searching for oil and natural gas, that shows the rock layers below Earth's surface. (Chap. 13, p. 396)

selective: type of pesticide that will kill or control only specific pests—an example of a selective rodenticide is one that will kill rats, but won't harm other rodents. (Chap. 10, p. 295)

series circuit: has only one path for current to flow through, and whose current decreases when resistance is increased. (Chap. 19, p. 580)

shear stress: results when opposite but equal forces, which are not directly aligned with each other, cause a solid to twist out of shape or break. (Chap. 16, p. 482)

simple machine: device, such as a wedge or pulley, that does work with one movement and can multiply a force, change its direction, or multiply its distance, but does not reduce the work required. (Chap. 17, p. 525)

soil: mixture that evolves from weathered rock and whose characteristics depend on rainfall, temperature, topography, type of parent material, soil organisms, and organic content. (Chap. 9, p. 264)

soil profile: vertical section of soil layers, called horizons, that show the different evolutionary stages of a particular soil based on color, organic content, texture, and moisture. (Chap. 9. p. 275)

solar energy: Earth's most important source of renewable energy, which can be harnessed for such uses as the production of electricity and the heating of homes. (Chap. 11, p. 340)

solute: substance that dissolves in a solvent—for example, powdered laundry detergent (the solute) dissolves when added to water (the solvent). (Chap. 4, p. 134)

solution: mixture in which one substance (the solute) is dissolved in another substance (the solvent). (Chap. 4, p. 134)

solvent: liquid in which a solute dissolves; water is called the universal solvent because so many different substances can dissolve in it. (Chap. 4, p. 134)

source reduction: reducing the amount of waste produced—buying one large size of a packaged item instead of many smaller sizes. (Chap. 14, p. 435)

source rocks: rocks in which petroleum is formed in small amounts over a long period of time. (Chap. 13, p. 386)

species: group of closely related organisms that interbreed and produce fertile offspring. (Chap. 4, p. 117)

specific heat: amount of energy that raises the temperature of 1 kg of a substance by 1 kelvin. (Chap. 18, p. 558)

specific impulse: measure, expressed in seconds, that is used to rate solid-fuel and liquid-fuel propellants. (Chap. 25, p. 782)

stages: series of fuel-containing rockets built one on top of the other to increase the amount of energy available to a spacecraft. (Chap. 25, p. 788)

station model: shows weather around a reporting station, represented by international symbols on a weather map. (Chap. 1, p. 39)

storm surge: wall of water formed when a mound of ocean water builds up in the low-pressure eye of a hurricane. (Chap. 3, p. 90)

substrate: specific molecule that fits into an area of an enzyme called the active site, and that can produce new substances through enzyme-assisted chemical reactions. (Chap. 7, p. 220)

succession: gradual change in the makeup of an ecological community as one set of populations slowly replaces another. (Chap. 6, p. 186)

symbiosis: long-term, close relationship between two or more species that often involves obtaining or conserving energy; parasitism, mutualism, and commensalism are symbiotic relationships. (Chap. 5, p. 154)

trophic level: feeding step in a food chain occupied by organisms that obtain energy in similar ways. (Chap. 5, p. 157)

tropical depression: low-pressure tropical air mass that may develop into a hurricane in the presence of light winds, warm water, and high humidity. (Chap. 2, p. 70)

vaccine: substance containing killed or weakened pathogens or their toxins; stimulates active immunity against disease. (Chap. 21, p. 648)

vector: insect or non-human animal that carries a disease-causing pathogen to a host. (Chap. 20, p. 614)

volt: unit that measures potential difference; the power rating of an appliance calculated by the following equation: Power = Current × Voltage. (Chap. 19, p. 569)

T cell: type of white blood cell, produced in the bone marrow and developed in the thymus; helper T cells, memory T cells, and killer T cells are important in cellular immunity. (Chap. 21, p. 640)

tensile stress: results when opposite but equal forces are applied, causing a solid to lengthen. (Chap. 16, p. 482)

terminal speed: constant falling speed of an object when all forces on it are balanced. (Chap. 23, p. 714)

thermal conductor: material, such as copper or gold, that transfers heat easily. (Chap. 18, p. 548)

thermal insulator: material, such as plastic foam or wool, that blocks conduction and heat transfer by air, which is trapped in small pockets. (Chap. 18, p. 548)

thin film: thin coating—usually of metal bonded to an underlying surface, such as glass—that is used to control energy transfer. (Chap. 16, p. 503)

thrust: the forward force of air on a plane's propeller, which is needed to balance drag. (Chap. 23, p. 708)

topography: natural features of a land surface, such as hills and valleys, which influence the rate of physical and chemical weathering and formation of soils. (Chap. 9, p. 272)

transpiration: in Earth's water cycle, the process of evaporation in which water absorbed by plant roots is released back into the atmosphere through plant leaves. (Chap. 5, p. 164)

weather: atmospheric conditions of a specific place on Earth at a given time; runs on energy from the sun. (Chap. 2, p. 52)

weathering: the first step in the formation of soil, which begins with the breaking down of rock and mineral matter by physical or chemical processes. (Chap. 9, p. 265)

weight: measure of the effect of gravity on an object, depending on its mass and location. (Chap. 17, p. 511)

wing loading: number that indicates how effectively the wing of a bird or plane produces lift, and that can be calculated by dividing the weight by the wing area. (Chap. 24, p. 737)

wingspan: the distance between both wing tips, which some planes and birds can reduce along with wing area, resulting in greater wing loading and higher speed. (Chap. 24, p. 738)

work: measure of the transfer of energy through motion, which can be calculated by the following equation: Work = Force × Distance. (Chap. 17, p. 520)

X ray: imaging technology that uses high-energy electromagnetic radiation to produce two-dimensional images of the body. (Chap. 22, p. 682)

xylem: tubelike cells strengthened by cellulose that carry water in plants; gives wood its strength. (Chap. 16, p. 485)

SPANISH GLOSSARY

This glossary defines each key term that appears in bold type in the text. It also indicates the chapter number and page number where you will find the word used.

abiotic factors/factores abióticos: características inanimadas en un ambiente (Cap. 4, pág. 126)

acceleration/aceleración: razón a la cual cambia la velocidad (Cap. 23, pág. 702)

acid/ácido: solución que contiene más iones de hidrógeno que de hidróxido (Cap. 4, pág. 136)

acid precipitation/precipitación ácida: precipitación, con alto contenido de óxidos nitroso y sulfuroso, que es más ácida que la precipitación que no ha sido contaminada (Cap. 6, pág. 189)

active immunity/inmunidad activa: ocurre cuando el cuerpo, por sí solo, produce sustancias llamadas anticuerpos que destruyen patógenos específicos a los cuales ha sido expuesto (Cap. 21, pág. 637)

active transport/transporte activo: proceso de bombear partículas desde un área de menor concentración hasta otra de mayor concentración (Cap. 22, pág. 675)

air mass/masa de aire: una gran cantidad de aire que posee características similares en toda su extensión (Cap. 2, pág. 69)

alleles/alelos: diferentes formas de un gene (Cap. 20, pág. 620)

alloy/aleación: mezcla de dos o más elementos en la que por lo menos uno de ellos es un metal (Cap. 14, pág. 427)

amino acids/aminoácidos: se forma cuando un átomo de carbono se enlaza covalentemente con un átomo de hidrógeno un grupo amino, un grupo carboxílico y uno R (Cap. 7, pág. 216)

ampere/amperio: cantidad usada para medir la corriente (Cap. 19, pág. 576)

anabolic reaction/reacción anabólica: reacción que requiere energía durante el metabolismo y que acumula moléculas complejas (Cap. 8, pág. 256)

analgesic/analgésico: grupo de drogas que alivian el dolor sin pérdida la conciencia (Cap. 21, pág. 654)

antibiotic/antibiótico: sustancia producida por microorganismos, generalmente bacterias u hongos, la cual mata o retarda el crecimiento de otros microorganismos (Cap. 21, pág. 652)

antibodies/anticuerpos: moléculas producidas, por ciertas clases de glóbulos blancos, las cuales neutralizan o destruyen químicamente los antígenos (Cap. 21, pág. 639)

antibody immunity/inmunidad humoral: uno de los métodos en que se usan los anticuerpos junto con células B para destruir patógenos específicos (Cap. 21, pág. 640)

antigen/antígeno: cualquier molécula extraña para el cuerpo (Cap. 21, pág. 639)

antioxidant/antioxidante: compuesto que previene o decelera las reacciones con el oxígeno (Cap. 10, pág. 302)

aspect ratio/proporción dimensional: razón entre el largo y el promedio del ancho de la envergadura (Cap. 24, pág. 738)

autoimmune disease/enfermedad autoinmunológica: condición en que el sistema inmunológico del cuerpo ataca sus propias células (Cap. 21, pág. 643)

autotroph/autótrofo: organismo que puede fabricar su propio alimento (Cap. 5, pág. 148)

barometric pressure/presión atmosférica: medida de la presión causada por el peso de la atmósfera (Cap. 1, pág. 27)

base/base: solución que contiene más iones de hidróxido que de hidrógeno (Cap. 4, pág. 136)

B cells/células B: glóbulos blancos especiales producidos en la médula ósea (Cap. 21, pág. 640)

Bernoulli effect/efecto de Bernoulli: dice que cuando el aire se mueve con más rapidez, ejerce menos presión (Cap. 23, pág. 722)

biological control/control biológico: método mediante el cual se utilizan organismos vivos, tales como predadores, parásitos y microbios, o productos extraídos de tales organismos, para controlar insectos nocivos (Cap. 10, pág. 299)

biotic factors/factores bióticos: organismos que forman la parte viva de un ecosistema (Cap. 4, pág. 116)

biotic potential/potencial biótico: la tasa más alta de reproducción bajo condiciones ideales (Cap. 6, pág. 174)

blocking high/zona anticiclónica bloqueante: masa de aire de alta presión que hace que un huracán cambie de dirección (Cap. 2, pág. 74)

Bowen's reaction series/serie de la reacción de Bowen: orden en que se cristalizan los minerales en el magma (Cap. 12, pág. 364)

calorie/caloría: cantidad de energía necesaria para aumentar, en un 1°C, la temperatura de un gramo de agua (Cap. 7, pág. 211)

Calvin cycle/ciclo de Calvin: conjunto de reacciones químicas que ocurren durante la fotosíntesis y que producen azúcares simples usando energía de las reacciones luminosas y CO_2 del aire (Cap. 8, pág. 255)

carbohydrate/carbohidrato: un azúcar simple o un polímero compuesto de azúcares simples (Cap. 7, pág. 212)

carrying capacity/capacidad de carga: el mayor número de individuos que un ambiente puede soportar continuamente (Cap. 6, pág. 175)

catabolic reaction/reacción catabólica: reacción durante la cual se libera energía, en forma de moléculas que almacenan energía, debido a la ruptura de moléculas complejas (Cap. 8, pág. 256)

cellular immunity/inmunidad celular: respuesta inmunológica que involucra macrófagos, antígenos y células T, pero no involucra ni células B ni anticuerpos que se disuelven en la sangre (Cap. 21, pág. 642)

cellular respiration/respiración celular: proceso que usa la mayoría de los organismos para convertir, en energía utilizable, la energía almacenada en la glucosa (Cap. 8, pág. 256)

cellulose/celulosa: carbohidrato formado por las plantas a partir de la glucosa; las moléculas de celulosa forman una estructura dura y rígida que compone las paredes celulares de las plantas (Cap. 8, pág. 241)

center of gravity/centro de gravedad: el centro de distribución de peso de un objeto (Cap. 17, pág. 514)

ceramic/cerámica: arcilla seca o materiales que parecen arcilla son duros y quebradizos y resisten el color y la intemperie (Cap. 16, pág. 500)

chemical sedimentary rock/roca sedimentaria química: se forma directamente de los minerales disueltos en agua (Cap. 12, pág. 369)

chemical weathering/meteorización química: ocurre cuando el agua, el aire y otras sustancias reaccionan con los minerales en las rocas y cambian la composición de estas últimas (Cap. 9, pág. 269)

chlorophyll/clorofila: pigmento verde en los cloroplastos de las células vegetales que absorbe energía solar y refleja ondas luminosas verdes (Cap. 8, pág. 254)

chloroplasts/cloroplastos: estructuras celulares vegetales que contienen el pigmento verde clorofila (Cap. 8, pág. 254)

clastic sedimentary rocks/rocas sedimentarias clásticas: las que se forman de fragmentos de rocas (Cap. 12, pág. 370)

climax community/comunidad clímax: una comunidad madura y estable que cambia muy poco (Cap. 6, pág. 186)

combustion/combustión: proceso de quema en que los hidrocarburos reaccionan con el oxígeno formando dióxido de carbono y agua, y en el cual se produce energía cuando los enlaces de carbonos se rompen y se forman nuevamente, produciendo monóxido de carbono como desecho (Cap. 13, pág. 404)

communicable disease/enfermedad contagiosa: enfermedad causada por patógenos que se puede difundir de una persona a otra (Cap. 20, pág. 607)

community/comunidad: un grupo de poblaciones en un área que interactúan entre sí (Cap. 4, pág. 123)

compression stress/estrés de compresión: resulta cuando se aplican dos fuerzas a través de un sólido, las cuales se empujan una hacia la otra (Cap. 16, pág. 482)

conduction/conducción: la transferencia de calor entre objetos en contacto (Cap. 2, pág. 52)

conodonts/conodontes: restos fósiles en forma de dientes que se encuentran en las rocas sedimentarias marinas que se formaron en el período entre hace 525 y 225 millones de años (Cap. 13, pág. 388)

contact metamorphism/metamorfismo de contacto: cuando el magma caliente de las intrusiones ígneas hace que se calienten las rocas de los alrededores, lo que causa el cambio o la fusión de los minerales en las rocas (Cap. 12, pág. 376)

convection/convección: transferencia de calor dentro de un fluido debido al movimiento del fluido desde áreas más calientes a áreas más frías (Cap. 2, pág. 56)

convection cell/célula de convección: región de un fluido en la cual se mantiene una corriente de convección (Cap. 2, pág. 57)

Coriolis effect/efecto de Coriolis: la desviación de un objeto que se mueve desde su posición original, vista por un observador desde la superficie terrestre (Cap. 2, pág. 60)

cracking/termofraccionamiento: proceso que usa altas temperaturas y sustancias químicas especiales para separar las cadenas largas de hidrocarburos en compuestos más útiles como la gasolina (Cap. 13, pág. 404)

creep/corrimiento: movimiento lento y fluido de tierra cuesta abajo (Cap. 15, pág. 453)

current/corriente: una medida del número de cargas que se mueven a través de cualquier lugar a lo largo de un circuito por segundo (Cap. 19, pág. 572)

D

decomposer/descomponedor: heterótrofo que descompone los compuestos complejos de organismos en proceso de descomposición o de decaimiento, en moléculas más simples (Cap. 5, pág. 150)

Delaney Clause/Cláusula de Delaney: regula más estrictamente el uso de sustancias químicas en la elaboración de alimentos (Cap. 10, pág. 303)

denaturation/desnaturalización: proceso mediante el cual se desenrollan las cadenas de aminoácidos cuando son sometidas al calor (Cap. 10, pág. 312)

dew point/punto de rocío: condensación formada cuando el aire se enfría a una temperatura en que ya no puede retener más humedad (Cap. 1, pág. 27)

digestion/digestión: proceso de descomponer el alimento en moléculas más pequeñas que pueden absorber las células corporales (Cap. 7, pág. 224)

disease/enfermedad: un cambio en el cuerpo que altera la homeostasis y perjudica una o más de las funciones esenciales del cuerpo (Cap. 20, pág. 604)

disease cluster/grupo de enfermedades: cuando las enfermedades ocurren con un patrón de distribución agregado y no al azar en la población (Cap. 22, pág. 666)

dispersal/dispersión: diseminación de semillas sobre una extensa área (Cap. 24, pág. 755)

diversity/diversidad: una medida del número de especies que moran en un ecosistema (Cap. 4, pág. 117)

Doppler radar/radar Doppler: usa señales radiales para detectar la ubicación, dirección y velocidad de los vientos en una tormenta y si la precipitación se mueve hacia la estación de radar o si se aleja de ella (Cap. 1, pág. 35)

drag/arrastre: la fuerza del aire sobre un objeto en movimiento (Cap. 23, pág. 715)

E

ecosystem/ecosistema: interacción de todos los organismos vivos con los factores inanimados en un área dada,

cuya energía proviene del flujo de energía (Cap. 4, pág. 116)

efficiency/eficiencia: describe la capacidad de una máquina para convertir el trabajo de entrada en trabajo de salida útil (Cap. 17, pág. 528)

electromagnetic spectrum/espectro electromagnético: colección de longitudes de ondas electromagnéticas (Cap. 25, pág. 766)

electromagnetic wave/onda electromagnética: alteración en los campos magnéticos y eléctricos que transmiten energía a través del espacio a la velocidad de la luz (Cap. 25, pág. 766)

electron-sea model/modelo del mar de electrones: una manera simple de explicar la mayoría de las propiedades metálicas como la resistencia, la flexibilidad y la durabilidad (Cap. 16, pág. 491)

electrophoresis/electroforesis: método de identificación de sustancias biológicas mediante el análisis de sus propiedades eléctricas y químicas o electroquímicas (Cap. 22, pág. 678)

endemic disease/enfermedad endémica: enfermedad que siempre está presente en una población (Cap. 22, pág. 672)

energy resources/recursos energéticos: incluyen todos los materiales usados para producir energía (Cap. 11, pág. 332)

enzyme/enzima: proteína que cataliza, o acelera, las reacciones químicas (Cap. 7, pág. 219)

epidemic/epidemia: ocurre cuando grandes números de personas que viven en la misma área contraen la misma enfermedad (Cap. 22, pág. 672)

erosion/erosión: proceso que mueve las rocas meteorizadas de un lugar a otro (Cap. 9, pág. 285)

evacuate/evacuar: cuando se le pide a la gente que abandone un área en donde ha ocurrido o posiblemente ocurra un desastre de la naturaleza (Cap. 3, pág. 85)

evaporation/evaporación: el cambio de un líquido en un gas (Cap. 2, pág. 58)

exponential growth/crecimiento exponencial: ocurre cuando una población aumenta un cierto porcentaje fijo cada año (Cap. 6, pág. 173)

extrusive igneous rock/roca ígnea extrusiva: se forma cuando la lava se enfría rápidamente sobre la superficie terrestre (Cap. 12, pág. 359)

F

fault/falla: una fractura grande en la corteza terrestre a lo largo de la cual ha ocurrido movimiento (Cap. 15, pág. 470)

floodplain/llanura aluvial: área llana y baja en las cercanías de una corriente de agua, la cual está cubierta de sedimentos provenientes de la corriente (Cap. 15, pág. 465)

food chain/cadena alimenticia: un modelo que usan los científicos para indicar cómo fluye la energía a través de los ecosistemas (Cap. 5, pág. 156)

food web/red alimenticia: un modelo que expresa todas las posibles relaciones alimenticias dentro de un ecosistema (Cap. 5, pág. 158)

fossil fuel/combustible fósil: combustible formado de los restos de organismos marinos enterrados debajo de capas de tierra durante millones de años (Cap. 11, pág. 332)

friction/fricción: una fuerza que se opone al movimiento entre dos superficies que están en contacto (Cap. 17, pág. 534)

G

geophone/geófono: detector especial que recoge las ondas sonoras reflejadas de las rocas debajo de la corteza terrestre en la exploración sísmica (Cap. 13, pág. 400)

geostationary satellite/satélite geodésico: satélite que permanece sobre el mismo punto por encima de la superficie terrestre (Cap. 1, pág. 33)

gravity/gravedad: fuerza de atracción hacia la Tierra que experimenta todo objeto con masa (Cap. 23, pág. 711)

gust/ráfaga (de viento): aumento repentino en la velocidad del viento que causa daño a los edificios y que puede arrancar árboles grandes del suelo (Cap. 3, pág. 87)

H

Haber process/proceso de Haber: proceso que utiliza tanto altas temperaturas como altas presiones, junto con un catalítico, para producir amoníaco directamente a partir de nitrógeno e hidrógeno (Cap. 8, pág. 248)

habitat/hábitat: la ubicación física en la cual viven los organismos (Cap. 5, pág. 145)

heat/calor: energía transferida desde un objeto con una temperatura mayor a otro con una temperatura menor (Cap. 2, pág. 52)

heat pumps/bombas de calor: aparatos que mueven el calor de un lugar a otro (Cap. 18, pág. 554)

heterotroph/heterótrofo: organismo que depende de otros organismos para obtener nutrientes y energía (Cap. 5, pág. 149)

heterozygous/heterocigoso: un organismo que tiene dos alelos diferentes para un rasgo y que es portador de dicho rasgo (Cap. 20, pág. 620)

homeostasis/homeostasis: capacidad que tienen los organismos vivos de mantener un ambiente interno estable sin importar los cambios en el ambiente externo (Cap. 20, pág. 600)

homozygous/homocigoso: un organismo que tiene dos alelos idénticos para un rasgo (Cap. 20, pág. 620)

humus/humus: material que consiste principalmente en plantas y animales muertos y en proceso de descomposición, los cuales una vez vivieron en el suelo (Cap. 9, pág. 273)

hydrolysis/hidrólisis: separación de una molécula por medio de una reacción química que involucra añadir agua (Cap. 7, pág. 225)

I

ice wedging/grietas debido al hielo: cuando el agua penetra en las grietas de las rocas y se congela y se expande (Cap. 9, pág. 268)

igneous rock/roca ígnea: se forma cuando el material caliente derretido se enfría y se solidifica en forma de roca sólida (Cap. 12, pág. 358)

incinerator/incinerador: hornos grandes en que se quema la basura sólida a temperaturas de casi 1300°C (2400°F) (Cap. 14, pág. 417)

inertia/inercia: la tendencia de un objeto a resistir cambios en su movimiento (Cap. 17, pág. 511)

inflammatory response/respuesta inflamatoria: primera reacción curativa local del cuerpo a una infección o daño (Cap. 21, pág. 635)

inhibitors/inhibidors: aditivos alimenticios comunes como el BHT y el BHA que retardan un proceso químico (Cap. 10, pág. 303)

insulator/aislador: material a través del cual el calor y la electricidad no pueden fluir fácilmente (Cap. 16, pág. 498)

interspecific competition/competencia entrespecífica: competencia entre diferentes especies (Cap. 6, pág. 179)

intrusive igneous rock/roca ígnea intrusiva: se forma cuando el magma se enfría debajo de la tierra (Cap. 12, pág. 362)

isobars/isobaras: líneas que se dibujan para conectar áreas que tienen la misma presión atmosférica, de acuerdo con el código meteorológico (Cap. 1, pág. 40)

kilowatt-hour/kilovatio-hora: energía eléctrica que usa un artefacto si recibe la energía a razón de 1000 W por hora (Cap. 19, pág. 576)

Koch's postulates/postulados de Koch: conjunto de cuatro pasos experimentales para determinar el tipo de patógeno que causa una enfermedad en particular (Cap. 22, pág. 668)

landslide/derrumbe: movimiento rápido cuesta abajo de tierra y rocas (Cap. 15, pág. 452)

law of action and reaction/ley de acción y reacción: tercera ley de Newton que dice que por cada fuerza de acción existe una fuerza de reacción igual y opuesta (Cap. 17, pág. 519)

law of conservation of energy/ley de conservación de la energía: establece que la energía no se puede crear ni destruir mediante procesos químicos común y corrientes, la energía simplemente cambia de forma (Cap. 8, pág. 251)

law of conservation of matter/ley de conservación de la materia: enuncia que los átomos no son ni creados ni destruidos durante una reacción química, simplemente son reordenados (Cap. 8, pág. 238)

lift/despegue: fuerza ascendente que el aire ejerce sobre las alas de un ave o avión (Cap. 23, pág. 719)

light microscope/microscopio óptico: instrumento que utiliza rayos de luz y lentes para producir una imagen aumentada de un objeto (Cap. 22, pág. 680)

light reactions/reacciones luminosas: la primera de las partes del proceso de fotosíntesis; resulta en la conversión de la energía luminosa en forma de energía química (Cap. 8, pág. 255)

lipid/lípido: categoría de alimentos que consisten en grasas y aceites ya sea saturados y sólidos o no saturados y líquidos a temperatura ambiente (Cap. 7, pág. 214)

lock-and-key model/modelo de llave y cerradura: modelo que utilizan los científicos para entender cómo interactúan las enzimas en una reacción química (Cap. 7, pág. 220)

macrophage/macrófago: el más grande de los fagocitos, traga tanto las células que han sufrido daño como también grandes cantidades de patógenos invasores (Cap. 21, pág. 635)

magma/magma: material derretido del cual se forman las rocas (Cap. 12, pág. 358)

magnetic resonance imaging/formación de imágenes mediante resonancia magnética: usa electricidad y magnetismo en lugar de rayos X u ondas sonoras para crear imágenes de órganos y tejidos excepcionalmente nítidas (Cap. 22, pág. 685)

mass/masa: una medida de la cantidad de materia en un objeto (Cap. 17, pág. 512)

mass wasting/erosión en masa: cualquier movimiento cuesta abajo de tierra o rocas debido a la gravedad (Cap. 15, pág. 452)

mechanical advantage/ventaja mecánica: el número de veces que una máquina multiplica el tamaño de la fuerza de esfuerzo (Cap. 17, pág. 525)

metabolism/metabolismo: la suma de todas las reacciones químicas tanto anabólicas como catabólicas dentro de un organismo (Cap. 8, pág. 256)

metamorphic rock/roca metamórfica: tipo de roca que se forma cuando las rocas se ven expuestas a altas presiones y altas temperaturas causando un cambio en sus propiedades y estructura (Cap. 12, pág. 376)

migration/migración: el movimiento de petróleo desde la roca madre hasta la roca almacén (Cap. 13, pág. 390)

momentum/momento: el producto de la masa y la velocidad de un objeto (Cap. 23, pág. 709)

mudflow/corriente de lodo: un tipo de movimiento de tierra que ocurre en laderas empinadas o en áreas con tierra empantanada (Cap. 15, pág. 456)

Newton's second law of motion/segunda ley de movimiento de Newton: relación entre la fuerza, la masa y la aceleración (Cap. 23, pág. 708)

niche/nicho: la forma en que una especie usa los recursos en su hábitat y su función en la comunidad (Cap. 5, pág. 146)

nitrogen fixation/fijación del nitrógeno: proceso que cambia el gas nitrógeno en compuestos que pueden utilizar las plantas (Cap. 8, pág. 245)

noncommunicable disease/enfermedad no contagiosa: enfermedad que no la causa un patógeno y que no se puede diseminar de una persona a otra (Cap. 20, pág. 616)

nonrenewable resources/recursos no renovables: recursos naturales que no se pueden reciclar ni renovar por la naturaleza (Cap. 11, pág. 331)

parallel circuit/circuito en paralelo: circuito que provee trayectorias múltiples para la corriente (Cap. 19, pág. 585)

parent material/material madre: tipo de roca del cual se origina el suelo (Cap. 9, pág. 272)

particulate/macropartículas: partículas pequeñas y sólidas de hollín que resultan de la quema de combustibles fósiles (Cap. 6, pág. 188)

passive immunity/inmunidad pasiva: ocurre cuando los anticuerpos son producidos por otra fuente y luego son transferidos dentro del cuerpo (Cap. 21, pág. 637)

passive transport/transporte pasivo: cuando la difusión se lleva a cabo a través de una membrana celular en el cuerpo desde un área de mayor concentración a otra de menor concentración (Cap. 22, pág. 674)

pasteurize/pasteurizar: tratamiento de someter la leche a altas temperaturas para retardar su deterioro y prolongar su frescura (Cap. 10, pág. 307)

pathogen/patógeno: virus u organismo microscópico que causa enfermedad (Cap. 20, pág. 607)

permeability/permeabilidad: la cantidad de conexiones entre los poros de un material (Cap. 13, pág. 394)

pesticide/insecticida: un agente químico que controla o elimina insectos nocivos o indeseados (Cap. 10, pág. 294)

petroleum/petróleo: reciclaje natural de los restos de organismos que una vez estuvieron vivos, la mayoría de los cuales eran microscópicos (Cap. 13, pág. 386)

pH/pH: unidad que se usa para medir la acidez o la basicidad de una sustancia (Cap. 4, pág. 136)

phagocyte/fagocito: glóbulos blancos sanguíneos que rodean, tragan y consumen partículas extrañas (Cap. 21, pág. 635)

photosynthesis/fotosíntesis: proceso mediante el cual las plantas y las algas verdes absorben energía luminosa y la convierten en energía química que es almacenada en las moléculas de glucosa en las células de estos organismos (Cap. 8, pág. 254)

physical weathering/meteorización física: cambia las rocas y los materiales minerales en fragmentos más pequeños, sin cambiarles su composición química (Cap. 9, pág. 268)

plastic/plástico: material orgánico sintético o natural al que se le puede cambiar fácilmente, de forma al aplicarle presión y calor (Cap. 16, pág. 498)

polar molecule/molécula polar: molécula que tiene una carga negativa en uno de sus extremos y una carga positiva en el otro (Cap. 4, pág. 134)

pollution/contaminación: introducción desfavorable en el ambiente de un exceso de materiales de desecho (Cap. 6, pág. 187)

population/población: un grupo de organismos de la misma especie que viven en un área específica (Cap. 4, pág. 116)

porosity/porosidad: porcentaje de espacios vacíos en una roca o sedimento (Cap. 13, pág. 391)

potential difference/diferencia de potencial: cambio de energía por cada unidad de carga eléctrica (Cap. 19, pág. 569)

power/potencia: razón a la que se realiza trabajo (Cap. 17, pág. 524)

primary succession/sucesión primaria: formación de una nueva comunidad en un área que comenzó como tierras baldías (Cap. 6, pág. 186)

propellant/propulsor: combustible y oxidante que se usan en la propulsión de cohetes (Cap. 25, pág. 779)

proteins/proteínas: polímeros de aminoácidos que ayudan a mantener saludable el cuerpo (Cap. 7, pág. 216)

radiation/radiación: la transferencia de energía en forma de ondas electromagnéticas (Cap. 2, pág. 53)

recyclable resource/recurso reciclable: recurso que se puede procesar de nuevo y volver a usar en vez de ser desechado (Cap. 11, pág. 345)

recycling/reciclaje: proceso de recoger y separar los materiales de desecho, los cuales son procesados en nuevos materiales que pueden ser usados nuevamente (Cap. 14, pág. 420)

regional metamorphism/metamorfismo regional: cuando una región entera de masa continental se ve expuesta a altas temperaturas y altas presiones, lo cual causa que las rocas sufran cambios en su composición mineral y en el tamaño de los cristales (Cap. 12, pág. 377)

reinforced concrete/hormigón armado: el que contiene varillas de acero a todo lo largo de su extensión para que pueda soportar fuerzas de tensión y compresión (Cap. 16, pág. 490)

relative humidity/humedad relativa: una medida de la cantidad de vapor de agua en el aire, comparada con la cantidad de vapor que el aire puede retener a esa temperatura (Cap. 1, pág. 26)

renewable resource/recurso renovable: recurso natural que es reciclado o reemplazado por procesos naturales en menos de 100 años (Cap. 11, pág. 335)

reservoir/roca almacén: capa amplia de roca porosa y permeable que permite la acumulación del petróleo, porque se encuentra rodeada por otra capa rocosa impermeable (Cap. 13, pág. 394)

resistance/resistencia: propiedad que tiene un conductor de convertir la energía eléctrica en energía térmica a medida que la corriente lo atraviesa (Cap. 19, pág. 584)

reusable resource/recurso que se puede volver a usar: recurso que se puede volver a usar una y otra vez en su forma original (Cap. 11, pág. 345)

rock cycle/ciclo de las rocas: transformaciones de un tipo de roca a otro (Cap. 12, pág. 379)

salinity/salinidad: concentración de sal en el ambiente (Cap. 3, pág. 98)

sanitary landfill/vertedero controlado: hueco enorme en la tierra cubierto con un plástico o arcilla densa en el cual la basura se arroja, se comprime y se cubre diariamente con una capa delgada de tierra o de plástico (Cap. 14, pág. 416)

secondary successión/sucesión secundaria: la secuencia de cambios que tienen lugar cuando una comunidad clímax se ve alterada por procesos naturales o por las acciones de los humanos (Cap. 6, pág. 186)

sedimentary rock/roca sedimentaria: la que se forma cuando los sedimentos se acumulan o cementan (Cap. 12, pág. 369)

seismic profile/perfil sísmico: fotografía de las rocas subterráneas generada por una computadora a partir de los datos recogidos en la exploración sísmica (Cap. 13, pág. 400)

seismic prospecting/exploración sísmica: uso de ondas sonoras para construir fotografías de las rocas debajo de la corteza terrestre en la exploración petrolera (Cap. 13, pág. 396)

selective/selectivo: que es efectivo o mata solo a ciertos insectos (Cap. 10, pág. 295)

series circuit/circuito en serie: circuito que solo tiene una trayectoria a través de la cual pueden fluir las cargas eléctricas (Cap. 19, pág. 580)

shear stress/estrés de cizallamiento: ocurre cuando fuerzas opuestas e iguales actúan para cambiar la forma de un objeto debido a que las líneas de fuerza no están directamente alineadas unas con otras (Cap. 16, pág. 482)

simple machine/máquina simple: dispositivo que realiza trabajo con un solo tipo de movimiento (Cap. 17, pág. 525)

soil/suelo: una combinación de fragmentos de rocas y de materia mineral y orgánica, aire y agua (Cap. 9, pág. 264)

soil profile/perfil del suelo: una sección vertical a través del suelo que muestra los distintos horizontes del mismo y el material precursor del cual se originó (Cap. 9, pág. 275)

solar energy/energía solar: energía proveniente del Sol y la fuente más importante de energía renovable (Cap. 11, pág. 340)

solute/soluto: la sustancia que se disuelve en una solución (Cap. 4, pág. 134)

solution/solución: acción y efecto de disolver o disolverse una sustancia en otra (Cap. 4, pág. 134)

solvent/disolvente: líquido en el cual se disuelve el soluto (Cap. 4, pág. 134)

source reduction/reducción de origen: quiere decir simplemente la aminoración de los desperdicios que se producen (Cap. 14, pág. 435)

source rock/roca madre: roca en que se origina el petróleo y el gas (Cap. 13, pág. 386)

species/especie: un grupo de organismos estrechamente relacionados y que pueden aparearse uno con otro para producir progenie fértil (Cap. 4, pág. 117)

specific heat/calor específico: cantidad de energía necesaria para elevar, en un kelvin, la temperatura de un kilogramo de material (Cap. 18, pág. 558)

specific impulse/impulso específico: razón de impulso a peso que se utiliza como unidad de medida en propulsores (Cap. 25, pág. 782)

stages/fases: se aplica a la serie de cohetes que se construyen uno encima del otro para aumentar la cantidad de energía accesible en una nave espacial (Cap. 25, pág. 788)

station model/código meteorológico: cada conjunto de datos que describe el tiempo en una de las estaciones meteorológicas y que se convierte en un grupo de símbolos que representan información climatológica alrededor de esa estación en un mapa meteorológico (Cap. 1, pág. 39)

storm surge/marejada de tempestad: elevación insólita en el nivel del océano, la cual produce una pared de agua (Cap. 3, pág. 90)

substrate/sustrato: molécula específica que una enzima reconoce químicamente (Cap. 7, pág. 220)

succession/sucesión: cambio gradual en la estructura de una comunidad ecológica (Cap. 6, pág. 186)

symbiosis/simbiosis: es una relación estrecha y de largo tiempo entre dos o más especies (Cap. 5, pág. 154)

T cells/células T: glóbulos blancos producidos en la médula ósea que, a diferencia de las células B, maduran en el timo, un órgano pequeño ubicado exactamente arriba del corazón (Cap. 21, pág. 640)

tensile stress/estrés de tracción: cuando se aplican fuerzas opuestas igualmente (Cap. 16, pág. 482)

terminal speed/rapidez terminal: en cualquier cosa que cae hacia la Tierra, la fuerza de ascenso ejercida por el aire y la Tierra, es igual a la fuerza de gravedad que lo hace descender (Cap. 23, pág. 714)

thermal conductor/conductor térmico: material que transfiere bien el calor (Cap. 18, pág. 548)

thermal insulator/aislador térmico: material que no transmite bien el calor (Cap. 18, pág. 548)

thin film/película delgada: una capa fina de una sustancia, tal como un metal, que se aplica y adhiere a un material subyacente como el vidrio (Cap. 16, pág. 503)

thrust/empuje: fuerza de movimiento hacia adelante (Cap. 23, pág. 708)

topography/topografía: configuración natural de la superficie terrestre (Cap. 9, pág. 272)

transpiration/transpiración: la evaporación de agua de las hojas de una planta (Cap. 5, pág. 164)

trophic level/nivel trófico: un nivel alimenticio en una cadena alimenticia, constituido por especies que obtienen energía de maneras similares (Cap. 5, pág. 157)

tropical depression/depresión tropical: una masa de aire tropical de presión atmosférica baja, la cual se puede convertir en un huracán (Cap. 2, pág. 70)

vaccine/vacuna: sustancia compuesta de partes de patógenos o antígenos debilitados o muertos y la cual estimula al cuerpo a que desarrolle inmunidad activa a una enfermedad (Cap. 21, pág. 648)

vector/vector: un insecto o animal que transmite una enfermedad de un huésped a otro (Cap. 20, pág. 614)

volt/voltio: unidad que se usa para medir la diferencia de potencial (Cap. 19, pág. 569)

weather/tiempo: las condiciones de la atmósfera terrestre en un lugar particular en un momento dado (Cap. 2, pág. 52)

weathering/meteorización: proceso por el cual las rocas y los materiales minerales se rompen en fragmentos mediante cambios mecánicos o químicos (Cap. 9, pág. 265)

weight/peso: en la Tierra, es una medida de la fuerza de gravedad entre la Tierra y un objeto (Cap. 17, pág. 511)

wing loading/carga alar: carga por unidad de superficie de ala; se obtiene al dividir el peso entre el área del ala de un ave o de un avión, e indica la eficiencia con que un ala produce despegue (Cap. 24, pág. 737)

wingspan/envergadura: distancia entre ambos extremos de las alas de un avión o un ave (Cap. 24, pág. 738)

work/trabajo: cuando una fuerza mueve un objeto en la dirección de la fuerza (Cap. 17, pág. 520)

X rays/rayos X: una forma de radiación electromagnética que se usa para producir imágenes bidimensionales del cuerpo (Cap. 22, pág. 682)

xylem/xilema: células vegetales que transportan agua a través de la planta (Cap. 16, pág. 485)

INDEX

The Index for *Science Interactions* will help you locate major topics in the book quickly and easily. Each entry in the Index is followed by the numbers of the pages on which the entry is discussed. A page number given in **boldface type** indicates the page on which that entry is defined. A page number given in *italic type* indicates a page on which the entry is used in an illustration or photograph. The abbreviation *act.* indicates a page on which the entry is used in an activity.

cellular, **642,** *642*

   passive, **637,** *638*

Immunization, 646-649, *646*

Immunization schedule, 649

Impulse, 781-783

Incinerators, **417**-419, *417, 419*

Inclined planes, *529*

Independent variable, 9, 829-830

Inductive reasoning, 6

Industrialized agriculture, 242-243, *259*

Inertia, **511**-512

Inferring, 377

Inflammatory response, 634-**635,** *635,* 636, *636*

Influenza, *598-599,* 606, *607,* 649, 672, *679*

Inhibitor, in food, **303,** *303*

Inhibitor molecules, 221, *221*

Insecticidal soap, 300

Insecticides, *294,* 297-298, *297. See also* Pesticides

Insects, *139*

   as biological control, 300, *300*

   light and, *126*

   migration of, 188-189, *188*

   population size of, *173, 197*

   spread of disease and, 611, 612

   symbiotic relationships of, *154, 167*

   in urban ecosystems, *122*

Insulation, 545-550, *545, act.* 546-547, *549, 550*

Insulator, **498,** *498*

   thermal, **548,** *549, 563*

Insulin, *605, 675*

Integrated pest control (IPC), 299-300, *299, 300*

Interactions among organisms, *143, act.* 143, 144-159

Intercropping, *242, 243, 259*

Interspecific competition, **179**-181

Intrusion, layered, 364, *364*

Intrusive igneous rocks, **362**-363, *363, act.* 363

Ionic bonding, *210*

Ionic compound, 134, *135,* 136

Irradiated food, 308-309, *308, 309*

Isobar, **40,** *40*

Jenner, Edward, 646, *648*

Jets, 696-699, *698-699,* 751, *751, 752. See also* Aerodynamics; Airplanes

Joule (J), 520, 574, *576*

Journals, scientific, 13, *13, 15*

Keating, Joe, 418

Kerosene, 752

Khosla, Nutan, 574-575

Kilogram (kg), 512

Kilowatt-hour (kWh), **576,** *576, 589*

Koch, Robert, 670

Koch's postulates, **668,** *668-669*

Krebs, Hans Adolf, 232

Krebs cycle, 232

Kudzu, 160-161, *160*

Lactobacillus bacteria, *609*

Lamm, Richard D., 689

Landfills, sanitary, *act.* 414, **416**-417, *416*

Land resources, *334,* 335

Landsat photograph, *768, 791*

Landsat wavelength bands, 769

Landscaping, 548-549, *548, 549*

Landslides, **452,** *452*

Lava, 358, *358, 362*

Law of action and reaction, 518, **519**-520, *520*

Law of conservation of energy, **251**

Law of conservation of matter, **238**

Law of motion (Newton's second), **708,** 781

Layered intrusion, 364, *364*

Leachate, 416

Lead, 368, 430

Leaf litter, 144-145, *act.* 144, *145, act.* 155

Legumes, 244-245, *244, 259*

LeMone, Margaret, 62-63, *62, 63*

Leukemia, 652-653

Levers, *529,* 534

Lichens, *184,* 270

Lifestyle diseases, *616,* 617-618

Lift, *act.* 718, **719**-724, *719*

   angle of attack and, 724, *724, 729*

   Bernoulli effect and, **722,** *722*

   Coanda effect and, 723, *723*

   increasing, 720

   producing, 736-739

   stall speed and, 721

Light

   oxygen production and, *act.* 252-253, 254-255

   spectrum of, *254,* 766, *766*

   See also Sunlight

Light microscope, **680**-681, *681*

Lightning, 65, *65,* 91, 92-93, *92, 93*

Light reactions, 254-**255,** *255*

Limestone, 272, 486, 487

Lind, James, 258

Lipids, **214**-215, *214, act.* 214, *215*

   in body fluids, *674*

   digestion of, 229, *229*

Liquid-fueled rockets, 785, *785*

Literature features, 76, 138, 352, 474

Living ecosystems, *act.* 115, 116-123

Lizards, *130, 139*

Lock-and-key model, **220**

Logging, *124, 187,* 338-339

"Logging the well," 400-401, *401*

Lorenz, Edward, 44

Lungs, asbestos in, *188*

Lyme disease, 608-609, 667

Machines

   compound, 529, *529,* 534-535

   efficiency of, **528,** *528*

   friction and, **535,** *535*

   ideal mechanical advantage of, **525**-526, *528, 529*

   simple, *act.* 509, **525**-527, *529, 534*

Macrophages, *630,* **635,** *636, act.* 638, *640*

Magma, **358,** *358, 362,* 364

Magnet, *act.* 686

Magnetic resonance imaging (MRI), **685**-689, *687, 688, 691*

Malaria, 611-612, *611*

Credits

Illustrations

Computer Group/Morgan-Cain & Associates (t) 137; **John Edwards** xii, 64, 71, 90, 159, 168, 272, 364, 365, 397, 416, 417, 419, 471, 510, 552, 554, 558, 559, 563, 564, 643, 741, 745, 770, 771, 779, 784, 785, 788-789, 833; **David Fisher/Morgan-Cain & Associates** 452, 466; **Chris Forey/Morgan-Cain & Associates** 358, 359, 367, 376, 379, 381; **Tom Galiano** 52, 58, 135, (t) 137, (b) 140, 208, 209, 210, 215, 203, 297, 317, 319, 366, 491, 569, 572, 573, 576, 580, 584, 586, 587, 589, (t) 595, 604, 619, 620, 654, 679, 680, 708, 711, 718, 720, 722, 723, 724, 725, 729, 780, 781, 808; **Barbara Hoops** 802; **Tom Kennedy/Romark Illustration** 5, 12, 14, 16, 39, 40, 47, 48, (t) 60, 69, 72, 73, 74, (bl) 77, 78, 83, 106, (t) 140, 155, 169, 173, 175, 177, 180, 198, 212-213, 214, 216, 217, 220, 221, 225, 233, 234, 238, 245, 249, 250, 254, 257, 260, 290, 333, 334, 353, 354, 377, 382, 391, 415, 437, 461, 465, (b) 471, 472, 483, 514, 518, 520, 525, 528, 529, 549, 575, 577, (b) 595, 622, 628, 646, 647, 655, 660, 664, (t) 665, 667, 673, 688, 692, 703, 714, 726, 727, 740, 750, 751, 754, 792; **Susan Moore/Lisa Freeman Inc.** 151, 184-185, 204-205; **Laurie O'Keefe** 146, 149, 167, 735; **Felipe Passalacqua/Worldwide Biomedic Images** 121, 110-111, 156-157, 158, 167, 179, 192-193, 270, 611, 614, 633, 635, 638, 670-671, 691; **Precision Graphics** 28, 34, 36, 53, 57, 59, (b) 60, 61, (tl) 77, (tr) 77, 109, 129, 130, 162, 164, 165, 224, 240, 248, 255, 256, 362, 390, 395, 404, 409, 426-427, 434, 439, 453, 457, 458, (t) 480, 482, 515, (t) 527, 545, 548, 550, 568, 579, 596-597, 600, 617, 627, 696-697, 698-699, 738, 739, 744, 746, 755, 766, 767, 769, 814-815; **Rolin Graphics** 178, 264, 268, 269, 271, 274, 275, 289, 348, 420, 430, (b) 527, 536, 639, 640, 642, 644, (b) 665, 674, 675, 709, 719, 803; **James Shough & Associates** 326-327, 406, 446-447, 681

Photographs

Cover, (eagle) Tom & Pat Leeson, (plane) John J. Cecchini/FPG International, (sunflower) Otto Rogge/The Stock Market, (bkgd) Richard Kaylin/Tony Stone Images; **x,** Stocktrek Photo Agency; **xi,** NASA/TSADO/Tom Stack & Associates; **xii,** S. Nielson/DRK Photo; **xiv,** (t) Rosalind Creasy/Peter Arnold, Inc., (b) Matt Meadows; **xv,** Glencoe file photo; **xvi,** Morton & White Photographic; **xvii,** Bob Daemmrich; **xviii,** Morton & White Photographic; **xix,** Mark Gibson; **xx,** (t) Ed Reschke/Peter Arnold, Inc., (b) Lennart Nilsson/Bonnier-Alba; **xxi,** Robert Chase/Science Source/Photo Researchers; **xxiii,** (t) Chip Clark, (b) Morton & White Photographic; **xxiv,** (l) STUDIOHIO, (r) Anthony Mercica/The National Audobon Society Collection/Photo Researchers; **xxv,** Spencer Grant/Photo Researchers; **xxvi,** (l) Matt Meadows, (r) Richard T. Nowitz; **1,** Ann Duncan/Tom Stack & Associates; **2,** (t) ©Leonard Lessin/Peter Arnold, Inc., (bl) Chip Clark, (bc, br) Matt Meadows; **3,** Morton & White Photographic; **4,** P. Breese/Gamma Liaison; **5,** Matt Meadows; **6,** ©Vic Cox/Peter Arnold, Inc.; **7,** (tl) ©David J. Cross/Peter Arnold, Inc., (tr) ©Ray Pfortner/Peter Arnold, Inc., (b) STUDIOHIO; **8, 9, 11,** Matt Meadows; **12,** (l) H. Corat Moran/Profiles West, (r) Wiley/Wales/Profiles West; **13, 14,** Matt Meadows; **15,** (t) Chip Clark, (c) P. Breese/Gamma-Liaison, (b) Matt Meadows; **18,** R. Lewis/Weatherstock; **19,** (l) National Baseball Library & Archive, Cooperstown, N.Y., (r) Robert Stottlemyer/Biological Photo Service; **20,** (t) Mark Burnett/Stock Boston, (b) Matt Meadows; **21,** Matt Meadows; **22-23,** Michael Gallacher/Gamma-Liaison, **23,** (t) Dr. E.R. Degginger/Color-Pic, (b) Stocktrek Photo Agency; **24,** (l) Morton & White Photographic, (r) Seth Resnick/Stock Boston; **25,** Matt Meadows; **26,** Kent Knudson/Stock Boston; **27,** Matt Meadows; **29,** (t) Barry L. Runk from Grant Heilman, (b) Jim Markham; **30,** (t,c) Dr. E.R. Degginger/Color-Pic, (b) Jeff Spielman/The Image Bank; **31,** (tl) Runk/Schoenberger from Grant Heilman, (tr) Earth Scenes/Patti Murray, (bl) Dr. E.R. Degginger/Color-Pic, (br) Phil Degginger/Color-Pic; **32,** (t) Earth Scenes/Breck P. Kent, (bl) John Masterson/NCAR, (br) Mark Burnett/Stock Boston; **33,** Warren Faidley/Weatherstock; **34,** Rick Kohrs, Space Science and Engineering Center/UW-Madison; **35,** Morton & White Photographic; **37,** Phil Degginger/Color-Pic; **39,** Earth Scenes/Francis Lepine; **41,** courtesy Kavouras, Inc.; **42,** Richard Pasley/The Stock Boston; **43,** Thomas Kitchin/Tom Stack & Associates; **44,** Matt Meadows; **45,** (l) Chris Sorensen, (r) Arthur C. Smith from Grant Heilman; **46,** (t) Richard Steedman/The Stock Market, (c) Ruth Dixon/Stock Boston, (b) W. Eastep/The Stock

Market; **47,** (l) Stocktrek Photo Agency, (r) Seth Resnick/Stock Boston; **49,** John Elk III/Stock Boston; **50-51,** ©1994 Jeff Foott; **51,** (t) Frank Rossotto/The Stock Market, (b) Morton & White Photographic; **54,** Morton & White Photographic; **55,** Sanford/Agiolo/The Stock Market; **62, 63,** NCAR; **65,** Tom Ives; **66,** Brownie Harris/The Stock Market; **67,** David R. Frazier Photolibrary; **68,** Warren Faidley/Weatherstock; **70,** Jack Dykinga; **72,** Photri/The Stock Market; **75,** Tom Ives; **76,** Gary Yeowell/Tony Stone Images; **77,** Tom Ives; **80-81,** AP/Wide World Photos; **81,** (t) Morton & White Photographic, (b) Matthew J. Atanian/Gamma Liaison; **82,** Matt Meadows; **84,** NASA/TSADO/Tom Stack & Associates; **85,** Gary Bohn/St. Louis Post-Dispatch; **87,** ©1992 David Butow/Black Star; **88,** AP/Wide World Photos; **89,** Jack W. Dykinga/Bruce Coleman, Inc.; **91,** NCAR; **92, 93,** Jeff Vanuga; **95,** (t) ©Haviv/Saba Press Photos, (bl) ©John J. Lopinto/The Palm Beach Post,(br) ©Larry Mayer/Gamma-Liaison; **96,** (t) Dominique Braud/Tom Stack & Associates, (b) Steve Mellon/Impact Visuals; **97,** ©Steve Leonard/Black Star; **99,** ©Mark Conlin; **100,** STUDIOHIO; **101,** ©1994 Tammy Peluso/Tom Stack & Associates; **102,** (t) ©Steve Starr/SABA Press Photos,(b) Reuters/Bettmann; **103,** Lannis Waters/The Palm Beach Post; **104,** Morton & White Photographic; **105,** (t) AP/Wide World Photos, (c) ©1992 David Butow/Black Star, (b) ©Mark Conlin; **108-109,** Glencoe file photo; **108,** (bl) Matt Meadows, (br)Tom Pantages; **110-111,** Norbert Wu; **111,** (tl) G. C. Kelley/The National Audubon Society Collection/Photo Researchers, (r) Michael P. Gadomski/The National Audubon Society Collection/Photo Researchers; **112,** Galen Rowell/Mountain Light; **113,** Stephen J. Krasemann/Peter Arnold, Inc.; **114-115,** Ann Duncan/Tom Stack & Associates; **115,** (t) Morton & White Photographic, (b) Bill Keogh; **116,** (l) Randy Brandon/Alaska Stock Images, (r) John Shaw; **117,** (t) Susan McCartney/Photo Researchers, (c) Joanne Lotter/Tom Stack & Associates, (b) Mike Bacon/Tom Stack & Associates; **118-119,** Craig J. Brown/Profiles West; **118,** (bl) T.J. Ulrich/VIREO, (br) Darrell Gulin/DRK Photo; **119,** (t) Jeff Foott, (c) Wayne Lankinen/DRK Photo, (b) Frank Staub/Profiles West; **120,** (t,bl) Norbert Wu, (br) Brian Parker/Tom Stack & Associates; **121,** Norbert Wu; **122,** (l) Runk/Schoenberger from Grant Heilman, (c) Michael Newman/PhotoEdit, (r) Larry Lefever from Grant Heilman; **123,** Larry Ulrich/Tony Stone Images, (inset) S. Nielson/DRK Photo; **124,** T.A. Wiewandt/DRK Photo; **125,** Sharon Gerig/Tom Stack & Associates; **127,** (tl) A.B. Dowsett/Science Source/Photo Researchers, (tr) Tony Stone Images, (bl) William E. Ferguson, (br) Stephen J. Krasemann/DRK Photo; **128,** Bob Daemmrich; **130,** (l) John Gerlach/Tony Stone Images, (r) Rod Planck/Tom Stack & Associates; **131,** Inga Spence/Tom Stack & Associates; **132,** Morton & White Photographic; **133,** David Cavagnaro/DRK Photo; **134,** (l) Michael J. Doolittle from Rainbow, (r) Andrew Kratter; **135,** M.P. Kahl/DRK Photo; **138,** Randy Wells/Tony Stone Images; **139,** (t) Craig J. Brown/Profiles West, (c) Runk/Schoenberger from Grant Heilman, (br) John Gerlach/Tony Stone Images; **142-143,** Earth Scenes/John Lemker; **143,** (bl) S. Nielson/DRK Photo, (t) Tom & Pat Leeson/DRK Photo; **145,** (t,c) Dr. E.R. Degginger/Color-Pic, (b) Leonard Lee Rue III/ The National Audubon Society Collection/Photo Researchers; **147,** Yoav Levy/Phototake; **148,** (t) Matt Meadows, (c) Dwight R. Kuhn, (b) Science VU-WHOI/Visuals Unlimited; **149,** (t) Dwight R. Kuhn, (c) Bob Daemmrich/Stock Boston, (b) Pat & Tom Leeson/The National Audubon Society Collection/Photo Researchers; **150,** F. Marquez/Peter Arnold, Inc.; **151,** Matt Meadows; **152,** (l) Matt Meadows, (r) Morton & White Photographic; **153,** Matt Meadows, **154,** (t) Rod Planck/Tom Stack & Associates, (c) Norbert Wu, (b) Michael Fogden/DRK Photo; **160,** Gilbert Grant/The National Audubon Society Collection/Photo Researchers; **161,** Tom McHugh/The National Audubon Society Collection/Photo Researchers; **163,** Matt Meadows; **166,** Artcetera; **167,** Rod Planck/Tom Stack & Associates; **170-171,** Bob Daemmrich; **171,** (t) Bob Daemmrich, (b) Matt Meadows; **172,** (t) Hans Pfletschinger/Peter Arnold, Inc., (b) H. Cruickshank/VIREO; **174,** Nigel Cattlin/The National Audubon Society Collection/Photo Researchers; **175,** Matt Meadows; **177,** (t) STUDIOHIO, (b) Alfred Pasieka/Peter Arnold, Inc.; **181, 182, 183,** Matt Meadows; **186,** (l) Jeff Henry/Peter Arnold, Inc., (r) Renee Lynn/The National Audubon Society Collection/Photo Researchers; **187,** (t) G. Colliva/The Image Bank, (b) Lawrence Migdale/Photo Researchers; **188,** (t) CNRI/Science Source/Photo Researchers, (b) Steve M. Alden/West Stock; **189,** Simon Fraser/The National Audubon Society Collection/Photo

Researchers; **190,** Rod Planck/The National Audubon Society Collection/ Photo Researchers; **191,** STUDIOHIO; **194-195,** Rob Simpson; **196,** David W. Hamilton/The Image Bank; **197,** Renee Lynn/The National Audubon Society Collection/Photo Researchers; **199,** Glencoe file photo; **200-201,** Miro Vintoniv/Stock Boston; **200,** (t) Miro Vintoniv/Stock Boston, (bl) Morton & White Photographic, (br) Matt Meadows; **201,** (t) Dr. E.R. Degginger/Color-Pic, (b) Glencoe file photo; **202,** Arthur C. Smith III from Grant Heilman; **203,** Wolfgang Kaehler, **206-207,** Erik Leigh Simmons/The Image Bank; **207,** (t) Morton & White Photographic, (b) STUDIOHIO; **211,** Bob Brooks/The Image Bank; **212, 213,** Matt Meadows; **215,** Morton & White Photographic; **218,** (tl) Biology Media/ Science Source/Photo Researchers, (tr) Gunter Ziesler/Peter Arnold, Inc., (bl) CNRI/SPL/Science Source/Photo Researchers, (br) Profs. P.M. Motta & S. Correr/ Science Source/Photo Researchers; **222,** STUDIOHIO; **223, 226, 227, 228,** Morton & White Photographic; **229,** Mary Lou Uttermohlen; **230, 231,** Holly Kuper; **232,** Science Photo Library/Photo Researchers; **233,** (t) STUDIOHIO, (c) Bob Brooks/The Image Bank, (b) Morton & White Photographic; **236-237,** Matt Meadows; **237,** (t) Matt Meadows, (b) STUDIOHIO; **239,** Rosalind Creasy/Peter Arnold, Inc.; **241,** William E. Ferguson; **242,** J.C. Allen & Son; **243,** David Sailors/The Stock Market; **244,** David M. Dennis/Tom Stack & Associates; **246, 247,** STUDIOHIO; **251,** Weinberg-Clark/The Image Bank; **253,** Matt Meadows; **255,** Biophoto Associates/Science Source/Photo Researchers; **258,** Matt Meadows; **259,** (t) Biophoto Associates/Science Source/Photo Researchers, (bl) J.C. Allen & Son, (br) David M. Dennis/Tom Stack & Associates; **262-263,** Kurgan-Lisnet/Gamma-Liaison; **263,** (t) STUDIOHIO, (b) Dr. E.R. Degginger/Color-Pic; **264,** STUDIOHIO; **265,** (t) G. Marche/FPG International, (bl) Gerry Ellis/Ellis Nature Photography; **266,** STUDIOHIO; **267,** Diana L. Stratton/Tom Stack & Associates; **268,** (l) William Felger from Grant Heilman, (r) Kevin Schafer/Tom Stack & Associates; **272,** (l) Michael Collier, (r) Rick McClain/Gamma-Liaison; **273,** Matt Meadows; **274,** Otis Imboden, ©National Geographic Society; **275,** William E. Ferguson; **276,** Matt Meadows; **277,** (bc) Earth Scenes/Doug Weschler, (others) Matt Meadows; **278,** (tl,tc) University of Idaho, Moscow, ID., (tr) Jerry Howard/Positive Images, (b) Morton & White Photographic; **279,** (t) William E. Ferguson, (tc,bc) University of Idaho, Moscow ID, (b) Patricia J. Bruno/Positive Images; **280,** Grant Heilman/Grant Heilman Photography; **281,** (t) Inga Spence/Tom Stack & Associates, (b) Dr. E.R. Degginger/Color-Pic; **282,** Mark Newman/Tom Stack & Associates; **283,** Grant Heilman/Grant Heilman Photography; **284,** (tl) Grant Heilman Photography, (tr, blc) STUDIOHIO, (bl) Larry Lefever from Grant Heilman, (brc) Morton & White Photographic, (br) Phil Degginger/Color-Pic; **285,** Grant Heilman/Grant Heilman Photography; **286,** Matt Meadows; **287,288,** STUDIOHIO; **289,** Dr. E.R. Degginger/Color-Pic; **292-293,** ©Greg Vaughn/Tom Stack & Associates; **293,** (t) Morton & White Photographic, (b) Glencoe file photo; **294,** (tl) Runk/Scheonberger from Grant Heilman, (tr) John Colwell from Grant Heilman, (bl) Alvin E. Staffan, (br) Grant Heilman/Grant Heilman Photography; **295,** STUDIOHIO; **297,** ©1979 Greg Vaughn/Pacific Stock; **298,** ©Lon E. Luaber/Alaska Stock; **299,** (t) STUDIOHIO, (others) Arthur C. Smith III from Grant Heilman; **300,** (tl) Dr. E.R. Degginger/Color-Pic, (tr) Runk/Schoenberger from Grant Heilman, (b) Matt Meadows; **301,** (t) Matt Meadows, (bl) ©Clark James Mishler/Alaska Stock Images, (br) Matt Meadows; **301,** Morton & White Photographic; **303-309,** Matt Meadows; **311,** Morton & White Photographic; **312,** ©Crandall/The Image Works; **313-315,** Morton & White Photographic; **316,** Paul G. Elson/The Image Bank; **318,** Dan McCoy from Rainbow; **319,** (l) Matt Meadows, (r) Grant Heilman/Grant Heilman Photography; **322-323,** Morton & White Photographic; **322,** (l) Morton & White Photographic, (r) STUDIOHIO; **323,** Morton & White Photographic; **324-325,** Sally Beyer/Greg Ryan; **325,** (l) Los Angeles Times Syndicate, (r) Spencer Grant/Photo Researchers; **328-329,** Peter Griffith/Masterfile; **329,** (t) Ron Kimball, (b) UPI/Bettmann; **330,** (t) Christopher S. Lobban/Biological Photo Service, (b) STUDIOHIO; **331,** (tl) Grant Heilman/Grant Heilman Photography,(tr) Matt Meadows, (b) Mark A. Leman/Tony Stone Images; **332,** (l) Superstock, (r) John Lamb/Tony Stone Images; **335,** Brenda L. Lewison/The Stock Market; **336-337,** STUDIOHIO; **338,** (t) David R. Frazier Photolibrary, (b) ©Mark Moffett/Minden Pictures; **339,** David R.

Frazier Photolibrary; **340,** (l) L.L.T. Rhodes/Tony Stone Images, (r) Thomas Braise/The Stock Market; **341,** (l) Superstock, (r) David R. Frazier Photolibrary; **342,** David R. Frazier Photolibrary; **343,** Montana Historical Society; **345,** (tl) Dr. E. R. Degginger/Color-Pic, (tr) Aaron Haupt, (c) Barbara Van Cleve/Tony Stone Images, (b) Matt Meadows; **346-347,** Matt Meadows; **348,** David R. Frazier Photolibrary; **349,** Photo Novovitch/Gamma-Liaison; **350-351,** Mark Burnett; **352,** Morton & White Photographic; **353,** (t) STUDIOHIO, (c) L.L.T. Rhodes/Tony Stone Images, (b) Matt Meadows; **356-357, 357,** Dr. E.R. Degginger/Color-Pic; **360,** (l) Morton & White Photographic, (others) Matt Meadows; **361,** Doug Martin; **362,** (l) Chip Clark, (r) Glencoe file photo; **363,** Chip Clark; **366,** Jason Laure/Laure Communications; **368,** (l) Chip Clark, (r) William E. Ferguson; **369,** (l) G. Tortoli/Photo Researchers, (r) Chip Clark; **370,** (l) John D. Cunningham/Visuals Unlimited, (r) Jack Dykinga; **371,** (l) Nancy L. Cushing/Visuals Unlimited, (r) Glencoe file photo; **372,** C. Nikolay Zurek/FPG International; **373,** ©Leonard Lessin/Peter Arnold, Inc.; **374,** (tl) Al Michaud/FPG International, (tr) Bruce Iverson, (b) Will & Deni McIntyre/Photo Researchers; **375,** (l) Tom Tracy/The Stock Market, (r) Tom Pantages; **378,** (t) Chip Clark, (c) Jim Zuckerman/Westlight, (b) Earth Scenes/Phil Degginger; **380,** Morton & White Photographic; **381,** (t) Chip Clark, (b) G. Tortoli/Photo Researchers; **384-385,** Arnulf Husmo/Tony Stone Images; **385,** Matt Meadows; **386,** Dr. E.R. Degginger/Color-Pic; **387,** Matt Meadows; **388,** courtesy Dr. Anita Harris; **391,** (t) Dr. E.R. Degginger/Color-Pic, (c) Matt Meadows, (b) Bob Daemmrich; **392-393,** Morton & White Photographic; **393,** Dr. E.R. Degginger/Color-Pic; **395,** Bob Daemmrich; **396,** courtesy Texaco; **397,** The Stockhouse Inc.; **399,** Matt Meadows; **400,** (l) courtesy Texaco, (r) Dr. Jeremy Burgess/Science Photo Library/Photo Researchers; **401,** Bob Daemmrich; **402,** Kaku Kurita/Gamma-Liaison; **403,** Mark A. Leman/Tony Stone Images; **405,** Morton & White Photographic; **406,** Matt Meadows; **407,** Bettmann Archive; **408,** Morton & White Photographic; **409,** (t) Bob Daemmrich, (b) Morton & White Photographic; **412-413,** ©Bruce Hands/The Image Works; **413,** (t) STUDIOHIO, (b) Dr. E.R. Degginger/Color-Pic; **414,** STUDIOHIO; **415,** Morton & White Photographic; **418,** Tom O'Keefe; **421,** (t) ©1991 Ford Motor Co./FPG International, (b) Tom DeFranco/©Mary Ann Evans; **422,** (tl) Dennis Barnes, (bl) ©Mary Ann Evans, (br,tr) STUDIOHIO; **424,** courtesy Tire Management Inc.; **425,** Hank Morgan/Photo Researchers; **427,** Matt Meadows; **429,** (tl,tr,br) courtesy Glass Packaging Institute, (bl) courtesy United Glass Limited; **430,** Matt Meadows; **431,** (t) Dennis Barnes, (bl) Matt Meadows, (br) ©Greg Vaughn; **432,** STUDIOHIO; **433,** Morton & White Photographic; **435,** Matt Meadows; **436,** Glencoe file photo; **438,** Phil Degginger/Color-Pic; **439,** (t) Morton & White Photographic, (b) Matt Meadows; **440,** Mark Burnett; **442-443, 442,** Morton & White Photographic; **443,** (tl) STUDIOHIO, (tr) Matt Meadows, (b) Morton & White Photographic; **444-445,** Ian Adams; **445,** (l) Matt Meadows, (r) Len Kaufman/Black Star; **447,** Tony Freeman/PhotoEdit; **448-449,** Bob Daemmrich; **449,** Morton & White Photographic; **450,** (l) Kevin Schafer/Tom Stack & Associates, (r) Starlene Frontino/Westlight; **451** Matt Meadows; **453,** Atwood/USGS; **454-455,** Morton & White Photographic; **456,** (t) Gamma-Liaison, (b) Reuters/Bettmann; **457,** Ric Ferro/Gamma-Liaison; **459,** Morton & White Photographic; **460,** (tl,tr) Reuters/Bettmann, (b) Andras Dancs/Gamma-Liaison; **462,** Morton & White Photographic; **463,** Jeff Smith/Science Source/Photo Researchers; **464,** Tom McHugh/Science Source/Photo Researchers; **466,** Stephen Rose/Gamma-Liaison; **467,** Kevin and Cat Sweeny; **468,** Charles O'Rear/Westlight; **469,** (l) Reuters/Win McNamee/Archive Photos, (r) Ben Van Hook/Black Star; **470,** G.K. Gilbert/USGS; **473,** Mark Gibson; **474,** ©Greg and Tim Hildebrandt; **475,** (tr) Kevin Schafer/Tom Stack & Associates, (l) Reuters/ Bettmann, (br) Charles O'Rear/Westlight; **476,** Mark Gibson; **478-479,** Earth Scenes/George H.H. Huey; **479,** (t) Morton & White Photographic, (b) Hugh Sitton/Tony Stone Images; **483,** Kevin Kolczynski/Silver Image; **485,** Bruce Iverson; **486,** (tl) David Sutherland/Tony Stone Images, (tr) Steve Elmore/Tony Stone Images, (bl) Mike Mazzaschi/Stock Boston, (br) Glencoe file photo; **487,** Matt Meadows; **488, 489,** Morton & White Photographic; **490,** (l) Portland Cement Association, (r) Concrete Reinforcing Steel Institute; **491,** (bl) Morton & White Photographic, (others) Matt Meadows; **492,** ©David Ball/The Stock Market; **493,** Morton & White

Photographic; **494,** (l) Morton & White Photographic, (r) John Lamb/Tony Stone Images; **495,** (br) Pete Saloutos/Tony Stone Images, (others) Matt Meadows; **496,** Lawrence Migdale/Stock Boston; **498,** (l) Matt Meadows, (r) Morton & White Photographic; **499,** (t) Matt Meadows, (b) Cathlyn Melloan/Tony Stone Images; **500,** STUDIOHIO; **501,** Earth Scenes/Breck P. Kent; **502,** (t) Photri, (others) Morton & White Photographic; **503,** ©1992 David Noble/FPG International; **504,** Galen Rowell/Mountain Light; **505,** (t) Portland Cement Association, (c) Morton & White Photographic, (b) Earth Scenes/Breck P. Kent; **506,** Duomo; **508-509,** Michael Dwyer/Stock Boston; **509,** (t) Matt Meadows, (b) STUDIOHIO; **511,** (l) George Mars Cassidy/Tony Stone Images, (r) Glencoe file photo; **512,** (l) Matt Meadows, (r) Guy Marche/FPG International; **513,** (t) David Austen/Tony Stone Images, (others) STUDIOHIO; **514,** (l) Matt Meadows, (r) STUDIOHIO; **516, 517,** courtesy Tsui Design and Research Inc.; **519,** STUDIOHIO; **521,** (tl) Morton & White Photographic, (tr) Bob Daemmrich/Tony Stone Images, (b) STUDIOHIO; **522,** (c) STUDIOHIO, (others) Morton & White Photographic; **523, 524,** Morton & White Photographic; **526,** Lucy Stone/Tony Stone Images; **530,** STUDIOHIO; **531, 532, 533,** Matt Meadows; **534,** (b) Morton & White Photographic, (others) Matt Meadows; **535,** Morton & White Photographic; **536,** Richard T. Nowitz; **537,** (t) Guy Marche/FPG International, (others) Morton & White Photographic; **538,** The Image Bank; **540-541,** ©Evan Agostini/Gamma-Liaison; **541,** Matt Meadows; **542,** (l) ©M. Sutton/FPG International, (r) Bryan F. Peterson/The Stock Market; **543,** Matt Meadows; **544,** Morton & White Photographic; **545,** Matt Meadows; **546, 547,** Morton & White Photographic; **549,** (t) Morton & White Photographic, (b) David Cavagnaro/DRK Photo; **552,** Matt Meadows; **553,** Bob Daemmrich; **555,** (l) ©Chip Simons/FPG International, (r) George Grigoriou/Tony Stone Images; **556,** (l) STUDIOHIO, (r) Glencoe file photo; **557,** Matt Meadows; **560,** ©Roy Morsch/The Stock Market; **561,** ©Andy Caulfield/The Image Bank; **562,** Matt Meadows; **563,** Morton & White Photographic; **566-567,** Mark Gibson; **567,** (t) STUDIOHIO, (b) Morton & White Photographic; **570,** STUDIOHIO; **571,** Matt Meadows; **574,** Mark Burnett; **578,** Michael J. Howell/Gamma-Liaison; **581,** Matt Meadows; **582,** (l) STUDIOHIO, (r) Matt Meadows; **583, 585, 588, 589, 590,** STUDIOHIO; **592, 593,** Morton & White Photographic; **594-595,** CNRI/Science Source/Photo Researchers; **596-597,** Morton & White Photographic; **598-599,** Matt Meadows; **599,** (t) Jim Solliday/Biological Photo Service, (b) Simon Fraser/RVI, Newcastle-Upon-Tyne/Science Source/Photo Researchers; **600,** Bob Daemmrich/Tony Stone Images; **602,** (c) Matt Meadows, (others) Morton & White Photographic; **603,** Matt Meadows; **605,** (tl) Will & Deni McIntyre/Science Source/Photo Researchers, (others) Matt Meadows; **607,** (l) CNRI/Science Source/Photo Researchers, (c) Visuals Unlimited/David M. Phillips, (r) Visuals Unlimited/Jerome Paulin; **608,** (tl) Visuals Unlimited/David M. Phillips, (tr) Visuals Unlimited/Science VU, (b) David York/Medichrome; **609,** (l) David Scharf/Peter Arnold, Inc., (c) Moredun Animal Health Ltd./Science Source/Photo Researchers, (r) Ed Reschke/Peter Arnold, Inc.; **610,** (t) James Solliday/Biological Photo Service, (cl) M.I. Walker/Science Source/Photo Researchers, (cr) Robert Brons/Biological Photo Service, (b) Matt Meadows; **613,** (l) Visuals Unlimited/Ken Greer, (r) Leonard Morse, MD/Medical Images Inc.; **615,** (tl) Glencoe file photo, (tr) Lennart Nilsson/Bonnier-Alba, (bl) Morton & White Photographic, (bc) Blair Seitz/Photo Researchers, (br) Grapes-Michaud/Science Source/Photo Researchers; **616,** (l) Matt Meadows, (r) ©1993 Bill Losh/FPG International; **617,** (l) Visuals Unlimited/Cabsico, (r) Martin M. Rotker/Science Source/Photo Researchers; **618,** STUDIOHIO; **623,** Biophoto Associates/Science Source/Photo Researchers; **624,** Matt Meadows; **625,** Visuals Unlimited/SIU; **626,** Nicole Duplaix/Peter Arnold, Inc.; **627,** (l) David Scharf/Peter Arnold, Inc., (r) Visuals Unlimited/SIU; **630-631,** Lennart Nilsson/Bonnier-Alba; **631,** (t) Matt Meadows, (b) STUDIOHIO; **632,** ©Biophoto Associates/ Science Source/Photo Researchers; **634,** (t) Visuals Unlimited/Michael G. Gabridge, (b) Lennart Nilsson/Bonnier-Alba; **636,** Lennart Nilsson/Bonnier-Alba; **637,** (l) Visuals Unlimited/Science VU, (r) Glencoe file photo; **638,** Glencoe file photo; **641,** Matt Meadows; **645,** Lennart Nilsson/Bonnier-Alba; **648,** Alfred Pasieka/Science Source/Photo Researchers; **650,** STUDIOHIO; **651,** Morton & White Photographic; **652,** (t) Visuals Unlimited/C.

Case, (b) Mark Burnett; **654,** Morton & White Photographic; **656, 657,** Mike Fitelson; **658,** Matt Meadows; **659,** (tl) Biophoto Associates/Science Source/Photo Researchers, (tr) Lennart Nilsson/Bonnier-Alba, (bl) Visuals Unlimited/VU, (br) Glencoe file photo; **662-663,** Blair Seitz/Science Source/Photo Researchers; **663,** (t) Ed Reschke/Peter Arnold, Inc., (b) Larry Mulvehill/ Science Source/Photo Researchers; **667,** Scott Camazine/Science Source/Photo Researchers; **668,** SIU/Science Source/Photo Researchers; **670,** (l) STUDIOHIO, (r) Matt Meadows; **671,** STUDIOHIO; **672,** UPI/Bettmann; **676, 677,** Morton & White Photographic; **678,** (l) Matt Meadows, (r) James Holmes/Cellmark/Science Source/Photo Researchers; **682,** Matt Meadows; **683,** (l) CNRI/Phototake, (r) Robert Chase/Science Source/Photo Researchers; **684,** (l) Will & Deni McIntyre/Science Source/Photo Researchers, (r) Howard Sochurek/The Stock Market; **685,** Morton & White Photographic; **687,** (l) Visuals Unlimited/SIU, (r) Michael Fisher/Custom Medical Stock Photos; **690,** Visuals Unlimited/Science VU; **691,** (t) Blair Seitz/Science Source/Photo Researchers, (bl) Michael Fisher/Custom Medical Stock Photo, (br) Visuals Unlimited/SIU; **694-695,** Matt Meadows; **694,** (t) Matt Meadowns, (b) Morton & White Photographic; **695,** Morton & White Photographic; **696-697,** Ed Boettcher/Airborne; **696,** Bettmann Archive; **697,** Mark R. Lawrence/The Stock Market; **698,** Joe Towers/The Stock Market; **700-701,** Jordan Coonrad; **701,** (t) Matt Meadows, (b) Bob Abraham/The Stock Market; **702,** Robert Morrison/FPG International; **704, 705, 706,** Matt Meadows; **707,** Matt Meadows; **710,** Chris Sorensen; **712, 713,** Morton & White Photographic; **714,** Jordan Coonrad; **715,** Focus On Sports; **716,** STUDIOHIO; **717,** Michael McGowan/ Gamma-Liaison; **718,** STUDIOHIO; **720,** Mark Burnett; **721,** Chris Sorensen; **724,** Jordan Coonrad; **727,** Manfred Kage/Peter Arnold, Inc.; **728,** Chris Sorensen; **729,** Jordan Coonrad; **731,** Chris Sorensen; **732-733,** Toyohiro Yamada/FPG International; **733,** (t) Mark Burnett, (b) Animals Animals/Ray Richardson; **734,** (l) Mike Vines/Tony Stone Images, (tr) Russell C. Hansen/Peter Arnold, Inc., (br) Gunter Ziesler/Peter Arnold, Inc.; **736,** Chris Sorensen; **738,** James R. Fisher/DRK Photo; **740,** Morton & White Photographic; **743,** John C. Beatty/Silverwing; **744,** Johnny Johnson/DRK Photo; **745,** David Pollack/The Stock Market; **746,** Stephen J. Krasemann/DRK Photo; **747,** Stephen Dalton/The National Audubon Society Collection/Photo Researchers; **748,** Bob Abraham/The Stock Market; **749,** (tl) S.R. Maglione/The National Audubon Society Collection/Photo Researchers, (tr) Wayne Lankinen/DRK Photo, (b) Anthony Mercica/The National Audubon Society Collection/Photo Researchers; **751,** William Taufic/The Stock Market; **752,** Jordan Coonrad; **753,** Christian Grzimek/Photo Researchers; **754,** Morton & White Photographic; **755,** (l) Earth Scenes/Breck P. Kent, (r) Jerome Wexler/Photo Researchers; **756,** Morton & White Photographic; **757,** Dick Canby/DRK Photo; **758,** (t) F. Collet/Photo Researchers, (b) Stephen P. Parker/Photo Researchers; **759,** (l) Dr. Jeremy Burgess/Science Source/Photo Researchers, (c) R. Cavignaux/Peter Arnold, Inc., (r) David Scharf/Peter Arnold, Inc.; **760,** Bruce Frisch/Photo Researchers; **761,** (tl) Chris Sorensen, (tr) Animals Animals/Ray Richardson, (bl) Anthony Mercica/The National Audobon Society Collection, Photo Researchers, (br) Dick Canby/DRK Photo; **762,** Russell C. Hansen/Peter Arnold, Inc.; **764-765,** NASA; **765,** (t) Frank Rossotto/The Stock Market, (b) NASA/Gamma-Liaison; **768,** (t) NASA, (b) Matt Meadows; **772,** (l) NASA, (r) NASA/Gamma-Liaison; **773,** NASA; **774,** Glencoe file photo; **775,** NASA; **776,** Superstock; **777,** The Everett Collection; **778,** Bettmann Archive; **782, 783,** NASA; **786,** (l) Glencoe file photo, (r) Morton & White Photographic; **787,** Morton & White Photographic; **790,** ©1983 Michael Whelan; **791,** NASA; **794-795,** (slide mount) Morton & White Photographic, (photo) David Smart/DRK Photo; **794,** (l) Aaron Haupt, (r) Elaine Shay; **795,** (slide mount) Morton & White Photographic, (photo) Dom Riepe/Peter Arnold, Inc., (br) Morton & White Photographic; **804,** (l) Fred Hossler/Visuals Unlimited, (c) Richard Kessler, (r) Runk/Schoenberger from Grant Heilman; **805,** (t) Dr. Jeremy Burgess/Science Photo Library/Photo Researchers, (bl) Matt Meadows, (br) G.R. Roberts; **806,** (tc) Norbert Wu, (tr) Lynn M. Stone, (cr) Sharon Kurgis, (bc) Geri Murphy, (others) Glencoe file photo; **807,** (tl) Kevin Barry, (tr) Nancy Sefton, (c) Mike Hopiak for the Cornell Laboratory of Ornithology, (bl) Glencoe file photo, (br) Geri Murphy; **817, 823, 824, 826, 827, 828, 831, 833, 834,** Glencoe file photo.

PERIODIC TABLE OF THE ELEMENTS

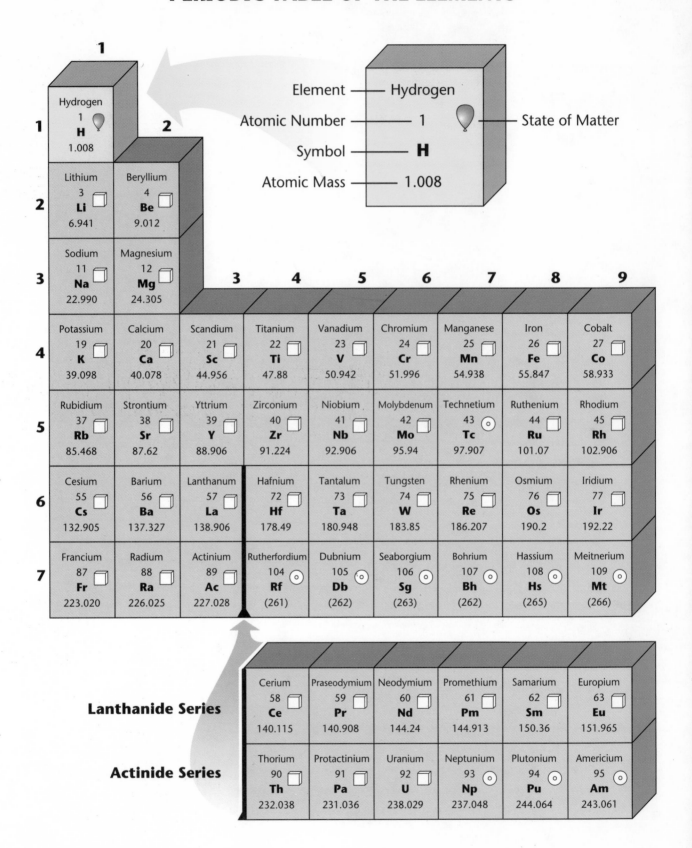